W9-BFJ-476

About Island Press

Island Press is the only nonprofit organization in the United States whose principal purpose is the publication of books on environmental issues and natural resource management. We provide solutions-oriented information to professionals, public officials, business and community leaders, and concerned citizens who are shaping responses to environmental problems.

In 2001, Island Press celebrates its seventeenth anniversary as the leading provider of timely and practical books that take a multidisciplinary approach to critical environmental concerns. Our growing list of titles reflects our commitment to bringing the best of an expanding body of literature to the environmental community throughout North America and the world.

Support for Island Press is provided by The Jenifer Altman Foundation, The Bullitt Foundation, The Mary Flagler Cary Charitable Trust, The Nathan Cummings Foundation, The Geraldine R. Dodge Foundation, The Charles Engelhard Foundation, The Ford Foundation, The German Marshall Fund of the United States, The George Gund Foundation, The Vira I. Heinz Endowment, The William and Flora Hewlett Foundation, The W. Alton Jones Foundation, The John D. and Catherine T. MacArthur Foundation, The Andrew W. Mellon Foundation, The Charles Stewart Mott Foundation, The Curtis and Edith Munson Foundation, The National Fish and Wildlife Foundation, The New-Land Foundation, The Oak Foundation, The Overbrook Foundation, The David and Lucile Packard Foundation, The Pew Charitable Trusts, The Rockefeller Brothers Fund, Rockefeller Financial Services, The Winslow Foundation, and individual donors.

Economic Losses from Marine Pollution

To all living things that provide us the
splendor and wonder of wetlands

To past, present, and future stewards of marine environments,
estuaries, and wetlands—your work is to be commended

*To Robin, Jonathan, and Laura and to the
memory of my parents Joe and Anne for everything*
—DDO

To Rosalind and Matthew
—JJS

Economic Losses from Marine Pollution

A Handbook for Assessment

Douglas D. Ofiara
and
Joseph J. Seneca

ISLAND PRESS
Washington • Covelo • London

Library of Congress Cataloging-in-Publication Data
Ofiara, Douglas D.
  Economic losses from marine pollution : a handbook for assessment / Douglas D. Ofiara and Joseph J. Seneca.
       p.   cm.
Includes bibliographical references and index.
  ISBN 1–55963–609–2 (cloth : alk. paper)
  1. Water—Pollution—Economic aspects—United States. 2. Marine pollution—Economic aspects—United States. 3. Water quality—United States—Measurement. 4. Welfare economics. 5. Environmental economics. I. Seneca, Joseph J., 1943– II. Title.
  HC110.W32 O37   2000
   363.739'4'0973—dc21

                                                              00–012385
                                                                   CIP
British Library Cataloging-in-Publication Data available.

Printed on recycled, acid-free paper

Manufactured in the United States of America
10 9 8 7 6 5 4 3 2 1

Contents

Part III. Applications

Preface

The idea for this book grew from experience and frustration we have had working in interdisciplinary fields and in team efforts that have addressed environmental issues. Experience has taught us how to communicate and combine efforts across many disciplines. Frustration about techniques, measures, and values in assessing effects was a primary reason for writing this book. In retrospect a number of environmental and natural resource allocation problems important several decades ago are still with us, examples being the collapse of important fisheries of Georges Bank off the New England coast and that of Atlantic billfish due to overfishing, and the increasing threat of historical "in-place" pollution and global warming. Could it be that the approach of the past, whereby individuals in their separate fields investigated a problem, offering solutions in a vacuum, is not sufficient to tackle problems that truly involve multidisciplines? It seems that what we have learned from past investigations is that these issues and problems are complex, have not gone away, and are probably best approached by involving interdisciplinary team efforts. This view was recently expressed by the director of the National Science Foundation, Dr. Rita Colwell, when she announced that the NSF would provide funding for more interdisciplinary research.

Marine pollution encompasses a variety of different causes and effects, and both the "hard" sciences (marine sciences, chemistry) as well as the "soft" sciences (economics and public policy analysis) have addressed various issues. Resulting economic effects can be quite varied. This book is one of the first attempts to identify the economic effects that can result from marine pollution that is specific to ecosystems and their organisms (e.g., specific effects on marine habitats and their organisms) as well as impacts to mankind (e.g., health, recreation, and production activities). Until now there has been a lack of a self-contained and systematic treatment of marine pollution and the resulting economic effects. The separate disciplines and professions examined marine pollution and its impacts in their own manner. This has created a gap in knowledge and communication among economists, environmental researchers, and practitioners. The primary motivation in writing this book was to fulfill both of these needs.

We designed this book to serve many purposes and to reach a wide audience and scientific community. In doing so, some sections will appeal to different disciplines, however, taken as a whole, the book provides a comprehensive and practical treatment of the economic consequences of marine pollution. We include discussions of economic principles and theory, substances involved in marine pollution, linkages between marine pollution and subsequent economic effects and losses, economic methods and techniques in use to assess economic losses, and potential issues regarding wetlands restoration and creation. We also provide extensive case studies that can further demonstrate the use of applications, sometimes better than a cookbook-style manual can do.

For those readers who use this book as a practical manual, the text can be viewed in two parts—the first a principles theory (Chapters 2–6) and the second an applications (Chapters 7–10). Some may choose to review the applications chapters first, however, our reasoning is that a firm basis in theory logically precedes any applications. Depending on the reader's interest and background, the applications chapters may offer the most appeal and value. However, if the reader needs to review some aspects of theory and principles, the principles theory chapters contain this material. We want this type of reader to know that there are rewards for wading through the theory and principles part, and this will come in the form of a better understanding and appreciation of the applications of economic methods and techniques and the case studies.

The book is written in a handbook style where all chapters are meant to stand alone and be comprehensive. The book contains extensive reviews of the literature and historical perspectives regarding the development of methods and techniques. Those already familiar with these topics can skim through those passages. For those interested or unfamiliar, the reviews should be a good introduction to the field. Without such a background, one will not appreciate why some techniques are favored over others in certain applications or why controversy surrounds the contingent valuation approach. Concerning the applications part, the level of statistical background is uneven across the techniques, mainly because some techniques are more empirically sophisticated than others. Here the reader with little background in statistics will need to advance his/her understanding in statistics to begin to appreciate the more advanced empirical techniques.

Lastly, the reader who is unfamiliar with economics may want to examine the case studies first for an overview of the issues and approaches involved, consult the theory section to understand what economic measures are being estimated, and then turn to the applications part to understand how specific techniques are applied. We envision such a process being repeated over and over. Both authors served equally on an earlier report that formed the basis for this book. Douglas Ofiara and Joseph Seneca prepared Chapters 4, 5, 6, 7, and 8 and the remaining chapters were prepared by Ofiara.

We would like to acknowledge a number of individuals who have provided us with comments and have shared research and concerns with us. First and foremost our thanks are extended to the members of our review board: Michael Grossman, City University of New York and National Bureau of Economic Research; Douglas Lipton, University of Maryland; Francis Schuler, National Sea Grant College Program; Larry Swanson, State University of New York-Stony Brook; Bob Abel, Stevens Institute of Technology; and Fred Grassle, Rutgers University. To the following individuals who either read parts or the entire manuscript or provided information and material we are also indebted: Arnold Aspelin, U.S. EPA; Monroe Berkowitz, Rutgers University; Bernard Brown, NJDEP; Edna Loehman, Purdue University; Peter Parks, Rutgers University; Mike Kennish, Rutgers University; Martin McHugh, NJDEP; Brian Julius, NOAA, Damage Assessment Center; Bill Desvousges, Triangle Research Institute; Robert Unsworth, Industrial Economics Inc.; Thomas O'Connor, NOAA; Jonathan Sharp, University of Delaware; Bill Hansen, U.S. ACOE, Institute for Water Resources; Merrill Leffler, Maryland Sea Grant College

Program; and John Charbonneau, U.S. DOI, Fish and Wildlife Service; and many individuals at the NOAA, Damage Assessment Center. We thank the U.S. Army Corps of Engineers, Philadelphia Region, who provided our initial funding in 1990 for a report that was expanded and updated into the present book. We also want to thank Island Press and Todd Baldwin, our editor, for believing in this project. It was a pleasure to work with so many talented individuals. Of course any errors that remain are our responsibility.

PART I

Background

CHAPTER 1

Introduction

The best way to understand the importance of economics in assessing losses from marine pollution is to see its application in the real world. New Bedford Harbor was among the first cases in which economic studies were conducted. Not coincidentally, it was one of the first marine areas for which the federal government sought monetary compensation for damages caused by industrial toxicants. It was designated as a Superfund site in 1983 because of the extent of its deterioration and the levels of toxic chemicals found in its sediment. What follows is a brief history of the events surrounding that designation, and the economic assessment of damages. This synopsis is intended to illustrate the scope and coverage of this book as well as a number of key issues: the stakes involved, the purpose and importance of biological and economic assessments, the governing regulatory and legal framework, the public policy implications, and the importance of assessment to cleanup and restoration.

1.1 New Bedford Harbor

New Bedford, Massachusetts, has a rich and diverse history as a seaport and industrial center throughout the birth and and growth of America. New Bedford was regarded as the whaling capital of America and the world during the ninteenth century and was made famous by a resident, Herman Melville, in *Moby Dick*. In 1774, over 50 whaling vessels claimed New Bedford as home port; by the 1850s, it was home to 426 vessels with over 10,000 seamen employed in their service. Discovery of cheap petroleum in Pennsylvania in 1859, coupled with an Arctic whaling disaster in 1871 (in which 29 whaling vessels were abandoned, frozen in the ice) and the development of alternatives to whalebone in corsets, sealed the fate of the whaling economy, and by 1905 the whaling era had ended (NBHTC 1997, *Providence Sunday Journal* 1998). In the meantime, however, New Bedford and other New England towns (e.g., Fall River, Lowell) became important textile centers, referred to locally as "mill towns." From 1870 to 1918, population in New Bedford grew by more than 686 percent (from 15,000 to 118,000) mainly from immigration due to the availability of jobs in the textile industry and mills. During its height in the early 1900s the textile industry employed over 35,000 individuals. But, as with the whaling era, the booming textile industry and New Bedford's economy experienced another bust, losing 21,000 jobs in the period from 1917 to 1937, and 19 percent of its population from 1924 to 1955 (from 130,000 to 105,000). More recently, New Bedford has returned to its maritime roots and is regarded as one of the most important commercial fishing ports in the United States, with almost 300 commercial fishing vessels claiming it as home port. In 1993, with the value of commercial landings exceeding $100 million, New Bedford was the second-largest fishing port in the United States (NBHTC 1997).

After World War II, as New Bedford was regaining its importance as a commercial fishing port, unbeknownst to all but a few, New Bedford Harbor and the surrounding Buzzards Bay were slowly becoming contaminated with industrial discharges, largely from electrical parts manufacturers, which had begun to replace textiles in the New Bedford industrial base. In the early 1950s little was known about the effects of toxic chemicals, nor was there much concern for the environment, which was taken for granted as a limitless resource base. It was not until the 1960s that environmentalists such as Rachel Carson revealed the dangers of highly persistent toxic chemicals in widespread use as pesticides. In New Bedford Harbor, the toxicant was polychlorinated biphenyls (PCBs), a chlorinated organic compound used by the electrical industry as an insulating product in electrical transformers and capacitors. Electricity does not pass through PCBs, and PCBs do not break down when exposed to heat, electricity, water, or other elements in the environment that cause it to persist (U.S. EPA 1984). Furthermore, PCBs are suspected carcinogens to humans and can biomagnify in the food chain (i.e., accumulate in increasing concentrations as they move up the food chain). From the late 1940s until 1977 (the year that PCBs were banned in the United States), PCBs were discharged directly and indirectly into New Bedford Harbor and the surrounding estuary (i.e., New Bedford Harbor and Buzzards Bay) by manufacturers of electric parts, specifically Aerovox Incorporated, Belleville Industries, AVX Corporation, Cornell-Dubilier Electronics (CDE), and Federal Pacific Electric Company (FPE) (NBHTC 1997)

Unlike oil spills like those of the *Exxon Valdez* and *Amoco Cadiz,* discharges of PCBs in marine and aquatic environments are not dramatic or visible forms of pollution. Many years can pass before we witness signs that the environment and living organisms are compromised. During the period from 1974 to1982 it was discovered that the bottom sediment of New Bedford Harbor contained some of the highest concentrations of PCBs found anywhere. Moreover PCBs discharged in New Bedford Harbor had spread to the more open waters of Buzzards Bay, although in lesser concentrations. It has been estimated that from 1958 to 1977, 145 tons of PCBs were discharged in the harbor area, and an estimated range of 200 to 700 pounds of PCBs were discharged annually from the late 1970s to early 1980s in New Bedford Harbor (Howes and Goehringer forthcoming).

Studies also documented high levels of heavy metals such as cadmium, chromium, copper, and lead in New Bedford Harbor. Its water, sediment, and marine life were found to contain these substances; edible fish tissue exceeded the U.S. Food and Drug Administration (FDA) guidelines of 5 parts per million (ppm). Then, in the late 1980s to early 1990s, additional studies confirmed the occurrence and distribution of PCBs and toxic metals within New Bedford Harbor Estuary and Buzzards Bay. Sediment concentrations of PCBs ranged from a few ppm to over 200,000 ppm in the estuary, and over 50 ppm in the Outer Harbor. In the water column PCB concentrations were found to range from 5 ng/l (nanograms/liter) to over 7500 ng/l within the New Bedford Harbor Estuary, levels that well exceed the federal ambient water quality standard of 0.03 ng/l, which is considered by the U.S. Environmental Protection Agency (U.S. EPA) to cause chronic effects on living marine organisms (NBHTC 1997, Ebasco 1990, U.S. EPA 1990a). Concentration levels of PCBs in bottom sediments, in tidal sediments, and in salt marshes of New Bedford Harbor and in parts of Buzzards Bay were found to range from 10 ppm to over 50 ppm—in some places in excess of 100–500 ppm and as high as over 200,000 ppm (NBHTC 1997, Pruell et al. 1990, VHB 1996).

The extent of injuries to the natural resources and living organisms in the New Bedford Harbor Estuary and in Buzzards Bay is not fully known—nor will it be, because this case was settled before federal rules were in place and before a natural resources damage assessment (NRDA) was completed. Because, the New Bedford Harbor Superfund site was one of the first cases to be prosecuted under the Comprehensive Environmental Response, Compensation, and Liability Act (CERCLA) of 1980, its legal outcomes and rulings have been instrumental in influencing the federal rules and procedures under CERCLA's domain.

However, before the case was settled, biologists did find mean concentrations of PCBs in edible tissue of 8 of 15 species of finfish (striped bass, cunner, summer flounder, winter flounder, windowpane flounder, scup, tautog, and bluefish) that exceeded the U.S. FDA action level of 2 ppm within New Bedford Harbor (NBHTC 1997, Weaver 1982, Kolek and Ceurvels 1981). Herring sampled in the harbor estuary contained mean PCB concentrations below the U.S. FDA level, but mean concentrations in roe and body tissue were over the FDA limit (MA DMF 1995). Mean concentrations of PCBs in edible tissue of American eel, oysters, soft-shelled clams, blue crabs, and lobsters were found to exceed the FDA action levels; for lobsters mean concentrations were 8.7 ppm, ranging from 0.1 to 87 ppm (NBHTC 1997, Weaver 1984).

Within the surrounding Buzzards Bay several studies assessed PCB concentrations. For a shorebird, a state coastal survey found that PCB concentrations in eggs of common terns were the highest for locations within Buzzards Bay and Boston Harbor (NBHTC 1997, Nisbet and Reynolds 1984). Similar patterns emerged for juvenile Atlantic silversides, mussels, and sand lance. In another study, concentrations of PCBs in lobster were found to range from 0.26 ppm to 1.66 ppm in edible tissue in Buzzards Bay, all within the U.S. FDA action level for PCBs of 2.0 ppm, and a level of 3.96 ppm within the Outer New Bedford Harbor. For winter flounder, concentrations ranged from 0.39 ppm to 0.52 ppm in edible tissue in Buzzards Bay and 1.60 ppm in the Outer Harbor (BBP 1988, Schwartz 1988). Both findings (lobster and winter flounder) exceeded the average for all of coastal Massachusetts.

On the basis of this evidence the New Bedford Harbor Trustee Council (NBHTC) concluded that the occurrence of PCBs in the water, sediments, and living resources within the New Bedford Harbor Estuary has contributed to:

- Reduction in the biodiversity of the harbor ecosystem
- Decrease in the level of benthic ecosystem health (e.g., biodiversity, community condition, and structure)
- Decrease in benthic organisms' survival
- Reduction in living resources' reproductive capabilities

- Increase in mortality of living resources such as finfish and shellfish
- Decrease in the abundance and diversity of benthic invertebrates, finfish, and shellfish
- Reduction in the diversity and abundance of marine birds dependent on diets of finfish and shellfish (e.g., osprey, terns, and herons)
- Lethal poisoning of birds and other predators such as common terns

These impacts bore direct consequences for the quality of the New Bedford environment and the health of the fisheries on which the town depended for a significant part of its livelihood.

1.1.1. The Economic Assessment

As damaging as these pollutants were (and still are) to the ecology of New Bedford Harbor, the biological assessment was only the first step in evaluating the problem from a legal and policy perspective. Serious questions remained: What action should be taken against the polluters? Who should pay to restore the harbor, and how much? Should the site be restored with funds from the public till, given competing claims on the limited tax dollars available? The loss of ecological and social value must be translated into monetary terms involving an economic assessment. Its purpose is to determine the extent of liability on the part of the manufacturers responsible and to determine the level of resources that society should allocate to restore the ecological integrity of the New Bedford Harbor Estuary.

Governments are not in the position to make open-ended commitments to projects involving cleanup and restoration, nor will courts assign liabilities and awards without estimates of actual damages. However, such assessments are often complicated and can be contentious. This is particularly true in an atmosphere of potential litigation in which the stakes are high and the information is likely to be contested. It is therefore of utmost importance that careful detail and application of appropriate methods be used to ensure that the analysis is thorough and accurate so that public policies can be formulated and implemented to address these resource damages. Underestimating or overestimating the economic losses can send both the wrong signal and the wrong incentive regarding the future actions of private agents and public policies. Perhaps the greatest challenge is to prepare such analyses in extremely short time frames.

When the New Bedford Harbor case was settled, economic analyses of three distinct uses and of private real estate were being prepared. They were completed in 1986 for:

- Commercial lobster fishery (McConnell and Morrison 1986)
- Sportfishing (McConnell and Morrison 1986)
- Recreational beach use (McConnell and IE 1986)
- Private real estate adjacent to New Bedford Harbor (Mendelsohn 1986).

These studies estimated losses at:

- $50,000/year for the commercial lobster fishery; a total discounted value of $2.0 million in 1986 dollars over a 106-year period (1980–2085) ($2.9 million in 1996 dollars [NBHTC 1997])
- $60,000/year for sportfishing; a total discounted value of $3.1 million in 1986 dollars over a 107-year period (1979–2085) ($4.4 million in 1996 dollars [NBHTC 1997])

- $68,100/year for recreational beach use; a total discounted value of $8.4 million to $11.4 million over a 107-year period (1979–2085) in 1986 dollars ($12 million to $16.3 million in 1996 dollars [NBHTC 1997])
- $5616/home to $6338/home (or 9.8 percent to 13.9 percent decrease in housing sales price) for private real estate adjacent to polluted waters; an estimated total discounted loss of $35.9 million in 1986 dollars ($45 million in 1996 dollars [NBHTC 1997]).

These represent losses of real economic value to each of the individual sectors or uses. If taken together, these studies suggest that economic losses were in excess of a discounted value of $50 million over a 107-year period (the time period initially assumed that it would take for natural recovery) in 1986 dollars (or $64.3 to $68.6 million in 1996 dollars).

But this represents a partial assessment. These figures do not account for the losses to other industries. Nor do they account for the loss in ecological functioning, of which the damages to the lobster fishery and sport fishing are only a symptom. If migrating terns and other species no longer stop in New Bedford Harbor, this represents a loss in value. How does one place a dollar value on a reduction in tern populations? Terns have no commodity value, but the loss of such a predator has an effect on ecosystem functions and productivity. Moreover, humans value the existence of such terns as part of a natural, functioning ecosystem. The task of assigning a specific dollar value to resources such as these is exceedingly difficult—though as we shall see in this book, economists are refining techniques to do the job.

But there is an additional shortcoming of these studies: They could overestimate the damages. How? Given that uses sometimes overlap (e.g., in the case of sportfishing and recreational beach use) double-counting can occur. Such summation (e.g., summing over piecemeal uses) of losses of economic value assumes that losses associated with single uses are independent of similar losses for other uses (Randall 1991). In general, to fairly and accurately assess economic losses, either for the purpose of assigning liability for damages or to make policy choices based on costs and benefits, one should conduct a comprehensive study that obtains losses for *all uses at the same time* so that losses from one use are conditional or dependent on losses from all other uses.

The economic assessment of the PCB contamination of New Bedford Harbor was conducted at a time before the economic methods described in this book had been fully developed. A number of issues were not resolved at that time, including the inaccuracy in summing over piecemeal uses versus the economic value obtained from a one-time comprehensive application. The actual damages assessed could have been higher (not all uses were assessed) or lower (due to double-counting). It is clear that had the advancements in these methods been available, the ultimate settlement would have been more fair, accurate, and defensible in both the courtroom and the legislative chamber.

1.1.2. Legal Settlement

With the passage of CERCLA (Comprehensive Environmental Response, Compensation, and Liability Act) in 1980 and the Superfund Amendments and Reauthorization Act (SARA) in 1986 (collectively referred to as the Superfund Act), the federal government began to pursue legal actions against parties responsible for pollution (although authority to do so had previously been provided for by the Clean Water Act and its subsequent amendments). Following passage of the Superfund Act, the U.S. EPA routinely sampled old and abandoned industrial sites and dumps to assess their relative environmental quality and safety to the public. In 1983 New Bedford Harbor was added to the Superfund site list (i.e., National Priorities List of Hazardous Waste Sites under the Superfund program) by the U.S. EPA, and the Commonwealth of Massachusetts regarded it as the most significant Superfund site in the state.

In 1983 complaints were filed in the federal district court of Boston under the CERCLA legislation against a number of electrical manufacturers, namely Aerovox Incorporated, Belleville Industries, AVX Corporation, Cornell-Dubilier Electronics (CDE), and Federal Pacific Electric Company (FPE), for allegedly causing injuries to natural resources and subsequent economic losses and damages from the discharge of PCBs (NBHTC 1997). This was one of the first NRDA cases to be prosecuted under CERCLA and the case was settled before economic guidelines and procedures were in place. As noted above, a full NRDA (both biological and economic components) could not be completed.[1] Nonetheless, the case made clear that the stakes involved in marine pollution events where high, and it forged new ground both in biological assessments of injuries to natural resources and in economic assessments of damages to several important uses. Many of the lessons learned and problems discovered from this exercise were helpful in developing the procedures.

As it happened, the federal district court issued a total of eight opinions in the New Bedford Harbor case, including another opinion issued by the First Circuit Court of Appeals. Based on the studies and assessments at the time, a substantial economic loss was established in court and resulted in the following settlements (NBHTC 1997):

- Aerovox and Belleville settlement of $13.15 million in June 1992
- AVX, Inc., settlement of $66 million in July 1992
- FPE and CDE settlement of $21 million in October 1992
- Total settlements of $100.15 million, earmarked as follows:
  - Natural resource damages: initially with interest $20.2 million; with interest from investment in the Court Registry Investment System the sum is currently $24 million (NBHTC 1998)
  - Cleanup costs—$59 million
  - Response costs—$10 million
  - Damage assessment costs (reimbursed to NOAA)—$815,000 plus interest
  - U.S. EPA–maintained joint registry account (for response or natural resource damages)—$10 million

Overall, $79 million is assigned for remediation and cleanup, and approximately $21 million for restoration of natural resources (currently $24 million with interest) (NBHTC 1997, 1998).

1.1.3. Cleanup and Restoration Actions

One of the main reasons to assess the magnitude of overall damages and the level of liability to assign to the individual polluters is to determine how much of society's resources to devote to restore the ecological integrity of a damaged ecosystem. The overall goal is to achieve the same level of *net* economic value from the restored/cleaned ecosystem equivalent as in its predamaged state (sometimes equated to the quantity of resources or services the ecosystem provides associated with its predamaged state). While the assessment of lost economic benefits in resource damage assessments is paramount to economists and has received the most attention in the federal rules and procedures, not much attention has been given to the actual costs of achieving the desired outcomes, the domain of restoration ecologists and environmental engineers. We are learning about the costs of restoring damaged ecosystems, but know less about whether the cleaned and restored ecosystems function equivalently to their predamaged state and hence provide equivalent economic benefits. We know more about revegetation efforts but have yet to learn about the accompanying functions revegetation performs vis à vis that of predamaged wetlands. This limitation is reflected in how the damage award must be used. The bulk of damage awards are meant for restoration-cleanup efforts, not monitoring efforts; very little monitoring is built into a restoration-cleanup plan because it is not required by federal policy. The new fields of ecological economics and restoration ecology are beginning to address these issues as discussed in more detail in Chapter 10. However, if we are to make advancements in the area of wetlands restoration, monitoring must become an integral part of the research design and should become integrated into federal policy.

As part of the settlement for New Bedford Harbor, the court established the NBHTC consisting of three trustees:

- The Commonwealth of Massachusetts
- The U.S. Department of the Interior (U.S. DOI)
- The U.S. Department of Commerce, National Oceanic and Atmospheric Administration (NOAA)

General goals of the restoration actions to be implemented by the NBHTC include restoring, replacing, or acquiring the equivalent of natural resources injured by discharges of PCBs in the New Bedford Harbor. Specific goals of restoration actions include: (1) restoring natural resources injured by PCBs, (2) restoring the habitats and ecological services of living resources, and (3) restoring human uses of the natural resources (NBHTC 1997). Because cleanup of the Superfund site (New Bedford Harbor) is ongoing and will continue until 2011 (approximately another 10 years) and will have further negative and beneficial impacts on natural resources within the New Bedford Harbor Estuary and Buzzards Bay, restoration efforts have to be coordinated with the cleanup and remediation efforts. As a result, the NBHTC has approved and implemented a number of near-term restoration projects supported by the current restoration fund of $24 million (NBHTC 1997). These involve:

- Hydrologically restoring wetlands
- Developing and improving new and existing coastal parks
- Restoring natural resources in New Bedford Harbor and nearby areas (e.g., eelgrass habitat, shellfish resources, herring runs, Buzzards Bay tern populations)
- Purchasing coastal property (160 acre tract)
- Coordinating efforts with open-space planning and use in the New Bedford/Fairhaven Harbors
- Inventorying all wetlands for future restoration work

Throughout the cleanup effort the NBHTC will periodically identify and implement other restoration projects, and upon completion of cleanup will identify and implement a final round of restoration projects so as to achieve the above stated objectives and goals of the restoration process (NBHTC 1997).

In 1990, the U.S. EPA began the cleanup phase by dredging an area of the harbor known as the "Hot Spot," where sediment contained PCB concentrations in excess of 4,000 ppm. This project was designed to remove and incinerate almost half of the estimated 145 tons of PCBs in the harbor sediment, but the sediment is now being stored due to public opposition over incineration (BBP 1990, NBHTC 1997). In 1994 another Hot Spot was dredged and the material was placed in storage in a confined disposal facility (CDF). Total costs of dredging 28,000 cubic yards were approximately $28 million and involved an area of over 5 acres. The U.S. EPA also plans to dredge about 118 acres in both the inner and outer harbor where concentrations in sediments exceed 50 ppm of PCBs, and to dredge areas in the upper estuary where sediment contains over 10 ppm of PCBs (NBHTC 1997). This phase of the remediation is expected to last at least a decade (until 2011) and use the remaining cleanup funds of approximately $51 million.

1.1.4. Conclusion

The New Bedford Harbor resource damage assessment case will be remembered as the first such case in the United States. This case and the assessment forged new ground in biological assessments of injuries to natural resources and in economic assessments of damages to several important uses. Many of the lessons learned and problems discovered during this effort were useful in developing the federal NRDA procedures. And this is the first time in which such a massive dredging project is used to address cleanup and remediation of contaminated bottom sediment. All will be watching and waiting for evaluations of key environmental parameters (e.g., presence of PCBs in water column, bottom sediment, and wetlands, and in various living organisms, shellfish, finfish, shorebirds) to determine the degree of success achieved and the potential for the use of dredging in future remediation.

This case will also be important and examined as to whether it successfully achieved the restoration goals, whether the damage award was administered properly and wisely, and in particular whether the settlement and damage award was sufficient to restore New Bedford Harbor and Buzzards Bay. An outcome of this case could involve changes in the handling and administering of damage awards, such as the use of annuities to provide for future resources for further restoration as needed and to provide for monitoring of restoration efforts. Extensive monitoring efforts of restored or created wetlands are needed so that we may ensure that public funds (society's resources) are put to their best use toward achieving what was intended. Simply put, without monitoring we will never know if a restored or created wetland achieves social values equal to those of the same wetland in its predamaged state. The concern is that we could shortchange future generations if restored or created wetlands return significantly less social value than wetlands in their predamaged or natural state.

1.2. Introduction to the Book

The stakes are high, and the economic values are difficult to determine. Cases like New Bedford Harbor are being replayed around the country, and increasingly society must make decisions about remedying past problems and restoring natural environs. Biologists, restoration ecologists, environmental engineers, and lawyers all play critical roles in these outcomes. But to act on their contributions, society must have an accurate and firm grasp of the values and costs involved. The purpose of this book is to provide a comprehensive and practical treatment of the economic consequences of marine pollution. It will enable communication between economists and other researchers in the environmental, marine, and ecological sciences as well as environmental policymakers and environmental lawyers. There is a need for communication among disciplines that are involved with NRDAs. If economists, for example, understand the specific effects of marine pollution on a particular resource (e.g., the effect of a decrease in productivity of an ecosystem on a particular fishery), they can design and apply appropriate economic techniques with which to best measure these effects. Likewise, if biologists are to provide appropriate information for assessment of damages and policy, they must understand the economics. Lawyers involved in litigation against (or on behalf of) marine polluters must also understand the basis for assessing damages and particular models used when they are put to the test in the courtroom.

Clear and open communication across disciplines about their respective tasks can result in efficiencies in both biological and economic assessments. Understanding assessment techniques and sharing information needs among disciplines can benefit all involved and can enhance the development and performance of assessment techniques and the overall NRDA process. This is essential for assessing subtle effects on marine organisms and humans over longer time periods. The bioaccumulation and biomagnification of toxic substances must be assessed both for their ecological effects and for subsequent risks to the public from seafood consumption. Biological, chemical, physical, medical, and economic sciences need to coordinate how to address matters such as acceptable risk levels from short-term and long-term exposure for various contaminant levels, either from consumption of seafood product or through direct contact at contaminated sites. The assessment of risk, for policy purposes, is expressed in economic terms, so it is necessary for all professionals involved to understand these terms.

This book focuses on marine pollution and the subsequent economic losses and damages. It systematically identifies various substances that degrade and contaminate the marine environment and categorizes them into generic groups based on their effects on marine organisms and, ultimately, on society. The book also addresses social well-being and welfare economic techniques that are used in the assessment of losses that may result from degradations in the marine environment. This book explains the theoretical underpinnings of these techniques and then describes their uses and methods of application. Some of these economic techniques have been in use for more than three decades, and some have become controversial. In general, the area of applied welfare economics is controversial because resource decisions are framed between public and private goods as well as across various policies, and hence tradeoffs between the interests of individuals and those of society as a whole become central in the evaluation of different goods and services (e.g., more prosperous corporations vs. a cleaner environment). It is because resources are scarce and must be allocated among competing uses that society must confront decisions regarding tradeoffs.

I.3. Public Policy and Economic Assessments

Almost every public policy has affected or has the potential to affect social well-being. Consider for instance, the space program, the food stamp program, the national park system, and endangered species programs. In evaluations of the merits of public policy actions and in situations that involve choices among a variety of public programs, there is a need for a methodology that can provide a common metric of the outcomes of proposed policies. Economic analysis of the full benefits and full costs of such programs can accomplish this. Furthermore, knowledge of all benefits and costs of public policies and specific economic activities can help achieve the most efficient use of society's scarce resources.

Production and consumption processes can affect individuals other than the individual or entity engaged in that activity. Spillovers (or *externalities* in economics terminology) from production processes are examples of situations where unwanted byproducts such as pollution are created from the production of certain goods. In addition to PCBs, examples are air and water pollution from paper and pulp mills that generate dioxin, a hazardous substance classified as a carcinogen that contaminates waterways and aquatic organisms. The burning of high sulfur coal in electric power generating plants has introduced sulfur particles into the atmosphere. Combined with water vapor, the sulfur has caused increased acidification of freshwater lakes and ponds via acid rain. Gasoline used as a fuel source for automobiles also causes air pollution. All these externalities create potential and unwanted damages to other members of society (e.g., consumers, households, firms).

In instances where spillovers occur, the primary production or consumption activity has effects on society that the primary economic agent (i.e., producer or consumer) has ignored or which are external to that agent's concern. In the case of pollution, this results in additional costs borne by society in the form of added health costs, reduced visits to and enjoyment of polluted sites, and added cleanup costs in restoring degraded environments. The capability to measure these costs allows policymakers to design policies that can cause primary agents to bear a portion or all of the costs from their activity. Such a practice causes spillovers to become internalized by the primary agent.

For instance, in the case of producing a good with damaging spillover effects (i.e., negative external effects) social costs exceed private costs; that is, the costs to society as a whole exceed those to the individuals producing the externality. This indicates that too much of the good associated with external effects is being produced from society's viewpoint. Typical policy approaches address and correct this by using either a quantity control to restrict or regulate the level of pollutant discharged, or a tax instrument. In each case, costs to the producer rise and output of the good falls. In the case of a quantity control, the regulator would limit the amount discharged via emission or discharge permits. In the case of taxes, a tax would be levied to equalize private costs with social costs and achieve a socially optimal or, in economic terms, efficient level of production (i.e., where benefits to society from producing an additional unit of the good equal the social costs of producing that unit). Different outcomes result, depending on the choice of the tax instrument. A lump-sum tax (flat tax) set equal to the spillover effect (i.e., cost of damage from pollution) can raise a tax revenue to offset it, but this may not change the level of production of the good, and the damage will continue. A unit tax, referred to as a Pigou tax, after the economist A.C. Pigou, or an effluent/emissions charge set equal to the marginal social damage per unit of discharge is designed to cause production costs to increase to the point where the agent must reduce output to socially efficient or economically efficient levels. When the full cost of the externality is known with certainty, both quantity controls and tax instruments can achieve the socially efficient level. But with uncertainty, the typical situation, results are not easily generalized and can become more complicated.

Although the economics profession has often been accused of neglecting the environment, a number of economic researchers have been working for many years to assign dollar values to environmental impacts and thereby ensure that they are given proper weight in policy decisions. This is particularly important because, since 1974, when President Ford implemented Executive Order 11281, analysis of the costs and benefits (initially referred to as inflationary impact analysis and now as regulatory impact analysis) has had to be performed for any federal regulation that would have a potential economic impact (Bentkover et al. 1986, Presidential Documents 1974). Each succeeding president has subsequently made changes to this process and analysis (Bentkover et al. 1986, Presidential Documents 1977, 1978, 1981, 1993). The U.S. EPA regularly examines the benefits and costs from proposed regulations and bans on the use of pesticides as part of the Federal Insecticide, Fungicide, and Rodenticide Act (FIFRA) (True 1997, Allison and Ofiara 1981, Ofiara et al. 1982). The Occupational Safety and Health Administration (OSHA) has also conducted economic analyses of the benefits and costs from regulating the use of hazardous substances in the workplace (Viscusi 1992, Lave 1981, 1982). The U.S. EPA has conducted extensive studies on investments in pollution control technologies in meeting environmental quality standards, and impacts on municipalities and others from pollution control technologies (U.S. EPA 1988, 1990b). The U.S. Congress must go through similar exercises in the approval of various public programs and in situations that involve tradeoffs among public programs.

These types of analyses are not limited to public policy issues. Private industry conducts similar analyses of whether they should undertake proposed investment decisions or create new product lines in which benefits and costs (i.e., discounted future flows of revenues and costs) of each undertaking are evaluated, comparisons made, and decisions reached. These analyses attempt to ensure that decisions are not made that reduce the profit potential of new initiatives in private industry; rather initiatives are undertaken that raise profits (i.e., net earnings). Increasingly, these economic methods have been used in policies that affect the degradation and management of marine waters.

1.4. Outline of the Book

The first part of this book introduces the economic principles and theory, coupled with the federal environmental legislation and rulemaking that produced the economic assessment procedures. It is designed to give the reader an appreciation of what lies ahead, to introduce the reader to important concepts and theories discussed later, and to show how the federal government has been involved in addressing and managing marine pollution and in developing uniform economic procedures for use in evaluating the effects of economic losses from marine pollution. This is followed by a brief overview of marine pollution in general terms. The discussion and treatment of measurable effects of marine pollution follows a systematic (i.e., taxonomic) approach to identify all possible effects of marine pollution.

Chapter 2 contains a primer on economic principles and theories to introduce the reader to important concepts and terminology, the field of environmental economics, and the controversy surrounding ex ante versus ex post measures of economic welfare. Chapter 3 is an overview of federal initiatives in two areas—environmental legislation as it pertains to marine pollution, and economic procedures and guidelines to assess federal policies and economic welfare in general as well as procedures specific to economic losses and damages from marine pollution. It contains a historical overview of federal rules pertaining to the use of economic methods in assessing benefits and costs, how these techniques have evolved, an overview of the NRDA process, and an overview of the National Estuary Program as an example of a federal initiative to manage the water quality of coastal waters. Chapter 4 begins the discussion of specific substances that cause degradations in the quality of marine waters and in the marine environment. This chapter treats the most important biological aspects of water quality degradations by first identifying and classifying substances into generic groups that cause degradations in marine water quality and their associated impairments. It then briefly identifies the corresponding effects or impacts on organisms, on the ecosystem, and on humans (in ascending order from simple to complex organisms). Chapter 4 sets the scope and coverage of all impacts and effects treated in the book. It serves as the first step in the process of identification of economic losses from water quality degradations.

Chapter 5, which begins Part II, introduces the economic principles and methods needed to understand and to assess economic losses and damages (i.e., losses of economic welfare). The material is divided into two sections, one devoted to a treatment of economic measures and methods, the other to an assessment of economic welfare. The chapter also contains brief discussions of economic welfare theory, externalities, and environmental economics concepts. It highlights problems dealing with the aggregation of economic welfare measures, the distinction between economic losses and economic impacts, the treatment of economic losses that occur over multiple time periods, the presence of uncertainty in the analysis, and NRDA procedures. Chapter 6 completes the taxonomic process. Biological effects of water quality impairments and degradations are identified and carried to the next level, where they are linked to their potential economic effects or impacts, and associated losses of economic welfare. The economic losses are expressed in terms of specific economic welfare measures (following the discussion in Chapter 5) where appropriate. The basic economic techniques used to measure changes in economic value, and in particular, economic losses from water quality degradations are introduced in Chapter 7. A brief history of each method is discussed, along with its advantages and disadvantages.

The third part of the book is about application and shows how to use these techniques along with case studies of damages from marine pollution. Chapter 8 explains how to apply the economic techniques from the previous chapter and discusses the use of benefit transfers in economic assessments, an important tool. Several examples give the reader some appreciation for the variety and complexity of the applications and for the levels of creativity needed to apply these techniques. Among other things, the chapter is meant to show practitioners, policymakers, environmental scientists, and economists from other fields the breadth and depth of their coverage and application. Issues such as study design, sample design, and survey design are not treated, since these are treated in more detail in their respective literatures. Practical applications is the focus of Chapter 9, which uses a series of case studies of actual assessments of impairments and damages to components of marine ecosystems from various types of marine pollution (e.g., damages to fish and shellfish from hypoxic events, pathogens, and hazardous substances; impairments to estuaries from hazardous substances, marine debris, and oil spills). These case studies are an extremely valuable teaching aid that can illustrate better than any general discussion how to apply economic methods.

Finally, Chapters 10 and 11 discuss future directions in economic theory relating to managing marine pollution and NRDA procedures, as well as to wetlands restoration and creation. Chapter 10 contains cutting edge material in subsequent fields (ecological restoration, ecological/restoration economics) that have grown as a result of the NRDA legal process, oil spills, and concern over degraded coastal environments and habitats. Topics involve wetland restoration and mitigation principles and efforts. Here we are concerned about factors critical to proposed restoration projects and selection criteria in such projects. Measures of wetland restoration efforts also form a crucial part of this discussion. Selected case studies are included to illustrate many of the principles and challenges facing this area. The role of overseers concludes the discussion in Chapter 10. Lastly, Chapter 11 examines the efficiency of liability rules, such as the NRDA rules, in controlling pollution.

This book is designed to meet multiple needs, from those of the novice seeking a quick overview, to those of experienced professionals. As such it proceeds from elementary discussions in Part 1 to progressively advanced economics. The discussion in this book uses graphical diagrams similar to those in elementary economic mathematics textbooks to develop the concepts presented; however, as the book progresses to the applications section (Part 3), formal training in statistics may be necessary to follow the discussion since detail is needed to motivate the material and each model and to illustrate its application.

1.5. Note

1. It was not until 1986 and 1987 that the U.S. Department of Interior, the agency responsible for promulgating procedures in performing Natural Resource Damage Assessments under CERCLA, finalized and published the first set of uniform rules and procedures, for Type B and Type A procedures, respectively (U.S. DOI 1986, 1987).

1.6. References

Allison, J.R. and D.D. Ofiara. 1981. *Preliminary Benefit Analysis of PCBN Use on Peanuts.* Prepared for Economic Analysis Branch, Office of Pesticide Programs, U.S. EPA: Washington, DC.

Bentkover, J.D., V.T. Covello and J. Mumpower (eds.). 1986. *Benefits Assessment: The State of the Art.* D. Reidel Publishing Co.: Dordrecht, Holland.

———. 1988. *Annual Report, 1987.* Buzzards Bay Project: So. Dartmouth, MA.

Buzzards Bay Project. 1990. *The Buzzards Bay Project Newsletter.* 5(2). Buzzards Bay Project: So. Dartmouth, MA.

Ebasco Services Inc. 1990. *Draft Final Baseline Ecological Risk Assessment.* New Bedford Harbor Site Feasibility Study. EPA Contract No. 68-01-725C.

Howes, B.L. and D.D. Goehringer. In Press. *Ecology of Buzzards Bay: An Estuarine Profile.* National Biological Service: Washington, DC.

Kolek, A. and R. Ceurvels. 1981. *Polychlorinated Biphenyl (PCB) Analyses of Marine Organisms in the New Bedford Area, 1976–80.* Massachusetts Division of Marine Fisheries: Boston, MA.

Kopp, R.J. and V.K. Smith (eds.). 1993. *Valuing Natural Assets: The Economics of Natural Resource Damage Assessment.* Resources for the Future: Washington, DC.

Lave, L.B. 1981. *The Strategy of Social Regulation: Decision Frameworks for Policy.* Brookings Institution: Washington, DC.

———. (ed.). 1982. *Quantitative Risk Assessment in Regulation.* Brookings Institution: Washington, DC.

Lipton, D.W., K.F. Wellman, I.C. Sheifer, and R.W. Weiher. 1995. *Economic Valuation of Natural Resources: A Handbook for Coastal Resource Policymakers.* NOAA Coastal Ocean Program Decision Analysis Series No. 5. U.S. Dept. of Commerce, NOAA: Silver Spring, MD.

Massachusetts Division of Marine Fisheries. 1995. *PCB Tissue Analysis Data Summary: Acushnet River.* Report #B010-011. Massachusetts Division of Marine Fisheries: Salem, MA.

McConnell, K.E. and Industrial Economics, Inc. 1986. *The Damages to Recreation Activities from PCBs in New Bedford Harbor.* Report to NOAA, Ocean Assessment Division: Rockville, MD.

McConnell, K.E. and B.G. Morrison. 1986. *Assessment of Economic Damages to the Natural Resources of New Bedford Harbor: Damages to the Commercial Lobster Fishery.* Report to NOAA, Ocean Assessment Division: Rockville, MD.

Mendelsohn, R. 1986. *Assessment of Damages by PCB Contamination to New Bedford Harbor Amenities Using Residential Property Values.* Report to NOAA, Ocean Assessment Division: Rockville, MD.

Nelson, W.G. et al. 1996. *New Bedford Harbor Long-Term Monitoring Assessment Report: Baseline Sampling.* EPA/600/R-96/097. U.S. EPA, NHEERL, AED: Narragansett, RI.

New Bedford Harbor Trustee Council. 1997. *New Bedford Harbor Trustee Council Restoration Plan Environmental Impact Statement.* U.S. DOC, NOAA, DARP: Silver Spring, MD.

———. 1998. *New Bedford Harbor Trustee Council Restoration Plan Environmental Impact Statement—Record of Decision.* U.S. DOC, NOAA, DARP: Silver Spring, MD.

Nisbet, I.C.T and L.M. Reynolds. 1984. "Organochlorine Residues in Common Terns and Associated Estuarine Organisms, Massachusetts, USA, 1971–81. *Marine Environmental Research* 11: 33–66.

Ofiara, D.D., J.R. Allison, G.V. McMahon, and B.D. Elias. 1982. *Preliminary Benefit Analysis of Captan Use on Peaches.* Prepared for Economic Analysis Branch, Office of Pesticide Programs, U.S. EPA: Washington, DC.

Presidential Documents. 1974. "Executive Order 11821—Inflation Impact Statements." *Federal Register* 39: 41501.

———. 1977. "Executive Order 11949—Economic Impact Statements." *Federal Register* 42: 1017.

———. 1978. "Executive Order 12044—Improving Government Regulations." *Federal Register* 43: 12661.

———. 1981. "Executive Order 12291—Federal Regulation." *Federal Register* 46(33): 13193–13198.

———. 1993. "Executive Order 12866—Regulatory Planning and Review." *Federal Register* 58(190): 51735–51744.

Providence Sunday Journal. 1998. "The New Bedford Whaling Era." August 2, Providence, RI.

Pruell, R.J., et al. 1990. "Geochemical Study of Sediment Contamination in New Bedford Harbor, Massachusetts." *Marine Environmental Research* 29: 77–101.

Randall, A. 1991. "Total and Nonuse Values." In Braden, J.B. and C.D. Kolstad (eds.). *Measuring the Demand for Environmental Quality.* North Holland: New York, NY: 303–321.

Schwatrz, J.P. 1988. *Distribution and Concentration of Polychlorinated Biphenyls in Lobster, Winter Flounder, and Quahogs from Buzzards Bay, Massachusetts.* Draft Report. MA Division of Marine Fisheries: Salem, MA.

True, L.P. 1997. "Agricultural Pesticides and Worker Protection." In Morgenstern, R.D. (ed.). *Economic Analyses at EPA: Assessing Regulatory Impact.* Resources for the Future: Washington, DC.

U.S. Department of Interior. 1986. "Natural Resource Damage Assessments; Final Rule." *Federal Register* 51(148), Friday, August 1: 27674–27753.

———. 1987. "Natural Resource Damage Assessments; Final Rule." *Federal Register* 52(54), Friday, March 20: 9042–9100.

U.S. Environmental Protection Agency. 1984. *PCBs and New Bedford Harbor: Clarifying the Issues.* EPA Circular. U.S. EPA, Region 1: Boston, MA.

———. 1988. *The Municipal Sector Study: Impacts of Environmental Regulations on Municipalities.* EPA-230-09: 88-038. U.S. EPA: Washington, DC.

———. 1989a. *Marine and Estuarine Protection: Programs and Activities.* EPA-503/9-89-002. U.S. EPA: Washington, DC.

———. 1989b. *Saving Bays and Estuaries: A Primer for Establishing and Managing Estuary Projects.* EPA-503/8-89-001. U.S. EPA: Washington, DC.

———. 1990a. *Feasibility Study of Remedial Alternatives for the Estuary and Lower Harbor/Bay, New Bedford, Massachusetts.* Volumes I and II. Draft Final. EPA Contract No. 68-01-7250. U.S. EPA: Boston, MA.

———. 1990b. *Environmental Investments: The Cost of a Clean Environment.* EPA-230-11-90-083. U.S. EPA: Washington, DC.

Vanesse Hangen Brustlin, Inc. 1996. *New Bedford Harbor: Historic Overview and Natural Resources and Uses Status Report.* Prepared for NBHTC: New Bedford, MA.

Viscusi, W.K. 1992. *Fatal Tradeoffs: Public and Private Responsibilities for Risk.* Oxford University Press: New York, NY.

Weaver, G. 1982. *PCB Pollution in the New Bedford, Massachusetts Area: A Status Report.* Massachusetts Coastal Zone Management: Boston, MA.

———. 1984. "PCB Contamination In and Around New Bedford, Mass." *Environmental Science and Technology* 18(1): 22–27.

CHAPTER 2

Primer on Welfare Economics and Environmental Economics

2.1. Background

Within economics there are two basic types of inquiry, known as positive economics and normative economics. Positive economics comprises the bulk of economic theory and applications involving theoretical and empirical comparisons across different outcomes (e.g., comparisons across different policy outcomes). It involves no value judgments. Normative economics involves comparisons across different outcomes where value judgments *are* made, that is, where societal benefits and costs are explicitly evaluated.

The field of economics that deals with normative economic inquiry is welfare economics (Boadway and Bruce 1989). Formally, welfare economics involves the ordering or ranking of alternative states of the world (i.e., alternative outcomes that result from different policy measures) based on a value judgment or criterion, such as *economic efficiency* or a specific social welfare function or goal. Welfare economics covers a broad field and it is in welfare economics that *externalities* are treated in addition to many of the tools to analyze public policy responses.[1] Most of the concepts of environmental economics, in turn, are derived from welfare economics.

In a public policy context, welfare economics can be extremely useful where one must make relative judgments about alternative public policies that affect society and select a "best" or a number of "bests." For example, proposed federal regulations and policies are usually examined in terms of the costs and benefits and/or economic impacts that would result from their implementation. With respect to natural resource damages, welfare economic theory and methods can be particularly useful in determining, for example, a "preferred" restoration project on the basis of its potential costs and benefits to society. To apply welfare economic techniques in a public policy context, an understanding of the relevant concepts, methods, and theory is necessary. In this chapter, we briefly discuss economic concepts and terminology that are important in the assessment of values for natural resources, services of natural resources, and measures of change in economic

activity. This will familiarize the reader with key points and issues and important terminology. Chapter 5 presents a more extensive discussion. Readers may wish to use the present chapter as a quick reference for these concepts.

2.2. Introduction to Welfare Economics

Welfare economics and its results rely on models, in particular *general equilibrium models,* that account for the behavior and actions of all individuals (e.g., consumers and producers) in an economy (Boadway and Bruce 1989, Bohm 1976, Johansson 1991, Kreps
1990, Myles 1995, Varian 1984). These models are used to determine the effect that policies, changes in market conditions, and the like (for example, the imposition of a tax) will
have on the (theoretical-hypothetical) equilibrium state. These models are necessary
because one seldom has the opportunity to conduct controlled experiments of economic
actions given variations in market scenarios, regulations and rules, prices, information,
and preference structures. Hence, economists must develop economic models and theories in an abstract world and test the models through empirical research where specific
effects and relations are isolated from all other effects.

Probably the single most important concept in welfare economics is that of *pareto
efficient (or optimal) allocation* of resources. In a perfectly competitive market structure,
in theory, pareto optimality is a powerful concept. In perfectly competitive markets all
agents (producers and consumers) are price-takers, that is individual producers and consumers have no control or influence over the price; the price is determined in the market
and given to these agents. It is further assumed that these agents act in a rational manner. The assumption in economics of rational economic behavior means that consumers
seek to attain the highest level of utility or well-being within the limits of their income,
and producers seek to maximize profits as well as minimize costs of production. Pareto
optimality involves trade or exchange between economic agents, consumers and producers, so that all are either in the same position or in improved positions and no one is in
a worse position. Therefore, in a pareto optimal allocation, producers and consumers
trade in their own best interests, and no one ends up worse off after the transaction. In
market economies with competitive behavior, the producer's profit is maximized when
price equals the extra cost of producing an additional unit of a good (this cost is known
as the marginal cost; for an explanation of *marginal value* see the glossary at the end of
this chapter). This can only occur if the value of that unit to the consumer (private marginal benefits) is equal to its cost to the producer (private marginal costs). In the absence
of market failures (e.g., externalities) private and social benefits and costs are identical;
that is, no individual firm benefits at the expense of society (e.g., by not cleaning up its
hazardous wastes and forcing society to foot the bill), and society does not benefit at the
expense of the individual.

The point of maximum profits (where price equals marginal cost) in a perfectly competitive market also has important implications regarding pareto optimal allocations. To
understand this we need to consider how prices (P) and marginal costs (MC) link the
consumer and producer together. In a general equilibrium model, the ratio of prices for
different goods can be interpreted as the rate at which consumers would trade one good
for another. These tradeoffs are made at the "margin" where economists are interested
only with how many units of good *y* (say Pepsi) are traded in return for an extra unit of

good x (say pizza), and the ratio of prices can measure such a tradeoff in the real world. In terms of production, the ratio of marginal costs can be interpreted either as the rate at which producers would trade inputs to achieve a specific level of output when inputs are the primary concern, or as the rate any two goods could be traded for one another (e.g., soda vs. pizza, here the tradeoff in costs is in terms of labor and capital used to produce both goods). As a result, the condition for profit maximization achieves equality between consumers and producers because the respective tradeoffs made by each (via the condition that the ratio of prices equals the ratio of marginal costs) achieves a pareto optimal allocation. All producers and all consumers of all goods and services are as well off as they can be.

In a perfectly competitive marketplace there is no difference between private and social measures of benefits and costs, and it therefore serves as a baseline model by which to compare all possible types of imperfections (e.g., market, price, externalities, etc.). This is the basis for the fundamental theorems of welfare economics: (1) The first fundamental theorem of welfare economics states that all competitive equilibriums are pareto optimal allocations. This coincides with a perfect competitive market outcome. Formally it refers to a situation in which perfect competitive equilibriums exist defined as a set of prices and consumption/production bundles (i.e., combinations of goods in consumption or combinations of inputs in production) where all markets clear, and an absence of departures from perfect competition (e.g., externalities). These conditions must hold for the first theorem to work; however, there is no mention about social desirability or fairness regarding pareto allocations of resources. The main point then is the efficiency of the perfect competitive market system rather than pareto optimal allocations. (2) The second fundamental theorem of welfare economics states that any pareto optimal allocation can be achieved as a competitive equilibrium given an appropriate reallocation of resources (endowments, income). The basic message of this second theorem is that given any pareto allocation (there are many possible such allocations, essentially infinite) there is a redistribution of resources (e.g., lump-sum taxes and transfers) that can achieve a pareto optimal allocation as a competitive equilibrium. Here the emphasis is placed on redistributing resources using lump-sum taxes and transfers across all agents and then letting the competitive market system work to reach an equilibrium. Since that equilibrium is reached via perfect competition, it is pareto optimal. Again, nothing said about social desires, this mainly gives weight to the idea of redistributing resources in society.

2.2.1. Prices and Distortions

In the real world there are only approximations to perfectly competitive markets; these markets in the pure sense do not exist. Distortions such as monopoly power, cartels, external effects, tariffs, and unequal or asymmetric information have effects on both competitive behavior and prices. To account for price distortions in assessments of economic value, economists have defined an ideal measure for price known as *shadow price*. The shadow price can differ from the equilibrium established market price under distorting conditions such as monopoly power, cartels, and externalities (Boadway and Bruce 1989, Mishan 1976, Sugden and Williams 1990). Shadow prices, in essence, are an attempt to represent the true or full marginal value of a good or resource. As already discussed, market prices in the presence of perfectly competitive markets will achieve pareto optimal resource allocation positions. That is, in a competitive equilibrium private marginal benefits (PMB) equal private marginal costs (PMC), social marginal benefits (SMB) equal social marginal costs (SMC), and all costs and benefits, private and social, are equal (i.e., formally stated as P = PMB = SMB = MC = PMC = SMC). This means that the economy is operating at the most *economically efficient* (or socially optimal) level of production and consumption (see Bohn 1976). Restated, neither society nor any individual in it could achieve a better operating level given their starting conditions (e.g., resource endowments and allocations).

Any deviations from competitive market structure and the free functioning of markets and prices implies that the market price will differ from the shadow price and that either the producer or the consumer is in a worse situation. For example, the presence of taxes, subsidies, price floors, price ceilings, and quantity rations, as well as institutions that restrict the level of equilibrium input prices (e.g., in the form of unions and minimum wage agreements), and imperfections in market structure in general (imperfect competitive markets in outputs and inputs), can all cause equilibrium prices to differ from prices that would be achieved under perfect competition.

2.2.2. Economic Value versus Economic Effects

In the field of welfare economics, *economic value* has a specific meaning and represents a unique, and to non-economists somewhat narrow, measure—the monetary value of *economic welfare* (well-being or satisfaction). This is also the same context and measure used in cost-benefit analysis, where net economic value represents the change in economic welfare or surplus as a result of a project (Boadway and Bruce 1989, Howe 1971, Gittinger 1972, Sugden and Williams 1990, U.S. EPA 1990). There are other monetary value measures that have from time to time been referred to as measures of economic value. For example, the market value of final goods and services produced by firms using domestic resources (gross domestic product), the value of fish landed (market price times quantity), sales and revenues of private firms (price times number of units sold), the value of inputs used in a manufacturing process (production costs); all of these measures are price times quantity measures. These kinds of measures are often confused with economic value in the popular press. In this book, however, "economic value" refers to the money value of economic welfare (or surplus). This is the meaning used in welfare economics and in environmental economics, and it is the meaning in the context of damage assessments pertaining to use values and nonuse values (i.e., compensable values) and subsequent damage awards.[2]

Economic losses and gains, in turn, represent the money value of changes in economic welfare (i.e., where, again, welfare represents a measure of well-being, satisfaction, or utility) (Boadway and Bruce 1989, Bohm 1976, Desvousges et al.1989, Freeman 1979, 1993, Johansson 1987, 1991, 1993, Just et al. 1982, Lipton et al. 1995, Mishan 1976). To consumers these losses and gains are defined in terms of changes in *consumer surplus* measures (i.e., net economic value), which refers to changes in the surplus that accrues to the consumer over and above the cost of buying the good. Technically consumer surplus or net economic value is derived as the area under a downward sloping *demand curve* above the cost to the consumer, that is the shaded area *a* in Figure 2.1.[3] In practice, net economic value to consumers is measured from changes in demand curves in which

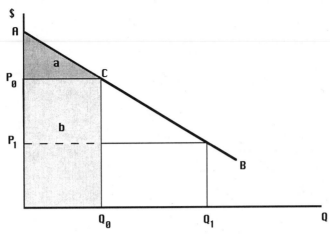

Figure 2.1
Demand Curve.

the utility to consumers from a good is held constant; these are known as compensated demand curves.

To producers (i.e., private firms, manufacturers, commercial fishermen) economic losses and gains are defined in terms of *producer surplus* measures, which represent a net economic value from production, a surplus that accrues to the producer over and above the variable costs of producing the good. In practice this is measured as the area above a *supply curve* (i.e., that portion of the marginal cost-curve above the minimum point on the average variable cost curve) or above the average variable cost curve depending on the context, up to the price received (see Chapter 5 for more detail). In Figure 2.2, producer surplus is represented by the shaded area *a* above the upward sloping supply curve, CD, and below the market price received OP_0. Figure 2.3 illustrates both demand and supply curves and the shaded area *a* represents consumer surplus, and *b* represents producer

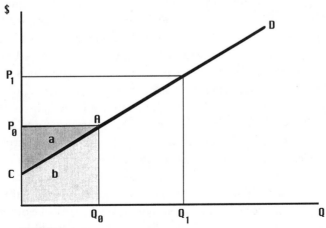

Figure 2.2
Supply Curve.

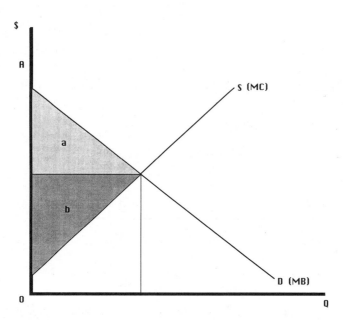

Figure 2.3
Consumer Surplus and
Producer Surplus.

surplus (this is a typical diagram in intermediate textbooks, for example, Nicholson 1997: 270). To reiterate in the strict sense of welfare economics, economic losses and gains refer to the money value of changes in economic welfare—consumer surplus measures for consumers and producer surplus measures for producers. In principle, one would sum consumer surplus over all consumers affected and producer surplus over all firms affected to estimate the total or aggregate net economic value.

But losses and gains in economic welfare are not the only change in economic activity that can occur from marine pollution. There are other impacts or effects that, in the public's opinion, should also be counted. We refer to these as economic effects (and sometimes as economic impacts or economic activity measures). These economic effects include such things as decreases in revenues and incomes to the tourism sector, decreases in the value of catch of commercial fish and shellfish, increases in production costs (for commercial fishermen, fish processors), and losses to local economies from reduced spending on goods and services as measured by multiplier effects. All of these effects represent price times quantity measures, and to the non-economist these measures are a fair accounting of economic losses attributable to pollution that economists seem to ignore. Actually, economists do not overlook these measures; rather, they approach the issue based on welfare economic criteria that involve a strict, and perhaps to others narrow, treatment of measures of economic losses, namely the monetary value of losses in welfare to an economy (i.e., sum of lost consumer surplus and producer surplus).

This is because economists assume that resources, such as labor, are mobile and can move from areas of low demand to areas of high demand (which are fundamental assumptions of general equilibrium models). In a practical sense this means that decreased spending in one sector or in a local economy will usually be offset by increased spending in another sector or in another local economy. For example, marine pollution that affects travel and use, and hence spending, at a particular site (e.g., a specific beach, water body, state, region) will result in local negative economic impacts at the polluted site that may be partially or totally offset from increased travel and use patterns at alternative clean sites. In the aggregate or at the national level we might see no appreciable change in economic effects such as spending and impacts from isolated and local marine pollution events, even though significant losses of economic welfare may have occurred at the local level.

To illustrate this point, consider the occurrence of marine pollution at a state in the Mid-Atlantic region that results in local beach closings and contaminated seafood. This may, if severe enough, cause individuals to change travel and visitation plans from local beaches in the affected state to beaches in nearby states or travel elsewhere. In terms of an analysis at the local level, negative economic impacts from lost tourism expenditures result in the affected state, while positive economic impacts are experienced in neighboring states or elsewhere. In the aggregate (i.e., at the regional or even national level) these losses and gains may partially or totally offset each other, resulting in no change in aggregate spending. Therefore, economists measure losses only by the value of lost surplus (economic welfare) that is not captured by consumer spending or by production costs. To include the monetary value of other effects and impacts (effects in addition to lost net economic value) would result in overstated measures of true economic losses. Furthermore, such a practice could possibly introduce double-counting of losses of economic activity (e.g., as in the case where both consumer expenditures and producer revenues are included).

Summation across economic effects and economic welfare is not appropriate for another reason. Economic welfare measures and measures of economic effects are different measures of gains and losses of economic activity, and adding across these measures essentially involves adding apples and oranges. In situations where economic effects occur and where there is a need to substantiate and quantify these effects, it is more appropriate to itemize the specific effects under consideration and include separate estimates of the monetary value of these effects along with estimates of the money value of economic welfare losses. Adding across effects will only add to the confusion of the true estimated monetary loss from marine pollution.

In this book we adhere to the strict measure of losses and gains in economic welfare when we refer to "economic losses and gains" from marine pollution. All other effects will be referred to as "economic effects" and itemized where they occur. This is to minimize any potential confusion that may arise, and at the same time educate the lay reader and reinforce both the approach used by economists and the strict meaning of "economic loss and gain."

2.3. Ex Ante versus Ex Post Economic Measures and Perspectives

Welfare economics poses the question, What would happen if . . . ? That is, this field of inquiry analyzes possibilities before they are (or could be) realized, before an economic change occurs. This involves the use of ex ante economic measures, all of which imply uncertainty and sometimes controversy. Most if not all publicly funded projects and many public policies are subjected to *cost-benefit analysis* (CBA) before they are approved. This is an attempt to measure costs and benefits before they are incurred and accrue, and an attempt to ensure that the greatest benefits to society from public money are possible. Some economic development projects and federal projects can take considerable time to complete; for example water resource projects in developing countries to provide irrigation, drinking water, electric power can take many years to complete (sometimes exceeding 10 years) before benefits can be attributed to the project. The CBA process must first examine the period involving project construction and estimate construction costs based on forecasts of the future cost of construction items and construction processes. It must then examine a projected time period following project completion associated with the life of the project to measure additional costs as well as contributions to economic activity and added economic benefits attributable to the completed project. This usually involves forecasts of future events, future economic activity, and economic benefits that would result with, as opposed to without, the completed project based on forecasts of future prices and costs. Hence, any analysis is only as good as its underlying assumptions and forecasts of future scenarios.

There are at least four key issues to keep in mind when using ex ante measures:

1. *There is a need to verify ex ante CBA with ex post CBA in order to assess the accuracy of ex ante CBA.* CBA is used to evaluate proposed projects. It is a tool developed by economists and policy planners to evaluate alternative investment decisions and decisions about alternative projects, usually supported by public funds. CBA is typically performed prior to any investment decision. It is based on hypothetical scenarios of what the proposed investment project is expected to achieve if completed. This scenario is in turn contrasted to a scenario without the completed project. Formally this process in CBA is referred to as a "with or without" rule, a scenario *with* the project versus a scenario *without* the project.

   It is usual practice to carefully scrutinize such analyses to verify the accuracy of the assumptions and any specific analysis used, and to perform what is known as a sensitivity analysis, in which various economic data and parameters such as interest rates, future price, and cost predictions are slightly changed, and revised CBAs are compared to a baseline or reference outcome. Oversensitivity to a single parameter change can indicate a dependency of the project's outcome to that parameter, and other factors should be incorporated into a decision regarding the project versus alternatives.

   Partly because economics is not an exact science and partly because our understanding of future economic activity is limited, and there are many assumptions and sometimes complex analyses used in cost-benefit analyses, two separate analyses should be performed, one based on an ex ante analysis (i.e., before) and the other based on an ex post analysis (i.e., after) once the project has been completed (Freeman 1993, Haveman 1972). This process serves to advance our knowledge in performing CBAs and in identifying specific assumptions or analyses that may be at fault in ex ante analyses. However, ex post analyses regarding investment decisions, public projects, and development projects are rarely performed, probably due to the costs of performing these analyses. But, especially with natural resource valuations and resource damage assessments, such a practice can be useful and can lower conflicts and expensive court and litigation time so that particular cases can be settled more expediently.

2. *The issue of uncertainty associated with future states of the world and with anticipated behavior, as in the case of proposed projects, has implications concerning the appropri-*

ate benefit measure to use. Some argue that in certain cases the appropriate ex ante benefit measure is option price *and in some other cases the expected value of contingent payments is appropriate.* A second context related to ex ante–ex post analyses in the literature concerns identification of an appropriate benefit measure with *uncertainty.* This section will alert the reader to some alternative measures of economic value that will be encountered in the literature and will help to dispel any confusion over them. Given the presence of uncertainty in assessments of economic values, the analysis to define monetary measures of economic value quickly becomes complicated and calls for somewhat complicated mathematics to express definitions and derivations. New information requirements become necessary consisting of future states of the world that can affect the good or proposed project under consideration, whether or not all individuals are similar, the type of risk facing affected individuals (collective versus individual), and the presence of insurance markets to cover risk (to allow an individual to purchase insurance for various states of the world to partially or totally reduce future potential risk). It is argued that the expected value of net benefits (i.e., expected value of *net* economic value measures) may not be an appropriate measure of benefits in the presence of uncertainty (Chavas et al. 1986, Freeman 1993, Graham 1981, Johansson 1993, Smith 1990). Furthermore, a consensus over the use of a specific economic value measure associated with uncertainty, *option value,* a value once thought to be important, has outright dismissed its importance and hence use in nonmarket good assessment (Freeman 1993, Randall 1991).[4]

3. *Nonmarket valuation techniques that obtain ex ante welfare or value measures are often subject to the criticism that such hypothetical behavior (i.e., stated preferences) will not match actual (i.e., observed) behavior or preferences.* Some economists criticize these nonmarket valuation techniques, such as contingent valuation, because they argue that such hypothetical behavior or stated preferences will not match actual (observed or revealed) behavior or preferences. Proponents of this view argue that there is no reason to believe and no evidence to support that anticipated behavior will actually result in observed behavior, and differences will usually exist. Such a view offers no support for methods and approaches based on hypothetical data and would likely dismiss the field of experimental economics outright, since it is based on hypothetical scenarios and data. In recent times experimental economics has seen considerable growth and interest among economists and has achieved important contributions to our understanding of economic processes and institutions (Davis and Holt 1993, Kagel and Roth 1995, Smith 1982).

    Rather than dismissing these approaches outright, we suspect that both views will always be with us and that there is room for approaches based on actual as well as hypothetical data. Through repeated testing and application of experimental economic methods, approaches such as contingent valuation can be refined and advanced and can contribute to our understanding of economic behavior. Due to the relative infancy of the field of experimental economics and of other techniques based on hypothetical data such as contingent valuation, we are just beginning to learn how these approaches can contribute to our understanding of economic behavior and the possibility of a link between anticipated and actual behavior. Further research is warranted.

4. *Some researchers argue that comparison studies of alternative nonmarket valuation techniques have little merit because ex ante welfare measures are not theoretically equiv-*

alent to ex post welfare measures and cannot be compared (e.g., ex ante measures from contingent valuation compared to ex post measures from travel cost demand models). This argument developed from the realization that there were faults with early comparison studies of contingent valuation (CV) with alternative approaches (Mitchell and Carson 1989). Early research proceeded on the notion that estimates of economic value from alternative nonmarket valuation methods were comparable and theoretically equal. It was reasoned that if estimates of economic value from the CV method were similar (i.e., where differences are not statistically significant) to estimates from alternative nonmarket valuation methods, this then provided evidence to support the validity of the CV method. Researchers subsequently learned that none of the alternative nonmarket valuation methods results in a superior measure of the theoretical construct (i.e., monetary value of preferences), and that researchers were often confused with the concept of validity (Mitchell and Carson 1989).

In early comparison studies correspondence of estimated welfare measures between CV methods and alternative valuation methods was interpreted as a strong form of validity, that is, criterion validity, whereby neither nonmarket valuation method results in a "truer" measure of the theoretical construct than the other; all are equal. It was subsequently learned that only a weak form of validity could be examined across alternative nonmarket valuation methods, that is, convergent validity, which examines the correspondence between economic value estimates from the alternative valuation methods. If one nonmarket valuation method could yield a superior measure of the theoretical construct, then a basis for comparisons would exist and one could examine how close estimates from alternative nonmarket valuation methods would be to those of a method that resulted in a superior measure. However, one can only establish credibility of the CV method in the sense of convergent validity. This realization weakens efforts to establish credibility of the CV method via comparison studies and underscores the need for further experimentation of the CV method.

2.4. Introduction to Environmental Economics

A concise introduction to environmental economics is included to show how the perfect competition market model is used as a reference case when it comes to measuring environmental impacts and economic losses, and to introduce the notion of optimal pollution levels and controls. Environmental economics is concerned with the application of economic theory and principles to environmental issues, namely pollution problems and quality of the environment.

2.4.1. Externality Theory

Externalities occur when the actions of primary producers or consumers have effects on other economic agents and society that the primary economic agent has ignored (Baumol and Oates 1988, Bohm 1976, Cornes and Sandler 1996, Hanley et al. 1997). Such effects in economics have been historically referred to as spillover effects, and such effects can be beneficial or detrimental. Externality theory concerns the occurrence, effects, and responses of economic agents, and the controls (e.g., instruments and incentives) that can cause an externality to become internalized, constrained, or managed. In the case of pollution, negative spillover effects result. The subsequent effect on all other agents, and to society in general, is that additional costs are borne by other agents and society such as cleanup costs, added health costs, reductions in the enjoyment of the degraded environment, and reduced visits and activities associated with polluted sites. It is important that these added costs be measured and assessed. Knowledge of the magnitude of these costs can allow public policymakers to design policies that can cause the primary agent to bear a portion or all of the costs from their activity. We use a simple example to illustrate these points.

Consider the production of paper products, or metal finishing, where a byproduct of the primary production process is the release of pollutants (e.g., both toxic and nontoxic substances) into a waterway. Downstream are other production facilities such as a beverage producer that relies on the waterway for clean freshwater as an input into canned beverages, a small city that relies on the waterway for its water supply, and recreational facilities such as parks. The occurrence of pollutants in the waterway causes the beverage plant to treat the water before it can be used as an input, and the same is true for the municipal water supply. As a result, added costs are borne by agents other than the polluter. The pollution also results in reduced enjoyment and visits at downstream recreational sites, and hence losses of economic welfare to users of these sites and associated recreational facilities. There may be a group of individuals from the city that do not visit the waterway and recreational sites but gain enjoyment from knowing that such places exist for future generations to use. Knowing that pollution is present could decrease their satisfaction and result in economic welfare losses related to *nonuse values;* these are known as *existence values.*

If the primary producer releases pollutants that are toxic to living organisms in the waterway and to humans, further costs are borne by society. Added costs can include added health costs associated with morbidity (treatment of illness) and mortality and lost welfare from injuries to the living resources. For instance, the waterway could have supported a valuable and popular, and now jeopardized, trout fishery, and a popular birdwatching site attracting common and endangered bird species that may be affected and further endangered by the toxic pollutants. Consider a more formal treatment of this scenario.

The metal finisher produces jewelry. The producer manufactures and sells the finished jewelry in a free market where the demand curve (*d*) is horizontal (i.e., perfectly elastic to indicate that the producer has no influence over the price, the producer is merely a price-taker) and represents a constant price level indicative of a perfectly competitive market. In a perfectly competitive market scenario the metal finisher maximizes profits by setting price (P) equal to its marginal costs of production (MC) and produces the quantity $0q_0$ illustrated in Figure 2.4. In the absence of externalities (i.e., a perfect market economy) the price represents the jewelry consumers' valuation of additional units (i.e., marginal increments) of the commodity jewelry. In the process the metal firm also produces an unwanted byproduct, pollution (metals and chemicals), which it discharges into the waterway. The corresponding effect on users of the waterway, its resources, and recreational activities and sites are decreases in the value (*v*) of these activities and services, as more jewelry is produced as shown in Figure 2.5. The total effect of metal finishing on jewelry consumers and on consumers of the waterway resource and its services is determined by a vertical summation of the two curves, *d* and *v*, which gives the P–*v* curve, as shown in Figure 2.6.

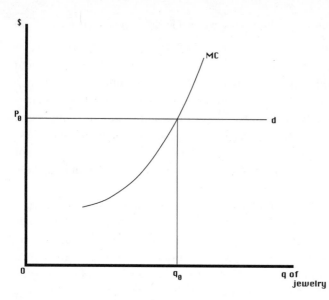

Figure 2.4
Profit Maximum Position in
Perfect Competition.

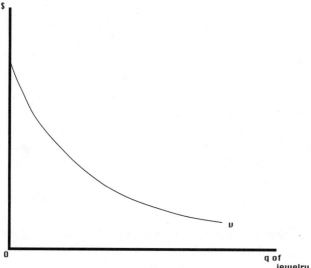

Figure 2.5
Value of Environmental Damages
from Jewelry Production.

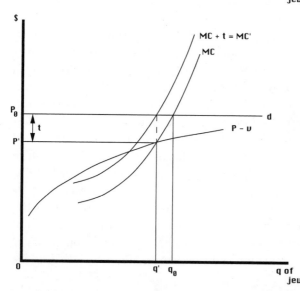

Figure 2.6
Socially Optimal Level of Jewelry
Production.

In the absence of externalities, market price represents social marginal benefits of the good and marginal cost represents social marginal costs. In Figure 2.4, the intersection of the demand and marginal cost curves represents the economically efficient production level where private marginal benefits equal private marginal costs. If there were no external effects, then this would also represent the *socially efficient* point where social marginal benefits and social marginal costs are equal. In a perfectly competitive market such a point achieves both economic efficiency and social efficiency (Bohm 1976, Rosen 1999). With external effects, the initial demand curve (*d*) no longer represents social marginal benefits, the adjusted demand curve (P-*v*) does (Figure 2.6). As a result private marginal benefits (i.e., the constant price P_0 associated with the elastic demand curve *d*) are greater than social marginal benefits, that is, all prices along the adjusted demand curve P–*v* are below P_0 (e.g., P' < P_0 at quantity 0q'); too much of the good is produced in society's view, that is, the quantity produced is in excess of that desired by society. The intersection of the adjusted demand curve (P–*v*) and the MC curve at p'q' represents the production point that is desired by society (i.e., the socially optimal or efficient level of production) and involves a smaller quantity of the good (0q' < $0q_0$). In essence, a negative externality results in production levels that exceed those socially desired, and positive externalities result in production levels below those that are socially desirable.

Knowing where such a socially optimal position is located can assist public policymakers to design policy instruments to cause polluters to internalize such spillover effects and bear the costs imposed on society. A per unit tax (i.e., a socially efficient tax) equal to the amount P_0–P' = t (where P' is the price received by the jewelry producer after the tax is paid), imposed on jewelry production will cause the MC curve to shift upward, parallel to the initial MC curve by the amount t. The result is that social marginal costs now equal private marginal costs (MC'), and in turn, equal both social marginal benefits and private marginal benefits (P_0 = P' + t) at 0q'; a smaller level of production with the presence of the externality. At 0q' economic efficiency and social efficiency coincide. This is why the perfect competitive market model is so compelling to economists.

2.4.2. Economic Efficiency

Economic efficiency can also be expressed and interpreted in terms of aggregate (market) demand and supply curves. A typical diagram used in environmental economics is a diagram of marginal benefits (MB) and marginal costs (MC) (see Field 1997). With the added assumption of perfect competition these curves in turn represent private as well as social MBs and MCs. Based on demand and supply curves, economic efficiency is expressed in the context of production of goods and services. Another context in which MB and MC curves are used concerns the optimal level of pollution reduction/control (the converse of each other) in terms of the additional benefits from reducing pollutants compared to the extra costs of doing so. The optimal level of reduction in pollution or the optimal level of pollution control is where the additional benefits from an extra unit of pollution controlled just equals its cost (or formally where MB = MC, Field 1997). In this section the same diagram (Figure 2.3) will be used in both contexts.

Individual demand-curves represent maximum amounts individuals are willing to pay to consume various quantities of a good, that is, demand curves can be thought of as marginal willing-to-pay (MWTP) curves. Aggregation of demand curves over all individuals yields an aggregate or market MWTP curve. Supply curves are derived from a producer's MC-curves above the minimum average variable cost point and summed over all producers. The aggregate supply curve then represents the marginal costs of producing various quantities of a good. In the absence of any imperfections, the demand curve measures both private and social marginal benefits, and the supply curve measures private and social marginal costs. The downward sloping demand curve, D in Figure 2.3, represents the MWTP curve as well as private and social marginal benefits. The upward sloping supply curve, S, represents both private and social marginal costs. The intersection of demand and supply curves for the market (i.e., market equilibrium) then yields the optimal level of a good to society; that is, the socially efficient level of production. Market equilibrium occurs where private and social marginal benefits are equated to private and social marginal costs (formally expressed as PMB = SMB = PMC = SMC).

Figure 2.3 can be also used to demonstrate the second context of the use of MB curves and MC curves in determining the optimum level of pollution reduction or control. In this context the demand curve, D, represents the MBs from reducing pollution (or providing pollution control) where the marginal benefits fall as increasing amounts of pollution are reduced (or MBs fall as increasing amounts of pollution control are provided) and explains why the MB curve is downward sloping. The supply curve, S, represents the MCs from reducing pollution (or providing pollution control) where the marginal costs rise as increasing amounts of pollution are reduced (or MCs rise as increasing amounts of pollution control are provided) and explains why the MC curve is upward sloping. The optimal level of pollution reduction/control is achieved where MB = MC, where the MB curve intersects the MC curve (where the demand curve intersects the supply curve).

2.5. Glossary of Economic Terminology, Measures, and Methods

2.5.1. Economic Terminology

Demand Curves. In terms of the consumer, the notion of economic value in economic theory is based on measures that involve demand curves. Demand curves can be interpreted in two different contexts. Anyone who has taken a first-year principles economics course knows that demand curves show how much of a good consumers will buy at various prices. Demand curves are derived from consumer theory on the principle that additional units of a good yield less and less satisfaction (the enjoyment from eating one steak is more than that from a second or third steak and so on), and consumers are willing to pay lower amounts for these additional units. Hence, consumers demand greater quantities of a good at lower prices, and demand curves are downward sloping (Figure 2.7). The second interpretation of demand curves is in the context of welfare economics. Demand curves show the maximum amounts individuals would be willing to pay for increasing quantities of a good. This is where the term "willingness to pay" is derived from.

Supply Curves. In terms of the producer or firm, economic value is based on measures that involve supply curves. As with demand curves there are two different contexts in which supply curves can be interpreted. Supply curves generally show how much of a

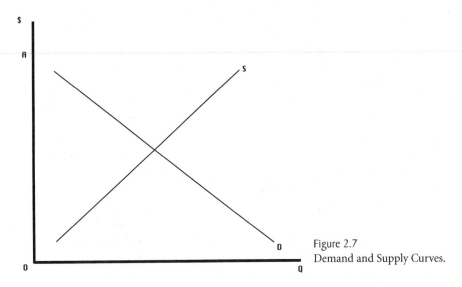

Figure 2.7
Demand and Supply Curves.

good producers are willing to produce at various prices. Supply curves are derived
from production and cost theory using the principle that additional units of a good
can only be produced at higher and higher costs reflecting the scarcity of inputs (the
additional costs are an increasing function of output). As a result, supply curves are
upward sloping (Figure 2.7). The second interpretation is in the context of welfare
economics where supply curves show the minimum amounts producers are willing to
accept for producing increasing quantities of a good.

Economic Value (Consumer Surplus, Producer Surplus). Also referred to as economic benefits in the literature, economic value is a central concept in welfare economics, cost-
benefit analysis, and Natural Resource Damage Assessments (NRDAs), however it is
often misunderstood in the popular press. It represents the monetary value of economic welfare (i.e., where welfare is well-being or satisfaction) and, with an exogenous
change (e.g., a change in behavior or policy not accounted for by the economic model)
the monetary value of changes in economic welfare. Consumer surplus represents a *net*
economic value to consumers from consuming a good, a surplus that accrues to the
consumer over and above the cost of buying the good (shaded area *a* in Figure 2.1,
shaded area *a* in Figure 2.3). It is often expressed as the difference between what a consumer would be willing to pay and what the consumer actually pays. Producer surplus
(or quasi-rent) represents a *net* economic value from production, a surplus that
accrues to the producer over and above the variable costs of producing the good
(shaded area *a* in Figure 2.2, shaded area *b* in Figure 2.3). It is often expressed as the
difference between what the producer receives (market price received) and the actual
cost of producing the good as measured by the supply curve.

Marginal Value. Simply stated marginal value reflects the additional value of an extra unit
(or marginal unit) of a good. To the consumer the marginal value of a good (or the
additional value from consuming one more unit of the good) is reflected in its price.
We can also specify the marginal net value of a good where this is the additional net
value (consumer surplus, producer surplus) from one more unit of the good.

Shadow Price. This reflects the true or full marginal value for any given good or service. It differs from the actual market price of any good or service where distortions or imperfections in markets exist. With distortions, such as taxes or monopoly power, the shadow price will differ from the established market price. With a tax, $p^* = p + t$, the price (p^*) including a tax per unit (t), then the shadow price is $p = p^*-t$. In the presence of monopoly power the effect is to result in a price higher than that determined by usual demand and supply forces. Where imperfections such as spillovers exist, the established market price will diverge from the shadow price (i.e., shadow price $<$ ($>$) equilibrium price with negative (positive) spillovers) and in these instances shadow prices are synonymous with social economic value or social benefits (i.e., the marginal value of the good to society). For example, if we were to factor in the damages caused by using a good (e.g., the use of electricity produced from hydropower plants that damage fisheries habitat, a negative externality), the shadow price would be lower than its established market equilibrium price; it would be the market price less the damage for a unit of the good purchased (if *v* is per unit damage and *p* the market price, then the shadow price is p–*v*). Conversely, in the case of goods that result in beneficial effects (e.g., the nonconsumptive good whale watching on a trip where individuals are given the rare display of multiple breachings) the shadow price will exceed the established market price, where shadow price is p + *u*, if *u* represents the per unit benefit (i.e., here consumer surplus). Given the added presence of price discounts that sometimes occur, the shadow price will equal p^*, that is, $p^* = p + d + u$, where *d* is per unit price discount, and *u* per unit benefit, and d + u would represent consumer surplus here (the consumer receives added surplus from the price discount).

Opportunity Cost. The opportunity cost is the value of a resource, good, or service in its best and most valuable use, that is, the highest possible value of a resource determined from all possible alternative uses. If the resource is labor, for example, the opportunity cost will differ depending on the skill and training of the worker. The opportunity cost a broker working on Wall Street incurs to mow his lawn is far greater than that of a hot dog vendor. The best use of a broker's time could yield him thousands of dollars, which he forgoes if he mows his lawn. Likewise, in investment decisions if the return on capital to fund a new project is compared to the opportunity cost of capital (e.g., the return on capital in the money market or from certificates of deposit), the investor can factor into his decision the opportunity cost of investing in the new project.

Externalities (Spillovers). These are either production or consumption processes that affect individuals other than the individual or entity engaged in that activity. Formally externalities are where the primary production or consumption activity has effects on society (others) that the primary economic agent (producer or consumer) has ignored. For example, spillovers from production processes constitute unwanted byproducts such as pollution that are created from the production of goods which, in turn, create unwanted effects and damages such as added health costs borne by other members of society.

General Equilibrium Models. Economic models that account for the behavior and actions of all consumers and producers in the economy are known as General Equilibrium Models (GEMs). In welfare economics, GEMs consist of simple models of two consumers with two goods and of two producers with two inputs involving barter economies (i.e., economies without prices and formalized markets) up to complex models of multiple agents and multiple sectors (e.g., consumption and production sectors combined) with prices and formalized markets. A key assumption of these models and of general equilibrium models is that all markets clear, which means that all resources (both goods and inputs) are used up.

Economic Efficiency. This is one of the more important concepts in welfare economics. There are two basic contexts in which it is used. In one context economic efficiency coincides with pareto efficiency where economically efficient allocations of resources are allocations that satisfy pareto optimal criteria. In another context, economic efficiency coincides with social efficiency (see Bohm 1976 for this usage). In market economies (i.e., economies with prices) economic efficiency is automatically achieved in perfectly competitive markets where price (i.e., marginal benefit—the additional benefit from an extra unit of the good) equals the true marginal cost (i.e., the additional cost from an extra unit of the good). When private marginal benefits and private marginal costs are equal to social marginal benefits (SMB) and social marginal costs (SMC), economic or social efficiency is achieved. In market economies with competitive behavior, the operating condition for profit maximization, where price (P) equals marginal cost (MC), P = MC, represents the equality of private marginal benefits (P) with private marginal costs (MC), and in the absence of market failures (e.g., externalities) private and social benefits and costs are identical. In other words, the condition for profit maximization coupled with an absence of market failures imply that P = SMB = MC = SMC (i.e., social efficiency occurs). Furthermore, where P = MC (profit maximization condition), a pareto optimal allocation between consumers and producers in a general equilibrium context is also achieved. Theoretically this is where the ratio of prices (P_x/P_y) for goods is equal to the rate at which consumers would trade one good for another (i.e., the marginal rate of substitution [MRS] between two goods), and the ratio of marginal costs (MC_x/MC_y) is equal to the rate at which producers would trade inputs to produce specific levels of output (i.e., the marginal rate of technical substitution [MRTS] when inputs are the primary determinant, and the marginal rate of transformation [MRT] when output or goods are the primary determinant). Formally, this condition is stated as follows, when P = MC this implies that $P_x/P_y = MC_x/MC_y$, and $P_x/P_y = MRS = MC_x/MC_y = MRT$, which only occurs as a pareto optimal allocation within a general equilibrium context.

Pareto Efficient Allocations. Pareto efficiency (optimality) is probably the single most important concept in welfare economic theory. Pareto efficient (or pareto optimal) allocations are allocations of resources such that it is not possible to improve the position of at least one economic agent (i.e., a consumer or producer) without decreasing the position of any other agent. Another way of stating the principle is to say that an allocation of resources is pareto optimal where one or more agents are made better off (i.e., improved) without anyone else being made worse off. For consumers, this implies a situation where it is not possible to increase the well-being of at least one individual from a reallocation without making any individual worse off. Pareto efficient allocations exist in pure barter economies (i.e., economies without prices) and in market economies (i.e., economies with prices).

Socially Efficient Levels. Social efficiency (also referred to as economic efficiency) is one of the more important concepts in welfare economics (see Bohm 1976). Socially efficient levels of consumption and production are levels preferred by society after all distortions and imperfections have been taken into account. In the presence of any imperfection, such as externalities or imperfect markets, the established equilibrium level will differ from the socially efficient level that is determined from perfect competitive behavior. For example, a firm that does not pay to keep its hazardous effluents within mandated levels (creating a negative externality or social cost) reduces its costs of production and creates a competitive advantage. This may result in too much of the good produced compared to a socially optimal level, at the expense of the environment. Socially efficient levels of production are determined on the basis of perfect competitive behavior and compared to models of imperfect competitive behavior. The latter results in too little of the good produced compared to the production from a firm characterized by perfect competition.

Damage Assessments. Damage assessments are assessments of the monetary losses of economic welfare (well-being) to society from damage or injury to the environment and natural resource. Damage assessments are formalized as NRDAs (see next entry).

Natural Resource Damage Assessments (NRDA). An NRDA is a formalized federal procedure to follow in the assessment of damages (i.e., economic losses) caused by injuries to natural resources as specified by federal law (either the Oil Pollution Act [OPA]–1990 or the Comprehensive Environmental Response, Compensation, and Liability Act [CERCLA]–1980/86; see Chapter 3 for more detail). It is based on lost use and nonuse values, or replacement costs, or restoration costs, whichever is less. This is the decision criteria to be followed for spills of hazardous substances, but for spills of oil, federal procedures circumvent this criteria and instead use criteria based on the lesser of replacement, or restoration, or acquisition cost of equivalent resources lost (based on the resource-to-resource approach) or equivalent services lost (based on the service-to-service approach). In all cases if a number of projects qualify as the "preferred" project, then the selection criterion becomes that project which is the least-cost (i.e., most cost-effective) to carry out. Recent advancements in the assessment procedure use compensable values and habitat equivalency analysis in determinations of replacement costs and restoration costs.

There are more terms and concepts that one needs to be aware of that are briefly described as follows:

Use Value. Net economic value derived from the use of a resource.

Nonuse Value. Net economic value that individuals derive from a resource, but that does not derive from actual use of the resource (i.e., where use is constrained to 0). It includes existence value. It is often thought of as the economic value of knowing a resource exists for others to use.

Option Price. Willingness to pay independent of state or outcome; that is, the amount an individual is willing to pay for a good/service/policy regardless of the state or outcome, formally the maximum economic value for uniform or independent contingent claims on both states affecting the good or outcome in question (see Johansson 1993).

Option Value. A nonuse value, originally defined as the value individuals would place on an option for future use of a resource above and beyond use values. Option value is now understood to be the algebraic difference between two different points on a willingness to pay locus: the expected value of consumer surplus less option price. Its use and importance in nonmarket good assessment has been dismissed in recent times.

Existence Value. A nonuse value; sometimes referred to as preservation value. A *net* economic value individuals derive from knowing that resources exist for future generations to enjoy.

Bequest Value. A nonuse value; an option value that reflects concerns across generations, especially future generations.

Total Value. The sum of use values and nonuse values.

Consumer Surplus. A net economic value (or surplus) to the consumer. Represents the (positive) difference between what a consumer would be willing to pay for a good and its actual cost to that consumer. It is measured by the area under an ordinary demand curve above the price paid. See *Economic Value.*

Producer Surplus. A net economic value to the producer; a surplus the firm realizes over and above the variable costs of the goods sold. Producer surplus represents the area above the producer's supply curve (i.e., marginal cost curve) and below the price received. See *Economic Value.*

Economic Welfare. The sum of consumer surplus and producer surplus. It represents a monetary measure of society's well-being.

Hicksian Variation Measures. Based on changes in economic welfare following price or income changes. See *Compensating Variation* and *Equivalent Variation* below.

Hicksian Surplus Measures. Based on changes in economic welfare following quantity or quality changes. See *Compensating Surplus* and *Equivalent Surplus* below.

Compensating Variation. Based on the original level of utility (i.e., the "pre-change" level) and represents the amount of compensation that must be taken away from an individual following a price or income change that would leave the consumer just as well off as before the change. In other words, it represents the maximum amount of income an individual would be willing to pay (WTP) for a price reduction.

Equivalent Variation. Uses the new level of utility (i.e., "post-change" level) as its reference point and reflects the amount of compensation that must be given to an individual in lieu of a price or income change that leaves the consumer just as well off after the change (i.e., "post-change" level). Thus, it measures the minimum amount of compensation an individual is willing to accept (WTA) to relinquish the lower price.

Compensating Surplus. The amount of money that must be taken away from an individual following a quantity increase that leaves the consumer just as well off as before the change. It represents the maximum amount of money an individual would be willing to pay (WTP) rather than give up the higher quantity.

Equivalent Surplus. The amount of money that must be given to an individual, providing the quantity change does not occur, leaving the consumer just as well off as if the change had occurred. It represents the minimum amount of money an individual is willing to accept (WTA) to forgo the higher quantity as if the change had not occurred.

Nonmarket Goods. These are a category of goods that are not sold via formal markets, hence the term "nonmarket," but possess some public good characteristics. Examples are recreation and leisure activities such as sportfishing, hunting, pleasure boating, exercise, and some sports activities. In addition the "good" environmental quality can be thought of as a nonmarket good, since it is not produced by anyone although the government implements policies to preserve its quality, and it satisfies nonexclusionary and nonrival characteristics of public goods (see *Public Goods* below).

Public Goods. Goods and services that posses the following characteristics: No one can be excluded from consuming or benefiting from the good (nonexclusionary characteristic), an individual's consumption does not reduce the amount of the good available to others (nonrival characteristic), and the extra cost of providing an additional unit of the good is zero (i.e., the marginal cost–MC is zero). Examples consist of national defense and public fire and police protection (although tax payers support these programs, which implies that these programs are not free; on a typical day the number of calls police or firefighters respond to does not affect their annual salaries and budgets, and it is in this sense that the marginal cost of providing an additional unit is zero). Pure public goods, furthermore, are not sold in the marketplace. There are public-type goods in which use is restricted, such as with member fees or entrance fees to sports facilities and parks, but once paid all members can consume as much as they want (the case of club goods). Private goods on the other hand are different. When an individual buys a good such as a can of soda, a car, or a house, the individual assumes ownership or the good becomes private property. Here the individual can exclude others from consuming the good and thereby decreases the amount available to others. Furthermore, the marginal cost of the good is nonzero; in the marketplace it is equated to the price of the good.

2.5.2. Economic Measures

There are several ways in which economists measure, represent, and conceptualize economic activity. Unfortunately, not all measures represent similar or equal economic activity, and this is one reason why economic measures are often used improperly and misquoted in the press. A clear understanding of the distinctions among measures is needed to avoid confusion.

National Income Accounting. National income accounting measures of aggregate economic activity are discussed in the press. These measures represent the total market value of all final goods and services produced in an economy for a given time period, usually a year. The measures gross national product (GNP, i.e., the value of all final goods and services produced in a country using resources located inside and outside the country) and gross domestic product (GDP, i.e., the value of all final goods and services produced in a country using resources located inside the country) are the best known. In principle these measures are equal to the price of all goods and services times the quantity produced of these goods and services. In recent times, economists have attempted to account for the full economic value of some goods such as pollution and have produced "Social Income Accounts" and "Green Accounts."

Economic Benefit. Economic benefits in the context of welfare economic theory are a measure of the monetary value of economic welfare (i.e., *net* economic value). These are associated with changes in economic welfare and represent either gains or losses in economic value to an individual or firm. Aggregate economic value is the sum of changes in the value of economic welfare to all agents involved (e.g., consumers and producers). Gross economic value to a consumer is the total welfare the consumer obtains from consuming a good. It is measured by the total area under a demand curve up to the level consumed (the shaded areas $a + b$ in Figure 2.1). Two examples will give perspective. If the good is thought of as a good meal in a restaurant and the consumer pays $19 for an exquisite seafood dish, the consumer may be willing to pay up to $25 for this meal; here expenditures are $19 (shaded area b in Figure 2.1) and consumer surplus $6 (shaded area a) yielding a *gross* economic value of $25. If the good is pizza and the consumer pays $2/slice and buys 3 slices, *gross* economic value represents the expenditure of $6 ($2 * 3) plus consumer surplus. If the consumer could have bought only one slice she might be willing to pay up to $4/slice, if only 2 slices she might be willing to pay up to $4 for the first and up to $3.50 for the second, and so on. For the case of 2 slices sold at $2/slice, expenses are $4, consumer surplus $3.50 ($2 + $1.50), and *gross* economic value $7.50.

For producers, *gross* economic value represents the total welfare from producing a good and is measured by the total area under the equilibrium price (i.e., price received here) and above the supply curve up to the level produced (shaded areas $a + b$ in Figure 2.2). In terms of Figure 2.2, the producer produces a quantity of OQ_1 units (say 5 cans of Pepsi) and receives a price of $1/can ($OP_1$). Revenues to the producer represent the price received times the quantity sold ($5 or shaded areas $a + b$ in Figure 2.2, this represents *gross* economic value). The price of $1/can also represents the minimum amount the producer must receive in order to produce 5 cans of Pepsi. However, because supply curves increase with output (due to increasing costs as more resources are used reflecting scarce resources) and represent the costs of producing more output, the producer can produce the first can of Pepsi at less than $1 (say $0.50), as well as the second can ($0.65) on up to the fourth can (e.g., $0.75–third can, $0.90–fourth can). The fifth can needed can only be produced at $1. The costs of production represented by the area under the supply curve (area b in Figure 2.2) equal $3.80 ($0.50 + $0.65 + $0.75 + $0.90 + $1.00, respectively, for the 1st, 2nd, 3rd, 4th, and 5th cans). The difference between what the producer receives and the cost of production is the surplus, shaded area a in Figure 2.2, equal to $1.20 when 5 cans are produced ($0.50 + $0.35 + $0.25 + $0.10 + 0, respectively, for the 1st, 2nd, 3rd, 4th, and 5th cans). The sum of production costs ($3.80) and producer surplus ($1.20) equal the revenue received ($5), hence profits in this simple example also equal producer surplus.

Net economic value is the same as consumer surplus to the consumer, and producer surplus to the producer, and usually represents the sum of both. That is, it is the difference between the *gross* economic value of a good or service to a consumer and the price (expenditures) of that good. For producers, it is the difference between the economic value of the good produced (i.e., market value without market failure/imperfections) and the cost to produce it.

Economic benefits in the context of cost-benefit analysis (CBA) refers to all changes in the net economic value (i.e., welfare component) that directly and indirectly result *with* a proposed project (as compared to a situation *without* the project). Within CBA, then, economic benefits represent the same measure as in an economic welfare context. However, the meaning of economic benefits has been used loosely in the past. In some cases, studies purporting to use CBA measure economic benefits to include changes in economic activity (e.g., changes in sales, income, employment, etc., i.e., nonwelfare components) in addition to the welfare component; this is not appropriate in a CBA context. In a CBA context, all benefits that result from the situation *with* the project over and above those benefits that would result *without* the project classify as total or gross benefits. All costs that result from the situation *with* the project over and above those costs that would result *without* the project classify as total costs. The difference between total benefits and total costs yields *net* economic benefits or *net* economic value, a measure identical to that in a welfare context (see Chapter 5 for further discussion). In some cases cost-savings are included as a benefit. The U.S. Army Corps of Engineers has closely followed the CBA approach and philosophy in its computation of National Economic Development (NED) benefits for water resource, flood control, and shore protection projects (Eckstein 1958, U.S. ACOE 1991).

Economic Impact Measure. Economic impact measures have been used loosely both by economists and in the popular press. The main reason is that economists approach assessments of economic impacts in two distinct ways in two different contexts: (1) they use a back-of-the-envelope approach frequently in public policy analysis or economic impact analysis, and (2) they use formal input-output economic models to evaluate direct and indirect impacts (e.g., changes to sales activities, employment) from structural changes (e.g., plant closings or openings).

A primary difference between benefit measures and impact measures is that benefit measures represent economic welfare, while impact measures represent changes of economic activity in observed markets; economic welfare is neither measured nor included in impact analyses. In the loose sense (back-of-the-envelope), impacts represent any quantifiable change in economic activity that can be attributable to a proposed action or from an actual event. Most individuals are familiar with "expenditure impacts" reported in the news media, impacts of consumer and tourism spending due to changes in policy or activity. However, in the formal sense, based on input–output models, impacts are expressed in terms of changes in sales (expenditures on goods and services), labor, and income. Many times these impacts are based on multipliers of direct effects (i.e., effects on primary and secondary sectors), to obtain indirect and induced effects. For example, a multiplier of 2.8 would imply that a change in economic activity of $5 million from a marine pollution event would result in total measurable impacts of $14 million.

2.5.3. Economic Methods

Several economic methods used to evaluate public policy issues suffer from a similar misuse in the press, and a clear understanding of the differences among them is useful.

Cost-Effectiveness Analysis. Cost-effectiveness analysis determines the minimum cost method to achieve a given objective. It ignores benefits (i.e., economic value) and does not address economic rationales for achieving a given objective. It is appropriate when considering how a project can be implemented in the least expensive way or when one or more projects achieve the same benefits. When more than one time period is involved one must express all dollar values in discounted terms. The decision criterion for cost-effectiveness analysis is to select that project with the smallest present value of costs (i.e., sum of discounted costs) over time.

Discounting. Discounting is the technique used when multiple time periods are involved to account for the difference between dollars in the present period and dollars in future periods. In practice one discounts future dollar values before summing them (e.g., for a 2-period case of $500 in both periods, the discounted value based on a discount rate of 3 percent in the second time period is computed as follows: $500/(1+0.03)^1 + 500/(1+0.03)^2$ which equals $956.73. For a project involving up to 4 time periods the discounted value is $500/(1+0.03)^1 + 500/(1+0.03)^2 + 500/(1+0.03)^3 + 500/(1+0.03)^4 = 1858.55$). Discounting is used to express future dollars in terms of present dollars. When monetary values are discounted they are also referred to as present value, because they represent the value in present terms. In some cases the monetary value may have to represent a value in future terms, referred to as future value, and instead of discounting, the value is compounded by $(1 + r)^i$ where *r* is the interest rate and *i* refers to the time period.

Cost-Benefit Analysis. Cost-benefit analysis (CBA) is the primary method by which both the benefits (i.e., economic value) and costs associated with a project are considered. In this method all benefits and all costs that occur in a situation *with* the proposed project (versus a situation *without* the proposed project) are accounted for. This results in the same measure of *net* economic benefits as if the *net* economic value for all uses that occur in a situation *with* the proposed project over and above those in a situation *without* the project were individually computed for each use and then summed over all uses, i.e., the sum of all consumer surplus and producer surplus welfare measures for the situation *with* the project versus those welfare measures that would occur *without* the project. It provides an economic rationale for the investment decision, i.e., whether the economic return (or outcome) of a project is worth the costs of achieving it. The decision criteria is to select that project that yields the maximum present value of net benefits (i.e., sum of discounted *net* economic value) over the appropriate life of the project.

Economic Impact Analysis—Public Policy Analysis. Economic impact analysis (EIA) is also referred to as regulatory impact analysis (RIA) and public policy analysis. One should think of this method of impact analysis as a "back-of-the-envelope" approach. In this context, this procedure is commonly used to analyze policy problems and proposed regulations at the federal and state levels of government to determine the effects of such actions. All quantifiable changes of economic activity in observed markets associated with a proposed action are identified and quantified.

Input–Output Analysis. This technique uses national or regional aggregate measures of economic activity such as sales revenues, income, and employment levels related to an economy defined by geographical–political boundaries (e.g., state, region, nation) that can serve as baseline conditions. The analyst then examines how changes in specific sectors (manufacturing, services, etc.), either from market events or proposed policies, affect the entire economy in question; that is, how economic activity differs from the baseline condition following a given change. I/O models, if properly applied, do not double-count economic activity measures; the value-added is summed across all components of the economy, for example, when output-sales is the relevant variable achieving a measure similar to that of national income accounts (see Section 5.2.2. for details).

2.6. Notes

1. All terms in italic type throughout this chapter are explained in a glossary at the end of the chapter
2. However, damage awards that are based solely on replacement costs, that is, the direct costs of attaining equivalent resources and services, that follow from NOAA procedures for oil spills may not be equivalent to economic value associated with their use or nonuse.
3. In graphs the convention used to measure distance along an axis is the distance from the origin to a point on one of the axes, hence the length of the distance $0q_0$ in Figure 2.1 could represent 5,000 units of jewelry.
4. There has been much debate about option price and option value (following Weisbrod 1964). The definition of option value (OV) is defined as the difference between option price (i.e., the maximum economic value for uniform or independent contingent claims on both states affecting the good or outcome in question, see Johansson [1993]) and the expected value of *net* economic value, that is OV = OP–E(WTP), where *OP* is option price, and *E(WTP)* is the expected value of net economic value (willingness-to-pay) to the consumer (see Smith and Desvousges [1986] for additional clarification). As Smith (1990) stresses only in conditions where the aggregate option price equals the sum of individual option price measures, will option price be the correct measure for individual benefits under uncertainty. Given situations of collective risk and where individuals are similar, option price is superior to the use of the expected value estimate of contingent payments (i.e., E[WTP]). In cases with individual risk and similar individuals the expected value of contingent payments associated with the fair bet point yield the largest expected value, and hence the expected value is the more appropriate measure of ex ante benefits (Graham 1981). However there are conditions that affect the use of the fair bet point as an appropriate measure of benefits. When individual risks could potentially support actuarially fair markets for contingent claims or payments, then the fair bet point becomes appropriate (Smith 1990). Using a total value framework, Randall (1991) has shown that a decomposition of compensated welfare measures (either from price or quantity changes) results in use value components and a nonuse value component, i.e., existence value. Such a result can be expressed as an aggregate measure or as a sequence of partial measures (of separate use values and existence value) of net economic value. Furthermore this result holds in the presence of uncertainty, and with uncertainty all economic values are in ex ante measures. The decomposition yields no place for other economic values such as option value, hence other economic values are not necessary in assessments of the total value of the good in question.

2.7. References

Baumol, W.J. and W.E. Oates. 1988. *The Theory of Environmental Policy.* Cambridge University Press: New York, NY.

Boadway, R.W. and N. Bruce. 1989. *Welfare Economics.* Basil Blackwell: Cambridge, MA.

Bohm, P. 1976. *Social Efficiency: A Concise Introduction to Welfare Economics.* Macmillan: London.

Chavas, J.P., R.C. Bishop and K. Segerson. 1986. "Ex Ante Consumer Welfare Evaluation in Cost-Benefit Analysis." *Journal of Environmental Economics and Management* 13: 255–268.

Cornes, R. and T. Sandler. 1996. *The Theory of Externalities, Public Goods and Club Goods.* Cambridge University Press: New York, NY.

Davis, D.D. and C.A. Holt. 1993. *Experimental Economics.* Princeton University Press: Princeton, NJ.

Desvousges, W.H., R.W. Dunford and J.L. Domanico. 1989. *Measuring Natural Resource Damages:*

An Economic Appraisal. API Publication No. 4490. American Petroleum Institute: Washington, DC.

Eckstein, O. 1958. *Water Resource Development—the Economics of Project Evaluation.* Harvard University Press: Cambridge, MA.

Field, B.C. 1997. *Environmental Economics: An Introduction.* Irwin/McGraw-Hill: New York, NY.

Freeman, A.M. 1979. *The Benefits of Environmental Improvement: Theory and Practice.* Johns Hopkins University Press: Baltimore, MD.

———. 1993. *The Measurement of Environmental and Resource Values: Theory and Methods.* Resources for the Future: Washington, DC.

Gittinger, G.P. 1972. *Economic Analysis of Agricultural Projects.* Johns Hopkins University Press: Baltimore, MD.

Graham, D.A. 1981. "Cost-Benefit Analysis under Uncertainty." *American Economic Review* 71(4): 715–725.

Hanley, N., J.F. Shogren and B. White. 1997. *Environmental Economics in Theory and Practice.* Oxford University Press: New York, NY.

Haveman, R.H. 1972. *The Economic Performance of Public Investments.* Johns Hopkins University Press: Baltimore, MD.

Howe, C.W. 1971. *Benefit–Cost Analysis for Water System Planning.* American Geophysical Union: Washington, DC.

Johansson, P.O. 1987. *The Economic Theory and Measurement of Environmental Benefits.* Cambridge University Press: New York, NY.

———. 1991. *An Introduction to Modern Welfare Economics.* Cambridge University Press: New York, NY.

———. 1993. *Cost–Benefit Analysis of Environmental Change.* Cambridge University Press: New York, NY.

Just, R.E., D.L. Hueth and A. Schmitz. 1982. *Applied Welfare Economics and Public Policy.* Prentice Hall: Englewood Cliffs, NJ.

Kagel, J.H. and A.E. Roth (eds.). 1995. *The Handbook of Experimental Economics.* Princeton University Press: Princeton, NJ.

Kreps, D.M. 1990. *A Course in Microeconomic Theory.* Princeton University Press: Princeton, NJ.

Lipton, D.W., K.F. Wellman, I.C. Sheifer, and R.W. Weiher. 1995. *Economic Valuation of Natural Resources: A Handbook for Coastal Resource Policymakers.* NOAA Coastal Ocean Program Decision Analysis Series No. 5. U.S. Dept. of Commerce, NOAA: Silver Spring, MD.

Mishan, E.J. 1976. *Cost–Benefit Analysis.* Praeger: New York, NY.

Mitchell, R.C. and R.T. Carson. 1989. *Using Surveys to Value Public Goods: The Contingent Valuation Method.* Resources for the Future: Washington, DC.

Myles, G.D. 1995. *Public Economics.* Cambridge University Press: New York, NY.

Nicholson, W. 1997. *Intermediate Microeconomic Theory and Its Application.* Dryden Press: Orlando, FL.

Randall, A. 1991. "Total and Nonuse Values." In Braden, J.B. and C.D. Kolstad (eds.). *Measuring the Demand for Environmental Quality.* North Holland: New York, NY: 303–321.

Rosen, H.S. 1999. Public Finance. Irwin, McGraw-Hill: New York, NY.

Smith, V.K. 1987a. "Nonuse Values in Benefit Cost Analysis." *Southern Economic Journal* 54: 19–26.

———. 1987b. "Uncertainty, Benefit-Cost Analysis, and the Treatment of Option Value." *Journal of Environmental Economics and Management* 14: 283–292.

———. 1990. "Valuing Amenity Resources under Uncertainty: A Skeptical View of Recent Resolutions." *Journal of Environmental Economics and Management* 19: 193–202.

Smith, V.K. and W.H. Desvousges. 1986. *Measuring Water Quality Benefits.* Kluwer–Nijhoff Publishing: Boston, MA.

Smith, V.L. 1982. "Microeconomic Systems as an Experimental Science." *American Economic Review* 72(5): 923–955.

Sugden, R. and A. Williams. 1990. *The Principles of Practical Cost–Benefit Analysis.* Oxford University Press: New York, NY.

U.S. Army Corps of Engineers. 1991. *National Economic Development Procedures Manual—An Overview Manual for Conducting National Economic Development Analysis.* IWR Report 91-R-11. Fort Belvoir, VA.

U.S. Environmental Protection Agency. 1990. *The Economics of Improved Estuarine Water Quality: An NEP Manual for Measuring Benefits.* EPA 503/5-90-001. Office of Policy, Planning, and Evaluation: Washington, DC.

Varian, H.R. 1984. *Microeconomic Analysis.* W.W. Norton & Co.: New York, NY.

Viscusi, W.K. 1992. *Fatal Tradeoffs: Public and Private Responsibilities for Risk.* Oxford University Press: New York, NY.

Weisbrod, B.A. 1964. "Collective-Consumption Services of Individual-Consumption Goods." *Quarterly Journal of Economics* 78: 471–477.

CHAPTER 3

Federal Legislation and Rulemaking: Marine Pollution and Economic Methods

3.1. Introduction

There are two areas in which federal initiatives are important in this book. One area concerns federal legislative efforts to manage hazardous/toxic substances in the environment and specifically in marine waters. This will be briefly discussed below. The other area is federal rulemaking pertaining to economic analysis of federal projects. This is embodied in a set of recommended uniform procedures to assess benefits and costs from federal construction projects that grew out of water resource development–river basin planning efforts (e.g., navigation, flood control, hydro power), and more recently to assess economic losses that result from spills of hazardous substances and oil and petroleum substances in waterways (i.e., Natural Resource Damage Assessment [NRDA] procedures). While other initiatives such as state legislation can affect the control of hazardous/toxic substances in the environment we only examine those at the federal level and note that in some cases state legislation can be more progressive than federal legislation and vice versa.

The purpose of this chapter is to provide a brief review of the federal laws applicable to the discharge of substances (all types) into the marine environment, their history, and the motivation behind them, as well as to survey and describe the motivation behind the development of a uniform set of recommended procedures for economic analysis of federal projects and resource damage assessments. Concerning the latter we provide an overview of the salient points and procedural steps along with a brief conclusion. We also discuss a federal initiative to address water quality issues of nationally significant estuaries, the relatively new National Estuary Program of the U.S. Environmental Protection Agency (U.S. EPA).

3.2. Federal Hazardous Substances Legislation

Federal efforts to manage hazardous/toxic substances consist of a variety of federal laws and statutes. These federal efforts date back to the creation of the U.S. EPA in June 1970, when this entity was given ultimate control of the protection of environmental quality. It was charged with overseeing, controlling, and implementing specific federal environmental legislation. Prior to the U.S. EPA, the Federal Water Pollution Control Authority, created by the Federal Water Pollution Control Act of 1956, was the sole body responsible for mitigating water pollution. The legislative acts relevant to water pollution are:

- Federal Water Pollution Control Act (33 U.S.C. 1251 et seq., Public Law 92-500) first enacted in 1972 and subsequently amended in 1977 (P.L. 95-217), 1987 (i.e., Water Quality Act of 1987, P.L. 100-4) known collectively as the Clean Water Act (CWA)
- Marine Protection, Research, and Sanctuaries Act (33 U.S.C. 1401 et seq., P.L. 92-532) enacted in 1972, amended in 1974 so as to be consistent with the London Dumping Convention, and in 1988 by the Ocean Dumping Ban Act (P.L. 100-688)
- Comprehensive Environmental Response, Compensation, and Liability Act (42 U.S.C. 9601 et seq., P.L. 96-510) of 1980, and amended in 1986 by the Superfund Amendments and Reauthorization Act (P.L. 99-499)
- Oil Pollution Act (33 U.S.C. 2701 et seq., P.L. 101-380) of 1990
- Toxic Substances Control Act (15 U.S.C. 2601 et seq., P.L. 94-469) first enacted in 1976 has been amended three times, and now includes four Acts: the Control of Toxic Substances–Title I, the Asbestos Hazard Emergency Response Act–Title II, the Indoor Radon Abatement Act–Title III, and the Residential Lead-Based Paint Hazard Reduction Act
- Resource Conservation and Recovery Act (42 U.S.C. 6901 et seq., P.L. 94-580) of 1976 amended a previous act known as the Solid Waste Disposal Act, and was subsequently amended in 1984 by the Hazardous and Solid Waste Amendments
- Low-Level Radioactive Waste Policy Amendments Act (42 U.S.C. 2021(b) et seq.)
- Food and Drug Administration's regulation and control of hazardous substances via action levels of poisonous or deleterious substances in human food and animal feed, which further identifies specific poisonous or hazardous substances pertaining to consumption

For the purposes of marine pollution, the following federal legislation and regulatory stipulations have the most bearing and are discussed in greater detail: Clean Water Act; Marine Protection, Research, and Sanctuaries Act of 1972 and the Ocean Dumping Ban Act of 1988; Comprehensive Environmental Response, Compensation, and Liability Act of 1980; Oil Pollution Act of 1990; Toxic Substances Control Act of 1976; Resource Conservation and Recovery Act of 1976; and the Food and Drug Administration's Action Levels.

3.2.1. Water Quality—Clean Water Act (CWA)

The Clean Water Act (CWA) as it is now known, has been around for some time (Dolin 1990, Evans 1997, Freeman 1990, U.S. Congress, OTA 1987, Ward and Duffield 1992). The Federal Water Pollution Control Act of 1948 (Public Law 80-485) was the first federal legislation that addressed the control of water pollution. It was subsequently amended in 1956 by the Federal Water Pollution Control Act (P.L. 84-660), which established the Federal Water Pollution Control Authority as the overseer. Then in 1965 the Water Quality Act (P.L. 89-234) was passed. It required states to establish standards and develop plans to meet those standards. These early federal actions and federal agencies followed a decentralized logic whereby the individual states assumed responsibility and were required to establish pollutant thresholds and manage and monitor the discharge of pollutants into the states' waterways, including the territorial seas (i.e., marine waters up to 3 miles from the mean low water line). It is generally agreed that this first variant of the CWA adopted a "laissez-faire" approach, and as a result the nation's and states' water bodies suffered water quality degradations.

In 1970 the Water Quality Improvement Act was enacted, partly in response to overall deteriorating water quality throughout the nation, and partly in response to an oil spill/discharge near Santa Barbara, California, from a pipe rupture in an offshore oil rig (Ward and Duffield 1992). The 1970 act contained provisions for the recovery of response costs of oil spills into navigable waters. It was subsequently revised in 1972 as the Federal Water Pollution Control Amendments–FWPCA (P.L. 92-500) and it is this version that is referred to as the Clean Water Act (CWA). In 1977 it was revised and amended by the Federal Water Pollution Control Act Amendments (P.L. 95-217) containing Section 311 provisions regarding liability of discharges of hazardous substances and/or oil into U.S. navigable waters and cost recovery of these discharges. Cost recovery included actual costs incurred for the removal of the substance (i.e., hazardous substance and/or oil), and costs incurred for the restoration or replacement of natural resources damaged and/or destroyed by the discharge of the substance into navigable waters. In 1987, the act was again amended as the Water Quality Act of 1987 (P.L. 100-4) and included a provision for the creation of the National Estuary Program to be administered by the U.S. EPA. Hazardous substances now regulated by the CWA now number 126 (40 C.F.R. Ch. I, Sect. 131.36).

The Water Quality Act of 1987 also revised financial limits concerning penalties and cost recovery (Ward and Duffield 1992, 33 U.S.C. Sect. 1321). It stipulated that the liability for an owner-operator of an inland oil barge (i.e., a non–self-propelled vessel carrying oil certified to operate in the inland waters of the United States) not exceed $125 per gross ton or $125,000, whichever is greater. For any other vessel carrying oil or a hazardous substance, liability was set at $150 per gross ton or $250,000, whichever is greater. And liability for owner-operators of an onshore/offshore facility was not to exceed a maximum of $50 million. These liability limits do not apply if the spill or discharge can be shown to be the result of willful negligence or willful misconduct on the part of the owner-operators responsible. Then the full amount of the actual costs of restoration can be sought. In addition to the above liability, owners-operators may face civil penalties (class I and/or class II civil penalties) resulting from spills or discharges of hazardous wastes or oil. Present limits on civil penalties via CWA were amended by the Oil Pollution Act (OPA) of 1990 and are a maximum penalty of $25,000 for a class I civil penalty and a maximum of $125,000 for a class II penalty (33 U.S.C. 2701, Sect. 4301). Furthermore additional penalties can be assessed due to failure to notify the appropriate agency of the state or federal government and failure to report a spill or discharge of oil or a hazardous substance. Such failure to report can result in a fine or imprisonment up to a maximum of 5 years (33 U.S.C. 2701, Sect. 1403).

Two laws were subsequently passed, the Comprehensive Environmental Response, Compensation, and Liability Act (CERCLA) in 1980 and OPA in 1990, that superseded the CWA regarding cost recovery of discharges of hazardous substances and oil, respectively. These new laws were written so that if a conflict between CERCLA and CWA were to arise, CERCLA would apply. And for any discharges of oil on or after August 18, 1990, OPA applies; CWA applies to pre-August 18, 1990, oil spills not covered by CERCLA. It is also possible that in the case of mixed spills or discharges (e.g., oil and hazardous substances) more than one law can prevail, e.g., both CERCLA and OPA.

3.2.2. Transportation and Ocean Dumping of Wastes (MPRSA [ODA])

The Marine Protection, Research, and Sanctuaries Act (MPRSA) of 1972 (Public Law 92-532) regulates and manages the transportation, disposal, and dumping of nondredged material such as sewage sludge, and of dredged material such as material dredged from deepening navigation channels into the territorial sea (i.e., 0–3 nautical miles), the contiguous zone (i.e., 3–12 nautical miles), and beyond these limits into the open ocean (U.S. Congress, OTA 1987, 33 U.S.C. 1401 et seq.). It has since become known as the Ocean Dumping Act (ODA). Any material that can adversely affect human health, the health of the marine environment, or the economic potential of the ocean is regulated under this act. Several federal agencies were given jurisdiction over ocean dumping; the National Oceanic and Atmospheric Administration (NOAA) and U.S. EPA have administration over ocean dumping of nondredged material, while the U.S. Army Corps of Engineers (ACOE) has administration over ocean dumping of dredged material. In addition, the MPRSA of 1972 required that the U.S. Department of Commerce (DOC) initiate and continue a comprehensive program of monitoring and research of the effects of dumping materials into ocean waters.

Congress amended this act in 1977 (P.L. 95-153) and imposed a statutory deadline to end ocean dumping of all sewage sludge by December 31, 1981 (U.S. Congress, OTA 1987, USCCAN 1988, 33 U.S.C. 1412a). However, municipalities in the New York metro area argued that they could not develop sufficient alternative plans by this date. The U.S. EPA tried to force New York City (the largest of these municipalities) to end ocean dumping of sewage sludge in 1981, the city sued the U.S. EPA and a federal court ruled in favor of the city (*City of New York v. EPA* 543 F. Supp. 1084, S.D.N.Y. 1981). The U.S. EPA did not appeal this decision. Federal legislation was introduced to reverse this decision and end sludge dumping at the 12-mile dumpsite in the New York Bight. Prompted by this action, the U.S. EPA promulgated a decision on April 1, 1985, to close the 12-mile dumpsite and move sewage sludge dumping to a new offshore site, the 106-Mile Ocean Waste Dump Site commonly referred to as the 106-mile dumpsite (also known as the Deepwater Municipal Sludge Site). In 1986, Congress passed the Water Resources Development Act (P.L. 99-962) that amended previous versions of MPRSA (33 U.S.C. 1414a). It stipulated that on December 15, 1987, the 12-mile dumpsite would be officially closed to sewage sludge dumping, which subsequently began at the 106-mile dumpsite on March 17, 1986, and ended at the 12-mile dumpsite on December 31, 1987 (USCCAN 1988).

The Ocean Dumping Ban Act of 1988 (P.L. 100-688) subsequently amended all previous federal ocean dumping statutes pertaining to the dumping of nondredged material (33 U.S.C. 1401); it phased out sewage sludge dumping at the 106-mile dumpsite by December 31, 1991, and it mandated that the governors of New York and New Jersey report annually to the U.S. EPA on progress toward a plan to develop alternative management and treatment of sewage sludge to replace ocean dumping, along with a scheduled phase out of ocean dumping. Furthermore it contained substantially revised penalties and civil penalties for not complying with the 1991 deadline. Prior civil penalties were limited to $50,000 per violation. In the case of New York City, it was estimated that the annual cost of operations and maintenance and the debt service from a land-based alternative could approach $60 million per year compared to a maximum civil penalty of $15 million if it continued to dump sludge 300 times a year (approximately 3.6 million wet tons). In this case there was insufficient financial incentive to cause the city to abide by the 1991 deadline, hence new penalties were subsequently set that would result in penalties to New York City from $72 million to $144 million per year if it continued such practice. Specific fees were set at $100 per dry ton (or equivalent) of sewage or industrial waste for violations up to January 1, 1990, $150 per dry ton after January 1, 1990, and up to January 1, 1991, and $200 per dry ton after January 1, 1991, and up to January 1, 1992. Civil penalties were also stipulated for violations and set at $600 per dry ton (or equivalent) for any sewage and industrial waste dumped in calendar year 1992. Thereafter, for any violation the civil penalty was set to equal the amount of the penalty per dry ton that occurred in the previous calendar year plus 10 percent of such amount plus 1 percent of such amount for each calendar year since December 31, 1991 (33 U.S.C. 1401, Sect. 1002). Specific trust accounts were designated to receive these penalties and specific uses were stipulated, such as reimbursement of costs incurred for issuing permits for sludge dumping, costs of any environmental assessment of the direct effects of dumping related to the permits, Coast Guard surveillance of transportation and dumping activities, and monitoring, research, and related activities.

In 1992 sludge dumping ceased at the 106-mile dumpsite. New York City was one of the last municipalities that continued sludge dumping after the 12-mile dumpsite was closed; it entered into a consent decree and enforcement agreement with the U.S. EPA on August 10, 1989, to cease sludge dumping on June 30, 1992 (Hunt et al 1996, Martin 1991). In addition to a timed phase out of ocean dumping of sewage sludge, the Ocean Dumping Ban Act of 1988 also contained amendments that addressed the disposal and dumping of medical wastes in ocean waters. Maximum civil penalties were set at $125,000 per violation, and criminal penalties were established up to a maximum of $250,000 per violation and/or imprisonment up to five years, and any property used in committing the violation would be forfeited to the U.S. government (33 U.S.C. 1401, Sect. 3201).

3.2.3. Brownfields—Contaminated Sites (CERCLA)

The Comprehensive Environmental Response, Compensation, and Liability Act (CERCLA) was enacted in December 1980 (P.L. 96-150) as a means to clean up the nation's most contaminated sites (mainly former industrial sites and properties, referred to as brownfields [Smary and Dewitt 1997]) and from public outrage over incidents such as Love Canal near Niagara Falls, New York (U.S. DOI 1994a, 1996a, 42 U.S.C. 9601 et seq.). It is administered by the U.S. EPA. CERCLA was designed to handle the discharge of hazardous substances and to address cleanup of highly contaminated sites, and it was the first act associated with uniform procedures used to assess natural resource damages that were subsequently developed and promulgated by the U.S. Department of the Interior

(DOI) (Anderson 1993, Bacher 1993, Campbell 1993, Dower and Scodari 1987, Evans 1997, Helton 1993, U.S. Congress, OTA 1987, U.S. DOI 1986, 1987, Ward and Duffield 1992).[1] CERCLA was subsequently amended in 1986 by the Superfund Amendments and Reauthorization Act (SARA), and now these highly contaminated sites are referred to as Superfund sites (e.g., New Bedford Harbor is designated as one such site, which has settled for $99.6 million in damages from hazardous substances discharge) (42 U.S.C. 9601). The term "Superfund" refers to a fund generated from taxes on the petroleum, chemical, and waste disposal industries. The U.S. EPA can use this fund to (1) pay for cleanups, (2) pay for U.S. EPA enforcement actions to monitor private-party cleanups, and (3) recover response costs from responsible parties (Hockley and Martin 1997). To avoid overlap and duplication with the CWA the following rule was used: Where CERCLA and the CWA are in conflict, provisions are such that CERCLA shall apply. And oil not covered by CERCLA is covered by OPA 1990.

CERCLA was designed to cover discharges of hazardous substances (i.e., all substances regulated under CWA, the Toxic Substances Control Act (TSCA), the Resource Conservation and Recovery Act (RCRA), Clean Air Act, and CERCLA, which now exceed several hundred in number [40 C.F.R. Sect. 302, Table 302.4 1996]), and some petroleum, including crude oil that had been designated as a hazardous substance under any of the above federal environmental statutes, including subsequent amendments (i.e., "hazardous substance" does not include petroleum, crude oil, or any fraction thereof, *which is not otherwise specifically listed or designated* as a hazardous substance under other federal statutes [42 U.S.C. Sect. 9601(14)]). It excludes other petroleum not so designated as a hazardous substance under the above federal statutes. This exclusion is referred to as the "petroleum exclusion."

Interpretation and application of the petroleum exclusion has been a controversial issue, and one must be careful in its application (Bacher 1993, Hockley and Martin 1997). The U.S. EPA has interpreted this exclusion as follows and courts appear to agree with this interpretation: Where hazardous substances have been mixed with or added to crude oil in the refining process or are indigenous to petroleum, the petroleum exclusion shall apply and these substances are not covered by CERCLA (OPA now covers this type of oil-petroleum). Petroleum that contains hazardous substances that have been added to or have increased in concentration from the use of oil (e.g., oil waste), from storage or any reason other than from the normal refining process is covered by CERCLA; the petroleum exclusion does not apply in these cases. Furthermore, the courts have taken this a step further based on communication with the U.S. EPA in the case of a "mixed spill." Where oil is contaminated with any amount of a hazardous substance the spill or discharge of the multiple substance may be covered under CERCLA (i.e., is "so commingled that ... they [i.e., oil and the hazardous substance] cannot be separated, the entire spill is governed under CERCLA," clarification added [Bacher 1993, Hockley and Martin 1997, U.S. EPA 1987]).

CERCLA established liability of potentially responsible parties from spills/discharges of hazardous substances into or upon the navigable waters of the United States including the territorial seas (i.e., ocean waters from mean low water to 3 nautical miles) and adjoining shorelines, waters of the contiguous zone (i.e., 3–12 nautical miles), or which may affect natural resources belonging to or under U.S. management, including natural resources within the exclusive economic zone (i.e., ocean waters up to 200 nautical miles) established by the Fishery Conservation and Management Act of 1976 (U.S.DOI 1994a, 1996a, 42 U.S.C. 9601, Sect. 1004). Such parties are liable for all removal and necessary response costs incurred, and damages to natural resources including reasonable assessment costs. This liability has become referred to as the sum of removal costs, compensable value from damages, and the reasonable costs of assessment.

Probably the most significant aspect of CERCLA was that it required the promulgation and development of a set of uniform procedures for use in assessing natural resource damages for the first time. Up to this point in time no such procedures existed. When Congress passed CERCLA it gave the U.S. DOI the responsibility to develop, promulgate, and implement uniform procedures to assess natural resource damages and to revise these procedures every two years (U.S. DOI 1986, 1987, 1994b, 1996b). In developing the procedures, two specific rules were formulated by the U.S. DOI associated with two discharge categories: small or less significant discharges and large or significant discharges (U.S. DOI 1986, 1987, 1994a, 1996a). These rules are known as type A rules for small spills or discharges and type B rules for large spills or discharges. Dollar limits are set for damage recovery for spills or discharges of hazardous substances. Spills or discharges from any facility are not to exceed $50 million relating to resource damages. As with the CWA, if such spills or discharges of hazardous substances can be shown to be the result of willful negligence or willful misconduct or caused by a violation of relevant safety, construction, or operating standards or regulations, the above limits on damage recovery are not applicable and the full amount of damages can be sought from the responsible party (42 C.F.R. Sect. 9607, Ward and Duffield 1992).

The Superfund amendments to CERCLA amended the limits of liability toward potentially responsible parties and penalties and established civil penalties as well (42 U.S.C. 9601, Sects. 107, 109). Limits on liability for any potentially responsible party were set at a maximum of (1) for any vessel that carries a hazardous substance as cargo or residue, the larger of $300 per gross ton or $5 million, (2) for any other vessel the larger of $300 per gross ton or $500,000, (3) for pipelines from $5 million to $50 million, and (4) for any facility the sum of all response costs plus $50 million. As in the case of CWA, if it can be shown that a spill or discharge was the result of willful neglect or willful misconduct or if potentially responsible parties fail or refuse to provide reasonable cooperation and assistance, the above liability limits do not apply and the liability is set at the full costs of removal plus damages in addition to the above preset limits. Furthermore, any claim that is authorized by Section 107 or 111 can be asserted directly against any guarantor that provides evidence of financial responsibility for a vessel and or facility. The limit of liability for any guarantor was set to equal the aggregate amount (sum) of the monetary limits of the following: insurance policy, guarantee, surety bond, letter of credit, or similar instrument obtained from the guarantor. Punitive damages also apply in the case where the person or party responsible fails to properly provide removal or remedial action if requested by presidential order (such as an Executive Order), an amount equal to the amount of any costs incurred by the Hazardous Substance Response Fund due to response activities up to a maximum of three times the amount of these costs.

Penalties from failure to notify appropriate government agencies of a spill or discharge, destruction of records, and false information were amended in 1986 to be punishable by imprisonment up to a maximum of 3 years (up to 5 years for a second or subsequent violation). Civil penalties were amended to include a class I penalty with a maximum of $25,000 per violation, a class I penalty with a maximum of $25,000 per day for each day the violation continues, and a judicial assessment for the purpose of assessment and collection of a penalty of a maximum of $25,000 per day for each day the violation (or failure or refusal) continues (a maximum of $75,000 per day for a second or subsequent violation).

3.2.4. Oil Spills (OPA)

Almost everyone in the United States has witnessed the publicity surrounding the *Exxon Valdez* oil spill in Prince William Sound, Alaska. This oil spill occurred on March 24, 1989, and involved 11 million gallons of Alaska crude oil. It is the largest oil spill to have occurred in U.S. waters. Later in 1989 another oil spill occurred in U.S. marine waters; the *Apex Houston* released crude oil in San Francisco Bay. In 1990 four additional oil spills occurred in U.S. marine waters, the *Nautilus* spill in the Kill Van Kull of New Jersey and New York, and within a 24-hour period, the *World Prodigy* oil spill in Rhode Island waters, the *Presidente Rivera* oil spill in the Delaware River, and the *Apex Galveston* oil spill in the Houston Ship Channel (U.S. DOC, NOAA 1996a, 1996b, Ward and Duffield 1992). The OPA of 1990 (P.L. 101-380) was enacted in direct response to these oil spills and was signed into law by President Bush (33 U.S.C. 2701). It defined the extent of liability of oil spills and discharges into or upon U.S. navigable waters, the territorial seas (i.e., to include ocean waters measured from the point of mean low water up to 3 nautical miles) and adjacent shorelines, and the exclusive economic zone (i.e., including ocean waters from territorial seas up to 200 nautical miles) (U.S. DOC, NOAA 1996, 33 U.S.C. 2701, Sect. 1002). OPA was designed to cover oil not already designated as a hazardous substance, which CERCLA covers, and applies to oil spills and discharges after August 18, 1990; prior to this date CWA applied. Similarly to CERCLA, it required the development and promulgation of specific procedures by NOAA, the responsible federal agency, for use in assessing natural resource damages attributable to oil spills. These procedures were published in 1996 (U.S. DOC, NOAA 1996a, 15 C.F.R. 990) and have been the source of much controversy.

In general, OPA provided for the liability for removal costs and damages resulting from an oil spill or discharge for responsible parties (owner-operators) (33 U.S.C. 2701, Sect. 1002). This liability is now treated as the sum of response costs incurred (i.e., removal costs), compensable value, and the reasonable costs of assessment. Limits on liability were also stipulated in OPA. The total of the liability of a responsible party is set at a maximum for a tank vessel of $1200 per gross ton or for a vessel greater than 3,000 gross tons $10 million or for a vessel smaller than 3,000 gross tons $2 million, whichever is greater. For any other vessel, maximum liability is set at the greater of $600 per gross ton or $500,000. For an offshore facility total liability is set at the sum of $75 million plus all removal costs, and for onshore facilities and deepwater ports maximum liability is not to exceed $350 million (33 U.S.C. 2701, Sect. 1004). The exceptions to this liability limit are: (1) if it can be shown that the spill was the result of willful gross negligence or willful misconduct or the violation of applicable federal safety, construction, or operations regulation; (2) if the responsible party fails or refuses (a) to report the spill incident where the responsible party knows or has reason to know of the incident, (b) to provide all reasonable cooperation and assistance requested pertaining to removal, or (c) does not comply with an order under other federal statues (CWA as amended by OPA, Intervention on the High Seas Act); and (3) for spills from Outer Continental Shelf facilities or vessels carrying oil as cargo from such facilities. In these cases the above liability limits do not apply and the full costs of recovery and damage can be sought.

The litigation of the *Exxon Valdez* oil spill involved widely varying assessments of damages and liability. This put economic analysis under a microscope. Several nonmarket valuation techniques used in the assessments, contingent valuation (CV) in particular, received a great deal of criticism and caused a split in the economics profession. As economists soon learned, litigation often involves pitting professionals against one another, as well as their research techniques and valuation methods. An economic valuation technique on shaky footing can become highly controversial in a court case. CV was highly criticized in terms of its assumptions, applications, and damage estimates with the result that it lost much credibility; to some researchers it has no bearing (Hausman and Diamond 1993). Nonetheless, a large number of economists are working to reestablish credibility of the CV method. This process could involve extensive experimental economics studies followed by field testing and applications. Only when the CV method has received acceptance through testing will it again be a valuable and useful tool in the field. Until then it will remain highly controversial, especially in litigation.

3.2.5. Toxic Substances (TSCA)

The Toxic Substances Control Act (TSCA) of 1976 (P.L. 94-469) was specifically designed to address the manufacture, processing, distribution, use, and disposal of manufactured chemicals (Brown and Johnston 1997, Shapiro 1990, 15 U.S.C. 2601). It is not a "cradle-to-grave" law (i.e., it does not cover substances from manufacture to disposal); it is designed to force the chemical industry to inform the U.S. EPA of what it is manufacturing. If a substance (i.e., individual chemical or mixture of chemicals) is potentially harmful to human health or the environment (i.e., poses a risk to human health or to the environment), the U.S. EPA must conduct studies and review industry studies to determine if the specific substance poses unacceptable risk. If so, the substance may undergo a regulatory action. There are more than 60,000 chemicals presently on the TSCA inventory; a number that could exceed effective management. For example, data limitations and deficiencies were found to exist for substances on the TSCA inventory from a sample of toxicity data conducted by the National Academy of Sciences (NAS 1984). However, progress has been made concerning specific chemical products and/or their variants such as asbestos, chlorofluorocarbon propellants, dioxin, hexavalent chromium, PCBs (banned by the TSCA when passed in 1976), certain metal-working fluids, lead-based paint, radon, and possibly formaldehyde (Brown and Johnston 1997, Shapiro 1990).

3.2.6. Solid and Hazardous Wastes Disposal (RCRA)

The Resource Conservation and Recovery Act (RCRA) of 1976 (P.L. 94-580) was enacted to deal with the generation and eventual disposal of solid and hazardous wastes (Dower 1990, 42 U.S.C. 6901). This legislation controls the handling and final deposition of solid and hazardous waste products in accepted or approved waste storage facilities. It was designed as a "cradle-to-grave" regulatory action for the generation, transport, treatment, storage, and disposal of hazardous wastes. It is meant to manage and control hazardous wastes once deposited at accepted sites. If hazardous substances infiltrate (immigrate) to waterways, it is a violation of RCRA, and subsequent laws such as CERCLA and OPA may apply concerning discharges into such waterways.

3.2.7. Food and Drugs

Besides the U.S. EPA, the Food and Drug Administration (FDA) of the U.S. Department of Health and Human Services (U.S. DHHS) has regulatory responsibility over various hazardous substances that have been found in edible human food and in animal feed (U.S. DHHS, FDA 1992). In amounts above the action level that the FDA has established, the FDA has authority to take legal action to remove the products from the market (40 C.F.R. 180.34[f]). Even in cases where an action level has not been established, the FDA can still pursue legal action based on a minimal detectable level of the contaminant. For fish products the FDA has established action levels for the substances aldrin and dieldrin, chlordane (including its residue products), chlordecone (or its tradename Kepone), DDT, DDE, and TDE, endrin, heptachlor and heptachlor epoxide, mercury, mirex, and toxaphene (U.S. DHHS, FDA 1992). For crabmeat products an FDA action level was established for chlordecone (Kepone). And for shellfish products, action levels have been established for chlordecone (Kepone), mercury, and paralytic shellfish toxin.

3.3. Water Resource Development and River Basin Planning

3.3.1. Introduction

The experience and knowledge gained from water resource development and river basin planning efforts and from uniform federal procedures to follow helped in the process of developing a similar set of rules and procedures for the assessment of economic losses that are now applicable to marine damage assessments. Benefit-cost guidelines and economic analyses were a key part to the federal government's role in developing water resources in the United States as early as the early 1800s (Eckstein 1958, Graves 1995, Holmes 1972). The purpose of projects then was to improve water transportation and navigation. This was expanded to include the provision of water supply for irrigation (mainly in western states), flood control, and electric power generation tied to electrification programs in the United States federal agencies involved include the U.S. ACOE for the areas of navigation, flood control, and power generation; the U.S. DOI, Bureau of Reclamation for the areas of irrigation and power generation; and the Federal Power Commission (FPC) for the marketing of hydroelectric power from U.S. ACOE projects.

3.3.2.1. U.S. Army Corps of Engineers

The U.S. ACOE became the first federal agency given sole responsibility over maintaining the nation's waterways and harbors. Efforts were primarily directed to improvements in water transportation and navigation in the nation's waterways and harbors. Public support for these efforts was stipulated by Congress and in legislation that evolved into modern-day versions of the Transportation Act (e.g., the Transportation Act of 1920 began a period of increased public support [Eckstein 1958]) and the Rivers and Harbor Act of 1927. Federal involvement and support for flood control projects began with passage of the Flood Control Act of 1936 (33 U.S.C.S. Sect. 701(a) 1980). Prior to this act, the Rivers and Harbor Act of 1927 requested that the U.S. ACOE prepare plans for the nation's waterways and harbors pertaining to flood control, irrigation, and electric power generation, and to improve navigation. In addition to the U.S. ACOE, the U.S. Department of Agriculture, Soil Conservation Service has responsibility for flood control on small tributaries upstream of large waterways (Eckstein 1958, Holmes 1972). Because federal waterway projects usually involved the construction of dams the U.S. ACOE became involved with the provision of hydroelectric power.

3.3.2.2. U.S. Department of Interiors, Bureau of Reclamation

The Bureau of Reclamation was created by the Federal Reclamation Act of 1902 (43 U.S.C.S. Sect. 371 et seq. 1980 and Supplement 1991). This federal agency was given sole responsibility for the provision of irrigation and water supply to the western United States and Alaska (Eckstein 1958, Holmes 1972). In the construction of irrigation projects, the Bureau of Reclamation constructed dams on western rivers and became involved with hydroelectric power generation. In addition to the U.S. ACOE, another large agency that provides hydroelectric power generation is the Tennessee Valley Authority (TVA) established in 1933 (Holmes 1972).

3.3.2.3. Other Agencies

Although not engaged with the construction of water resource projects that involved hydroelectric power generation, the FPC was created to examine the economic feasibility and justification of proposed U.S. ACOE hydroelectric projects and the marketing of some U.S. ACOE hydropower projects, and was given regulatory authority over all hydroelectric power projects (Eckstein 1958). Several agencies were created to market the electric power generated from U.S. ACOE projects; the Southwestern Power Administration and Southeastern Power Administration within the U.S. DOI, and the Bonneville Power Administration for electric power from federal projects in the Pacific Northwest (both U.S. ACOE projects and U.S. DOI, Bureau of Reclamation projects). In addition, the U.S. DOI, Bureau of Reclamation markets electric power from U.S. ACOE projects in the Missouri River Basin as well as its own. Lastly, the TVA is responsible for marketing its own electric power.

3.4. Federal Rulemaking

3.4.1. Analysis of Federal Water Resource Projects

Concern over the efficient use of public capital in federal initiated development projects has been around since the 1930s. The Flood Control Act of 1936 contained the first mention of benefit-cost analysis in justifying projects; it simply required that benefits exceed costs, "to whomsoever they may accrue" (Eckstein 1958: 47). However, a set of uniform procedures and standards pertaining to economic analysis of benefits and costs did not exist at the time and was needed (Eckstein 1958). It has always been unclear whether the use of economic analysis is intended to justify proposed projects on their merits or to provide evaluations, that is to measure projects against alternative projects and criteria so as to choose among them. Concern over the lack of uniform procedures and standards resulted in the formation of the Federal Inter-Agency River Basin Committee (FIARBC) in 1946 that consisted of all relevant agencies responsible for water resource development (Eckstein 1958). This committee worked toward advancing procedures in economic analyses of water resource projects and in developing uniform procedures (FIARBC 1947, 1948). It ultimately produced what is referred to as the "Green Book," a manual of recommended procedures to follow in performing economic analyses of water resource development projects (FIARBC 1950). Mainly because this interagency was not given any federal power to enact or require that the recommended procedures be followed, compliance among agencies was "uneven" (Eckstein 1958: 13).

At about the same time the Bureau of Reclamation developed its own manual of economic procedures for irrigation projects and for electric power projects (U.S. DOI 1952a). Following criticism over the treatment of indirect or secondary benefits the Bureau changed its procedures for hydroelectric power projects in 1952 (FIARBC 1952, U.S. DOI 1952b, 1952c).

Federal government and academic economists continued to pursue the goal of uniform procedures and standards in economic analyses of water resource development projects (Ciriacy-Wantrup 1952, 1955; Eckstein 1957, 1958; Heady 1950; Hirshleifer et al. 1960; Krutilla and Eckstein 1958; Maass 1962; Margolis 1957, 1959; McKean 1958; President's Advisory Committee 1955; Regan and Greenshields 1951; Regan and Weitzell 1947). Two laws were introduced and passed by Congress in the mid-1960s that committed the federal government to maintaining the development and use of a set of uniform procedures in future pursuits of water resource projects. The Water Resources Research Act of 1964 provided for funding of Water Resource Research Institutions at land grant universities (Holmes 1979, Reuss 1992). Then the Water Resources Planning Act was passed in 1965 (P.L. 89-80). This act was debated for four years before the Johnson administration lent support, from which the U.S. Water Resources Council (U.S. WRC) was created in 1968, along with the creation of river basin commissions for each major national watershed (Graves 1995, U.S. ACOE 1996). At the same time, parallel efforts within the U.S. ACOE resulted in the establishment of the Institute of Water Resources in 1969 to provide input and direction to policy and procedures to U.S. ACOE water resource projects (Graves 1995). Unlike previous federal efforts, the U.S. WRC was given federal power and authority to require federal agencies to use the uniform set of procedures in proposed water resource projects. The U.S. WRC subsequently developed a set of recommended uniform procedures for federal agencies to follow known as the *Principles and Standards* for water resource planning and development (U.S. WRC 1973). The *Principles and Standards* received public comment and review over time and has been updated and revised to incorporate new developments and techniques (U.S. WRC 1973, 1979a, 1979b). The Reagan administration felt the current version of the *Principles and Standards* contained regulations that delayed and even stopped federal water projects. It set up a Cabinet Council Working Group on Water Resources to develop a simpler set of procedures than those of the *Principles and Standards* (Graves 1995). Its *Principles and Guidelines* for water resource planning and development were published in 1983 and superseded the *Principles and Standards* (U.S. WRC 1983).

Federal projects for which these procedures (both the *Principles and Standards* and the *Principles and Guidelines*) were recommended comprised the traditional areas: (1) water transportation (navigation), (2) flood damage (agricultural and urban), (3) agricultural water supply (irrigation), and (4) hydro power, and new areas: (5) municipal and industrial water supply, (6) agricultural drainage, (7) water transportation (deep water ports), (8) recreation, (9) beach erosion control, and (10) commercial fishing and trapping. The procedures were required for all water resource projects conducted by the (1) U.S. ACOE, (2) U.S. DOI, Bureau of Reclamation, (3) TVA, and (4) USDA, Soil Conservation Service. Decision criteria pertaining to federal projects were to select those projects that yielded a maximum of net National Economic Development (NED) benefits consistent with the federal objective (i.e., protecting the nation's environment). The conceptual basis of NED benefits in these guidelines represented society's willingness to pay (WTP) for the goods and services provided by the proposed project. In 1983, President Reagan and then secretary of interior, James Watt, effectively closed down the U.S. WRC by eliminating its staff; technically it still exists on paper.[2]

Professional staff of the U.S. ACOE served on the U.S. WRC and relied on the published guidelines in their evaluation of water related projects during the tenure of the U.S. WRC. At about the same time that the Reagan administration shut down the U.S. WRC, the staff within the U.S. ACOE and the ACOE's Institute of Water Resources (IWR) continued their work of expanding, updating, and developing a set of manuals of recommended NED benefit procedures to follow in ACOE water resource projects (Graves 1995). Over time the NED Procedures Manual Work Unit, U.S. ACOE Planning Methodologies Research Program at the IWR developed a set of recommended uniform procedures for economic analysis of federal projects that the U.S. ACOE was involved with; 13 manuals of procedures were developed (U.S. ACOE 1986a, 1986b, 1987, 1988, 1990, 1991a, 1991b, 1991c, 1991d, 1991e, 1993a, 1993b, 1995).

Project areas included traditional areas: (1) inland water transportation (navigation); (2) flood control (agriculture and urban), and new areas: (3) recreation; (4) water transportation (deep-draft); and (5) coastal shore protection and erosion control. Presently, the U.S. ACOE is involved with (1) navigation and water transportation (both inland and deep-draft), (2) flood damage reduction (agricultural and urban), and (3) environmental restoration; the ACOE budget for coastal shore protection was eliminated at the direction of the Clinton administration in 1996 and 1997, and ACOE shore protection projects are now conducted on a piecemeal basis via congressional mandate.[3] The category of recreation benefits remains a present concern of the U.S. ACOE, although recreation benefits represent secondary benefits and not primary benefits. Decision criteria follow that of the early procedures and are based on net NED benefits, whereby a project must stand alone on the basis of priority benefits (i.e., navigation, flood damage reduction, or environmental restoration). In addition, the emphasis of U.S. ACOE's water resource programs presently has shifted away from construction of new projects to improvements and modifications of existing projects. This shift from new construction to primarily maintenance and upgrading has affected procedures, with more emphasis placed on cost-effectiveness analysis and incremental cost analysis and less emphasis on the more traditional NED benefit-cost analyses (U.S. ACOE 1995).

Economic techniques recommended in the *Principles and Standards,* the *Principles and Guidelines,* and current U.S. ACOE NED Benefit Procedural Manuals, consist of market-based techniques and nonmarket-based techniques. Market-based techniques were developed to estimate NED benefits for water transportation (navigation), flood control, hydropower, water supply, and specific shore protection benefit components. Examples of market-based benefits might be defined as alternative costs (i.e., costs associated with the most likely alternative project), cost savings (e.g., cost savings in production and transportation with the proposed project versus without), the value of damages averted, gains in net income (i.e., profit) to businesses, and gains in consumer surplus and producer surplus with the project. In some cases the technique to measure these benefits is obvious: business records to determine gains in profits, and cost savings; insurance records to measure flood damage prevented, changes in assessed real estate values, and estimation of demand and supply curves to determine economic surplus measures. These appear to be the most commonly defined benefits and techniques cited.

The nonmarket-based benefits and techniques treated in the federal procedures include only those to assess impacts on recreational activities. Development of valuation methods for nonmarket goods (recreational uses) created a challenge because these goods were not market goods and could not be measured by market-based techniques (U.S. WRC 1979a, 1979b, 1983). In these instances, benefits were represented by willingness to pay for recreational goods and services produced from the proposed project. These benefits were to be measured from willingness to pay, which included entry and use fees plus consumer surplus but not expenses such as food, transportation, lodging, and equipment. The techniques recommended comprised three methods:

1. Travel cost approach
2. Contingent valuation method
3. Unit-day value approach

The travel cost method involves a survey to collect observed data on expenses, travel time and distance, and entry or use fees from which travel cost demand curves are estimated. Then consumer surplus can be estimated from the area under statistical travel cost demand curves. Contingent valuation involves the use of surveys to obtain direct hypothetical responses of consumer surplus for proposed changes in quality and quantity of goods produced from a proposed project. Lastly, the unit-day value method relies on professional judgment in determining estimates of recreational benefits on the basis of a variety of recreational activities and published values associated with those activities, together with estimates of gains in user days. In principle it can be considered a crude version of a benefit transfer approach. More detailed descriptions are contained in Chapters 7 and 8.

3.4.2. Federal Economic Regulatory Analysis Procedures

In addition to federal initiatives and rulemaking concerning water resource projects, another effort was pursued by the federal government that began with environmental regulations in the 1960s shortly after the U.S. EPA was formed during the Nixon administration (Rusin et al. 1996). This early initiative began with a "Quality of Life" review issued by President Nixon, which involved the assessment of available alternatives and cost comparisons for proposed regulations by the Occupational Safety and Health Administration (OSHA), U.S. EPA, and several other agencies. By the mid-1970s the use of economic procedures and analyses was expanded to include all "major" regulations issued by all federal agencies as specified in Executive Order 11281 (Presidential Documents 1974) issued by President Ford and referred to as Inflation Impact Statements. Procedures for performing these assessments were developed by the Office of Budget and Management (OMB) in Circular No. A-107. Inflation Impact Statements were the first time an executive rule required the assessment and comparison of costs and benefits, risks, and inflationary impacts of the proposed action or regulation and any alternatives to be used in policy decisions.[4] These rules were extended by Executive Order 11949 in 1977 (Presidential Documents 1977) issued by President Ford and referred to as Economic Impact Analyses.

In 1978, economic analyses of proposed regulations were required under Executive Order 12044 issued by President Carter and were referred to as Regulatory Analyses (Presidential Documents 1978). Differences with previous Executive Orders included: (1) the emphasis was placed on calculating economic impacts rather than benefits and costs of proposed actions and any alternatives (agencies were not required to calculate benefits); (2) proposed regulations that required economic analyses had to have potential annual impacts of $100 million or more or had major increases in prices-costs (previous rules did not specify a dollar amount associated with proposed regulations); and (3) agencies were to choose the regulation with the "least-burdensome" economic impact when faced with alternative choices (Rusin et al. 1996).

President Carter's Regulatory Analyses were superseded by Regulatory Impact Analyses (RIAs) in 1981, when President Reagan issued Executive Order 12291 (Presidential Documents 1981). Analyses of proposed regulations/actions were required by all federal agencies and expanded to include those that had annual impacts of $100 million or more or had major increases in prices-costs or significant impacts to the economy. RIAs reintroduced the calculation of benefits and costs and introduced benefit-cost principles in regulatory decision making (e.g., implement the action when benefits exceed costs, or the action with the maximum net benefits). To assist federal agencies in preparing RIAs, the OMB developed revised procedures that superseded those from Circular A-107. Presently, Executive Order 12866 issued by President Clinton has revised RIAs (Presidential Documents 1993) and the OMB, in turn, has periodically revised procedures to conduct RIAs (OMB 1996). The requirement of RIAs for proposed regulations remains essentially the same (actions that result in at least $100 million of economic effects or cause significant adverse impacts). Benefit-cost analyses of all proposed actions are required; however, the decision criteria have been changed (benefits should justify costs, and other factors, such as equity considerations and cumulative impacts of proposed regulations, can be considered). The new rules then contain a mix from Executive Orders 12291 and 12044, without a strict reliance on benefit-cost principles in decision making. And in some sense the current RIA with the use of economic analysis to justify costs rather than the use of benefit-cost analysis to provide criteria in selecting actions, reverts back to a procedure that economists objected to in early economic analyses of water resource projects, that is, the use of economic analysis and procedures to *justify* projects as opposed to *evaluate* projects.

While the above Executive Orders required the use of economic analyses to evaluate proposed regulations and actions, they did not require the development of specific procedures how to assess benefits, costs, or impacts. This type of initiative was quite different than the federal laws of CERCLA-1980 and OPA-1990 in performing Natural

Resource Damage Assessments (NRDAs). Rather than take an indirect and passive role in developing procedures, in these two recent laws the federal government has taken an active and direct role in the development of a uniform set of procedures to assess benefits and costs, and related damages of natural resources.

3.5. U.S. DOI Procedures for Natural Resource Damage Assessments

In what follows, the U.S. DOI procedures apply to NRDAs from spills of hazardous chemicals and specific types of oil in all navigable waterways of the United States. These procedures were the first of their kind in which a uniform set of federal rules was developed that detailed how to assess resource damages. These rules predated the NOAA NRDA procedures by some 10 years.

3.5.1. Introduction

Federal procedures for the assessment of damages to natural resources commonly referred to as Natural Resource Damage Assessments (NRDAs), were developed by two separate federal agencies. The U.S. DOI was (1) given responsibility and authority to develop and promulgate procedures to use in the case of spills of hazardous substances and oil in all navigable waters of the United States under the Comprehensive Environmental Response, Compensation, and Liability Act of 1980 (CERCLA) and amendments from the Superfund Act of 1986 (SARA), and (2) given authority to seek legal means to recover assessed economic damages that can result from spills of hazardous substances. The legal liabilities and responsibilities were stipulated in CERCLA of 1980 and SARA of 1986, both of which are most often referred to as CERCLA by practitioners. As such, oil was not included within CERCLA; at the time it was covered under the Clean Water Act, although the procedures (i.e., type A and type B rules) developed by the U.S. DOI also referred to oil spills (U.S. DOI 1986, 1987, 1996a, 1996b). For both the CWA and CERCLA, these laws provided that natural resource damages are to be compensatory and not punitive, following common law principles relating to damages (compensatory damages are favored over punitive damages). Then in 1990, the Oil Pollution Act (OPA) was passed, which gave the U.S. Department of Commerce (U.S. DOC), National Oceanic and Atmospheric Administration (NOAA), legal responsibility and liability over oil spills in the nation's waterways. For all oil spills that occurred after August 1, 1990, OPA 1990 superseded the regulations, responsibilities, and liabilities stipulated in the CWA. However, OPA does not regulate crude oil and petroleum products that were either treated as hazardous substances under CERCLA or under the CWA; this has become known as the "petroleum exclusion" (Kenefick 1997).

The U.S. DOI as required by law subsequently developed a set of uniform procedures to use in the assessment of damages of natural resources and their services known as type A and type B rules, pertaining to, respectively, "small" and "large" spills of hazardous substances. The final rules were published in the *Federal Register* in 1986 for type B procedures, and in 1987 for type A procedures (U.S. DOI 1986, 1987). The type A rules were designed for a more simplistic, straightforward application that pertained to relatively simple and small spills. It relies on a computer model that determines an estimate of natural resource damages depending on various characteristics of the spill, weather and water conditions, shoreline environment, and location. It was developed so that anyone could use it. The estimate of economic damages in the model was based on use values from the most current relevant economic studies in the published literature and adjusted to current dollars. The type A model, referred to as the Natural Resource Damage Assessment Model for Coastal and Marine Environments (NRDAM/CME), was released in 1987 and updated in 1996 (another computer model for the Great Lakes Environment was developed in 1996—the NRDAM/GLE model), was in principle based on a benefits transfer approach, where estimates of the damage were based on the product of average use value (i.e., use value from previous published studies averaged over pertinent geographical areas) associated with a specific natural resource and physical measures of the resource injured, killed, or spoiled, adjusted to current dollars. The type B procedures were designed for more complex spills or relatively large spills. They allow flexibility in the assessment of injuries to the natural resource and its services and in assessments of economic damage.

For both rules (type A and type B), the U.S. DOI acknowledged that willingness to accept (WTA) was theoretically the correct welfare concept to measure the monetary value of injuries to natural resources; however, because few empirical studies measured WTA, the procedures for NRDA were based on WTP welfare measures. The initial procedures developed for the type B rules included lost nonuse values (i.e., option and existence values) as part of recoverable damages for natural resources but not for type A rules. The reason was that there were no empirical studies that reported nonuse values for natural resources and their services for the marine and coastal environment in the literature at the time (U.S. DOI 1986, 1987). In the 1986 published procedures for the type B rules, the U.S. DOI limited these measures of nonuse value by stipulating that nonuse values could only be used when use values could not be determined. In the 1994 published procedures for the type B rule, the U.S. DOI revised its definition of nonuse values to include existence value and bequest value, and dropped option value (U.S. DOI 1994a).

When the initial versions of the type A and type B procedures were published, the U.S. DOI advanced two slightly different decision criteria that would become challenged in court. In the type B rule published first, the decision criterion was that *the lesser of the amounts of restoration costs or replacement costs or use values be used to represent the monetary value of damages that could be recovered.* The criterion for the type A procedures gave the impression that it considered only use values, since the computer model designed for type A rules only included use values in the economic component of the model. Published comments criticized the U.S. DOI for this dual criterion because it did not agree with the CWA criterion on recoverable damages, and because the common law principle of damages (to make the injured party whole) was not followed in the type A procedures. Criteria specific to the CWA allowed damages to be recovered based on restoration costs (or replacement costs) actually incurred for injuries caused by oil discharges; hence the type A rules could not be used for oil spills under provisions of the CWA. The interpretation and use of the common law principle of damage by the courts is to focus on restoration and replacement of injured resources, and damages should be based on this view. The response to these criticisms of the type A procedures by the U.S. DOI was that "adequate data were not available to create a standardized model" associated with restoration and replacement costs so as to be incorporated within the type A computer model (U.S. DOI 1987: 9051).

In 1989, both the type B and type A rules were challenged in the courts by several groups. A combination of state, industry, and environmental groups challenged the type B procedures in *State of Ohio v. United States Department of the Interior* (*Ohio v. Interior*), 880F.2d 432 (D.C. Cir. 1989; U.S. DOI 1996b: 20561). The court ordered the U.S. DOI to revise the type B procedures so that the measure of natural resource damages would be based on restoration costs (i.e., the cost of restoring, rehabilitating, replacing, or acquiring the equivalent of natural resources injured). In addition, the court ordered the U.S. DOI to develop a procedure so that trustees could include all reliably calculated lost values from injury to natural resources as part of damages; hence, the limitation on incorporating nonuse values in damage assessments was struck down: Both lost use values and lost nonuse values could now be included as part of damages to be recovered (U.S. DOI 1994a: 14264-5). All other aspects of the type B procedures developed by the U.S. DOI were upheld by the court.

In 1989, state, industry, and environmental groups concurrently challenged the published final rules for type A procedures for coastal and marine environments in *State of Colorado v. United States Department of the Interior* (*Colorado v. Interior*), 880 F.2d 481 (D.C. CIR. 1989; U.S. DOI 1996b: 20561). The court remanded the U.S. DOI to develop damage measures based on restoration costs following the decision in *Ohio v. Interior*, and that the computer model consider calculation of restoration costs. In addition, the court urged that additional type A procedures be developed to account for as many different types of situations as possible. New final rules were developed and published in 1994 for type B procedures and in 1996 for type A procedures by the U.S. DOI that incorporated the 1989 court decisions (U.S. DOI 1994a, 1996b).

3.5.2. U.S. DOI NRDA Rules and Procedures

Under the final published U.S. DOI rules, damages were primarily based on the costs of restoration, rehabilitation, replacement, and/or acquiring the equivalent of injured resources, with the lesser of these categories to represent the "preferred" project. In addition, discretion was given to the trustees to include the value of services lost to the public from the time the spill/discharge occurred until the injured resource has been returned to baseline conditions. The value of these lost services was referred to as compensable value; that is, all lost public economic value including lost use values and lost nonuse values such as existence and bequest values. Recoverable damages were now defined to include restoration costs (i.e., the costs of restoration, rehabilitation, replacement, and/or acquisition of equivalent resources) plus compensable value plus the reasonable costs of assessment:

$$damages = restoration\ costs + compensable\ value + assessment\ costs.$$

The NRDA procedures consist of four general phases that trustees are to follow: a Pre-assessment Phase, an Assessment Plan Phase, an Assessment Phase based on a type A rule or type B rule, and a Post-Assessment Phase. It is worth noting that the emphasis appears to be on how to conduct assessments; most of the written procedures and rules published by the U.S. DOI reflect this emphasis, rather than restoration and monitoring activities of restored resources. In contrast, the NRDA procedures written by NOAA appear to deal more equally with all phases involved (preassessment phases, assessment phases, and restoration phases).

3.5.2.1. Preassessment Phase

The purpose of the Preassessment Phase is for trustees to decide if an NRDA should be performed, on the basis of preliminary evidence and information, and subject to specific criteria (U.S. DOI 1986, 1994a, 1994b, 1996b). The Preassessment Phase consists of four steps:

1. Notification and detection
2. Emergency restorations
3. Sampling of potentially injured natural resources
4. Preassessment screen

3.5.2.1.1. Notification, Detection, and Emergency Restorations

The first part of the process involves notification and detection, whereby trustees (federal or state and local government have responsibility over injured resources; in some cases tribal communities are included as in the *Exxon Valdez* NRDA process) are notified, usually by the U.S. Coast Guard, of a spill or discharge of a hazardous substance or oil in marine waters that either has injured or could injure natural resources. Included in notification and detection is the situation where a trustee either has noticed or has been informed that natural resources have been injured from hazardous substances or oil without being notified that a spill or discharge occurred. The next step involves emergency activities and restorations, which could include preventing or reducing the threat of injury to natural resources and preventing or reducing migration of the spill/discharge through containment, removal, and cleanup measures.

3.5.2.1.2. Sampling of Potentially Injured Natural Resources

This phase includes preliminary field sampling of biological organisms and water samples and counts of injured and dead birds, mammals, and fish. This step is deemed necessary to determine the extent of the spill and concentration of the substance in the water column prior to evaporation, dilution, mixing, and sinking. The concentration detected in biological organisms can degrade over time, and hence emergency sampling can be justified to aid in determining the extent of injury and level of concentration. Moreover, remains of larger organisms such as birds, mammals, and fish can disappear as a result of decomposition and scavengers or they may sink or migrate from the initial area in which the spill or discharge occurred; hence emergency sampling is justified.

3.5.2.1.3. Preassessment Screen

Following these preliminary steps, the trustees prepare a preassessment screen, which consists of a quick review of available information and an assessment as to the likelihood of a successful claim before further effort and money are expended. The trustee's determination whether to conduct an NRDA is crucial to this component. Such a decision is documented in a Preassessment Screen Determination, which is to be included in a Report of Assessment in the Post-Assessment Phase. The trustees must perform the preassessment screen subject to specific criteria from on-site information (amount and occurrence of spill, identification of substance(s) spilled or discharged, history of the spill site, potentially responsible parties [PRP], and whether the release or spill was authorized or covered by federal/state legislation). They must also determine resources at or potentially at risk (i.e., identification of exposure pathways, estimate of exposed areas, exposed water estimates, concentration estimates, and potentially affected resources). Before an assessment is conducted, it must be determined that: (1) a spill or discharge of a hazardous substance or oil has occurred, (2) natural resources in which a state or federal agency can assume trusteeship under CERCLA either have or are likely to be injured from the spill, (3) the substance spilled is of sufficient concentration and quantity to cause injury to resources, (4) data necessary to conduct an NRDA can be gathered at reasonable costs, and (5) emergency response actions ongoing or planned would not provide remediation to the injured resources without further action. Once these criteria have been met and the trustees determine that an NRDA is justified, they advance to the next phase of the assessment process.

3.5.2.2. Assessment Plan Phase

The Assessment Plan Phase is meant to guide the trustee in the assessment of injury and damages so that the assessment is conducted in a planned and systematic manner and the methodologies chosen satisfy reasonable costs. This phase consists of the following five steps:

1. Designation of lead trustee
2. Assessment plan preparation
3. Decision to perform type A or type B assessment or some combination thereof
4. Confirmation of exposure
5. Preliminary estimate of damage

3.5.2.2.1. Designation of Lead Trustee

As a first step in preparation of the Assessment Plan, all affected trustees and potential trustees must mutually designate a lead authorized official (lead trustee) to act as coordinator and lead contact in all aspects of the assessment. This lead trustee will act as a final arbitrator in the event of disputes and if consensus cannot be reached among all other trustees concerning the Assessment Plan and its implementation. The lead trustee is to administer the assessment. Once chosen, the lead trustee must send a Notice of Intent to Perform an Assessment to all potentially responsible parties that have been identified in the Preassessment Phase. The lead trustee has considerable power and autonomy over the preparation of the Assessment Plan and the procedure chosen. The lead trustee also has final approval over the appropriate methods to include in the assessment and Assessment Plan as well as any changes in the Assessment Plan. The Assessment Plan must be made available to the public for review and comment. The lead trustee then decides upon implementation of the Assessment Plan and is free to select any party to implement the assessment plan, which is to be documented in this report. The lead trustee provides direction and guidance and must monitor the actions of the selected party in this implementation. At any time during the assessment, the Assessment Plan may be modified based on new information. The lead trustee has final authority on any such modifications and must notify all appropriate parties (other responsible trustees, PRP, and the public) and invite review and comments of such changes.

3.5.2.2.2. Assessment Plan Preparation

The trustee must prepare an Assessment Plan in order to document all relevant information, including why a type A or type B procedure is to be used and the specific requirements for type B assessments if selected. Here the trustee must: (a) identify all scientific and economic methods to be used in the assessment procedure chosen (either type A or type B), (b) assist in determining if the approach(es) identified are cost-effective and meet the definition of "reasonable costs," (c) provide a statement of authority for trusteeship, (d) show that the ongoing NRDA has been coordinated with other investigations via the National Oil and Hazardous Substances Pollution Contingency Plan (NCP), and (e) generate plans for sharing the data with all parties concerned if needed. If a type B procedure is to be used, the trustee must report the results of a confirmation of exposure (see type B assessment procedure below) and prepare a Quality Assurance Plan and Restoration and Compensation Determination Plan, both of which are subject to public review and comment.

3.5.2.2.3. Decision to Perform Type A or Type B Assessment

If the decision is to perform a type B assessment, the lead trustee must examine specific information relevant to the type B procedure. Briefly, the type B procedure comprises an Injury Determination Phase, Quantification Phase, and Damage Determination Phase. After the Injury Determination Phase has been completed the lead trustee must review the decisions incorporated into the Assessment Plan. This provides confirmation and ensures consistency with various methods selected for the determination of injury, quantification, and damage, and for economic assessments of resource injury.

The choice of using procedures from a type A rule or type B rule is the next component of the Assessment Plan Phase. The lead trustee must document the decision to use a specific rule and procedure at this point. Specific criteria that can be used to assist in this decision are as follows. A type A rule can be used if (1) the spilled or discharged substance has entered a location covered by the NRDA computer models, (2) the particular substance is specified in the NRDA computer model, (3) the spill or discharge occurred at or near the surface of the water, (4) winds were fairly uniform in the area of the release at the time of the spill or discharge, (5) the lead trustee determines that the injury is within the bounds estimated by the NRDA computer models and does not exceed these bounds, (6) subsurface currents are either fairly uniform in the water column in the area of the release or are not expected to further impact threatened resources, and (7) on the basis of a preliminary run, estimated damages do not exceed $100,000 (if damages do, then a type B assessment should be performed since recoverable damages for a type A rule are limited to $100,000).

The decision to use a type A versus a type B procedure is determined by evaluating whether the type B procedure can be conducted at "reasonable costs" and whether the increase in accuracy from the type B rule outweighs the increase in costs. In addition, a type B procedure can be used if preliminary damage estimates based on the type A NRDA computer model indicate that damages will likely exceed $100,000. Furthermore, a type B assessment must be conducted if (1) a PRP requests in writing that a type B procedure be used, (2) a PRP advances all reasonable assessment costs of the type B procedure in an acceptable time period, (3) the type A procedure does not apply to the spill or discharge or to the substance spilled (e.g., the location of the spill and substance is not contained in the NRDA model; if these conditions are not satisfied, one would use the type A model), and (4) the lead trustee can select a type B rule based on comments to the

Assessment Plan but cannot reverse this decision (e.g., select a type A rule at a later date) if exposure cannot be confirmed.

The lead trustee furthermore can use both a type A and a type B procedure for the same spill provided that (1) the type B assessment is cost-effective (i.e., the least cost) and can be conducted at a reasonable cost, (2) no double recovery can occur, and (3) the type B rule is to be used for determination of damages and compensable values for injuries that the type A NRDA computer model does not cover. Selection of one procedure or combination of both procedures must be documented in the Assessment Plan by the lead trustee.

3.5.2.2.4. Confirmation of Exposure

In the next step in this phase, the lead trustee must confirm that at least one of the natural resources previously identified as injured or potentially injured from the preassessment screen phase has been exposed to the spilled or discharged substance. Positive confirmation is required before a type B assessment can be performed. As mentioned above in the procedure selection decision, if a type B rule is selected, the successful application and assessment hinge on a positive confirmation finding. Without such a finding the lead trustee cannot conduct an NRDA and loses potentially recoverable money to return the injured resources to their baseline condition. This confirmation is to be based on chemical analyses of actual data collected from field samples, or where field samples are not available, the use of methods from the Injury Determination Phase may be used.

3.5.2.2.5. Preliminary Estimate of Damage

The last component of the Assessment Plan Phase concerns a preliminary estimate of damages. In this part, the lead trustee must develop estimates of the anticipated restoration costs (i.e., costs of restoration, rehabilitation, replacement, and/or acquisition resources equivalent to those injured), and estimates of the compensable value (i.e., lost use value and lost nonuse value to the public for the period from the date of the spill or discharge to the date natural resources are returned to baseline or pre-spill conditions) if this component is to be included in damages to be recovered. These estimates (anticipated restoration costs and compensable value) are referred to as preliminary estimates and are to be measured in constant dollars and expressed in expected present value terms. Regarding restoration actions, the preliminary estimate of damages (i.e., costs) should represent a range of possible alternatives for restoration, rehabilitation, replacement, and/or acquisition of equivalent resources, as well as for natural recovery. Furthermore, estimates of the compensable value should reflect the possible alternative actions as well as the situation without any action (i.e., natural recovery). The preliminary estimates of damage are to be estimated before the completion of the Assessment Plan, although the lead trustee does not have to disclose these preliminary estimates until the conclusion of the final assessment. The preliminary estimates together with all documentation must be included in the Report of the Assessment. The lead trustee can revise these preliminary estimates based on new information from the Injury Determination and Quantification Phase components of the type B assessment phase.

3.5.2.3. Assessment Phase

The Assessment Phase consists of the use of either a type A rule or a type B rule to conduct an assessment of the damages to the injured natural resources. In both cases, similar steps are followed:

1. Injury determination phase
2. Quantification phase
3. Damage determination phase

3.5.2.3.1. Type A Assessment

The procedures specified in the latest version of the type A rules use a computer model to determine and estimate damages from spills/discharges to coastal and marine environments (NRDAM/CME—natural resource damage assessment model, version 2.4), and those to the Great Lakes environment (NRDAM/GLE—model, version 1.4). This procedure represents a standardized methodology that requires minimal field data and is meant to provide a fairly simplified straightforward procedure for use in NRDAs. The NRDAM consists of four linked submodels: (1) physical fates submodel, (2) biological fates submodel, (3) restoration submodel, and (4) compensable value submodel. Unlike earlier procedures, the new procedures include restoration actions as a major component of the type A procedures incorporated in a new submodel, the restoration submodel. Also, the earlier economic damages submodel has been completely revised as the new compensable value submodel. Briefly, the physical fates submodel is designed to determine the distribution of the spilled or discharged substance in the water and on its surface, along shorelines, and in sediments over time. The biological fates submodel incorporates the previous information to determine and quantify injuries to natural resources and associated services. Estimates of the cost of restoring the injured natural resources are determined by the restoration submodel, based on average costs of previous restoration efforts. Decision criteria built into the restoration submodel evaluate specific restoration actions by comparing costs with benefits based on input from the compensable value submodel. The compensable value submodel then estimates the sum of specific economic use values lost to the public from the time the spill occurred to the return of the resources to baseline conditions. It should be noted that these lost use values are developed for public resources and facilities where applicable. For example, lost beach use value is based on the lost use value at public beaches (i.e., national seashore facilities and state public beaches); local beach use (i.e., town beaches) and private beach use are excluded. Lost use value from marine recreational fishing is distributed throughout a state and is not dependent on a public facility, therefore use values are based on state statistical data collected as part of the National Marine Fisheries Service Marine Recreational Fishing Survey efforts. In the 1996 published type A rules, nonuse values were excluded, and this remains an issue for future rulemaking.

Decision criteria are built into the restoration submodel. Habitat restoration actions constitute the first level of restoration actions considered. Restocking fish and wildlife constitute the second level of restoration actions. For first level restoration actions, the total estimated costs of a particular habitat restoration are compared with the compensable value (i.e., lost use value) that action would achieve. If the specific restoration action results in lower compensable value than that achieved under natural recovery (i.e., lost use values are lower with the specific action compared to lost use values from natural recovery), then the decision is that that action is preferred to natural recovery, and the NRDAM computes the total costs of the specific restoration. If the compensable value is higher for a restoration action than for natural recovery, then natural recovery is the preferred action, and the NRDAM does not compute any restoration costs.

For restocking actions (i.e., second level restoration actions), the NRDAM estimates total restocking costs if similar stocks are available compared to injured resources. The final comparison involves combined habitat and restocking actions, where the decision criteria involve comparison of total estimated costs of restoration actions with benefits of such actions (i.e., the difference in compensable value with natural recovery less compensable value with the specific action). If estimated costs exceed estimated benefits by a factor of 10 (i.e., costs are 10 times greater than benefits), then the decision is that natural recovery is the preferred action and no restoration action is to be taken to return injured resources to baseline conditions. If not, then the decision is that the restoration action is the preferred action and such restoration and restocking will be undertaken.

To implement the NRDAM computer model, the lead trustee must provide a variety of data to describe the characteristics of the substance (specific type, characteristic of oil or hazardous substance) spilled or discharged, information about the spill or discharge, weather and water conditions, emergency response actions, and habitat type if known, or if not, the characteristics of the resource affected by the spill or discharge. This allows the computer model to estimate as accurately as possible pertinent information about Injury Determination, Quantification, and Damage Determination Phases of the Assessment Phase.

Specific data requirements include:

- Identity of spilled substance
- Mass or volume of substance spilled
- Duration, time, and location of spill/discharge
- Wind conditions
- Emergency response actions
- Extent of closure(s)
- Price deflator (i.e., an overall price index used to deflate goods and services)
- Currents and tide conditions for the marine model (NRDA/CME)
- Presence of ice
- Specific information if known (i.e., air and water temperature, total suspended sediment concentration, mean settling velocity of suspended solids, and habitat type)

The lead trustee then must apply the model (i.e., run/execute the computer model); information about using the model is provided in the technical manuals that come with the NRDAM computer model. If more than one substance was spilled or discharged in the initial spill or discharge the trustee must choose one of the substances and can run the NRDAM computer model only once. The rules stipulate that the lead trustee cannot run the NRDAM for each identified substance for the purpose of determining which would result in the highest damage; hence the trustee must be cautious in the use of the NRDAM and must choose the substance believed to result in the most significant injuries and damages.

Once a preliminary run is conducted to determine an initial estimate of damages, and the lead trustee decides to continue using the type A model, the lead trustee must prepare an Assessment Plan that is available to all interested parties for review and comment. The lead trustee can then modify the Assessment Plan and either continue to use the type A rule or choose to use the type B rule. If the type A rule is selected, the lead trustee conducts a final run of the NRDAM and prepares a Report of Assessment that includes the printout of the final run, along with the Preassessment Screen Determination and Assessment Plan. The lead trustee then prepares a demand on the basis of this assessment, and if the final run of the NRDAM estimates damages that exceed $100,000, the lead trustee must limit the demand to $100,000.

3.5.2.3.2. Type B Assessment

The latest published type B procedures consist of three key elements: (1) injury determination, (2) quantification, and (3) damage determination (U.S. DOI 1994a). The purpose of injury determination is to verify that a natural resource(s) has been injured from the spill or discharge incident. The quantification component is to estimate the extent of injuries to the natural resource(s) in the context of services lost relative to baseline conditions (i.e., pre-spill conditions or conditions without the spill). The purpose of damage determination is to establish the amount of compensation for injuries to natural resources. The latest version of the type B rule differs from earlier versions in that restoration actions are included as a major component in the procedures, and restoration costs are now included in the definition of damages to be recovered.

3.5.2.3.2.1. INJURY DETERMINATION SUBPHASE

The Injury Determination Subphase consists of three components to assist in verifying if one or more natural resources were injured or impaired as a result of the spilled or discharged substance. For injury to occur to a natural resource under either CERCLA or the CWA, the lead trustee must determine and document that at least one of the definitions of injury to resources stipulated in the type B rule has occurred. Injuries are defined for the following categories of resources: surface water, ground water, air, geologic resources, and biological resources. Once satisfied, the lead trustee must establish the exposure pathway to verify that the injury resulted from the spilled or discharged substance for the above natural resource categories. Regarding both injury determination and exposure pathway determination, the lead trustee can only use the specific tests and methods listed in the published type B rule.

3.5.2.3.2.2. QUANTIFICATION SUBPHASE

The Quantification Subphase is meant to establish the extent of the injury(ies) to the natural resource(s) determined to be injured and to be included in a damage claim. This quantification is expressed in terms of reductions in the quantity and quality of services from baseline conditions caused by the spilled substance. As part of the Service Reduction Quantification component, the lead trustee must determine the extent of the injury to all relevant resources relative to baseline conditions and must quantify the reduction in services relative to baseline conditions as a result of the spilled substance. Regarding the Baseline Services Determination component, the lead trustee must determine the physical, chemical, and biological baseline conditions and identify services associated with injured resources relative to baseline service conditions. Then the lead trustee must estimate the time for each injured resource to recover and return to baseline conditions in the Resource Recoverability Analysis component. This must include all alternative restoration plans under consideration and a natural recovery (i.e., no restoration action) case to serve as a reference point.

3.5.2.3.2.3. DAMAGE DETERMINATION SUBPHASE

Once the Quantification Subphase has been completed, the lead trustee proceeds to the Damage Determination Subphase in which the monetary claim is to be determined for compensation of injuries to natural resources from a spilled substance. Damages may include the cost or restoration, rehabilitation, replacement, and/or acquisition of equivalent natural resources for those resources injured. The lead trustee has the discretion to include the compensable value of all or some portion of the associated services lost to the public for the time when the spill occurred to when the injured resources are returned to baseline or pre-spill conditions. Furthermore the reasonable costs of assessment can also be included in the damage claim. In general recoverable damages are:

$$\text{damages} = \text{restoration costs} + \text{compensable value} + \text{assessment costs.}$$

The Damage Determination Subphase includes the following components:

Restoration and Compensation Determination Plan. The lead trustee must first prepare a Restoration and Compensation Determination Plan. This plan is to describe a range of possible alternative restoration, rehabilitation, etc. actions, describe the related services lost to the public associated with each alternative plan (services lost will differ across alternative plans because each plan could return the injured resources to baseline conditions in different amounts of time), select a preferred plan and provide reasons for this choice, and identify appropriate methods that will be used to determine costs of the preferred alternative and possibly the compensable value.

Alternatives for Restoration. Next, the procedures stipulate that the lead trustee must develop a reasonable number of possible alternative plans for the restoration, rehabilitation, replacement, and/or acquisition of equivalent resources so as to return the injured resource(s) to baseline conditions. Similar information must also be developed in terms of associated services. The selection of the alternative (i.e., preferred) plan, is to be based on the following criteria: technical feasibility, expected costs and expected benefits, cost-effectiveness, effects of emergency response actions, potential for additional injury from implementing alternative plans, natural recovery period, ability of resource recovery with and without further action, effects on human health and safety, and compliance with relevant policies and laws.

Cost Estimation and Valuation Methods. This component contains specific methods that the lead trustee must use to estimate costs of all possible alternative plans as well as to estimate compensable value. Regarding restoration cost methods, the procedures stipulate that only those methods that (1) are feasible and reliable associated with a specific incident and type of damage, (2) can be conducted at a reasonable cost, (3) avoid double counting, and (4) are cost-effective can be used. Specific definitions and categories of direct costs and indirect costs are provided. The methods that can be used include (1) comparison method, (2) unit method, (3) probability methods, (4) factor methods, (5) standard time method, (6) cost- and time-estimating relationships, and (7) any other cost method that meets the stated criteria.

Regarding compensable value estimates the following methods can be used, as well as any other methods that are cost-effective in estimating compensable value:

- Market price method
- Appraisal method
- Factor income method
- Travel cost model
- Hedonic price method
- Unit value method
- Contingent value method

In the 1994 published procedures for type B rules, the above methods were listed as well as any other methods that are cost-effective to measure use values based on willingness to pay (U.S. DOI 1994a). The inclusion and estimation of nonuse values is an issue for future federal rulemaking. We are only interested, at this point, in noting which techniques were listed and that they involve both market-based methods and nonmarket-based methods. Examining this type of information reveals the importance of economic techniques in federal rulemaking and how up to date specific federal rules and procedures are. Detailed discussion of these particular techniques is covered in Chapters 7 and 8.

Implementation Guidance. The last step of the Damage Determination Phase concerns the Implementation Guidance component. This consists of checks and criteria that the lead trustee must incorporate into the damage determination that include (1) determining use, (2) double counting, (3) uncertainty, (4) discounting, (5) substitutability, and (6) scope of analysis (i.e., whether scope of analysis is federal, state, local, or tribal). Once all these checks have been verified and the above steps completed in the type B assessment, the lead trustee has completed the Assessment Phase and can advance to the Post-Assessment Phase.

3.5.2.4. Post-Assessment Phase

The Post Assessment Phase consists of four elements:

1. Report of assessment
2. Demand for recoverable damages
3. Restoration account
4. Restoration plan

These are meant to fulfill the final step of the NRDA process. All findings are incorporated into the final Report of Assessment, the PRP is presented with a demand for recoverable damages, a restoration account is set up to administer the recovered sum so as to carry out the restoration plan, and the preferred or recommended restoration plan is described in detail in the Restoration Plan. The Report of Assessment contains the following elements: the Preassessment Screen Determination; the Assessment Plan; the results of the assessment for either a type A rule or type B rule, and if a type B rule, all documentation and findings from the Injury Determination Phase, Quantification Phase, and Damage Determination Phase; and a Restoration and Compensation Determination Plan (when the measure of damages is based on restoration or replacement costs).

The lead trustee then prepares and presents a "Written Demand" (i.e., a claim for the recoverable damages including the reasonable costs of assessment) to the potentially responsible party. The responsible party is given at least 60 days to acknowledge and respond to the demand. Following the demand, the lead trustee establishes a Restoration Account from which the Restoration Plan will be administered and paid for. All sums recovered are either placed in a separate account in the U.S. Treasury if the lead trustee is a federal agency, a separate account in a state treasury or an interest bearing account payable in trust to the lead trustee if such trustee is a state agency, or some combination thereof if a decision to divide the assessment between federal and state agencies is reached in the Assessment Plan Phase. Sums are to be paid out of the account for only those items specified in the Restoration Plan, such as the acquisition of land, reimbursement of reasonable costs of conducting the assessment and carrying out the restoration plan, and payment of compensable values. In the restoration process, the lead trustee can also make appropriate modifications to the restoration plan as restoration proceeds and must then document such changes in the Restoration Plan and make this available to the public for review and comment.

3.6. U.S. DOC (NOAA) Procedures for Natural Resource Damage Assessments

3.6.1. Introduction

The Oil Pollution Act of 1990 (OPA 1990) was passed by Congress on August 19, 1990. It stipulated that the U.S. DOC was the agency responsible for developing, implementing, and promulgating federal NRDA rules and procedures concerning oil spills in navigable water of the United States, adjoining shorelines, or the Exclusive Economic Zone (i.e., a territorial boundary extending out to 200 miles from the coastline) (U.S. DOC, NOAA 1996a, Kenefick 1997). This act was limited to spills of oil and did not include spills of crude oil or petroleum products, which were either treated as hazardous substances under CERCLA or under the CWA (Kenefick 1997). OPA 1990 required that federal procedures be developed within two years of its effective date. NOAA began a process of developing interest in and soliciting comments for NRDA rules and procedures, however NOAA failed to develop NRDA rules and procedures by the time limits stipulated in OPA 1990. The Natural Resources Defense Council subsequently sued NOAA for failure to develop and publish final rules and procedures by the time limit stipulated in OPA 1990. A new time limit was determined in the court judgment (*NRDC v. United States Coast Guard*, No. CV-94 4892 [E.D.N.Y. 1994]), it was extended several times due to public comments and requests, and final rules and procedures were published in 1996, six years later (Kenefick 1997, U.S. DOC, NOAA 1996a).

There are slight differences in the purposes and emphases of NRDA procedures developed by NOAA compared to those of U.S. DOI. One should keep these in mind when using and referring to them. The overall purpose of NOAAs NRDA procedures is that of restoration of the injured natural resource. Specifically, the goal of the federal NRDA rules and procedures developed by NOAA is to make the environment and public whole from injuries to natural resources and associated services as a result of an oil spill (i.e., discharge of oil or substantial threat of a discharge of oil). There is an obvious parallel to common law principles in this goal, to make the injured party whole. Achievement of the goal is met from the return of resources and their services to baseline conditions together with compensation for interim losses of resources and resource services for the period covering the date of the spill or discharge until recovery of the resource and resource services. The emphasis in NOAAs NRDA procedures is placed on restoration rather than on compensation of losses and damages (the latter being the emphasis of U.S. DOI procedures). The basis for this approach was to avoid controversy, disputes, and litigation over economic assessments and economic methods, namely the CV method, and to proceed quickly with restoration efforts rather than involve court time (Kenefick 1997).

The rules and procedures state that claims (i.e., a demand) can recover three monetary components similar to U.S. DOI published procedures:

recoverable sums = restoration costs + compensable values +
                     reasonable assessment costs, or

recoverable sums = primary restoration + compensatory restoration +
                     reasonable assessment costs.

Restoration costs include the costs of restoration, rehabilitation, replacement, or acquisition of equivalent natural resources and services (i.e., primary restoration); when two or more alternatives exist, the most cost-effective alternative is to be chosen. Compensable values (i.e., compensatory restoration), the second component of a claim, includes the value of lost interim uses from the date of the incident to recovery to baseline conditions to be compensated. Lost interim uses are both use values and passive use values (i.e., nonuse values) associated with knowing that such resources exist and are protected. The last component, consists of the reasonable costs of assessing damages and restoration alternatives.

It should be noted that because the emphasis of NOAA NRDA rules and procedures concerns restoration of injured natural resources and services, approaches were developed to determine and assess the scale (i.e., size) of suitable restoration projects and/or acquisition of equivalent resources and services so as to make the public and resources whole (U.S. DOC, NOAA 1996a). Among these are the economic approaches of nonmarket valuation methods (travel cost method, contingent valuation) and market methods (factor income approach, demand and supply market models, hedonic price approach), benefit transfer, conjoint analysis, and habitat equivalency analysis. In all cases the goal of these approaches is to aid in determining the appropriate scale of the restoration project that will return the injured resource and associated services to their baseline or provide an equal value of resource and associated services to the public. We now consider an overview of the NRDA rules and procedures.

3.6.2. NOAA NRDA Rules and Procedures

Three phases compose the NOAA procedures and rules. These include:

- Preassessment Phase
- Restoration Planning Phase
- Restoration Implementation Phase

3.6.2.1. Preassessment Phase

This phase determines whether appropriate trustees can and should take actions regarding restoration of injured natural resources and services due to an oil spill. This process begins when emergency response agencies, usually the U.S. Coast Guard in cases concerning marine waters, notifies the appropriate trustees that an oil spill or discharge has resulted. Trustees must then determine whether there is jurisdiction via OPA to pursue a Restoration Plan and NRDA. The next step involves a Preliminary Determination to verify that resource injury has occurred, and whether emergency response actions and restoration actions have the potential to eliminate the threat of further injury and return the resource to pre-spill conditions. If the decision is made to proceed, trustees can generate an NRDA and Restoration Plan in which the public must be notified with a Notice of Intent to Conduct Restoration Planning, and the trustees must concurrently open an Administrative Record in which to place all relevant documents, communications, decisions, and findings that must be available to the public. They then advance to a Restoration Planning Phase. If the decision is made not to proceed because evidence and information do not support a violation of the OPA or indicate continued resource injury that cannot be addressed by cleanup-response parties, the trustees cannot take any additional action, but they can recover all reasonable costs of assessment up to this point.

3.6.2.2. Restoration Planning Phase

The Restoration Planning Phase consists of six steps:

1. Injury determination
2. Quantification of injury
3. Development of restoration alternatives
4. Evaluation of alternatives
5. Development of restoration plan
6. Implementation of a regional restoration plan

3.6.2.2.1. Injury Determination

This phase consists of two key components, injury assessment and restoration selection. The trustees must determine the nature and extent of injuries, quantify these injuries, and subsequently determine the need for and scale of restoration actions. They must determine whether injuries to natural resources and associated services have occurred from the spill or discharge incident. They must then identify the nature of the injury; establish exposure, concentration, and a pathway to link the injuries to the spill or discharge incident; determine any injuries to resources and services from the emergency response and cleanup actions; and then select which injuries the NRDA and restoration plans are to address.

3.6.2.2.2. Quantification of Injury

In this phase, trustees must provide estimates of the degree and extent (in spatial and temporal contexts) of the injuries to natural resources and services identified and selected for the NRDA and Restoration Plan relative to baseline or pre-spill conditions. Trustees must also provide estimates of the time associated with natural recovery of the injured resources and services in the case of no emergency response actions (i.e., without response actions).

3.6.2.2.3. Development of Restoration Alternatives

The next component of the Restoration Planning Phase involves restoration selection. There are four potential components for restoration selection: primary restoration actions, compensatory restoration actions, quantity-based scaling approaches, and valuation-based scaling approach. The first, Development of Restoration Alternatives, requires trustees to decide whether to proceed. If prior information to this phase warrants restoration actions, trustees can proceed forward, otherwise they cannot take further actions but can recover all reasonable costs of assessment (incurred) up to this point. This step begins a complex process in which the trustees identify a "reasonable range" of alternative restoration plans before a preferred plan(s) is selected. The set of alternative restoration plans must contain information in the context of primary restoration and compensatory restoration actions that are associated with one or more injury(ies) previously identified and selected for the assessment (NRDA and Restoration Plan) that are a result of the spill or discharge incident. Each alternative plan must be designed in such a way that the set of alternative plans could make the environment and public whole, that is, to return the injured resource and service to baseline conditions. The alternatives that are technically feasible and are in accordance with environmental laws, regulations, and permits can only be considered further; the previous characteristics identify a set of technically feasible and environmentally acceptable restoration alternatives. Primary restoration actions consist of (1) a natural recovery (i.e., no intervention) alternative for comparison purposes, and (2) restoration actions that would return the injured resource and associated services to baseline conditions sooner than natural recovery (i.e., accelerated time frames)—referred to as active primary restoration actions. Compensatory restoration actions are relatively complex in comparison because they account for a variety of possible scenarios. The preferred level of restoration actions trustees must consider are those that provide "services of the same type and quality, and of comparable *value* as those injured," (U.S. DOC, NOAA 1996a: 507, emphasis added). If not of comparable value, the next level of restoration actions are those that provide resources and services of "comparable *type and quality* as those provided by the injured natural resources," (ibid., emphasis added). Only in this case (i.e., where injured and alternative resources and services *are not* of comparable value), trustees must incorporate values of lost and replacement services in scaling of restoration alternatives.

Following identification and evaluation of primary and active primary restoration actions, trustees must determine the scale of the restoration actions that can satisfy the goal of OPA to make the environment and public whole. Two basic scaling approaches are available in the rules and procedures, resource-to-resource and/or service-to-service scaling approaches (i.e., quantity-based scaling approaches), and a valuation-based scaling approach. The quantity-based scaling approaches are relatively straightforward where the trustee determines the scale or size of restoration alternatives so as to provide natural resources and associated services equal in quantity to those injured and lost, i.e., quantity (of resources) restored equals quantity (of resources) injured and lost. In cases where quantity-based scaling approaches are not appropriate, trustees can base restoration actions on a valuation scaling approach. Basically the approach involves a determination of the scale of restoration alternatives that could provide natural resources and associated services of the same or equal value of those resources and services injured or lost.

The valuation-based scaling approach involves several steps. The trustee must measure the value of injured or lost resources and services, and then determine the scale of alternatives that can achieve resources and services of equal value to those injured or lost to the public. In the case that valuation of injured or lost resources and services is practicable, but that valuation of replacement or restored resources and services cannot be "performed within a reasonable time frame or at a reasonable cost," trustees can adapt the valuation scaling approach to scale restoration alternatives based on the cost of the provision of resources and services. The criteria would be based on scaling alternatives where the cost of providing resources and services is equal to the value of those injured or lost. Lastly, trustees must express all values and quantities in discounted terms, and consider the effect of uncertainties on the outcome of restoration actions.

3.6.2.2.4. Evaluation of Alternatives

In the second component of restoration selection, Evaluation of Alternatives, trustees must conduct an evaluation of all restoration alternatives based on various factors. These factors include: (1) implementation cost, (2) extent to which the alternative plan could return injured resources and services to baseline conditions and compensate for interim losses, (3) likelihood of success, (4) extent to which the alternative plan will prevent future injury and avoid collateral injury from implementation, (5) extent to which the alternative plan benefits more than one natural resource and service, and (6) effect of the alternative plan on public health and safety. On this basis trustees will then select a "preferred" restoration alternative(s), and where more than one alternative plan is equally preferable, the selected plan will be the most cost-effective, that is, the least costly plan to carry out.

3.6.2.2.5. Development of Restoration Plans

The third component of restoration selection, Developing Restoration Plans involves developing a Draft Restoration Plan available for public comment, and then a Final Restoration Plan. It is in this phase that trustees must consider monitoring and develop specific criteria to assess the success of the preferred restoration plan. Such information must be contained within the Draft Restoration Plan. The purpose is to document restoration effectiveness, an area that has become controversial and has grown in popularity in recent times. This in turn will be used to determine the success of restoration and the need for corrective action. Specific performance criteria must be identified for this purpose.

3.6.2.2.6. Implementation of a Regional Restoration Plan

The last component of restoration selection, Implementation of a Regional Restoration Plan or Existing Restoration Project, appears to be a logical choice when a spill or discharge repeatedly occurs in the same location or in close proximity to a location undergoing an existing restoration plan. In these cases the preferred restoration plan could be either a Regional Restoration Plan or an Existing Restoration Plan if all of the above criteria have been met. If repeated spills or discharges happen in the same area it makes sense to develop restoration plans that can cover a larger area that has or could experience injury; such efforts could provide cost and performance efficiencies if economies of scale are present in restoration projects. A second aspect of this component involves the demand (i.e., a claim for recoverable monies). If a Regional Restoration Plan is the preferred alternative, then the trustee would present a demand to the responsible party. This demand would invite the responsible party to either implement the component of the Regional Restoration Plan relevant to the injury that resulted from the party's actions or advance the cost of implementing the relevant component of the Regional Restoration Plan to the trustees.

3.6.2.3. Restoration Implementation Phase

This phase represents the last part of the NRDA and restoration process and begins implementation of the preferred restoration plan. It consists of five steps:

1. Closing the administrative record and presenting a demand
2. Discounting and compounding
3. Determining unsatisfied demands
4. Opening an account for recoverable damages
5. Additional considerations

3.6.2.3.1. Closing the Administrative Record and Presenting a Demand

The first component involves closing of the Administrative Record created in the Pre-assessment Phase. The second component involves presenting the responsible party with a Demand, i.e., monetary claim. In this written demand, trustees invite the responsible party to implement the preferred restoration plan subject to trustee oversight and to reimburse the trustees for costs of assessment and oversight or advance a sum of money to cover assessment costs and all costs of implementation of the preferred restoration plan that have been discounted to the trustees. The responsible parties have a 90-day period to respond in writing to this demand.

3.6.2.3.2. Discounting and Compounding

The third component, Discounting and Compounding, is for the purposes of providing more detail for discounting estimated future restoration costs (these must be discounted back to the date the demand is presented, because a future dollar will be smaller than a dollar now in discounted or present value terms), and compounding past assessment and emergency restoration costs (these incurred costs are to be compounded forward to the date the demand is presented, where a past dollar will be larger than a dollar now in present value terms).

3.6.2.3.3. Unsatisfied Demands

The forth component, Unsatisfied Demands, is for further action against the responsible party if the party does not agree to the written demand within a 90-day period. Trustees have two options: (1) to file a judicial action for damages within a three-year period after the Final Restoration Plan or Notice of Intent to Use a Regional Restoration Plan or Existing Restoration Plan is made publicly available, or (2) to seek an appropriation from the Oil Spill Liability Trust Fund. At this point the U.S. Coast Guard, the agency that oversees the Oil Spill Liability Trust Fund, can seek monetary damages from the guarantor of the vessel or facility involved in the spill or discharge similar to the process discussed under CERCLA (Section 3.1.1.3).[5]

3.6.2.3.4. Opening an Account for Recoverable Damages

The fifth component, Opening an Account for Recoverable Damages, stipulates that trustees must place all monetary sums recovered from NRDA claims in a revolving trust account. Sums recovered can first be used to reimburse trustees for past assessment costs and emergency restoration costs; the remainder must be used to implement the preferred restoration plan. Any sums that remain in such an account after the preferred restoration plan has been implemented and monitoring of the implemented restoration plan has been completed and judged successful to make the environment and public whole must be deposited into the Oil Spill Liability Trust Fund.

3.6.2.3.5. Additional Considerations

The last component of this phase, Additional Considerations, is meant to help trustees facilitate implementation of the preferred restoration plan.

3.6.2.4. Restoration Scaling Procedures

A number of procedures are listed in the published rules and procedures for determining the scale of restoration projects for NRDA under OPA. Trustees are not bound to use only these procedures, but instead may select any procedure that is appropriate to the particular situation as long as the selected procedures satisfy the above federal rules and procedures (specifically Section 990.27, U.S. DOC, NOAA 1996a). These procedures are:

- Habitat equivalency approach
- Travel cost method
- Factor income approach
- Hedonic price model
- Market models of demand and supply
- Contingent valuation
- Conjoint analysis
- Benefits transfer approach

At this point, we are interested only in noting which techniques were listed and that they involve both market-based methods and nonmarket-based methods. Examining this type of information enables one to observe the importance of economic techniques in federal rulemaking and how up to date specific federal rules and procedures are. Detailed discussion of most of these particular techniques is covered in Chapters 7 and 8.

3.7. Summary of Federal NRDA Rules and Procedures

3.7.1. NRDA Procedures

The process of developing and promulgating federal NRDA procedures has been lengthy. The U.S. DOI developed final rules in 1994 for type B assessments and in 1996 for type A assessments, some 14 and 16 years, respectively, after passage of CERCLA in 1980. The most recent version of the published final rules was based on initial procedures developed in 1986 and 1987, which were challenged in court in 1989 and had to be revised subject to the court decision. It took NOAA six years to finalize a uniform set of procedures to assess injury, damages, and restoration actions. This was a tremendous effort in developing these federal procedures and an effort that proceeded as quickly as our knowledge in science and economics would allow. NOAA benefited tremendously from hindsight and the procedures the U.S. DOI had developed. One could compare the development of these procedures with those developed for water resource projects. In the late 1950s (1956–58), both academic economists and individuals elected to public office (senators, representatives) pursued the goal of a set of uniform procedures for water resource projects. With the publication of these procedures in 1972 and 1979, over 20 years later, tremendous progress had been made in our ability to respond, develop, and promulgate uniform procedures at the federal level. That is not to say that these procedures are accepted universally, but the procedures are needed, and they represent the latest knowledge in science and economics. They reflect the acceptance as well as the controversies among the professionals who use them. The continuing process of critiquing these procedures is healthy and will push practitioners and researchers to iron out the rough spots. Procedural recommendations and field applications of particular techniques and methods should never supersede further systematic theoretical development and field testing of a particular technique. Some would admit this may have happened in the development of the contingent valuation technique (Randall 1991, Mitchell and Carson 1989).

Because the NRDA process involves the responsible parties in cleanup, restoration, damage assessment activities, and payment of monetary claims, the government hopes to have created incentives to discourage such behavior. This is the extent of incentives that was created in the CWA, CERCLA, and OPA. Further research is needed to determine the effectiveness of such liability rules relative to other economic policies (e.g., effluent taxes).

The U.S. DOI and NOAA NRDA procedures and rules now contain many parallels, the most important of which is the definition of damages. Both use the following definition:

damages = restoration costs + compensable value + assessment cost,

where restoration costs refer to the costs of restoration, rehabilitation, replacement, or acquisition of equivalent natural resource and services, compensable value for the U.S. DOI procedures refers to lost use value and lost nonuse value to the public (included at the discretion of the lead trustee), compensable value for the NOAA procedures refers to lost interim values to the public (lost use value and lost passive use value, i.e., the nonuse values of existence and bequest values), and assessment costs refer to the reasonable costs of assessment. Both procedures also include restoration actions, costs of restoration actions, and methods to estimate restoration costs as a major component of the procedure and damage estimate. Both techniques share a similar procedural approach that involves a Preassessment Phase, an Assessment Phase, and a Post-Assessment Phase. Both procedures select the "preferred" restoration plan based on technical feasibility, reasonable costs, and cost-effectiveness where appropriate; more sophisticated and alternative approaches are used only when they can be applied at reasonable cost, and when the extra cost from their use would be exceeded by additional benefits these techniques can measure and estimate. The U.S. DOI NRDA rules and procedures are heavily weighted toward the measurement and estimation of injury(ies), restoration costs, and compensable value. The NOAA NRDA rules and procedures are weighted toward scaling restoration projects (i.e., choosing the appropriate size of restoration projects), estimating and basing the scale of restoration projects on restoration costs and damages, and including monitoring actions as a component of restoration actions in the Post-Assessment Phase. Concerning monitoring, the NOAA procedures contain specific procedures to evaluate such restoration actions. Monitoring and the use of scaling procedures are not treated or are treated minimally in the U.S. DOI rules. It remains an issue for future rulemaking whether these issues will be incorporated in both federal rules and procedures on a consistent and equal basis.

3.7.2. Future Issues

There are five key issues and concerns in federal NRDA procedures to be resolved:

1. The NRDAM computer model to be used for type A assessments, and possibly the use of standardized restoration tables and costs in NOAAs NRDA (U.S. DOC, NOAA 1996a). Effort here will be to expand the NRDAM to cover more scenarios and improve both use value estimates and restoration cost estimates.
2. The contingent valuation technique will remain controversial until adequate testing has resolved all aspects of its application. This will require use of experimental economic techniques in the laboratory and in field environments and applications.
3. Restoration and monitoring must become more important as researchers and practitioners learn more about restoration methods.
4. The area of nonuse values will remain controversial in NRDA procedures due to limited field applications (and especially their use and incorporation into the NRDAM computer model), and because of theoretical difficulties. Theoretical issues must be resolved among economists before field applications can proceed. We envision that the area of NRDA and development of techniques and methods will see explosive growth and will generate new contributions to our limited knowledge in assessments of resource damages and in the general area of environmental and resource economics.
5. More attention must be given to the use of liability rules in controlling negative externalities such as random spills or discharges as in CERCLA, the CWA, and OPA.

3.7.3. Progress and Cases to Date

As of November 1992, the Damage Assessment and Restoration Program of NOAA reported $120.7 million in marine resource damage settlements (Anderson 1993). A total of 22 cases involving $195.9 million in marine resource damage claims ($199.7 million including two settlements from groundings and damage to coral reefs at Key Largo National Marine Sanctuary, a total of $3,825,000) had been settled (US DOC, NOAA 1996b). Based on more recent data up to 1998, 42 cases involving $213.3 million in NRDA claims ($229.35 million including 7 settlements from groundings and damage to coral reefs at Key Largo National Marine Sanctuary, a total of $16.02 million) has been settled (Appendix A). None of these figures contain the $900 million settlement for resource damages (out of a $1.125 billion settlement) in 1991 that involved the *Exxon Valdez* oil spill in Prince William Sound, Alaska. Of those listed in Appendix A, those that involved oil spills included locations along the West Coast (CA, WA), East Coast (DE, PA, NJ, NY, CT, RI, FL), and Gulf of Mexico (LA, TX). Hazardous substance spills included locations along the West Coast (CA, WA), East Coast (DE, NJ, MA), and Gulf Coast (TX). Locations in New Jersey and New York contained the most incidents of oil spills, while locations in Washington contained the most incidents of hazardous substance spills or discharges.

Concerning specific federal statues, for the most recent case histories reported, 12 or 28.6 percent were applied under CERCLA, 6 or 14.3 percent under OPA, 8 or 19.1 percent under the CWA, 8 or 19.1 percent under NMSA (National Marine Sanctuaries Act) (note some individual cases involved multiple statues). The largest oil spill case settled (other than the *Exxon Valdez* oil spill) was for $15 million from the Exxon Bayway spill in New York–New Jersey, followed by $9 million in damages from the *Tenyo Maru* in Washington, and $6.4 million from the *Apex Houston* oil spill in San Francisco Bay, California. The largest hazardous substance spill or discharge case settled was for $99.6 million for cleanup of New Bedford Harbor, Massachusetts, followed by $24.25 million in *re US v. The City of Seattle, et al.* located in Elliott Bay, Washington, and $12 million in *re US v. Montrose Chemical Corp.* located near the Palos Verdes Shelf, California.

3.8. National Estuary Program Overview

3.8.1. Introduction

The National Estuary Program (NEP) is a fairly recent federal policy initiative designed to manage and protect the water quality of estuaries of significant national importance as well as the Great Lakes. It is administered by the U.S. EPA. Established in 1987 via the Water Quality Act of 1987, the NEP uses a decentralized policy approach that integrates and directs state governments and the federal government in identifying pollution problems and sources, quantifying and measuring pollution problems, and developing policies to reduce and reverse the pollution problems (including financial commitment to achieve recommended actions). The overall goal of the NEP is "the protection and improvement of water quality and enhancement of living resources," of nationally significant estuaries that are "threatened by pollution, development, or overuse" (U.S. EPA 1989b: 1).

Prior to the NEP, and the formal inclusion of specific estuaries within this program, Congress had directed the U.S. EPA to take steps to protect several estuaries and coastal waters that were becoming severely polluted. The two earliest such programs, the Great Lakes Program (1970) and the Chesapeake Bay Program (1977), continue to serve as examples of the type of success achievable from state–federal cooperative efforts. In 1984, the U.S. EPA created the Office of Marine and Estuarine Protection (OMEP) to centralize efforts concerning the nation's ocean and coastal waters (U.S. EPA 1989a). At the time, two federal statutes gave the OMEP the power to protect the nation's ocean and coastal waters, the Marine Protection, Research, and Sanctuaries Act of 1972, and the CWA. In 1985, Congress directed the U.S. EPA to implement programs for four estuaries of national significance (Narragansett Bay in Rhode Island, Buzzards Bay in Massachusetts, Long Island Sound that borders Connecticut and New York, and Puget Sound in Washington). Two estuaries were added in 1986 (San Francisco Bay/San Joaquin Delta, and Albemarle/Pamlico Sounds in North Carolina).

In 1987 amendments to the CWA were passed by Congress and became known as "The Water Quality Act." The Water Quality Act expanded the nation's commitment to protect and manage pollution in surface water, lakes, and estuaries, and it created new efforts directed at the protection and restoration of important coastal resources, specifically the National Estuary Program (which included Narragansett Bay, Buzzards Bay, Long Island Sound, Puget Sound, San Francisco Bay/San Joaquin Delta, and Albemarle/Pamlico Sounds), the Great Lakes Program, and the Chesapeake Bay Program, to be administered by the OMEP, U.S. EPA. These specific initiatives became part of the U.S. EPA's Near Coastal Waters Activities, which included coastal waters not designated under the NEP, e.g., New York Bight, Gulf of Mexico, and Oregon Coast (U.S. EPA 1989a).

The NEP was modeled after two well-established comprehensive ecological and environmental programs, the Great Lakes Program and the Chesapeake Bay Program. These landmark programs achieved dramatic improvement in the health of these water bodies, and from them, lessons on organization, management, and approach to pollution problems and control were incorporated into the NEP. In particular, the program borrows the useful "phased program approach," whereby pollution problems and their causes are systematically identified and alternative strategies for solving them are developed. In addition, the NEP borrowed the "collaborative problem-solving process," where all parties (i.e., stakeholders) are involved in each step and make a financial commitment to achieve recommended actions (U.S. EPA 1989b).

In 1987 and 1988, six new estuaries were added to the NEP, respectively, from the 1987 amendments to the CWA and 1988 Appropriations Act (U.S. EPA 1989a). These new estuaries were New York–New Jersey Harbor, Delaware Bay, Delaware Inland Bays, Sarasota Bay in Florida, Galveston Bay in Texas, and Santa Monica Bay in California, bringing the total to 12 estuaries under the NEP. In 1988, as part of U.S. EPA's Near Coastal Water Activities, the Ocean Dumping Ban Act of 1988 identified four new water bodies to be included in the NEP, Massachusetts Bay, Barataria-Terrebone Bay in Louisiana, Indian River Lagoon in Florida, and Peconic Bay in New York (U.S. EPA 1989a, 1996). In addition, the U.S. EPA identified the Gulf of Mexico to be included in its overall activities to protect the nation's coastal waters and estuaries (U.S. EPA 1989a). Continuing efforts of the OMEP concern the examination of some 90 estuaries within the United States regarding possible protection efforts and inclusion in the NEP.

The types of concerns and environmental problems pertaining to coastal waters and estuaries the U.S. EPA faces encompass six major areas: (1) toxic contamination, (2) pathogen contamination, (3) eutrophication, (4) habitat loss and alteration, (5) changes in living resources, and (6) persistent marine debris (U.S. EPA 1989a). All are potential concerns for estuaries that become designated as nationally significant and included within the NEP. In addition, these environmental concerns can also exist in other coastal water areas such as the New York Bight and the Gulf of Mexico. For the 12 estuaries in the NEP, toxic contamination, pathogen contamination, eutrophication, and changes in living resources were the most commonly cited concerns (U.S. EPA 1989a).

3.8.2. Approach to Estuary Projects Under the NEP

The NEP is a decentralized policy approach that integrates and directs the cooperation and involvement of state governments and the federal government in approaching identification of pollution problems and sources, quantification and measurement of the pollution problem, and policy approaches to reduce and reverse pollution problems (U.S. EPA 1989b; this section borrows heavily from that reference). The first part of this process begins at the state level whereby a governor will nominate an estuary for inclusion in the NEP. The U.S. EPA administrator will review the nomination and make a determination. If selected, a State–EPA Conference Agreement is prepared to list program activities, products, and a timetable in order to meet completion of a Comprehensive Conservation and Management Plan (CCMP) within a five-year period. There are four basic phases that each estuary follows within the NEP:

1. Planning Initiative Phase
2. Characterization and Problem Definition Phase
3. CCMP Development Phase
4. CCMP Implementation Phase

3.8.2.1. Planning Initiative Phase

In the Planning Initiative Phase committees are developed composed of all interested and knowledgeable individuals (e.g., citizens, scientists, and other professional–technical individuals at the federal, state, local, and private level). It is in this phase that all stakeholders in an estuary are included so that concerns can be aired and decisions can be made that will be acceptable to all parties. These stakeholder groups include (1) elected and appointed policymakers representing all levels of government, (2) environmental managers at the federal, state, and local level, (3) individuals from the local scientific and academic communities, and (4) citizens from public and user interest groups. The various committees can include the following: (1) a policy committee, (2) a management committee, (3) a scientific and technical advisory committee, (4) a citizens advisory committee, (5) a local government committee, and (6) a financial planning committee. These are convened in a Management Conference, the purpose of which is to build a management framework to identify and solve problems and to build a constituency for the individual estuary. It is during the conference that an estuary's problems are identified, specific areas are selected for further study, and a workable timetable is set to meet the CCMP within five years.

3.8.2.2. Characterization and Problem Definition Phase

Characterization involves a historical overview of the health and quality of the estuary and its living resources together with a history of notable problems (e.g., nutrient overloads, excessive levels of toxic contaminants, hypoxic conditions, notable declines in fishery resources), and pollution loadings. Probable causes are suggested and tested for each specific problem. This phase provides the objective basis on which action strategies are developed. The information generated in this phase comprises (1) pollutant loadings and sources to the estuary, (2) circulation patterns, (3) distribution of pollutants in water and sediment, (4) distribution of living resources, (5) rates of biological processes, (6) factors critical to environmental and human health, (6) geographic areas of special importance, and (7) the economic importance of specific uses and their distribution and use patterns. Historical data are collected and analyzed in addressing these areas, and where gaps in data and knowledge exist, further study may be warranted.

3.8.2.3. Comprehensive Conservation and Management Plan Development Phase

The goal in developing a CCMP is to identify the most relevant problems in an estuary and offer ways to alleviate or correct them. The CCMP contains specific action plans in order to address priority problems so as to protect and enhance the estuary and its living resources. The CCMP also addresses funding strategies and sources so that the policies proposed can be implemented.

3.8.2.4. Comprehensive Conservation and Management Plan Implementation Phase

The last, and probably the most important, phase involves implementation of the CCMP, specifically the action plans and policies to which all constituencies have agreed. The CCMP will be more likely to succeed if it has identified appropriate funding sources and a funding strategy. The following tools are suggested to acquire resources for the recommended policies: tax instruments (i.e., taxes on income, property, overall sales, and specific commodity taxes), collection of fees (i.e., fees from pollution of the estuary), intergovernmental transfers of tax-based revenues, debt financing from issuance of municipal bonds, and private capital resources. Along with funding, the last phase must also periodically conduct reviews to evaluate each action plan and redirect efforts when necessary. Monitoring the quality of the estuary (its waters and sediments) and its living resources becomes a necessary component of this phase and the only manner by which to gauge progress and success.

3.9. Notes

1. Although the CWA addressed resource damages from hazardous substances and oil it did not require development of specific procedures and guidelines to assess such damages.
2. Personal communication with W. J. Hansen, U.S. ACOE, Institute of Water Resources on 12/11/97.
3. Personal communication with N.P. Psuty, Rutgers University, Institute of Marine and Coastal Sciences on 12/17/97.
4. It may be entirely coincidental, but the title of these procedures issued under President Ford, inflation impact statements, probably was related to an objective of the chief economic advisor to the president at the time, Alan Greenspan, currently the chairman of the Federal Reserve Board, well known for his anti-inflation emphasis.
5. Personal communication with B.E. Julius, U.S. DOC, NOAA, Office of Ocean Resources and Damage Assessments on 2/10/98.

3.10. References

Anderson, F.R. 1993. "Natural Resource Damages, Superfund, and the Courts." In Kopp, R.J. and V.K. Smith (eds.). *Valuing Natural Assets: The Economics of Natural Resource Damage Assessment.* Resources for the Future: Washington, DC: 26–62.

Bacher, L.O. 1993. "When Oil Is Not Oil: An Analysis of CERCLA's Petroleum Exclusion in the Context of a Mixed Oil Spill." *Baylor Law Review* 45(2): 233–242.

Brown, E.C. and T.B. Johnston 1997. "Toxic Substances Control Act (TSCA)." In Stern, C. and C. Volz (eds.). *1997 Wiley Environmental Law Update.* John Wiley and Sons: New York, NY: 157–175.

Campbell, T.A. 1993. "Natural Resource Damage Assessments: A Glance Backward and a Look Forward." *Baylor Law Review* 45(2): 221–232.

Ciriacy-Wantrup, S.V. 1952. *Resource Conservation Economics and Policies.* University of California Press: Berkeley, CA.

———. 1955. "Benefit–Cost Analysis and Public Resource Development." *Journal of Farm Economics* (November): 676–689.

Dolin, E.J. 1990. *Dirty Water/Clean Water: A Chronology of Events Surrounding the Degradation and Cleanup of Boston Harbor.* MIT Sea Grant Report No. MITSG 90-21. MIT Sea Grant College Program: Cambridge, MA.

Dower, R.C. 1990. "Hazardous Wastes." In Portney, P.R. (ed.). *Public Policies for Environmental Protection.* Resources for the Future: Washington, DC: 151–194.

Dower, R.C. and P.F. Scodari. 1987. "Compensation for Natural Resource Injury: An Emerging Federal Framework." *Marine Resource Economics* 4(3): 155–174.

Eckstein, O. 1957. "Investment Criteria for Economic Development and the Theory of Intertemporal Welfare Economics." *Quarterly Journal of Economics* (February): 56–85.

———. 1958. *Water Resource Development: The Economics of Project Evaluation.* Harvard University Press: Cambridge, MA.

Evans, P.B. 1997. "The Clean Water Act." In Stern, C. and C. Volz (eds.). *1997 Wiley Environmental Law Update.* John Wiley and Sons: New York, NY: 41–69.

Federal Inter-Agency River Basin Committee. 1947. *Qualitative Aspects of Benefit–Cost Analysis.* Subcommittee on Benefits and Costs: Washington, DC, April.

———. 1948. *Measurement Aspects of Benefit–Cost Analysis.* Subcommittee on Benefits and Costs: Washington, DC, November.

———. 1950. *Proposed Practices for Economic Analysis of River Basin Projects.* Subcommittee on Benefits and Costs: Washington, DC, May.

———. 1952. *Revised Statement on Secondary Benefits.* Subcommittee on Benefits and Costs: Washington, DC.

Freeman, A.M. III. 1990. "Water Pollution Policy." In Portney, P.R. *Public Policies for Environmental Protection.* Resources for the Future: Washington, DC: 97–149.

Graves, G. 1995. *Pursuing Excellence in Water Planning and Policy Analysis: A History of the Institute for Water Resources, U.S. Army Corps of Engineers.* U.S. Army Corps of Engineers: Alexandria, VA.

Hausman, J.A. and Diamond, P.A. 1993. "On Contingent Valuation of Nonuse Values." In Hausman, J.A. (ed.). *Contingent Valuation: A Critical Assessment.* North Holland: New York, NY: 3–38.

Heady, E.O. 1950. "Some Fundamentals of Conservation Economics and Policy." *Journal of Farm Economics* (November): 1182–1195.

Helton, D. 1993. "Oil Spill Scenario." *Baylor Law Review* 45(2): 215–220.

Hirshleifer, J., J.C. DeHaven, and J.W. Milliman. 1960. *Water Supply: Economics, Technology and Policy.* University of Chicago Press: Chicago, IL.

Hockley, M.D. and C.Y. Martin. 1997. "The Comprehensive Environmental Response, Compensation, and Liability Act." In Stern, C. and C. Volz (eds.). *1997 Wiley Environmental Law Update.* John Wiley and Sons: New York, NY: 105–155.

Holmes, B.H. 1972. *A History of Federal Water Resources Programs, 1800–1960.* Miscellaneous Publication No. 1233. U.S. Department of Agriculture, Economic Research Service: Washington, DC.

———. 1979. *History of Federal Water Resources Programs and Policies, 1961–70.* Miscellaneous Publication No. 1379. U.S. Department of Agriculture, Economic Research Service: Washington, DC.

Hunt, C.D., D. Redford, H. White, A. Robertson, F. Aikman III and D. Pabst. 1996. "Transport, Fate and Effects of Sewage Sludge Disposal at the 106-Mile Site: A Summary and Synthesis of Findings." *Journal of Marine Environmental Engineering* 3(2–4): 313–326.

Johansson, P.O. 1993. *Cost–Benefit Analysis of Environmental Change.* Cambridge University Press: New York, NY.

Kenefick., A.M. 1997. "Oil Pollution Act of 1990." In Stern, C. and C. Volz (eds.). *1997 Wiley Environmental Law Update.* John Wiley and Sons: New York, NY: 193–224.

Krutilla, J.V. and O. Eckstein. 1958. *Multiple Purpose River Development: Studies in Applied Economic Analysis.* The Johns Hopkins University Press: Baltimore, MD.

Maass, A. 1962. *Design of Water Resource Development.* Harvard University Press: Cambridge, MA.

Madden, G.J. 1997. "Resource Conservation and Recovery Act." In Stern, C. and C. Volz (eds.). *1997 Wiley Environmental Law Update.* John Wiley and Sons: New York, NY: 71–103.

Margolis, J. 1957. "Secondary Benefits, External Economies, and the Justification of Public Investment." *Review of Economics and Statistics* (August): 284–291.

Martin, J.H. 1991. "New York City Agrees to End Dumping of Sludge in Ocean by June 30, 1992." *Waste Management Research Report* 3(2): 14.

McKean, R.N. 1958. *Efficiency in Government through Systems Analysis with Emphasis on Water Resources Development.* J. Wiley & Sons, Inc.: New York, NY.

National Academy of Sciences. 1984. *Toxicity Testing: Strategies to Determine Needs and Priorities.* National Academy Press: Washington, DC.

———. 1994. *Managing Wastewater in Coastal Urban Areas.* National Academy Press: Washington, DC.

Office of Management and Budget. 1996. *Economic Analysis of Federal Regulations under Executive Order 12866.* Executive Office of the President: Washington, DC.

President's Advisory Committee on Water Resource Policy. 1955. *Water Resources Policy.* Washington, DC, December.

Presidential Documents. 1974. "Executive Order 11821—Inflation Impact Statements." *Federal Register* 39: 41501.

———. 1977. "Executive Order 11949—Economic Impact Statements." *Federal Register* 42: 1017.

———. 1978. "Executive Order 12044—Improving Government Regulations." *Federal Register* 43: 12661.

———. 1981. "Executive Order 12291—Federal Regulation." *Federal Register* 46(33): 13193–13198.

———. 1993. "Executive Order 12866—Regulatory Planning and Review." *Federal Register* 58(190): 51735–51744.

Randall, A.J. 1991. "Total and Nonuse Values." In Braden, J.B. and C.D. Kolstad (eds.). *Measuring the Demand for Environmental Quality.* North-Holland: New York, NY: 303–321.

Regan, M.M. and E.L. Greenshields. 1951. "Benefit–Cost Analysis of Resource Development Programs." *Journal of Farm Economics* (November): 866–878.

Regan, M.M. and E.G. Weitzell. 1947. "Economic Evaluation of Soil and Water Conservation Measures and Programs." *Journal of Farm Economics* (November): 1275–1294.

Reuss, M. 1992. "Coping with Uncertainty: Social Scientists, Engineers, and Federal Water Resource Planning." *Natural Resources Journal* 32(1): 101–135.

Rusin, M., R.C. Anderson, T.J. Lareau, G.P. Rao and A. Wiese. 1996. *Analysis of the Costs and Benefits of Regulations: A Review of Historical Experience.* Discussion Paper #084R. American Petroleum Institute: Washington, DC.

Shapiro, M. 1990. "Toxic Substances Policy." In Portney, P.R. *Public Policies for Environmental Protection.* Resources for the Future: Washington, DC: 195–241.

Smary, E.E. and D.K. DeWitt. 1997. "Learning from Our Mistakes: Brownfields Redevelopment." In Stern, C. and C. Volz (eds.). *1997 Wiley Environmental Law Update.* John Wiley & Sons: New York, NY: 267–288.

U.S. Army Corps of Engineers. 1951. "Report of the Civil Works Program as Administered by the Corps of Engineers." In *Annual Report of the Chief of Engineers, U.S. Army.* Part 1, Volume 3. Fort Belvoir, VA.

———. 1986a. *National Economic Development Procedures Manual—Recreation: Volume I: Recreation Use and Benefit Estimation Techniques.* IWR Report 86-R-4. Fort Belvoir, VA, March.

———. 1986b. *National Economic Development Procedures Manual—Recreation: Volume II: A Guide for Using the Contingent Value Methodology in Recreation Studies.* IWR Report 86-R-5. Fort Belvoir, VA.

———. 1987. *National Economic Development Procedures Manual—Agricultural Flood Damage.* IWR Report 87-R-10. Fort Belvoir, VA.

———. 1988. *National Economic Development Procedures Manual—Urban Flood Damage.* IWR Report 88-R-2. Fort Belvoir, VA.

———. 1990. *National Economic Development Procedures Manual—Recreation: Volume III: A Case Study Application of Contingent Value Method for Estimating Urban Recreation Use Benefits.* IWR Report 90-R-11. Fort Belvoir, VA.

———. 1991a. *National Economic Development Procedures Manual—Coastal Storm Damage and Erosion.* IWR Report 91-R-6. Fort Belvoir, VA.

———. 1991b. *National Economic Development Procedures Manual—Recreation: Volume IV: Estimating Changes in the Quality of the Recreation Experience.* IWR Report 91-R-7. Fort Belvoir, VA.

———. 1991c. *National Economic Development Procedures Manual—Urban Flood Damage: Volume II: Primer for Surveying Flood Damage for Residential Structures and Contents.* IWR Report 91-R-10. Fort Belvoir, VA.

———. 1991d. *National Economic Development Procedures Manual: An Overview Manual for Conducting National Economic Development Analysis.* IWR Report 91-R-11. Fort Belvoir, VA.

———. 1991e. *National Economic Development Procedures Manual—Deep Draft Navigation.* IWR Report 91-R-13. Fort Belvoir, VA.

———. 1993a. *National Economic Development Procedures Manual—Public Surveys: Volume I: Use and Adaptation of Office of Management and Budget Approved Survey Questionnaire Items for the Collection of Planning Data.* IWR Report 93-R-2. Fort Belvoir, VA.

———. 1993b. *National Economic Development Procedures Manual—National Economic Development Cost Manual.* IWR Report 93-R-12. Fort Belvoir, VA.

———. 1995. *Evaluation of Environmental Investments Procedures Manual—Interim: Cost Effectiveness and Incremental Cost Analysis.* IWR Report 95-R-1. Fort Belvoir, VA.

———. 1996. *Planning Manual.* IWR Report 96-R-21. Fort Belvoir, VA.

U.S. Congress, Office of Technology Assessment. 1987. *Wastes in the Marine Environment.* U.S. GPO: Washington, DC.

U.S. Department of Commerce, National Oceanic Atmospheric Administration. 1993. "Natural Resource Damage Assessments: Advance Notice of Proposed Rulemaking, Extension of Comment Period, and Release of Contingent Valuation Methodology Report." *Federal Register* 58(10), Friday, January 15: 4600–4614.

———. 1996a. "Natural Resource Damage Assessments: Final Rule." *Federal Register* 61(4), Friday, January 5: 439–510.

———. 1996b. *Damage Assessment and Restoration Program: Settlements and Restoration Status.* Office of Ocean Resources, Conservation and Assessments: Rockville, MD.

U.S. Department of Health and Human Services. Food and Drug Administration. 1992. *Action Levels for Poisonous or Deleterious Substances in Human Food and in Animal Feed.* Washington, DC.

U.S. Department of Interior. 1952a. *Reclamation Manual, Volume XIII, Benefits and Costs.* Bureau of Reclamation: Washington, DC, March.

———. 1952b. *Report of Panel of Consultants on Secondary or Indirect Benefits of Water-Use Projects to Michael W. Straus, Commissioner.* Bureau of Reclamation: Washington, DC, June.

———. 1952c. *Reclamation Manual, Volume XIII, Benefits and Costs.* Bureau of Reclamation: Washington, DC, Revision of October.

———. 1986. "Natural Resource Damage Assessments; Final Rule." *Federal Register* 51(148), Friday, August 1: 27674–27753.

———. 1987. "Natural Resource Damage Assessments; Final Rule." *Federal Register* 52(54), Friday, March 20: 9042–9100.

———. 1994a. "Natural Resource Damage Assessments; Final Rule." *Federal Register* 59(58), Wednesday, October 19: 14261–14288.

———. 1994b. "Natural Resource Damage Assessments: Advance Notice of Proposed Rulemaking." *Federal Register* 59(201), October 19: 52749–52759.

———. 1996a. "Natural Resource Damage Assessments: Type A Procedures; Final Rule." *Federal Register* 61(89), Tuesday, May 7: 20559–20614.

———. 1996b. "Natural Resource Damage Assessments: Second Advance Notice of Proposed Rulemaking." *Federal Register* 61(137), July 16: 37031–37032.

U.S. Environmental Protection Agency. 1987. EPA Memorandum from Francis S. Blake, General Counsel of the EPA to J. Winston Porter, Assistant Administrator for Solid Waste and Emergency Response Re: Scope of the CERCLA Petroleum Exclusions Under Sections 101(14) and 104(a)(2).

———. 1989a. *Marine and Estuarine Protection: Programs and Activities.* EPA 503/9-89-002. Office of Marine and Estuarine Protection: Washington, DC.

———. 1989b. *Saving Bays and Estuaries: A Primer for Establishing and Managing Estuary Projects.* EPA 503/8-89-001. Office of Marine and Estuarine Protection: Washington, DC.

———. 1990. *The Economics of Improved Estuarine Water Quality: An NEP Manual for Measuring Benefits.* EPA 503/5-90-001. Office of Marine and Estuarine Protection: Washington, DC.

———. 1996. *EPA National Estuary Program: 1996 Summary of Projects.* EPA Contract No. 68-C2-0134. Oceans and Coastal Protection Division: Washington, DC.

U.S. Senate. 1962. *Policies, Standards, and Procedures in the Formulation, Evaluation, and Review of Plans for Use and Development of Water and Related Land Resources.* Senate Document 97, 87th Congress, 2nd Session, Washington, DC, May 29.

———. 1988. *Senate Report No. 100-431.* In U.S. Code, Congressional and Administrative News. 1988. *100th Congress - Second Session, Vol. 3.* West Publishing Co.: St. Paul, MN: 5867–5906.

U.S. Water Resources Council. 1973. "Principles and Standards for Planning of Water and Related Land Resources." *Federal Register* 38(174), September 10: 24778–24869.

————. 1979a. "Procedures for Evaluation of National Economic Development (NED) Benefits and Costs in Water Resources Planning (Level C) and Proposed Revisions to the Standards for Planning Water and Related Land Resources." *Federal Register* 44(102), May 24: 30193–30258.

————. 1979b. "Procedures for Evaluation of National Economic Development (NED) Benefits and Costs in Water Resources Planning (Level C), Final Rule." *Federal Register* 44(242), December 14: 72892–72977.

————. 1983. *Economic and Environmental Principles and Guidelines for Water and Related Land Resources Implementation Studies.* U.S. Government Printing Office: Washington, DC.

Ward, K.M. and J.W. Duffield. 1992. *Natural Resource Damages: Law and Economics.* John Wiley & Sons: New York, NY.

CHAPTER 4

Water Quality Degradations in Marine Environments: Impairments and Effects

4.1. Introduction

This chapter describes and summarizes the most important biological aspects of water quality degradations. Substances that can impair and degrade marine water quality are first identified and classified into generic groups following an approach similar to that used by the (former) Office of Technology Assessment (OTA) in their assessment of marine pollution (U.S. Congress, OTA 1987). We then identify and briefly describe the corresponding effects or impacts on organisms, ecosystems, and humans (in ascending order from simple organisms up to complex organisms). In addition to historical data, recent evidence of hazardous substances in coastal waters based on the National Status and Trends Program of the National Oceanic and Atmospheric Administration (NOAA) (O'Connor 1990, 1996) is included to give perspective concerning the presence and distribution of hazardous substances and their temporal trends in U.S. coastal waters.

This chapter identifies the scope and coverage of all impacts and effects treated in this book and serves as the first step in the systematic process of identification of economic effects and losses from water quality degradations. A review of the biological effects of hazardous substances, petroleum and oil, sewage sludge dump sites, pathogens, or metals on marine resources and organisms is beyond the scope of this treatment, and many good reviews of these effects already exist (French et al. 1996; Kennish 1992, 1997, 1998; NRC 1985, U.S. Congress, OTA 1987). Further, although toxicity effects from exposure to "pure" forms of specific toxicants and pollutants are well-known from chemical handbooks, specific toxic effects of the same substances that are found in the marine environment are less known or not known for a variety of reasons: (1) "Pure" forms are rarely found in the marine environment (due to contamination from exposure to air, sunlight, and marine water—weathering effects and dilution), and toxic effects of impure forms can vary considerably; and (2) toxic substances have different effects on different organisms, not all of which have been explored by researchers, nor are researchers in uniform agreement about these effects.

To understand degradations, impairments, and subsequent effects beyond this generic level of analysis requires some knowledge of basic oceanographic principles. For example, factors such as water temperature, salinity levels, tides, wind, water currents, waves, and depth can all affect mixing and settling rates of pollutants in marine waters. A good place to start is Bishop (1983), Carter (1988), and Clarke (1997).

4.2. Identifiable Substances

A variety of substances can degrade and impair marine water quality and sediments, and in excessive amounts can impair marine resources, living organisms, and, ultimately, humankind. Substances (classified in terms of their generic nature) that have effects on water quality include: (1) oxygen-demanding substances (e.g., primary effluent, raw sewage); (2) nutrients (e.g., nitrogen, phosphorous); (3) suspended solids (e.g., sewage sludge, dredged material); (4) pathogens (e.g., bacterial—coliform, *Streptococcus;* viral-hepatitis; parasitic—nematodes); (5) organic chemicals (e.g., halogenated and chlorinated hydrocarbons—tDDT [i.e., DDT and all of its derivatives], tPCB [i.e., PCB and all of its cogeners], organophosphate substances, and carbamates); (6) petroleum and oils (e.g., petroleum hydrocarbons—aromatic hydrocarbons); and (7) metals (e.g., mercury, lead) (U.S. Congress, OTA 1987) (Table 4.1).

Table 4.1. General Categories of Marine Pollutants.

Categories	Examples	Sources
Oxygen-demanding substances	Waste material, sewage sludge, primary/raw sewage	Industrial waste, sewage treatment plants, septic systems, vessel sewage
Nutrients	Nitrogen, phosphorous	Sewage treatment plants: effluent discharge, agricultural runoff, septic system runoff
Suspended solids	Particulate matter, e.g., sewage sludge, dredged material (sediment)	Sewage treatment plants, harbor/channel dredging
Pathogens	Bacteria (coliform, streptococcus), viruses (hepatitis), parasites (nematodes), fungi	Sewage treatment plants: salmonella, effluent, combined sewage overflows, agricultural runoff, septic system runoff
Organic chemicals and metals (Toxicants)	Metals (mercury, lead, cadmium, tin), Petroleum hydrocarbons (alkanes, cycloalkanes, aromatic hydrocarbons—organic com pounds (halogenated hydrocarbons, chlorinated hydrocarbons, tDDT, tPCB, dioxin)	Manufacturers: industrial wastes/sludge, petroleum products, agricultural pesticide runoff, vessel—tanker (benzene), spills/discharges, oil well blowouts
Solid waste, plastics	Metal cans, glass bottles, plastic bottles, bags, balloons	Recreational boats, combined sewer outflows, landfills, negligent waste disposal, general population

Source: Bishop 1983; Clark 1997; U.S. Congress, OTA. 1987.

Table 4.2. Water Quality and Water-Related Degradations.

Result	Cause
Excessive enrichment	Oxygen-demanding substances; organic matter and nutrients Eutrophication: excess nutrient levels Hypoxia: low oxygen levels
Pollutants in water column	Toxicants (hazardous/toxic substances) metals, petroleum substances, organic compounds
Pathogens	Bacteria, raw and partially treated sewage
Turbidity	Suspended solids, plankton blooms from nutrients
Noxious odors	Raw and partially treated sewage, industrial waste, decaying matter
Sediment decomposition, contaminated sediment	Particulate matter: sewage sludge, dredged material; toxicants
Marine debris, floatables	Nondegraded solid waste products: plastic bags and bottles, ballons, tampon applicators, tires, glass bottles, aluminum and tin cans, abandoned and lost fishing nets and lines.

Source: Bishop 1983; Clark 1997; U.S. Congress, OTA. 1987.

4.3. Types of Impairments

Impairments caused by the substances mentioned earlier are varied, and for some, only excessive amounts result in biological impairments (Bishop 1983; Clarke 1997, 1994; French et al. 1996; Kennish 1992, 1997, 1998; NRC 1985; U.S. Congress, OTA 1987). For example, nutrients such as nitrogen are essential to life, but excessive enrichment caused by oxygen-demanding substances and nutrients can result in eutrophication. This, in turn, can degrade water quality by producing hypoxic conditions (i.e., low oxygen levels) and anoxic conditions (i.e., an absence of oxygen) that can damage living organisms in the marine environment (Table 4.2). In addition, excessive nutrients can promote plankton and algal "blooms" and affect the turbidity of the water (i.e, cloudiness). Suspended solids can also affect water turbidity. Increased turbidity can restrict sunlight penetration in the water column, impair photosynthesis in aquatic vegetation, and has been associated with declines in aquatic vegetation (e.g., submerged aquatic vegetation [SAV]) in marine ecosystems such as the Chesapeake Bay (U.S. Congress, OTA 1987).

Elevated levels of organic chemicals, petroleum and oils, and metals, collectively referred to as "toxicants" (i.e., hazardous–toxic substances) in this book, are present in both the water column and bottom sediment. Absorption of these hazardous substances, in turn, can adversely affect living organisms. Pathogens from raw or partially treated sewage can occur in water and in sediment and can affect public health from the consumption of contaminated shellfish. Noxious or foul odors can also be an effect of degraded water quality. While not degrading water quality, per se, marine debris and floatable waste are visible and can result in injuries to living organisms and a variety of economic damages.

4.4. Ecosystem Health and Productivity: Impacts on Organisms

Numerous effects on marine organisms and marine ecosystems can result from the above types of water quality and water-related impairments. Researchers naturally describe these in terms of their effect on the simplest of organisms on up to more complex organisms, the ecosystem, and human society (U.S. Congress, OTA 1987). We follow this general outline.

Marine sediments are contaminated from the accumulation of toxicants and pathogens in sediment (Table 4.3). In addition, physical, chemical, and biological alteration of sediment can be caused by deposition of particulate matter, sewage sludge, and

Table 4.3. Impairments to Ecosystem Health and Productivity and Man.

Ecosystem Health and Productivity — Impairments to Organisms
Impairments to Sediments
  • Contamination and accumulation of toxicants (hazardous/toxic substances and metals) and pathogens
  • Physical, chemical, biological alterations

Impairments to Benthic Organisms (Bottom-Dwelling Plants and Animals)
  • Mortality(from hypoxic bottom-waters, acute levels of toxicants, suffocation from particulate/sludge deposition)
  • Long-term contamination (bioaccumulation of toxicants)
  • Disease and abnormalities
  • Alteration of abundance and distribution
  • Alteration of community structure

Impairments to Aquatic Vegetation (Submerged Aquatic Vegetation, Seagrasses and Other Aquatic Vegetation
  • Decline and loss of abundance and distribution (from increased turbidity, hypoxic conditions, eutrophication)

Impairments to Habitat
  • Decline in benthic organisms and change in structure
  • Decline in aquatic vegetation
  • Decline in food sources
  • Increased levels of toxicants in water column and sediment
  • Hypoxic water
  • Excessive nutrients
  • Floatable surface trash/plastics

Impairments to Fish and Shellfish
  • Harvest closures/restrictions
  • Change in site-specific productivity (from habitat impairments)
  • Mortality (from hypoxic waters, acute levels of toxicants)
  • Bioaccumulation and biomagnification of toxicants
  • Physiological effects: disease and abnormalities (e.g., fin rot, shellburn, tumors, lesions); increased susceptibility to disease; impaired growth, weight gain; impaired reproduction
  • Behavioral effects: avoidance of hypoxic waters and contaminated waters during seasonal migrations, and feeding range
  • Changes in abundance, distribution, and diversity
  • Alteration of community structure

Impairments to Birds, Mammals, Sea Turtles
  • Bioaccumulation and biomagnification of toxicants
  • Physiological effects: disease and abnormalities; impaired reproduction

• Mortality (acute levels of toxicants; marine debris [plastic products, lost fishing nets and lines]: ingestion, blockage and resulting starvation in mammals and sea turtles, and entanglement and suffocation in all)
• Alteration in abundance and distribution
• Alteration of community structure

Impairments to Humans — Economic Activities
Impairments to Human Health (from toxicants and pathogens; contact, ingestion, and consumption of contaminated water, contaminated seafood products)
• Impaired behavioral and motor responses
• Physiological effects: occurrence of disease (gastroenteritis, hepatitis); increased cancer risk; premature mortality; threat and/or occurrence of birth abnormalities

Consumption Sector Activities — Recreational Activities
• Use restrictions/closures of specific areas/waterbodies
• Beach use (from contamination of sediment and water, washups of marine debris)
• Swimming and water sports (from contamination of sediment and water)
• Recreational fishing (from fish and shellfish impairments)
• Pleasure boating (from contaminated water, floatable waste)
• Nonconsumptive activities, e.g., birdwatching (from impairments to resources)
• Reductions in demand for seafood products (both contaminated and noncontaminated product)
• Increased travel and avoidance of polluted or closed areas
• Decreases in all marine-related recreational activities
• Reduced demand in marine-related recreational activities

Production Sector Activities
• Seafood Industry Sector (from fish and shellfish impairments): commercial fishing harvesters (finfish and shellfish, aquaculture operations); processors; wholesale/retail trade establishments; restaurant trade; decreased demand for seafood product (decrease in market prices)
• Wholesale and Retail Trade Sector: manufacturers of marine recreational equipment: decreased demand for marine recreational equipment
• Travel and Tourism Industry (from beach closings): retail trade establishments, service establishments (e.g., hotel, motel, restaurants), transportation, reduced demand for these goods and services
• Real Estate, Housing Industry Sector (from contamination of sediment and water): residential housing, decreased demand for residential housing in contaminated areas
• Commercial and Pleasure Vessels (from floatable waste): increased frequency of repairs and downtime

Note: Abundance refers to the quantity or biomass of organisms, distribution refers to the occurrence of organisms throughout an ecosystem, diversity refers to the variety of organisms (i.e., number of different species in an ecosystem), community structure refers to both the distribution and diversity of organisms and their interaction within an ecosystem.

dredge material as well as by the process of dredging channels and harbors to deepen them (Bishop 1983, Clarke 1997, NRC 1989, U.S Congress, OTA 1987).

These impacts on sediments, in turn, have both direct and indirect effects on bottom-dwelling (i.e., benthic) plants and animals (flora and fauna). One effect on benthic animals is mortality caused by acute levels of toxicants and possibly from suffocation due to particulate deposition (e.g., where particulates from repeated sludge dumping covers the bottom in a thick layer) (Table 4.3). Mortality can also result from hypoxic bottom-waters; such an event occurred off the northern coast of New

Jersey in 1976 (Swanson and Sindermann 1979). Long-term contamination as a result of bioaccumulation of toxicants (i.e., the process whereby a substance enters an organism and becomes stored within its tissues) is another effect. Disease and abnormalities, such as cancer and mutagenesis, can result from long-term contamination and can affect reproductive capabilities (e.g., fecundity, maturity), and may ultimately lead to premature mortality. All of these effects on benthic organisms alter their abundance (i.e., quantity or biomass) and distribution (i.e., occurrence of organisms throughout an ecosystem) and, hence, their community structure (see Kennish 1992 and Day et al. 1989 for a good summary of ecological principles for marine environments).

Impacts on aquatic vegetation (e.g., submerged aquatic vegetation, seagrasses, and other aquatic vegetation) can occur from increased levels of turbidity and hypoxia and result in decreased abundance and distribution. This has been a problem in the Chesapeake Bay and has been cited as a problem in many of the estuaries within the U.S. Environmental Protection Agency's (U.S. EPA's) National Estuary Program (e.g., Long Island Sound, Delaware Bay) (U.S. Congress, OTA 1987, U.S. EPA 1989).

These impacts have effects on habitats of marine environments. In addition, elevated levels of hazardous substances in the water column could also damage habitats by reducing abundance of the food supply, an effect also caused by hypoxic waters (Table 4.3).

Considering the next trophic level of organisms (i.e., successive levels of a food chain web within an ecosystem) a wide variety of effects on shellfish and finfish have been identified in the literature. Impacts include the presence of pathogens, bioaccumulation of toxicants, biomagnification of toxicants (i.e., increases in concentrations of bioaccumulated substances in tissues of consumers and predators occupying higher trophic levels), mortality from hypoxic conditions and acute levels of hazardous substances, and physiological and behavioral effects (Table 4.3). Physiological effects such as disease and abnormalities (e.g., finrot, increased tumor incidence) can further increase the susceptibility of fish and shellfish to disease and can diminish growth and weight gain as well as impair reproduction. In addition, researchers have observed fish species avoiding hypoxic and contaminated waters, a behavioral effect (U.S. Congress, OTA 1987). All of these effects ultimately can change the abundance, distribution, and diversity of fish and shellfish resources in marine environments associated with impaired water quality.

Birds, mammals, and sea turtles are affected by degraded water quality in many ways. Impacts on this category of organism are especially important because many such species are considered threatened and endangered (e.g., the Kemps ridley sea turtle, piping plover, osprey, and many species of whales). All are affected by bioaccumulation and biomagnification of toxicants, which can result in physiological effects, disease and other abnormalities, and impaired reproduction. Mortality has occurred as a result of acute levels of toxic substances and from starvation due to blockage of the throat and mouth from ingestion of floatable trash that resembles food (e.g., plastic bags and balloons have reportedly been mistaken as jellyfish by sea turtles) (U.S. Congress, OTA 1987, WMI–SUNY 1989). All of these factors, in turn, ultimately affect and change the abundance and distribution of birds, mammals, and sea turtles within marine environments associated with impaired water quality.

4.5. Present State of Marine Water Quality in the United States

This section is included to provide the reader with an assessment of the present state of marine water quality in U.S. waters. Knowledge of baseline conditions of marine water quality is important for assessing and comparing relative changes; for assessing and comparing remedial, cleanup, and restoration efforts; and for noting areas in need of remedial measures, further research, and suspected problems.

Public policies and the current level of technology of municipal and industrial wastewater treatment facilities can help to influence the overall level of coastal water quality. Advances in cleanup technologies of Superfund sites and in estuaries subject to highly urbanized and industrialized development will aid in decisions regarding cleanup of contaminated bottom sediment. Such a situation faces the U.S. EPA in the cleanup of New Bedford Harbor, a Superfund site. Does one remove the bottom sediment and perhaps on the one hand permanently remove the source of the problem, while on the other hand risk contamination from resuspension and disturbance of the bottom sediment? Does one place a nonpermeable cap over the entire bottom to prevent further contact of water and living organisms with the contaminants? Is it preferable to develop organisms capable of consuming the contaminants via bioremediation (as in the case of petroleum and hydrocarbon products)? Or does one simply do nothing? Sufficient funds must be available to allow researchers to explore these issues and their relative effectiveness and success, and to thereby facilitate researchers' participation in public policy decisions.

An indication of recent water quality trends is based on evidence from reported fish kills that show an increase in the frequency of occurrence of fish kills in U.S. coastal waters (i.e., coastal rivers, streams, and estuarine waters) of the Northeast, the Mid-Atlantic, the South Atlantic, the Gulf of Mexico, and the Pacific, over the period from 1980 to 1989 (Lowe et al. 1991). The largest increases occurred in the Mid- and South Atlantic regions (Table 4.4). Information collected that associates specific causes for these fish kill events shows that low-dissolved oxygen accounted for the majority (41%) of these events, followed by wastewater, eutrophication, and pesticides (4.9%, 4.5%, and 4.0%, respectively, for a total of 13.4%) (one should note that 21% of the fish kill events did not specify a particular cause) (Table 4.5).

The National Status and Trends (NS&T) Program administered by the U.S. Department of Commerce, NOAA, composed of the Benthic Surveillance Project and the Mussel Watch Project, was designed to provide monitoring of ambient environmental quality in the nation's coastal waters to determine trends of chemical contamination over space and time and to assess biological effects of that contamination. Such a national pro-

Table 4.4. Fish Kill Events (Numbers) in Coastal Waters, 1980–89.

Region	1980	1981	1982	1983	1984	1985	1986	1987	1988	1989
New England	12	12	5	12	11	17	12	18	18	12
Mid-Atlantic	81	78	45	41	44	93	162	151	168	120
Southeast	50	123	99	114	98	151	241	159	166	218
Gulf	92	96	97	96	82	52	82	58	94	79
Pacific	43	49	37	19	28	27	22	38	18	12
Total	278	358	283	282	263	340	519	424	464	441

Source: Lowe et al. 1991.

Table 4.5. Direct Cause of Fish Kill Events, 1980–89.

Direct Cause	New England	Mid-Atlantic	Southeast	Gulf	Pacific	Total No.	Total %
Low DO	29	282	831	321	33	1496	40.96
Temperature	4	40	35	41	8	128	3.50
Sedimentation	0	8	2	11	1	22	0.60
Eutrophication	1	9	126	26	3	165	4.52
Disease	5	83	8	15	7	118	3.23
Stranding	3	20	14	16	12	65	1.78
Storm event	1	12	14	48	1	76	2.08
Wastewater	16	45	34	71	14	180	4.93
Animal waste	1	11	7	7	26	52	1.42
pH	4	9	1	4	3	21	0.58
Organic chemicals	2	8	4	7	9	30	0.82
Inorganic chemicals/ metals	13	27	3	26	16	85	2.33
Mixed chemicals	9	11	12	24	13	69	1.89
Pesticides	5	31	56	26	27	145	3.97
Nutrients	1	0	16	19	1	37	1.01
Salinity changes	0	2	29	6	2	39	1.07
Petroleum	3	33	8	23	15	82	2.25
Chlorine	4	41	1	2	24	72	1.97
Red Tide	0	4	1	9	0	14	0.38
Predation	0	3	0	0	0	3	0.08
Unspecified	28	307	217	126	78	756	20.70
Total	129	986	1419	828	293	3652	100.00

Note: Percent may not add precisely due to rounding. Low DO refers to low dissolved oxygen.
Source: Lowe et al. 1991.

gram is necessary because most coastal environmental monitoring in the United States is mainly for compliance monitoring (NRC 1990).

The NS&T Program began in 1984 with the Benthic Surveillance Program to monitor chemical contamination in sediment and in marine fish at almost 300 sites around the U.S. coastline (Atlantic, Gulf, and Pacific Coasts) (O'Connor 1990). In 1986 the NS&T Program was expanded to examine chemical contamination in mussels and oysters, referred to as the Mussel Watch Program (O'Connor 1996). Data are collected from mollusks (mussels and oysters) and from bottom sediment in which concentration levels of 13 elemental metals (aluminum, arsenic, cadmium, chromium, copper, iron, lead, manganese, mercury, nickel, selenium, silver, zinc) and organic compounds (18 cogeners of polychlorinated biphenyls (PCB), 6 derivatives of DDT, 4 derivatives of chlordane, 2 types of dieldrin compounds, 3 butyltin compounds, and 24 [polycyclic aromatic hydrocarbons] (PAH) compounds) were measured over the period from 1986 to 1993; however not all chemicals were sampled in early years (O'Connor 1990, 1996). There were up to 287 coastal sites sampled in the Benthic Surveillance Project from 1984 to 1987 and from 145 to 214 sites in the Mussel Watch Project in the period from 1986 to 1993 (O'Connor 1990, 1996; O'Connor and Beliaeff 1994).

4.5.1. Historical Evidence of Occurrence of Hazardous Substances: Evidence from the National Status and Trends Program

Results from the sediment sampling efforts indicate that chemical contamination is primarily associated with urbanized areas in the Northeast (e.g., Boston, New Haven, New York, Baltimore) and on the Pacific Coast (specifically, San Francisco, Los Angeles, San Diego, and Seattle) and is less frequent along the Southeast and Gulf Coasts. Coupled with historical data from other studies for the Pacific Coast (Southern California, Puget Sound), evidence indicates that chemical concentrations in general increased up to the year 1970 and thereafter began to decrease (O'Connor 1990). However, recent levels have not returned to baseline levels (i.e., levels when first measured) for tDDT (total DDT compounds; "t" stands for "total"), tPCB, tPAH in Puget Sound, and for lead and chromium in Southern California marine waters. In Southern California marine waters, zinc has returned to relative baseline levels, copper could show signs of increasing change, and DDT has almost returned to a relative baseline level over the period from 1951 to 1982. Conclusions reached by O'Connor (1990) were that higher levels of contamination are characteristic of urbanized estuaries, that these high levels were lower than levels thought to cause sediment toxicity, and that evidence of sediment toxicity and tumors in fish (e.g., liver tumors) were not commonly found. In addition coupled with historical data from other studies, concentrations of most contaminants measured in the NS&T Program may be falling.

The Mussel Watch Program expanded the number of substances measured over those mentioned above, and results are based on eight years of annual data (1986–94). Table 4.6 shows the results of trends (i.e., the correlation between ranking of concentrations and time) based on nonparametric Spearman correlations at the 95 percent confidence level (O'Connor and Beliaeff 1994). For all organic compounds in which use has been banned (i.e., chlordane compounds, DDT compounds, dieldrin compounds, PCB cogeners, butyltins-BT), findings indicate that concentrations have decreased over time and the number of sites with a downward trend overwhelms the number of sites with increasing trends of concentrations; few cases of increasing trends were, in fact, found (Table 4.6). The elements cadmium and arsenic, the use of which has been restricted, also show decreasing trends in concentrations. O'Connor (1996) further examined national trends based on annual geometric mean concentrations from 1986 to 1993, and findings confirmed the nonparametric Spearman tests; for example, from 1986 to 1993, geometric concentrations decreased from 39 ng/g (nanograms/grams; ng is one billionth of a gram) to 25 ng/g for tDDT , from 180 ng/g to 82 ng/g for tPCB, 350 ng/g to 300 for tPAH, 120 to 32 ng/g for tBT, 16 to 7.2 ng/g for tCDANE, 6.6 to 3.7 ng/g for tDIELD and from 10.2 µg/g (microgram/gram; µg is one millionth of a gram) to 8.5 µg/g for arsenic, and 3.1 to 2.5 µg/g for cadmium (Table 4.6). Overall findings show that concentrations have significantly decreased (or equivalently, that significant decreasing trends exist) for chemicals whose use has either been banned or restricted.

For most remaining metals, temporal trends have decreased. However, for lead, copper, and zinc measured in oysters and for mercury, temporal trends have increased; this trend was strongest for lead in oysters, and for mercury (O'Connor 1996, Table 5: 197). From a public health perspective, it might be useful to determine the quantity of oysters

Table 4.6. Trends of Toxicants in Mollusks (Mussels and Oysters) as Part of the Mussel Watch Program: Numbers of Sites with 95 Percent Confidence of Increases/Decreases in Trends Based on Mean Concentration Levels, Annual Geometric Mean Concentrations, and Spearman Rank Correlation Coefficient, 1986–1993.

Chemical	Increase	Decrease	1986	1987	1988	1989	1990	1991	1992	1993	r_s
Arsenic	5	14	10.2	9.8	9.4	8.5	9.5	9.1	9.3	8.5	−0.786*
Cadmium	3	20	3.1	2.9	2.7	2.6	2.8	2.7	2.1	2.5	−0.857*
Copper	5	17									
Copper (mussels)			9.9	9.9	9.3	10	8.9	9	8.7	8.1	−0.810*
Copper (oysters)			110	110	130	120	150	120	130	1200	.294
Mercury	7	8	0.11	0.11	0.11	0.12	0.09	0.11	0.11	0.120	.429
Nickel	4	5	2.1	2.1	1.9	1.7	1.7	2.1	2.3	1.7	−0.333
Lead	7	8									
Lead (mussels)			2.1	2.2	2.1	1.7	1.9	2.1	1.6	1.7	−0.571
Lead (oysters)			0.42	0.53	0.49	0.45	0.55	0.60	0.5	0.59	0.667
Selenium	2	12	2.5	2.6	2.9	2.2	2.4	2.6	2.5	2.4	−0.381
Zinc	6	7									
Zinc (mussels)			140	130	130	120	140	130	130	130	−0.291
Zinc (oysters)			1,800	1,700	2,100	2,100	2,300	1,700	2,000	1,900	0.133
tCDANE	0	43	16	19	14	14	14	6.2	7.3	7.2	−0.886*
tDIELD	0	19	6.6	8.6	5.4	5.4	3.7	3.0	4.4	3.7	−0.786*
tDDT	0	24	39	46	39	42	36	20	26	25	−0.878*
tPCB	0	26	180	140	130	140	110	67	86	82	−0.833*
tPAH	2	3			350	310	270	250	280	300	−0.486
tBT	0	11				120	78	71	47	32	−1.000*

Note: "Increase" refers to numbers of sites showing increasing trends, "Decrease" the number of sites with decreasing trends, concentration units were measured in μg/g-dry for elements and ng/g for organic compounds with tBT in units of Sn/g-dry, "r_s" refers to the Spearman correlation coefficient of concentration versus year, tCDANE refers to total chlordane (sum of concentrations of 4 compounds), tDIELD total dieldrin (sum of 2 compounds), tDDT total DDT and its metabolites, tPCB total PCB and its cogeners (twice the sum of 18 cogeners), tPAH total polycyclic aromatic hydrocarbon compounds (sum of 24 compounds), and tBT total tributyltin and its metabolites (3 compounds).
*Statistically significant at .95 confidence level.
Source: O'Connor and Beliaeff 1994.

(i.e., volume of oyster meats) that would have to be consumed before those substances with increasing trends would pose a public health threat. In addition, because the organic chemical compounds include halogenated hydrocarbons and chlorinated hydrocarbons that have been shown to biomagnify in predators and consumers, it might be useful to determine consumption levels that would begin to pose a public health threat.

4.5.2. Unsafe Seafood and Fish Consumption Advisories

Although the U.S. Food and Drug Administration continually monitors the safety of seafood for toxic contaminants (i.e., metals, chlorinated hydrocarbons, pathogens, etc.), the increase in fish and shellfish health advisories over the past two decades, while justifying the importance of such monitoring programs, brings into question the overall health and safety of certain seafood (e.g., striped bass and bluefish, shellfish, crustaceans such as crabs and lobsters, certain bottom feeding fish, and large pelagic fish). It seems possible that fish and shellfish caught in unsafe waters could enter the pool of available seafood product to consumers, which may suggest that monitoring efforts be expanded in the future. And what of new threats? Fish farming practices commonly use antibiotics in fish feed and in other ways (e.g., treating cages with antibiotics) (IOM 1991). One must wonder if similar issues will arise as with the use of antibiotics in animal feed, as in beef and poultry. The occurrence of virus strains resistant to most or all antibiotics in current times (e.g., a virus known as DT104 resistant to most common antibiotics may pose a threat to less than 1 percent of the population) presents the possibility that the widespread use of antibiotics in animal feed, with residues in edible meat products and now in fish feed, is a contributing factor to the generation of resistant viruses. The effects of such food products on young children, and on subsequent generations, are unknown, but it appears that there could be tremendous public health impacts both in terms of health care costs and in terms of preventative measures, and the adverse impacts could outweigh the benefits from using antibiotics in animal and fish feed (e.g., a population of 200 million with less than 1 percent at risk involves almost 2 million individuals, a sizable number). These types of issues and concerns should be continually monitored so that public policy decisions can determine the path society should follow.

Fish consumption advisories issued by state governments are another approach and a tool for dealing with unsafe seafoods by restricting or banning the consumption of seafood taken from specific waters. Thirty-seven states currently have some form of advisory limiting fish–shellfish consumption targeting specific groups (Cunningham et al. 1990). Although well intended, fish consumption advisories or health advisories have become a lesson in risk communication and risk management (Reinert et al. 1991). It is generally agreed that early advisories communicated incomplete or poor information that resulted in confusion among the public. Differences in risk assessment methods across states have also led to confusion. A major shortcoming of advisories regards compliance among the public and targeted population (usually recreational fishermen and new mothers). Poorly communicated information and poor or incomplete information in advisories can affect compliance as found by Knuth and Connelly (1992).

Unsafe seafood incidents and fish health advisories justify and underscore the importance of efforts such as the National Estuary Program that seek to restore the health of coastal water quality. Federal funds should continue to support these types of efforts because it may take longer than currently believed to achieve restoration of marine water quality, and in turn coastal ecosystems.

4.5.3. Marine Debris and Floatable Waste

For years the random and now illegal practice of disposal of trash that now is referred to as marine debris and floatable waste was left unchecked without monitoring or policies to address it. It took a number of years to bring attention to the problem of marine debris and floatable waste, and the efforts of three International Conferences on Marine Debris (Coe and Rogers 1997, Farris and Hart 1995, Shomura and Godfrey 1990, Shomura and Yoshida 1985) and a SUNY Conference on Floatable Wastes in the New York Bight (WMI, SUNY 1989) are to be applauded. Researchers learned that these problems were widespread throughout the world's oceans. They are responsible for marine mammal mortalities in both threatened and endangered status categories and can result in sizable economic effects (both in terms of lost economic value and negative economic impacts [CMC 1989; Haab et al. 1995; Kahn et al. 1989a, 1989b, 1989c, 1989d; Ofiara and Brown 1988, 1999; Smith et al. 1996; Swanson et al. 1991; U.S. MMC 1988; Wagner 1990]).

Public policy now exists to control some of the sources of marine debris and floatable wastes, for example MARPOL V (the International Convention for the Prevention of Pollution from Ships [1973] and its 1978 Protocol are referred to collectively as MARPOL 73/78; V refers to the fifth amendment [NRC 1995]) (MEPC 1988, NRC 1995), and in the United States, more advanced waste facilities should be provided in more marinas available to recreational boat users to further expand these efforts.

4.6. References

Berger, J. 1997. *Oil Spills*. Rutgers University Press: New Brunswick, NJ.

———. (ed.). 1994. *Before and After an Oil Spill: The Arthur Kill*. Rutgers University Press: New Brunswick, NJ.

Bishop, P.L. 1983. *Marine Pollution and Its Control*. McGraw-Hill: New York, NY.

Bruno, M.S. 1996. (ed.) "Offshore Disposal: Results of the 106-Mile Dumpsite Study—Part 1: Transport Processes." *Journal of Marine Environmental Engineering* 2(1–2); "Offshore Disposal: Results of the 106-Mile Dumpsite Study—Part 2: Water Column and Sediment Fates." *Journal of Marine Environmental Engineering* 2(3–4); and "Offshore Disposal: Results of the 106-Mile Dumpsite Study—Part 3: Biological Fates and Effects." *Journal of Marine Environmental Engineering* 3(2–4).

Capuzzo, J.M., A. McElroy and G. Wallace. 1987. *Fish and Shellfish Contamination in New England Waters: An Evaluation and Review of Available Data on the Distribution of Chemical Contaminants*. Coast Alliance: Washington, DC.

Carter, R.W.G. 1988. *Coastal Environments: An Introduction to the Physical, Ecological and Cultural Systems of Coastlines*. Academic Press: New York, NY.

Center for Marine Conservation. 1989. *Cleaning America's Beaches: 1988 National Beach Cleanup Result*. Center for Marine Conservation: Washington, DC.

Clarke, R.B. 1994. *Marine Pollution*. 3rd ed. Oxford University Press: New York, NY.

———. 1997. *Marine Pollution*. 4th ed. Oxford University Press: New York, NY.

Coe, J.M. and D.B. Rogers (eds.). 1997. *Marine Debris: Sources, Impacts, and Solutions.* Springer-Verlag: New York, NY.

Cunningham, P.A., J.M. McCarthy and D. Zeitlin. 1990. *Results of the 1989 Census of State Fish/Shellfish Consumption Advisory Programs.* Research Triangle Institute Report. Research Triangle Institute: Research Triangle Park, NC.

Day, J.W., C.A.S. Hall, W.M. Kemp and A. Yanez-Arancibia. 1989 *Estuarine Ecology.* John Wiley & Sons: New York, NY.

Farris, J. and K. Hart. 1995. *Seas of Debris: A Summary of the Third International Conference on Marine Debris.* UNC-SG-95-01. North Carolina Sea Grant College Program: Raleigh, NC.

French, D.P., M. Reed, K. Jayko, S. Feng, H. Rines, S. Pavignano, T. Isaji, S. Puchett, A. Keller, F. Freruh III, D. Gifford, J. McCue, T. Opishinski, G. Brown, E, MacDonald, J. Quirk, S. Natzke, B.S. Ingram, R. Bishop, M. Welsh and M. Phillips. 1996. *The CERCLA Type A Natural Resource Damage Assessment Model for Coastal and Marine Environments (NRDAM/CME), Technical Documentation.* Prepared for Office of Environmental Policy and Compliance, U.S. Department of the Interior: Washington, DC.

Haab, T., K.E. McConnell, M. Devitt, Q. Fong, J. Sutinen and J. Kirkley. 1995. *Economic Aspects of Marine Debris.* Project No. NA90AA-D-SG810 and SC3527887. National Sea Grant Program: Silver Spring, MD.

Institute of Medicine. 1991. *Seafood Safety.* National Academy Press, Washington, DC.

Kahn, J., D. Ofiara and B. McCay. 1989a. "Economic Measures of Beach Closures." In WMI, SUNY. *Use Impairments and Ecosystem Impacts of the New York Bight.* SUNY: Stony Brook, NY: 96–103.

———. 1989b. "Economic Measures of Toxic Seafoods." In WMI, SUNY. *Use Impairments and Ecosystem Impacts of the New York Bight.* SUNY: Stony Brook, NY: 121–126.

———. 1989c. "Economic Measures of Pathogens in Shellfish." In WMI, SUNY. *Use Impairments and Ecosystem Impacts of the New York Bight.* SUNY: Stony Brook, NY: 147–149.

———. 1989d. "Economic Measures of Commercial Navigation and Recreational Boating—Floatable Hazards." In WMI, SUNY. *Use Impairments and Ecosystem Impacts of the New York Bight.* SUNY: Stony Brook, NY: 162–167.

Kennish, M. 1992. *Ecology of Estuaries: Anthropogenic Effects.* CRC Press: Boca Raton, FL.

———. (ed.). 1997. *Practical Handbook of Estuarine and Marine Pollution.* CRC Press: Boca Raton, FL.

———. 1998. *Pollution Impacts on Marine Biotic Communities.* CRC Press: Boca Raton, FL.

Knuth, B.A. and N.A. Connelly. 1992. "Is New York's Health Advisory on Fish Consumption Making a Difference?" *Coastlines* 22(4): 4–5.

Lowe, J.A., D.R.G. Farrow, A.S. Pait, S.J. Arenstam and E.F. Lavan. 1991. *Fish Kills in Coastal Waters 1980–1989.* U.S. Department of Commerce, National Oceanic and Atmospheric Administration, Strategic Environmental Assessments Division: Rockville, MD.

Marine Environment Protection Commission of the International Maritime Organization. 1988. *Marine Environment Protection Committee Resolution 31(26) Adopted on 9 September 1988 and Implementation of Annex V and IV of MARPOL 73/78.* 26th Session, Agenda Item 10. International Maritime Organization: London, UK.

Myers, E.P. (ed.). 1983. *Ocean Disposal of Municipal Wastewater: Impacts on the Coastal Environment,* 2 Vols. MITSG 83-33. MIT Sea Grant: Cambridge, MA.

National Academy of Sciences. 1976. *Disposal in the Marine Environment: An Oceanographic Assessment.* National Academy Press: Washington, DC.

National Research Council. 1975. *Petroleum in the Marine Environment.* National Academy Press: Washington, DC.

———. *Disposal of Industrial and Domestic Wastes: Land and Sea Alternatives.* National Academy Press: Washington, DC.

———. 1984b. *Ocean Disposal Systems for Sewage Sludge and Effluent.* National Academy Press: Washington, DC.

———. 1985. *Oil in the Sea: Inputs, Fates, and Effects.* National Academy Press: Washington, DC.

———. 1989. *Contaminated Marine Sediments—Assessment and Remediation.* National Academy Press: Washington, DC.

———. 1990. *Managing Troubled Waters: The Role of Marine Environmental Monitoring.* National Academy Press: Washington, DC.

———. 1993. *Managing Wastewater in Coastal Urban Areas.* National Academy Press: Washington, DC.

———. 1995. *Clean Ships, Clean Ports, Clean Oceans: Controlling Garbage and Plastic Wastes at Sea.* National Academy Press: Washington, DC.

O'Connor, T.P. 1990. *Coastal Environmental Quality in the United States, 1990.* NOAA 20th Anniversary Report. National Status and Trends Program, U.S. DOC, NOAA: Silver Spring, MD.

———. 1996. "Trends in Chemical Concentrations in Mussels and Oysters Collected along the U.S. Coast from 1986 to 1993." *Marine Environmental Research* 41(2): 183–200.

O'Connor, T.P. and B. Beliaeff. 1994. *Recent Trends in Coastal Environmental Quality: Results from the Mussel Watch Project 1986 to 1993.* National Status and Trends Program, U.S. DOC, NOAA: Silver Spring, MD.

O'Connor, T.P., A. Okubo, M.A. Champ and P.K. Park. 1983. "Projected Consequences of Dumping Sewage Sludge at a Deep Ocean Site Near New York Bight." *Canadian Journal of Fisheries and Aquatic Sciences* 40(2): 228–241.

Ofiara, D.D. and B. Brown. 1988. *Economic Assessment of New York Bight Use Impairments on the State of New Jersey.* Institute of Marine and Coastal Sciences, Rutgers University: New Brunswick, NJ.

———. 1999. "Assessment of Economic Losses to Recreational Activities from 1988 Marine Pollution Events and Assessment of Economic Losses from Long-Term Contamination of Fish within the New York Bight to New Jersey." *Marine Pollution Bulletin* 38(11): 990–1004.

Pearce, J.B., D.C. Miller, and C. Berman (eds.). 1983. *106-Mile Site Characterization Update.* NOAA Technical Memorandum NMFS-F/NEC-26. Northeast Fisheries Center: Woods Hole, MA.

Reinert, R.E., B.A. Knuth, M.A. Kamrin and Q.J. Stober. 1991. "Risk Assessment, Risk Management, and Fish Consumption Advisories in the United States." *Fisheries* 16(6): 5–12.

Shomura, R.S. and M.L. Godfrey (eds.). 1990. *Proceedings of the Second International Conference on Marine Debris 2–7 April 1989, Honolulu, Hawaii.* U.S. Department of Commerce. NOAA Technical Memorandum NMFS. NOAA-TM-NMFS-SWFC-154. Southwest Fisheries Science Center: Honolulu, HI.

Shomura, R.S. and H.O. Yoshida (eds.). 1985. *Proceedings of the Workshop on the Fate and Impact of Marine Debris, 26–29 November 1984, Honolulu, Hawaii.* U.S. Department of Commerce. NOAA Technical Memorandum NMFS. NOAA-TM-NMFS-SWFC-54. Southwest Fisheries Science Center: Honolulu, HI.

Simon, A.W. and P. Hauge. 1987. *Contamination of New England's Fish and Shellfish: A Report to the Governors and the Public.* Coast Alliance: Washington, DC.

Smith, V.K., X. Zhang and R.B. Palmquist. 1996. "Marine Debris, Beach Quality, and Non-Market Values." Department of Economics, Duke University: Durham, NC. Unpublished Paper.

Squires, D.F. 1983. *The Ocean Dumping Quandary: Waste Disposal in the New York Bight.* State University of New York Press: Albany, NY.

Studholme, A.L., J.E. O'Reilly, and M.C. Ingham. 1995. *Effects of the Cessation of Sewage Sludge Dumping at the 12-Mile Site.* NOAA Technical Report NMFS 124. U.S. Department of Commerce, National Marine Service: Seattle, WA.

Swanson, R.L. and C.J. Sindermann (eds.). 1979. *Oxygen Depletion and Associated Benthic Mortalities in New York Bight, 1976.* NOAA Professional Paper No. 11. U.S. GPO: Washington, DC.

Swanson, R.L., T.M. Bell, J. Kahn, and J. Olga. 1991. "Use Impairments and Ecosystem Impacts of the New York Bight." *Chemistry and Ecology* 5: 99–127.

U.S. Congress, Office of Technology Assessment. 1987. *Wastes in Marine Environments.* U.S. Government Printing Office: Washington, DC.

———. 1987. *Ecological Consequences of Waste Disposal in Marine Environments.* NTIS: Washington, DC.

U.S. Environmental Protection Agency. 1989. *Marine and Estuarine Protection: Programs and Activities.* EPA 503/9-89-002. Office of Marine and Estuarine Protection: Washington, DC.

U.S. General Accounting Office. 1977. *Problems and Progress in Regulating Ocean Dumping of Sewage Sludge and Industrial Wastes.* U.S. Government Printing Office: Washington, DC.

U.S. Marine Mammal Commission. 1988. *Report of the Interagency Task Force on Persistent Marine Debris.* U.S. Marine Mammal Commission, Office of Domestic Policy: Washington, DC.

Wagner, K.D. 1990. "Medical Wastes and Beach Washups of 1988: Issues and Impacts." In Shomura, R.S. and M.L. Godfrey (eds.). *Proceedings of the Second International Conference on Marine Debris 2–7 April 1989, Honolulu, Hawaii.* U.S. Department of Commerce. NOAA Technical Memorandum NMFS. NOAA-TM-NMFS-SWFC-154. Southwest Fisheries Science Center: Honolulu, HI: 811–823.

Waste Management Institute, SUNY. 1989. *Use Impairments and Ecosystem Impacts of the New York Bight, Phase I Preliminary Report for the New York Bight Restoration Plan.* Marine Sciences Research Center, State University of New York: Stony Brook, NY.

4.7. Further Reading

Here we briefly list and summarize some of the more important books that the reader can turn to for in-depth material and coverage. For comprehensive and authoritative overviews the three volumes by Kennish are the most up-to-date and by far the most comprehensive:

Kennish, M. 1992. *Ecology of Estuaries: Anthropogenic Effects.* CRC Press: Boca Raton, FL.

———. (ed.). 1997. *Practical Handbook of Estuarine and Marine Pollution.* CRC Press: Boca Raton, FL.

———. 1998. *Pollution Impacts on Marine Biotic Communities.* CRC Press: Boca Raton, FL.

CERCLA Type A model report: French, D.P., M. Reed, K. Jayko, S. Feng, H. Rines, S. Pavignano, T. Isaji, S. Puchett, A. Keller, F. Freruh III, D. Gifford, J. McCue, T. Opishinski, G. Brown, E, MacDonald, J. Quirk, S. Natzke, B.S. Ingram, R. Bishop, M. Welsh and M. Phillips. 1996. *The CERCLA Type A Natural Resource Damage Assessment Model for Coastal and Marine Environments (NRDAM/CME), Technical Documentation.* Prepared for Office of Environmental Policy and Compliance, U.S. Department of the Interior: Washington, DC.

A fairly up-to-date treatment and assessment of the effects and fates of a variety of marine pollutants that are regulated by CERCLA-1980 and to some extent by OPA-1990 (oil spills and petroleum products are included) on living marine organisms and the marine environment in general are covered. A must for those who need to use the CER-CLA Type A computer model (NRDAM/CME) for relatively small spills. Older works include a series of three published multiple volumes on most aspects of marine pollution:

Wastes in the Ocean. 1983–1985. 6 vols. John Wiley and Sons: New York, NY. (See below for complete citation.) Republished in 1990 as *Oceanic Processes in Marine Pollution.* R.E. Krieger: Melbourne, FL.

Oceanic Processes in Marine Pollution. 1987. 5 vols. R.E. Krieger: Melbourne, FL. (See below for complete citation.)

For oil and petroleum products:

NRC. 1985. *Oil in the Sea: Inputs, Fates, and Effects.* National Academy Press: Washington, DC.

An update of an earlier state-of-the-art 1975 volume by the National Research Council. As stated in this updated version it contains significant new data and information since publication of the 1975 publication. By now it, too, is somewhat outdated, but remains the most authoritative treatment of the effects of oil in marine environments. No other treatment rivals this volume. The effects of several oil spill events are summarized as case histories (e.g., the barge *Florida*, the tankers *Arrow*, *Argo Merchant*, *Amoco Cadiz*, and *Zoe Colotroni*, and the Ixtox I undersea oilwell blowout).

NRC. 1975. *Petroleum in the Marine Environment.* National Academy Press: Washington, DC.

A review and summary of state-of-the-art material that predates a 1973 conference on which this publication is based.

Berger, J. 1997. *Oil Spills.* Rutgers University Press: New Brunswick, NJ.

A general treatment and overview of the effects of oil in marine environments. Evidence presented from the *Exxon Valdez* spill in Alaska, and the Exxon-Bayway spill in the Arthur Kill, NY–NJ.

Berger, J. (ed.). 1994. *Before and After an Oil Spill: The Arthur Kill.* Rutgers University Press: New Brunswick, NJ.

A summarization of the impacts of the Exxon Bayway spill in the Arthur Kill on biological organisms and animals.

For municipal wastewater, effluent:

NRC. 1993. *Managing Wastewater in Coastal Urban Areas.* National Academy Press: Washington, DC.

A summary of current practices of municipal wastewater treatment facilities in the United States as of 1993.

NRC. 1990. *Managing Troubled Waters: The Role of Marine Environmental Monitoring.* National Academy Press: Washington, DC.

Argues the need for routine monitoring of coastal waters.

Myers, E.P. (ed.). 1983. *Ocean Disposal of Municipal Wastewater: Impacts on the Coastal Environ-ment.* 2 vols. MITSG 83-33. MIT Sea Grant: Cambridge, MA.

For sewage sludge dumping, ocean dumping:

Studholme, et al. 1995. *Effects of the Cessation of Sewage Sludge Dumping at the 12-Mile Site.* NOAA Technical Report NMFS 124. U.S. Department of Commerce, National Marine Service: Seattle, WA.

The most authoritative and current summary and collection of technical papers pre-sented at a conference convened to determine the effects of termination of sewage sludge dumping at the 12-mile dumpsite in New York Bight. Papers examine the recovery of this site related to various biological parameters for various living organisms.

Bruno, M.S. (series ed.). 1996. "Offshore Disposal: Results of the 106-Mile Dumpsite Study—Part 1: Transport Processes." *Journal of Marine Environmental Engineering* 2(1–2); "Offshore Dis-posal: Results of the 106-Mile Dumpsite Study—Part 2: Water Column and Sediment Fates." *Journal of Marine Environmental Engineering* 2(3–4); and "Offshore Disposal: Results of the 106-Mile Dumpsite Study—Part 3: Biological Fates and Effects." *Journal of Marine Environmental Engineering* 3(2–4).

A series of special issues, and the most authoritative and current summary and collection of technical papers (29 in all) concerning results of the 106-Mile Dumpsite Study in the New York Bight conducted by NOAA and U.S. EPA.

Other publications regarding ocean dumping include:

NAS. 1976. *Disposal in the Marine Environment: An Oceanographic Assessment.* National Academy Press: Washington, DC.

NRC. 1984a. *Disposal of Industrial and Domestic Wastes: Land and Sea Alternatives.* National Acad-emy Press: Washington, DC.

———. 1984b. *Ocean Disposal Systems for Sewage Sludge and Effluent.* National Academy Press: Washington, DC.

O'Connor, T.P., A. Okubo, M.A. Champ and P.K. Park. 1983. "Projected Consequences of Dump-ing Sewage Sludge at a Deep Ocean Site Near New York Bight." *Canadian Journal of Fisheries and Aquatic Sciences* 40(2): 228–241.

Pearce, J.B., D.C. Miller, and C. Berman. 1983. (eds.). *106-Mile Site Characterization Update.* NOAA Technical Memorandum NMFS-F/NEC-26. Northeast Fisheries Center: Woods Hole, MA.

Squires, D.F. 1983. *The Ocean Dumping Quandary: Waste Disposal in the New York Bight.* State Uni-versity of New York Press: Albany, NY.

U.S. GAO. 1977. *Problems and Progress in Regulating Ocean Dumping of Sewage Sludge and Indus-trial Wastes.* U.S. Government Printing Office: Washington, DC.

For contaminated bottom sediment:

NRC. 1989. *Contaminated Marine Sediments—Assessment and Remediation.* National Academy Press: Washington, DC.

For marine debris and floatable waste:

Coe, J.M. and D.B. Rogers (eds.). 1997. *Marine Debris: Sources, Impacts, and Solutions*. Springer-Verlag: New York, NY.

Proceedings from the Third International Conference on Marine Debris; first proceedings to contain papers dealing with economic and pubic policy issues.

Farris, J. and K. Hart. 1995. *Seas of Debris: A Summary of the Third International Conference on Marine Debris*. UNC-SG-95-01. North Carolina Sea Grant College Program: Raleigh, NC.

NRC. 1995. *Clean Ships, Clean Ports, Clean Oceans: Controlling Garbage and Plastic Wastes at Sea*. National Academy Press: Washington, DC.

Shomura, R.S. and M.L. Godfrey (eds.). 1990. *Proceedings of the Second International Conference on Marine Debris 2–7 April 1989, Honolulu, Hawaii*. U.S. Department of Commerce. NOAA Technical Memorandum NMFS. NOAA-TM-NMFS-SWFC-154. Southwest Fisheries Science Center: Honolulu, HI.

Shomura, R.S. and H.O. Yoshida (eds.). 1985. *Proceedings of the Workshop on the Fate and Impact of Marine Debris, 26–29 November 1984, Honolulu, Hawaii*. U.S. Department of Commerce. NOAA Technical Memorandum NMFS. NOAA-TM-NMFS-SWFC-54. Southwest Fisheries Science Center: Honolulu, HI.

U.S. Marine Mammal Commission. 1988. *Report of the Interagency Task Force on Persistent Marine Debris*. U.S. Marine Mammal Commission, Office of Domestic Policy: Washington, DC.

For general overviews and coverage:

Berger, J. 1997. *Oil Spills*. Rutgers University Press: New Brunswick, NJ.

Bishop, P.L. 1983. *Marine Pollution and Its Control*. McGraw-Hill: New York, NY.

Carter, R.W.G. 1988. *Coastal Environments: An Introduction to the Physical, Ecological and Cultural Systems of Coastlines*. Academic Press: New York, NY.

An introduction to basic ocean processes and oceanography principles.

Clarke, R.B. 1997. *Marine Pollution*. 4th ed. Oxford University Press: New York, NY. (See also earlier editions.)

NRC. 1990. *Managing Troubled Waters: The Role of Marine Environmental Monitoring*. National Academy Press: Washington, DC.

Demonstrates and argues for the need for routine monitoring of coastal water quality.

U.S. Congress, Office of Technology Assessment. 1987. *Wastes in Marine Environments*. U.S. Government Printing Office: Washington, DC and NTIS: Washington, DC.

An authoritative overview of the dimensions and problems of marine pollution.

U.S. Congress, Office of Technology Assessment. 1987. *Ecological Consequences of Waste Disposal in Marine Environments*. NTIS: Washington, DC.

The citation for the older multivolume series mentioned earlier follows:

Wastes in the Ocean. 1983–1985. J. Wiley & Sons and republished in 1990 by R.E. Krieger.

Duedall, I.W., D.R. Kester, B.H. Ketchum and Park, P.K. (eds.). 1983. Volume 1: *Industrial and Sewage Wastes in the Ocean*.

Kester, D.R., I.W. Duedall, B.H. Ketchum and Park, P.K. (eds.). 1983. Vol. 2: *Dredged Material Disposal in the Ocean.*

Park, P.K., D.R. Kester, I.W. Duedall and B.H. Ketchum (eds.). 1983. Vol. 3: *Radioactive Waste in the Ocean.*

Duedall, I.W., et al. (eds.). 1985. Vol. 4. (Publisher could not provide a citation to this volume).

Kester, D.R., Burt, J.M. Capuzzo, I.W. Duedall, B.H. Ketchum and Park, P.K. (eds.). 1985. Vol. 5: *Deep Sea Waste Disposal.*

Kester, D.R., Burt, J.M. Capuzzo, I.W. Duedall, B.H. Ketchum and Park, P.K. (eds.). 1985. Vol. 6: *Near Shore Disposal.*

Oceanic Processes in Marine Pollution. R.E. Krieger: Melbourne, FL.

Capuzzo, J.M. and D.R. Kester. 1987. Volume 1: *Biological Processes and Wastes in the Ocean.*

O'Connor, T.P., et al. (eds.). 1987. Volume 2: *Physical and Chemical Processes.*

Champ, M.A., P.K. Park, et al. (eds.). 1987. Volume 3: *Marine Waste Management: Science and Policy.*

Volume 4 (Publisher could not provide a citation to this volume).

Wolfe, D.A. and T.P. O'Connor. 1987. Volume 5: *Urban Wastes in Coastal Marine Environments.*

PART II

Principles and Theory

CHAPTER 5

Economic Damages and Losses:
Principles and Methods of Assessments

5.1. Introduction

This chapter provides the basic economic theory and principles for understanding economic damages and losses. It introduces the fundamental concepts pertaining to a variety of economic measures, economic methods, and economic welfare measures used to assess changes in general, and to assess economic damages (i.e., losses of economic welfare). The level of explanation is slightly above a good principles (first-year college) level, and material in appendices is more advanced because it is expressed using formal mathematics. The theoretical framework is essential to gain an understanding of the application of cost–benefit analysis to evaluate public sector policy programs, such as improvements in water quality. Thus, although this chapter is theoretical, it represents the basis of conventional cost–benefit analysis applied to public programs, and in evaluating private sector activities as well (e.g., gains to commercial fishing following improvements in water quality). This chapter also covers the topics of input/output analysis, alternative measures of economic welfare, aggregation of economic welfare over individuals, economic losses versus impacts, scope of analysis and transfers, intertemporal losses, economic value from a total value perspective, federal natural resource damage assessments, and the issue of sequencing changes in economic welfare given multiple sites.

A discussion of terms and concepts will be useful at this point to dispel any contradictory and unnecessary meanings and to define the context in which we refer to them in this book, building on the discussion in Chapter 2. Several terms and concepts have been widely used by economists and in the popular press to represent different meanings and concepts. "Net economic value" refers to the monetary value of changes in economic surplus/welfare to consumption and production activities following a change in the quality of the environment (i.e., the sum of changes in consumer surplus and producer surplus), and when losses of economic surplus occur it is referred to as lost net economic value. But losses in economic surplus are not the only adverse change in economic activity that can occur from marine pollution. To the public there are other impacts or effects that should also be counted. We refer to such effects as adverse economic effects or economic impacts following degradations of the environment, and they can be thought of as decreases in measurable economic activity (e.g., sales, output, employment, income, etc.) and conceivably could include all possible economic effects that can be quantified—nonwelfare measures. These measures of effects are sometimes referred to as economic activity measures. Economic losses can then be thought of as decreases in measurable economic activity (e.g., sales, output, employment, income, etc.) from marine pollution. Economic losses have also been used to represent lost net economic value (i.e., the value of lost economic surplus or welfare) from marine pollution. "Economic losses" and "lost net economic value" represent different concepts; the former represents a nonwelfare measure and the latter a welfare measure. There is another context in which "economic impacts" is used, in conjunction with input/output (I/O) models to examine proposed policy and other changes in economic activity (e.g., structural change, a plant closing). In this context "economic impacts" refers only to those changes in economic activity (e.g., the sum of value-added throughout the economy where sales–output is the relevant variable) that are estimated from an I/O model where impacts to output or sales, income, and employment can be measured. Economic surplus or welfare is ignored. In this book we systematically identify all measurable economic effects (when appropriate) that can result from marine pollution, referring to them as either economic effects or economic impacts, and then further identify all losses of economic surplus from marine pollution, referring to these as economic losses.

The terms "benefits" and "economic benefits" suffer from a similar problem; they can have different meanings in various contexts. In the context of economic welfare theory and for the purposes of this book, "economic benefits" means gains in net economic value (i.e., gains in money measures of economic welfare or surplus). From the perspective of economic impacts (e.g., back-of-the-envelope impact analyses of proposed policies, environmental degradations), "benefits" refers to gains in economic activity that can be quantified and can include gains in economic welfare or surplus. In a CBA (cost–benefit analysis) context, economic benefits refer to all gains in the net economic value (i.e., welfare component) that directly and indirectly result with a proposed project/policy/etc. (as compared to a situation without the project/policy/etc.). Within CBA, then, economic benefits represent the same measure as in an economic welfare context.

5.2. Economic Measures*

A number of different economic measures exist that are conceptually separate. From a national income accounting perspective, measures of economic activity represent total expenditures on final goods and services produced by a country and are usually separated into distinct sectors (i.e., consumption, production, government, and foreign trade sector), for example gross domestic product (GDP) measures. The literature on I/O analysis treats economic measures as the change in the dollar amount of output (sales), income (wage-income), the number of individuals (employment levels), and the dollar amount of tax revenue (taxes) that results from a proposed outside change. In economic

---

* Sections 5.2 and 5.3 draw heavily from Ofiara (1996).

welfare theory, economic benefits and economic losses are other types of economic measures that represent gains or losses, respectively, in economic welfare or surplus (i.e., net economic value). Lastly, from the CBA literature, economic benefits and economic losses are measures that represent gains or losses, respectively, in economic surplus and are equivalent to the measures from economic welfare theory. In some cases economic benefits have been loosely used to include changes in economic activity (e.g., changes in sales, income, employment, etc., which are nonwelfare components); this is not appropriate in a CBA context. These concepts are treated in more detail in the following text.

5.2.1. Aggregate Economic Activity

Aggregate economic activity at the national level or macroeconomic measures are usually referred to as GDP or gross national product (GNP). These measures represent the total value of all final goods and services produced in an economy for a given time period, usually a year. The distinction between GDP and GNP is due to the origin of resources used in the production of goods. If one is concerned with the value of all final goods produced from resources within the boundaries of a country or region, GDP is the relevant measure (e.g., value of Coca Cola produced in the United States). But if we are concerned with the value of all final goods produced from resources located inside and outside a country, then GNP is the relevant measure (e.g., value of Coca Cola produced worldwide). Because prices can change over time, the above measures need to be adjusted to yield real GDP (gdp) and real GNP (gnp), which represent the value of all final goods and services produced in an economy in terms of constant dollars (i.e., dollars adjusted for inflation). As such, changes in gdp or gnp will reflect changes in real output.

GDP (or GNP) can be measured by two basic approaches, the flow of expenditures approach and the flow of earnings approach, because economic activity can be represented as a circular flow. This means that final goods and services are produced by firms using inputs (e.g., labor, capital, land, entrepreneurial skill) usually provided by households. These inputs are, in turn, paid compensation (e.g., wages, interest, rent, and profits, respectively), which constitutes the income that is used to finance spending on goods and services. As a result, the sum of spending will equal the sum of compensation, by definition. Basically, the flow of expenditures approach defines GDP as the amount of spending on consumption (C); private business investment (I); government services—federal, state, and local (G); and, if there is foreign trade, exports (X) less imports (M). Hence, GDP = C + I + G + X – M. The flow of earnings approach takes the sum of compensation paid to all inputs: wages (for labor), interest (for capital), rent (for land), and profits (for entrepreneurial skill) as national income. Given several adjustments (these include depreciation and indirect business taxes), aggregate earnings will equal aggregate spending on goods and services. Another technique known as the value-added approach also yields national income measures where the value-added at each step of the production process is summed to yield GDP. It is shown in Section 5.2.2 that the value-added approach and the flow of expenditures approach yield identical measures.

5.2.2. Economic Impacts

Economic impact measures have been used loosely both by economists and popular press. The main reason is that economists approach assessments of economic impacts in two distinct ways in two different contexts: (1) They use a "back-of-the-envelope" approach frequently in public policy analysis or economic impact analysis, and (2) they use formal I/O economic models to evaluate direct impacts (e.g., changes to sales activities, employment) from structural changes (e.g., plant closings or openings). As already discussed, adverse economic impacts or economic effects can be thought of as decreases in measurable economic activity (e.g., sales, output, employment, income, etc.) and conceivably could include all possible economic effects that can be quantified—nonwelfare measures. These measures of effects are sometimes referred to as economic activity measures.

In the context of I/O models, "economic impacts" has a different and specialized meaning. In this context, the term refers only to those changes in economic activity (e.g., the sum of value-added throughout the economy where sales–output is the relevant variable) that are estimated from an I/O model where impacts to output or sales, income, and employment can be measured. Economic surplus or welfare is ignored. Impacts can also measure changes in the amount of output or sales ($s), income ($s), employment (Nos.), and sometimes tax revenues ($s) that are associated with a change in the economy (e.g., structural change—plant closings, reduced demand, increased demand) or policy change (e.g., proposed regulation). Many times they are based on multipliers that not only account for direct effects (direct expenditures on goods and services), but also indirect and induced effects. Economic impact measures in this context reflect the effect that changes in a particular sector have on economic activity (e.g., sales, employment, etc.) in other sectors within a study economy.

The overall effect consists of several rounds of impacts that can be described as a multiplier effect. The first round of impacts involves only the sector of interest (i.e., primary sector) and sectors that directly interact with the primary sector (i.e., secondary sectors). Subsequent rounds involve impacts based on the interaction of secondary sectors with still other sectors (tertiary sectors) (i.e., responding activity), and then the interaction of these other sectors with still other sectors until the effect originating in the designated primary sector has been transmitted throughout the economy in question. In the context of a formal I/O analysis, then, when sales–output are the relevant variable, the analysis computes the value-added at each stage of analysis (e.g., primary stage, secondary stage, etc.) and for each sector of the economy (e.g., agricultural sector, manufacturing sector, wholesale–retail sector, etc.) that results from an initial change. The value-added is then summed to measure the total change in value-added for the entire economy, a measure equivalent to that based on the value-added approach from national income accounting, hence a formal I/O analysis does not double-count economic activity. The multiplier, when used correctly, captures the final change relative to the initial situation, and in principle represents (final change)/(initial position). If this is $255/$110 (in millions), the multiplier is equal to 2.3182. Therefore, in principle, if one were to examine a change in a given economy from a policy change using either a formal I/O analysis or a national income accounting approach (e.g., value-added approach), one would obtain identical measures of the change to value-added from the policy change.

Note that the above "back-of-the-envelope" economic impact measures differ from aggregate measures such as GDP, which measure net changes in the value of final activity without double-counting and differ from impact measures based on formal I/O models. The "back-of-the-envelope" economic impact measures can contain some double-counting in the summation of the effects throughout the economy that are precipitated by an initial change. However, care should be taken to avoid the problem of double-counting as much as possible or altogether. To give some appreciation for this, consider an abstract example followed by an applied example. Let primary economic impacts be calculated as the sum of sales of output and expenses for inputs for a given industry or sector. This is a measure of partial economic activity generated by the study sector rather than one of total economic activity. This is because it considers only the direct economic activity generated from the effect of the primary sector on secondary sectors, and not the effects of interactions among secondary sectors with still other sectors in the economy; that is, multiplier effects are not included. Once we include the secondary sector and beyond, and calculate economic impacts as the sum of sales and expenses from the primary sector and sales from the secondary sector, we begin to double-count economic activity because the sales from the secondary sector are used as inputs in the primary sector and represent expenses in the primary sector. From a national accounting perspective, by including the full value of input expenses and output sales rather than just input expenses and the value-added (from further processing by the primary sector), as is done in GDP measures, we have double-counted by some degree and have overstated the true measure of economic activity throughout the production process. This error is compounded when the effects of multipliers are considered. To avoid the problem of double-counting, one should consider expenses of the primary sector or sales of the secondary sector but not both.

An arithmetic example will provide further illustration of the problem of double-counting and how to avoid it. Consider the production of a cigar (from Ekelund and Tollison 1991). Here the first stage consists of a farmer selling tobacco to a cigar maker for $3. The value-added to the farmer is $3 which covers his costs of production (returns to labor, land, capital, and entrepreneurial ability). The second stage in the process consists of the cigar maker. Here he manufactures and sells cigars to a cigar store for $8. Now the value-added at the second stage is $5 ($8 − $3, i.e., sales less expenses). In the final stage, the cigar store sells these cigars to consumers for $15; the value-added is now $7 ($15 − $8). The measure of GDP in this example based on the value-added approach would be the sum of the value-added at each stage, $15. (Note this is equal to the value of final sales, i.e., GDP measured by the flow of expenditures approach.) But by summing sales and expenses at each stage of production ($3 + $8 + $15) we have double-counted the true measure of economic activity; GDP is $15 and not $26. In this simple example, the measure of primary economic impacts overstates the true measure of economic activity by a factor of 1.73 times, excluding multiplier effects. Therefore, without evidence of the magnitude of the error involved, expenditure impacts should be treated with caution, and one should be concerned about the approach used, whether it is a "back-of-the-envelope" impact analysis or a formal I/O analysis.

5.2.3. Benefits in an Economic Welfare Context

Specific measures of changes in economic welfare are quite theoretical concepts and are covered in more detail in various textbooks (see Boadway and Bruce 1989; Dinwiddy and Teal 1996; Freeman 1979, 1993; Johansson 1987, 1991, 1993; Just et al. 1982; Sugden and Williams 1990). These measures are associated with losses and gains in economic welfare and represent lost economic value and gains in economic value, respectively. In the production sector, the measure of lost (gains in) economic value is economic rent or producer surplus (i.e., the reduction [gains] in profit plus the surplus above variable costs or above the supply curve) (see Section 5.5.2 for further detail). Both measures represent a monetary surplus that accrues to the producer (i.e., the firm or entrepreneur) over and above the value of goods and services provided, and are more appropriate measures of producer welfare than profits alone (Just et al. 1982). Both measures are equivalent in the short run and are regarded as a measure of the net economic value to the producer from the production and sale of goods and services.

In the consumption sector a measure of lost (gains in) economic value is the reduction (gain) in consumer surplus, a monetary surplus that accrues to the consumer over and above expenditures from consumption of a good (Just et al. 1982). It represents a net economic value that accrues to consumers from their consumption activities. Any reduction (gain) in it can be considered a loss (gain) in economic value. At this point it should be stressed that the measure of consumer surplus is not very accurate, especially if income effects are present (where positive income effects can result in overstated measures of consumer surplus); then more specific consumer welfare measures are appropriate (Auerbach 1985; Freeman 1979, 1993; Just et al. 1982).

In practice, marine pollution can affect many consumers and producers, and economic welfare analysis of the changes at the individual level are both impractical and burdensome. To be useful to public officials, economic welfare analysis requires aggregation over individual economic units (i.e., consumers and producers) that are affected. This can be accomplished by analyzing the change in economic welfare at the market level since the aggregation process yields the economic surpluses associated with the market or total demand and supply of private goods and services. Under competitive conditions, economic welfare at the market level is equivalent to the sum of economic surpluses over all consumers and producers in the market (Just et al. 1982). Hence, the change in aggregate welfare will reflect the sum of changes in individual welfare under competitive conditions.

Unlike private goods and services, various goods and services such as recreational activities are not rationed by price; for example one does not buy the good "sportfishing," "birdwatching," or "swimming." Because one does not observe market prices and quantities of these nonmarket goods, changes in economic welfare resulting from changes in levels of the nonmarket good must be determined at the individual user level and then aggregated over all users. This involves the use of various nonmarket valuation or indirect market valuation techniques based on representative samples of individuals to obtain estimates of economic welfare associated with the good in question, and then expanded to represent the population of interest (these techniques are treated in the following text and in the textbooks previously referenced).

In order to evaluate changes in economic welfare that result from marine pollution, two situations must be compared, the economic welfare of the economy that results with the presence of marine pollution, and the economic welfare of the economy that would occur without it (i.e., in the absence of marine pollution). The net change represents the change in economic welfare attributable to the presence of marine pollution (a parallel use of these two situations can also be used to measure the welfare attributable to efforts that reduce marine pollution, i.e., welfare with partial/complete pollution control [or with partial or no pollution] versus welfare without pollution control [or with pollution]). A procedure known as the "with and without" rule commonly used in CBA can assist in this process and avoids attributing effects to an event that are not caused by it (Gittinger 1972, Howe 1971, Kohli 1993, Sugden and Williams 1990).

5.2.4. Benefits in a Cost–Benefit Analysis Context

Benefits in CBA represent the same measure as in an economic welfare context. In CBA, economic benefits refer to all gains in economic value (welfare component) that directly and indirectly result with a proposed project (as compared to a situation without the project) (Boadway and Bruce 1989, Gittinger 1972, Howe 1971, Sugden and Williams 1990, U.S. EPA 1990). In some cases, studies purporting to use CBA measure economic benefits to include changes in economic activity (e.g., changes in sales, income, employment, etc.—nonwelfare component) in addition to changes in net economic values—welfare component; this is not appropriate in a CBA context.

In CBA, all benefits that result from a situation with the project over and above those benefits that would result without the project classify as total or gross benefits. All costs that result from the situation with the project over and above those costs that would result without the project classify as total costs. The difference between these benefits and costs yields net economic benefits or net economic value, a measure identical to that in a welfare context. This process (aggregate or total approach) results in the same measure of net economic benefits as if one were to compute the net economic value for each use individually, and then sum over all uses (i.e., the sum of consumer surplus and producer surplus welfare measures across all uses). The individual or per use approach is discussed in the following text. However, in any application of CBA care must be used to avoid any double-counting of benefits. Section 5.9 contains a discussion of CBA relative to federal criteria that federally sponsored projects must satisfy.

An example will demonstrate the application of the "with and without" rule in CBA, and the equivalency of net economic value using an aggregate or total approach versus an individual or per use approach. Consider a water resource project that is primarily designed to produce hydroelectric power and to provide irrigation water to local agricultural producers. First some of the direct costs consist of the investment and capital construction costs to build the project (i.e., capital costs that would occur with the project versus a situation without the project). We would add to this annual maintenance and repair costs that would occur over and above a situation without the project. We will further assume that this project is not large enough to affect the market for electricity or that for agricultural crops so the prices are not affected. Benefits can be identified as either direct (or primary) benefits or indirect (or secondary) benefits; these are referred to as use benefits (i.e., benefits that result from use of the resource) as opposed to nonuse benefits (i.e., benefits associated with nonuse, and sometimes referred to as intrinsic benefits, measured by existence value). The most obvious are the primary or direct benefits. These represent the total production of new electricity valued at the market price (i.e., the value of electricity production—total revenue—that would occur with the project vs. a situation without the project), and the value of increased crop production—total revenue—that would occur over and above a situation without the project. In addition, where entrance fees apply for recreational activities (we assume they do in this example), benefits would represent total revenues collected at specific sites. Having treated the production sector, we will examine the consumption sector. Here it is assumed that in both cases new electricity generation and increased crop yields are not sufficient to change the market prices, but only change the availability and abundance in the local area. Primary benefits to the consumption sector would then include the total economic value (i.e., the total area under the demand curve) to consumers from the added availability of electricity and that from increased crop abundance over and above a situation without the project.

Before examples of indirect benefits are discussed, we want to adjust the cost side by the costs incurred from bringing the added electricity to the market (e.g., costs of additional transmission lines, staff to operate the dam and generators and their servicing) compared to a situation without the project, additional production costs farmers would incur with the project versus a situation without the project, and the costs of collecting entrance fees that would result with the project versus without it. Costs from the consumption sector include the direct costs of new electricity purchased and direct costs of crops purchased for that additional portion of electricity and crops compared to a situation without the project. In this example the only indirect benefits we consider are lake-based recreation activities (e.g., water sports, swimming, water skiing, recreational boating, fishing, etc.). In each case economic benefits are equal to the total or gross economic value (i.e., the total area under the respective demand curve comprising the sum of total costs and consumer surplus). To the analysis we would also include the costs that recreationists would incur with the project versus a situation without the project (e.g., travel costs, entrance fees, lodging if appropriate, etc.). One would then compute the difference in benefits and costs in each period to determine net economic benefits. This example involving the total or aggregate approach is summarized in the top half of Table 5.1.

An alternative approach to this example was mentioned above and involves computing the economic benefits and costs for each use separately, obtaining a measure of net economic value for each use, and then summing across all uses (the individual or per unit approach); each of these two basic approaches computes the same measure of net economic value. For primary uses, net economic benefits equal benefits of new electricity production (i.e., total revenues) less the relevant portion of capital construction costs and the annual maintenance and repair costs that would occur with the project versus a situation without the project (i.e., producer surplus from new electricity production). For the agricultural sector, net economic benefits equal benefits of increased crop production (i.e., total revenue) less the relevant portion of capital construction costs and annual maintenance and repair costs, and added production costs of farmers that would occur with the project versus a situation without the project (i.e., producer surplus from new crop production). Regarding the consumption sector, net economic benefits are equal to the total economic value of increased electricity availability (i.e., the total area under the demand curve) less the direct costs of the amount purchased (i.e., consumer surplus from new electricity), and total economic value of increased abundance of crops less direct costs of that bought (i.e., consumer surplus from added crop abundance), in both cases over and above a situation without the project. And for recreational activities, net economic benefits equal total benefits (i.e., total revenues collected) at all recreation sites less the costs involved with fee collection for a situation with the project versus a sit-

Table 5.1. Hypothetical Example of Cost-Benefit Analysis: Hydroelectric and Agriculture Irrigation Water Resource Project.

Primary (Direct) Benefits

Production Sector

- Value of new electricity *with* project less that *without* the project (i.e., total revenues received associated with new electricity production)
- Value of increased crop yields as opposed to a situation *without* the project (i.e., total revenues associated with added crop abundance)
- Value of entrance fees charged for recreational activities *with* project less that *without* the project

Consumption Sector

- Total economic value of increased availability of electricity over and above a situation *without* the project (i.e., total area under the demand curve)
- Total economic value of increased abundance of agricultural crops over and above a situation *without* the project.

Secondary (Indirect) Benefits

- Total economic value of water-based recreation activities (e.g., swimming, boating, fishing) over and above a situation *without* the project (i.e., total area under the demand curve).

Primary (Direct) Costs

Production Sector

- Capital construction costs to build the project
- Annual maintenance and repair (M & R) costs incurred as opposed to a situation *without* the project
- Costs to bring new electricity to market (e.g., cost of new transmission lines, staff to operate the dam and generators and servicing)
- Construction costs and annual M & R costs, and staffing costs (to collect fees) associated with recreational access facilities incurred as opposed to a situation *without* the project

Consumption Sector

- Direct costs of electricity purchased associated with that portion of new electricity generation over and above a situation *without* the project
- Direct costs of agricultural crops purchased associated with that portion of increased crop yields over and above a situation *without* the project

Secondary (Indirect) Costs

- Additional production costs farmers incur as opposed to a situation *without* the project
- Recreational costs (e.g., travel costs, user fees, lodging, and food) incurred as opposed to a situation *without* the project.

Summary[b]

$$\text{Total Benefits} = (\text{Benefits}_{electricity} + \text{Benefits}_{irrigation} + \text{Benefits}_{recreation})_{production\ sector}$$
$$+ (\text{Benefits}_{new\text{-}electricity} + \text{Benefits}_{more\text{-}crops})_{consumption\ sector},$$

$$\text{Total Costs} = \text{Capital Costs} + \text{Annual Maintenance and Repair Costs} +$$
$$\text{Costs (bringing electricity to market)} + (\text{Added Production Costs})_{irrigation}$$
$$+ \text{Capital Costs}_{recreation\ facilities} + (\text{Annual Maintenance and Repair Costs})_{recreation\ facilities}$$
$$+ (\text{Direct Costs}_{new\ electricity} + \text{Direct Costs}_{more\ crops}$$
$$+ \text{Direct Costs}_{recreation\text{-}participation})_{consumption\ sector},$$

Net Economic Benefits = Total Benefits − Total Costs.

(continues)

ALTERNATIVE APPROACH (INDIVIDUAL/PER USE APPROACH)[c]

Primary (Direct) Net Benefits (Net Economic Value)
- Value of electricity (revenues) less portion of capital construction costs, annual maintenance and repair costs, and costs of bringing electricity to market associated with new electricity production as opposed to a situation *without* the project—Producers Surplus (PS) (i.e., total revenue less total variable costs)
- Value of increased crop yields less portion of capital construction costs and annual maintenance and repair costs, associated with agriculture irrigation, and additional production costs farmers incur as opposed to a situation *without* the project—PS
- Value of recreation fees (revenues) less portion of recreation facility construction costs, annual maintenance and repair costs, and staffing costs associated with operation of recreational facilities incurred as opposed to a situation *without* the project—PS
- Total economic value of new electricity to consumers less their direct costs incurred as opposed to a situation *without* the project—Consumers Surplus (CS) (i.e., total economic value less direct costs)
- Total economic value of increased abundance of agricultural crops less the direct costs incurred as opposed to a situation *without* the project—CS

Secondary (Indirect) Net Benefits (Net Economic Value)
- Total economic value of water-based recreation activities (e.g., swimming, boating, fishing) less associated recreational costs (e.g., travel costs, user fees, lodging and food) incurred as opposed to a situation *without* the project—Consumers Surplus (CS) (i.e., total economic value less costs)

SUMMARY[d]

Aggregate Net Economic Value $= PS_{\text{new-electricity}} + PS_{\text{irrigation}} + PS_{\text{recreation facilities}}$
$$+ CS_{\text{new-electricity}} + CS_{\text{more crops}} + CS_{\text{recreation}}$$
$$\text{where } CS_{\text{recreation}} = CS_{\text{swimming}} + CS_{\text{boating}} + CS_{\text{fishing}} + \dots$$

Assumptions: Electricity generation will not affect the market price, only provides increased availability; increased crop yields will not affect market prices, only provides added abundance.
[a]Total economic value (benefits) and total costs are computed and summed, and then the difference is taken to determine net economic value.
[b]All for the situation with the project vs. the situation without the project.
[c]Net economic value computed for each use and then summed or aggregated over all uses.
[d]All for the situation with the project vs. the situation without the project

uation without the project. Concerning indirect uses and benefits, for each recreational activity net economic benefits equal the benefits from the specific activity (i.e., total benefits, sum of costs and consumer surplus, which is the total area under the demand curve) less the costs incurred to participate in the activity that would occur with the project versus a situation without the project (i.e., the consumer surplus for each activity). The bottom half of Table 5.1 summarizes the second or individual per use approach.

5.3. Economic Methods*

5.3.1. Present Value Analysis

Present value analysis is the technique that economists use to compare costs and benefits of various projects over time, to choose among projects given limited budgets, and

---

* Sections 5.2 and 5.3 are from Ofiara (1996).

to select a "best" or several "bests." In other words, it allows for changes in value over time so that policymakers can compare different projects over time. There are two variations of present value analysis commonly used by economists: cost-effectiveness analysis and CBA. Cost-effectiveness analysis concerns the minimum cost method to achieve a given objective. CBA, however, considers both the benefits and the costs associated with a particular project. More detailed explanations of these two versions will be discussed here.

It is important to note that CBA has a slightly different meaning in the field of economics than it has in finance. In economic theory, CBA is a technique used to evaluate the economic feasibility of public projects (i.e., projects financed with public funds) (Bohm 1976, Kohli 1993, Sugden and Williams 1990). CBA is referred to as capital budgeting, financial analysis, or investment analysis in finance theory and is used to evaluate investment decisions such as plant expansions and new product development (Brealey and Myers 1991, Levy and Sarnat 1994); we will refer to its use in finance theory as financial analysis in the remainder of this book. The difference between CBA in economic theory and financial analysis in finance theory is due to the treatment and measurement of benefits and costs that accrue to the project. In financial analysis, benefits are treated as all additional income (e.g., sales revenues) that result from a project (i.e., gross benefits), and costs are direct costs (e.g., costs of producing a new product line). From direct benefits and direct costs, net returns are derived (i.e., net benefits, the difference between returns and costs including initial investment). The criterion used in financial analysis is to undertake a project where the present value of net returns or net present value (i.e., net sales less initial investment and costs) is greater than zero, and in the case of multiple projects to select that project which yields the maximum present value of net returns. This criterion can also be expressed, in some cases, as undertaking a project where the internal rate of return from net returns less initial investment at current market prices is greater than the prevailing market interest rate (which represents the opportunity cost of capital).

Regarding CBA, benefits are based on the additional economic surplus (in all economic sectors affected by the project, e.g., sum of consumer surplus and producer surplus of all agents affected) that is attributable to a project. Costs sometimes include opportunity costs if direct costs are not representative of the full costs attributable to a project. The criterion in CBA is to undertake a project if the present value of net benefits or net economic value (benefits less project costs, discounted) exceeds zero, or equivalently, if the ratio of the present value of benefits to the present value of costs exceeds one. In sum, financial analysis considers the direct effects of a project, that is, direct net benefits measured as additional sales-returns less costs from a project. CBA is based on all direct and indirect effects attributable to a project, or all direct and indirect net benefits (benefits less costs) due to a project. It is argued that financial analysis is inappropriate in evaluations of public projects because governments are not in the business of maximizing profits, and scrutiny of the use of public funds requires greater accounting. Furthermore, because public projects involve public funds an objective such as to maximize social welfare (i.e., the welfare of society, sum of societies' consumer surplus and producer surplus) is a more appropriate decision criterion than profit maximization or maximization of private benefits.

Investment decisions and the choice among various projects involve a time element in most cases, and a concern among economists is to properly evaluate present and future dollars. The issue is that price levels change over time due to inflation and, because one can earn the market rate of return on investments, one must use a common measure to equate present and future dollars. This is usually accomplished through the mechanism of discounting, to express all dollars as present dollars (commonly referred to as the present value). (In much the same manner one could express all dollars in terms of future dollars, the future value of a project via compounding [see Brealey and Myers 1991]). In simple terms this means to divide the measure, be it benefits or costs, by the sum of one plus the discount rate all raised to a power to correspond to a specific time period (e.g., $B_2/(1+r)^2$ means that total benefits in the second period of the project are being discounted by the discount factor squared [i.e., raised to the second power] which corresponds to the discount factor in the second period).

The basic present value (PV) concept for CBA is the sum of discounted net benefits over the life of the project. This is expressed for each period by way of a formula as follows:

(5.1) $PV = -C_0 + (B-C)_1/(1+r)^1 + (B-C)_2/(1+r)^2 + \cdots + (B-C)_n/(1+r)^n$, or

(5.2) $PV = -C_0 + \sum_{i=1}^{n}(B-C)_i/(1+r)^i$,

where "$-C_0$" refers to the initial cost outlay, B the benefit in each period, C the cost in each period, r the discount rate, and n the time period, where the subscripts on the net benefit terms correspond to a specific time period as do the superscripts on the discount factor (Herfindahl and Kneese 1974, Kohli 1993). These formulas are appropriate for projects that realize costs and benefits over any time period. The manner in which the formulas are written with the first element "$-C_0$" represents a situation where a project involves front-end investment before the project can generate a return or benefit (such as when a municipality begins construction of a wastewater treatment facility). In some cases, there is no front-end investment and then the term "$-C_0$" is simply dropped (such as when a municipality contracts wastewater treatment with an independent supplier or with a nearby municipality that has idle capacity). The present value of net benefits (benefits less costs, discounted) is the appropriate measure for comparing projects over time given equal scale (i.e., size) and time period.

5.3.1.1. Cost-Effectiveness Analysis

Cost-effectiveness analysis concerns the minimum cost method to achieve a given objective. By definition, it ignores benefits and, thus, does not address economic rationale to achieve a given objective. It is appropriate when considering how a project can be implemented in the least expensive way. The procedure is to estimate all costs for a particular project over time, discount these costs, and then sum the discounted costs (discounted costs represent the total cost in today's dollars); the sum of discounted costs is referred to as the present value of costs. Expressed in terms of a formula, project costs are discounted in each period over the life of the project and then summed such as:

(5.3) $PV = -C_0 + \sum_{i=1}^{n}(C)_i/(1+r)^i$,

to represent cost-effectiveness analysis. The decision criterion is to select that project with the smallest present value of costs over time. This formula can also be used in comparing projects when the benefits realized from alternative projects are equal; hence one only needs to consider comparative costs since the only concern is to provide a project in the cheapest way possible.

5.3.1.2. Cost–Benefit Analysis

CBA is the primary method in which both the benefits and the costs associated with a project are considered. It is based on economic justifications in determining the implementation of a project; that is, whether the outcome of a project is worth the costs of achieving it. Here the analyst must identify, quantify, and value all possible benefits and costs associated with the presence of the project as opposed to a situation without the project, choose a time horizon and discount rate, and face an investment constraint. This technique has two variations commonly used. One is to examine the difference among benefits and costs (benefits less costs) for each time period, discount it, and then sum it, giving the present value of net benefits over time (i.e., Equation [5.2]). The decision criterion is to select that project that yields the maximum present value of net benefits over time. The second version involves the benefit to cost (B/C) ratio, where the sum of discounted benefits is divided by the sum of discounted costs. Expressed in terms of a formula, the sum of discounted benefits over the project's life is divided by the sum of discounted costs over the project's life and is represented as:

(5.4) $\text{B/C ratio} = \sum_{i=1}^{n}(B)_i/(1+r)^i / \sum_{i=1}^{n}(C)_i/(1+r)^i.$

When discounted benefits equal discounted costs this ratio will equal 1, hence if this ratio is greater than 1, benefits will be above costs. The decision criterion is to select that project that yields the maximum B/C ratio. The use of this ratio is quite controversial among economists. A brief summary will suffice. Most agree that selection of a project should not be based solely on the B/C ratio, it should be used in conjunction with discounted net benefits to rank alternative projects (Herfindahl and Kneese 1974, Margolis 1959). Also most agree that maximizing the B/C ratio in order to select a project is inappropriate. Most economists discourage the use of the B/C ratio in benefit–cost comparisons of projects at the aggregate (i.e., total) level; conversely most agree that the B/C ratio is useful in examining incremental (i.e., an extra unit or marginal) benefits and costs associated with a project in each period (Eckstein 1958, Herfindahl and Kneese 1974). The association between total benefits and costs with marginal benefits and costs in project choice will lend perspective on these points. Recall the decision criterion for CBA based on net benefits, to choose that project with a maximum of discounted net benefits. Maximization of discounted net benefits (total benefits less total costs) occurs where discounted marginal benefits (MB) equal discounted marginal costs (MC) or where the ratio of discounted MB to discounted MC is equal to 1. Hence, concerning incremental benefits and costs a B/C ratio not equal to 1 implies a situation where discounted net benefits are not at a maximum.

Further complications arise when comparing projects of unequal scale and time frame. The following points apply because the decision criterion for both CBA and cost-effectiveness analysis changes. The B/C ratio, Equation (5.4), is useful in comparing alternative projects of unequal scale only when no extreme variation in scale (referred to as capital intensity) is present (Eckstein 1958). In a sense the B/C ratio reduces the scale factor; consider two projects, one twice the size of the other so that all proportions are equal, then the ratios will be the same. But, this raises another issue concerning the use of capital investment in a project; that is, front-end investment versus rationing of capital investment among various periods through the project's life similar to annual operating expenses. Then the criterion and comparison become more complicated (see Eckstein 1958 for more detail). When faced with unequal time frames in comparing projects, the time frames should be made compatible. This can be accomplished by using a least common denominator (LCD) to determine equivalent time periods (e.g., a 3-year and a 5-year project have an LCD of 15 years). And finally, the literature is rich with discussion of the appropriate discount rate to use, usually the rate on long-term Treasury bills (see Bohm 1976, Herfindahl and Kneese 1974, Just et al. 1982, Kohli 1994, Mishan 1976).

Much of the debate over the appropriate discount rate centers on several theoretical issues (Just et al. 1982). One issue is that the discount rate is essentially an exchange rate between individuals' time preferences and the productivity of investments. Too high a rate will favor present consumption over future consumption and too little investment would be made for future generations. Economists advocate a low rate for public projects (e.g., water quality improvements) because of the view that public investments are less risky than private investments. However, some advocate use of higher discount rates because future resource use is uncertain enough that a lower risk premium may not be appropriate (Yang et al. 1984). (It should be pointed out that a risk premium is that portion of the total interest rate that compensates for risk, and low discount rates correspond to low risk premiums and vice versa, other things equal.) In addition, some argue that a discount rate should be based on the opportunity cost of private investment displaced by the public project. In sum, there is no consensus over the appropriate discount rate to use. Yang et al. (1984) note that some applications have used a rate equal to a long-run nominal interest rate (e.g., 30-year U.S. Treasury Bond rate) less the long-run inflation rate.

5.3.2. Economic Impacts: Economic Impact Analysis (Public Policy Analysis)

Economic impact analysis (EIA) also needs clarification. Many applied policy problems and proposed federal regulations use variations of EIA commonly referred to as Public Policy Analysis (OMB 1996, Weimer and Vining 1991). Here the analyst conducts an economic analysis to determine the effects (impacts) of proposed policy changes on all appropriate economic units (consumers, producers) and/or economic sectors (consumption, production, government) where the economic effects associated with the policy are identified and quantified. Such an approach will be referred to as a public policy analysis in the remainder of this book. Furthermore, the meaning of economic impacts and of economic impact analysis based on this technique is different and must not be confused with similar terminology used in the context of an I/O analysis discussed in the next section.

5.3.3. Economic Impacts: Input/Output Analysis

I/O analysis is a specific technique developed by an economist (Leontieff 1966, 1986) and is based on an input/output model of economic activity, usually at an aggregate level, based on some standard industrial classification system (e.g., agricultural sector, manufacturing sector, etc.). Economic activity is expressed as dollar expenses (inputs) used to realize dollar output measured as sales revenues related to an economy defined by geographic–political boundaries (state, region, nation). Other measures of economic activity used are in terms of income and employment. A main feature of this technique is to determine "multipliers," which can be thought of as how changes in primary economic activity translate into final economic activity, and to examine how changes in specific sectors (manufacturing, services) of an economy affect the entire economy in question. When one examines such changes throughout the economy based on an I/O model, such an analysis is referred to as an impact analysis. I/O analysis was primarily developed to address policy questions concerning the effects on sales, income, and employment resulting from various structural changes in the economy (e.g., plant closings/openings, changes in local infrastructure investment, reduced demand) and from proposed policies (e.g., different minimum wage policies, proposed regulations/deregulations).

The following discussion will describe some of the reasoning behind the I/O approach. The basic premise is that each dollar of expenditure or sales in an industry or sector has an effect on other industries and sectors as well as on regional (or state and national—whatever the study area is defined as) output, income, and employment. Any change in economic activity (e.g., sales, investment, employment, technology) will produce a change in a sequential manner throughout a study economy ("study economy" is used in the same context as that of a study area used in research statistics, i.e., it is defined as the boundary of a particular economy in question, e.g., state economy, regional economy, or possibly county economy). Such a change is represented by multiplier effects. The magnitude of impacts within an economy resulting from such a change is influenced by the degree of interdependency that exists among the various sectors within that economy (i.e., represented by technical I/O coefficients). These I/O models can then be solved for sector outputs (i.e., sales), income, employment, and tax revenues in some cases. Based on an I/O model solved for sales, the economic impacts that correspond to the level of activity in a final demand sector on the level of outputs of the other sectors and on the economy as a whole can be estimated.

These impacts in turn are characterized as either direct, indirect, or induced effects. (Similar remarks can be developed for I/O models solved for income and employment.) Direct effects represent the change in demand of industries or sectors directly affected by a change in the demand of a given primary sector. Suppose demand increases for certain recreational activities such as marine fishing and boating, as well as for fresh-caught seafood in a specific coastal area. The effect would show up as increases in participants, trips, and more equipment and vessels needed in the recreational sector and as increases in price and immediate shortages in fresh seafood. The response in the recreational sector to this increased sportfishing and boating activity would result in an increased supply of fishing equipment, trips, and boats to meet the demand represented by increased sales and expenses. The commercial fishing sector would also respond by increases in its activity (i.e., increases in trips and more equipment and vessels) to meet the increased demand for local seafood. Both types of activity, in turn, will increase intermediate producers' purchases of inputs (goods and services) used in the manufacture of both recreational and commercial fishing equipment and vessels. Here, an increase in the demand for recreational sportfishing and seafood has resulted in a direct effect on those industries and sectors (secondary sector) that supply the primary recreational and commercial sector.

Indirect effects measure the effect of secondary sectors' increased purchases of the inputs necessary to meet the increased demand for their products. The effect of income generated from this increased activity that is re-spent in the study economy is defined as an induced effect.

Aggregate economic impacts on a given economy are referred to as multiplier effects that can measure output, income, and employment (and sometimes tax revenue) effects. Output multipliers measure the total change in the economic activity associated with output (sales) of all sectors of the economy (e.g., primary and secondary sectors and beyond) that is generated from an additional dollar of final demand (e.g., goods and services of the primary sector). The total change in income that occurs in a given economy due to a dollar change in final demand is reflected by the income multiplier. Employment multipliers, have a slightly different interpretation because they are not in terms of dollars. They show the change in a given economy's employment generated by a change in output that causes an employment change of one unit.

Two types of multipliers are estimated in I/O studies to project the total economic impacts created by a change in final demand (sales) per dollar of direct change in the primary sector within the economy. Type I multipliers are defined as (D+I)/D, where D refers to direct and I refers to indirect effects, and represent the combined direct and indirect effects of economic activity within a given economy per dollar of direct change in the designated primary sector. Type II multipliers, (D+I+IN)/D where D and I are already defined, and IN refers to induced effects, measure the combined direct, indirect, and induced effects of economic activity throughout the economy per dollar change in the primary sector within the economy. It is the product of these multipliers with sales (for output and income effects), and employment in the primary sector (for employment effects) that results in projections of economic impacts.

In practice economists are quite careful with the application of formal I/O models to avoid the problem of double-counting. The multipliers discussed above represent all activity that is generated from an initial change and is only appropriate to use in the context of the specific initial change. These models and the multipliers measure and represent the sum of the value-added at each stage of the analysis and for each sector of the economy without double-counting.

One actually measures these changes with an I/O model and analysis in one of two ways. Both involve comparisons to a baseline situation (e.g., economic activity without a change) so as to isolate the effects of a proposed change or effect. Without comparison to a reference or baseline situation one has no basis to judge the relative effects or changes. One way is to compare the impacts with the proposed change to those without the change (i.e., baseline impacts). The difference is then attributable to the proposed change summarized as:

Impacts from proposed change/effect = $IM_{w\ change} - IM_{w/o\ change}$ for both positive and negative effects, where $IM_{w\ change}$ refers to impacts associated with the proposed change and $IM_{w/o\ change}$ impacts without the change. The other way is to compare the multipliers generated from the I/O models; the multiplier associated with a baseline situation versus one associated with the proposed change. The difference is then attributable to the proposed change as:

$M_{w\ change} - M_{w/o\ change}$ where $M_{w\ change}$ refers to the multiplier associated with the proposed change and $M_{w/o\ change}$ that without the proposed change (i.e., the baseline situation). For example, let's assume that direct expenditure activity is \$123.7 million. This represents the information the I/O model is based on without any new changes or effects. As the I/O model is "run" on a computer, expenditure impacts of \$235 million are generated representing direct and indirect activity (or $IM_{w/o\ change}$ = \$235 million). The type I multiplier is 1.899 (\$235/\$123.7) associated with the baseline situation. If the I/O model measures expenditure–sales impacts of \$284.1 million due to the proposed change ($IM_{w\ change}$ = \$284.1 million), then one can determine the additional expenditure impacts attributable to the proposed change of \$49.1 million (an additional \$49.1 million in expenditure impacts is attributable to the proposed change, i.e., (ΔIM = \$49.1 million, where (Δ refers to "the change in" IM). Considering the change in multipliers, the second method, $M_{w/o\ change}$ is 1.899 and $M_{w\ change}$ is 2.296, the multiplier associated with the proposed change (i.e., type I multiplier associated with the proposed change is \$284.1/\$123.7). The proposed change is responsible for additional economic activity equivalent to an additional multiplier effect of 0.397 (i.e., ΔM = 0.0397). Either way, both give equivalent results; to see this we compute 0.397*\$123.7 million which gives \$49.1 million in additional economic activity (additional expenditure–sales impacts). Hence, results are compared to a baseline situation, and it is best to think of these comparisons as with versus without the proposed change similar to the rule used in CBA.

5.4. Economic Welfare Measures: Consumption Sector

5.4.1. Demand and the Concept of Economic Benefits

The measurement of economic benefits in the consumption sector (sometimes referred to as the public sector) is based on the premise that consumers derive satisfaction and enjoyment from participation and consumption of goods and services. A basic premise of consumer demand theory is that the consumers objective is to maximize satisfaction (i.e., utility) subject to budgetary limits. Economic benefits represent a money measure of this derived satisfaction. Although satisfaction, represented by utility, is not observed nor measurable, a money measure of satisfaction can be determined from demand theory. A demand curve is a downward sloping schedule of quantities demanded at various prices and reflects prices an individual would be willing to pay rather than forgo consumption of that unit of a good or service in question. All other variables that affect demand (the determinants of demand) such as income, tastes and preferences, and the price of related goods (e.g., substitutes and complements) are held constant, a condition referred to as *ceterius paribus* (all other things remaining equal). At a specific price–quantity combination, a surplus accrues to the consumer since there usually exists a higher price the consumer would have been willing to pay instead of refraining from consumption. This surplus represents an income gain to the consumer by not having to pay a higher price than the price actually paid. It is referred to as consumer surplus and represents a money measure of net economic value (or net economic benefits). These concepts are easily illustrated by way of Figure 5.1. One should note from this discussion that there are four variables that can influence a demand relation: the price of the good itself (i.e., known as "own" price), the price of related goods, tastes–preferences, and income. To graph a demand curve with all of these variables one would require a five-dimensional graph (i.e., a graph in five-space), one axis for each variable including the quantity demanded. However it is usual to graph a typical demand curve with price versus quantity demanded on two axes (i.e., a graph in two-space) and to hold all other variables constant.

In Figure 5.1, the demand curve is represented by the downward sloping line AB, which depicts a linear relationship between the price of the good and the quantity demanded, holding all other factors constant. For the price–quantity combination of $Q_0 P_0$, gross benefits are approximated by the area $OACQ_0$ (i.e., the total willingness-to-pay for OQ_0 units of the good). The difference between gross benefits and costs represent net economic benefits, area $P_0 AC$, and is referred to as consumer surplus; this is the surplus that accrues to the consumer as a net economic value. This surplus (or net economic value) represents the difference between what the consumer is willing to pay and the actual amount paid.

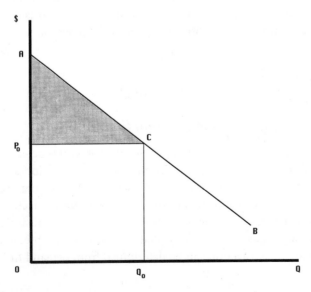

Figure 5.1
Demand and Consumer Surplus.

5.4.2. Ordinary Consumer Surplus as a Benefit Measure

Although consumer surplus appears fairly straightforward and easy to estimate, it is not an "ideal" measure of economic benefits. One of the reasons is that utility is not constant along a demand curve, although money income is. One way to show this follows. Consider the ordinary demand curve (or Marshallian demand curve) in Figure 5.2 represented by AD. At the price–quantity combination of P_0Q_0, consumer surplus, which we refer to as ordinary consumer surplus (OCS) is measured by area a, and costs by area $b+d$. With a price reduction from P_0 to P_1, the consumer's purchasing power or real income increases and in turn the consumer will increase consumption to OQ_1 units of the good. Had the consumer continued to consume the "pre-change" quantity, OQ_0, he would have to spend an amount equal to area d, and hence, a savings in cost results equal to area b. In other words, the value of area b accrues to the consumer in the form of a cost savings (an income gain) that can be spent on other goods and services. This, in turn, raises the amount of satisfaction received by the consumer from consuming OQ_0 units of the good. At the quantity of OQ_1 units, the gain in income to the consumer is equal to areas $b+c$ from the price reduction, and OCS becomes equal to areas $a+b+c$. As a result the consumer gains added utility from a movement down the demand curve. Another and perhaps more intuitive way to demonstrate the utility changes along an ordinary demand curve is from a decomposition of a price change into substitution effects and income effects (in Section 5.4.3).

Income effects can influence the ordinary demand curve and, in turn, measures of OCS. Hicks (1943) first proposed that OCS may actually overstate net benefits. A positive income effect (i.e., as income increases, more of the good will be demanded) will cause the demand curve to pivot to the left and represent an income-compensated demand curve (see the following discussion below on income-substitution effects for the rationale behind income-compensated demand curves). OCS, based on the initial, uncompensated demand curve will tend to overstate net economic benefits in this case. To resolve this theoretical dilemma, a strict condition must be imposed to ensure uniqueness of the benefit measures. When the income effect associated with a welfare change is zero (i.e., change in

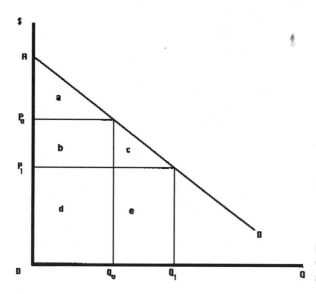

Figure 5.2
Consumer Surplus Resulting from a Price Decrease.

quantity consumed, Δq, corresponding to a change in income, Δm, that is, $\Delta q/\Delta m$ is zero) the income-compensated demand curve will coincide with the ordinary demand curve. This condition also corresponds to a zero income elasticity (i.e., the proportional change in quantity consumed resulting from a proportional change in income).

Furthermore, Just et al. (1982) demonstrate the difficulties in measuring the change in OCS associated with a multiple price change or simultaneous price–income change. This is called the path-dependency problem. Ambiguous measures result, depending on how the order of events (i.e., adjustment path) is chosen to examine the overall welfare change. The relative change in the income effect resulting from a price change or price–income change is the crux of the issue.

In response to these problems Willig (1976) developed boundary conditions under which commonly observed OCS may be used to approximate the theoretically correct Hicksian measure for price–income changes. His results showed that for price changes for goods in which expenditures are a small proportion of total household expenditures (or income), the difference between OCS and Hicksian welfare measures will be small. Hence, either OCS or Hicksian measures may be used (Hausman 1981, confirms this with an example, pgs. 672–3). Randall and Stoll (1980) adapt Willig's results to measure welfare changes induced by quantity changes (e.g., changes in the level of provision of the good following quality improvements) since these types of changes are more common than price–income changes in public sector benefit–cost applications.

Although the Willig results hold for specific cases (i.e., goods that form a small proportion of total expenditures), Hausman (1981) demonstrates that in calculating a deadweight loss from the imposition of a tax (i.e., the difference between tax revenue and welfare loss suffered on the part of consumers and producers), OCS can be a poor approximation of the correct Hicksian measures. This is a more important shortcoming of the use of OCS, and it follows that the usefulness of the Willig technique suffers equally.

Subsequent research (Bergland and Randall 1984, Hanemann 1981, Hausman 1981, McKenzie and Ulph 1982, Vartia 1983) produced operational techniques to calculate exact Hicksian welfare measures. All employ the use of duality theory of consumer behavior (see Deaton and Muellbauer 1980, Varian 1984) in deriving exact measures from observable ordinary demand functions (Section 5.12 formally treats this). The basic technique begins with empirically estimated ordinary demand functions. Indirect utility functions are derived via integration of ordinary demand curves, then inverted and solved to derive expenditure or income-compensation functions. Exact Hicksian measures defined in terms of these expenditure or income-compensation functions are then estimated. There is no need for approximations.

It must be emphasized that these techniques are based on the existence and identification of demand curves, and hence, assume that price–quantity information is available. In the case of nonmarket-public goods, because price–quantity information are not observed, the researcher must first gather this data based on nonmarket valuation techniques, and then exact Hicksian welfare measures can be calculated (e.g., Bockstael [1984] uses a travel cost derived demand function from which Hicksian measures are calculated for recreational fishing).

5.4.3. Income and Substitution Effects of Price Changes

Knowledge of income and substitution effects following price changes will lead to a clearer understanding of the concept of income-compensated (Hicksian) demand curves, which are the basis of measures of consumer welfare. The conventional theory of consumer behavior assumes that an individual consumer maximizes utility from the consumption of goods and services subject to prices, tastes, and a constraint on money income. The change in consumption (purchases) following a price reduction can be decomposed or separated into what economists refer to as a substitution effect and an income effect (Henderson and Quandt 1971, Just et al. 1982, Nicholson 1989). The following discussion will be confined to the case of positive income effects (i.e., when income increases, more of the good is purchased) and relates to the concerns raised by Hicks (1943) above that OCS will overstate economic welfare.

As the price of a good, say good x, decreases relative to all other goods, the consumer will now find good x to be a better buy (i.e., cheaper relative to other goods) and will correspondingly increase his or her purchases of it by lowering the consumption of other goods. This is called the substitution effect. In addition, the consumer will experience a gain in the purchasing power of his or her income (i.e., a gain in real income) following a price reduction, allowing the consumer to increase consumption of all goods. This is the income effect. The substitution effect involves a movement along an initial indifference curve so that utility is held constant, and the income effect involves a shift to a higher indifference curve due to the gain in real income and higher utility.

In the upper diagram of Figure 5.3, the initial indifference curve is represented by U_1, the subsequent higher indifference curve by U_2, the initial price line, EF, represents the budget constraint in this two-good diagram (Q_1, Q_2). The initial point of utility maximization occurs at point A, where the indifference curve, U_1, is tangent to the price line. Now consider a reduction in the price of Q_1. This causes the price line to pivot outward to the right from point E to the new price line EG. The consumer can now purchase OG units of Q_1 if all of the income is spent on Q_1. However, because of the convexity of the indifference curves the consumer maximizes utility by purchasing the bundle of goods represented by point B. The total effect of the price decrease is the movement from point A to point B, whereby the consumer increases her consumption of Q_1 from OA' units to OB' units (a gain of A'B' units). Following this price reduction and subsequent consumption decisions, an ordinary demand curve, D, can be constructed as depicted in the lower diagram of Figure 5.3. It shows the amount of Q_1 demanded at the initial price P_1, OA' units, and the subsequent amount following the price decrease to P_2, OB' units. The gain in OCS following the fall in price is represented by the areas $x+y+z$. As one moves along the ordinary demand curve, D, from point A to point B, notice in the top diagram that point A is associated with a level of utility of U_1 and point B a level of U_2, hence utility changes along an ordinary demand curve (it increases as one moves down the ordinary demand curve).

However, the total effect of the price reduction can be decomposed into a substitution effect and an income effect. Recall that the substitution effect of a price reduction shows the amount of the good purchased in substitution against other good(s) whose price has not fallen. To observe this in Figure 5.3, the gain in real income must be taken away from the consumer so as to leave the consumer just as well off as before the price reduction, that is, to hold utility constant by leaving him or her on the same indifference curve prior

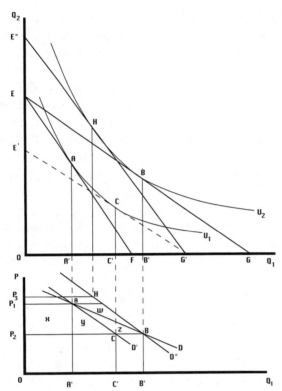

Figure 5.3
Income and Substitution Effects of a
Price Decrease.

to the price change. This is accomplished by taking away sufficient income so that the price line EG shifts downward to E′G′. The amount of real income relinquished by the consumer is equal to the distance between the price lines EG and E′G′. The substitution effect can then be defined as the change in the quantity of Q_1 bought as the consumer moves along the initial indifference curve as Q_1 becomes a better buy relative to Q_2. (The rate at which one good is substituted for another by moving along the indifference curve is the marginal rate of substitution, the slope of the indifference curve. Any movement along the indifference curve shows combinations of goods that yield the same utility to the consumer, i.e., total utility is constant.) At point C, the consumer maximizes utility.

In the lower diagram, a demand curve can be constructed to reflect the necessary reduction in real income so as to leave the consumer just as well off as before the price reduction (that is, to hold utility constant). The demand curve, D′, is referred to as an income-compensated (or Hicksian) demand curve. Following the price decrease, the substitution effect accounts for OC′ units of Q_1, and economic welfare is measured by the area under the Hicksian demand curve, D′, areas $x+y$ (referred to as *compensating variation*). Ordinary consumer surplus overstates the welfare measure by area z in this case. A second measure of economic welfare (referred to as *equivalent variation*) can be defined based on the "post-change" level or final state of utility represented by U_2. If the initial price line is shifted outward represented by E″G′ so that the gain in real income is given back to the consumer, the optimal position is represented by point H, and a second income-compensated demand curve can be constructed as D″ in the lower diagram. Using the price change of P_1 to P_2, economic welfare measured under the Hicksian demand curve D″ (i.e., equivalent variation) is equal to the areas $x+y+z+w$ and is greater than OCS by the area w.

Consider now the income effects of the price reduction. The income effect represents the increase in goods purchased following a gain in real income as a result of a price decrease. Starting at point C, if real income is increased from E'G' to EG the consumer's new utility maximizing position is at point B. Compared to the position at point C, the individual consumes more of both goods at the new position at point B. Thus the total effect of a price decrease of Q_1 increases consumption of Q_1 from OA' units to OB' units, a gain of A'B' units. The substitution effect accounts for A'C' units of Q_1 and the income effect C'B' units of Q_1. But, more importantly, these effects illustrate how ordinary and Hicksian demand curves can be constructed, and introduce alternative measures of economic welfare (discussed in detail in the next section). They also provide an intuitive explanation of the welfare measures associated with Hicksian demand curves and show that utility changes along an ordinary demand curve.

5.4.4. Alternative Consumer Welfare Measures

As previously discussed, OCS is not an "ideal" measure of economic benefits since utility is not constant along an ordinary (or Marshallian) demand curve. By constructing income-compensated (or Hicksian) demand curves one can satisfy such a condition and obtain utility-constant measures of economic benefits. Consider the corresponding welfare effects from a price decrease in Figure 5.4.

Following Smith and Desvousges (1986a) the ordinary demand curve is shown as D and the Hicksian demand curves that correspond to a price decrease from P_0 to P_1, holding utility constant, are H_0 and H_1, the "pre-change" and "post-change" levels of utility, respectively. The addition to OCS from the decrease in price is equal to area $a+b$, i.e., the area under the ordinary demand curve. The Hicksian measures of welfare corresponding to a price reduction are known as compensating variation (CV) equal to area a, and equivalent variation (EV) equal to areas $a+b+c$. The difference between these measures and OCS relate to the Willig conditions discussed above. On the basis of the price reduction from P_0 to P_1, OCS is greater than CV by area b and less than EV by area c, and thus OCS overstates CV and understates EV. In order to interpret the Hicksian welfare measures one must keep in mind the

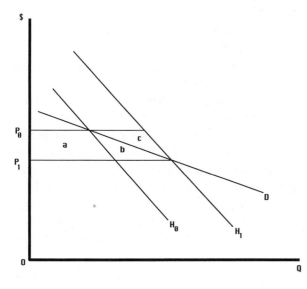

Figure 5.4
Comparison of Alternative Welfare Measures Corresponding to a Price Change.

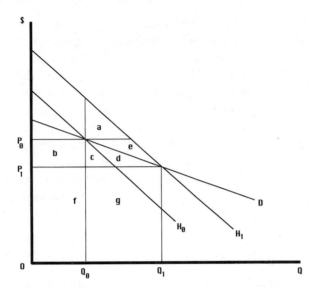

Figure 5.5
Comparison of Alternative Welfare
Measures Corresponding to a Quantity
Change.

level of utility used as a reference point. The CV measure is based on the original level of utility (i.e., the "pre-change" level) and represents the amount of compensation that must be
taken away from an individual following a price or income change that would leave the consumer just as well off as before the change (i.e., at the original utility level). In other words,
it represents the maximum amount of income an individual would be willing to pay (WTP)
for a price reduction. EV uses the new level of utility (i.e., "post-change" level) as its reference point and represents the amount of compensation that must be given to an individual
in lieu of a price or income change that leaves the consumer just as well off after the change
(i.e., "post-change" level). Thus it measures the minimum amount of compensation an individual is willing to accept (WTA) to relinquish the lower price (Just et al. 1982: 84–87).

Now consider the welfare effects of a quantity increase of an environmental good
(e.g., an increase in water quality). Following Just et al. (1982) in Figure 5.5, D refers to
the ordinary demand curve, and H_0 and H_1 the income-compensated demand curves
corresponding to the initial and final states, respectively. An increase in quantity from
OQ_0 to OQ_1 results in a change in OCS equal to the areas $b+c+d$. The Hicksian welfare
measures relative to a quantity *change* are known as compensating surplus (CS) and
equivalent surplus (ES). In our example of a quantity increase, CS is represented by the
areas $b+c$ and ES by the areas $b+c+d+e$. Thus OCS is greater than the compensating surplus by area d and less than the equivalent surplus measure by area e (Desvousges et al.
1983). The interpretation of the compensating surplus measure for a quantity increase is
the amount of money that must be taken away from an individual following the quantity
increase that leaves the consumer just as well off as before the change, that is, it represents
the maximum amount of money an individual would be willing to pay (WTP) rather
than give up the higher quantity. Interpretation of equivalent surplus in lieu of a quantity increase represents the amount of money that must be given to an individual, providing the quantity change does not occur, leaving the consumer just as well off as if the
change had occurred. That is, it represents the minimum amount of money an individual is willing to accept (WTA) to forgo the higher quantity as if the change had not

Table 5.2. Theoretical Welfare Measures and Corresponding Operational Measures for Price Changes and Quantity Changes.

	Price Decrease	Price Increase	Qunatity Decrease	Quantity Increase
WTP	CV; CS	EV; ES	ES	CS
WTA	EV; ES	CV; CS	CS	ES

occurred (Just et al. 1982: 10–11, 84–87, 136–139). It should be noted that the NRDA procedures discussed in Chapter 3 recognize that given a quantity decrease, CS or WTA measures are the theoretically correct welfare measures; following a quantity increase, CS measures become represented by WTP measures, and WTP is then the theoretically correct welfare measure (see Table 5.2).

Although the commonly cited theoretical rationale explaining the source of discrepancy between exact welfare measures exists due to income effects, another reason has been advanced by Knetsch (1984, 1985) and Knetsch and Sinden (1984). They point out that the above conventional beliefs are not consistent with observed behavior. Results of empirical studies provide evidence of consistent differences between exact welfare measures for goods that represent a small proportion of total expenditures (Bishop and Heberlein 1979, Gordon and Knetsch 1979, Loehman 1984). It is posited that this divergence has little to do with income effects but is the result of two characteristics of rational behavior. The first is that individuals assess changes in welfare (gains and losses) from a neutral reference point rather than from comparisons among final states. The second reason is that evidence would suggest that losses from this reference point are of greater importance than gains. Kahneman and Tversky (1979) elude to this latter point, concluding that the aggravation experienced from losses of money appear to be greater than the pleasure associated with gaining the same amount. Evidence by Knetsch (1985) illustrates this asymmetric behavior and concludes that a discontinuity in the value function must exist at the reference point, hence, movements along indifference curves are not reversible and different indifference curves exist for acquisition versus disposal behavior.

Some economists, in addition, have interpreted the empirical evidence to mean that individuals do not behave as utility maximizers and therefore act irrationally (see Opaluch 1984 for a summary). If tastes (i.e., descriptions of what individuals like) and values (i.e., description of the way the world ought to be) both influence consumer behavior, that is, enter the utility function, and if tastes and values are not comparable, the relative influence of values on consumer behavior may offer an explanation of the above asymmetry in preferences. In fact, some researchers believe that preferences revealed through a CV approach, because of the hypothetical nature of the questions, are more influenced by values rather than by tastes (Cummings et al. 1986a). Smith and Desvousges (1986b) further examined disparities among welfare measures and perceived entitlements to risk and provide a different explanation than does Knetsch. Disparities were noticed among WTP bids to avoid increases in environmental risk and WTP bids to obtain equivalent risk levels from reductions in risks. The reason for the difference results from traditional utility and welfare maximization whereby this process does not reflect an individual's perceived entitlements to various nonmarket goods. Hence, they suggest a reformulation of perceived constraints in utility maximization. Further experimental research will determine which interpretation holds.

5.5. Economic Welfare Measures: Production Sector

5.5.1. Profit as a Measure of Producer Welfare

Compared to welfare measures in the consumption sector, measures of welfare in the production sector (sometimes referred to as the "private sector") are relatively straightforward. One of the basic economic premises of the theory of the firm is that firms maximize profits. Based on this, one could reason that profits are a valid measure of economic welfare to producers. Just et al. (1982) explore this issue and show that profit is equal to both the compensating and the equivalent variation measures of economic welfare for a price change. They conclude that profit can serve as a measure of economic welfare in some cases.

In Figure 5.6, average costs are represented by the curve AC and marginal costs by the curve MC. At price P_0, the firm is earning a profit, measured by the area below marginal costs and above average costs, area P_0DCB. When price rises from P_0 to P_1, profit becomes equal to area P_1FEA, and the gain in profit is represented by area P_0GFP_1. The compensating variation of the price increase is the monetary amount that can be taken away from the firm so that the firm is just as well off as it would have been if the price did not change. Thus, area P_0GFP_1 is equal to the compensating variation. The equivalent variation measure is defined as the monetary amount that, if given to the firm, leaves it just as well off without the price change as it is with the price change (Just et al. 1982). It is equal to the area P_0GFP_1. Thus the change in profit following a price change provides an exact measure of both the compensating and equivalent variation welfare measures.

However, in cases when a firm is not producing (i.e., idle or shut-down) or when it is operating at a loss, profit is not an appropriate measure of economic welfare. This is illustrated in Figure 5.7. Marginal cost, MC, average cost, AC, and average variable cost, AVC,

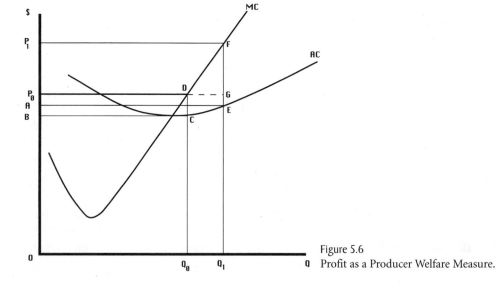

Figure 5.6
Profit as a Producer Welfare Measure.

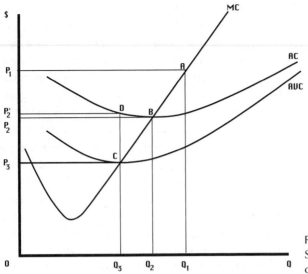

Figure 5.7
Shortcomings of Profit as a Measure of Producer Welfare.

curves are depicted. At price P_1, or point A on the MC curve, the firm is earning profits. If prices decrease to P_2, the firm will operate at point B on the MC curve and produce an output of OQ_2. At this position revenues simply equal costs, and profits vanish. Thus, at prices equal to or less than P_2 profits are zero or negative, respectively. At prices less than P_2 but greater than P_3, the firm will continue to operate earning losses. By operating though, the firm minimizes its losses because the losses are less than total fixed costs, represented by the vertical distance between the AC and AVC curve times quantity, that would result from shutting down. At prices equal to P_3 the firm is indifferent about operating. If it operates it will produce OQ_3, earn revenues that equal its variable costs, and realize a loss equal to its fixed costs (i.e., loss is equal to area $OQ_3DP_{2'}$ less area OQ_3CP_3 or area $P_3CDP_{2'}$, that is, total costs less total variable costs, or total fixed costs). Alternatively, if it shuts down the loss will be the same and equal to its fixed costs. By operating at prices less than P_3 its losses will be greater than losses incurred had it shut down. Therefore, at prices equal to or greater than P_3 (the firm's shut-down point) and less than or equal to price P_2 (the firm's break-even point) profits can no longer measure welfare changes.

5.5.2. Alternative Producer Welfare Measures

Two alternative measures of producer welfare were advanced by Marshall (1930), quasi-rent and producer surplus. Both are similar in concept to consumer surplus in that the firm realizes a surplus over and above the value of the goods sold. *Quasi-rent* is defined as the difference between revenues and variable costs (i.e., TR–TVC). *Producer surplus* represents the area above the producer's supply curve (i.e., marginal cost curve) and below the price line; a geometric measure of the economic concept of quasi-rent. However, as with consumer surplus, welfare measures of the effects of price and quantity changes on the producer are complex.

Currie et al. (1971) show that confusion has resulted over the meaning of the producer. In our case it represents the owner of a firm or business. More importantly, debate over producer surplus has focused on its measurement. The traditional measure of producer surplus is defined as the area above the producer's supply curve and below price (Marshall 1930). However, in the short run the supply curve of a firm coincides with its marginal cost curve. For a perfectly competitive firm in the short run, the surplus that accrues to the firm represented by the area above the marginal cost curve and below the price line measures the excess of revenues less prime costs. This surplus represents both producer surplus and quasi-rent. But what is meant by "prime costs"? In an early article, Marshall (1893) describes prime costs as the extra costs that a firm incurs from operating which would not have been incurred had the firm halted production. That is, they are the total variable costs of production, since these costs vanish when a firm shuts down. Hence, quasi-rent and producer surplus coincide for perfectly competitive firms in the short run and therefore represent equivalent measures of producer welfare. For the purposes of this book, economic damages (gains) to businesses are measured as reductions (increases) in economic welfare to the producer (i.e., producer surplus) that result from water quality impairments (improvements). In the case of impairments to water quality, businesses that suffer losses are assumed to satisfy the conditions of a perfectly competitive firm operating in the short run.

More formally, by definition, quasi-rent (QR) is:

$$QR = TR - TVC,$$

and producer surplus (PS) is:

$$PS = \pi + TFC \quad \text{(in the short run)};$$

where   TR = total revenue,

TVC = total variable costs,

TFC = total fixed costs,

TC = total costs, and

π = profit.

To show that PS = QR, rewrite PS:

$$PS = \pi + TFC$$

$$= [TR - TC] + TFC,$$

$$= [TR - (TVC + TFC)] + TFC,$$

$$= TR - TVC - TFC + TFC,$$

$$= TR - TVC, \text{ since the TFC terms cancel, and}$$

$$PS = QR.$$

Hence, the two measures are equal.

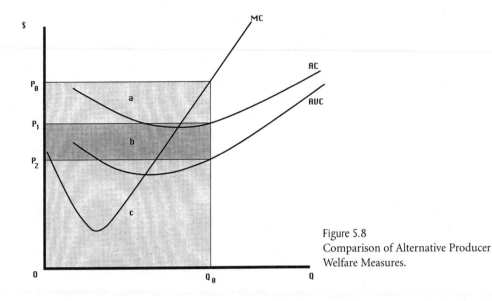

Figure 5.8
Comparison of Alternative Producer
Welfare Measures.

The measures of profit, quasi-rent, or producer surplus are illustrated in Figure 5.8. At the price–quantity combination, P_0Q_0, total revenue is equal to areas $a+b+c$, total cost, areas $b+c$, (i.e., total variable cost, area c, plus total fixed cost, area b) and profit, area a. Quasi-rent is equal to the areas $a+b$ (TR–TVC) which is producer surplus as well (π + TFC). From this illustration it should be clear that profit understates producer welfare by the amount incurred from shutting down, total fixed costs or area b. It is concluded that producer surplus or quasi-rent are more "ideal" measures of producer welfare.

5.6. Economic Welfare Aggregation over Individual Consumers and Producers

The previous sections examine economic welfare measures in terms of the individual consumer and producer. In practice, environmental quality degradations and public policies affect many individuals, and economic welfare analysis of the changes at the individual level are both impractical and burdensome. To be useful to public officials and policymakers welfare analysis of environmental degradations and policies requires aggregation over the individual economic units (consumers and producers) that are affected.

5.6.1. Private Sector/Goods Aggregation

As shown in the previous chapters, degradations of marine water quality can affect economic activities in both the private and the public sectors. Individual consumer demand curves are added horizontally to yield an aggregate or "market" quantity demanded (see Henderson and Quandt 1971, Nicholson 1994 for a diagrammatic explanation). At a given price the quantity demanded by each consumer is added over all consumers, and by repeating this for all prices a demand curve can be traced that represents the aggregate or "market" demand curve at various prices. Therefore, aggregate demand can be defined as:

(5.5) $D_m = \Sigma_{i=1}^{n}\ d_i(p)$ for i=1, ... , n consumers,

where *p* is the price of the good in question.

Aggregate supply is derived in a similar manner. The supply curve for each producer, represented by the marginal cost curve above average variable cost (i.e., shut-down point) in the short run and above the minimum point on the average costs (i.e., break-even point) in the long run (Henderson and Quandt 1971, Varian 1984, 1990) is summed horizontally at a given price to determine an aggregate or "market" quantity supplied (see Just et al. 1982 for a graphical analysis). By repeating this process over all prices, a supply locus can be traced that reflects an aggregate or "market" supply curve (i.e., aggregate quantity supplied at various prices). Aggregate supply can be defined as:

(5.6) $S_m = \Sigma_{j=1}^{q}\ s_j(p)$ for j=1, ⋯ , q producers.

Just et al. (1982) demonstrate that under conditions of perfect competition, the aggregation process will yield economic surpluses associated with market demand and supply equivalent to the sum of economic surpluses (consumer and producer surpluses) over all individuals in the market. Welfare analysis of policies or other exogenous effects that affect the demand or supply of private goods and services can then be analyzed from the change in economic welfare at the market level. That is, the change in welfare resulting from a movement along or a shift in the market demand/supply curve (i.e., aggregate welfare) will reflect the sum of changes in individual welfare under competitive conditions.

5.6.2. Public Sector/Goods Aggregation

Public goods and services are those for which an individual's consumption does not reduce the availability of the good to others (the characteristic of nonrival), and no one can be excluded from using them (the characteristic of nonexclusion). Furthermore, the added costs of providing an extra unit of a public good to an additional individual is zero (marginal costs are zero), and hence the unit price is negligible. As a result, the demand for public goods must be aggregated in a different manner than for private goods. Aggregate demand for public goods is determined from the summation of individuals' marginal valuations of the good; that is, the vertical summation of individuals' demand. At a given quantity (i.e., provision of the public good), the marginal value represented by consumer surplus for each individual is summed over all individuals. By repeating this process for various quantities, a demand curve is defined that represents aggregate demand, which is the aggregate willingness-to-pay (value) associated with various quantities. Aggregate demand or total value (TV) can be defined as:

(5.7) $TV = \Sigma_{i=1}^{n}\ MV_1(q)$ for i=1, ⋯ , n individuals,

where marginal value (MV) is a function of the level of provision (quantity) of the public good.

Unlike private goods and services, public goods and services are usually provided at zero cost to individuals and are not rationed in markets. If one could observe prices and quantities of the public good, one could use a market demand approach to determine changes in aggregate economic welfare. However, changes in economic welfare resulting from changes in levels of a public good must be determined at the individual user level and then aggregated over all users. This involves the use of nonmarket valuation techniques or indirect market valuation techniques (discussed in Chapter 7) based on a representative sample of individuals in order to obtain estimates of economic welfare associated with the good in question. These sample estimates are then projected, or aggregated, over all users to obtain an aggregate measure for the population in question.

5.7. Economic Losses versus Impacts: Measuring Net Losses due to Marine Pollution

Economic damage caused by water quality impairments in marine environments can lead to both economic losses and economic impacts. Based on economic theory lost economic value is the equivalent of lost aggregate economic welfare. As already discussed, aggregate welfare losses can be assessed in terms of consumer surplus measures of consumption activities of private and public goods summed over all individuals, and producer surplus summed over all producers.

Economic impacts such as lost business volume (sales), idle investment, unemployment, and added expenses to pursue recreational activities can result from marine pollution. An issue is whether to consider these impacts as losses in any economic assessment of impairments. On the basis of the economic welfare measures of surplus discussed above, that portion of lost sales or revenues equal to expenditures on inputs cannot be considered as part of economic losses. Why? Recall that consumer surplus measures the surplus net of expenditures. The portion of consumer expenditures or, equivalently, the portion of producer revenues that can be considered as economic losses, is the amount of revenues net of variable costs. The remaining amount of sales revenues (or, equivalently, consumer expenses) cannot be considered as economic losses (i.e., revenues equal in amount to variable costs).

To gain an understanding of why variable costs of inputs, that is, payments to inputs are not considered as losses it is useful to think in terms of opportunity costs (i.e., the value of an input in its next best alternative use). Under conditions of efficient markets, inputs will move to employment opportunities in which the highest opportunity cost can be gained. It is assumed that inputs can move effortlessly and with zero cost from one firm to another or from one area to another. It follows that in an economy with efficient markets, inputs normally move from one producer to another and if there is no overall growth in the economy, the value of input payments are simply transferred within the economy with the total value of input payments remaining constant. In an area that experiences marine pollution the private sector may experience a loss of business volume, and inputs may become idle if any firms shut down (worst case scenario) or experience a drop in activity (both drop in sales and employment) and payments to the inputs are not made. Assuming efficient market conditions these inputs can relocate elsewhere and the value of the factor payment is transferred, thus remaining within the economy (assuming no growth).

Therefore, input payments such as labor are not considered as losses of economic welfare because the inputs have opportunity costs and can relocate elsewhere (and the monetary value is not lost from the economy). However, this is not the case in the real world and a given economy may experience lumpy transfers (where not all inputs and business activity are transferred instantly) and costly transfers (where transfers of inputs and business activity are associated with real costs) and may not be able to absorb input transfers efficiently resulting in unemployment, for example. A loss does occur to inputs, such as labor, from remaining idle, and the issue becomes how much and how long to compensate the employee for the loss (see Mishan 1976 for further insights).

This does not mean that assessments of detrimental impacts are to be ignored when considering damages that result from water quality impairments. They are a meaningful measure of economic damage. Detrimental economic impacts measure the monetary loss to a particular segment of the economy. That is, they represent the aggregate flow of capital that has left an economic sector due to an outside (exogenous) effect, such as marine-related pollution. This is equal to the sum of revenues plus costs to producers (i.e., decrease in revenues and increase in costs from degradations, increase in revenues and decrease in costs from improvements) or the sum of consumer surplus and expenses to consumers (i.e., reductions in consumer surplus and expenditures from degradations, increases in consumer surplus and expenditures from improvements). When both producers and consumers are included, it is equal to the sum of revenues and costs from the production sector plus consumer surplus from the consumption sector. Consumer expenditures are not included because they represent purchases of goods and appear in the production sector as revenues. Including both consumer expenditures and producer revenues would be double-counting.

It should be clear that in most cases, economic losses defined as the sum of consumer surplus and producer surplus represent all lost net economic values that result from water quality impairments—welfare component. The process of making an actual assessment of the economic losses caused by an exogenous effect such as marine pollution can become complicated. For example, it is possible that other influences may be affecting economic welfare during the same time. One has to identify first the suspected effects caused by marine pollution, and then these effects on economic activities must be separated from other possible influences. For example, marine pollution that results in beach closings causes attendance to drop (both supply and demand effects). But weather conditions such as cloudy and rainy weather can also cause attendance to drop. Decreases in fish stock abundance (i.e., supply effects) can be the result of long-term chronic pollution that impairs reproduction and growth, or an acute oil or chemical spill that results in kills, or the alteration and loss of habitats by real estate development, or natural fluctuations in the food source, or climate, or overfishing, or even a combination of all of these reasons. Furthermore in the case of fish found to be contaminated with pollutants (i.e., unsafe seafood), economic losses may occur from the public's concern over the safety of seafood generally resulting in avoidance of seafood (a demand effect). A simple comparison of changes in economic activities and changes in producer and consumer welfare before and after a pollution event has occurred will capture not only the effects of marine pollution but any of these other influences as well. The challenge to the researcher is to isolate the individual influences from one another in order to calculate as precise an estimate as possible of the economic damage and losses attributable to marine pollution.

One approach that can be used to accomplish this is taken from CBA. Similar problems to those just outlined arise in CBA when one is identifying the benefits and costs that would result from proposed public projects such as water development and flood control projects (Eckstein 1958, Gittinger 1972). The "with and without" rule is commonly used in CBAs of such projects and it can also be used in assessing losses due to marine pollution. To evaluate losses of economic welfare that result from marine pollution two situations must be compared: the economic welfare of the economy that results with the presence of marine pollution, and the economic welfare of the economy that would occur without it. This comparison is central to any CBA application. The "with and without" rule is simply a restatement of this central concept in CBA: that any action or economic effect, here the presence of marine pollution, be evaluated "in terms of the effects which it specifically causes," (Eckstein 1958: 52). Use of this rule prevents attributing effects to an action (or affect) that are not caused by it.

By adopting this rule, one is forced to identify only those effects due to marine pollution. In some cases, the rule will require a more restrictive research design (e.g., sample and study design) in order to achieve more precise estimates of economic damage and losses from marine pollution. Use of the "with and without" rule should result in more accurate estimates than estimates obtained from a comparison of changes before and after a pollution event. It should be noted that the two approaches, "with and without" and "before and after" will give the same answer only when changes in economic welfare occur in a given time period when marine pollution occurs, while all other effects remain constant. Changes in economic activity and losses based on a "before and after" comparison may include many more exogenous influences on economic activity and losses.

The "with and without" rule is not a perfect procedure that will consistently isolate only the effects attributable to marine pollution time after time. Although it can isolate those effects mainly attributable to marine pollution and do so more accurately than a "before and after" comparison, it cannot isolate the exact effects of marine pollution when other influences are occurring simultaneously. This must be accomplished through careful detail in research design and empirical techniques adopted.

Estimates of the net economic welfare due to marine pollution (i.e., net welfare lost) can then be defined as the sum of consumer surplus and producer surplus associated without pollution less the sum of consumer surplus and producer surplus with pollution. Such a measure will represent the net change in economic welfare attributable to marine pollution. Formally we write this as:

(5.8a) $\Delta W = (CS + PS)_{\text{w/o pollution}} - (CS + PS)_{\text{w pollution}}$, or

(5.8b) $\Delta W = (CS + PS)_{\text{pre-spill state}} - (CS + PS)_{\text{post-spill state}}$,

where Δ refers to "the change in," W equals economic welfare, CS equals consumer surplus, and PS equals producer surplus. Several of these effects are illustrated with demand and supply effects diagrams. First consider demand effects alone when the supply curve is horizontal (i.e., perfectly elastic). In general a demand curve can shift downward as a parallel downward shift, or it can pivot inward from the intercept. Figure 5.9 illustrates the case of a downward parallel shift in demand and subsequent economic losses. Economic losses result from a loss of consumer surplus, the area represented by P_0ABP_1, as the original demand curve P_0D_0 has shifted down to P_1D_1. Figure 5.10 illustrates the case where the demand curve pivots inward. Subsequent economic losses represent the loss of consumer surplus equal to the area P_0AB. Because of the shape of the supply curve, producer surplus does not exist. The net economic welfare (i.e., the loss of CS) in both of these cases is expressed formally by Equations (5.8a) and (5.8b).

Now consider supply effects alone given the special case of a horizontal demand curve (i.e., perfectly elastic). As in the case of demand effects, decreases in supply curves can also be represented by a parallel shift or by a pivoting of the supply curve. Figure 5.11 illustrates the case of a decrease in supply where the supply curve shifts parallel inward (i.e., a leftward shift). The economic loss in welfare is represented by a loss in producer surplus, the area P_0ABP_1. Figure 5.12 illustrates the case of a supply decrease given a pivot

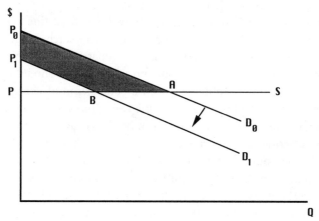

Figure 5.9
Loss of Consumer Surplus from a Decrease in Demand.

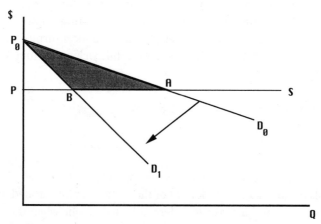

Figure 5.10
Loss of Consumer Surplus from a Decrease in Demand.

inward. The loss in producer surplus is represented by the area P_0AB. In this special case consumer surplus does not exist. The net economic welfare (i.e., the loss of PS) from supply reductions is also formally expressed by Equations (5.8a) and (5.8b). Both equations, in addition account for the case where both demand and supply effects simultaneously occur, and represent the net change of consumer surplus and producer surplus.

Because the above diagrams represent simple cases where it is assumed that one of the demand or supply curves has constant slope or is a horizontal line, the following set of diagrams shows the more realistic case where the demand and supply curves have the usual shape: downward sloping for demand and upward sloping for supply. Although this is more realistic, it adds a level of complexity and is now possible double-counting because of transfers of surplus. Hence, care must be used in applications. Figures 5.13 and 5.14, show, respectively, the lost consumer surplus for the consumer alone and the lost producer surplus for the producer alone, represented

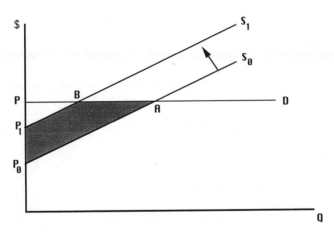

Figure 5.11
Loss of Producer Surplus from a Decrease in Supply.

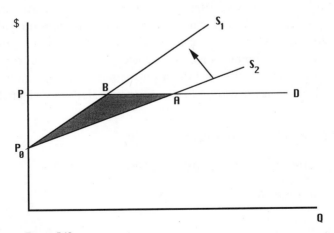

Figure 5.12
Loss of Producer Surplus from a Decrease in Supply.

by the shaded areas in both from a downward shift in the demand curve. When both consumption and production sectors are combined, there is a transfer of surplus from producer to consumer, hence lost surplus is not simply the sum of the shaded areas. First, the lost consumer surplus for the consumer alone (see Figure 5.13) is as follows:

initial CS = area P_2P_0D = 1/2(5)(15) = $37.50

−new CS = area P_3P_1C = 1/2(3)(12) = $18.00

lost CS = area P_1P_0DE = $19.50.

Second, the lost PS for the producer alone (see Figure 5.14) is as follows:

initial PS = area P_4P_2D = 1/2(5)(15) = $37.50

−new PS = area P_4P_3C = 1/2(4)(12) = $24.00

lost PS = area P_3P_2DC = $13.50.

Now the sum of lost CS and lost PS when both the consumption and production sectors are included as follows:

lost CS = area P_1P_0DE = $19.50

+ lost PS = area P_3P_2DC = $13.50

−transfer = area P_3P_2EC = $10.50

                  $22.50, and not $33 (i.e., $19.50 + $13.50).

Hence, $22.50 represents the lost net economic value (after the transfer is netted out) as formally stated in Equations (5.8a) and (5.8b) relative to a decrease in the demand curve when both consumers and producers are combined.

As a result of a decrease in the supply curve (i.e., an inward shift), Figures 5.15 and 5.16, show, respectively, the loss of consumer surplus for the consumer alone and producer surplus for the producer alone as the shaded areas. When both consumption and production sectors are combined, there is a transfer of surplus from consumer to producer (the transfer reverses); hence, lost surplus is not simply the sum of the shaded areas. First, the lost consumer surplus for the consumer alone (see Figure 5.15) is as follows:

initial CS = area P_2AC = 1/2(5)(15) = $37.50

−new CS = area P_3AB = 1/2(4)(10) = $20.00

lost CS = area P_2P_3BC = $17.50.

Second, the lost PS for the producer alone (see Figure 5.16) is as follows:

initial PS = area P_0P_2C = 1/2(5)(15) = $37.50

−new PS = area P_1P_3B = 1/2(2)(10) = $10.00

lost PS = area P_0P_1EC = $27.50.

Now the sum of lost CS and lost PS when both the consumption and production sectors are included is as follows:

lost CS = area P_2P_3BC = $17.50

+ lost PS = area P_0P_1EC = $27.50

−transfer = area P_2P_3BE = $7.50

$37.50, and not $45 (i.e., $17.50 + $27.50).

Hence, $37.50 represents the lost net economic value (after the transfer is netted out) as formally stated in Equations (5.8a) and (5.8b) relative to a decrease in the supply curve when both consumers and producers are combined.

Furthermore, to dispel any confusion, Figure 5.17 illustrates that consumer surplus and producer surplus always decrease given a decrease in supply no matter what the degree of elasticity of demand (graphically depicted by the relative steepness of the demand curve). For a relatively elastic demand curve (i.e., one in which quantity is very sensitive to small price changes), D_0 in Figure 5.17, a reduction in supply causes the area under demand and above price P_0 to decrease. In the case of a relatively inelastic demand curve (i.e., one in which quantity is insensitive to small price changes), D_1 in Figure 5.17, a reduction in supply causes the area under demand and above price P_1 to decrease. However, depending on the elasticity of demand, total expenditures can change given a decrease in supply; increase with an inelastic demand, and decrease with an elastic demand.

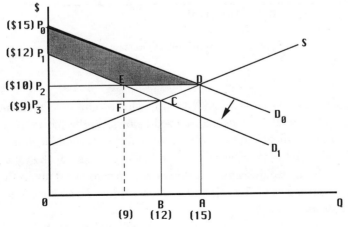

Figure 5.13
Loss of Consumer Surplus from a Decrease in Demand.

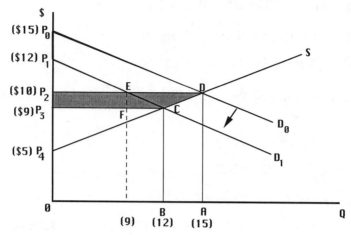

Figure 5.14
Loss of Producer Surplus from a Decrease in Demand.

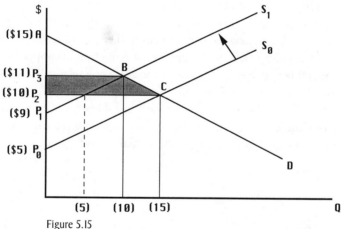

Figure 5.15
:Loss of Consumer Surplus from a Decrease in Supply.

In some cases additional costs are added to these losses. One case is when the costs of relocating inputs are nonzero. This is discussed below. Another concern is the public health aspects of impairments. In these cases economic losses would include the medical costs incurred, plus the lost earnings had the individual worked or the value of the lost productivity. An alternative measure is willingness-to-pay to avoid illness or premature death, such as in estimates of the value of a statistical life. These concepts will be discussed in more detail in Chapter 7.

In the preceding discussion we have simplified the approaches to account for cases where substitute sites do not exist; that is, the discussion and treatment pertains to the case of a single site that experiences pollution at some time. The presence of

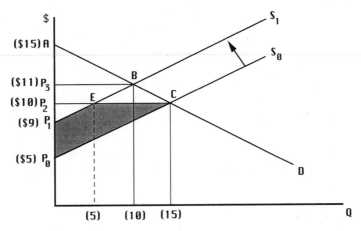

Figure 5.16
Loss of Producer Surplus from a Decrease in Supply.

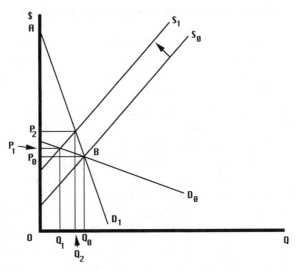

Figure 5.17
Graphic Proof That Only Total Expenditure Can Change Depending on Elasticity of Demand Given a Decrease in Supply; Consumer Surplus and Producer Surplus Decrease in All Cases.

multiple substitute sites complicates the task of assessing economic losses for a particular site that has experienced a pollution event, further assuming that the substitute sites remain unpolluted. In these cases one must determine the influence of the demand for clean substitute sites on the demand for the polluted site and the demand for the clean substitute sites given the demand for the polluted site based on a particular use activity. Formally the complication involves sequencing of the disaggregated (i.e., individual) welfare effects so that one site is conditional on each relevant substitute site. A formal discussion of this problem is discussed in Section 5.14 following McConnell and Industrial Economics (1986) and Bockstael and McConnell (1990).

5.8. Intertemporal Economic Losses

Economic damage resulting from marine pollution often occurs over a substantial period of time. The different types of impairments identified earlier can range from short-term effects to long-term effects. For example, excessive levels of bacteria and washups of marine debris can result in short-term, acute damages to marine environments. Contamination of water and bottom sediment with toxic substances can result in long-term, chronic damages to marine environments. When evaluating losses over time, both losses in the present period and losses in future periods must be considered. In order to combine losses that occur in future periods with those of the present period, future losses must be discounted to their present value. The PV formula for evaluating welfare losses is:

$$(5.9) \qquad PV = \Sigma_{i=1}^{n} \, WL_i \, / \, (1 + r)^i$$

where WL is the welfare loss in each period, r the discount rate, and i=1, ... , n the time period.

The literature contains a discussion of the appropriate discount rate to use (see Bohm 1976, Herfindahl and Kneese 1974, Just et al.1982, Kohli 1993, Mishan 1976). Generally, if losses are in real terms (constant dollars) an inflation adjusted discount rate should be used; if losses are in nominal terms (current dollars) a nominal discount rate should be used (Just et al. 1982). Real rates of discount from empirical economic studies are in the range of 0 to 4 percent, and nominal rates range from 8 to16 percent (Just et al. 1982: 305–306). Current dollars reflect the prices that exist in each time period (e.g., losses in 1986$, 1987$, etc.). If, however, the stream of losses were adjusted for inflation using an index (e.g., the consumer price index or producer price index from the *Survey of Current Business,* U.S. Department Commerce), then losses could be indexed to 1967 dollars or 1986 dollars, or any year for that matter, and represent a constant dollar measure. That is, constant dollars are current dollars adjusted for inflation.

Much of the debate over the appropriate discount rate centers on several theoretical issues (Just et al. 1982) (what follows is a brief version of the discussion in Section 5.3.1.2). The discount rate is essentially an exchange rate between individuals' time preferences and the productivity of investments, and too high a rate will favor present consumption over future consumption with too little investment made for future generations. A low rate for public projects (e.g., water quality improvements) is suggested because of the view that public investments are less risky than private investments (i.e., low risk premium). However, some suggest higher discount rates because future resource use is uncertain and a low risk premium may be inappropriate (Yang et al. 1984). (It should be pointed out that a risk premium is that portion of the total interest rate that compensates for risk, and low discount rates correspond to low risk premiums and vice versa, other things being equal.) Furthermore, some suggest that a discount rate should be based on the opportunity cost of private investment displaced by the public project. In sum, there is no consensus over the appropriate discount rate to use. Yang et al. (1984) note that some applications have used a rate equal to a long-run nominal interest rate (e.g., 30-year U.S. Treasury Bond rate) less the long-run inflation rate.

5.9. Scope of Analysis, Federal Criteria, and Transfers

5.9.1. Scope of Analysis

In applications of CBA and Natural Resource Damage Assessments (NRDAs) the scope of analysis must be determined, and appropriate welfare measures are assessed relative to this scope. NRDAs are usually defined by the area affected by an oil spill or historical release of toxic chemicals as determined from biological and environmental monitoring. For example, the U.S. EPA Long Island Sound Study encompasses Long Island Sound; the New Bedford Harbor Superfund site is included within the U.S. EPA Buzzards Bay Program. In applications of CBA the scope can depend on the jurisdiction that provides support for a project (e.g., federal support, local support), the jurisdiction of the agency or entity that oversees or manages the project, and/or the jurisdiction(s) affected by the project—the area affected. In some cases this could be at a local, state, regional, or national level.

5.9.2. Federal Criteria

Concerning federally funded projects, these projects must be based on national economic development (NED) criteria in CBA. These criteria consider contributions to NED as increases in the net economic value of the national output of goods and services; in other words, the net economic value the proposed project contributes to national output (U.S. WRC 1983). Those projects are selected that maximize NED benefits.

5.9.3. Transfers

In applications of welfare economics and in CBA the issue of transfers (e.g., transfer payments from one area to another because a project may have detrimental effects in an area) is not appropriate (Kohli 1993, Sugden and Williams 1990). However, in terms of economic effects or economic activity measures, such as impacts where a project or an environmental hazard (spill or release) has different effects across areas, it may be appropriate to evaluate these effects. For example in the case of a proposed project, given two areas where one area benefits from the project and the other area experiences losses, situations are possible where the gains in spending in area B are greater than, equal to, or less than the loss in spending at area A. In the case of environmental-resource damages, a similar situation can exist where losses in economic activity (e.g., spending) due to marine pollution in one geographic area or community are greater than, equal to, or less than gains in economic activity at a nearby unpolluted area or community. This is an instance where beach users avoid closed beaches in a community that has experienced marine pollution, and travel to clean, open beaches in nearby communities. Site-specific areas may suffer economic losses such as lost economic activity, whereas others may experience gains, with the net effect over both areas, or a larger region may differ and show net gains, no net change, or net losses. Again evaluation of these effects only makes sense if one is concerned with changes in economic activity or impacts.

5.10. Economic Value in a Total Valuation Framework

Stimulated by a concern among economists that after all the economic value from all possible uses has been accounted for in CBA and in economic assessments, there may be some residual value not accounted for, various economic values have been proposed for consideration. Several researchers have explored various frameworks to examine these issues (Randall and Stoll 1983; Randall 1991; Smith 1987a, 1987b). The two basic areas this research has addressed include the implications of economic value in a total valuation framework (Randall and Stoll 1983, Hoehn and Randall 1989, Randall 1991) and concerns over option value (Smith 1987a, 1987b; Randall 1991).

Randall (1991) showed that a decomposition of Hicksian welfare measures (either from price or quantity changes) results in a use value component and a nonuse value component (i.e., existence value) (Section 5.13 contains a formal treatment.) Such a result can be expressed as an aggregate measure or as a sequence of partial measures (i.e., individual use values and existence value) of net economic value. Furthermore, this result holds in the presence of uncertainty, and with uncertainty all economic values are in ex ante measures. More importantly, the decomposition yields no place for other economic values such as option value, hence other economic values are not necessary in assessments of the total value of the good in question. And lastly, results emphasize that assessments based on piecemeal research (i.e., summing individual economic values across separate uses based on previous research), as is sometimes done for public policy evaluations, can lead to overestimates of the net economic value and should be avoided or used with caution. Research should instead be designed from the outset to assess the total value for a given resource or service versus separate, disjointed research projects that individually assess economic value on a piecemeal basis.

The importance of Smith's (1987a, 1987b) research was to show that option value, previously deemed an important component of economic value, was in fact the algebraic difference between two different points on a willingness to pay locus, the expected value of consumer surplus and option price (i.e., amount of willingness to pay independent of state or outcome).

Both findings have led researchers to drop option value as a component of economic value in future assessments of resource and environmental goods (Freeman 1993, Randall 1991), and we follow suit.

5.11. Simplified NRDAs (Natural Resource Damage Assessments)

5.11.1. Introduction

In this brief section we examine the relation of federal procedures of NRDAs to common law principles of damages, and then consider whether the use of such liability rules and common law principles of damages achieves economic efficient allocations of resources and socially optimal levels of resources. Federal procedures of NRDA via the Comprehensive Environmental Response, Compensation, and Liability Act (CERCLA) (U.S. DOI) and the Oil Pollution Act (OPA) (National Oceanic and Atmospheric Administration [NOAA]) that pertain to compensable values (or recoverable damages) are based on common law principles of damages (U.S. DOI 1986: 27680, 1987, U.S. DOC, NOAA 1996). Common law theories state that damages are recoverable to the extent and for the purpose that the injured party and/or natural resource is made whole again (U.S. DOI 1986: 27688), and that damages are compensatory and not punitive (U.S. DOI 1986: 27680). This partially explains why current NOAA federal procedures emphasize restoration costs and/or replacement costs as the basis for measurement of damages and not values of economic welfare. Here a seemingly subtle conflict is present between economic theory and legal theories. A central issue is that there may be little or no basis from empirical research to gauge whether damages based on restoration costs versus damages based on the value of decreased economic welfare are similar or diverge from one another nor information of their relative magnitudes. This should concern economists because of the implications for economic efficiency and the socially optimal allocation of resources. If restoration costs significantly understate damages relative to welfare measures, then the NOAA federal rules as designed could promote economically inefficient allocations of resources.

Economists can help to effect future changes in NRDA procedures through research that examines and compares the value of lost economic welfare with that of restoration and replacement costs to determine if similarities or differences occur across various resources and services as evidence becomes available. On this basis, efficient liability rules that can attain economically efficient resource allocations and social optimums can be developed.

5.11.2. Economic Damage Assessments in Federal NRDAs

In Chapter 3, federal NRDA procedures as developed by the U.S. Department of Interior (U.S. DOI) and U.S. Department of Commerce (U.S. DOC, NOAA) were discussed with an emphasis placed on how one would follow and conduct an NRDA. Here we briefly want to emphasize the component of the NRDA procedures based on the determination of economic damages. As previously noted, both the U.S. DOI and U.S. DOC, NOAA NRDA procedures and rules contain many parallels. The most important is the definition of damages. Both use the following definition:

$$\text{damages} = \text{restoration costs} + \text{compensable value} + \text{assessment cost,}$$

where restoration costs refer to the costs of restoration, rehabilitation, replacement, or acquisition of equivalent natural resources and services, compensable value for the U.S. DOI procedures refers to lost use value and lost nonuse value to the public (included at the discretion of the lead trustee), compensable value for the NOAA procedures refers to lost interim values to the public (i.e., lost use value and lost passive use value, where passive use values consist of the nonuse values of existence value), and assessment costs refer to the reasonable costs of assessment. Both procedures also include restoration actions, costs of restoration actions, and specific methods to estimate restoration costs as a major component of the procedure and damage estimate. Both techniques share a similar procedural approach that involves a preassessment phase, an assessment phase, and a post-assessment phase. Both procedures also contain criteria in which to select a "preferred" restoration plan based on (1) technical feasibility, (2) reasonable costs, (3) cost-effectiveness where appropriate, and (4) the use of more sophisticated or alternative approaches only when they can be applied at reasonable cost, and where the extra cost from their use is exceeded by the additional benefits these techniques can measure and estimate.

Where the U.S. DOI NRDA rules and procedures appear to be heavily weighted and emphasize specific detail is in the application of various techniques to measure and estimate injury(ies), restoration costs, and compensable value. The NOAA NRDA rules and procedures appear weighted toward scaling restoration projects (i.e., choosing the appropriate size of restoration projects) and estimating and basing the scale of restoration projects on restoration costs and damages. They include monitoring actions as a component of restoration actions in the post-assessment phase. Concerning monitoring, the NOAA procedures contain specific procedures to evaluate such restoration actions (Chapter 10 contains a discussion of this). Monitoring and the use of scaling procedures are either not treated or are treated minimally in the U.S. DOI rules. It remains an issue for future rulemaking whether these issues will be incorporated in both federal rules and procedures on a consistent and equal basis.

We want to emphasize the importance of compensable value because it involves well established economic principles and theory. Compensable values consist of use values and nonuse values associated with a resource and its services. These values represent measures of changes in economic welfare to users of a resource and to nonusers. Assessment costs are relatively straightforward. The other component, restoration costs involve habitat and resource restoration using cost effectiveness techniques, that is, the least costly means of achieving restoration. The area of resource restoration is a new area and much needs to be learned here before formal models based on economic theory can be developed and become useful. Chapters 7 and 8 discuss and show how economic welfare associated with use values can and has been determined.

5.12. Technical Appendix to Chapter 5: Exact Hicksian Welfare Measures

Although the discussion in this chapter has presented the basic notion of net economic value it is given a more formal and precise definition in advanced textbooks and in the professional literature. The purpose of this technical appendix is to expose the reader to this literature. This requires knowledge and familiarity of mathematics (see Chiang 1984, McKenna and Rees 1992).

Consumer Theory

In basic consumer theory, the agent (consumer) is assumed to derive utility (i.e., satisfaction) from the consumption of goods and services. This is formally represented by an expression for the utility function:

(5.10) $U = U(x_1, x_2)$, in the two-good case,

where x_1 and x_2 could be substitute or complement goods or independent goods, U is the utility function expressed by U(.) assumed to have the typical properties of utility functions in consumption theory and the dot "." refers to the arguments of the utility function. In Equation (5.10) x_1 and x_2 are these arguments.

The agent's problem is to derive the highest level of satisfaction from those goods desired, limited by a fixed income. This problem is referred to as the primal problem in consumer theory, where the agent chooses to maximize U relative to a linear budget/income constraint. Formally this is expressed as:

$$\max_{x_1, x_2} U = U(x_1, x_2)$$

subject to $p_1 x_1 + p_2 x_2 \leq M$,

where p_1, p_2 are the respective prices of the goods, and M is money income (i.e., nominal income). The solution yields ordinary or Marshallian demand curves of the form:

(5.11) $x_1 = x_1(p_1, p_2, M)$, and

(5.12) $x_2 = x_2(p_1, p_2, M)$.

It should be pointed out that these Marshallian demand curves are based on and influenced by several variables or determinants of demand such as the price of the good itself, the price of related goods, tastes–preferences, and income. The area under this curve between two prices (p^0 to p^1) gives us consumer surplus:

(5.13) $CS = \int_{p^0}^{p^1} x_1(p_1, p_2, M) dp_1,$

where dp_1 represents the change in the price for x_1. A similar expression holds for the second good if we are interested in determining welfare changes from price changes. It is noted that Marshallian demand curves are structured whereby quantity is dependent on (i.e., a function of) prices and money income. In graphical analyses it is common to express and graph these demand curves where price is dependent on quantity (i.e., inverse demand curves) while holding all the remaining factors of demand constant. Consumer surplus can be determined from inverse demand curves as the area under the inverse demand curve between two quantities (since quantities would be on the x [or horizontal] axis); more importantly both approaches yield the same result.

The agent also faces a dual problem, to minimize expenses relative to achieving a given level of utility (U^*). This dual problem is expressed formally as:

$$\min_{x_1, x_2} p_1 x_1 + p_2 x_2$$

subject to $U(x_1, x_2) \geq U^*$.

The solution yields compensated or Hicksian demand curves, expressed as:

(5.14) $x_1 = h_1(p_1, p_2, U)$, and

(5.15) $x_2 = h_2(p_1, p_2, U)$.

Substituting these compensated demand expressions into the budget constraint yields:

(5.16) $p_1 x_1 + p_2 x_2,$

(5.17) $p_1 h_1(p_1, p_2, U) + p_2 h_2(p_1, p_2, U)$, by substitution.

This last expression is defined as an expenditure function which depends only on prices and utility:

(5.18) $e(p_1, p_2, U) = p_1 h_1(p_1, p_2, U) + p_2 h_2(p_1, p_2, U).$

It is from this expression, the expenditure function, that Hicksian welfare measures can be defined exactly. Consider first price changes of only a single good (p^0 to p^1, where $p^1 > p^0$).

Compensating variation (CV) is:

(5.19) $CV = e(p^1, U^0) - e(p^0, U^0),$

where the subscript on price has been dropped and U^0 refers to the initial level of utility. A similar expression for equivalent variation (EV) is:

(5.20) $EV = e(p^1, U^1) - e(p^0, U^1)$, where U^1 is the new level of utility and $U^1 > U^0$.

Here CV refers to the minimum amount an individual is willing to accept as compensation to avoid the price change and maintain the initial position, (i.e., the same level of utility: U^0). EV refers to the maximum amount an individual would be willing to pay for the price change that would achieve a new and higher level of utility, (i.e., U^1).

For quantity changes (x^0 to x^1, where $x^1 > x^0$), Hicksian surplus measures are expressed as:

(5.21) $CS = e(p^0, x^1, U^0) - e(p^0, x^0, U^0)$, and

(5.22) $ES = e(p^0, x^1, U^1) - e(p^0, x^0, U^1)$, where U^1 is the new level of utility.

Now compensating surplus (CS) refers to the minimum amount an individual is willing to accept as compensation to avoid the quantity change and maintain the initial position. Equivalent surplus (ES) refers to the maximum amount an individual would be willing to pay for the quantity change that would achieve a higher level of utility.

5.13. Technical Appendix to Chapter 5: Economic Value in a Total Valuation Framework

To begin, we use the expenditure function as in Equation (5.18) and following Randall (1991) define total value (TV) of natural resource services in the context of Hicksian compensating welfare changes as:

$$(5.23) \qquad TV = e(p_e^*, p_s^*, p_1^*, p_2^*, x^0, U^0) - e(p_e^0, p_s^0, p_1^0, p_2^0, x^0, U^0),$$

where the subscript e equals existence, s equals site experience, 1 equals activity 1, 2 equals activity 2, p^* equals a "choke" price where the price is high enough so that demand is zero, p^0 equals a base or initial price level, x^0 equals an initial level of resource quality. It is noted that the price for existence is a virtual price similar to a shadow or true price (i.e., the marginal valuation of a service that would be determined in a market had a market existed, usually under perfect competitive conditions). But there are no markets for "existence" of resources. Equation (5.23) represents the aggregate measure of total value. Randall shows that this can be decomposed into a sequence of price changes as follows:

$$(5.24a) \qquad TV = e(p_e^*, p_s^*, p_1^*, p_2^*, x^0, U^0) - e(p_e^0, p_s^*, p_1^*, p_2^*, x^0, U^0)$$

$$(5.24b) \qquad + e(p_e^0, p_s^*, p_1^*, p_2^*, x^0, U^0) - e(p_e^0, p_s^0, p_1^*, p_2^*, x^0, U^0)$$

$$(5.24c) \qquad + e(p_e^0, p_s^0, p_1^*, p_2^*, x^0, U^0) - e(p_e^0, p_s^0, p_1^0, p_2^*, x^0, U^0)$$

$$(5.24d) \qquad + e(p_e^0, p_s^0, p_1^0, p_2^*, x^0, U^0) - e(p_e^0, p_s^0, p_1^0, p_2^0, x^0, U^0),$$

where total value consists of several components of economic value. Equation (5.24a) represents the nonuse value component, existence value; Equation (5.24b) is the economic value associated with site experience; and Equations (5.24c) and (5.24d) are the economic value for activities 1 and 2, respectively. In other words, Equation (5.24a) represents existence value (nonuse value), and Equations (5.24b–5.24d) represent a variety of use values. Hence, total value can be decomposed into use values and existence value. One can see there is no need to include any other economic value concepts for fear that some value component has been missed. As Randall (1991) further shows, this result holds in the presence of uncertainty where the consumer maximizes expected utility limited by income; a parallel or equivalent expression is obtained to that above.

5.14. Technical Appendix to Chapter 5: Problem of Sequencing Losses or Gains in Economic Welfare Given Multiple (Substitute) Sites

This section serves to further elaborate the discussion where environmental quality has changed at more than one recreational site and that changes in economic welfare where multiple (and sometimes alternative) sites are present now depend on a sequence of changes in economic welfare summed across all sites. This is because the quality level at one site influences the demand at the other $m-1$ sites, e.g., the demand for site 1 is dependent or conditional on the environmental quality at site 1 as well as on the level of quality at site 2, and vice versa for the demand for site 2. Given this situation economic value is based on a sequencing of quality changes, where economic value is now represented by the sum of the economic value at site m when quality changes from the initial level to a new level at site m holding quality constant (i.e., at initial levels) at all $m-1$ sites, the economic value at the $m-1$ site when quality changes at the $m-1$ site given the new level at site m and again holding quality at all remaining $m-2$ sites at initial levels, and the economic value at the $m-2$ site when quality at the $m-2$ site changes given the previous changes in quality at sites m and $m-1$ while holding quality at the remaining $m-3$ sites at initial (before change) levels and so on. Such a sequencing problem in economic welfare also arises in the case of evaluating welfare changes from multiple price changes (see Just et al. 1982).

The following discussion follows from McConnell (1986). Following the notation used in Equation (5.21) economic value after a change in environmental quality from α^0 to α^1 where $\alpha^1 < \alpha^0$ in the case of a decrease in quality can be represented as:

$$(5.25) \qquad CS^* = e(p^0, \alpha^1, U^0) - e(p^0, \alpha^0, U^0),$$

a quasi-compensating surplus analog given a decrease in quality, and in the case of two sites:

$$(5.26) \qquad CS^* = e(p_1^0, p_2^0, \alpha_1^1, \alpha_2^0, U_1^0, U_2^0) - e(p_1^0, p_2^0, \alpha_1^0, \alpha_2^0, U_1^0, U_2^0)$$

$$+ e(p_1^0, p_2^0, \alpha_1^1, \alpha_2^1, U_1^0, U_2^0) - e(p_1^0, p_2^0, \alpha_1^1, \alpha_2^0, U_1^0, U_2^0),$$

$CS^* =$ economic value at site 1 given the change in quality at site 1, holding quality at site 2 at initial levels

+ economic value at site 2 given the change in quality at site 2, when quality at site 1 is at the new level.

Using Shepard's lemma, that the partial derivative of the expenditure function with respect to price is the Hicksian demand curve, i.e., $\partial e / \partial p_i = h_i(p, \alpha, U)$, Equation (5.26) can be expressed as:

$$(5.27) \quad CS^* = \int_{p_1^0}^{p_1^*} h_1(p_1, p_2^0, \alpha_1^1, \alpha_2^0, \alpha^*, U_1^0, U_2^0) dp_1$$

$$-\int_{p_1^0}^{p_1^{**}} h_1(p_1, p_2^0, \alpha_1^0, \alpha_2^0, \alpha^*, U_1^0, U_2^0) dp_1$$

$$+\int_{p_2^0}^{p_2^*} h_2(p_2, p_1^0, \alpha_1^1, \alpha_2^1, \alpha^*, U_1^0, U_2^0) dp_2$$

$$-\int_{p_2^0}^{p_2^{**}} h_2(p_2, p_1^0, \alpha_1^1, \alpha_2^0, \alpha^*, U_1^0, U_2^0) dp_2$$

where $\alpha^* = (\alpha_3^0, \alpha_4^0, \dots, \alpha_n^0)$ refers to the initial quality at sites 3 to n (or sites m-3 to m-n), and p_1^*, p_1^{**}, p_2^*, and p_2^{**} are the choke prices for sites 1 and 2, respectively, and represent that price where demand becomes zero (i.e., a price so high that no one will pay it). Equation (5.27) shows that the choke prices will depend on both quality and price, and will differ for the same site as the demand curves change following a change in quality. This equation states that changes in economic welfare attributable to quality changes at several sites is evaluated as the sum of the areas under the appropriate Hicksian demand curves (i.e., economic value when utility or real income is held constant) for site 1 and for site 2. Equation (5.27) can be further expressed assuming weak complementarity between α_j and site j, so in the case where there are no visits to the jth site the individual is indifferent between quality levels at the jth site, following integration as:

$$(5.28) \quad CS^* = e(p_1^*, p_2^0, \alpha_1^1, \alpha_2^0, \alpha^*, U_1^0, U_2^0) - e(p_1^0, p_2^0, \alpha_1^1, \alpha_2^0, \alpha^*, U_1^0, U_2^0)$$

$$-[e(p_1^{**}, p_2^0, \alpha_1^0, \alpha_2^0, \alpha^*, U_1^0, U_2^0) - e(p_1^0, p_2^0, \alpha_1^1, \alpha_2^0, \alpha^*, U_1^0, U_2^0)]$$

+ a similar symmetrical expression pertaining to site 2,[1]

$$= e(p_1^0, p_2^0, \alpha_1^1, \alpha_2^0, \alpha^*, U_1^0, U_2^0) - e(p_1^0, p_2^0, \alpha_1^1, \alpha_2^0, \alpha^*, U_1^0, U_2^0)$$

+ a similar symmetric expression pertaining to site 2,

because $e(p_1^*, p_2^0, \alpha_1^1, \alpha_2^0, \alpha^*, U_1^0, U_2^0) = e(p_1^{**}, p_2^0, \alpha_1^1, \alpha_2^0, \alpha^*, U_1^0, U_2^0)$ by the assumption of weak complements. In words, the expenditure function is not responsive to changes in quality or in prices that change due to quality levels where demand is zero. Therefore Equation (5.28) can be rewritten in simplified form as:

(5.29) $CS^* = e(p_1^0, p_2^0, \alpha_1^1, \alpha_2^0, \alpha^*, U_1^0, U_2^0) - e(p_1^0, p_2^0, \alpha_1^1, \alpha_2^0, \alpha^*, U_1^0, U_2^0)$

$\qquad + e(p_2^0, p_1^0, \alpha_1^1, \alpha_2^0, \alpha^*, U_1^0, U_2^0) - e(p_2^0, p_1^0, \alpha_1^1, \alpha_2^1, \alpha^*, U_1^0, U_2^0).$

Equation 5.29 is a substantial help in the evaluation of economic value. It shows that one does not need to calculate all the changes in behavior and demand affected by a change in quality at site *j*, all one needs to do to develop benefit estimates is to determine how the demand curve at each site (i.e., site *2* or at *m-1* through *m-n* sites) changes relative to the base site (i.e., site *1* or site *m*).

5.15. Note

1. $e(p_2^*, p_1^0, \alpha_1^1, \alpha_2^1, \alpha^*, U_1^0, U_2^0) - e(p_2^0, p_1^0, \alpha_1^1, \alpha_2^1, \alpha^*, U_1^0, U_2^0)$

   $- [e(p_2^{**}, p_1^0, \alpha_1^1, \alpha_2^0, \alpha^*, U_1^0, U_2^0) - e(p_2^0, p_1^0, \alpha_1^1, \alpha_2^0, \alpha^*, U_1^0, U_2^0)]$

   $= e(p_2^0, p_1^0, \alpha_1^1, \alpha_2^0, \alpha^*, U_1^0, U_2^0) - e(p_2^0, p_1^0, \alpha_1^1, \alpha_2^1, \alpha^*, U_1^0, U_2^0),$

   because $e(p_2^*, .) = e(p_2^{**}, .)$ and cancel by weak complementarity.

5.16. References

Auerbach, A.J. 1985. "The Theory of Excess Burden and Optimal Taxation." In Auerbach, A.J. and M. Feldstein (eds.). *Handbook of Public Economics,* vol. 1. North-Holland: New York, NY: 61–127.

Bergland, O. and A.J. Randall. 1984. *Operational Techniques for Calculating the Exact Hicksian Variations from Observable Data.* Staff Paper 177. Department of Agricultural Economics, University of Kentucky: Lexington, KY.

Bishop, R.C. and T.A. Heberlein. 1979. "Measuring Values of Extra-Market Goods: Are Indirect Measures Biased?" *American Journal of Agricultural Economics* 61: 926–30.

Boadway, R.W. and N. Bruce. 1989. *Welfare Economics.* Basil Blackwell Publishers: Cambridge, MA.

Bockstael, N.E. 1984. Valuing Natural Resource and Environmental Amenities: Can Economic Valuation be Made Defensible? *Northeastern Journal of Agricultural and Resource Economics* 13(2): 129–137.

Bohm, P. 1976. *Social Efficiency: A Concise Introduction to Welfare Economics.* Macmillan: Surry, Great Britain.

Brealey, R.A. and S.C. Myers. 1991. *Principles of Corporate Finance.* McGraw-Hill: New York, NY.

Burt, O.D. and D. Brewer. 1971. "Evaluation of Net Social Benefits from Outdoor Recreation." *Econometrica* 39: 813–827.

Chiang, A.C. 1984. *Fundamental Methods of Mathematical Economics.* 2nd ed. McGraw-Hill: New York, NY.

Cummings, R.G., D.S. Brookshire and W.D. Schulze. 1986a. *Valuing Public Goods: The Contingent Valuation Method.* Rowman and Allenheld Publishers: Totowa, NJ.

Cummings, R.G., L.A. Cox and A.M. Freeman. 1986b. "General Methods for Benefits Assessment." In Bentkover, J.D., V.T. Covello and J. Mumpower (eds.). *Benefits Assessment: The State of the Art.* D. Reidel: Boston, MA.

Currie, J.M., J.A. Murphy and A. Schmitz. 1971. "The Concept of Economic Surplus and Its Use in Economic Analysis." *Economic Journal* 8(324): 741–799.

Deaton, A. and J. Muellbauer. 1980. *Economics and Consumer Behavior.* Cambridge University Press: New York, NY.

Desvousges, W.H., V.K. Smith and M.P. McGivney. 1983. *A Comparison of Alternative Approaches for Estimating Recreation and Related Benefits of Water Quality Improvements.* EPA-200-05-83-001. Office of Policy Analysis, U.S. Environment Protection Agency: Washington, DC.

Dinwiddy, C. and F. Teal. 1996. *Principles of Cost–Benefit Analysis for Developing Countries.* Cambridge University Press: New York, NY.

Eckstein, O. 1958. *Water Resource Development—the Economics of Project Evaluation.* Harvard University Press: Cambridge, MA.

Ekelund, R.B. and R.D. Tollison. 1991. *Economics.* HarperCollins: New York, NY.

Freeman, A.M. 1979. *The Benefits of Environmental Improvement.* Johns Hopkins University Press: Baltimore, MD.

———. 1993. *The Measurement of Environmental and Resource Values: Theory and Methods.* Resources for the Future, Inc.: Washington, DC.

Gittinger, J.P. 1972. *Economic Analysis of Agricultural Projects* Johns Hopkins University Press: Baltimore, MD.

Gordon. I.M. and J.L. Knetsch. 1979. "Consumer's Surplus Measures and the Evaluation of Resources." *Land Economics* 55: 1–10.

Hanemann, W.M. 1981. *Some Further Results on Exact Consumer's Surplus.* Working Paper No. 190. Department of Agricultural and Resource Economics, University of California, Berkeley, CA.

Hausman, J.A. 1981. "Exact Consumer's Surplus and Deadweight Loss." *American Economic Review* 71: 662–676.

Henderson, J.M. and R.E. Quandt. 1971. *Microeconomic Theory: A Mathematical Approach.* McGraw-Hill: New York, NY.

Herfindahl, O.C. and A.V. Kneese. 1974. *Economic Theory of Natural Resources.* Charles E. Merrill: Columbus, OH.

Hicks, J.R. 1943. "The Four Consumers' Surpluses." *Review of Economic Studies* 11(1): 31–41.

Hoehn, J.P. and A. Randall. 1989. "Too Many Proposals Pass the Benefit Cost Test." *American Economic Review* 79: 544–551.

Howe, C.W. 1971. *Benefit–Cost Analysis for Water System Planning.* American Geophysical Union: Washington, DC.

Johansson, P.O. 1987. *The Economic Theory and Measurement of Environmental Benefits.* Cambridge University Press: New York, NY.

———. 1991. *An Introduction to Modern Welfare Economics.* Cambridge University Press: New York, NY.

———. 1993. *Cost–Benefit Analysis of Environmental Changes.* Cambridge University Press: New York, NY.

Just, R.E., D.L. Hueth and, A. Schmitz. 1982. *Applied Welfare Economics and Public Policy.* Prentice-Hall: Englewood Cliffs, NJ.

Kahneman, D. and A. Tversky. 1979. "Prospect Theory: An Analysis of Decision Under Risk." *Econometrica* 47: 263–291.

Kaldor, N. 1939. "Welfare Propositions of Economics and Interpersonal Comparisons of Utility." *Economic Journal* 49(195): 549–52.

Knetsch, J.L. 1984. "Legal Rules and the Basis for Evaluating Economic Losses." *International Review of Law and Economics* 4: 5–13.

———. 1985. "Values, Biases and Entitlements." *Annals of Regional Sciences* 19: 1–9.

Knetsch, J.L. and J.A. Sinden. 1984. "Willingness to Pay and Compensated Demand: Experimental Evidence of an Unexpected Disparity in Measures of Value." *Quarterly Journal of Economics* 99: 507–521.

Kohli, K.N. 1993. *Economic Analysis of Investment Projects: A Practical Application.* Oxford University Press: New York, NY.

Leontieff, W. 1966. *Input/Output Economics.* Oxford University Press: New York, NY.

———. 1986. *Input/Output Economics.* Oxford University Press: New York, NY.

Levy, H. and M. Sarnat. 1994. *Capital Investment and Financial Decisions.* Prentice-Hall: Englewood Cliffs, NJ.

Little, I.M.D. 1957. *A Critique of Welfare Economics.* Oxford University Press: Oxford, Great Britain.

Loehman, E.T. 1984. *Willingness to Pay for Air Quality: A Comparison of Two Methods.* Staff Paper 84-18. Department of Agricultural Economics, Purdue University: West Lafayette, IN.

Margolis, J. 1959. "The Economic Evaluation of Federal Water Resource Development." *American Economic Review* 49 (1): 96–111.

Marshall, A. 1893. "On Rent." *Economic Journal.* Vol. 3.

———. 1930. *Principles of Economics.* Macmillan: London, Great Britain.

Mas-Colell, A., M.D. Whinston, and J.R. Green. 1995. *Microeconomic Theory.* Oxford University Press: New York, NY.

McConnell, K.E. and Industrial Economics, Inc. 1986. *The Damages to Recreational Activities from PCBs in New Bedford Harbor.* Ocean Assessment Division, NOAA: Rockville, MD.

McKenna, C.J. and R. Rees. 1992. *Economics: A Mathematical Introduction.* Oxford University Press: New York, NY.

McKenzie, G.W. 1983. *Measuring Economic Welfare: New Methods.* Cambridge University Press: New York, NY.

McKenzie, G.W. and D. Ulph. 1982. *An Exact Welfare Measure.* Discussion Paper No. 8121. Department of Economics, Southampton University, Great Britain.

Mishan, E.J. 1976. *Cost–Benefit Analysis.* Praeger: New York, NY.

Nicholson, W. 1989. *Microeconomic Theory: Basic Principles and Extensions.* The Dryden Press: Orlando, FL.

———. 1994. *Intermediate Microeconomics and Its Applications.* Dryden Press: Orlando, FL.

Office of Management and Budget. 1996. *Economic Analysis of Federal Regulations under Executive Order 12866.* Executive Office of the President: Washington, DC.

Ofiara, D.D. 1996. *Coastal Value: A White Paper on Economic Assessment and Its Application for Management.* Prepared for Coastal Hazard Management Plan, NJDEP. Institute of Marine and Coastal Sciences, Rutgers University: New Brunswick, NJ.

Opaluch, J.J. 1984. "Valuing Natural Resource and Environmental Amenities: Can Economic Valuation Techniques be Made Defensible: Discussion." *Northeastern Journal of Agricultural and Resource Economics* 13: 138–141.

Randall, A. 1991. "Total and Nonuse Values." In Braden, J.B. and C.D. Kolstad (eds.). *Measuring the Demand for Environmental Quality*. North Holland: New York, NY: 303–321.

Randall, A. and J.R. Stoll. 1980. "Consumer's Surplus in Commodity Space." *American Economic Review* 70: 449–455.

———. 1983. "Existence Value in a Total Valuation Framework." In Rowe, R.D. and L.G. Chestnut. (eds.). *Managing Air Quality and Scenic Resources at National Parks and Wilderness Areas*. Westview Press: Boulder, CO.

Smith, V.K. 1987a. "Nonuse Values in Benefit Cost Analysis." *Southern Economic Journal* 54: 19–26.

———. 1987b. "Uncertainty, Benefit–Cost Analysis, and the Treatment of Option Value." *Journal of Environmental Economics and Management* 14: 283–292.

Smith, V.K. and W.H. Desvousges. 1986a. *Measuring Water Quality Benefits*. Kluwer, Nijhoff: Boston, MA.

———. 1986b. "Asymmetries in the Valuation of Risk and the Siting of Hazardous Waste Disposal Facilities." *American Economics Review* 76: 291–294.

Sugden, R. and A. Williams. 1990. *The Principles of Practical Cost–Benefit Analysis*. Oxford University Press: Oxford, Great Britain.

U.S. Department of Commerce, National Oceanic Atmospheric Administration. 1996. "Natural Resource Damage Assessments: Final Rule." *Federal Register* 61(4), Friday, January 5: 439–510.

U.S. Department of Interior. 1986. "Natural Resource Damage Assessments; Final Rule." *Federal Register* 51(148), Friday, August 1: 27674–27753.

———. 1987. "Natural Resource Damage Assessments; Final Rule." *Federal Register* 52(54), Friday, March 20: 9042–9100.

U.S. Environmental Protection Agency. 1990. *The Economics of Improved Estuarine Water Quality: An NEP Manual for Measuring Benefits*. EPA 503/5-90-001. Office of Policy, Planning, and Evaluation: Washington, DC.

U.S. Water Resources Council. 1983. *Economic and Environmental Principles and Guidelines for Water and Related Land Resources Implementation Studies*. Washington, DC.

Varian, H.R. 1984. *Microeconomic Analysis*. W.W. Norton: New York, NY.

———. 1990. *Intermediate Microeconomics: A Modern Approach*. W.W. Norton & Co.: New York, NY.

Vartia, Y. 1983. "Efficient Methods of Measuring Welfare Change and Compensated Income in Terms of Ordinary Demand Functions." *Econometrica* 51(1):79–98.

Weimer, D.L. and A.R. Vining. 1991. *Policy Analysis: Concepts and Practice*. Simon & Schuster, Prentice Hall: Englewood Cliffs, NJ.

Willig, R.D. 1976. "Consumer's Surplus without Apology." *American Economics Review* 66(4): 589–597.

Yang, E.J., R.C. Power and M. Menefee. 1984. *The Use of Economic Analysis in Valuing Natural Resource Damages*. Environmental Law Institute: Washington, DC, Prepared for Ocean Assessment Division, NOAA: Rockville, MD.

Identification of Biological Effects and Subsequent Economic Effects and Losses from Water Quality Impairments and Degradations in Marine Environments

6.1. Introduction and Linkages

We are now in a position to build upon the economic concepts and apply these ideas in the context of marine pollution impacts. We begin a systematic process in this chapter that builds from Chapter 4 by sketching out possible biological effects and associated economic effects and economic losses at different levels (or groupings) of ecosystems and organisms first delineated in Table 4.3. The purpose of this chapter is twofold: first to identify specific and generic types of biological effects from pollution in marine environments; second to associate these biological effects with specific economic effects and economic losses.

A clarification of terminology is useful here. "Economic effects" refers to specific losses of economic activity (e.g., losses of revenues–sales) and economic losses such as lost net economic value (e.g., net economic value to consumers—consumer surplus, and to producers—producer surplus). As previously argued, economists usually consider changes in economic welfare as the appropriate measure, but in certain instances adverse economic effects involving specific losses of economic activity and their subsequent indirect and induced effects have been used. Concerning the producer, the terms "producer surplus" and "quasi-rent" are used interchangeably in the literature; in this book we will use "producer surplus." And aggregate net economic value refers to the sum of producer surplus and consumer surplus less any transfers in the case of both sectors.

In addition, the term "damages" is often used to represent impairments to resources and their services from degraded water quality, which includes injuries, mortality, and soiled resources. Note that this use of these terms differs from that in federal Natural Resource Damage Assessment (NRDA) procedures, which refers to impairments associated with resources as injuries (i.e., biological losses), and economic losses of use and nonuse activities as damages.

Many of the adverse economic effects and losses can be classified as supply effects, that is, changes that reduce the abundance and distribution of economically important organisms such as fish and shellfish. In addition, supply effects can occur for organisms that are ecologically, but not economically, important (e.g., rare and endangered species) such as the Kemp's ridley sea turtle and various seabirds. These supply effects can be measured by both use and nonuse values (e.g., existence value) related to the respective demand curves (e.g., demand for current participation in nonconsumptive recreational activities such as birdwatching, and the value of preserving the existence of unique species and habitats for future generations) (Krutilla and Fisher 1976). Demand effects of economically important organisms such as fish can also occur due to changes in the quality of seafood products and also from perceived changes in quality. There can be demand effects associated with both marketed and nonmarketed activities that rely on coastal ecosystems, such as the demand for partyboat fishing and the demand for sport-fishing, birdwatching, and beach use. Both supply effects and demand effects can result in measurable losses of net economic value as described in Chapter 5. It is then the task of the economist to conduct empirical research to isolate and develop estimates of these losses.

Because we have already isolated the losses of net economic value from decreases in the demand and supply curves in Chapter 5 the reader may want to return to that discussion in Section 5.7. Briefly, following an effect caused by marine pollution that results in a *decrease in demand* (i.e., an inward shift in the demand curve) the lost net economic value is represented by the sum of lost consumer surplus and lost producer surplus less any transfer, as formally stated in Equations (5.8a) and (5.8b). In turn, marine pollution that causes a *decrease in the supply curve* (i.e., an inward shift in the supply curve) results in lost net economic value composed of the sum of lost consumer surplus and lost producer surplus less any transfer as formally stated in Equations (5.8a) and (5.8b). If these types of losses occur over multiple time periods, then the losses in future periods must be expressed in discounted values before being summed (as in Equation [5.9], Chapter 5). The simplest way to begin to isolate economic losses is to think of the net economic value (NEV) that would have occurred *without* marine pollution less that *with* marine pollution (i.e., $NEV_{w/o} - NEV_w$). When both consumption and production sectors are included, one must be careful not to double-count and to net out any transfers of surplus. By using this "with and without" rule, the task can be greatly simplified. The following treatment of economic losses uses this approach.

6.1.1. Linkages

To simplify the identification of potential economic effects and economic losses it is instructive to link them to the possible impairments and degradations of ecosystem health and productivity. The approach we follow in linking the resource effects with associated economic effects is referred to as physical linkages (or a damage function approach) for a number of reasons. First, most of the impairments and effects on the marine environment and living organisms are more appropriately thought of and modeled as supply effects, which in turn affect agents' behavior from decreases in resource supplies. In a general equilibrium framework an agent's behavior is modeled based on specific variables that enter their utility function (usually multiple goods that the individual agent desires) plus constraints on a monetary budget due to limited income and available supply of the goods in question. Such an approach has been used in bioeconomic models of resource decisions and in modeling the effects of pollution (Conrad and Clark 1987, Fisher 1981, Hanley et al. 1997, McConnell and Strand 1989). Second, federal NRDA procedures to assess compensable values from resource injuries (i.e., economic damages) are essentially based on physical linkages (i.e., the monetary value of injured or dead or soiled resources). And third, while marine scientists and researchers acknowledge that it is often difficult to establish precise links between specific hazardous substances and effects on the marine environment and marine resources, there is general agreement that the introduction of hazardous substances in the marine environment through accidental spills and releases and waste disposal activities has contributed to substantial declines in the quality of marine waters and has harmed marine organisms with adverse effects on humans (U.S. Congress, OTA 1987). The recent federal initiative of the U.S. Environmental Protection Agency (U.S. EPA) to address degraded water quality in estuaries and coastal waterbodies of national significance via the National Estuary Program and the finding that a variety of substances has contributed to this problem demonstrate that substances in excessive amounts do result in degraded water quality (U.S. EPA 1989). Furthermore another federal initiative to assess the quality of marine waters over time, the Mussel Watch Program of the National Status and Trends Program of NOAA, has used one measure (i.e., the presence of hazardous substances from repeated samples of shellfish at specific locations over time) to document trends in the occurrence of hazardous substances in marine waters (O'Connor and Beliaeff 1994). Such evidence and recognition are, we believe, convincing support that hazardous substances do cause degradations in marine water quality and impairments in marine organisms and the marine environment in general.

An alternative approach advanced by some economists is based on behavioral linkages and was developed to provide a theoretical basis for such nonmarket valuation methods as the Contingent Valuation (CV) method. CV is based on a form of behavioral linkage between a change in an amenity (e.g., environmental quality) and subsequent effects on economic behavior and value. However, a true theoretical model capable of describing such a behavioral linkage was absent. But such an approach also has limits. For example, in consumer theory, agents' behavior determines demand responses and most of the effects on marine organisms, and ecosystems can be treated as supply-effects; two distinct economic concepts. Demand-response is relevant in cases where impairments result in decreased demand for such goods as (1) recreational activities dependent on the the marine environment (e.g., beach use, marine sportfishing, water contact sports), (2) travel and tourism at marine based resorts, and (3) edible seafood products contaminated with hazardous substances. We incorporate such demand behavior in our treatment of linking and associating economic effects to effects on the marine environment and its resources when appropriate.

In sum, we believe that those linkages which are supply oriented be accounted and treated as such, and the linkages that are demand oriented be similarly recognized. We also encourage efforts that attempt to provide a theoretical basis for nonmarket valuation techniques that link changes in environmental quality (amenities) with changes in agents' behavior and values such as the CV method. Such work is at an early stage and further work can develop an acceptable theory of agents' behavior.

6.2. Impairments in Marine Environments and Subsequent Economic Effects and Economic Losses

6.2.1. Damage to Habitat

6.2.1.1 Biological Effects/Impairments

The first level of damages that can occur to marine habitats can decrease the productivity of habitats (Table 6.1). Such effects could be the result of degraded sediment and decreases in benthic organisms and aquatic vegetation. Decreases in habitat productivity could be measured as a decrease in the quantity and weight of living organisms (i.e., biomass) produced by a habitat. Alternatively, changes in habitat productivity might be measured in terms of a decrease in the amount of nutrients cycled (i.e., change in functions or services) in a given habitat. Extreme levels of impairments could damage habitat sufficiently to result in a loss of benthic organisms and aquatic vegetation, in turn affecting the food source and habitat of aquatic and terrestrial organisms. If degradations are severe enough, changes in habitat structure and food source can contribute to a decline in the distribution of aquatic organisms such as fish, shellfish and crustaceans, and terrestrial organisms such as birds. Furthermore some organisms may avoid specific areas that were once important along their migratory routes.

Changes in habitat structure and habitat loss over a large enough area or long enough time period could result in declines in the distribution (i.e., occurrences of organisms throughout an ecosystem) and abundance (i.e., quantity or biomass) of organisms (both aquatic and terrestrial). For example, researchers attribute a large portion of the decline in Atlantic coast striped bass during the early 1980s to degradations that occurred in estuary habitats (e.g., spawning grounds) important to striped bass (Rago et al. 1989, U.S. Congress, OTA 1987).

Additional damage to habitat can result from chronic, hypoxic bottom waters creating an environment in which organisms cannot survive. Short-term hypoxic events result in much publicized fish kills and are treated in the following text. Chronic hypoxic conditions result in similar economic effects, such as habitat loss, as well as site-specific productivity losses.

6.2.1.2 Economic Effects and Losses

Economic assessments of marine wetland ecosystems have considered those products that are sold in markets (e.g., the contribution to commercial fisheries) (Bell 1989), real estate (Batie and Mabbs-Zeno 1985), and nonmarket products such as storm damage or prevention and recreational use (Farber 1987, Farber and Costanza 1987). Little is known about the "services" and their respective values produced by marine ecosystems such as nutrient uptake and cycling, maintenance of biological diversity, flood control, and climate regulation in general, although in some cases these services are known for very specific coastal wetlands (Mitsch and Gosselink 1993, NRC 1995, U.S. Congress, OTA 1987). Hence, impairments that reduce the productivity of marine wetlands and habitats can only be partially addressed with our present knowledge.

Table 6.1. Impairments, Economic Activities Impacted, and Possible Economic Effects Attributable to Degradations in Water Quality in Marine Environments.

Impairments	Economic Activities Impacted	Possible Economic Effects	Lost Economic Value, Welfare Losses
(1) DAMAGE TO HABITAT Decrease in Productivity and Biological Value; e.g., Chesapeake Bay—striped bass fishery decline in 1980s	Commercial Fishery, Recreational Fishery, Wholesale/Retail Trade, Consumers, Other Recreational Uses	*Generic Effects:* Refer to Fish and Shellfish below *Specific Effects:* decrease in value of productivity/biomass; decrease in value of "services" provided; decrease in catch per unit effort (CPUE); increase in effort per vessel/angler; increase in costs per unit of output (catch, trips); increase in costs (re travel, time, congestion); decrease in economic surplus, (i.e., rent, producer surplus, consumer surplus)	Lost value from decline in productivity biomass; lost value from decline in "services"; decrease in producer surplus (PS)–rent from all commercial activities; decrease in consumer surplus (CS) from consumer-recreational activities (use values); decrease in CS associated with existence of habitat (existence value; nonuse value)
(2) DAMAGE TO FISH AND SHELLFISH (a) Harvest Closures/Restrictions on Specific Waterbodies: e.g., New Bedford Harbor and Buzzards Bay, MA; Raritan Bay, NJ; Santa Monica Bay, CA	Commercial Fishery, Recreational Fishery, Wholesale/Retail Trade	*Generic Effects:* refer to "Abundance and Distribution" *Specific Effects* *Commercial Fisheries:* value of forgone harvest; harvest costs lost regarding forgone harvest; economic rent (i.e., profit, producer surplus) lost regarding forgone harvest; opportunity cost (OC) of fishermen that exit; increase in production costs, travel costs for fishermen that remain; decrease in rents (profit, PS) for those who remain *Recreational Fisheries:* economic surplus (CS) lost regarding forgone harvest; fishing expenses lost regarding forgone harvest; increase in costs (travel, time, congestion); decrease in CS regarding present catch *Seafood Industry:* possible supply reduction if severe; possible increase in local market price from decrease in local supply	*Commercial Fishing Losses:* lost PS regarding forgone harvest; decline in PS due to increased travel costs, and other production costs to alternative fishing grounds regarding present catch *Recreational Fishing Losses:* lost CS (use value) regarding forgone harvest; decrease in CS (use value) due to increase in travel costs and congestion costs to alternative sites regarding present catch *Seafood Market—Consumer Losses:* lost CS from decrease in supply and higher prices

(continues)

Table 6.1. Continued

Impairments	Economic Activities Impacted	Possible Economic Effects	Lost Economic Value, Welfare Losses
(b) Decrease in Site-Specific Productivity: e.g., Upper Delaware Bay; estuaries in Gulf of Mexico	Commercial Fishery, Recreational Fishery	*Generic Effects:* refer to "Abundance and Distribution" *Specific Effects:* decrease in value of productivity; evaluation of reduced productivity (refer to "Damage to Habitat")	*Commercial and Recreational Fisheries:* decrease in economic surplus (PS, CS) regarding decline in productivity
(c) Mortality—Fish–Shellfish Kills: e.g., 1976 incident off NJ Coast; western Long Island Sound incidents	Commercial Fishery, Recreational Fishery, Wholesale/Retail Trade, Processors, Consumers	*Generic Effects:* refer to "Abundance and Distribution" *Specific Effects* *Commercial Fisheries:* lost market value of portion of product killed that would have been harvested; lost harvest expenditures regarding portion of harvestable product that was killed; lost economic surplus regarding portion of harvestable product that was killed; OC of fishermen that exit if kill is severe; if kill is minor to moderate, possible increases in costs (harvest) and decrease in PS *Recreational Fisheries:* lost CS of portion of harvestable product that was killed; lost harvest expenditure regarding portion of harvestable product that was killed; if kill is minor to moderate, possible increases in costs (travel, time, congestion) from reduced abundance; if kill is minor to moderate, possible decrease in CS from reduced abundance *Seafood Market/Industry:* lost handling/processing costs of portion of harvestable product that was killed; lost economic rent of portion of harvestable product that was killed; aggregate supply effects if severe (refer to "Abundance and Distribution"); possible increase in local market price if severe (refer to "Abundance and Distribution"); possible decrease in CS to consumers from decline in supply and higher prices	*Commercial and Recreational Fisheries:* lost economic surplus (PS, CS) from portion of harvestable product that was killed; if minor to moderate kill, decrease in PS, CS from reduced abundance and from increased harvest (effort) costs *Seafood Market/Industry-Consumers:* lost CS from decrease in supply if severe

(d) Disease and Abnormalities: e.g., fin rot/erosion in winter flounder, shell burn in lobsters/crabs, liver tumors in flounder/sole; Boston Harbor, San Francisco Bay, Puget Sound	Commercial Fishery, Recreational Fishery, Wholesale/Retail Trade, Processors, Consumers	*Generic Effects*: refer to "Abundance and Distribution" if severe *Specific Effects*: relative to % population affected; evaluation of this % (refer to "Mortality—Kills"); increase in labor costs to process diseased portion *Demand Effects*—possible decrease in local demand; possible decrease in local market price; decrease in revenue, economic surplus in seafood industry; possible decrease in revenue, profit, economic surplus to local fishermen; possible decrease in vessels in fishery; OC of fishermen that exit fishery; lost CS from consumers that completely avoid seafood product; increase in CS from consumers that continue consumption due to effect of decreased demand and lower prices	Lost PS from increased processing costs, and from decreased demand to commercial fishermen and seafood industry net change (gain/loss) in CS to consumers due to combined effect of those that avoid the product (loss in CS), and those that continue to consume the product (gain in CS) as a result of the fall in demand and price; possibly reduced CS to sport anglers from reduced enjoyment from catching diseased fish
(e) Impaired Reproduction: e.g., striped bass—Chesapeake Bay and San Francisco Bay	Commercial Fishery, Recreational Fishery, Wholesale/Retail Trade, Consumers	*Generic Effects*—refer to "Abundance and Distribution" if severe *Specific Effects*—refer to "Disease/Abnormalities"	If severe refer to "Abundance and Distribution" below; if moderate effects, effects could be decreases in PS from commercial activities (commercial fishing, seafood industry) due to possible reduced supply; if moderate, possible decrease in CS from consumers due to reduced supply; if moderate, decrease in CS from sportfishing due to reduced abundance, and from increased effort to offset reduced abundance; if slight effects, welfare losses expected to be negligible
(f) Abundance and Distribution: e.g., Atlantic Coast Striped Bass	Commercial Fishery, Recreational Fishery, Wholesale/Retail Trade, Processors, Consumers	*Harvest Supply Effects*: summed over all units involved *Commercial Fisheries*: decrease in overall catch (and hence, catch per unit of effort [CPUE]); decrease in revenues, profit, economic surplus due to reduced catch possible decrease in vessels, if severe; increase in effort per vessel to offset reduced abundance; increase in production costs to offset reduced abundance; possible decrease in revenues, profit, economic surplus regarding efforts to offset reduced abundance	If slight, welfare effects expected to be negligible; if moderate, possible decrease in PS from commercial activities due to reduced supply; if moderate, possible decrease in CS from consumers due to reduced supply; if moderate, decrease in CS from sportfishing due to and from increased effort to offset reduced abundance; if severe, decrease in PS from commercial activities (commercial fishing, seafood industry) due to supply effect (reduced supply and higher prices); if severe, decrease in CS from consumers

(continues)

Table 6.1. *Continued*

174

Impairments	Economic Activities Impacted	Possible Economic Effects	Lost Economic Value, Welfare Losses
		Seafood Market/Industry—Consumers: possible decrease in local catch/supply from minor to moderate reduction in stock-population abundance; possible increase in price from supply effect (reduced supply); decrease in CS to consumers from supply effect (reduced supply and higher prices); decrease in market supply, if severe effects; increase in market price, if severe effects; net change (gain/loss) in revenues, profit, economic surplus from reduced production capacity (decrease) versus supply effect (revenues and profit may increase if demand is inelastic given higher prices, and decrease when demand is elastic)	due to reduced supply; if severe, decrease in CS from sportfishing due to reduced abundance, reduced success, and from increased effort to offset reduced abundance; if severe, decrease in economic surplus (nonuse values), existence values, from knowing that the existence of a particular fish stock has been compromised
		Recreational Fishery: (summed over all units involved); decrease in CPUE and success rates (catch/effort); decrease in CS from reduced abundance, success, and overall fishing experience; reduction in participation rates; increase in effort per angler to offset reduced abundance; increase in costs (travel, time, congestion) to offset reduced abundance; decrease in CS regarding increased efforts to offset reduced abundance	
(3) DAMAGE TO BIRDS, MAMMALS, SEA TURTLES (a) Mortality: e.g., entanglement and suffocation from plastic—marine debris; ingestion and starvation from blockage caused by plastic bags, balloons—sea turtles	Public—Recreational Participation	Value of units involved (killed); expenses and CS forgone regarding nonconsumptive activities, e.g., birdwatching, whale-watching; replacement costs of units killed; existence value (EV) forgone	If moderate to severe, refer to "Abundance and Distribution" below; if slight, CS and EV forgone per individual lost
(b) Disease and Abnormalities: e.g., deformities, tumors	Biological Diversity, Preservation of Species, Public Participation	Refer to "Mortality-Birds, Mammals, etc."	Refer to "Mortality-Birds, Mammals, etc."
(c) Impaired Reproduction: e.g., decreased rates and birthing difficulties.	Biological Diversity, Preservation of Species, Public Participation	Refer to "Mortality-Birds, Mammals, etc."	Refer to "Mortality-Birds, Mammals, etc."
(d) Abundance and Distribution: e.g., Kemp's ridley sea turtle, osprey, piping plover, various whales (many of these are threatened or endangered species)	Biological Diversity, Preservation of Species, Public Participation	Reduction in recreational (nonconsumptive use) participation; decrease in participation expenditure totals; loss in CS associated with decreased enjoyment from reduced	Decrease in PS from commercial activities that provide viewing trips due to decreased participation—demand; decrease in CS to public (consumers) from reduced

(continues)

		abundance and associated with a decrease in participation (i.e., decrease in demand); loss in EV (nonuse value) regarding a decline in species; loss in revenues, profit, and economic surplus to commercial activities that provide trips to view shorebirds, whales from reduced participation (i.e., demand)	enjoyment as a result of reduced abundance, and from reduced demand; decrease in economic surplus (non-use value), existence value from knowing these organisms have been compromised
(4) DAMAGE TO PUBLIC HEALTH			
(a) Pathogens in Water: e.g., 1987–89 beach closings in NJ, Long Island; Southern CA beach closings	Public Health	Increase in incidence of gastrointestinal disease, number of cases; costs of medical treatment incurred; sick days from work; value of lost earnings or opportunity cost of sick days; value of lost productivity to employer; economic value to avoid illness.	Costs of medical treatment incurred, plus value of lost earnings, or value of lost productivity; or value of economic surplus (WTP—willingness-to-pay) to avoid illness
(b) Unsafe Seafood—Pathogens: e.g., 103 cases of gastroenteritis reported in NY in 1982; several dozen cases of cholera in LA; economic impacts on market (Capps et al. 1984, Brown and Folson 1983)	Public Health	*Health Effects:* refer to "Public Health—Pathogens in Water"	Refer to "Public Health—Pathogens in Water" above
(c) Unsafe Seafood—Toxicants: e.g., excess cancer mortality from: PCB (Belton et. al. 1986); dioxin (Belton et. al. 1985); various toxicants (Conner et al. 1984)	Public Health	*Health Effects—Illness:* increased additive risk of cancer (excess cancer mortalities); costs of medical treatment incurred; sick days; value of lost earnings from sick days or opportunity costs of sick days; value of lost productivity regarding sick days. *Premature Mortality Effects*—present value of lost earnings; present value of lost productivity; economic welfare to avoid premature mortality	*Assessment of Illness:* refer to "Public Health—Pathogens in Water" above. *Premature Mortality Effects:* discounted costs of medical treatment, plus present value of lost earnings; or present value of value of lost productivity, or value of economic surplus (WTP) to avoid premature mortality
(d) Unsafe Seafood—Demand Effects: e.g., mercury in swordfish (Lipton 1986); kepone in oysters (Swartz and Strand 1981)	Commercial Fishery, Recreational Fishery, Wholesale/Retail Trade, Processors, Consumers	*Demand Effects*—possible decrease in demand; possible decrease in market price; possible decrease in revenue, economic surplus in seafood industry; possible decrease in vessels in fishery affected; lost CS from consumers that avoid product; increase in CS from consumers that continue consumption. *Recreational Fishery*—decrease in effort; forgone decrease in participation rates; forgone fishing expenditures, travel costs; forgone economic surplus	Possible decrease in PS from all commercial activities due to demand effect (i.e., reduced demand and lower prices); net change in CS from consumers due to demand effect (net decrease if number of consumers that avoid product exceeds number of consumers that continue to consume product; net increase if number of consumers that avoid product is less than number of consumers that continue consumption); possible decrease in CS from sportfishing due to reduced enjoyment in knowing catch is contaminated

Table 6.1. *Continued*

Impairments	Economic Activities Impacted	Possible Economic Effects	Lost Economic Value, Welfare Losses
(5) DAMAGE TO BEACH USE (a) Pathogens in Water: e.g., 1987–89 beach closings in NJ; Southern CA beach closings	Public Health, Recreational Activities, Travel and Tourism Industry	*Health Effects:* refer to "Public Health—Pathogens in Water" *Effects on Recreation:* decrease in attendance at affected beaches or net change in attendance with multiple beaches; decrease in expenditures at affected beach communities or net change in expenditures with multiple beaches; possible increase in travel costs and opportunity costs of travel time if unaffected beaches are located farther from population centers; possible increase in congestion cost at unaffected beaches due to increased use; lost economic surplus at affected beaches or decrease associated with multiple beaches *Travel and Tourism Industry Effects:* decrease in tourism volume at affected communities; decrease (or lost) expenditures at affected communities; decrease in demand, revenues, and economic surplus associated with affected communities (these are primary effects); decreases in multiplier or secondary effects (consisting of spending and respending effects as defined by indirect and induced effects) in affected economy; with multiple communities: the net change in primary expenditures, revenues, and surplus, and in multiplier effects (net losses if losses in affected communities outweigh gains in unaffected communities, net gains if gains in unaffected communities outweigh losses in affected communities).	*Health Effects:* refer to "Public Health—Pathogens in Water" above *Other Effects (Recreation, Travel and Tourism):* net change in PS from commercial activities (net loss if lost PS associated with affected communities exceeds gains in PS associated with unaffected communities; net gain if lost PS associated with affected communities is offset by gains in PS associated with unaffected communities); net change in CS from beach use activities (net loss if lost CS associated with affected beaches exceeds gains in CS associated with unaffected beaches, net gain if lost CS associated with affected beaches is offset by gains in CS associated with unaffected beaches)
(b) Washups of Marine Debris, Floatable Waste: e.g., 1988 beach closings in NJ; 1987 and 1988 beach closings in NY	Recreational Activities, Travel and Tourism Industry	*All Effects (Recreation, Travel and Tourism)* refer to "Beach Use—Pathogens in Water" above	Refer to "Beach Use—Pathogens in Water" above

(c) Washups of Algal Blooms: e.g., 1988 beach closings in NJ	Recreational Activities, Travel and Tourism Industry	Refer to "Beach Use—Pathogens in Water" above	Refer to "Beach Use—Pathogens in Water" above

(6) DAMAGE TO COMMERCIAL AND PLEASURE VESSELS

(a) floatable hazards: e.g., NY–NJ Harbor floatables cleanup	Commercial Navigation, Boating Public	*Combined Effects:* Number of vessels with damage/repairs; increase in repair costs; opportunity costs or value of lost productivity of down-time of vessel in repair; lost revenues, profit, and economic surplus and operating expenses from down-time for commercial vessels; lost economic surplus, and operating expenses from down-time for pleasure vessels *Commercial Vessels:* increase in annual costs (repair costs); reduction in economic surplus due to down-time *Recreational Boating:* reduction in pleasure boating satisfaction (economic surplus) compared to an absence of floatable hazards. *Aesthetic:* reduction in economic surplus compared to an absence of odors	Lost PS from commercial activities due to down-time from damage and repair to vessel; lost CS from pleasure boating compared to an absence of floatable hazards
(b) Noxious, Foul Odor	Boating Public		Lost CS from pleasure boating compared to an absence of odors

(7) DAMAGE TO PROPERTY VALUE via Use Restrictions/ Closures on Specific Water Bodies: e.g., New Bedford, MA (Mendelsohn 1986)

	Private Property Owners, Real Estate Market	Decrease in demand for housing and real estate in close proximity to closed–contaminated waterbody (demand for property may be inversely related to the distance to the waterfront–shoreline of contaminated waterbody); annual and/or present value of reduction in value and sales price of housing and real estate in close proximity to closed-contaminated waterbody; lost economic surplus due to location effect (i.e., reduced satisfaction from close proximity to contaminated waterbody) and from decrease in demand	Lost CS (present value of lost CS if over multiple years) compared to an absence of contamination in the waterbody (reduced value of amenities associated property in close proximity to contaminated waterbody)

Note: Unless noted, all examples are from U.S. Congress, OTA. 1987. *Wastes in Marine Environments.* U.S. Government Printing Office, Washington, DC. "Abundance" refers to the quantity or biomass of organisms and "distribution" refers to the occurrence of organisms throughout an ecosystem.

The specific economic effects and economic losses that are described in this section are the result of *minor* damage. More severe damage that results in short-term hypoxic conditions and declines in the abundance of fish and shellfish and damage to birds, mammals, and sea turtles is discussed in Sections 6.2.2 and 6.2.3, respectively.

Economic effects resulting from a decrease in the productivity of marine habitats and distribution of organisms could adversely affect the consumptive uses of commercial fishing and shellfishing activities, recreational fishing activities, and nonconsumptive activities such as birdwatching, exploring, and educational uses (Table 6.1). Economic effects could be local in nature at this level of damage, but are directly related to the severity of damage. Severe damages could result in regional and national effects to these activities, such as with the Chesapeake Bay and the decline in striped bass along the East Coast in the early 1980s. Possible economic effects include a decrease in the value of productivity and "services" provided by the habitat (Table 6.1). For commercial and sport activities (e.g., fishing, hunting) a decrease in habitat productivity and distribution of organisms can cause a decline in the catch per unit of effort (CPUE) and can result in higher costs per unit of output (i.e., catch, trips) and a subsequent decrease in net economic value (i.e., producer surplus for commercial fishermen, and consumer surplus from sportfishing). As the severity of damage increases, supply reductions could affect the market supply and price of the species involved. In general, it is unknown whether increases in price (as supply decreases relative to demand) can offset higher production costs to maintain, increase, or decrease revenue and profit levels (one needs information of the relative elasticity of the demand curve). For nonconsumptive uses, severe impairments of habitat productivity can decrease the net economic value resulting from decreases in supply and demand.

In the case of minor effects, specific losses of net economic value from damage to marine habitats consist of lost aggregate producer surplus (from the combination of decreased revenues and increased production costs), assuming individual producers do not change their behavior. For those that do change their behavior (referred to as averting behavior), such as switching to species not affected or traveling to areas that remain unaffected, aggregate producer surplus is further reduced due to increased costs from increased travel, assuming revenues do not change. However if relative productivity is less at the new sites, then revenues can also decrease, which further decreases producer surplus. Hence, losses of net economic value *with* averting behavior will also include losses of economic welfare equivalent to the increase in costs and the possible decrease in revenues. Similar losses exist for consumptive and nonconsumptive recreational activities. Losses consist of lost consumer surplus (from less satisfaction due to decreases in the habitat's productivity and quality) for those that do not change their behavior. For those that do, lost consumer surplus is equivalent to additional costs from increased travel to new and unaffected sites, including possible increased congestion at these new sites.

6.2.2. Damage to Fish and Shellfish

6.2.2.1. Biological Effects/Impairments

Damage to fish and shellfish is by far the largest category because there are many types of damage and because of their economic importance. In this section generic economic effects resulting from supply-type reductions (i.e., reductions in abundance) can occur for virtually all the specific impairments identified (e.g., harvest closures, decrease in site-specific productivity, mortality, and disease and impaired reproduction), providing that the damage is severe enough or is over a long enough time period (Table 6.1).

6.2.2.2. Harvest Closures and Restrictions

Closures and restrictions of fish and shellfish harvesting in specific waterbodies primarily cause localized economic effects and losses. In general, greater effects will occur from outright closures and lesser effects from restrictions on use. For example, the closure of parts of Buzzards Bay, Massachusetts, to shellfish and fish harvesting has severely affected the local lobster fishery and has caused some lobstermen to exit the fishery (McConnell and Morrison 1986). The recreational fishery and sport anglers have also been adversely affected (McConnell and IE 1986).

Commercial fishing operations (both fish and shellfish), recreational fisheries, and components of the local seafood industry (wholesale and retail trade establishments) can be affected by harvest closures and restrictions (Table 6.1). These effects are considered to be local in scope since the size of the effect will be related to the size and importance of the waterbody affected. It is quite possible that effects could also be regional.

Specific economic effects related to a commercial fishery are the quantity and value of landings forgone from harvesting in these waters, that is, the amount and value that would have been harvested had the waterbody(ies) remained open (Table 6.1). Associated with the landings forgone are expenditures that would have resulted in these waters without harvest restrictions, and economic rents such as profit and producer surplus (PS). For those fishermen that exit the fishery the opportunity costs (OC) of their labor must also be considered. For those fishermen that remain in the fishery, specific effects comprise an increase in production costs and subsequent decline in profit, producer surplus, and possibly a decrease in catch per unit of effort. If the effect of the harvest restriction is large enough to reduce local landings, local and possibly regional markets could experience supply reductions and possibly higher prices.

In terms of the sportfishery, specific economic effects are most likely associated with those anglers that would have fished in the restricted waterbody(ies) but no longer can do so. This results in lost consumer surplus and costs. These effects consist of expenditures associated with forgone fishing activities and the corresponding decline in net economic value, which is measured as consumer surplus (CS). Other specific effects relate to increased travel costs, both the costs of travel and the time that anglers must spend traveling to more distant sites. In addition, it is possible that congestion and further costs may result at these new sites as more anglers seek fewer clean local sites.

Economic losses specific to harvest closures and restrictions in sum, are related to the amount of fish–shellfish that would have been harvested had the waterbody(ies) not been closed (i.e., forgone harvest), a supply effect. Losses represent lost producer surplus from the forgone harvest to the commercial fishery and similarly lost consumer surplus to the sportfishery (that is the lost net economic value as a result of a supply-curve type decrease to both users). The increased costs of travel for those who must travel to new fishing grounds or sites would reduce overall net economic value (PS + CS) and it is possible to use these increased costs to represent the lost net economic value as McConnell and Morrison (1986), and McConnell and IE (1986) have. In addition, it is possible that congestion and further costs may result at these new sites (from the transfer of effort). What one wants to keep in mind is at what level of economic activity losses are identified, if one always uses the market level of aggregation, then the lost net economic value from decreases in either demand or supply curves captures all of the losses without double-counting. If losses are not at the market level, one must be careful not to double-count.

6.2.2.3. Decrease in Site-Specific Productivity

Decreases in site-specific productivity can be caused by a variety of impairments. The resulting damage to fish and shellfish is similar to that discussed in Section 6.2.1, "Damage to Habitat," but the areas involved will be smaller in size (see Table 6.1). As a result, effects on economic activities will tend to be more local in scope. Economic effects that can result include increased effort to offset lower productivity and catch, and increased travel to alternative sites. Both effects will increase fishing costs and could lower profits if revenues remain constant.

Economic losses are lost aggregate producer surplus in commercial fisheries and lost aggregate consumer surplus in sportfishing due to the reduction in productivity (a supply type effect). Formally they are equal to the economic welfare *without* the decrease in productivity less the economic welfare *with* the decrease in productivity.

6.2.2.4. Mortality-Fish–Shellfish Kills

Outright mortalities reduce the abundance and distribution of fish and shellfish stocks. The size of the kill, both in terms of the number and weight of fish–shellfish and the area involved, becomes a critical factor. Sporadic kills that are minor in size probably have little effect on fish stocks and are of negligible economic importance, but kills that occur frequently within a given area can affect the site-specific productivity of the area. The resulting economic effects will tend to be local in nature. If severe enough, these effects could be regional and possibly national in scope.

Economic activities that can be affected by kills include commercial fisheries, recreational fisheries, wholesale–retail trade establishments and processors, and possibly consumers. The nature of the impact will, again, depend on the magnitude of the kill. One of the most extensively examined kills occurred off the New Jersey coast in 1976 (Swanson and Sindermann 1979). As a result of a severe hypoxic event, a massive kill occurred, valued at a loss of $11.6 million to the commercial and recreational fishery and $62.5 million to the resource (in 1976 dollars, Figley et al. 1976). Losses in future time periods due to reduced densities of the resource were estimated at $498.6 million. In terms of weight, this event killed from 8.8 to 12.9 percent of the New Jersey sea scallop resource, 32 percent of the state's lobster resource, and an estimated 283 million pounds of surf clam meats and 102 million pounds of ocean quahogs; the effects were greater for the latter two resources (Figley et al. 1979). Compared to the 5-year average harvest of surf clams prior to this event in the United States, 76 million pounds per year and that for ocean quahogs 1 million pounds per year, these losses represent several magnitudes above the average U.S. harvest.

Subsequent economic effects and losses should be assessed in terms of the portion of the killed product that normally would have been harvested. This assumption implies that if the amount of product killed significantly exceeds the amount that would have been harvested, only a portion of the lost resource that is potentially harvestable should be assessed as an economic loss. The remaining amount could be assessed, but its effects on market supply and price must be considered. A situation could occur where some of the killed resource is not considered because it could glut the market and cause the price to collapse (see the preceding discussion of the shellfish kill in New Jersey).

Specific economic effects of kills involve an assessment of the product killed and projections of future supply reductions (Table 6.1). They consist of the market value of the product killed for the portion that would have been harvested by commercial fishermen, forgone costs associated with harvesting the lost product, and forgone producer surplus. In the remainder of the seafood industry economic effects can include forgone costs associated with processing the lost product, the marginal value added (price margin above the ex-vessel price times quantity processed) that would have accrued to whole-sale–retail trade establishments and processors, or alternatively the producer surplus that would have accrued to wholesale–retail establishments and processors. In the recreational fishery, economic effects are the sum of forgone costs associated with the portion of the fish killed potentially harvested by sport anglers, and the subsequent lost consumer surplus.

If the kill is severe enough and it affects the present and future abundance of fish and shellfish, a decrease in supply could occur with a corresponding increase in market price over time until the resource recovers. Specific economic effects that can result (e.g., a loss of consumer surplus for those who buy the product) are discussed in Section 6.2.2.6., "Abundance and Distribution."

In sum, economic losses in the commercial fishery consist of lost aggregate producer surplus in the present time period and discounted losses over future time periods. Producer surplus can be measured in terms of the net change in producer surplus (i.e., producer surplus without the kill less producer surplus with the kill), or equivalently as the forgone producer surplus associated with the kill. Similar losses occur in the remaining sectors of the seafood industry. Losses of consumer surplus also occur to consumers that pay higher prices as a result of a decrease in the supply curve. For the recreational fishery, economic losses comprise lost aggregate consumer surplus in present and discounted losses in future time periods. It is possible that increased travel costs for anglers that travel to sites not affected by the kill can represent lost consumer surplus for those anglers that travel to such sites. Lost consumer surplus can be thought of as the consumer surplus *without* the kill less consumer surplus *with* the kill, or, equivalently, as the forgone consumer surplus associated with the kill.

6.2.2.5. Disease, Abnormalities, and Impaired Reproduction

6.2.2.5.1. Biological Effects—Impairments

Disease, abnormalities, and impaired reproduction could affect the overall biomass of fish–shellfish stocks by causing direct mortalities, decreases in recruitment (i.e., the process whereby new members replenish a resource stock, such as a fish stock) and weight gain (McVicar 1980, 1981; Tibbo and Graham 1963; Van den Brock 1978). In addition, disease and abnormalities can result in decreases in marketable product. For example, fin rot (or fin erosion) may only affect the edible portion of fish and hence average meat yield per fish. With shellfish, it is suspected that fishermen are discarding the affected catch, since diseased products such as lobster with shellburn have not reached the market.

6.2.2.5.2. Economic Effects and Losses

Economic activities that can be affected involve the commercial fisheries, recreational fisheries, the seafood industry, and consumers (Table 6.1). If the incidence of disease and abnormalities is small and the effect of impaired reproduction on recruitment is small, economic effects and impacts on the above activities will be negligible. As the individual effects increase in severity, economic effects could range from local to possibly regional in scope.

Economic assessment of the decrease in marketable product is similar to the methodology used in assessing kills already described. On the basis of an estimate of the population affected, one can assess the value of the product lost. This will differ between fish and shellfish because it is suspected that for fish the diseased portion is simply cut off and discarded resulting in a lower meat yield per fish, whereas for shellfish the entire product is discarded resulting in a lower total catch. Thus, for fish, economic effects are equal to the value of the discarded product, additional labor costs necessary to process the fish (that is, costs of labor necessary to cut off the diseased portion of the fish), and the forgone producer surplus associated with the discarded product had it not been diseased. With a low incidence of disease, these effects would only affect the commercial harvesting sector. A high incidence of disease could reduce catch, increase costs, reduce profit and producer surplus, and possibly force some vessels out of the fishery.

6.2.2.5.2.1. SUPPLY-RELATED EFFECTS

Other effects of disease that affect reproduction and growth are supply effects that reduce fish–shellfish stocks (Strand and Lipton 1986). If disease is great enough to reduce biomass, both CPUE and total catch will decline and costs per unit of catch will increase, with the result of lower revenues, higher costs, and a decline in economic rents (profits and producer surplus). Less efficient vessels may exit the fishery, and if the effect of disease is severe enough, market supply of those species affected could decrease. The result could be a higher market price providing demand remains constant relative to the supply change. The corresponding effect on revenues is ambiguous and depends on the relative elasticity of demand (if inelastic, revenues will rise and if elastic, revenues will fall) and coupled with the increase in costs, profits may or may not increase. In any event, following a decrease in supply, producer surplus will fall.

Economic effects in the seafood industry could range from negligible effects to a decrease in supply and corresponding price increase. In the recreational fishery, if disease and impaired reproduction are minor, there will be little effect on effort and satisfaction, but if decreases in biomass occur, economic effects will result. These comprise a decline in CPUE, increased fishing costs (from increased effort and travel), and a decrease in net economic value (consumer surplus). As a result, participation rates could also fall.

6.2.2.5.2.2. DEMAND EFFECTS

Disease in fish–shellfish could affect consumer demand if the disease results in any noticeable effects (e.g., color, taste, texture of flesh) related to quality. It could also affect consumers' perception of quality. If these quality effects are perceived as detrimental, the result can be reduced demand for seafood products relative to supply. This will cause the market price of seafood and, eventually, the ex-vessel price (i.e., the price paid to fishermen) to fall. Short-term losses could be experienced in both the seafood industry and the commercial fishery. In the seafood industry, lower price margins would cause revenues to drop relative to costs resulting in lower economic rents. In the commercial fishery, a decrease in ex-vessel prices received means lower revenues and a decrease in profits and producer surplus. This may cause vessels to leave the fishery. Regarding consumers, a fall in market price generally will increase consumer surplus to those that continue consumption, but for those that avoid the product, lost consumer surplus will result; here one needs to segment the population of consumers accordingly (those that avoid the product and those that continue to consume the product).

It is difficult to summarize the exact losses due to variability in these effects but in general, losses can occur due to supply reductions if severe and reductions in demand due to concern and perceptions over the quality of seafood. One can measure losses in economic value in two ways: as the net economic value *without* the effect less net economic value *with* the effect, or equivalently as the forgone net economic value associated with the portion of the resource affected. Due to supply reductions, losses in aggregate producer surplus in both the commercial fisheries and the seafood industry would occur (refer to Figure 5.16, Chapter 5). In the sportfishery, losses in consumer surplus could occur from a decline in effort and participation. If not all species are affected, anglers can simply switch effort to alternative species, and assuming equally preferred alternative species, no net change in surplus benefits would occur; however, if not, losses comprise the lost consumer surplus. Losses to consumers include lost consumer surplus following a supply reduction (refer to Figure 5.15, Chapter 5). Furthermore, losses as a result of reduced demand include lost producer surplus in all sectors of the seafood industry, from a decrease in price and revenues relative to costs as well as lost consumer surplus (refer to Figures 5.13 and 5.14, Chapter 5).

6.2.2.6. Abundance and Distribution

6.2.2.6.1. Biological Effects—Impairments

Impacts of marine pollution that affect the abundance (i.e., quantity or biomass of organisms) and distribution (i.e., occurrence of organisms throughout an ecosystem) of fish–shellfish stocks are considered supply reductions. These could be outright reductions in biomass from kills, loss of habitat and spawning-nursery grounds, and decreases in recruitment and growth. An example is the decline in the Atlantic coast striped bass fishery in the early 1980s.

6.2.2.6.2. Economic Effects and Losses

Economic activities that could be affected by minor reductions in abundance and distribution are commercial and recreational fisheries. These types of effects will tend to be local in scope. If reductions in abundance and distribution are severe, all components of the seafood industry, both regional and national, could be affected along with the recreational fishery and consumers (Table 6.1). The following discussion will first examine minor impacts and then severe impacts.

Minor biomass reductions will lower CPUE and raise the cost per unit of output. This will increase operating costs, and at first, vessels may increase effort to offset the lower catch, raising costs even further. The overall result will be a decrease in profit and producer surplus, which, if great enough, will cause less efficient vessels to exit the fishery. Fishing effort would adjust until revenues equal costs for all vessels in an open-access fishery (Anderson 1986). It is expected that the decrease in catch would not be sufficient to impact the market or regional supply. However, the supply of locally caught product could be reduced resulting in increases in the local price. This rise in price may not be great enough to offset the increase in production costs, and vessels may experience a decrease in profits and producer surplus. In addition, the slightly higher price of locally caught product will decrease consumer surplus to consumers of seafood.

In terms of the recreational fishery a minor reduction in biomass will cause a lower catch per unit effort (i.e., person or trip). Some less successful anglers could reduce their effort or stop fishing entirely. Those that remain would incur higher costs per unit of output and may increase effort to maintain the same catch rate as before the biomass reduction occurred. This would raise fishing costs further. The overall result would be to lower both average and aggregate net economic value.

Now consider the effects from a *severe* reduction in biomass (Table 6.1). In the commercial fishery this would translate to a decrease in CPUE; reduction in total catch; increases in effort, cost per unit of output, total production costs; and a decline in profits and producer surplus. The first level of changes could result in less efficient vessels exiting the fishery until zero profits (i.e., where revenue equal costs) are realized. The reduction in catch, if severe enough, may cause supply to shift relative to demand resulting in a higher price. The effect on revenue will depend on the degree of elasticity of demand; if inelastic (relatively steep) the higher price will increase revenues, and if elastic (relatively flat) it will decrease revenues. If the increase in revenues is enough to offset the increase in costs, profits will increase, otherwise profits will fall. Furthermore, a supply reduction will result in lost producer surplus no matter what the elasticity of demand (refer to Figures 5.16 and 5.17, Chapter 5).

In the seafood industry sector a supply decrease and corresponding price rise will result in a change in revenues and profits; revenues increase if demand is inelastic or decrease if demand is elastic. Profits could rise if the increase in revenues offsets the increase in costs. In any event, producer surplus is lost given a supply reduction. Regarding the consumption sector or the demand side, a decrease in the supply-curve would result in lost consumer surplus (refer to Figure 5.15, Chapter 5).

Effects in the recreational fishery would result in lower CPUE or success rate of anglers and an increase in costs per unit of output. Two different behavioral responses could occur as a result of lower CPUE and average catch per angler. Less successful anglers may reduce their effort and participation in marine sportfisheries, stop entirely, or possibly switch to freshwater fisheries. More successful anglers could increase their effort and subsequent costs (expenses and opportunity costs associated with travel and time spent fishing) in order to maintain catch at previous levels, travel to more productive areas, or switch to freshwater fisheries. If these cost increases are large enough to offset the marginal gain in consumer surplus from an additional fish caught, a net decrease in consumer surplus will result. If the cost increase is equal to the surplus gain the net effect will be constant, and the net effect will increase if costs are less than the surplus gain. For those anglers that remain in the fishery, although less fish caught per angler would result in greater marginal consumer surplus compared to a situation with a higher catch rate (because the demand curve is downward sloping), average consumer surplus per angler probably would decrease. Therefore, it is expected that a net decrease in aggregate consumer surplus would result in the sportfishery, consisting of lost economic surplus from a reduction in effort and participation, and the net change in consumer surplus of anglers attempting to maintain previous catch rates.

In general with a severe reduction in biomass, it is expected that the supply curve will decrease, and that economic losses will include lost aggregate producer surplus from the commercial fishing and seafood processing sectors, lost aggregate consumer surplus from consumers of seafood, and lost consumer surplus from the sportfishery (as a result of less satisfaction from lower catch and increased effort and costs).

6.2.3. Damage to Birds, Mammals, Sea Turtles

Economic assessments of damage to birds, mammals, and sea turtles due to marine pollution are complicated because some of these species are considered threatened or endangered species (e.g., ospreys, piping plover, various whales, and Kemp's ridley sea turtles). Furthermore, the reason for death is uncertain in some cases. Marine pollution in sufficient amounts and toxic composition can cause outright mortality, but in smaller, diluted amounts the effect is not so obvious (Table 6.1). Weight gain, reproduction, and health can be affected by low levels of toxic substances, which can change the abundance and distribution of the affected organisms.

6.2.3.1. Mortality

6.2.3.1.1. Biological Effects—Impairments

Sufficient amounts of toxic substances and oil spills can cause outright mortality. A new form of pollution, floatable plastic debris, discarded synthetic fishing nets, and monofilament fishing line, has caused mortality due to entanglement (suffocation and starvation) and ingestion (starvation from blockage due to plastic bags and balloons) (MMC 1988, Shomura and Yoshida 1985).

6.2.3.1.2. Economic Effects and Losses

Economic activities affected by outright mortalities consist of recreational nonconsumptive activities such as birdwatching and whale watching. Impacts are expected to be local and possibly regional in scope from random mortalities. More severe impacts are discussed in the following text. Specific economic effects due to mortalities involve an assessment of the damage, which includes the lost expenses and net economic value that would have accrued from nonconsumptive recreational activities had the mortalities not occurred. Some assessments have valued the lost organisms at the average cost it would take to replace or restore the lost organisms (Yang et al. 1984). However, this approach has been criticized since it only considers the supply side; nevertheless it is a possible component of the damage estimate. An added value, along with the forgone expenses and consumer surplus, could be the product of the number of organisms lost and their respective existence values; that is, the value that society places on knowing that a species, such as blue whales, is preserved for future generations (Krutilla and Fisher 1975).

Outright mortality of these organisms can range from a small area and number of organisms to a large area and many organisms. Examples of the first are oil spills in the Arthur Kill area of the New York–New Jersey Harbor Estuary; and at the other extreme, the *Exxon Valdez* oil spill in Prince William Sound in Alaska. Welfare losses from these events consist of losses of aggregate consumer surplus associated with a decrease in non-consumptive recreational activities, such as birdwatching (Table 6.1). Other losses include an assessment of the value of the species killed in terms of their existence value.

6.2.3.2. Abundance and Distribution

6.2.3.2.1. Biological Effects—Impairments

Severe impacts from marine pollutants may affect the abundance (i.e., quantity or biomass of organisms) and distribution (i.e., occurrence of organisms throughout an ecosystem) of birds, mammals, and sea turtles. The organisms and species that have been, and currently are, considered as threatened and endangered species, such as sea birds and whales, are examples of this level of impact.

6.2.3.2.2. Economic Effects and Losses

Again, while not affecting a great number of economic activities compared to the case of mortalities just discussed, experts consider impacts in terms of losses in the biological diversity of nature and in terms of the extinction of species (Bishop 1978, Krutilla and Fisher 1975, Soule and Kohm 1989) (Table 6.1). Both of these effects could have regional and national implications. Specific economic effects could include a reduction in non-consumptive recreation activities such as birdwatching, a decrease in participation expenses, and a decrease in consumer surplus. In addition, the loss in existence value associated with a decline in abundance must be included (Krutilla and Fisher 1975).

In sum, economic losses can result in a decrease in aggregate consumer surplus from nonconsumptive recreation and a decrease in existence values associated with the population decrease.

6.2.4. Damage to Public Health

Pathogens in marine water, pathogens in seafood, and toxic substances in seafood can affect public health (Table 6.1). Pathogens in marine waters would primarily affect public health, whereas pathogens and toxic substances in seafood would affect both public health and the seafood industry, the latter from demand-type effects (Table 6.1).

In evaluating economic losses to public health it is relatively easy to identify certain types of diseases, such as gastrointestinal diseases, attributable to acute water quality impairments. Assessments of these are relatively straightforward as will be shown here. It is much harder to evaluate losses associated with chronic diseases that take many years to develop. We will identify such losses and how they can be assessed. Discussion of the cause–effect relationship is beyond the scope of this book.

6.2.4.1. Pathogens in Water

Pathogens in water affect public health through water contact activities and from ingestion of water. The pathogens are responsible for gastrointestinal disease in the public.

Outbreaks of gastrointestinal disease are usually local (U.S. Congress, OTA 1987), and the resulting economic effects are expected to be local and possibly regional in scope.

Specific economic effects as a result of disease and sickness consist of the number of individuals (or cases) of gastrointestinal disease from water-related activities. An assessment of the economic effect would include both direct and indirect costs. Direct costs are actual costs of medical treatment incurred. Indirect costs are the value of lost earnings or, equivalently, the opportunity costs of sick days and the value of lost productivity (incurred by the employer). In terms of losses, if the value of lost productivity from the employer's perspective is included, we double-count losses. In terms of opportunity costs, employers pay employees on the basis of their relative productivity, that is, their contribution to production at the margin, equal to the wage rate. Hence the value of lost productivity can be assessed as a reduction in the value of the marginal product (i.e., decrease in revenues and producer surplus), and opportunity costs of sick days can be assessed as the number of days absent times the wage rate. All represent losses since they relate to specific illnesses caused by pathogens in the water and are borne by the individuals that contract the disease and represent lost economic welfare for the economy. An alternative approach to measuring the value of illness–morbidity that is not dependent on measures of lost earnings is the willingness of individuals to pay to avoid the illness (i.e., consumer surplus or net economic value to avoid the illness).

6.2.4.2. Unsafe Seafood—Pathogens

Impairments of water quality can also result in illness to the public from the consumption of seafood containing bacterial organisms. Most often these organisms are associated with shellfish consumption, rather than fish consumption, and have been reported to cause hepatitis and gastroenteritis (Brown and Folson 1983, Hughes et al. 1977). As a result, public health officials have established guidelines for bacteria levels in coastal waters. Violations of these guidelines have resulted in harvesting closures of shellfish. In many areas of the U.S. coast, state health officials routinely test and order closures or openings of shellfish beds. However, the system is not foolproof, and outbreaks of illness occasionally occur, although the magnitude and frequency have declined in recent times. Impacts to public health are expected to be local and possibly regional in scope and result in similar economic effects as with pathogens in water.

Evaluation of economic losses due to consumption of unsafe seafoods that contain pathogens depends on the number of cases of gastrointestinal disease. Losses include the cost of medical treatment and the value of lost earnings. These losses represent additional costs society must bear and lost economic value from the economy. Alternatively, these losses could be assessed as the economic value individuals would be willing to pay to avoid the illness.

6.2.4.3. Unsafe Seafood—Hazardous–Toxic Substances

Another public concern is the increased health risk from long-term consumption of seafood containing toxic substances. Illness from consuming seafood containing toxic substances (e.g., DDT, PCB, mercury found in bluefish and striped bass) has become an important research topic in recent times compared to illness caused from shellfish containing bacteria. This is due to the nature of the health effects and the chronic persistence and occurrence of toxic substances in the food chain. Some studies have estimated excess cancer risks that can result from consumption of contaminated seafood product (Belton et al. 1983; Belton et al. 1985a, 1985b; Connor et al. 1984; IOM 1991). During the past two decades, general public awareness about environmental and health issues associated with toxic substances has increased. At the same time, the public is becoming educated about nutritional benefits of seafood (Lands 1986, Standsby 1987). The overall effect of this mix of information has probably resulted in confusion over the safety of seafood consumption.

Economic effects to public health could range from local to national depending on the severity of the problem and the area involved. In this case, an assessment of the economic losses would be based on estimates of the increased or additive risk of cancer, that is, estimates of excess cancer mortalities from consuming a particular contaminated seafood product. Economic effects include the direct costs of medical treatment incurred, plus indirect costs associated with sick days and premature mortalities. These indirect costs consist of the value of lost earnings and the value of lost productivity associated with illness (i.e., morbidity effects) for all individuals involved, and the present value of lost earnings and productivity from premature mortality over the productive life of the individual had the person remained in the workforce. An alternative measure of the economic cost of sickness and premature mortality is the net economic value individuals would pay to avoid sickness and premature death.

Economic losses that can occur from the consumption of seafood containing toxicants can be separated into losses due to illness and losses due to premature mortality. The losses related to morbidity effects (i.e., illness) are identical to the evaluation of losses from consumption of seafood containing pathogens already described in Section 6.2.4.2. Losses related to premature mortality include the costs of medical treatment *plus* the value of lost earnings had the individual remained in the labor force *or* the value of lost productivity to the employer. When multiple time periods are involved losses are the present value of medical expenses *plus* the present value of lost earnings *or* lost productivity (had the individual remained in the labor force). An alternative measure is the net economic value associated with avoiding illness or premature mortality discounted over time when necessary. Both approaches will be treated in more detail in Chapter 7.

6.2.4.4. Unsafe Seafoods—Demand Effects (Perceived Quality Effects)

News of illness resulting from the consumption of unsafe seafood and reports of contaminated seafood product with hazardous substances could have economic effects on the demand and price of seafood. If seafood is perceived to cause detrimental health effects, consumers may become alarmed and limit or stop their consumption of the seafood in question. This reportedly happened during the 1988 marine pollution events in New Jersey (Ofiara and Brown 1999). When adverse health effects are at issue, it is reasonable to expect that risk-averse individuals will choose to avoid contaminated seafood products. If information is incomplete or in error, consumers will respond rationally and avoid both contaminated and uncontaminated seafood products. Opposite effects will occur when reports of beneficial effects from seafood consumption are publicized or, for that matter, reports of previously contaminated products are deemed safe for consumption.

If risks are publicized widely, coupled with vague information about the location of the contaminated product or vague health effects, economic effects could be noticed in local markets and possibly in regional markets (Table 6.1). Economic activities affected could include all components of the seafood industry, consumers, and the recreational fishery. Specific economic effects result from a downward shift in demand for seafood product in the market accompanied by depressed prices in local and regional markets. These factors will lead to a decline in producer surplus to wholesale–retail trade establishments and processors. In the commercial fishery sector, effects of lower prices will cause a reduction in revenues and profits and producer surplus. If the drop in price is great enough or lasts long enough, vessels may exit the fishery and enter other fisheries that are not affected. Regarding consumers, a decrease in consumer surplus will result for those that stop or reduce their consumption of the affected seafood product or switch to less preferred seafood products. For those individuals that continue to consume the affected product an increase in net economic value will result from lower prices. Overall, there could be a net decrease, no net change, or a possible increase in consumer surplus.

In the recreational fishery, news of illness or contaminated fish species may or may not affect participation rates and subsequent consumer surplus. A number of possible scenarios exist because sport anglers are a diverse group. Some sport anglers are subsistence-type fishermen with an objective to catch fish for home consumption to supplement a limited food budget. If these sport anglers are risk-averse, one may expect a decline in participation and effort and subsequent losses in consumer surplus for the species in question. However, anglers can simply switch effort to another species that is unaffected. (Several northeastern states, New Jersey, New York, and Connecticut, have issued health advisories and warnings against consuming large bluefish and striped bass, American eels, blue crabs, white catfish, and white perch [U.S. Congress, OTA 1987]. Species not named in these advisories and warnings are treated as being unaffected for the purposes of this book.) The net effect over multiple species could be no change in consumer surplus in the fishery. The sport angler could also opt to catch and release the species in question, hence, a slight decrease in consumer surplus may be possible for those anglers that wish to consume caught fish. However, no change is expected for those anglers that fish strictly for sport (i.e., catch and release fishing). We would expect no change in participation and effort and consumer surplus for all sport anglers who are not risk-averse. They would continue to harvest and consume (for subsistence-type anglers) the affected species as if it did not pose a health threat. For those sport anglers who are not subsistence-type anglers and are risk-averse, there may not be any net decrease in effort or consumer surplus since these anglers can catch and release the affected species or switch to alternative species. To measure the above effects the total recreational fishery should be considered in order to examine whether or not decreases in effort and consumer surplus associated with the affected species are offset by equal gains in effort and consumer surplus in other, alternative species. Again, the net effect could be no change.

In sum, news of unsafe seafood can affect demand. Economic losses consist of decreases in aggregate producer surplus in all sectors of the seafood industry due to a decrease in demand and price (due to the downward shift in demand relative to supply). On the consumption side, losses in aggregate consumer surplus will occur from consumers who avoid the product, i.e., consumers who are risk-averse. This could be offset by gains in aggregate consumer surplus due to lower prices for consumers that are not risk-averse and who continue consumption, however this will depend on the number of individuals affected in both cases. Welfare losses will result if the losses are greater than gains where the portion of the loss not offset by gains is an economic loss (we assume this to be the case). For recreational fisheries, aggregate consumer surplus losses could result if anglers reduce effort and participation based on a perception that the fish are unsafe, resulting in lost consumer surplus, and if those remaining anglers travel to areas unaffected (increased travel costs) and switch to less preferred species (further reducing consumer surplus).

6.2.5. Damage to Beach Use

An assessment of the economic consequences of marine pollution on beach use is complicated due to various factors. First, marine pollution in some areas (for instance the New York Bight region) is not a new occurrence; it has been present for many years. It is therefore difficult to construct a data set and establish a baseline from which to evaluate changes in beach use resulting from changes in pollution levels. Second, two types of effects on beach use are discernible: long-term (or chronic) effects that result in degradation of water quality (e.g., bacteria, turbidity, odor, etc.) and short-term (or periodic) effects, such as the washups of marine debris and medical waste along New York and New Jersey beaches in 1988. This requires data in sufficient detail to measure the relative impacts of each of these effects. Third, there are many factors that affect beach use and attendance. Some relate to the physical characteristics of the beach, proximity of facilities and concession stands, relative distance and travel costs to the site, beach fees, weather conditions, and characteristics of beach users. Lastly, there is the question of whether beach users can distinguish between various levels of marine pollution and the long-term versus short-term effects just mentioned. Since many forms of marine pollution are not detectable by sight (e.g., levels of coliform bacteria), public officials intervene and limit beach use based on public health criteria.

Economic effects and losses are further complicated because beach users have multiple beaches to choose from, and when one beach is closed, they can travel to an alternative beach, perhaps in another community. Specific effects on the travel and tourism industry result from a decrease in tourist volume attributable to a fall in beach use and participation levels. Prolonged beach closings may reduce vacation plans in both the short run (present season) and the long run (future seasons) and may thus reduce demand for travel- and tourism-related services in communities near the affected beaches. This will decrease revenues, profits, and producer surplus to travel- and tourism-related establishments and will create multiplier effects of reduced economic activities throughout the local economy compared to a situation without the presence of marine pollution. In communities near the unaffected beaches opposite effects may occur. Demand for travel- and tourism-related services may increase causing revenues, profits, and producer surplus to increase and result in ripple effects of increased economic activity throughout the local economy. The net effect due to a beach closing will depend on whether the decrease in economic activity in communities near the affected beach is less than, equal to, or greater than the increase in economic activity in communities near unaffected beaches.

Effects on recreational beach use and related activities include decreases in attendance and participation, corresponding decreases in travel- and tourism-related expenditures in nearby communities and a decrease in consumer surplus from beach use and associated recreational activities at those beaches closed. At beaches that are unaffected and remain open, economic effects could consist of the opposite effects; an increase in attendance and participation, corresponding increases in expenditures in nearby communities, and an increase in consumer surplus if additional costs from travel to alternative open beaches and congestion costs remain negligible (in general, the effect of congestion on satisfaction is inversely related, i.e., as congestion increases, satisfaction declines, as does consumer surplus). Considering just economic losses, the effect of multiple beaches complicates assessments of net economic value because the demand for a specific beach will depend on its quality (i.e., own site quality) as well as the quality at other beaches. Hence, net economic value depends on a sequence of consumer surplus estimates for the primary and each alternative beach site.

In sum, losses of aggregate producer surplus will depend on the scope of the study, losses at "closed" beach communities, and gains at "open" beach communities. To beach users or tourists (the consumption sector), losses of consumer surplus can occur due to a decrease in the supply of "open" beaches and can depend on the effect of multiple beach sites.

6.2.5.1. Pathogens in Water

Economic damage to beach use from pathogens in water will be noticed in the public health sector, recreation activities, and the travel and tourism industry (Table 6.1). Economic effects may be influenced by the geographic areas experiencing a problem, specific beaches closed or restricted to use, how long the problem is present, and news coverage. Effects will tend to be local in scope for a small area, few beaches affected, and short time period. As the area, number of beaches, and time period increase, impacts could range from local to regional effects. News reports could cause local impacts to become more regional in scope and affect areas that are not experiencing a water quality problem, as demonstrated in a study of marine pollution in New York in 1976 (ERA 1979).

Specific economic effects and losses consist of health effects, effects on recreational use, and effects on travel and tourism establishments. Health effects are similar to those discussed in Section 6.2.4.1, "Pathogens in Water." Briefly, assessments consist of the costs of medical treatment, the value of lost earnings, and lost productivity associated with sick days from work for all individuals that experience sickness. And specific economic effects and losses regarding recreational beach use and travel–tourism activities are similar to those already discussed in Section 6.2.5, "Damage to Beach Use."

6.2.5.2. Washups of Marine Debris, Floatable Waste

Washups of marine debris and floatable waste primarily cause aesthetic degradations (Table 6.1). In addition, medical waste washups could result in perceived detrimental health effects. Economic impacts from beach closures and restrictions due to washups of marine debris and floatable waste would affect recreational activities and beach use and the travel and tourism industry. Impacts, again, will depend on the area affected, the length of closure, and the available alternatives. Specific economic effects concerning recreational use and the travel and tourism industry are similar to those covered in Section 6.2.5, "Damage to Beach Use."

6.2.5.3. Washups of Algal Blooms

Washups of algae from algal blooms also cause aesthetic degradations and can result in beach closings. Economic effects could affect both recreational activities and the travel and tourism industry. The scope of the impact will be influenced by the area affected more than anything else, and effects will tend to be local in scope. Specific economic effects to recreational activities and travel–tourism industries would be similar to those covered in Section 6.2.5, "Damage to Beach Use," however the effects may be negligible.

6.2.6. Damage to Commercial and Pleasure Vessels

Damage to commercial and pleasure vessels from water quality impairments result from floatable hazards (debris) that damage the hull, propulsion system, guidance system, and so forth. Impairments from noxious, foul odors could cause aesthetic losses primarily to recreational boaters (Table 6.1).

6.2.6.1. Floatable Hazards

Floatable marine debris such as rotted pilings and timbers from decaying and abandoned piers, construction materials, plastic bags, balloons, and discarded fishing nets and ropes all can cause damage to vessels (Bell 1989). Large floatable objects can damage a vessel's hull as well as the propeller and rudder. Other damage can result when an engine's cooling intake system becomes blocked by plastic bags and rubber balloons, leading to engine overheating. Economic effects are expected to be local in scope.

Specific economic effects include the sum of the direct costs of damage (i.e., additional costs of repairs); the indirect costs of damage (i.e., the opportunity costs or value of lost productivity) from down-time of the vessel in repair for commercial vessels; lost revenues, production costs, and lost producer surplus from down-time for commercial vessels; and the lost consumer surplus associated with down-time for pleasure vessels. Economic losses can be thought of as the sum of lost producer surplus and consumer surplus in a situation *without* this impairment less the economic value *with* this impairment or, equivalently, as the net economic value associated with vessel down-time.

6.2.6.2. Noxious, Foul Odor

This type of impairment is expected to result in aesthetic damages to recreational boaters only. Effects are expected to be local in scope, with changes in the areas visited rather than in the number of trips. Hence, economic effects to recreational boaters would result in a decrease in surplus benefits from boating compared to a situation without the presence of odor.

Economic losses involve a decrease in aggregate consumer surplus from pleasure boating with the presence of odor, compared to a situation with an absence of the odor. Some boaters may avoid the affected water or site as a result and this could involve relocating the vessel to an alternative marina. However, any gains in welfare could be offset by increased costs of travel or mooring. Losses are expected to result in decreases in aggregate consumer surplus.

6.2.7. Damage to Property Value

The economic damage to housing and property values are based on the notion that property and homes located near a highly valued amenity (e.g., waterfront location on the seacoast and lakeside property) are valued more highly compared to property without this amenity. Impairments that degrade these amenities in turn affect the value of the property and home. Water quality degradations that result in accumulations of hazardous substances that contaminate bottom sediment in coastal areas have caused public officials to restrict and sometimes ban certain uses of specific waterbodies. For example, areas of New Bedford Harbor in Massachusetts are presently closed to water-contact activities (swimming and bathing) as well as harvests of fish and shellfish. In addition, oil and chemical spills can also affect the use of specific waterbodies.

Economic damage attributable to these types of water quality impairments can affect the value of adjacent and nearby property. Frequent occurrences of impairments and long-term, chronic effects are expected to result in greater damage to property value relative to a one-time pollution event and short-term, acute effects.

The specific economic effects would include a decrease in the current and present value (when more than one time period is involved) of housing and property located in close proximity to the area restricted or the site of the spill. Economic impacts of this nature will affect property owners as well as the general real estate market and can lead to a local effect (Table 6.1). (Such impairments do not affect other property markets located beyond the immediate area, and hence, this damage should be considered as a local effect at most.) The effect will be a reduction in property value attributable to the impairment and a downward shift in demand for housing and property located in the area (areas in close proximity to the affected site or waterbody as well as adjacent areas), thus affecting local real estate markets.

In sum, economic losses to property and real estate attributable to water-quality impairments are the result of two effects. One is due to the degradation of an amenity that once had a premium effect on the value of the property (i.e., consumer surplus associated with this amenity). When water quality becomes degraded, corresponding losses in property value can occur. These losses are borne by the private owners and are not transmitted as gains elsewhere. A secondary effect due to degradations of the shoreline or adjacent waterbody is that demand for housing and property in areas located close to the degraded amenity falls. The effect is to further reduce the sale price of homes and property, a direct loss to property owners and a subsequent loss in aggregate consumer surplus from the decrease in demand (refer to Figure 5.13, Chapter 5).

6.3. References

Anderson, L.G. 1986. *The Economics of Fisheries Management.* Johns Hopkins University Press: Baltimore, MD.

Batie, S.S. and C.C. Mabbs-Zeno. 1985. "Opportunity Costs of Preserving Coastal Wetlands: A Case Study of a Recreational Housing Development." *Land Economics* 61(1): 1–9.

Bell, T. 1989. "Commercial Navigation and Recreational Boating." In WMI, SUNY. *Use Impairments and Ecosystem Impacts of the New York Bight. Phase I Preliminary Report for the New York Bight Restoration Plan.* Marine Sciences Research Center, SUNY: Stony Brook, NY.

Belton, T.J., B.E. Ruppel, M. Lockwood and M. Boriek. 1983. *PCBs in Selected Finfish Caught Within New Jersey Waters 1981–82 (With Limited Chlordane Data).* Office of Science and Research, New Jersey Department of Environmental Protection: Trenton, NJ.

Belton, T.J., R. Hazen, B.E. Ruppel, K. Lockwood, R. Mueller, E. Stevenson and J.J. Post. 1985a. *A Study of Dioxin (2,3,7,8-tetrachlorodibenzo-p-Dioxin) Contamination in Select Finfish, Crus-*

taceans and Sediments of New Jersey Waterways. Office of Science and Research, New Jersey Department of Environmental Protection: Trenton, NJ.

Belton, T.J., B. Ruppel, K. Lockwood, S. Shiboski, G. Burkowski, R. Roundy, N. Weinstein, D. Wilson, H. Whelan. 1985b. *A Study of Toxic Hazards to Urban Recreational Fishermen and Crabbers.* Office of Science and Research, New Jersey Department of Environmental Protection: Trenton, NJ.

Bishop, R.C. 1978. "Endangered Species and Uncertainty: The Economics of a Safe Minimum Standard." *American Journal of Agricultural Economics* 57: 10–18.

Brown, J.W. and W.D. Folson. 1983. "Shellfish Associated Gastroenteritis: A Case Study on the Economic Impact of the Hard Clam Associated Outbreaks of Gastroenteritis in New York State, May to September, 1982." NOAA: Washington, DC. Unpublished Paper.

Connor, M.S., C.E. Werme, and K.D. Rosenmann. 1984. "Public Health Consequences of Chemical Contaminants in the Hudson Raritan Estuary." In Brateler, R.J. (ed.). *Chemical Pollution of the Hudson Raritan Estuary*. NOAA/NOS Technical Memorandum OMA-7, NOAA: Rockville, MD.

Conrad, J.M. and C.W. Clark. 1987. *Natural Resource Economics: Notes and Problems.* Cambridge University Press: New York, NY.

Economic Research Associates. 1979. *Cost Impact of Marine Pollution on Recreational Travel Patterns*. PB-290655. National Technical Information Service: Springfield, VA.

Farber, S. 1987. "The Value of Coastal Wetlands for Protection of Property against Hurricane Wind Damage." *Journal of Environmental Economics and Management* 14: 143–151.

Farber, S. and R. Costanza. 1987. "The Economic Value of Wetlands Systems." *Journal of Environmental Management* 24: 41–51.

Figley, W., B. Pyle and B. Halgren. 1979. "Socioeconomic Impacts." In Swanson, R.L. and C.J. Sindermann (ed.). *Oxygen Depletion and Associated Benthic Mortalities in New York Bight, 1976.* NOAA Professional Paper 11. U.S. Government Printing Office: Washington, DC.

Fisher, A.C. 1981. *Resource and Environmental Economics.* Cambridge University Press: New York, NY.

Freeman, A.M. III. 1979. *The Benefits of Environmental Improvement: Theory and Practice.* Resources for the Future: Washington, DC.

———. III. 1993. *The Measurement of Environmental and Resource Values: Theory and Methods.* Resources for the Future: Washington, DC.

Hanley, N., J.F. Shogren and B. White. 1997. *Environmental Economics in Theory and Practice.* Oxford University Press: New York, NY.

Hughes, J.M., M.H. Merson and E.J. Gargarosa. 1977. "The Safety of Eating Shellfish." *Journal of the American Medical Association* 237: 1982–1983.

Institute of Medicine. 1991. *Seafood Safety.* National Academy Press: Washington, DC.

Just, R.E., D.L. Hueth and, A. Schmitz. 1982. *Applied Welfare Economics and Public Policy.* Prentice-Hall: Englewood Cliffs, NJ.

Krutilla, J.V. and A.C. Fisher. 1975. *The Economics of Natural Environments.* Resources for the Future: Washington, DC.

Lands, W.E.M. 1986. *Fish and Human Health.* Academic Press: New York, NY.

Marine Mammal Commission. 1988. *Annual Report of the Marine Mammal Commission, Calender Year 1987, a Report to Congress.* Washington, DC.

McConnell, K.E. and Industrial Economics, Inc. 1986. *The Damages to Recreational Activities From PCBs In New Bedford Harbor.* Prepared for Ocean Assessment Division, NOAA: Rockville, MD.

McConnell, K.E. and B.G. Morrison. 1986. *Assessment of Economic Damages to the Natural Resources of New Bedford Harbor: Damages to the Commercial Lobster Fishery.* Prepared for Ocean Assessment Division, NOAA: Rockville, MD.

McConnell, K.E. and I. E. Strand. 1989. "Benefits for Commercial Fisheries When Demand and Supply Depend on Water Quality." *Journal of Environmental Economics and Management* 17(3): 284–292.

McVicar, A.H. 1980. "The Effects of *Ichthyophonous* Infection in Haddock *Melanogrammus aeglefinus* and Plaice *Pleuronectes platessa* in Scottish Waters." *International Council for the Exploration of the Sea.*

———. 1981. "An Assessment of Icthyophonous Disease as a Component of Natural Mortality in Plaice Populations in Scottish Waters." *International Council for the Exploration of the Sea CM* 1981/G: 49. Demersal Fish Committees.

Mitsch, W.J. and J.G. Gosselink. 1993. *Wetlands.* John Wiley and Sons: New York, NY.

National Research Council. 1995. *Wetlands: Characteristics and Boundaries.* National Academy Press: Washington, DC.

Ofiara, D.D. and B. Brown. 1989. "Marine Pollution Events of 1988 and Their Effect on Travel, Tourism and Recreational Activities in New Jersey." In *Proceedings of the Conference on Floatable Waste in the Ocean: Social, Economic, and Public Health Implications.* SUNY University Press: Stony Brook, NY.

———. 1999. "Assessment of Economic Losses to Recreational Activities from 1988 Marine Pollution Events and Assessment of Economic Losses from Long-Term Contamination of Fish Within the New York Bight to New Jersey." *Marine Pollution Bulletin* 38 (11): 990–1004.

Rago, P.J., R.M. Dorazio, R.A. Richards and D.G. Deuel. 1989. *Emergency Striped Bass Research Study Report for 1988.* U.S. Dept. of Interior, Fish and Wildlife Services, and U.S. Dept. of Commerce, NOAA, National Marine Fisheries Service: Washington, DC.

Shomura, R.S. and H.O. Yoshida (eds.). 1985. *Proceedings of the Workshop on the Fate and Impact of Marine Debris.* NOAA Technical Memorandum NMFSSWFC-54, PB86-14694, Southwest Fisheries Center: Honolulu, HA.

Smith, V.K. and J.V. Krutilla. 1982. "Towards Reformulating the Role of Natural Resources in Economic Models." In Smith, V.K. and J.V. Krutilla (eds.). *Explorations in Natural Resource Economics.* Johns Hopkins University Press: Baltimore, MD.

Soule, M.E. and K.A. Kohm. 1989. *Research Priorities for Conservation Biology.* Island Press: Covelo, CA.

Stansby, M. 1987. "Nutritional Properties of Recreationally Caught Marine Fishes." *Marine Fisheries Review* 49: 118–121.

Strand, I.E. and D.W. Lipton. 1986. "Disease Organisms, Economics and the Management of Fisheries." In *Transactions of the Fiftieth North American Wildlife and Natural Resources Conference— the Role of Disease in Marine Fisheries Management.* March 15-20, 1985: 655–674.

Swanson, R.L. and C.J. Sindermann (ed.). 1979. *Oxygen Depletion and Associated Benthic Mortalities in New York Bight, 1976.* NOAA Professional Paper No. 11. U.S. Government Printing Office: Washington, DC.

Tibbo, S.N. and T.R. Graham. 1963. "Biological Changes in Herring Stocks Following an Epizootic." *Journal of the Canadian Fisheries Research Board* 20(2): 435–449.

U.S. Congress, Office of Technology Assessment. 1987. *Wastes in Marine Environments.* U.S. Government Printing Office: Washington, DC.

U.S. Environmental Protection Agency. 1989. *Marine and Estuarine Protection: Programs and Activities*. EPA 503/9-89-002. Office of Marine and Estuarine Protection: Washington, DC.

Van den Brock, W.L.F. 1978. "The Effects of Lernaeocera branchialis on the *Merlangius merlangus* Population in the Medway Estuary." *Journal of Fishery Biology* 13: 709–715.

Yang, E.J., R.C. Power and M. Menefee. 1984. *The Use of Economic Analysis in Valuing Natural Resource Damages*. Environmental Law Institute: Washington, DC, Prepared for Ocean Assessment Division, NOAA: Rockville, MD.

CHAPTER 7

Evaluation of Economic Techniques to Assess Economic Welfare Losses

7.1. Introduction

The second part of the book begins with this chapter, which introduces the basic economic techniques that have been developed and used to measure changes in economic value, and in particular, economic losses from water quality degradations. A brief history of each method is discussed, and the advantages and disadvantages of each method are described.

The assessment of lost economic value (welfare losses) in the public sector for recreational activities such as recreational fishing; beach use; and nonconsumptive viewing of birds, mammals, and sea turtles, and marine habitats is complicated. These, and similar activities are characterized as nonmarket goods. Further, they share similar attributes common to public goods and services. The most noteworthy of these attributes is that these goods and services are not sold in a private market. The absence of a formal market complicates assessments of the economic value and collective decisions about their provision, because price and quantity information, which is normally used to determine demand and the associated value of goods, is missing.

In response to the lack of price–quantity data for such activities, a variety of economic techniques have been developed to assess nonmarket goods. Among the best known and widely used methods are the travel cost approach (TCA) (Clawson and Knetsch 1966), and the hedonic price approach (HPA) (Griliches 1971, Rosen 1974). A third technique, the household production framework (HPF) (Becker 1965) has been applied to recreation decisions (Bockstael and McConnell 1981, Ralph 1979, Strong 1983). All of these approaches rely on indirect means to value economic benefits based on observed behavior. However, another technique that has received attention and use recently is the contingent valuation (CV) approach (Freeman 1979, 1993, Mitchell and Carson 1989). This approach obtains direct measures of economic benefits based on survey data. A difference between the indirect methods and the CV approach is the context in which economic welfare is measured. Indirect (or imputed) techniques obtain ex post measures of welfare, that is, welfare measures based on activity that has already occurred (i.e., observed behavior), while the CV approach elicits ex ante measures of welfare based on anticipated behavior. This has led to some controversy (as will be described here). Several researchers have also questioned whether welfare measures based on anticipated behavior can accurately reflect "true" behavior (see Cummings et al. 1986a, and Mitchell and Carson 1989 for a summary of these arguments).

All of these nonmarket valuation techniques obtain dollar measures of unobserved utility or satisfaction. For example, the TCA accomplishes this by estimating ordinary demand curves, from which Hicksian (or exact) welfare measures can be estimated (Bockstael 1984). The hedonic price approach has been applied mainly to housing property value data, and economic losses are estimated for alternative states of environmental degradation. Although the household production framework has been used to value recreational activities (McConnell 1979, Ralph 1979, Strong 1983) and can be also used to value changes in environmental quality (Hueth and Strong 1984), researchers now recognize that it is more useful in understanding household behavior (i.e, individual decision making) than in assessing economic value (Bockstael et al. 1986, Cummings et al. 1986b, and Smith and Palmquist 1988). The CV approach obtains direct estimates of Hicksian welfare measures (e.g., equivalent and compensating measures), associated with the level of recreational use, and for changes in recreational use due to environmental quality changes. Each of these techniques will be discussed here. Emphasis is placed on recent developments and the next chapter provides examples of their application.

7.2. Direct Nonmarket Valuation Methods

7.2.1. Contingent Valuation Approach

7.2.1.1. Background

The roots of the CV approach can be traced to public choice theory (Mueller 1979, Freeman 1979). One aspect of public choice theory concerns the provision of public goods in order to achieve socially acceptable levels. Because public goods are not produced and sold in a market, researchers faced a problem in terms of evaluating present and proposed levels of public goods. As a result, a number of methods were developed to induce individuals to reveal their preferences toward public goods (i.e., preference revelation techniques). Freeman (1979) describes three basic approaches: (1) voting on referendums, (2) revealed preferences for the quantity of public goods, and (3) revealed preferences for the money value of public goods. Of these, the CV approach falls under the third case. It involves directly asking individuals to state their willingness-to-pay (WTP) for a given amount or a change in the amount of a public good.

The CV approach has evolved into a much more sophisticated technique, however, than simply asking WTP questions. The first level of CV studies basically asked WTP questions (e.g., What is the maximum dollar amount you would be willing to pay for a specific good?) (Bohm 1972; Davis 1963, 1964; Hammack and Brown 1974; Knetsch and Davis 1966; McConnell 1977). The next level of CV studies began a series of methodological developments concerning various limitations-biases of the CV approach. For example variations in question formats (e.g., iterative bidding questions, closed-ended questions, use of payment cards), more descriptive definitions of the hypothetical good (involving photographs), variations in payment vehicles (e.g., donations, taxes, utility fees), variations in information, variations in sequencing of questions and information (Brookshire et al. 1976, 1979, 1981, 1982; Loehman 1984; Loehman et al. 1981, 1982; Mitchell and Carson 1981, 1984; Randall et al. 1974, 1978, 1983; Rowe et al. 1980; Schulze et al. 1981; Schulze and Brookshire 1983; Thayer 1981). Randall et al. (1974) are credited with advancing the iterative bidding question along with early contributions from Brookshire et al. (1976) and Rowe et al. (1980). The work of Hanemann (1983, 1984a, 1984b, 1985) is credited with advancing the use of the closed-ended question format and use of referendum type CV models. The combined work of Brookshire et al. (1976, 1979, 1981, 1982), Loehman (1984), Loehman et al. (1981, 1982), Mitchell and Carson (1981, 1984), Randall et al. (1978, 1983), Rowe et al. (1980), Schulze et al. (1981), Schulze and Brookshire (1983), and Thayer (1981) has contributed to refinements in descriptions of the hypothetical good, payment vehicle, and relative importance of inherent biases associated with the CV approach.

Another level of CV studies examined and compared it to other nonmarket valuation approaches and to experimental economic techniques and assessment methods (Bishop and Heberlein 1979, Bishop et al. 1983, Brookshire et al. 1979, 1982, Coursey et al. 1987, Coursey and Schulze 1986, Desvousges et al. 1983, Knetsch and Sinden 1984, Loehman 1984, Schulze et al. 1981, Seller et al. 1985). The experimental economic studies involving CV are useful to note because some found evidence of convergence between WTP and WTA (willingness-to-accept) measures (Coursey et al. 1987), and that the CV approach compared favorably with alternative methods (Brookshire et al. 1979, 1981, 1982, Cummings et al. 1986a, Randall et al. 1983, Schulze et al. 1981, Seller et al. 1985).

The present level of CV studies involves numerous comparisons, tests, and refinements to reexamine many of the earlier concerns, biases, and subsequent issues (Adamowicz et al. 1993; Bateman and Willis 1999; Boyle et al. 1994, 1996; Cameron 1992; Carson et al. 1996a; Desvousges et al. 1993, 1996; Diamond et al. 1993; Loomis 1989; Randall and Hoehn 1996; Ready et al. 1996; Reiling et al. 1990; Schulze et al. 1996; Shogren et al. 1994; Smith and Osborne 1996; Stevens et al. 1994; Whitehead et al. 1995; Willis 1995). One reason for the renewed interest was to rebut claims that the CV approach has no basis in measuring nonuse values or in cost–benefit analysis (CBA) (Diamond and Hausman 1993, 1994), and to rebut recommendations from a National Oceanic and Atmospheric Administration (NOAA) panel on CV approach (U.S. DOC, NOAA 1993) (see Carson et al. 1996b, 1996c; Bjornstad and Kahn 1996; Willis and Corkindale 1995 for recent summaries).

A major assumption of the CV approach is that individuals can reveal their WTP for nonmarket goods contingent on a hypothetical market transaction (Freeman 1979, 1993). The mechanics of the approach are as follows. The CV approach is based on the premise of a realistically designed, though hypothetical, market setting. An individual is asked to reveal his or her preference, via a survey, in the form of a bid (e.g., maximum amount willing to pay) contingent on the availability of the good in question. Thus it is as if an individual faces an experimental market and reacts in terms of consumption behavior to the changes specified by the researcher.

The basic types of valuation questions that have been used and currently are in use are referred to as open-ended CV questions, closed-ended CV questions, and iterative bidding CV questions. Open-ended CV questions ask individuals for their maximum WTP or minimum WTA, and sometimes both, associated with a specific level of the hypothetical good. Iterative bidding CV questions start from a preset price and ask for economic values (i.e., maximum WTP or minimum WTA) corresponding to a specific level of the good in an iterative manner. If the individual responds "yes" to an initial price, the price is increased for WTP (and decreased for WTA) by some increment and the question is repeated. This process is repeated in an iterative manner until a "no" response is reached and the process is stopped. The last yes response is taken to be the max-WTP or min-WTA amount. Closed-ended questions (also known as referendum or discrete CV questions) were first based on asking individuals to reveal their preference by voting (yes/no) for a specific level of the good if available at a predetermined price (Hanemann 1984a). Later versions involved splitting the sample into several equal parts, assigning a different random price for each group, and then asking the individual to vote (yes, no) for a specific level of the good at the stated price, where all individuals face the same quantity of the good. This was an attempt to introduce price variation into closed-ended or referendum formats. The closed-ended or referendum data are evaluated using a number of discrete-choice models because the responses follow binary data (1, 0 for yes, no responses, respectively). The work of Hanemann (1983, 1984a, 1984b, 1985) developed procedures for estimating welfare measures from discrete-choice models and was a major factor in the popularity of the referendum CV approach. One issue that remains unresolved concerns the superiority of open-ended question formats versus closed-ended question formats (Bateman and Willis 1999, Boyle et al. 1996, Loomis 1990, Willis 1995).

The CV approach is composed of four critical, interrelated elements: the hypothetical market, the good to be valued, the payment method, and the valuation questions. Great care must be taken in advancing both the good and the market setting in the questionnaire design in a manner that is realistic and credible, and above all, easily understood by the survey respondent. The valuation questions must also be unambiguous and appear credible to the respondent. It is especially important to achieve these questionnaire design objectives by introducing as little as possible bias or offense (preferably none) to the respondent (Dillman 1978, Desvousges et al. 1983, Rowe and Chestnut 1983). Carelessness in any of the above components will cast doubt on the survey application and add to the skepticism associated with the CV approach and its results.

Advantages of the CV approach are that it is the most versatile of the nonmarket valuation techniques in assessing the value of a wide range of goods. It allows for flexibility in the good to be valued, and it can be used to assess nonuse values (i.e., existence values). The CV approach has been used in a wide range of applications, for example it has been used to value improvements in environmental quality (clean air, clean water); aesthetic goods (visibility, scenic views); recreational activities and experiences (sportfishing, recreational beach use, boating); protection of endangered species; preservation of unique habitats and environments; public pest control; and health-risk issues (comprehensive reviews are in Cummings et al. 1986a, Mitchell and Carson 1989, Schulze et al. 1981, Bjornstad and Kahn 1996). In contrast, the TCA and HPF have been confined to value recreational activities and experiences, while the HPA has been used chiefly to value changes in environmental quality and housing characteristics.

Disadvantages and shortcomings of the CV approach regard its basic premise and the difficulties of obtaining valid responses. Its major weakness, as previously mentioned, is whether values based on expected behavior can accurately reflect true behavior, that is, can ex ante values represent values of actual behavior (i.e., ex post values)? This concern involves two separate issues—strategic bias and hypothetical bias. The first involves whether respondents try to influence the outcome of survey results by not stating their "true" preferences. Individuals can understate or overstate their "true" preferences if they believe either that the response they give will influence the price they will have to pay, or that no matter what their response is they will not have to pay for the good. The second concern, hypothetical bias, results from the contention that because WTP or WTA amounts are not actually paid, but are hypothetical, individuals lack incentives to determine and reveal their "true" preferences. Research has shown that for both of these possible biases, if care is taken in designing the market, the good, and valuation questions so the survey is realistic and credible, these biases can be minimized. These efforts will increase the likelihood that revealed preferences obtained via such surveys will approach individuals' "true" preferences (Cummings et al. 1986a, Mitchell and Carson 1989, Randall et al. 1983, Schulze et al. 1981).

Other shortcomings of the CV approach concern questions related to aspects of the survey design such as the framing of questions, payment mode, information, starting bids (i.e., initial preset prices), and interviewer biases. Again, research has shown that well designed surveys and questions can minimize the effects of these problems on survey results (Cummings et al. 1986a, Mitchell and Carson 1989, Randall et al. 1983, Schulze et al. 1981).

In response to the major concern of the hypothetical nature of the CV approach, early research compared the economic value estimates obtained by the CV approach with those obtained from the indirect valuation methods, namely the TCA and HPA. Evidence showed that under appropriate applications, the CV approach produces economic values that compare well with the economic values obtained from indirect valuation methods (see Cummings et al. 1986a for a thorough discussion). However, as Mitchell and Carson (1989) realized in their assessment of the CV approach, early comparison studies were at fault and researchers often confused various validity criteria measures (see Section 7.2.1.2). Present research involves comparisons and tests of validity that attempt to address the shortcomings of previous research.

In addition, present concerns with the CV approach involve whether revealed bids will vary over time given experience and familiarity with the CV approach and public good in question (Adamowicz et al. 1993, Brookshire and Coursey 1987, Coursey et al. 1987, Hanemann 1991, Ofiara 1998, Shogren et al. 1994). Recent research has demonstrated that active participants or users participating in CV markets and games do revise their bids over multiple time periods (Ofiara 1998). Based on time-series techniques, results indicated that the WTP-series exhibited more evidence of convergence in a time-series sense relative to WTA-series; this result was fairly robust across various data subsets, subsets without $0 bids, subsets without large bids relative to income, and observations with excessive noise (Ofiara 1998). Although this behavior has been demonstrated in controlled laboratory environments (Adamowicz et al. 1993, Shogren et al. 1994) it has not been well established in applied field work (Brookshire and Coursey 1987 is the only study to date). This bid revision behavior could be due to an individual's familiarity with the CV game over time, changes in individuals' tastes and in repeated thinking about their true preferences, and in their success or failure with the good in a particular time period. Such findings suggest profound effects on future work in CV methods and in experimental methods that elicit preferences for nonmarket-public type goods. This evidence also suggests that single point estimates based on one-time application of the CV approach may not be appropriate in field studies designed to assess values for purposes of NRDAs, no matter how good the application is. Because of tastes and experience respondents can and will revise their CV bids in repeated game playing, discounting CV research based on test–retest criteria. Furthermore these findings suggest the need for continued experimental evidence in the CV approach; to advance the technique and to establish credibility and recommendations for its use. Researchers are advised to approach applications cautiously.

7.2.1.2. Controversy over Contingent Valuation*

In spite of extensive research involving tests and comparisons, the CV approach remains controversial. This controversy is associated with the following characteristics of the CV approach: (1) the method assesses values based on hypothetical data or responses, (2) the method obtains ex ante welfare measures rather than ex post welfare measures, and (3) the CV approach is claimed to be the only method available to obtain nonuse values— part of the controversy regarding nonuse values is that the CV method is essentially unverifiable regarding estimates of nonuse value (Cummings et al. 1986a, Diamond and Hausman 1994, Freeman 1993, Hausman 1993, Mitchell and Carson 1989). In attempts to gain credibility for the CV approach among peers, numerous research was conducted to examine limitations of the CV approach, and comparisons with alternative valuation methods (Mitchell and Carson 1989 contain a summary of this research). In addition, several conferences and workshops were convened to critically assess the current state of the CV approach (a U.S. Environmental Protection Agency [EPA] conference in 1983–84, an NOAA panel in 1992, and a joint U.S. EPA and U.S. Department of Energy [DOE] conference in 1994).

The first assessment of the CV approach commissioned by the U.S. EPA in 1983–84, involved a state-of-the-art assessment and conference of the CV approach (Cummings et al. 1986a). The overall conclusion reached was that the CV approach shows promise, but faces some real challenges. In 1992, prompted by the *Exxon Valdez* oil spill and subsequent economic analysis and settlement, and the Oil Pollution Act of 1990, the U.S. Department of Commerce (DOC), NOAA was directed to assemble an expert panel to provide advice to NOAA and conduct a current assessment of the CV approach with particular attention to nonuse values. They were specifically to assess whether the CV approach is capable of providing estimates of lost nonuse values "that are reliable enough" for natural resource damage assessments (Portney 1994: 8). The NOAA panel concluded that the CV approach "can produce estimates reliable enough to be the starting point of a judicial process of damage assessment, including lost passive nonuse values" (Ibid: 8, U.S. DOC, NOAA 1994). In addition, Exxon convened its own conference and team of economists to provide a critical assessment of the CV approach in 1992, with the conclusion that the CV approach should not be used to assess environmental dam-

---

* Section 7.2.1.2. is from Ofiara (1998).

ages nor used in CBA (Hausman 1993, Diamond and Hausman 1994). Then in 1994, the U.S. DOE and U.S. EPA cosponsored a workshop on the CV approach to address its status on assessments of nonuse values and to develop a research agenda for future CV research. Although much discussion concerned the NOAA panel recommendations and findings, conclusions reached were (1) that the CV approach would require a great deal of research effort to address its inherent characteristics and limitations so as to advance the technique, and (2) many researchers disagreed with the NOAA panel's recommendation that referendum type (i.e., closed-ended format) CV questions be used instead of open-ended formats, and that personal interviews be used instead of telephone and mail interviews.

Researchers now acknowledge that there were faults with early comparison studies (Mitchell and Carson 1989). Comparison studies were developed to provide support of the validity, and hence credibility, of the CV approach. This early research proceeded on the notion that estimates of economic value from alternative nonmarket valuation methods were comparable and theoretically equal. It was reasoned that if estimates (i.e., means) of economic value from the CV approach were similar (i.e., not statistically different) to estimates from alternative nonmarket valuation methods, this then provided evidence to support the validity of the CV approach.

Researchers subsequently learned that none of the alternative nonmarket valuation methods results in a superior measure of the theoretical construct (e.g., monetary value of preferences), and that researchers were often confused with the concept of validity. If one nonmarket valuation method results in a superior measure of the construct, then a basis for comparisons would exist, and one could examine how close alternative nonmarket valuation methods would be to the method that results in a superior measure. In early comparison studies, correspondence between CV methods and alternative valuation methods was interpreted as evidence of validity in the truest sense—criterion validity (i.e., whereby measures of economic value from alternative nonmarket valuation methods are neither a truer measure of the theoretical construct [monetary value of preferences] than one another). However, correspondence across methods is associated with the notion of convergent validity (i.e., correspondence between economic value estimates from alternative nonmarket valuation methods), a weak form of validity. Hence, one can only establish credibility of the CV approach in the sense of convergent validity. This realization weakens efforts to establish credibility of the CV approach via comparison studies. Probably a better approach would be to examine estimates of ex post welfare measures across alternative methods, and ex ante welfare measures across methods, as well as to investigate the correspondence in welfare measures (ex ante versus ex post) for a particular method from controlled experimental economic studies.

Litigation that involved the *Exxon Valdez* oil spill and federal rulemaking associated with the Oil Pollution Act of 1990 has reopened the status of the CV approach and created added controversies among the public, environmentalists, and economists. Legal proceedings concerning economic assessments of the environmental damage challenged economists to critically evaluate the CV approach, and at the same time resulted in a split in the profession concerning the use and credibility of the CV approach and its value estimates (see Carson et al. 1996a, 1996b; Diamond and Hausman 1993, 1994; Hausman 1993; Portney 1994). The current debate involves two polar views; those who advocate the CV approach and those who do not. While most of the criticism involves using the

CV approach for nonuse values, Diamond and Hausman do not recommend the CV approach for use in CBA, and conclude that the CV approach does not measure what it purports to measure and that use of the CV approach in government decision making "is basically misguided" (Diamond and Hausman 1994: 46). Hence, the CV approach is also suspect in estimating use values (Diamond and Hausman 1994, Hausman 1993).

It is surprising that economists were so taken with such controversy and polar views over the CV approach. In instances of divorce trials and litigation and with estate settlements it is common for both sides to hire experts to assess the value of an individual's or estate's holdings and future income potential, and reach positions quite different from one another. The simple fact that once a case enters a legal environment and courtroom, differences and polar views will arise resulting in controversy and debate and positions that become challenged in court and are often negotiated out of court.

7.2.2. Simulated Markets

In 1978, Bishop and Heberlein (1979, 1986) and Bishop et al. (1983) developed an experiment in which hunting permits could be bought and sold in a simulated market setting. This was a bold new experiment and had a profound impact on nonmarket valuation techniques. They conducted these experiments in another hunting application (Bishop et al. 1988). The approach of the simulated market experiment was basically a variation of the CV approach, but with an important difference. A market experiment was conducted where actual cash offers were made and permits were surrendered if accepted, and where permits were also sold and cash accepted. These responses from actual cash offers and selling of permits were interpreted as actual or observed behavior (i.e., ex post behavior) and could be compared to CV questions of ex ante values. Results were surprising. In their first study of goose hunting, Bishop and Heberlein (1979) found differences between the CV approach and simulated market experiment; estimated total consumer surplus was $63 for actual cash offers to buy hunters permits, $101 for WTA and $21 for WTP. They concluded that CV estimates could be in error by at least 50 percent. In another study using simulated markets, Bishop and Heberlein (1986) and Bishop et al. (1988) conducted experiments to buy and sell deer-hunting permits in 1983 and 1984 hunting seasons. Results of the 1983 experiment based on selling four permits yielded the following: (1) for a sealed bid auction experiment the mean cash bid offered was $24, WTP for a permit was $32; (2) for an auction experiment that used a telephone follow-up where the initial bid could be changed, the mean cash bid offered was $19 compared to $43 for WTP; (3) for a different auction experiment based on starting point bids and telephone follow-up, the mean cash bid was $24 compared to $43 for WTP; and (4) for a sealed bid auction where four highest bids would be accepted, the mean cash bid was $25 and WTP $42. Results for 1984 based on selling permits at a preselected price found that the mean cash offer was $31 compared to $35 for WTP for a permit. Results based on buying permits yielded a mean compensation of $153, compared to mean WTA of $420. In three of the experiments in 1983 (the latter three experiments) cash offers were roughly 50 percent of WTP, while for the first 1983 experiment the cash offer represented 75 percent of the WTP bid amount, a difference of $8. In the 1984 experiment results from selling permits found a difference of $4 while a greater difference was found in buying permits.

It is from these experiments (primarily the goose hunting study) that recommendations to adjust WTP estimates downward by at least 50 percent are based (U.S. DOC, NOAA 1993). It is emphasized that simulated market experiments are primarily an experimental approach to examine the issue of discrepancy between WTP and WTA, and between hypothetical economic value and actual economic value, and at this time are not advanced nor tested enough to be used in practical applications. This type of research is where simulated market experiments have their greatest benefit. Because of these reasons, we do not discuss this technique further.

7.3. Indirect or Imputed Market Valuation Methods

7.3.1. Travel Cost Approach

The travel cost approach (TCA) was originally developed to determine the demand for recreation sites from various geographic zones on the basis of their proximity to the site (Clawson and Knetsch 1966, Dwyer et al. 1977, Freeman 1979, Smith and Palmquist 1988). It assumes that demand for a recreation site based on participation rates (visits) varies inversely with travel distance, so demand (or trips) is low for individuals located far from the site, and relatively high for those located closer. It further assumes that the amount of distance traveled is responsible for most of the trip expenses, and the dollar values of these trip costs are measures of the satisfaction derived from the visit at the margin (i.e., trip costs represent measures of satisfaction in the context of an additional trip) and therefore can serve as a proxy for the price or participation fee of recreation activities at the site. On the basis of this information, travel cost demand curves could be estimated, and in turn, the area under the demand curve could yield an estimate of consumer surplus conditioned on the number of trips taken. Early applications were based on this zonal approach (see Bockstael et al. 1986 for a discussion).

The zonal approach to the travel cost demand method regresses per capita visitation in each zone on the per capita travel cost corresponding to each zone and other explanatory variables for the zone measured in per capita terms. The "zone" referred to in this approach could be a geographic area (e.g., municipality, county); region (e.g., northwest corner of state, Midwest); or an area defined by political boundaries (e.g., voting districts) or by some other means. The result is an estimated relationship that represents a "site–demand curve." There are several shortcomings to this approach. Other costs that influence travel behavior such as food, lodging, and equipment were not included in early models. It was assumed that utility and income were constant across zones, which researchers found introduced heteroscedasticity in the error term of the model (i.e., where the error term is related with one of the independent variables), resulting in inefficient variances of the regression parameter estimates. Furthermore, the time spent in travel to the site was not included in early applications (McConnell 1975, 1976). Lastly, travel cost demand models, while attempting to describe recreation behavior, had little connection to an underlying theoretical model (Bockstael et al. 1986, Smith and Palmquist 1988).

Further applications have examined each of these problems and have introduced rationale for the inclusion of variables not originally used. This has resulted in the addition of the following variables in the travel cost demand model as regressors (i.e., independent or right-hand-side variables), income, travel time or the cost of travel time, congestion, and substitute sites (Yang et al. 1984). However, shortcomings of the TCA still involved the restrictive assumptions of the zonal approach, the constancy of tastes and income across zones, and the missing theoretical link. It was felt that the zonal approach was less than "ideal."

Researchers acknowledge that models of recreational decision making are consistent with an HPF (Bockstael et al. 1986, Smith and Palmquist 1988). The HPF serves as the connection between recreation behavior based on utility maximization and travel cost demand models. Furthermore, it provides support to use data based on individual observations, instead of per capita visitation rates from a geographic zone, in the TCA since the HPF is based on individual behavior. An immediate advantage to using individual observations compared to zonal averages, is that tastes and income can vary across individuals and zones and this will eliminate an inherent heteroscedasticity problem. It also allows for an increase in the number of observations increasing the degrees of freedom in the model.

A general specification of the TCA based on individual observations is:

$$(7.1) \qquad T_{ij} = f(X1,X2,X3,X4,X5,X6,X7)_{ij},$$

where T_{ij} is the number of trips by the *ith* individual to the *jth* site, *X1* is the money costs of the trip (sum of expenses of travel, food and beverages, lodging, variable equipment, and entrance fees), *X2* the distance to the site or the opportunity costs of time in travel (round-trip), *X3* on-site time or the opportunity costs of on-site time, *X4* household income, *X5* a vector of socioeconomic attributes (education, age, ethnic background), *X6* a vector of other pertinent variables such as years of experience, measures of success (e.g., catch rate for sportfishing), and a measure of congestion (number of people encountered at the site), and *X7* money costs to alternative substitute sites for all *i* individuals. Sometimes the number of trips to alternative sites is included instead of costs, and sometimes a series of binary variables (0,1) are included to represent costs to alternative sites.

In sum, the overall strength of the TCA as specified above is that it is based on observed individual behavior of recreational decision making.

7.3.2. Household Production Framework

Researchers have come to recognize that the household production framework (HPF) is a methodology that describes individual decision making rather than an estimation technique to estimate and predict demand (Bockstael et al. 1986, Smith and Palmquist 1988). Applied to recreation behavior the HPF assumes that the purchases of inputs (equipment) and the use of time (on-site time) result in the production of a commodity. For example, expenses of fishing gear and travel, plus time spent in travel and fishing, produce both fishing trips and caught fish. The economic benefits of the recreational activity is the joint (or sum) of the value of the trip and output (or success) of the activity (e.g., catch rate) (Bockstael and McConnell 1981, Hueth and Strong 1984).

The formulation of the HPF is credited to Becker (1965) who viewed the household as a producer, purchasing inputs, supplying labor, and producing commodities (via a technological transformation), which are then consumed by the household to obtain utility. This process can be formulated as a utility optimization model (following Bockstael et al. 1986) such as:

(7.2) $\displaystyle \max_{z_i} U = u(z_1, \ldots, z_n)$, subject to:

(7.3) $z = f(x_1, \ldots, x_m, t_x)$,

(7.4) $Y(t_w, w) + R - p_i x_i = 0$,

(7.5) $T - t_w - t_x = 0$,

where U is utility or satisfaction, z commodities produced by the household, x inputs (market goods), p input prices, t_x time spent producing commodities, t_w time spent working, w the wage rate, Y wage income (endowment income), R nonwage income, and T total time (endowment time). The optimization problem the household faces is to maximize utility from the consumption of commodities, Equation (7.2), subject to the following constraints, the specific production technology facing the household that allows the transformation of inputs and time into commodities, Equation (7.3), an income constraint, Equation (7.4), and a time constraint Equation (7.5).

Advantages of the HPF are that it is based on observed behavior, it represents individual decision-making behavior, and it uses individual observations as opposed to the zonal averages used in the early travel cost demand models. However, because of its restrictive assumptions (production technology) and burdensome estimation technique (see Ralph 1979, Strong 1983 for applications), it is not suggested for use as a nonmarket valuation technique, but rather as a model to describe individual behavior (Bockstael et al. 1986, Cummings et al. 1986b).

7.3.3. Travel Cost—Varying Parameter Model

A modification of the travel cost model that is used to assess variation in site quality is referred to as the varying parameter model (VPM). The VPM introduces quality characteristics of alternative recreation sites based on a two-step estimation process. The first step involves the estimation of individual site demand equations as a function of prices and income. In the second step the estimated parameters from the first step are then regressed on the quality characteristics. The formal expression of the VPM is as follows.

In the first step, the trip demand equations, assuming linearity, are estimated:

(7.6) $x_1 = \beta_{01} + \beta_{11}p_1 + \beta_{21}p_2 + \beta_{31}y + e_1$

$$\vdots$$

$$x_n = \beta_{0n} + \beta_{1n}p_1 + \beta_{2n}p_2 + \beta_{3n}y + e_n,$$

for each *n*th site, where *x* represents the number of trips, *p* the prices for various sites (own-site, alternative sites), and *e* the error term. The second step involves estimation of the following equations:

(7.7) $\beta_{0i} = \mu_{01} + \mu_{02}q_i + u_i$

$\beta_{1i} = \mu_{11} + \mu_{12}q_i + u_i$

$\beta_{2i} = \mu_{21} + \mu_{22}q_i + u_i$

$\beta_{3i} = \mu_{31} + \mu_{32}q_i + u_i,$

where the estimated parameters from the first step are regressed on the site quality characteristics (q) for *i* characteristics, assuming linear equations.

Several versions of this basic model have been estimated. Bockstael et al. (1988, 1989) modified the VPM by using a Tobit model for the first step (to account for censored trips) and examined water quality in the Chesapeake Bay, while Smith and Desvousges (1986) examined water quality in the Monongahela River and modified the second step to account for heteroscedasticity of the form u = f(q). These modified travel cost models have been developed to examine the effect of site quality characteristics on recreational travel demand, but involve a two-step estimation procedure. Such a technique holds promise but should be used in consultation with a professional economist who can readily estimate such models if so desired.

7.3.4. Hedonic Travel Cost Approach

The hedonic travel cost approach (HTCA) is an attempt to modify the travel cost approach to account for site characteristics and possibly environmental quality characteristics (Brown and Mendelsohn 1984, Hueth and Strong 1984, Mendelsohn 1984). It draws on the travel cost approach and the hedonic price approach, where travel costs of individuals for alternative sites, site characteristics, and environmental attributes of sites are used to generate marginal costs associated with each characteristic and quality attribute, and ultimately to derive demand equations for each characteristic or attribute. The following discussion will be brief because the approach readily follows the hedonic price approach discussed in detail in Section 7.4.1.

The first stage of the HTCA involves estimating marginal costs associated with each characteristic or attribute researchers wish to examine. Here travel costs of individuals are regressed on measures of these site characteristics and environmental quality attributes. The marginal costs are used in the second stage where the levels of each characteristic or attribute are regressed on their marginal costs to derive demand equations associated with each characteristic or attribute.

A number of problems with the HTCA have limited their applications (see Hueth and Strong 1984, Smith and Desvousges 1986, Bockstael et al. 1991 for a summary). There are conceptual problems and empirical problems, and its relevance for public policy may be questionable. Bockstael et al. (1991) note that following initial efforts and research with the HTCA in the 1980s, the HTCA has, since then, received little attention. We will follow suit and defer further interest to the literature.

7.3.5. Random Utility Models

Researchers began to apply and extend random utility models (RUM) to problems involving recreation behavior and behavior given multiple sites where site characteristics were available. Previous models were either limited or inadequate to account for interaction between multiple sites of an individual's behavior in recreation activities or consumption activities of nonmarketed goods. Although RUMs are well suited to handle multiple sites and tradeoffs among such substitutes, it is not a technique that can estimate demand for sites or uses, just the probability that a particular site or use would be selected. Some researchers have developed hybrid models where a demand equation is coupled to the RUM as a second stage. In such a model the RUM is estimated as the first step, and the results used in estimating a demand equation in the second step. Such models still have limitations and are computationally sophisticated. But research in this direction can assist efforts in developing methods and demand models that can incorporate multiple site choice under specific quality conditions.

To many econometricians, random utility models are more appropriately thought of and treated as econometric models of individual choice behavior where individual choice is represented by discrete data, where characteristics either vary over the individual making the choice (which yields a multinomial choice model) or characteristics vary over specific choices made (which yields a conditional choice model) or possibly a hybrid model of both such as a mixed choice model (a mixed conditional choice model or perhaps a mixed multinomial choice model). In both cases individual choice is modeled as the dependent variable and the characteristics as the independent variables. These models are based on discrete data, rather than on continuous data, which distinguishes them from the class of ordinary regression models. In particular, the dependent variable, which reflects an individual's choice, is represented by 0,1 data associated with a "no" or "yes" response, respectively, regarding the particular choice (e.g., participate or not participate in a recreational activity). With multivariate choice models the individual has two or more options to choose from (e.g., the choice between several alternative recreation sites). It is these types of multivariate choice models that have been used in the recreation literature and specifically with the multivariate logit form.

These models take on a specific form based on the particular form the error term is assumed to follow (e.g., if the error term is assumed to follow a Weibull distribution the model is a multivariate logit model, if a Normal distribution the model is a multivariate probit model). We will confine our discussion to logit-type models as most of the recreation literature concerns these models. Within this class of discrete choice models, it is important to note whether individual choice reflects ordered data or unordered data. If unordered data, multivariate logit models are appropriate (either the multinomial logit [ML] model or the conditional logit [CL] is appropriate); if ordered then ordered probit or logit models are appropriate.

A limitation of these multivariate choice models is that they do not estimate trip demand behavior as do models based on continuous data, such as travel cost demand models as stated earlier. These choice models can only account for the probability that an individual makes a specific choice that depends on an individual's characteristics (e.g., age, education, income, etc.), characteristics of the particular activity (e.g., marine fishing vs. beach use vs. boating), or the particular site chosen for the activity the individual pursues. Both the ML and CL models have particular attributes, limitations, and particular uses that must be kept in mind, however applications and a complete understanding of these models involves a good foundation of statistical and econometric theory (for more detail the reader is referred to Mittelhammer et al. 2000, Greene 1993, Fomby et al. 1988, Judge et al. 1988).

Both the ML model and the CL model are used when the choice data are unordered; that is, in situations where the order of the choice is not important (e.g., the choice among alternative recreation sites). The difference between them concerns whether the data are individual-specific (i.e., characteristics vary across individuals making the choice) or are choice-specific (i.e., characteristics vary across specific choices, recreational sites). If data are individual-specific one would use the ML model, and it further assumes that the estimated parameters can change over the choice outcomes (a version based on this model used in the recreation literature is referred to as the varying parameter model). Furthermore, the ML model can only be estimated when the data are normalized or conditioned for all the estimated parameters to be uniquely identified. It is common to normalize on the basis of the first outcome, usually $ß_1$ (e.g., the parameter estimate associated with site 1). The ML model is then estimated and interpreted relative to the first outcome. The estimated coefficients associated with the choice selected are interpreted as the log-odds of choosing site 2 relative to site 1 given a unit change in one of the independent variables. The estimated coefficients can also be expressed in terms of probabilities (e.g., the probability of choosing site 3 relative to site 1, given a unit change in some independent variable).

If the data are choice-specific then the CL model should be used and a further assumption is that the estimated parameters cannot vary across outcomes. CL models must also be normalized in order to be estimated and are estimated for each of the alternative choices (i.e., a model for the first alternative choice, a model for the second alternative choice, and so on). Interpretations are on the basis of the normalized choice (e.g., the probability of site 2 relative to site 1, the probability of charter fishing given shore-based fishing, etc.) given a unit increase in one of the independent variables. In addition, one can determine individual probabilities for each of the choices selected (e.g., for site 1 to site 4, if four individual sites). However, a problem exists specifically with the CL model, referred to as independence of irrelevant alternatives where the relative odds of choosing any relative pair of alternative choices are constant over the remaining alternatives (i.e., where one of the subsets associated with a choice outcome is irrelevant and removal of it has little effect on the remaining estimated parameters) and in turn on the relative odds; one could say the subset is superfluous. If such a condition is violated then researchers have developed nested choice models that consist of a series of hierarchical choices (e.g., the choice to recreate, the choice to go fishing rather than use the beach, the choice to fish for striped bass, and so on) (Bockstael et al. 1991).

The two general models (ML model, CL model) are described below but estimation and application procedures are referred to more advanced econometric textbooks because of the difficulty in estimating and interpreting such models. We begin with a random utility model:

$$(7.8) \qquad U_{ij} = xß_{ij} + \varepsilon_{ij},$$

which describes utility of choice j for the *ith* individual faced with J choices, and ε is the disturbance term. When the individual chooses the *jth* choice, it is assumed that U_{ij} is the maximum utility of all *J* choices. The RUM is then modeled as the probability that choice *j* is selected as:

$$(7.9) \qquad \text{Prob}(U_{ij} > U_{ik}) \text{ for all other } k \neq j.$$

The RUM is then made operational by choosing a distribution for the disturbance term; a normal distribution yields the multivariate probit model, the Weibull distribution the multivariate logit model.

The ML model in general is:

$$(7.10) \qquad \text{Prob}(Y_i = \text{jth choice}): P_{ij} = \exp(x_i \text{ß}_j) / \sum_{k=0}^{m} \exp(x_i \text{ß}_k),$$
$$\text{for i individuals and j outcomes,}$$

where the probability of the *jth* outcome for the *ith* individual (P_{ij}) follows a logit model, outcomes are j = 1, 2, ..., m, and exp( ) is the exponential function. Here x_i are characteristics of the individuals and vary across individuals, but are constant across outcomes.

The CL model in general is:

$$(7.11) \qquad \text{Prob}(Y_i = \text{jth choice}): P_{ij} = \exp(z_{ij}\text{ß}) / \sum_{j=1}^{m} \exp(z_{ij}\text{ß}),$$
$$\text{for i individuals and j outcomes,}$$

where z_{ij} are characteristics of the outcomes and vary across outcomes. Note that the estimated parameters, ß's, are constant over *j* outcomes, whereas they could vary in the ML model.

If independent variables consist of both characteristics of outcomes and the characteristics of individuals, a mixed model is obtained:

$$(7.12) \qquad \text{Prob}(Y_i = \text{jth choice}): P_{ij} = \exp(z_{ij}\text{ß} + x_i\text{ß}_j) / \sum_{j=1}^{m} \sum_{k=0}^{m} \exp(z_{ij}\text{ß} + x_i\text{ß}_k),$$
$$\text{for i individuals and j outcomes.}$$

We emphasize that these models are somewhat complicated, estimation and interpretations are not straightforward, the CL model has high data requirements, and these models do not estimate the demand for trips but were initially developed to estimate individual choice behavior. Only with modifications that are not linked to utility theoretic behavior have researchers been able to use such random utility models to address demand issues. We recommend the reader pursue these issues from the following: Bockstael et al. (1988, 1989, 1991), Greene (1993), Fomby et al. (1988), Mittelhammer et al. (2000), Strand et al. (1985, 1986).

7.4. Property Valuation Techniques

The effects of environmental quality degradations are not strictly limited to reductions in the consumption of environmental amenities, such as recreational activity. Incidents such as the discovery of toxic wastes at Love Canal, New York, and radon in the Pennsylvania–New Jersey area have depressed the market value of housing in those areas. In both cases, housing values were affected in areas where high levels of pollution were discovered. The basic premise established earlier remains the same. Pollution that degrades the environment lessens the public's enjoyment and satisfaction from the consumption of those goods and activities that are affected.

The effects of air quality degradations on house or property values were the first to receive attention from economists (see Freeman 1979 for a review). In the South Coast Air Basin of the greater Los Angeles area and also in San Francisco, air quality degradations have long been a fact of life. Economists successfully demonstrated that residential housing values were influenced by air quality levels (Brookshire et al. 1979, 1982; Loehman et al.1981). As expected, consumers in the housing market gained more satisfaction, and hence benefits, from housing located in cleaner areas and lower values from areas associated with poorer air quality.

However, empirical research to examine the effects of water quality degradations on housing values has not received much attention. The issue of water quality degradation in the marine environment is even less researched. Wilman's (1984) study is probably the first study that assessed the social costs of pollution due to an oil spill on the basis of seasonal rental housing and hotel/motel rentals. Annual damages for the Cape Cod, Massachusetts, area were estimated to range from $192,848 to $278,664 in 1978 dollars due to an oil spill. Mendelsohn's (1986) study is the only other study that examined the impact of marine pollution, in this case PCBs, on residential property values in the New Bedford, Massachusetts, area. Results indicated that PCB contamination had a statistically significant negative effect on residential housing values in the New Bedford, Massachusetts, area. In two of the most polluted zones of New Bedford Harbor, housing values were from 9.8 percent to 13.9 percent lower than equivalent homes located near cleaner waters, all other things being equal (this is an average of $5,500 to $6,400 per home for a total damage estimate of $27.3 million to $39.7 million, in 1985 dollars).

Two approaches based on residential property values have been used to evaluate economic benefits and damage attributable to improvements and degradations of environmental quality. One is the hedonic price approach (HPA) and the other the repeat sales approach (RSA). Both of these approaches value the satisfaction derived from characteristics related to the location of residential housing (i.e., amenities). The overall advantage of both approaches is that they are based on observed behavior and thus derive estimates of ex post changes in property values that result from changes in housing amenities. However, they involve fairly sophisticated econometric techniques. These two approaches are discussed below.

7.4.1. Hedonic Price Approach

Rosen (1974) is credited with developing the theory associated with the hedonic price approach (HPA). He proposed that consumers perceive the value of a good to be based on the number and quality of characteristics embodied within the good. By obtaining measures of these characteristics and incorporating them into a regression model, the implicit prices associated with each characteristic can be determined. These prices then measure the economic value these attributes contribute to the overall value of the good. In general the formal model is,

(7.13a) $p = z_i \beta + u$, for $i = 1, \dots, n$ attributes, or

(7.13b) $p = h(z_i; \beta)$

where p is the price of the good in question, z_i a vector of attributes of the good, β the parameters of the hedonic model and u a disturbance term. The first step is to estimate Equation (7.13a). To determine the marginal value of each attribute, the partial derivative of Equation (7.13a) is used:

(7.14) $\partial p / \partial z_i = \partial h(z_i; \beta) / \partial z_i$ for $i = 1, \dots, n$.

Equation (7.14) shows the marginal value that consumers place on each attribute. In equilibrium, the consumer's marginal value or "price" for the *ith* attribute will equal its marginal cost. The second step is to formulate and estimate the following relation:

(7.15) $\partial h(z_i; \beta) / \partial z_i = g_i(z,y; \mu)$ for $i = 1, \dots, n$,

where y is income, μ parameters describing tastes–preferences, and the rest are defined above for all i attributes. Therefore, a marginal price function (Equation [7.15]) is obtained for each attribute where the marginal price is a function of the attribute and income. Equation (7.15) represents an equilibrium condition for individual buyers in the hedonic market (McConnell 1985a: 13).

The hedonic price approach, Equation (7.13b), can be used to test the hypothesis that water quality degradations, or a marine pollution event, has a negative effect on housing prices. The formal hypothesis to test is:

$$H_0: \beta_i \geq 0, \text{ versus } H_1: \beta_i < 0,$$

that is, whether the estimated parameter for the pollution variable is negative versus not negative; if negative, the null hypothesis is rejected and the alternative hypothesis is accepted. In the second step of the HPA, Equation (7.15), the marginal price for each attribute is estimated. This means that the second step procedure estimates the value of the reduction in house prices attributable to marine pollution. To determine aggregate economic damage estimates, the value of the absolute (or percentage) reduction in housing sales is multiplied by the value of all residences included in the study area.

A large number of studies have examined the effect of air pollution on housing values (see Freeman 1979, Rowe and Chestnut 1982, and McConnell 1985a for a summary). Applications have been made to other environmental effects, such as noise (Nelson 1979, O'Byrne et al. 1985), a nuclear accident (Nelson 1981), threat of earthquakes (Brookshire et al. 1985), accessibility to lakefront shoreline (Brown and Pollakowski 1977, Blomquist 1984), accessibility to marine coastlines (Edwards and Anderson 1984, Milon et al. 1984), proximity to water pollution (Epp and El-Ani 1979, Rich and Moffit 1982), and coastal zone restrictions pertaining to housing access along the seacoast (Hughes 1988, Parsons 1987).

In most of the above studies economists have augmented the basic hedonic model to include a vector of environmental quality measures (i.e., accessibility or distance to an environmental effect) in addition to normal housing attributes. Equation (7.13a) can then be rewritten as:

(7.16a) $p_i = z_i \beta + x_j \mu + u$, or in general

(7.16b) $p_i = h(z_i, x_j; \beta, \mu)$,

where x_j represents a vector of environmental quality measures and μ the associated parameters.

In spite of its appeal, the HPA, and specifically the Rosen model, is not without its problems. A basic requirement of the hedonic approach is that the variables (i.e., the environmental quality measures) exist for a wide range of values. Some measures of environmental quality and housing characteristics are only available in discrete values (e.g., number of rooms, the presence of air conditioning, swimming pools, location in a pollution zone, and neighborhood characteristics such as high school quality and the quality of police and fire protection). Both the aspect of lack of continuity for some variables and the lumpy combinations of other variables violate basic assumptions of the Rosen and hedonic models (Cropper 1985, McConnell 1985b). The significance of these violations is that an individual home buyer cannot make marginal adjustments in quantities consumed (i.e., Equations (7.14) and (7.15) do not exist for specific attributes).

The Rosen model also assumes that each attribute of a particular good can be varied independently of the other attributes subject only to a budget constraint. As Cropper (1985) correctly points out in the location choice problem, the choice of geographical location is a two-dimensional problem (i.e., latitude and longitude) and since certain attributes are embedded within the location decision, these attributes cannot be varied independently of one another. In other words, locational attributes may tend to be relatively constant for all housing within a particular location (e.g., a neighborhood). In order to model this situation, a constraint must be placed on the Rosen model with the result that the equilibrium conditions specified in Equation (7.14) are not satisfied (Cropper 1985). Therefore, the two-stage procedure cannot be applied.

Another difficulty of the HPA regards the potential confusion over the interpretation of the implicit prices, known as the identification problem. McConnell (1985b) intuitively describes the identification problem as one of obtaining estimates of μ (i.e., the parameters associated with the marginal bid function) when in fact what is actually obtained is a combination of μ and β. If we reconsider Equation (7.13b) and rewrite Equation (7.15):

(7.13b) $p = h(z_j; \beta)$

(7.15) $\partial h(z_j; \beta)/\partial z_i = g_i(z, y; \mu)\ i \neq j$.

we can express the identification problem as occurring when the parameters of preferences (μ) from the marginal bid function Equation (7.15) are confused with observed hedonic prices (β), the parameters of the hedonic price equation, Equation (7.13a) Research in this area has shown that the identification problem can be treated, under certain conditions, by the imposition of restrictions on the functional form of the model (McConnell et al. 1985, Cropper et al. 1988, McConnell and Phipps 1987). The restrictions are arbitrary in the sense that there is no prior knowledge about the functional form.[1] In most empirical applications, these types of restrictions are commonly tested for their validity, but with hedonic models there is no basis in which these restrictions can be evaluated.

Other research has shown that identification problems can be treated with the use of separability assumptions (McConnell and Phipps 1987). However, one cannot test for separability in hedonic models, and McConnell notes that "Our knowledge of behavior is not sufficient for us to argue that separability of the preference function is plausible" (1985b: 107).

Lastly, less severe problems usually exist with multicollinearity among the independent variables in hedonic models (e.g., as house size increases, number of rooms, baths, etc. also increases). Also cited as potential problems are specification of the model, measures of environmental attributes (can households perceive quality differently?), the aggregation of sample estimates from hedonic models to a population, how to derive specific welfare measures from the hedonic model, exactly what the hedonic approach measures in terms of economic welfare (is there double-counting of benefits?), and a household's lack of full information of the housing market. In addition, if individuals cannot distinguish between differences in quality, then market data will not reflect these attributes; that is, the implicit market will not develop (Blomquist 1984). To see how these factors can affect empirical applications, consider the following two examples.

Violations pertaining to the basic assumptions of the Rosen model (e.g., lack of continuous measures for some variables, lumpy combinations inherent with other variables, and the two-dimensional location–choice characteristic), and a household's inability to understand and distinguish among various levels of environmental quality are among potential reasons why Willis and Foster (1983) did not have success in applying the HPA to value water pollution in Massachusetts. But, because of exactly the opposite situation pertaining to these factors, Brookshire et al. (1982) were quite successful in valuing benefits of air quality improvements using an HPA in the Los Angeles area.

Due to these difficulties, researchers caution against the use of the hedonic price approach in evaluating environmental amenities in general at this time, and suggest alternative approaches that control for some of the problems inherent with the hedonic approach and Rosen model. An alternative approach that has seen a successful application is the repeat sales approach. In the only study to date, Mendelsohn (1986) measured economic damages from coastal marine pollution (PCB contamination) in the New Bedford, Massachusetts, area using this method, which is discussed in the following text.

7.4.2. Repeat Sales Approach

Both the repeat sales approach (RSA) and the hedonic price approach share similar theoretical grounds, although mechanically they are somewhat different. Both approaches are based on the notion that property and homes located near a highly valued amenity (e.g., waterfront location on the seacoast, lakeside property, waterfront views, and proximity to the waterfront) are valued more highly compared to similar property without this amenity. Degradations that affect this amenity, in turn, affect the value of the property. For example, water pollution due to toxic chemicals or an oil spill that closes a waterbody to swimming and fishing, can have an impact on the value of adjacent and nearby property. Frequent pollution occurrences and chronic effects are expected to have greater negative impacts of property values relative to a one-time-only pollution event.

The repeat sales approach controls for housing characteristics using a sample of paired observations of residential property (i.e., observations of repeat sales of the same property). By using samples of property that were sold repeatedly (more than once) over the study period, the approach automatically controls for factors (e.g., housing characteristics, location, access) that influence real property values. However, it allows some factors to change over time (e.g., environmental quality, or alternatively, measures of pollution). Because of the nature of the data, both the repeat sales and the hedonic methods control for factors that influence house and property values in different ways in order to measure the effect that changes in environmental quality have on property values. The hedonic approach is not limited to cross-sectional data though. It can be based on time-series and moving cross-section. A hedonic model using time-series data estimated before an environmental change occurred and another model estimated after the change would resemble the repeat sales approach (Mendelsohn 1986).

The repeat sales approach is ideally suited to measure the effect of an environmental change when a chronic degradation or pollution event has occurred at a point in time. Whether or not the RSA can measure short-term effects of one-time events (e.g., a two-week beach closing resulting from high bacteria levels in the summer) or short-term continual occurrences (e.g., repeated beach closings from high bacteria levels throughout a summer season) has not been determined.

The approach requires a sample of residential property that has been sold at two points in time, ideally a sale before a degradation and one after. Factors that can influence property values over time (e.g., inflation, changes in mortgage interest rates, and housing quality improvements) must be controlled. The process results in a data set of paired observations (i.e., observations of the same property unit at two points in time) in which all factors that influence its value are held constant over time, except for degradations of environmental quality.

In general, it is assumed that the value of a house (V) is influenced by its characteristics (z_i), or formally:

$$(7.17) \qquad V = h(z_i; \text{ß}),$$

where ß refers to the parameter estimates. This is the now familiar hedonic price model. The repeat sales approach then compares changes in property value in one time period (V_0) to another (V_1). The model then becomes (the following notation is adapted from Mendelsohn [1986]):

$$(7.18) \qquad V_1 - V_0 = h(z_{i1} - z_{i0}; \text{ß}).$$

In linear form this is:

$$(7.19) \qquad V_1 - V_0 = \text{ß}_0 + \text{ß}_1(z_{11} - z_{10}) + \dots + \text{ß}_i(z_{i1} - z_{i0}), i = 1, \dots, n,$$

where the subscript on z_{ij} refers to housing characteristic i, and j is time ($j = 0$ and 1). When a particular characteristic is the same in both periods, the characteristic and its subsequent effect on housing cancels in the above model. Thus only variables that change across time periods will affect value (i.e., have non-zero coefficients) and belong in the model.

The basic repeat sales model in Equation (7.19) tests the hypothesis that a specific marine pollution event has a negative impact on the absolute (or the percent) change in house prices before and after the event. The primary hypothesis to test is:

$$H_0: \text{ß}_i \geq 0, \text{ versus } H_1: \text{ß}_i < 0,$$

that is, whether the estimated parameters for the variables that represent the change in sale price attributable to pollution are negative versus not negative; if negative, the null hypothesis is rejected and the alternative hypothesis is accepted.

On the basis of the repeat sales approach, aggregate damage estimates attributable to a pollution event are estimated from the coefficients corresponding to the pollution variables multiplied by the total number of single family residences within municipalities included in the study area, times the average sale price of these residences based on sample results; that is, the product of the percentage (or absolute) change in sale price attributable to pollution and the value of all single family homes included in the study area.

7.5. Economic Methods to Value Morbidity and Mortality Health Effects

As noted in Chapters 4 and 6 marine pollution can indirectly cause health effects due to the consumption of contaminated seafood (from pathogens and toxicants) and from water contact activities. Economic damages that result stem from illness (e.g., gastrointestinal disease), and possibly premature death (e.g., increased cancer risk). There are two basic approaches that have developed over the years to measure the costs of illness and death, the human capital (HC) approach (also referred to as the cost-of-illness approach) and the WTP or CV approach (Blomquist 1981; Freeman 1979, 1993; Scitovsky 1982). Both of these approaches are based on different theoretical foundations and provide different measures of the economic damage.

7.5.1. Human Capital or Cost-of-Illness Approach

The HC or cost-of-illness approach is designed to provide a direct measure of the cost of illness or death (Cooper and Rice 1976; Freeman 1979, 1993; Hodgson and Meiners 1982; Rice 1966). Rice is credited with its development. The technique assesses the economic cost as the value of lost earnings had the individual remained in the labor force. When more than one time period is involved, economic costs are equivalent to the present value of lost earnings over the respective time periods. The value of lost earnings can be viewed from the perspective of the individual (employee) or the employer (producer). To the individual, the value of lost earnings is equal to the opportunity costs of his or her labor for the duration of time the individual is not at work. On the basis of opportunity costs, individuals will seek employment to obtain their maximum payment for their labor.

Thus the value of lost earnings is equal to the wage rate times the number of days absent from work. To the employer, the economic costs of illness and death are equal to the value of the lost productivity had the individual remained at work. This can be assessed as the value of the individual's productivity at the margin (i.e., the value of the marginal product of labor). At a profit maximum position, assuming competitive markets, the value of the marginal product of labor is equal to its marginal input costs, here, the wage rate. Thus the value of lost productivity is equal to the value of the marginal product times the period of time that the labor input (employee) is idle from work, or equivalently the period of time the employee is idle from work (days absent) times the wage rate.

There are two costs not included in assessing the economic costs of illness and death. One is the direct costs of medical treatment, and the other concerns the costs of recruitment and training that the employer must spend to fill the vacant position. These direct costs can be added to the above costs to yield an estimate of the economic costs of illness and death. On the basis of the HC approach, economic welfare measures of health effects attributable to marine pollution, then, are the sum of the indirect costs (i.e., either value of lost earnings or value of lost productivity) plus direct costs (i.e., costs of medical treatment and costs for recruitment and training). The advantage of the HC approach is its relative ease of application. As a result it has been used extensively and applied to assess the economic costs attributable to such illnesses as influenza, respiratory and circulatory diseases, and cancer. Another advantage is that the HC approach obtains ex post measures of the costs of health effects and thus is based on observed behavior, in contrast to the WTP approach.

However, there are severe and telling criticisms of the HC approach. Most importantly, its theoretical basis is suspect (i.e., that "earnings reflect an individual's marginal productivity" and are a measure of the value of life [Freeman 1979: 170]). It is also argued that the HC approach ignores the value of leisure, pain, and suffering. Proponents of it argue that it has the ability to consider these, but has not in the past due to a lack of measured data (Rice and Hodgson 1982). Scitovsky (1982) argues that estimates of the HC approach contain errors, where expenditures for hospital care are overstated and expenses for health care professionals, drugs, equipment are understated. In addition errors result in the presence of treatment for multiple conditions (Kenkel 1994, Scitovsky 1982). Hodgson and Meiners (1982) are concerned that some double-counting of expenses of nonpersonal health care services may be present in HC estimates. Furthermore, the HC approach does not include a factor for risk in assessing costs for illness and death (Landefeld and Seskin 1982).

7.5.2. Willingness-to-Pay or Contingent Valuation Approach

The WTP or CV approach proposes that what an individual is willing to pay to reduce the probability of an event such as illness or death determines how individuals value health or sickness and death (Freeman 1979, 1993; Hodgson and Meiners 1982; Jones-Lee 1976, 1982). In addition the WTP or CV approach has been used to value what is referred to as a statistical life (i.e., equal to aggregate economic value for a policy that saves a given number of lives divided by the number of lives saved, meaning a policy that reduces the probability of death by the number of lives saved [b] divided by the number of individuals affected [H; b/H]) (Johansson 1995, Freeman 1979). The notion that individuals not only choose between health-related events based on risk, but also implicitly place values on these events and weigh the tradeoffs between the pluses and minuses of a risky event is a reasonable assumption regarding individuals' preferences. An example is the decision to smoke. This decision involves an evaluation of the tradeoff between the satisfaction derived from smoking against a reduction in life expectancy. The ability to reflect an individual's preference along with the associated ties to utility theory and welfare maximization are reasons why the WTP approach is so conceptually attractive (Freeman 1979).

Disadvantages of the WTP approach are based on its measure and its assumptions. The WTP approach must rely on survey instruments and the CV method. The economic costs of illness, disease, and reductions in life expectancy represent ex ante measures, and as such, the approach suffers from the biases present in the CV approach, namely strategic and hypothetical bias. Applications of the WTP approach based on surveys have been applied in order to value the costs of various diseases and consumption activities, for instance heart and circulatory disease, traffic accidents and seat belt use, air travel safety, mortality, and recently a variety of nonfatal injuries (Rice et al. 1989). Other applications have obtained values of marginal willingness-to-pay associated with job risk based on revealed preferences such as differentials in wage rates using hedonic wage models. This approach avoids many of the shortcomings mentioned here. Critics claim that the WTP approach represents an aggregate level of welfare ignoring issues of welfare distribution, it assumes that individuals have perfect knowledge and can make rational decisions about their utility, and it assumes that the marginal utility of income is constant (Rice and Hodgson 1982). Other problems facing the WTP approach concern individuals' abilities to distinguish a particular outcome from among a set of risky outcomes. If individuals are unable to differentiate among various outcomes of a set of possible outcomes, then the WTP approach may suffer from the lack of being able to single out a specific outcome, for instance, death due to circulatory disease versus death caused by car accidents. The major concern between the two measures (HC vs. WTP) is that they are not simply alternatives, they measure different economic values of health effects.

7.5.3. Adjusted Health Value Approaches

In attempts to reconcile differences between these two different methods to value public health and risk, a number of researchers have proposed adjusted methods (Bailey 1980, Landefeld and Seskin 1982; Kenkel 1994 summarizes this). Landefeld and Seskin (1982) developed an adjusted approach to combine the advantages of both the HC and the WTP approaches: the adjusted WTP/HC approach. This measure allows for the fact that a person may be willing to pay more than his or her forgone income to avoid the risk of some event. The method provides an estimate of an average value of a statistical life, although it is limited to outcomes associated with mortality (Rice and Hodgson 1982).

Empirically the WTP/HC approach is similar to the HC approach except for two points. First, an individual's opportunity cost of investing in risk-reducing activities determines the choice of a discount rate. Since this is measured by the "real" rate of return on investment, after-tax income is used to represent labor income. Second, a risk-aversion factor is included in the adjusted WTP/HC model to reflect the assumption that persons should be at least as risk-averse with respect to loss of life as to other financial assets. Given this latter assumption, the adjusted WTP/HC estimates represent a lower bound of the value of risk reduction activities. Landefeld and Seskin (1982) demonstrate that the adjusted WTP/HC approach produced estimates that were consistently larger than those based on the HC approach (e.g., the adjusted WTP/HC approach estimates for the expected life of a male aged 40–44 is $660,193 versus $108,052 using an HC approach in 1987 dollars). The reason for the difference is because of a discount rate adjusted for a risk-aversion factor.

Bailey (1980) approached the problem from the opposite perspective. Rather than adjusting the HCA estimates upward, he proposes to adjust the WTP estimates downward. Specifically, the WTP estimate is modified to account for future direct taxes and indirect business taxes on labor that would be lost from premature death as well as from prolonged illness (that which requires disability). In addition, WTP estimates are adjusted to account for direct costs of a fatality (and prolonged illness) not paid by the victim's family or heirs.

The issue of trying to resolve differences between both approaches, the HC and the WTP or CV approach, will remain a concern for economists. As evidenced by the two adjustment procedures, we have just begun to address these issues.

7.6. Market Valuation of Rents in the Production Sector

Although the calculation of economic rents (i.e., profit and producer surplus) may seem relatively straightforward, estimating the reduction in rents attributable to marine pollution can be complicated. One of the first problems is having a private business divulge sensitive cost and revenue information. The next problem involves determining the amount of business activity and rents lost due to the occurrence of pollution. This is a two-step procedure: (1) estimate the amount of business activity that would have occurred had marine pollution not been present, and (2) estimate the absolute or percent change in economic rents attributable to marine pollution. One must then project these losses to aggregate economic damage estimates.

The following is a suggested procedure. Conduct a survey of businesses by industry type or standard industrial classification codes in a specific location that experienced a marine pollution problem (i.e., a sample set with pollution). Collect information on costs and revenues for the time period that coincides with the occurrence of marine pollution as well as for previous time periods. A second sample of businesses should be conducted in an area that possesses similar characteristics to the polluted area but has not experienced pollution (i.e., a sample set without pollution). Examination of sales and other factors in previous time periods for both areas will determine whether the businesses are similar in the two areas (e.g., if business growth is the same, if sales are growing at the same rate). This will provide justification for the comparison between areas. If the assumption that businesses in both areas are similar, then the absolute (or percentage) change in sales and economic rents can be determined from taking the difference in sales and rents of the set without pollution less sales and rents of the set with pollution. This absolute or percentage decrease in rents of the sample of businesses can be expanded to all businesses in the area affected by pollution in order to determine the aggregate economic welfare losses attributable to pollution in the production sector in the following manner:

$$\sum_{j=1}^{m} (\sum_{i=1}^{n} \Delta \text{ sales and rents } * \text{ No. firms}_i)_j,$$

for i=1, ... , n industry types, and j=1, ..., m business units, where the expansion is first within industry type and then summed over all industry types in the area affected by marine pollution. Complications arise if a two-sample procedure cannot be conducted or if the sampled businesses are not comparable in scale of operation.

7.7. Note

1. Researchers generally concur that a Box–Cox transformation and estimation procedure whereby the data aid in determining the functional form of hedonic models is the accepted correction (Milon et al. 1984, McConnell and Phipps 1987). However, it should be emphasized that a mechanical procedure to determine the functional form is not a perfect substitution for theoretical and a priori knowledge of a models form (McConnell and Phipps 1987).

7.8. References

Adamowicz, W.L., V. Bhardwaj and B. Macnab. 1993. "Experiments on the Difference Between Willingness to Pay and Willingness to Accept." *Land Economics* 69(4): 416–427.

Bailey, Martin J. 1980. *Reducing Risks to Life: Measurements of the Benefits.* American Enterprise Institute, Washington, DC.

Bateman, I.J. and K.G. Willis (eds.). 1999. *Valuing Environmental Preferences: Theory and Practice of the Contingent Valuation Method in the US, EU, and Developing Countries.* Oxford University Press: New York, NY.

Batie, S.S. and C.C. Mabbs-Zeno. 1985. "Opportunity Costs of Preserving Coastal Wetlands: A Case Study of a Recreational Housing Development." *Land Economics* 61(1): 1–9.

Becker, G.S. 1965. "A Theory of the Allocation of Time." *Economic Journal* 75: 493–617.

Bishop, R.C. and T.A. Heberlein. 1979. "Measuring Values of Extra-Market Goods: Are Indirect Measures Biased?" *American Journal of Agricultural Economics* 61: 926–930.

———. 1986. "Does Contingent Valuation Work?" In Cummings, R.G., B.S. Brookshire and W.D. Schulze (eds.). *Valuing Public Goods: The Contingent Valuation Method.* Rowman and Allanheld: Totowa, NJ: 123–147.

Bishop, R.C., T.A. Heberlein, and M.J. Kealy. 1983. "Contingent Valuation of Environmental Assets: Comparison with a Simulated Market." *Natural Resources Journal* 23 (3): 619–634.

Bishop, R.C., T.A. Heberlein, D. McCollum and M.P. Welsh. 1988. *A Validation Experiment for Valuation Techniques.* School of Natural Resources, University of Wisconsin: Madison, WI.

Bjornstad, D.J. and J.R. Kahn (eds.). 1996. *The Contingent Valuation of Environmental Resources: Methodological Issues and Research Needs.* Edward Elger: Brookfield, VT.

Blomquist, G. 1981. "The Value of Human Life: An Empirical Perspective." *Economic Inquiry* 19 (January): 157–164.

———. 1984. *Measuring the Benefits of Public Goods Provision Using Implicit and Contingent Markets.* Working Paper EF-74-84. Department of Economics, University of Kentucky: Lexington, KY.

Bockstael, N.E. 1984. "Valuing Natural Resource and Environmental Amenities: Can Economic Valuation be Made Defensible?" *Northeastern Journal of Agricultural and Resource Economics* 13(2): 129–137.

Bockstael, N.E. and K.E. McConnell. 1981. "Theory and Estimation of the Household Production Function for Wildlife Recreation." *Journal of Environmental Economics and Management* 8:199–214.

Bockstael, N.E. and I.E. Strand. 1987. "The Effect of Common Sources of Regression Error on Benefit Estimates." *Land Economics* 63(1): 11–20.

Bockstael, N.E., W.M. Hanemann and I.E. Strand (eds.). 1986. *Measuring the Benefits of Water Quality Improvements Using, Recreational Demand Models, Volume II.* Prepared for Office of Policy Analysis, Office of Policy and Resource Management, U.S. Environmental Protection Agency: Washington, DC.

Bockstael, N.E., K.E. McConnell and I.E. Strand. 1988. *Benefits from Improvements in Chesapeake Bay Water Quality, Volume III.* Prepared for Office of Policy Analysis, Office of Policy and Resource Management, U.S. EPA: Washington, DC.

———. 1989. "Measuring the Benefits of Improvements in Water Quality: Chesapeake Bay." *Marine Resource Economics* 6: 1–18.

———. 1991. "Recreation." In Braden, J.B, and C.D. Kolstad (eds.). *Measuring the Demand for Environmental Quality.* North Holland: New York, NY: 227–270.

Bohm, P. 1972. "Estimating the Demand for Public Goods: An Experiment." *European Economic Review* 3: 111–130.

Boyle, K.J., W.H. Desvousges, F.R. Johnson, R.W. Dunford and S.P. Hudson. 1994. "An Investigation of Part–Whole Biases in Contingent Valuation Studies." *Journal of Environmental Economics and Management* 27: 64–83.

Boyle, K.J., F.R. Johnson, D.W. McCollum, W.H. Desvousges, R.W. Dunford and S.P. Hudson. 1996. "Valuing Public Goods: Discrete versus Continuous Contingent-Valuation Responses." *Land Economics* 72(3): 381–396.

Brookshire, D.S. and D.L. Coursey. 1987. " Measuring the Value of a Public Good: An Empirical Comparison of Elicitation Procedures." *American Economic Review* 77(4): 554–566.

Brookshire, D.S., B.C. Ives and W.D. Schulze. 1976. "The Valuation of Aesthetic Preferences." *Journal of Environmental Economics and Management* 3(4): 325–346.

Brookshire, D.S., R.C. d'Arge, W.D. Schulze and M.A. Thayer. 1979. *Methods Development for Assessing Tradeoffs in Environmental Management, Vol. II, Experiments in Valuing Non-Market Goods: A Case Study of Alternative Benefit Measures of Air Pollution Control in the South Coast Air Basin of Southern California.* EPA-600/6-79-001b. Prepared for Office of Research Development, U.S. EPA: Washington, DC.

Brookshire, D.S., R.C. d'Arge, W.D. Schulze and M.A. Thayer. 1981. "Experiments in Valuing Public Goods." In Smith, V.K. (ed.). 1981. *Advances in Applied Microeconomics.* JAI Press: Greenwich, CT: 123 –172.

Brookshire, D.S., M.A. Thayer, W.D. Schulze and R.C. d'Arge. 1982. "Valuing Public Goods: A Comparison of Survey and Hedonic Approaches." *American Economic Review* 72(1): 165–177.

Brookshire, D.S., M.A. Thayer, J. Tschirhart and W.P. Schulze. 1985. "A Test of the Expected Utility Model: Evidence from Earthquake Risks." *Journal of Political Economy* 93: 369–389.

Brown, G.M. and R. Mendelsohn. 1984. "The Hedonic Travel Cost Method." *Review of Economics and Statistics* 66(3): 427–433.

Brown, G.M. and H.D. Pollakowski. 1977. "Economic Valuation of Shoreline." *Review of Economics and Statistics* 59:272–278.

Burt, O.D. and D. Brewer. 1971. "Evaluation of Net Social Benefits from Outdoor Recreation." *Econometrica* 39: 813–827.

Cameron, T.A. 1992. "Combining Contingent Valuation and Travel Cost Data for the Valuation of Nonmarket Goods." *Land Economics* 68(3): 302–317.

Carson, R.T., W.M. Hanemann, R.J. Kopp, J.A. Krosnick, R.C. Mitchell, S. Presser, P.A. Rudd, and

V.K. Smith. 1995. *Temporal Reliability of Estimates from Contingent Valuation*. Discussion Paper 95–37. Resources for the Future: Washington, DC.

Carson, R.T., N.E. Flores, K.M. Martin and J.L. Wright. 1996a. "Contingent Valuation and Revealed Preference Methodologies: Comparing the Estimates for Quasi-Public Goods." *Land Economics* 72(1): 80–99.

Carson, R.T., W.M. Hanemann, R.J. Kopp, J.A. Krosnick, R.C. Mitchell, S. Presser, P.A. Rudd, V.K. Smith, M. Conaway and K. Martin. 1996b. *Referendum Design and Contingent Valuation: The NOAA Panel's No-Vote Recommendation*. Discussion Paper 96-05. Resources for the Future: Washington, DC.

Carson, R.T., W.M. Hanemann, R.J. Kopp, J.A. Krosnick, R.C. Mitchell, S. Presser, P.A. Rudd, V.K. Smith, M. Conaway and K. Martin. 1996c. *Was the NOAA Panel Correct about Contingent Valuation?* Discussion Paper 96-20. Resources for the Future: Washington, DC.

Clawson, M. and J. Knetsch. 1966. *Economics of Outdoor Recreation*. Johns Hopkins University Press: Baltimore, MD.

Cooper, B.S. and D.P. Rice. 1976. "The Economic Cost of Illness Revisited." *Social Security Bulletin* 39(February): 21–36.

Coursey, D.L. and W.D. Schulze. 1986. "The Application of Laboratory Experimental Economics to the Contingent Valuation of Public Goods." *Public Choice* 49(1): 47–68.

Coursey, D.L., J. Hovis and W.D. Schulze. 1987. "The Disparity between Willingness to Accept and Willingness to Pay Measures of Value." *Quarterly Journal of Economics* 102: 679–690.

Cropper, M.L. 1985. "Should the Rosen Model be Used to Value Environmental Amenities?" Chapter 7. In McConnell, K.E., M. Cropper and T.T. Phipps (eds.). *Identification of Preferences in Hedonic Models, Volume I*. Prepared for Office of Policy Analysis, Office of Policy and Resource Management, U.S. EPA: Washington, DC.

Cropper, M.L., L.B. Deck and K.E. McConnell. 1988. "On the Choice of Functional Form for Hedonic Price Functions." *Review of Economics and Statistics* 70: 668–675.

Cummings, R.G., D.S. Brookshire and W.D. Schulze. 1986a. *Valuing Public Goods: The Contingent Valuation Method*. Rowman and Allanheld: Totowa, NJ.

Cummings, R.G., L.A. Cox and A.M. Freeman. 1986b. "General Methods for Benefits Assessment." In Bentkover, J.D., V.T. Covello and J. Mumpower (eds.). *Benefits Assessment: The State of the Art*. Boston, MA: D. Reidel Publishing Co.

Davis, R.K. 1963. "The Value of Outdoor Recreation: An Economic Study of the Maine Woods." Ph.D. Dissertation. Harvard University: Cambridge, MA.

———. 1964. "The Value of Big Game Hunting in a Private Forest." In *Transactions of the 29th North American Wildlife and Natural Resources Conference*. Wildlife Management Institute: Washington, DC.

Desvousges, W.H., S.P. Hudson and M.C. Ruby. 1996. "Evaluating CV Performance: Separating the Light from the Heat." In Bjornstad, D.J. and J.R. Kahn (eds.). *The Contingent Valuation of Environmental Resources: Methodological Issues and Research Needs*. Edward Elger: Brookfield, VT: 117–144.

Desvousges, W.H., V.K. Smith and A. Fisher. 1987. "Option Price Estimates for Water Quality Improvements: A Contingent Valuation Study for the Monongahela River." *Journal of Environmental Economics and Management* 14: 248–267.

Desvousges, W.H., V.K. Smith and M.P. Mc Givney. 1983. *A Comparison of Alternative Approaches for Estimating Recreation and Related Benefits of Water Quality Improvements*. Prepared for Office of Policy Analysis, U.S. Environment Protection Agency: Washington, DC.

Desvousges, W.H., F.R. Johnson, R.W. Dunford, K.J. Boyle, S.P. Hudson and K. W. Wilson. 1993. "Measuring Natural Resource Damages with Contingent Valuation: Tests of Validity." In Hausman, J.A. (ed.). *Contingent Valuation: A Critical Assessment.* North Holland: New York, NY: 91–164.

Diamond, P.A. and J.A. Hausman. 1993. "On Contingent Valuation of Nonuse Values." In Hausman, J.A. (ed.). *Contingent Valuation: A Critical Assessment.* North Holland: New York, NY: 3–38.

———. 1994. "Contingent Valuation: Is Some Number Better than No Number?" *Journal of Economic Perspectives* 8(4): 45–64.

Diamond, P.A. and J.A. Hausman, G.K. Leonard and M.A. Denning. 1993. "Does Contingent Valuation Measure Preferences? Experimental Evidence." In Hausman, J.A. (ed.). *Contingent Valuation: A Critical Assessment.* North Holland: New York, NY: 41–90.

Dillman, D.A. 1978. *Mail and Telephone Surveys: The Total Design Method.* John Wiley & Sons: New York, NY.

Dwyer, J.F., J.R. Kelly and M.D. Bowes. 1977. *Improved Procedures for Valuation of the Contribution of Recreation to National Economic Development.* WRC Research Report No. 128. Water Resources Center, University of Illinois: Urbana, IL.

Edwards, S.F. and G.D. Anderson. 1984. "Land Use Conflicts in the Coastal Zone: An Approach for the Analysis of the Opportunity Costs of Protecting Resources." *Journal of Northeastern Agricultural Economics Council* April: 73–81.

Epp, D.J. and K.S. El-Ani. 1979. "The Effects of Water Quality on Rural Residential Property Values." *American Journal of Agricultural Economics* 61: 529–533.

Fomby, T.B., R.C. Hill and S.R. Johnson. 1988. *Advanced Econometric Methods.* (Corrected edition). Springer-Verlag: New York, NY.

Freeman, A.M. 1979. *The Benefits of Environmental Improvement: Theory and Practice.* Resources for the Future, Inc.: Washington, DC.

———. 1993. *The Measurement of Environmental and Resource Values: Theory and Method.* Resources for the Future, Inc.: Washington, DC

Gordon. I.M. and J.L. Knetsch. 1979. "Consumer's Surplus Measures and the Evaluation of Resources." *Land Economics* 55: 1–10.

Greene, W.H. 1993. *Econometric Analysis.* Macmillan: New York, NY.

Griliches, Z. (ed.). 1971. *Price Indexes and Quality Change.* Harvard University Press: Cambridge, MA.

Hammack, J. and G.M. Brown, Jr. 1974. *Waterfowl and Wetlands: Toward Bioeconomic Analysis.* Johns Hopkins University Press: Baltimore, MD.

Hanemann, W.M. 1981. *Some Further Results on Exact Consumer's Surplus.* Working Paper No. 190. Department of Agricultural and Resource Economics, University of California: Berkeley, CA.

———. 1983. "Marginal Welfare Measures for Discrete Choice Models." *Economic Letters* 13: 129–136.

———. 1984a. "Welfare Evaluation in Contingent Valuation Experiments with Discrete Responses." *American Journal of Agricultural Economics* 66(3): 332–341.

———. 1984b. "Discrete/Continuous Models of Consumer Demand." *Econometrica* 52(3): 541–561.

———. 1985. "Some Issues in Continuous- and Discrete-Response Contingent Valuation Studies." *Northeastern Journal of Agricultural and Resource Economics* 14(1): 5–13.

Harrison, D. and D.L. Rubinfeld. 1978. "Hedonic Housing Prices and the Demand for Clean Air." *Journal of Environmental Economics and Management* 5: 81–102.

Hausman, J.A. (ed.). 1993. *Contingent Valuation: A Critical Assessment.* North Holland: New York, NY.

Hodgson, T.A. and M.R. Meiners. 1982. "Cost-of-Illness Methodology: A Guide to Current Practices and Procedures." *Milbank Memorial Fund Quarterly/Health and Society* 60: 3:429–462.

Hueth, D.L. and E.J. Strong. 1984. "A Critical Review of the Travel Cost, Hedonic Travel Cost, and Household Production Models for Measurement of Quality Changes in Recreational Experiences." *Northeastern Journal of Agriculture and Resource Economics* 13: 187–198.

Hughes, M.A. 1988. "CMS Economist Studies Coastal Development: The Coastal Price Tag." *At Sea, The Delaware College of Marine Sciences Newsletter* 8(3): 1–6.

Johansson, P.O. 1995. *Evaluating Health Risks: An Economic Approach.* Cambridge University Press: New York, NY.

Jones-Lee, M.W. 1976. *The Value of Life.* University of Chicago Press: Chicago, IL.

———. 1982. *The Value of Life and Safety.* Geneva Association Conference Proceedings. North-Holland: New York, NY.

Judge, G.G., W.E. Griffiths, R.C. Hill and T.C. Lee. 1988. *Introduction to the Theory and Practice of Econometrics.* John Wiley & Sons: New York, NY.

Kenkel, D. 1994. "Cost of Illness Approach." In Tolley, G. D. Kenkel and R. Fabian. (eds.). *Valuing Health for Policy: An Economic Approach.* Chicago University Press: Chicago, IL: 42–71.

Knetsch, J.L. and R.K. Davis. 1966. "Comparisons of Methods for Recreation Evaluation." In Kneese, A.V. and S.C. Smith (eds.). *Water Research.* Johns Hopkins University Press: Baltimore, MD.

Knetsch, J.L. and J.A. Sinden. 1984. "Willingness to Pay and Compensated Demand: Experimental Evidence of an Unexpected Disparity in Measures of Value." *Quarterly Journal of Economics* 99: 507–521.

Krutilla, J.V. and A.C. Fisher. 1975. *The Economics of Natural Environments.* Resources for the Future: Washington, DC.

Landefeld, J.S. and E.P. Seskin. 1982. "The Economic Value of Life: Linking Theory to Practice." *American Journal of Public Health* 72(6): 555–566.

Loehman, E.T. 1984. *Willingness to Pay for Air Quality: A Comparison of Two Methods.* Staff Paper 84–18. Department of Agricultural Economics, Purdue University: West Lafayette, IN.

Loehman, E.T. and V.H. De. 1982. "Application of Stochastic Choice Modeling to Policy Analysis of Public Goods: A Case Study of Air Quality Improvements." *Review of Economics and Statistics* 64(3): 474–480.

Loehman, E.T., D.Boldt and K.C. Chaikin. 1981. *Measuring the Benefits of Air Quality Improvements in the San Francisco Bay Area.* SRI Report No. 8962. Stanford Research Institute International: Menlo Park, CA.

Loomis, J.B. 1989. "Test-Retest Reliability of the Contingent Valuation Method: A Comparison of General Population and Visitor Responses." *American Journal of Agricultural Economics* 71(February): 76–84.

———. 1990. "Comparative Reliability of the Dichotomous Choice and Open-Ended Contingent Valuation Techniques." *Journal of Environmental Economics and Management* 18: 78–85.

McConnell, K. 1975. "Some Problems in Estimating the Demand for Outdoor Recreation." *American Journal of Agricultural Economics* 57 (2): 330–334.

———. 1976. "Some Problems in Estimating the Demand for Outdoor Recreation: Reply." *American Journal of Agricultural Economics* 58 (3): 598–599.

———. 1977. "Congestion and Willingness to Pay: A Study of Beach Use." *Land Economics* 53(2): 185–195.

———. 1979. "Values of Marine Recreational Fishing: Measurement and Impact of Measurement." *American Journal of Agricultural Economics* December: 921–925.

———. 1985a. "Hedonic Models: Current Research Issues." Chapter 2. In McConnell, K. E., M. Cropper and T.T. Phipps (eds.). *Identification of Preferences in Hedonic Models, Volume I.* Prepared for Office of Policy Analysis, Office of Policy and Resource Management, U.S. EPA: Washington, DC.

———. 1985b. "Summary and Assessment." Chapter 8. In McConnell, K.E., M. Cropper and T.T. Phipps (eds.). *Identification of Preferences in Hedonic Models, Volume I.* Prepared for Office of Policy Analysis, Office of Policy and Resource Management, U.S. EPA: Washington, DC.

McConnell, K.E. and N.E. Bockstael. 1984. "Aggregation in Recreation Economics: Issue of Estimation and Benefit Measurement." *Northeastern Journal of Agriculture and Resource Economics* 13(2): 181–186.

McConnell, K.E. and T.T. Phipps. 1987. "Identification of Preference Parameters in Hedonic Models: Consumer Demands with Nonlinear Budgets." *Journal of Urban Economics* 22: 35–52.

McConnell, K.E., M. Cropper and T.T. Phipps (eds.). 1985. *Identification of Preferences in Hedonic Models, Volume I.* Prepared for Office of Policy Analysis, Office of Policy and Resource Management, U.S. EPA: Washington, DC.

Mendelsohn, R. 1984. "An Application of the Hedonic Travel Cost Framework for Recreation Modeling to the Valuation of Deer." In Smith, V.K. (ed.). *Advances in Applied Microeconomics.* JAI Press: Greenwich, CT.

———. 1986. *Assessment of Damages by PCB Contamination to New Bedford Harbor Amenities Using Residential Property Values.* Prepared for Ocean Assessment Division, NOAA: Rockville, MD.

Milon, J.W., J. Gressel and D. Mulkey. 1984. "Hedonic Amenity Valuation and Functional Form Specification." *Land Economics* 60(4):378–387.

Mitchell, R.C. and R.T. Carson. 1981. *An Experiment in Determining Willingness to Pay for National Water Quality Improvements.* Draft Report. Prepared for Office of Research and Development, U.S. Environment Protection Agency: Washington, DC.

———. 1984. *A Contingent Valuation Estimate of National Freshwater Benefits.* Final Report. Prepared for Office of Research and Development, U.S. Environmental Protection Agency: Washington, DC.

———. 1989. *Using Surveys to Value Public Goods: The Contingent Valuation Method.* Resources for the Future: Washington, DC.

Mittelhammer, R.C., G.G. Judge and D.J. Miller. 2000. *Econometric Foundations.* Cambridge University Press: Cambridge, MA.

Mueller, D.C. 1979. *Public Choice.* Cambridge University Press: New York, NY.

Nelson, J.P. 1979. "Airport Noise, Location Rent, and the Market for Residential Amenities." *Journal of Environmental Economics and Management* 6: 320–331.

———. 1981. "Three Mile Island and Residential Property Values: Empirical Analysis and Policy Implications." *Land Economics* 57(3): 363–372.

O'Byrne, P.H., J.P. Nelson and J.J. Seneca. 1985. "Housing Values, Census Estimates, Disequilibrium, and the Environmental Cost of Airport Noise: A Case Study of Atlanta." *Journal of Environmental Economics and Management* 12: 169–178.

Ofiara, D.D. 1998. *Quasi-Experimental Evidence in Valuing Nonmarket/Public Goods: Consistency and Behavior of Intertemporal Bids in Contingent Valuation Techniques.* Ph.D Dissertation, PhD Program in Economics, CUNY: New York, NY.

Opaluch, J.J. 1984. "Valuing Natural Resource and Environmental Amenities: Can Economic Valuation Techniques Be Made Defensible: Discussion." *Northeastern Journal of Agricultural and Resource Economics* 13: 138–141.

Parsons, G.R. 1987. "The Opportunity Costs of Residential Displacement Due to Coastal Land Use Restrictions: A Conceptual Framework." *Marine Resource Economics* 4: 111–122.

Portney, P.R. 1994. "The Contingent Valuation Debate: Why Economists Should Care." *Journal of Economic Perspectives* 8(4): 3–18.

Ralph, W.L. 1979. "Estimation of the Demand and Value of Marine Recreational Fishing in Rhode Island with the Household Production Function." M.S. Thesis. University of Rhode Island: Kingston, RI.

Randall, A. and J.P. Hoehn. 1996. "Embedding in Market Demand Systems." *Journal of Environmental Economics and Management* 30: 369–380.

Randall, A., J.P. Hoehn and D.S. Brookshire. 1983. "Contingent Valuation Surveys for Evaluating Environmental Assets." *Natural Resources Journal* (23): 635–648.

Randall, A.B.C. Ives and C. Eastman. 1974. "Bidding Games for Valuation of Aesthetic Environmental Improvements." *Journal of Environmental Economics and Management* 1: 132–149.

Randall, A., O. Grunewald, A. Pagoulatos, R. Ausness and S. Johnson. 1978. "Reclaiming Coal Surface Mines in Central Appalachia: A Case Study of the Benefits and Costs." *Land Economics* 54(4): 427–489.

Ready, R.C., J.C. Buzby and D. Hu. 1996. "Differences between Contingent and Discrete Contingent Value Estimates." *Land Economics* 72(3): 397–411.

Reiling, S.D., K.J. Boyle, M.L. Phillips and M.W. Anderson. 1990. "Temporal Reliability of Contingent Values." *Land Economics* 66(2): 128–134.

Rice, D.P. 1966. *Estimating the Cost of Illness.* Health Economics Series No. 6, Publication No. 947-6. Washington, DC: U.S. Public Health Service.

Rice, D.P. and T.A. Hodgson. 1982. "The Value of Human Life Revisited." Editorial. *American Journal of Public Health* 72(6): 536–537.

Rice, D.P., E.J. Mackenzie and Associates. 1989. *Cost of Injury in the United States: A Report to Congress.* Institute for Health & Aging, University of California, San Francisco, ICA; and Injury Prevention Center, John Hopkins University: Baltimore, MD.

Rich, P.R. and L.J. Moffitt. 1982. "Benefits of Pollution Control on Massachusetts' Housatonic River: A Hedonic Pricing Approach." *Water Resources Bulletin* 18: 1033–1037.

Ridker, R.G. and J.A. Henning. 1967. "The Determinants of Residential Property Values with Special Reference to Air Pollution." *Review of Economics and Statistics* 49: 246–257.

Rosen, H. S. 1974. "Hedonic Prices and Implicit Markets: Product Differentiation in Price Competition." *Journal of Political Economy* 82: 34–55.

Rosenthal, D.H. and J.C. Anderson. 1984. "Travel Cost Models, Heteroskedasticity, and Sampling." *Western Journal of Agricultural Economics* 9(1): 58–65.

Rowe, R.D. and L.G. Chestnut. 1982. *The Value of Visibility.* Abt Books: Cambridge, MA.

———. 1983. "Valuing Environmental Commodities: Revisited." *Land Economics* 59: 404–410.

Rowe, R.D., R.C. d'Arge and D.S. Brookshire. 1980. "An Experiment on the Economic Value of Visibility." *Journal of Environmental Economics and Management* 7(1): 1–19.

Schulze, W.D. and D.S. Brookshire. 1983. "The Economic Benefits of Preserving Visibility in the National Parks of the Southwest." *Natural Resources Journal* 23: 149–173.

Schulze, W.D., R.C. d'Arge and D.S. Brookshire. 1981. "Valuing Environmental Commodities: Some Recent Experiments. *Land Economics* 57:151–172.

Schulze, W.D., G. McClelland, D. Waldman and J. Lazo. 1996. "Sources of Bias in Contingent Valuation." In Bjornstad, D.J. and J.R. Kahn (eds.). *The Contingent Valuation of Environmental Resources: Methodological Issues and Research Needs.* Edward Elger: Brookfield, VT: 97–116.

Scitovsky, A.A. 1982. "Estimating the Direct Costs of Illness." *Milbank Memorial Fund Quarterly/Health and Society* 60(3): 463–491.

Seller, C., J.R. Stoll and J.P. Chavas. 1985. "Validation of Empirical Measures of Welfare Change: A Comparison of Nonmarket Techniques." *Land Economics* 61(2): 156–175.

Shogren, J.F., S.Y. Shin, D.J. Hayes and J.B. Kliebenstein. 1994. "Resolving Differences in Willingness to Pay and Willingness to Accept." *American Economic Review* 84(1): 255–270.

Smith, V.K. and W.H. Desvousges. 1985. "The Generalized Travel Cost Model and Water Quality Benefits: A Reconsideration." *Southern Economic Journal* 52: 371–381.

———. 1986. *Measuring Water Quality Benefits.* Kluwer, Nijhoff Publishing: Boston, MA.

Smith, V.K. and Y. Kaoru. 1990. "Signals or Noise? Explaining the Variation in Recreation Benefit Estimates." *American Journal of Agricultural Economics* May: 419–433.

Smith, V.K. and L.L. Osborne. 1996. "Do Contingent Valuation Estimates Pass a "Scope" Test? A Meta-Analysis." *Journal of Environmental Economics and Management* 31: 287–301.

Smith, V.K. and R.B. Palmquist. 1988. "Models for Valuing Marine Recreational Fishing: An Overview." Department of Economics, North Carolina State University: Raleigh, NC, Unpublished Manuscript..

Smith, V.L. 1986. "Comments." In Cummings, R.G., D.S. Brookshire, and W.D. Schulze (eds.). *Valuing Environmental Goods: An Assessment of the Contingent Valuation Method.* Rowman & Allanheld: Totowa, NJ: 197–204.

Soule, M.E. and K.A. Kohm. 1989. *Research Priorities for Conservation Biology.* Island Press: Washington, DC.

Stevens, T.H., T.A. More and R.J. Glass. 1994. "Interpretation and Temporal Stability of CV Bids for Wildlife Existence: A Panel Study." *Land Economics* 70(3): 355–363.

Strand, I.E., K.E. McConnell and C.G. Hall. 1985. *Measuring Benefits from Improvements in Chesapeake Bay Water Quality, Some Preliminary Findings.* Paper Presented at the 8th Biennial Estuarine Research Federation Meeting, Durham, NH; Dept. of Food & Resource Econ, University of Maryland: College Park, MD.

Strand, I.E., N.E. Bockstael and C.L. Kling. 1986. *Chesapeake Bay Water Quality and Public Beach Use in Maryland.* Paper presented at the Conference on Economics of Chesapeake Bay Management II, Annapolis, MD; Dept. of Food & Resource Econ., University of Maryland: College Park, MD.

Strong, E.J. 1983. "Measuring Benefits of Outdoor Recreation Services: An Application of the Household Production Function Approach to the Oregon Steelhead Sport Fishery." M.S. thesis. Oregon State University: Corvallis, OR.

Thaler, R. and S. Rosen. 1975. "The Value of Saving a Life: Evidence from the Labor Market." In Terleckj, N.E. (ed.). *Household Production and Consumption,* No. 4. Columbia University Press: New York, NY: 265–298.

Thayer, M.A. 1981. "Contingent Valuation Techniques for Assessing Environmental Impacts: Further Evidence." *Journal of Environmental Economics and Management* 8: 27–44.

Tullock, G. 1969. "Problems in the Theory of Public Choice, Social Cost and Government Action." *American Economics Review* 59:189–197.

U.S. Department of Commerce, National Oceanic Atmospheric Administration. 1993. "Natural Resource Damage Assessments: Advance Notice of Proposed Rulemaking, Extension of Comment Period, and Release of Contingent Valuation Methodology Report." *Federal Register* 58(10), Friday, January 15: 4600–4614.

Whitehead, J.C., G.C. Blomquist, T.J. Hoban and W.B. Clifford. 1995. "Assessing the Validity and Reliability of Contingent Values: A Comparison of On-Site Users, Off-Site Users, and Nonusers." *Journal of Environmental Economics and Management* 29: 238–251.

Willis, C.E. and J.H. Foster. 1983. "The Hedonic Approach: No Panacea for Valuing Water Quality Changes." *Journal of the Northeastern Agricultural Economics Council* 12(1): 53–57.

Willis, K.G. 1995. "Contingent Valuation in a Policy Context: The National Oceanic and Atmospheric Administration Report and Its Implications for the Use of Contingent Valuation Methods in Policy Analysis in Britain." In Willis, K.G. and J.T. Corkindale (eds.). *Environmental Valuation: New Perspectives.* CAB International: Wallingford, U.K: 118–143.

Willis, K.G. and J.T. Corkindale (eds.). 1995. *Environmental Valuation: New Perspectives.* CAB International: Wallingford, UK.

Wilman, E.A. 1984. *External Costs of Coastal Beach Pollution: A Hedonic Approach.* Resources for the Future: Washington, DC.

Yang, E.J., R.C. Power and M. Menefee. 1984. *The Use of Economic Analysis in Valuing Natural Resource Damages.* Environmental Law Institute, Washington, DC, Ocean Assessment Division, NOAA: Rockville, MD.

Zeckhauser, R. 1975. "Procedures for Valuing Lives." *Public Policy* 23: 4: 419–464.

PART III

Applications

Application of Economic Techniques to Assess Economic Losses: Examples

8.1. Introduction

This chapter discusses how to apply the economic techniques from the previous chapter. We focus on the most commonly used methods, rather than all possible methods previously discussed. Although this is limiting, there is enough variety and discussion to introduce the reader to application techniques. Several examples are discussed to give the reader some appreciation for the variety of applications and for the levels of creativity and complexity in the approach of these techniques. The chapter is meant to show practitioners, policymakers, environmental scientists, and economists from other fields the breadth and depth of coverage and application. Issues such as study design, sample design, and survey design are not treated, since these are treated in more detail in the literature.

This chapter presents application of the techniques in a "how-to-do" outline. Details concerning sampling plans and techniques and survey design are not treated because they are covered elsewhere (Cochran 1977, Cummings et al. 1986a, Dillman 1978, Ostle and Mensing 1975, Smith and Desvousges 1986) and are beyond the scope of this book. A detailed example will be given for each technique. It is the intent of this chapter to give the reader a "hands-on" background so that one can interpret, understand, and perhaps apply these techniques. It must be recognized that the examples are not comprehensive in dealing with the multitude of problems that can arise in applied studies and are no substitute for field experience and comprehensive readings. The examples are meant to illustrate the techniques, how they have been applied, and how to interpret the results. Actual application and econometric models may be quite different from the examples discussed due to different underlying circumstances. Thus the examples are not to be taken literally. It is suggested that any application be conducted with the consultation of economists experienced with such techniques.

8.2. Contingent Valuation Approach

8.2.1. Application of the Contingent Valuation Approach

Application of the contingent valuation (CV) approach consists of the following elements: survey design elements, CV approach design elements, sampling design elements, and preparation of the data for data entry. To apply the CV approach one should follow the below outline proceeding in a systematic manner through all the steps: begin with the survey design elements, draft a questionnaire, develop the CV questions, and determine a sample plan. It is also helpful to field test the questions and survey instrument prior to administering the survey in the field, such as a pretest.

Survey design elements consist of the following:
- Selection of the survey mode
  - Face-to-face, telephone, or mail
- Design and layout of the survey instrument (questionnaire)
  - Introduction
    - Reason and importance of the study
    - Reason and incentive to participate
    - Stress confidentiality of results and voluntary participation
  - Background information on use—output of activity (success measures)
    - Number and weight of individual species caught fishing
    - Number and weight of individual species bagged hunting
    - Number of species sighted (birds, whales) while birdwatching, whalewatching
    - Number of days spent on a recreational activity (camping, canoeing, hiking, skiing)
    - Number of miles covered on trip (miles hiked, miles boated, etc.)
  - CV approach section (described in detail later)
  - Background—demographic information
    - Years participating in recreational activity—the "public good" in question (in order to establish respondent's experience and familiarity with good)
    - Age of respondent
    - Sex of respondent
    - Ethnic background of respondent
    - Years of education, or last grade completed by respondent
    - Household income before taxes
    - Size of household
    - Number of household members that participate in the recreational activity in question
    - Total amount of leisure time (per week, per month) of respondent
    - Amount of leisure time of respondent spent in participating in recreational activity (or consumption of "good") in question
  - Expenditure patterns
    - Round-trip travel costs (fuel, tolls, parking)
    - Food and beverages
    - Lodging
    - Equipment expenses (variable expenses of equipment)
    - Entrance fees if appropriate

- Guide service fees if appropriate
- Trip information
  - Length of stay
  - Number of people in party that share expenses (pro-rate expenses for respondent)
  - If trip was part of a larger trip or vacation (isolate and pro-rate costs to specific activity in question, e.g., fishing trip represents 15 percent of overall travel and trip costs)
- Cover letter if mail survey
  - Refer to Introduction above
  - Thank respondent(s) for their help
  - Train interviewers
  - Pretest survey instrument
  - Modify survey instrument based on pretest
  - Administer/implement survey
  - Follow up as needed per survey mode
    □ Mail survey (see Dillman 1978)
    □ Initial mailing
    □ Postcard follow-up in one to two weeks
    □ Second mailing to those not responding
    □ Third mailing to those not responding
    □ Telephone survey (see Dillon 1978)
      ■ Three to four callbacks

Contingent valuation approach elements consist of the following:
- Description of market, market setting
- Description of "good" to be valued
- Development of valuation questions
  - Open-ended CV questions: maximum WTP to consume an incremental unit of "good"
  - Open-ended CV questions: minimum WTA to give up an incremental unit of "good"
  - Iterative bidding question–yes/no responses to preset prices for a specific unit of the "good." The price is changed (increased-WTP, decreased-WTA) by some increment and the question repeated. This process is repeated in an iterative manner until a "no" response is reached and the process is stopped.
  - Closed-ended CV questions—early versions: involved voting (yes/no) on a preset price for a specific unit of the "good." The question is only asked once per individual.
  - Closed-ended CV questions—current version: current versions involve splitting the sample into several equal parts, assigning a different random price for each group and then asking the individual to vote (yes/no) for a specific level of the good at the stated price, where all individuals face the same quantity of the good but with different prices.
  - Variations of the preceding five items using predetermined starting points, and/or a payment card (see Mitchell and Carson 1989)
- Selection of the mode of payment (payment vehicle) used in valuation question(s)
  - Taxes, utility fees, user fees, prices, or contribution to a special exclusive fund

- Selection of unit economic value is to be specified in
    - $/person, $/household
    - $/year, $/month, $/trip, $/visit

Sampling elements include:
- Definition of the study area
- Choice of unit of respondent
    - Per person, per visitor, per household
- Selection of sampling plan
    - Simple random sample
    - Stratified random sample

The step following implementing or administering the survey and before analysis involves preparing the data for entry, editing the questionnaires for errors, and then inputting the data (usually computer entry and verification).

8.2.2. Contingent Valuation Approach—Examples

8.2.2.1 Benefits of Water Quality Improvements in the Monongahela River Basin— Open-Ended and Iterative Bidding CV Experiment

One of the best examples of the CV approach is a study by Desvousges, Smith, and McGivney (DSM) (1983) to estimate the economic surplus resulting from improvements in freshwater quality. The study used state-of-the-art concepts at the time in advancing the market, and especially the "good" to be assessed. As a result, key sections of the survey instrument used in the study are reproduced along with a discussion that draws heavily from DSM pertaining to the individual sections.

In Appendix B, Part B of their survey is reproduced. The section (Part B) discusses the methods used to measure benefit of water quality changes; it contains the description of the hypothetical market setting, the "good" to be valued, and the payment vehicle, and it develops the market valuation experiment. Because the hypothetical market is in fact hypothetical, care must be taken in designing a market that appears both realistic and credible to the respondent and represents a concept that can be easily understood. These efforts will assist in reducing hypothetical bias and increase the realism of the CV experiment.

The background section labeled "B-1" in Appendix B introduces the conceptual setting of the hypothetical market (refer to the first two paragraphs in B-1); then the "good" to be valued is introduced and described in the last two paragraphs. Note that these last two paragraphs refer to a "water quality ladder," in describing the "good"-"water quality" (see Figure 8.1). A key advancement in many recent CV experiments involves the use of graphic aids to assist in describing the "good." In some cases photographs are used (see Brookshire et al. 1979) and in others, diagrams (see Mitchell and Carson 1981, 1989). The "water quality ladder" used by DSM was developed at Resources for the Future for a study by Mitchell and Carson (1981). It depicts the four major standards of freshwater quality as set forth by the U.S. Environmental Protection Agency (EPA): boatable, fishable, swimmable, and drinkable, and the ladder places these standards on a 1 to 10 scale (called anchoring). The significance of this "ladder" is that it allows the respondent to understand the link between water quality and recreational activities in a straightforward visual diagram. The combination of this graphic aid and the description in the text of the

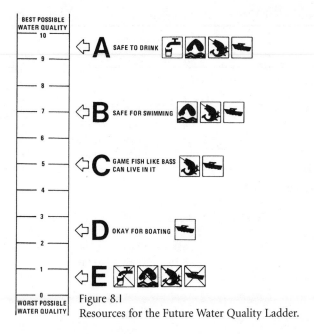

Figure 8.1
Resources for the Future Water Quality Ladder.

questionnaire (the last two paragraphs of "B-1" in Appendix B) helps maintain a realistic and credible description of the "good."

The next parts of the survey instrument (section B-1: a, b, and c) add to the realism of the overall experiment by allowing the respondent to become familiar with the "good" by determining a rating for the water quality of the Monongahela River (the river in the study area) or a particular section of it with which the respondent had some experience.

The next section of the questionnaire, labeled "B-2" is included because one objective of the study was to obtain economic values relating to both "use" (see B-2.a.), and "nonuse" values (i.e., option value) (see B-2.b.), and existence value (see B-2.c.).[1]

The next section (Introduction to Question B-3 in Appendix B) introduces the payment vehicle used by DSM, which is higher taxes or higher prices (see the first two paragraphs of B-3). The third paragraph was included in order to have the respondents focus on the specific good in the experiment and the "payment" for that good; that is, the economic value elicited from them. The fourth paragraph reminds respondents of their present and future uses of the river, and the last paragraph establishes the present average water quality of the river as a whole (i.e., it establishes the base from which the CV experiment begins).

The next sections (B-3.a to B-3.e) contain the actual market valuation experiment. The hypothetical goods that were valued involved (1) avoiding a decrease in water quality (i.e., a movement from "D" to "E" on the water quality ladder); (2) an increase in water quality from boatable to fishable (i.e., a movement from "D" to "C"); and (3) a further increase in water quality from fishable to swimmable (i.e., a movement from "C" to "B"). A number of types of valuation questions were used by DSM to examine obvious differences and specific biases, such as starting-point bias. The various types of valuation questions used were: (1) an open-ended question (the first set of B-3 questions); (2) an open-ended question together with a payment card (on which an array of annual amounts from $0 to $775/year were listed) (the second set of B-3 questions); (3) an iterative bidding question, using $25 as a starting point (third set of B-3 questions) as well as $125 as a starting point.

Table 8.1. Estimated User Values—Protect Bids and Outliers Excluded.

	User Only			Combined		
	Mean	S.D.	N	Mean	S.D.	N
ITERATIVE BIDDING FRAMEWORK						
$25 starting point (C)						
D to E	6.59	12.59	19.00	2.16	7.73	58.00
D to C	4.21	7.68	19.00	1.38	4.76	58.00
C to B	5.00	7.99	19.00	1.64	5.08	58.00
D to B	10.53	14.43	19.00	3.45	9.52	58.00
Combined: all levels	17.11	25.13	19.00	5.60	16.28	58.00
ITERATIVE BIDDING FRAMEWORK						
$125 starting point (D)						
D to E	36.25	58.98	16.00	12.08	37.52	48.00
D to C	20.31	42.67	16.00	6.77	25.98	48.00
C to B	20.00	42.82	16.00	6.66	25.99	48.00
D to B	48.75	87.87	16.00	16.25	54.81	48.00
Combined: all levels	135.11	85.00	16.00	28.33	87.90	48.00
DIRECT QUESTION (B)						
D to E	19.71	37.85	17.00	6.57	23.38	51.00
D to C	21.18	42.22	17.00	7.06	25.93	51.00
C to B	10.00	29.10	17.00	3.33	17.14	51.00
D to B	31.18	64.63	17.00	10.39	39.46	51.00
Combined: all levels	50.88	77.46	17.00	16.96	50.07	51.00
DIRECT QUESTION: PAYMENT CARD (A)						
D to E	19.71	34.30	17.00	6.20	20.99	54.00
D to C	30.88	74.57	17.00	9.72	43.45	54.00
C to B	19.71	49.42	17.00	6.20	28.68	54.00
D to B	51.18	122.88	17.00	16.11	71.65	54.00
Combined: all levels	70.88	127.61	17.00	22.31	77.59	54.00

Note: S.D. refers to standard deviation, and N the number of observations.
Source: Desvousges et al. (1983).

Estimates of use values that represent marginal surplus benefits per household for specific water quality changes (in 1981$) are in Table 8.1. Examining the results for the "direct question," shows that users' valued a decrease in water quality (D to E) at $19.71/household, and increase in water quality to fishable (D to C) at $21.18/household, an additional increase in water quality to swimmable levels (C to B) at $10/household; a total value for the increase in water quality from boatable to swimmable (D to B) at $31.18/household per year. Expansion of these estimates on the basis of the sampling design or estimated number of users would follow for this specific study area, a step that DSM did not address.

8.2.2.2. Benefits of Water Quality Improvements in the Chesapeake Bay— Closed-Ended CV Experiment

Bockstael et al. (1988, 1989) conducted a study that assessed the economic value of improvements of water quality in the Chesapeake Bay based on a closed-ended CV question where random dollar amounts were split across several sample groups. Many recent

CV studies have adopted this question format. Households were randomly sampled and asked: "Do you consider the water quality in the Chesapeake to be acceptable or unacceptable for swimming and/or other water activities?"

For those households that said it was unacceptable, the following question was asked: "Would you be willing to pay ($A) in extra state or federal taxes per year if the water quality were improved so that you found it acceptable to swim in the Chesapeake?"

The researchers varied the amount of money specified by ($A) randomly from $5 to $50. A yes/no response to this valuation question was then analyzed based on a logit model for discrete-choice responses from which economic welfare was estimated following Hanemann (1984). Specifically the following logit model was estimated:

$$\text{Prob(accept tax to achieve swimmable water)} = \exp(x'\text{ß}) \, / \, [1+ \exp(x'\text{ß})],$$

where $x'\text{ß} = a + a_2 D_1 - \text{ß}_1 A - \text{ß}_2 D_2 A$, a represents a constant term ($a_1 - a_0$ in their article), D_1 a binary variable for users ($D_1 = 1$ if users, 0 otherwise), A represents the dollar amount of the hypothetical tax in the closed-ended question, $D_2 A$ represents the product of $D_2 a$ binary variable for white (=1 if white, 0 otherwise) versus nonwhite and A (i.e., a slope shift term that must be subtracted from the ß_1 coefficient for the racial composition of white, see example below), and a, a_2, and ß's represent the parameter estimates. The estimated equation was:

$$x'\text{ß} = 0.385 + 1.084^*D_1 - 0.043^*A - 0.035^*D_2 A,$$
$$\quad\;\; (0.222) \quad (0.202) \qquad (0.009) \qquad (0.007)$$

where the standard errors are in parentheses.

The expected value of the dollar amount of the hypothetical tax was computed to determine average willingness to pay as $E[A] = a/\text{ß}$. Results of estimated net economic value were determined by participation status and racial composition. For example, for "White Users" $E[A] = (0.385 + 1.084) / (0.043 - 0.035) = \$183.63$, and for "Nonwhite, Nonusers" $E[A] = (0.385) / (0.043) = \$8.95$. Overall these results along with estimates of standard deviations (in parentheses) in 1984 dollars were (see Bockstael et al. 1988 for greater detail than their article):

	White	Nonwhite
User	$183.63	$34.16
	(55.12)	(10.40)
Nonuser	$48.13	$8.95
	(10.25)	(2.53)

Thus, a white user is willing to pay an average of $183.63 per household and a nonwhite $34.16 (1984$) for improving the water quality in Chesapeake Bay so that it is swimmable. Estimated standard deviations were used to derive aggregate benefit estimates for a pessimistic case (minus 1 standard deviation from the average case), an average case, and an optimistic case (plus 1 standard deviation from the average case). For example, for the category "white users" the aggregate estimate for an average case was ($183.625^*304.079 thousand individuals = ~$55,838 (thousand), for an optimistic case $55,838 +

$55.12*304.079 thousand individuals = ~$72,595 (thousand), and for a pessimistic case $55,838 − $55.12*304.079 thousand individuals = ~$39,081. Overall expansion of the sample to represent the entire Baltimore–Washington SMSA (Standard Metropolitan Statistical Area) population led to an aggregate benefit estimate of $83.6 million for an average case, $106,976 for the optimistic case, and $60,275 million for the pessimistic case (1984$).

8.3. Travel Cost Approach

8.3.1. Application of the Travel Cost Approach

Application of the travel cost approach consists of the following elements: survey design elements, travel cost approach (TCA) elements, sampling design elements, and preparation of the data for data entry. To apply the travel cost approach one should use the following outline proceeding in a systematic manner through all the steps beginning with the survey design elements, drafting a questionnaire, developing questions to collect information necessary to the TCA (see below), and determining a sample plan. It is also helpful to pretest the survey instrument prior to application.

Survey design elements consist of the following:
- Selection of the survey mode
  - Face-to-face, telephone, or mail
- Design and layout of the survey instrument
  - Introduction
    - Reason and importance of the study
    - Reason and incentive to participate
    - Stress confidentiality of results, and voluntary participation
  - Background information on use–output of activity (success measures)
    - Number and weight of individual species caught fishing
    - Number and weight of individual species bagged hunting
    - Number of species sighted (birds, whales) while birding, whalewatching
    - Number of days spent on a recreational activity (camping, canoeing, hiking, skiing)
    - Number of miles covered on trip (miles hiked, miles canoed, etc.)
  - TCA section covered in detail later
  - Background—demographic information
    - Years coming to site
    - Years participating in recreational activity—"the public good" in question
    - Age of respondent
    - Sex of respondent
    - Ethnic background of respondent
    - Years of education, or last grade completed of respondent
    - Household income before taxes
    - Size of household
    - Number of household members that participate in recreational activity in question
    - Total amount of leisure time (per week, per month) of respondent
    - Amount of leisure time of respondent spent in participating in recreational activity in question

- Cover letter if mail survey
  - Refer to Introduction above
  - Thank respondent(s) for their help
  - Train interviewers
  - Pretest survey instrument
  - Modify survey instrument based on pretest
  - Implement survey
  - Follow up as needed, per survey mode
    - Mail survey (refer to Dillman 1978)
      - Initial mailing
      - Postcard follow-up in one to two weeks
      - Second mailing to those not responding
      - Third mailing to those not responding
    - Telephone survey (Dillman 1978)
      - Three to four callbacks

Travel cost approach elements consist of the following:
- Use–participation patterns corresponding to the activity or "good" in question
  - Frequency of trips (number of trips if individual observation approach or number of site-specific trips and alternative substitute-site trips if zonal approach) in a selected time period (per month, per year)
    - Number of species-specific trips (blue marlin, striped bass, deer, goose)
    - Number of activity-specific trips (fishing, birdwatching, hunting, canoeing)
  - Expenditure patterns
    - Round-trip travel costs (fuel, tolls, parking)
    - Food and beverages
    - Lodging
    - Equipment expenses (variable expenses of equipment)
    - Entrance fees, if appropriate
    - Guide service fees, if appropriate
  - Trip information
    - Round-trip travel distance
    - Round-trip travel time
    - On-site time
    - Length of stay
    - Number of people in party that share expenses (prorate expenses for respondent)
    - If trip was part of a larger trip or vacation (isolate and prorate costs to specific activity in question, e.g., fishing trip represents 15 percent of overall travel and trip costs)

Sampling design elements include:
- Definition of the study area
- Choice of unit of respondent
  - Per person, per visitor, per household
- Selection of sampling plan
  - Simple random sample
  - Stratified random sample

The step that follows implementing or administering the survey and precedes the analysis involves preparing the data for entry, editing the questionnaires for errors, and then inputting the data (usually computer entry and verification).

The main difference between the zonal approach and the individual observation approach of the TCA concerns the formulation and specification of travel cost demand models. The zonal approach uses per capita averages that correspond to distinct zones on the basis of proximity to the recreation site in question. The "zone" referred to in this approach could be a geographic area (e.g., municipality, county), region (e.g., northwest corner of state, Midwest), or an area defined by political boundaries (e.g., voting districts), or by some other means. The individual observation approach avoids the restrictive assumptions and model specification of the zonal-TCA and allows for flexibility in measuring economic benefits of a specific site, as well as a specific recreational activity.

A basic specification of a travel cost demand model is:

$$T_{ij} = f(X1, X2, X3, X4, X5, X6, X7)_{ij},$$

where T_{ij} is the number of trips by the *ith* individual (or individuals from the *ith* zone) to the *jth* site, *X1* is the money costs of the trip (i.e., sum of expenses of travel, food and beverages, lodging, variable equipment, and entrance fees), *X2* the distance to the site or the opportunity costs of time in travel (round-trip), *X3* on-site time or the opportunity costs of on-site time, *X4* household income, *X5* a vector of socioeconomic attributes (e.g., education, age, ethnic background), *X6* a vector of other pertinent variables such as years of experience, measures of success (e.g., catch rate for sportfishing), and a measure of congestion (e.g., number of people encountered at the site), and *X7* money costs to alternative substitute sites (sometimes the number of trips to alternative sites is included instead of costs, and sometimes a series of binary variables (0,1) are included to represent visits to alternative sites).

The method as expressed is a system of demand equations, one for each site, thus incorporating the effects of multiple sites on trip behavior (Burt and Brewer 1971). Prices of the alternative substitute sites (i.e., *X7*) must be included within these equations to avoid cross-price variable bias (Burt and Brewer 1971). In some cases the model is estimated as a single equation with binary-shift variables to account for the site if based on individual observations (McConnell and Strand 1981). If a zonal average approach is used the above variables are specified in terms of per capita averages per zone (e.g., per capita trips from the *ith* zone to the *jth* site, per capita trip costs, per capita income and so on [Clawson and Knetsch 1966, Freeman 1979]). Using this zonal average approach will cause the disturbance term to be heteroscedastic across zones (Rosenthal and Anderson 1984). Variable transformations or weights are suggested remedies. However, as noted in Chapter 5, if travel cost demand models are based on individual observations, as opposed to a zonal average, the model and estimation can be simplified (Bockstael et al. 1986).

Two common specifications of the above travel cost demand model are the linear and semi-log model. The linear model is:

(8.1) $T_i = \beta_0 + \beta_1 X1_i + \beta_2 X2_i + \beta_3 X3_i + \beta_4 X4_i + \beta_5 X5_i + \beta_6 X6_i + \beta_7 X7_i + e_i,$

where the variables are described above for the *ith* individual, the ßs are the parameter estimates, and *e* is the error term, which is assumed to be normally distributed with a mean value of zero and a constant variance. The semi-log model is:

$$(8.2) \qquad \ln(T_i) = ß_0 + ß_1 X1_i + ß_2 X2_i + ß_3 X3_i + ß_4 X4_i + ß_5 X5_i + ß_6 X6_i + ß_7 X7_i + e_i,$$

where *ln( )* is the natural logarithm operator.

The above models are then estimated by ordinary least squares (OLS) regression techniques. Generalized least squares (GLS) techniques are used in cases where the model must be corrected for heteroscedasticity. Current work in recreational demand behavior has shown that the above travel cost demand models will result in biased parameter estimates because recreational decision making involves a yes/no choice and thus does not consider nonparticipants (McConnell and Bockstael 1984, McConnell and Kling 1986). Theorists maintain that recreation demand behavior is more aptly based on models that consider censored or truncated sample data. A standard econometric model that accounts for participants and nonparticipants based only on a sample of individuals (i.e., truncated sample data) is as follows:

$$T_i = X_{ij}ß + e_i, \text{ if } X_{ij}ß + e_i > 0$$

$$= 0, \qquad \text{if } X_{ij}ß + e_i \leq 0,$$

where X_{ij} refers to the *jth* variable for the *ith* individual, and *e* is the error term, which is assumed normal with zero mean and constant variance. This model is the familiar Tobit model and provides unbiased parameter estimates compared to OLS estimates based on a truncated sample (Greene 1993, Judge et al. 1988). Discussion of these more complex recreation demand models as well as more sophisticated travel cost demand estimation issues are beyond the scope of this book. However, in any specific application these issues must be examined.

8.3.2. Travel Cost Approach—Examples

Several examples are presented here to illustrate the versatility of the TCA.

8.3.2.1. Recreational Fishing for Winter Flounder in Rhode Island— Individual Observation Approach

From a survey of recreational anglers fishing for winter flounder in Rhode Island, McConnell (1979) estimated the following travel cost demand model based on an individual or unit observation approach:

$$t_i = 7.1 - 0.085^* X1_i + 0.015^* X2_i + 0.012^* X3_i, \text{Adjusted } R^2 = 0.11, n = 56,$$
$$ (-2.58) \qquad (0.14) \qquad (0.42)$$

where t_i is the number of trips of the *ith* individual, *X1* is the cost per trip, *X2* is the number of fish caught per trip, and *X3* is the number of years fished (a proxy for experience).

The numbers in parentheses are t-statistics and the estimated model explains 11 percent of the variation based on a sample of 56 anglers. The signs on the three variables are consistent with expectations: The cost per trip is inversely related to the number of trips, and both catch rate and experience have a positive influence on trips. Using the mean value of trips (6.3) and the following formula for OCS: OCS = $(t_i)^2/-2\beta$, OCS is estimated at $233 per angler for the 1978 season. This formula is defined for a linear demand curve, where the number of trips is a function of the price of trips, here the cost per trip, therefore the coefficient for trip cost is used in the formula: $(6.3)^2/-2(-0.085)$. The formula for calculating OCS is a rule-of-thumb used to estimate the area under a linear demand curve (Bockstael and Strand 1987). It is equal to the area under a linear demand curve and above price for an individual (e.g., it equals the shaded area a in Figures 2.1 and 2.3 of Chapter 2, and is approximated by the area of a triangle). Because the OCS measure is in terms of one angler, it is necessary to sum over individuals in order to determine a measure of aggregate surplus benefits for these types of public sector goods and services. On the basis of the estimated number of anglers in Rhode Island in 1978, aggregate surplus benefits for winter flounder fishing trips become $103,685 (i.e., $233/angler * 445 anglers).

We can extend this example to account for the effects of marine pollution for illustrative purposes. Suppose it is assumed that the presence of marine pollution results in fewer trips taken, (e.g., a mean value of only 4 trips—a 27% reduction in trips/angler), and a 30 percent reduction in angler participation (445 * 0.70 = 312 anglers). On the basis of the previous estimated model, annual surplus benefits become $94/angler, and aggregate surplus benefits are $29,328. The conclusion would be that the occurrence of such a marine pollution event resulted in lost surplus benefits equal to $139/angler and $74,357 for all anglers. Hence the above formula for OCS can be modified to account for the change in the initial state to the final state; that is, OCS = $[(t_i^1)^2-(t_i^0)^2] / -2\beta$, where t_i^1 refers to the mean number of trips associated with the final state (post-change level) and t_i^0 the number of trips associated with the initial state (prechange level) (e.g., $[(4)^2-(6.3)^2] / [-2(-0.085)] = -\$139$/angler). The above is an oversimplification and one should ideally estimate two separate travel cost demand curves, one for the initial state and one for the final state, and then estimate the OCS for each where the net change in OCS = $OCS^1 - OCS^0$.

8.3.2.2. Travel Cost Demand—Zonal Approach

A simplified travel cost demand model using the zonal approach is illustrated in Table 8.2 from an example in Dwyer et al. (1977).

The following trip demand equation represents this data.

$$t_{ij} = 10 - X1_{ij},$$

where t_{ij} is per capita trips from origin i to site j and $X1_{ij}$ is the per capita trip cost. If we use the weighted average per capita trip estimate of 5.67, OCS is estimated at $16.07 per capita trips using the above formula for linear demand, $x^2/-2\beta$, $[5.67^2/-2(-1) = \$16.07]$. Aggregated to the three zones, OCS is $546,531 (i.e., $16.07 * 34,000).

Table 8.2. Travel Cost Data Based on Zonal Approach.

Zone of Origin	Population	No. of Trips	Trips per Capita	Trip Cost	Total Cost
A	1,000	2,000	2	$8	$16,000
B	2,000	8,000	4	$6	$48,000
C	3,000	24,000	8	$2	$48,000
Total	6,000	34,000	–	–	$112,000
Weighted Avg.	–	5.67	–	–	$18.67
					(per capita trip cost)

8.3.2.3. Travel Cost Demand for Recreational Partyboat Fishing in California—Zonal Approach

The next example is of an application of a TCA using a zonal approach, for recreational fishing trips on partyboats. Huppert and Thompson (1984) estimate a per capita travel cost demand model for seven sites in California (San Diego, Newport, Los Angeles, Santa Monica, Santa Barbara, Morro Bay, and San Francisco), on the basis of trip information from 96 residence zones defined by zip codes. Per capita measures were used as the unit of observation of each variable in each zone. The following semi-log model was estimated for each site:

San Diego $\ln(t_{ij}) = -4.01 - 0.099 {}^{*} X1_{ij} + 0.000059 {}^{*} X2_{ij}$, Adjusted $R^2 = 0.64$,
(-8.80) (1.87) $n = 43$;

Newport $\ln(t_{ij}) = -7.54 - 0.025 {}^{*} X1_{ij} + 0.000073 {}^{*} X2_{ij}$, Adjusted $R^2 = 0.09$,
(-0.87) (1.67) $n = 25$;

Los Angeles $\ln(t_{ij}) = -3.95 - 0.11 {}^{*} X1_{ij} + 0.0000044 {}^{*} X2_{ij}$, Adjusted $R^2 = 0.13$,
(-2.36) (0.13) $n = 27$;

Santa Monica $\ln(t_{ij}) = -10.10 - 0.13 {}^{*} X1_{ij} - 0.000027 {}^{*} X2_{ij}$, Adjusted $R^2 = 0.26$,
(-2.38) (-2.68) $n = 46$;

Santa Barbara $\ln(t_{ij}) = -4.55 - 0.12 {}^{*} X1_{ij} - 0.000058 {}^{*} X2_{ij}$, Adjusted $R^2 = 0.60$,
(-6.72) (-7.96) $n = 58$;

Morro Bay $\ln(t_{ij}) = -0.82 - 0.055 {}^{*} X1_{ij} - 0.000092 {}^{*} X2_{ij}$, Adjusted $R^2 = 0.60$,
(-3.21) (-0.82) $n = 12$; and

San Francisco $\ln(t_{ij}) = -5.39 - 0.062 {}^{*} X1_{ij} + 0.000069 {}^{*} X2_{ij}$, Adjusted $R^2 = 0.89$,
(-10.62) (4.18) $n = 25$;

where t_{ij} is the number of partyboat fishing trips per capita from the *ith* zone to the *jth* site, $\ln(\ )$ is the natural logarithm operator, *X1* the per capita travel cost from the *ith* zone to the *jth* site, and *X2* median family income of the *jth* zone. *T*-statistics appear in parentheses.

We next examine consumer surplus estimates based on the following rule of thumb

Table 8.3. Estimated OCS Based on a Travel Cost Model–Zonal Approach

	OCS/trip	No. of trips	Aggregate OCS
San Diego	$10.10	156,737	$1,583,044
Newport	40.00–10.44	26,042	271,878
Los Angeles	9.09	104,360	948,632
Santa Monica	7.69	112,464	864,848
Santa Barbara	8.33	96,913	807,285
Morro Bay	18.18	33,973	617,629
San Francisco	16.13	77,882	1,256,237
Other areas	10.44	177,967	1,858,069
Total	–	786,338	8,207,622

formula for semi-log demand models, $t_i/-\beta$, where t_i is trips and ß the travel cost parameter estimate. This formula approximates the area under a semi-log demand curve (Bockstael and Strand 1987). The formula gives an estimate of OCS for trips taken, and an estimate of OCS per trip is obtained by dividing the estimate by t, $[(t/-B) * (1/t) = 1/-B]$. Estimates of OCS per trip are shown in Table 8.3.

Because the OCS/trip estimate for Newport is greater than the rest by at least an order of magnitude, Huppert and Thompson use an estimate of OCS for "Other Areas" (i.e., Oceanside and Monterey) in which insignificant numbers of anglers were sampled. On the basis of the zonal approach aggregate OCS is the product of OCS per capita trip times the number of trips taken in the *jth* site. (Compare this to the aggregation of OCS based on the individual observation approach shown in Section 8.3.1.)

These examples are meant to give the reader an appreciation of the mechanics of the TCA and the versatility of the TCA. The examples are only illustrative and these specific numbers for these study areas cannot be interpreted strictly as recommended numbers for other areas. Other issues must also be considered in any application, and the examples given have been simplified for the purposes of this book.

8.3.2.4. Benefits for Water Quality Improvements in Chesapeake Bay— Varying Parameter Model

The study described earlier by Bockstael, McConnell, and Strand (1988, 1989) (BMS) in Section 8.2.2.2 used both a CV approach and travel cost demand model, specifically a VPM, to examine the benefits from water quality improvements in Chesapeake Bay and to compare the two approaches. Their application of the VPM will be discussed here. They examined the benefits of water quality improvements for three recreational activities: beach use, pleasure boating, and sportfishing. Hence, similar forms of the VPM were estimated and net economic value was then derived. In general the following linear travel demand model was estimated for the first stage:

(8.3) $x_i = \beta_{0i} + \beta_{1i}p_i + \beta_{si}p_s + \beta_{yi}y + \varepsilon, i = 1, ..., n,$

where x_i is the number of trips to the *ith* site, p_i is the own site price, p_s is the price of the nearest substitute site, y represents money income, the ßs represent the estimated parameters, and ε is the error term. In the second stage the estimated parameters, β's, were assumed to be linear functions of water quality at the *ith* site, the product of nitrogen and phosphorous (TNP) and estimated as follows:

(8.4a) $\beta_{0i} = a_0 + a_1 q_i,$

(8.4b) $\beta_{1i} = c_0 + c_1 q_i,$

(8.4c) $\beta_{si} = d_0 + d_1 q_i,$

(8.4d) $\beta_{yi} = e_0 + e_1 q_i,$

where a, c, d, and e represent the estimated parameters in the respective models and q_i the water quality measure. The reason why the quality measure is a product term and not individual terms for nitrogen and phosphorous was to eliminate multicollinearity estimation problems, because high collinearity between nitrogen and phosphorous would make it difficult to separate individual nutrients' effects from one another. Besides the product term can capture the interactive nature between both nutrients. The choice of the regression model BMS used in the first stage was a Tobit model to account for censored dependent data (i.e., the fact that a large number of 0's occurs).

Beach Use. Data for this application comes from a survey of 484 individuals at 11 public beaches on the western shore of Maryland over the summer of 1984. For the first stage Tobit models of Equation 8.3 were estimated. The results of the first stage regression equations are contained in Table 8.4. Demand coefficients for own-price (travel cost) all have a negative sign as expected, and most are statistically significant. The second stage regression models were estimated via a Generalized Least Squares (GLS) model with weights equal to $1/S.E.(\beta)$; that is, the inverse of the standard error (SE) of the parameter estimate (β) for each beach to account for heteroscedasticity problems. These results yielded:

own-site price: $\beta_{1i} = -0.308 - 0.0002 * TNP_i,$
$\qquad\qquad\qquad (-0.04) \quad (-2.22)$

constant: $\beta_{0i} = -2.66 - 0.00016 * TNP_i,$
$\qquad\qquad\qquad (-1.1) \quad (-0.001)$

where *t*-statistics are in parentheses. The main purpose of these estimated equations is to derive benefit estimates.

Pleasure Boating. The data for this application comes from a mail survey of 2,515 registered boat owners, which resulted in 496 observations of boaters who used trailers to access boating sites (this characteristic was to allow boaters to visit different sites). Results of the first stage Tobit demand models are contained in Table 8.5. Estimated parameters for own-site price (cost/trip) are all negative and exhibit significant association; substitute price coefficients are all positive except for Somerset County and fairly significant (8 out of 12 are significantly different from zero). Results of the second-stage models are:

Table 8.4. Estimated Tobit Regression Demand Coefficients for Beach Use in Maryland, 1984.

Beach	Constant	(Own) Beach Access Costs	(Own) Beach Access Time	(Substitute) Beach Access Costs	(Substitute) Beach Access Time	Boat	Ownership Recrea. Vehicle	Ownership Swim. Pool	σ	Nonlimit/Limit Observations
Sandy Point	8.17 (2.83)	-0.35 (-4.07)	-4.85 (-3.61)	0.24 (2.86)	2.47 (1.15)				14.85 (57.59)	243/139
Fort Smallwood	0.16 (0.05)	-0.53 (-2.96)	-4.24 (-2.58)	0.34 (1.14)					9.52 (11.61)	41/198
Rod & Reel	-10.44 (-2.28)	-0.10 (-0.84)	-1.51 (-1.28)	0.29 (1.25)					9.72 (5.47)	22/201
Rocky Point	10.29 (2.04)	-0.47 (-1.45)	-5.63 (-2.38)					3.55 (1.36)	12.41 (19.00)	87/66
Chesapeake Beach	-3.96 (-1.89)	-0.18 (-2.19)	-1.19 (-1.76)	0.19 (1.80)			3.23 (2.58)		6.16 (10.00)	46/272
Porter's New Beach	-0.70 (-0.31)	-0.29 (-2.21)	-1.28 (-1.28)	0.31 (1.10)		1.54 (1.32)		-2.04 (-1.31)	3.43 (5.15)	25/118
Point Lookout	-3.49 (-2.72)	-0.05 (-5.62)	-1.72 (-4.27)	0.12 (3.35)	4.55 (5.41)	2.19 (1.69)	2.98 (2.50)	-1.76 (-1.21)	5.96 (15.14)	82/262
Miami	-2.20 (-1.45)	-0.09 (-1.35)	-1.27 (-1.18)				4.37 (2.46)		7.42 (10.06)	50/121
Bay Ridge	-6.98 (-1.16)	-0.78 (-4.90)	-9.63 (-3.50)	0.83 (3.19)	7.40 (1.96)	-6.19 (-1.00)	7.55 (1.50)	-5.67 (-1.13)	18.06 (17.56)	61/292

Note: Asymptotic t-statistics contained in parenthesis under the null hypothesis of no association.
Source: Bockstael et al. (1988).

own-site price: $\beta_{1i} = -0.0887 - 0.000102*TNP_i$,

$\qquad\qquad\qquad$ (−4.29)   (−3.54)

substitute price: $\beta_{2i} = -0.0682 - 0.00016*TNP_i$,

$\qquad\qquad\qquad$ (−7.47)   (−1.73)

constant: $\beta_{0i} = -19.41 - 0.007338*TNP_i$,

$\qquad\qquad\qquad$ (−4.14)   (1.93)

where t-statistics are in parentheses. The main purpose of these estimated equations is to derive benefit estimates.

Sportfishing for Striped Bass. Data for this application is based on 760 individuals, of which 184 fished for striped bass in 1980 in the Chesapeake Bay, from the National Survey of Fishing, Hunting, and Wildlife-Associated Recreation conducted by the U.S. Fish and Game Service, U.S. Department of Interior. A pooled travel cost demand model was estimated as a Tobit model for the first stage of the following form:

Table 8.5. Estimated Tobit Regression Demand Coefficients for Pleasure Boating in Maryland, 1983.

County	X1	X2	X3	Constant	Nonlimit Observations
Anne Arundel	-0.13	0.03	1.29	-2.21	142
	(-8.75)	(3.42)	(5.94)	(-1.61)	
Baltimore	-0.44	-0.02	1.78	-1.94	75
	(-9.21)	(1.13)	(4.01)	(-0.77)	
Calvert	-0.14	0.08	1.84	-27.14	44
	(-4.14)	(13.70)	(3.45)	(-7.21)	
Cecil	-0.22	0.04	2.12	-16.44	17
	(-4.84)	(1.54)	(3.09)	(-3.97)	
Charles	-0.34	0.07	2.75	0.49	38
	(-8.41)	(3.77)	(6.79)	(0.19)	
Dorchester	-0.09	0.08	0.66	-34.39	30
	(-2.98)	(2.69)	(0.78)	(-6.69)	
Harford	-0.15	0.05	-1.51	-12.21	36
	(-5.55)	(2.63)	(-1.67)	(-3.74)	
Kent	-0.25	0.11	0.14	-18.25	28
	(-4.94)	(3.57)	(0.14)	(-3.45)	
Queen Anne's	-0.27	0.07	0.12	-3.83	36
	(-6.17)	(2.89)	(-0.19)	(-1.03)	
St. Mary's	-0.11	0.05	1.25	-9.46	67
	(-6.40)	(3.12)	(2.94)	(-3.31)	
Somerset	-0.12	-0.03	2.81	-37.20	24
	(4.76)	(0.58)	(3.13)	(-6.64)	
Wicomico	-0.15	0.05	1.02	-7.03	26
	(-6.93)	(1.58)	(1.71)	(-2.02)	

Note: Asymptotic t-statistics are contained in parentheses under the null hypothesis of no association, X1 refers to the cost/trip (i.e., own price variable), X2 the cost/trip to a substitute boating site (i.e., substitute price variable), X3 is the value of the boat in thousands.
Source: Bockstael et al. (1989).

$$x_i = \text{ß}_0 + \text{ß}_1 p_i + \text{ß}_2 q_i + \text{ß}_3 y + \text{ß}_4 IB_i + \text{ß}_5 OB_i + \varepsilon, \text{ for } i = 1, \ldots 760,$$

where all variables are defined as before and *IB* represents a binary variable (=1) if an inboard motor, and *OB* also represents a binary variable (=1) if an outboard motor, but *q* represents the catch rate (no. fish caught/day). Results are as follows:

$$x_i = -10.60 - 0.34^* p_i + 0.34^* q_i + 12.65^* y + 6.66^* IB_i + 1.40^* OB_i ,$$
$$(-5.79) \ (-7.52) \ \ (2.13) \ \ \ (4.49) \ \ \ (3.47) \ \ \ (3.04)$$

where asymptotic *t*-statistics are in parentheses. Data limitations precluded estimation of second-stage models to relate water quality to trip behavior.

Benefits Calculation. BMS choose to examine benefits from a 20 percentage hypothetical reduction and from a 20 percentage hypothetical improvement in water quality based on the formula for OCS:

$$OSC_{ij} = x_{ij}^2 / -2\text{ß}_{ij}, \text{ corresponding to individual } i\text{'s demand for trips to site } j.$$

The above formula was slightly modified to represent a weighted average of OCS as follows:

$$WOCS_{ij} = \sum_{i=1}^{n} \{ x_{ij} (q_{j}^1)^2 / [-2\text{ß}_{ij} (q_{j}^1)] - x_{ij} (q_{j}^0)^2 / [-2\text{ß}_{ij} (q_{j}^0)] \} * k_i / N,$$

where *N* is the sample size, k_i is the sampling weight determined by the sample design, $x_{ij}(q_j)$ and $\text{ß}_{ij}(q_j)$ reflect that both the number of trips (quantity demanded) and the ß parameter are functions of the level of water quality. To derive OCS estimates one needs values for $x^0 = x(q^0)$, $\text{ß}^0 = \text{ß}(q^0)$, $x^1 = x(q^1)$, and $\text{ß}^1 = \text{ß}(q^1)$ to represent the "before" (q^0) and "after" (q^1) scenarios associated with changes in water quality.

One must first reestimate the second-stage model, Equation (8.4), to obtain predicted values of the ß_{ij} parameters following changes in water quality, and then use these predicted parameters to develop estimates for the trip variables pertaining to "before" and "after" scenarios. A Tobit predicting equation is used to obtain trip estimates accounting for the fact that trips was treated as a censored variable (i.e., both zero values and non-zero values occurred) of the form:

$$x_{ij}(\text{predicted}) = \Phi(\text{ß}z/\sigma)\text{ß}z + \sigma\phi(\text{ß}z/\sigma),$$

where ϕ and Φ represent the density and cumulative distribution functions, respectively, of the standard normal distribution (see Judge et al. 1988).

Furthermore, BMS used two methods for calculating trip demand associated with the "before" and "after" scenario; one method uses the Tobit predicting equation to predict trips for both scenarios, the other method uses observed trips as the "before" case and estimates trips for the "after" case by the following adjustment:

$$x_{ij}(\text{after}) = \text{observed } x_{ij} + \text{predicted } x_{ij}(\text{after}) - \text{predicted } x_{ij}(\text{before})$$

Table 8.6. Aggregate Economic Value from Changes in Chesapeake Bay Water Quality, 1987.

Activity	Net Economic Value ($thousands)		
	Pessimistic	Average	Optimistic
	ANNUAL GAINS, 20% IMPROVEMENT		
Beach Use[a]	15,352*	34,658	44,950
Pleasure Boating[b]	654	4,717	8,129
Sportfishing: Striped Bass[c]	663	1,368	2,071
Total Uses	16,669	40,743	55,150
	ANNUAL LOSSES, 20% DECREASE		
Beach Use[a]	11,991	23,789	34,288
Pleasure Boating[b]	478	3,312	6,327
Sportfishing: Striped Bass[c]	582	686	789
Total Uses	13,051	27,787	41,404

*Bockstael et al. (1988, 1989) reported a value of $16,853 (thousands). This estimate could not be duplicated following their explanation in footnote a of their original Table 7 (Bockstael et al. 1989: 16); 20% improvement values for Sandy Point were $14,084 (method A) and $9,967 (method B) in 1984 dollars (Table 4.6, Bockstael et al. [1988]). Adjusted to 1987 dollars by 1.09 yields $15,352 (method A) and $10,864 (method B); the larger estimate is used.
[a]From Table 4.6 Bockstael et al. (1988).
[b]From Table 5.13 Bockstael et al. (1988).
[c]From Table 6.4. Bockstael et al. (1988).

(the reader should consult Bockstael et al. 1988, 1989 for details). Unfortunately this procedure requires the original data and estimation software; furthermore not enough estimated values at each of the intermediate steps is given to illustrate the mechanics of obtaining OCS estimates by hand. Once per unit OCS estimates are estimated (annual OCS per user) for each use (e.g., OCS for each beach pertaining to beach users, OCS for each county pertaining to recreational boating), the OCS estimates are expanded to represent statewide populations that use the Chesapeake Bay, and then aggregated over all three uses. Aggregate net economic value (i.e., OCS) from a 20 percentage improvement and a 20 percentage decrease in Chesapeake Bay water quality is presented in Table 8.6 in 1987 dollars.

The reader should consult Section 8.2.2.2 for comparison with the aggregate CV estimates. BMS conclude that the CV estimates "are not vastly overstated" when compared to the TCA estimates (Bockstael et al. 1989: 16). Furthermore, BMS conclude that it "seems plausible" that the annual economic value from improving the water quality of the Chesapeake are within a $10 million to $100 million range.

8.4. Hedonic Price Approach

8.4.1. Introduction

The hedonic price approach (HPA) uses a statistical model to control for housing characteristics and other factors that influence property values (or housing sales prices) in order to measure the effect of changes in environmental quality. The HPA is most often applied to cross-sectional data, but is not limited to cross-sectional data. It could be used for time-series and/or moving cross-section data as well.

8.4.2. Structure of Approach

8.4.2.1. Assumptions and Model

The model postulates that the value of a good (V) is based on its attributes (z_i):

$$V = h(z_i; \text{ß}), \text{ for } i = 1, \dots, n \text{ attributes,}$$

where ß are parameters of the model. The first step is to estimate the above model. The second step is to take the partial derivatives of the model with respect to the z_i's which give the marginal value individuals place on each attribute, that is:

$$\partial V/\partial z_i = \partial h(z_i; \text{ß})/\partial z_i, \text{ for } i = 1, \dots, n,$$

and then one must formulate and estimate the following relation for each attribute (z_i's):

$$\partial h(z_i; \text{ß})/\partial z_i = g_i(z, y; \mu) \text{ for } i = 1, \dots, n,$$

where y is income, μ parameters describing tastes–preferences, and the rest are defined above for all i attributes. This relation is a marginal price function defined for each attribute where the marginal price is a function of the attribute and income. This relation represents an equilibrium condition for individual buyers in the hedonic market.

A specific model form of the HPA is the linear model:

$$V = \text{ß}_0 + \text{ß}_1 z_1 + \text{ß}_2 z_2 + \text{ß}_3 z_3 + \text{ß}_4 z_4 + e,$$

or in general:

$$V = \text{ß}_0 + \text{ß}_1 z_1 + \dots + \text{ß}_n z_n + e,$$

where e is the error term of the model and is assumed to be normally distributed with zero mean and constant variance.

The next step involves estimating the marginal price functions:

$$\partial V/\partial z_1 = \mu_0 + \mu_1 z_1 + \mu_2 y + e,$$

$$\partial V/\partial z_2 = \mu_0 + \mu_1 z_2 + \mu_2 y + e,$$

$$\cdot \qquad\qquad \cdot$$

$$\partial V/\partial z_4 = \mu_0 + \mu_1 z_4 + \mu_2 y + e,$$

or in general:

$$\partial V/\partial z_i = \mu_0 + \mu_1 z_i + \mu_2 y + e, \text{ for each } i = 1, \dots, n \text{ attributes,}$$

where y is income, μ parameters, and $\partial V/\partial z_i = g(z_i, y; \mu)$ is the relation between the attribute in question and income. The marginal price function above could be linear (as shown), semi-log, or log–linear in form.

Another specific model is the semi-log model:

$$V = \exp(\text{\ss}_0 + \text{\ss}_1 z_1 + \text{\ss}_2 z_2 + \text{\ss}_3 z_3 + \text{\ss}_4 z_4 + e),$$

where exp(.) is the exponential operator. In semi-log form this is expressed as :

$$\ln(V) = \text{\ss}_0 + \text{\ss}_1 z_1 + \text{\ss}_2 z_2 + \text{\ss}_3 z_3 + \text{\ss}_4 z_4 + e,$$

or in general:

$$\ln(V) = \text{\ss}_0 + \text{\ss}_1 z_1 + ... + \text{\ss}_n z_n + e.$$

The next step involves estimating the marginal price function:

$$\partial \ln(V)/\partial z_i = g(z_i, y; \mu)$$

for each of the *ith* attributes as shown in the example of the linear model.

A further specification of the HPA model is the log–linear model (sometimes referred to as the log–log model or double-log model):

$$V = \text{\ss}_0 z_1^{\text{\ss}1} z_2^{\text{\ss}2} z_3^{\text{\ss}3} z_4^{\text{\ss}4} \exp(e), \text{ or in log–linear form:}$$

$$\ln(V) = \ln(\text{\ss}_0) + \text{\ss}_1 \ln(z_1) + \text{\ss}_2 \ln(z_2) + \text{\ss}_3 \ln(z_3) + \text{\ss}_4 \ln(z_4) + e.$$

The general specification of this model is:

$$V = \text{\ss}_0 \prod_{i=1}^{n} z_i^{\text{\ss}i} \exp(e), \text{ or}$$

$$\ln(V) = \ln(\text{\ss}_0) + \text{\ss}_1 \ln(z_1) + ... + \text{\ss}_n \ln(z_n) + e.$$

8.4.2.2. Variable and Data Requirements

The following is a list of variables most likely to be included in the HPA.

- Housing characteristics:
  - Value or sales price of housing unit (in constant dollars)
  - Sales date
  - Value of any housing improvements
  - A measure of size of house—area in square feet, or number of rooms
  - Lot or property size—area
  - Number of bathrooms
  - 1-story or 2-story
  - Presence of basement
  - Age of house, or date of construction
  - Presence of pool
  - Exterior of house—brick, wood
  - Presence of garage
  - Presence of central air conditioning

- Length of time between sales
- Length of time on the market
- Neighborhood—municipal characteristics:
  - Education—percentage of adults that completed high school; or per pupil expenditure on K through 12 education
  - Employment/unemployment—percentage of population employed or unemployed
  - Owner occupied—percentage of owner-occupied dwellings
  - Racial/ethnic characteristics of neighborhood
  - Crime rate
  - Housing density (number homes per area)
  - Public safety expenditures—per capita expenditures
  - Distance to employment or employment centers
  - Tax rate per mil or aggregate property tax rate
- Environmental characteristics:
  - Measures of environmental quality that vary within a community, across communities, or across time, or equivalently, pollution levels that vary within a community, across communities, or across time
  - Continuous measures, or if not available, discrete measures, of pollution levels with the occurrence of a pollution event such as an oil/chemical spill or the closure of a waterbody, a (0,1) measure
  - Proximity of house to coastline of waterbody (or sometimes the inverse of this distance, as used by Mendelsohn [1986])

As discussed previously, the hedonic price model applied to property values and environmental degradations can be based on cross-sectional data, time-series data, and moving cross-sectional data. The following discussion serves to motivate these applications.

8.4.2.3. Cross-Sectional HPA

Up to now, the above standard forms of the HPA have been confined to a micro examination of residential homes within a specific community. However, the HPA has considerable flexibility. A simple application of the HPA across m municipalities could involve the data shown in Table 8.7, where the higher the pollution measure the lower the water quality, and average data is used across the m municipalities. The general linear form of the hedonic model is:

$$V_i = ß_0 + ß_1 z_{1i} + \ldots + ß_n z_{ni} + e_i, \text{ for } i=1, \ldots, m \text{ communities, and } n \text{ attributes.}$$

8.4.2.4. Time-Series HPA

A simple application of the HPA across time periods within a municipality could involve the data values shown in Table 8.8, where the higher the pollution measure the lower the water quality and average data used across the t time periods within a municipality. The general linear form of the hedonic model is:

$$V_i = ß_0 + ß_1 z_{1i} + \ldots + ß_n z_{ni} + e_i, \text{ for } i=1, \ldots, t \text{ time periods, and } n \text{ attributes.}$$

Table 8.7. Data Requirements for Cross-Sectional HPA.

| Municipality | Water Pollution Measure | Municipality Average | | | |
		Avg. Sales Price	Tax rate	Education	Race
	(coliform level)				
1	55	150,000	.	.	.
2	20	180,000	.	.	.
3	10	170,000	.	.	.
.	.	.	.	.	.
.	.	.	.	.	.
.	.	.	.	.	.
m	25	170,000	.	.	.

Table 8.8. Data Requirements for Time-Series HPA.

| Municipality | Water Pollution Measure | Municipality Average | | | |
		Avg. Sales Price	Tax rate	Education	Race
	(coliform level)				
1960	10	.	.	.	.
1961	10	.	.	.	.
.	.	.	.	.	.
.	.	.	.	.	.
.	.	.	.	.	.
t	55	.	.	.	.

8.4.2.5. Moving Cross-Section HPA

An application of the HPA to moving cross-section, that is, time-series across municipalities combining the above two applications could involve the range of values shown in Table 8.9. The general linear form of the hedonic model is:

$$V_{ij} = \beta_0 + \beta_1 z_{1ij} + ... + \beta_n z_{nij} + e_{ij}, \text{ for } i=1, ... , t \text{ time periods, } j=1, ... ,$$
m municipalities, and n attributes;

where average data is used across municipalities within a time period and over t time periods. Of course, the above model could be applied to the set of conditions in Table 8.10, where a sample of residences across three communities is examined (P1 from municipality 1, P2 from municipality 2, and P3 from municipality 3). The total sample size is the sum of the residences over the 3 municipalities, P1 + P2 + P3 (or in general $\sum_{j=1}^{m} \sum_{i=1}^{n} P_{ij}$).

Also, in cases involving two elements (i.e., municipalities across time periods, and individual residences across municipalities), one could estimate separate hedonic models for each.

Table 8.9. Data Requirements for Moving Cross-Section HPA.

Time Period	Municipality	Water Pollution Measure	Municipality Average			
			Avg. Sales Price	Tax rate	Education	Race
		(coliform level)				
1	1	10	.	.	.	.
1	2	20	.	.	.	.
.	.	.	.	.	.	.
.	.	.	.	.	.	.
.	.	.	.	.	.	.
1	m	15	.	.	.	.
2	1	12	.	.	.	.
2	2	18	.	.	.	.
.	.	.	.	.	.	.
.	.	.	.	.	.	.
.	.	.	.	.	.	.
2	m	15	.	.	.	.
.	.	.	.	.	.	.
.	.	.	.	.	.	.
.	.	.	.	.	.	.
t	m	25	.	.	.	.

Table 8.10. Data Requirements for Moving Spatial Cross-Sectional HPA.

Municipality	Sampled Residences	Water Pollution Measure	Municipality Average			
			Avg. Sales Price	Tax rate	Education	Race
		(coliform level)				
1	1	10	.	.	.	. .
1	1	20	.	.	.	. .
.	.	.	.	.	.	. .
.	.	.	.	.	.	. .
.	.	.	.	.	.	. .
1	P1	15	.	.	.	. .
2	1	12	.	.	.	. .
.	.	.	.	.	.	. .
.	.	.	.	.	.	. .
.	.	.	.	.	.	. .
2	P2	15	.	.	.	. .
3	1	.	.	.	.	. .
.	.	.	.	.	.	. .
.	.	.	.	.	.	. .
.	.	.	.	.	.	. .
3	P3	25	.	.	.	. .

8.4.3. Hedonic Price Approach—Examples

8.4.3.1. Benefits from Improvements in Air Quality

In an application to examine the economic value attributable to improvements in air quality in the Boston, Massachusetts, area, Harrison and Rubinfeld (1978) studied census tracts in the Boston SMSA in 1970. One of the hedonic models estimated was the following:

$$\log(MV) = 9.76 + 0.0063^*RM^2 + 0.0000898^*AGE - 0.19^*\log DIS + 0.096^*\log RAD$$
$$(65.22)\ (4.83) \qquad\qquad (1.7) \qquad\qquad (-5.73) \qquad (5.00)$$

$$-0.00042^*TAX - 0.031^*PTRATIO + 0.36^*(B-0.63)^2 - 0.37^*LogLSTAT$$
$$(-3.43) \qquad\qquad (-6.21) \qquad\qquad (3.53) \qquad\qquad (-14.84)$$

$$-0.012^*CRIM + 0.0000803^*ZN + 0.000241^*INDUS + 0.088^*CHAS$$
$$(-9.53) \qquad\qquad (0.16) \qquad\qquad (0.10) \qquad\qquad (2.75)$$

$$-0.00064^*NOX^2,\ R^2 = 0.81,$$
$$(-5.64)$$

where the numbers in parentheses are t-statistics, and the variables are defined as:

log MV = log of median value of owner-occupied homes.

RM = average number of rooms in owner units. The RM^2 form was found to provide a better fit than either the linear or the logarithmic forms.

AGE = Proportion of owner units built prior to 1940.

DIS = Weighted distances to five employment centers in the Boston region.

RAD = Index of accessibility to radial highways.

TAX = Full value property tax rate ($10,000).

PTRATIO = Pupil-teacher ratio by town school district.

$(B-0.63)^2$ = Proportion of population that is black "B." Harrison and Rubinfeld expected a parabolic relationship between "B" in a neighborhood and housing values (see their paper for more detail).

LSTAT = Combined proportion of adults without high school education and proportion of male workers classified as laborers.

CRIM = Crime rate per town.

ZN = Proportion of a town's residential land zoned for lots greater than 25,000 square feet.

INDUS = Proportion of nonretail business acres per town.

CHAS = Binary variable (0,1) if home is located along Charles River or not.

NOX^2 = Nitrogen oxide concentrations in pphm (annual average concentration in parts per hundred million).

This estimated model is a "hybrid," that is, a model containing mixed variable formulations (e.g., standard measures, log measures, and variables expressed as equations). Discussion of the logic behind hybrid models, and in particular this model, is beyond the scope of this book and the reader is referred to Harrison and Rubinfeld (1978). However, the following variables were found to have a positive influence on the median housing value: RM (average number of rooms), AGE (proportion of homes built prior to 1940), RAD (index of accessibility to radial highways), ZN (residential land zoned greater than 25,000 sq. ft.), INDUS (proportion of nonretail business acres per town), and CHAS (location on Charles River). For all variables except AGE and INDUS, a positive influence on housing value is expected. That is, as the number of rooms, the amount of residential land zoned in large parcels (large residential lots would decrease the density of residences, a favorable amenity), and accessibility to highways increases, the house value rises. Also, if a house is located on the Charles River the value of the house is expected to increase. The estimated coefficient on INDUS is also positive, but contrary to expectations.

The following variables had a negative influence on housing values: DIS (distance to employment), TAX (property tax rate), PTRATIO (pupil–teacher ratio), LSTAT (combined proportion of adults without high school education and male workers classified as laborers), CRIM (crime rate), and NOX (nitrogen oxide concentrations). In all cases these variables influence housing values as expected. As distance increases commuting is long and results in disutility; higher taxes would have a negative influence on housing value; a negative sign on PTRATIO implies a low pupil-teacher ratio and this is inversely related to housing value; the crime rate has a negative influence on values, the proportion of adults without high school education and male workers classified as laborers serves as an inverse proxy for socioeconomic status (as this proportion increases, socioeconomic status decreases as would housing values), and, hence, this proportion is inversely related to housing values (as shown by the negative sign); and the pollution variable NOX has a negative influence on housing value (the greater the air pollution as measured by NOX, the lower the housing value).

In order to interpret the NOX variable and estimate the change in housing value from a 1 pphm change in NOX, Harrison and Rubinfeld incorporate the mean values of the variables into the model and estimate a reduction of $1,613 in the median house value for a 1 pphm decrease in NOX.

In the next step, Harrison and Rubinfeld estimate a marginal price function for NOX levels. This is done as follows:

$$\log W = 1.08 + 0.87 * \log NOX + 1.0 * \log INC, \quad R^2 = 0.62,$$

where W represents marginal willingness-to-pay (marginal value associated with changes in the NOX attribute), and INC is household income (t-statistics or standard errors were not included in the original paper). The positive sign on the NOX variable suggests that households believe larger damages will occur at higher pollution levels, and it follows that economic surplus for marginal reductions in NOX will increase as pollution levels increase. For a typical household earning $11,500/year, there would be a gain in surplus benefits of $800 from a 1 pphm reduction in NOX levels when NOX levels are "anchored" at 3 pphm. Conversely, this household would be willing to pay $800 for a 1 pphm reduction in NOX starting from an initial point of NOX equal to 3 pphm. The same household would gain surplus benefits equal to $2,200 for a 1 pphm reduction in NOX given an initial level of 9 pphm.

8.4.3.2. Effects of Airport Noise on Housing Values

The following example examines the effect of airport noise on housing values in the Atlanta, Georgia, area (O'Byrne et al. 1985). Data consisted of 126 property sales for the 1979–80 period. One of the models estimated based on 96 observations (30 surveys were not usable) is as follows:

log SALES = 10.0971 – 0.0067*LDN + 0.0294*TIME + 0.0003*SIZE + 0.0847*BATHS

        (42.60)   (–2.23)   (4.90)   (3.00)   (2.35)

       + 0.1219*BASE + 0.1307*BEXT, Adjusted-R^2 = 0.7077, n=96,

         (4.20)   (9.34)

where the numbers in parentheses are t-statistics, and the variables are defined as:

log SALES = the common log value of house sales price in the 1979–80 period

LDN = day-night sound level ranging from 65 to 80 decibels (db) in 1980

TIME = time of sale

SIZE = square feet of living space

BATHS = number of bathrooms

BASE = binary variable (0,1) if presence of basement (= 1)

BEXT = binary variable (0,1) if exterior of house is brick (= 1)

This model explained 71 percent of the variation in the log value of housing sales price, and all variables have the expected signs. The variables that represent the housing characteristics have a positive influence on housing sales. The variable TIME reflects the inflation rate in the example. Of interest is the effect of noise, LDN which has a negative influence on housing sales. The interpretation of the parameter estimate suggests a reduction in housing sales price of 0.67 percent per decibel of airport noise. For example, a $30,000 house would sell for $2010 less if it were located in an area in which the sound averaged compared to 65 db. This study did not explore, nor estimate, marginal price functions as in the Harrison and Rubinfeld example.

8.5. Repeat Sales Approach

8.5.1. Introduction

The repeat sales approach controls for housing characteristics using a sample of paired observations of residential property that were sold repeatedly (more than once) over the study period (i.e., at least two observations per home). The approach controls for factors (e.g., housing characteristics, location, access) that influence real property vales. However, it allows some factors (e.g., environmental quality) to change with time.

8.5.2. Structure of Approach

8.5.2.1. Assumptions and Model

Assume that the value of a house (V) is influenced by its characteristics (z_i):

$$V= h(z_i; ß),$$

where ßs are parameters of the model. The repeat sales approach (RSA) compares changes in property value in one time period (V_0) to another (V_1) that straddles a pollution event:

$$V_1 - V_0 = h(z_{i1} - z_{i0}; \text{ß}),$$

where subscripts on z_{ij} refer to characteristics i and time j ($j = 1$ or 0 corresponding to time periods after an event and before an event, respectively).

A specific model form of the RCA is the linear model:

$$V_1 - V_0 = \text{ß}_0 + \text{ß}_1(z_{11} - z_{10}) + \text{ß}_2(z_{21} - z_{20}) + \text{ß}_3(z_{31} - z_{30}) + \text{ß}_4(z_{41} - z_{40}) + e,$$

or in general:

$$V_1 - V_0 = \text{ß}_0 + \text{ß}_1(z_{11} - z_{10}) + \ldots + \text{ß}_n(z_{n1} - z_{n0}) + e,$$

where e is the error term of the model which is assumed follows a normal distribution with zero mean and constant variance.

Another specific model is a semi-log model:

$$\log(V_1 / V_0) = \text{ß}_0 + \text{ß}_1(z_{11} - z_{10}) + \text{ß}_2(z_{21} - z_{20}) + \text{ß}_3(z_{31} - z_{30}) + \text{ß}_4(z_{41} - z_{40}) + e,$$

or in general:

$$\log(V_1 / V_0) = \text{ß}_0 + \text{ß}_1(z_{11} - z_{10}) + \ldots + \text{ß}_n(z_{n1} - z_{n0}) + e,$$

following Mendelsohn (1986).

8.5.2.2. Variable and Data Requirements

The following is a discussion about groups of variables most likely to be included in the repeat sales approach. It should be noted that because the RSA is based on observations of repeat sales, information about housing characteristics common in hedonic approaches is not needed. Sales information on the same house is collected when it was sold before a pollution event as well as after a pollution event. Only homes that satisfy this condition are included in the sample. Thus housing characteristics such as number of rooms, bathrooms, square feet, number of stories, for each home in the sample are not likely to change over time. In a sense, the RSA controls for housing characteristics as well as other characteristics such as neighborhood and municipal characteristics through its sampling design.

Variables most likely to be included in an RSA are:

- Housing sales information:
  - Difference in the sales price of a housing unit that straddles a pollution event, adjusted for inflation; that is, later period sales price less earlier period sales price in real dollars (sales deflated or inflated to a constant year)
  - Value of housing improvements and what the improvements were
  - Length of time between sales
  - Length of time on the market
  - Change in interest rate from the initial sales date to the later sales date
- Neighborhood—municipal characteristics:
  - Education—percentage of adults that completed high school, or per pupil expenditure on K through 12 education
  - Employment/unemployment—percentage of population employed or unemployed

- Income of household in real dollars
- Owner-occupied—percentage of owner-occupied dwellings
- Racial–ethnic characteristics of the neighborhood

- Environmental characteristics:
  - Measures of environmental quality that changed over time, or equivalently, changes in pollution levels over time (e.g., decreases in environmental quality or increases in pollution levels)
  - Discrete measures, when continuous measures are unavailable, of the occurrence of a pollution event such as an oil or chemical spill or closure of a waterbody, a (0,1) measure, where measures of pollution levels are not available
  - Proximity of house to coastline of polluted waterbody (sometimes the inverse of the distance), as used by Mendelsohn (1986)

Measures of the Neighborhood–Municipal Characteristics, in the context of the RSA, have to correspond to the time periods of the housing sales dates. Measuring the percentage change in these characteristics from the initial sales date to the later sales date is one way to accomplish this.

8.5.3. Repeat Sales Approach—Economic Damage from PCB Contamination in New Bedford Harbor, Massachusetts

Mendelsohn (1986) conducted an examination of the economic damage to single-family residential homes caused by PCB contamination in New Bedford Harbor, Massachusetts. The 1979–80 period was chosen as the time period when most residents became aware of the problem. A sample of single-family, owner-occupied residences that sold at least twice since 1969 resulted in 1,030 observations. A complete history of sales for this sample of residences was then obtained for the 1969–85 period. Many different variations of paired sales were then possible for residences that sold once, twice, or three or more times within this period. In addition, these paired sales could have occurred anytime within this period. The data set, then, is composed of observations of paired sales that sold before and after the 1979–80 period (i.e., sales that straddled the 1979–80 period) and observations of paired sales that did not straddle the 1979–80 period. Because the objective of the study and structure of the model was to examine the difference in sales for residences that sold before the 1979–80 period and after the 1979–80 period, observations of sales were identified and distinguished among paired sales that did not straddle the 1979–80 period by using a binary-shift variable. (Unfortunately, the original report does not list the breakdown of the number of observations that fall into these groups.)

Both linear and semi-log models were estimated. The linear model used to estimate the economic damage of marine pollution to residential homes was:

DIFFERENCE = 4470 + 1079*IMPROVE – 2711*INTEREST – 1024*LENGTH1

(6.12)   (6.68)   (–13.18)   (–3.49)

– 839*LENGTH3–4 + 16900*EVENT – 5616*EVPCBZONE1

(–3.55)   (8.90)   (–1.94)

– 6338*EVPCBZONE2 + 490*HIGHSCHOOL, Adjusted R^2 = 0.218,

(–2.43)   (2.12)

where the numbers in parentheses are *t*-statistics, and the dependent variable is:

DIFFERENCE = Later market sale price minus earlier market sale price in constant dollars (using the GNP residential nonfarm price deflator)

The independent variables are:

IMPROVE = Value in thousands of dollars of home improvements made, measured in real 1985 dollars between the first and second sale

INTEREST = The difference in annual effective mortgage interest rates between the sale dates

LENGTH1 = Time, in years, between first and second sale multiplied by PCBZONE1, a binary variable to indicate whether the property is located in PCB Zone I or not

LENGTH3–4 = Time, in years, between first and second sale multiplied by PCB-ZONE3–4, a binary variable to indicate whether the property is located in PCB Zone III or in PCB Zone IV

EVENT = Binary variable (0,1) for whether earlier or later sale dates straddle the 1979–80 period;

EVPCBZONE1 = Binary variable (0,1) for whether the sale dates straddle 1979–80 and also whether the nearest water is in PCB Zone I (the product of EVENT times PCB-ZONE1)

EVPCBZONE2 = Binary variable (0,1) for whether the sale dates straddle 1979–80 and also whether the nearest water is in PCB Zone II (the product of EVENT times PCB-ZONE2)

HIGHSCHOOL = The change in the percentage of adults in the census tract who completed high school in 1970 versus 1980 weighted by the length of sale

PCBZONE1 = Binary variable (0,1) for those properties whose nearest water lies within PCB Zone I

PCBZONE2 = Binary variable (0,1) for those properties whose nearest water lies within PCB Zone II.

This particular model was chosen on the basis of statistical tests, best fit, and a priori expectations. Many different model forms and variable combinations were examined to arrive at this equation; see Mendelsohn (1986) for more detail. In all, 17 regression models were estimated in addition to the above linear model—similar remarks apply to the semi-log model. The base models included the following variables (IMPROVE, INTEREST, LENGTH1, LENGTH3–4, EVENT, HIGHSCHOOL), the variables EVPCBZONE1 and EVPCBZONE2 were in most of the models, however, the variables EVPROXPCB, EVPROXSHORE, EVPROXSHPCB were substituted for the EVPCBZONE1 and EVPCB-ZONE2 variables in some models, and in others combinations of these variables were used. In some models the variables INCOME, UNEMPLOY, and OWNER were included. All of these efforts were to establish which variables explained the effects on the long-term contamination on the New Bedford area housing market and which model met a priori expectations and fit the data better. In general, many different model forms and variable combinations were explored on the basis of economic theory in order to arrive at an "acceptable" model. Economic theory provides a starting point for a general model specification and which variables should be included, but may not offer direction about the models statistical form (linear vs. semi-log).

Examining the above estimated model, one can see that all variables are statistically significant and have the expected signs. For every thousand dollars spent on housing improvements, the net effect is to raise housing value about $1,080. The sign on INTEREST is negative implying that as nominal interest rates increase the real value of homes decrease. Interpretation of LENGTH1 and LENGTH3–4 suggests that homes located in PCB Zone I and in PCB Zones III and IV, experienced a long-term decrease in prices over the study period. Mendelsohn cautions the reader in interpreting the variable HIGHSCHOOL. Although, at first, it suggests that as the percentage of high school graduates increases in a census tract the tendency is to raise housing values, it could simply be serving as a proxy for a general improvement in the socioeconomic status of a neighborhood.

Now consider the pollution variables. The variable EVENT, which represents homes that sold before and after 1980 (i.e., homes that straddle 1980—homes sold during 1980 are not included), suggests a positive trend in sales prices, other things being equal. That is, sales prices in general increased for homes that sold before and after 1980 in the New Bedford region. Although house prices rose, we would expect that the increase would have been greater had the pollution event not occurred, and this is the effect that Mendelsohn measures using house sales in constant terms. Lastly, the coefficients on the two variables EVPCBZONE1 and EVPCBZONE2 are both negative and significant. This suggests that real housing prices for residences located in PCB Zone I and PCB Zone II dropped after 1980, the time period when most residents became aware of the pollution problem. This occurred despite the general increase in housing prices in the New Bedford region. The estimated coefficients suggest that the average loss in housing value was $5,616 in PCB Zone I and $6,338 in PC Zone II, other things being equal.

On the basis of the RSA, aggregate damage estimates attributable to a pollution event are estimated from the coefficient corresponding to the pollution variable multiplied by the product of the population of single-family residences within municipalities included in the study area times the average sales price of these residences; that is, the product of the absolute change in sales price attributable to pollution and the value of all single-family homes in the study area. Based on the above estimated coefficient (–$5,616 in PCB Zone I and –$6,338 in PCB Zone II), Mendelsohn estimates aggregate damages of $27.3 million (in 1985$)—see Table 8.11 for detail.

Table 8.11. Estimate of Damages to Single-Family Residential Home Values from PCB Pollution to the New Bedford, MA Region, by Municipality (in millions of 1985 dollars).

PCB Zone	Dartmouth	Fairhaven	New Bedford	Total
I	—	9.5	—	9.5
II	5.7	6.9	5.2	17.8
Total	5.7	16.4	5.2	27.3

Source: Mendelsohn (1986).

8.6. Insights on Use of Benefits Transfer

Benefits transfer has become a workhorse in assessments of resource damages. A fairly large benefits transfer literature exists (see Bingham et al. 1992 regarding a 1992 workshop on benefits transfer, a special issue of *Water Resources Research* [March 1992 edition] containing nine articles, Naughton and Desvousges 1985, Unsworth and Petersen 1995). The reason it is so commonly used is that time constraints and financial constraints limit preparation of economic assessments of resource damages. Not only is time extremely critical in the rehabilitation of spoiled wetlands, but the legal process can become time consuming. A timely economic assessment keeps the process moving fast and allows for quick responses to restoration. This sometimes means there is not sufficient time to conduct original economic analyses for specific spills, and one must rely on previous studies and the literature to develop economic assessments of damages. Financial limitations are also a problem in economic assessments of resource damages. In cases of oil and hazardous substance spills or discharges government representatives that serve as trustees of the natural resource have no readily available funds to draw upon to conduct NRDAs. In the case of the Exxon Bayway Arthur Kill Oil Spill, the State of New Jersey, acting as the lead trustee, used a state law, the New Jersey Spill Compensation and Control Act, to have Exxon immediately release money that could be used to perform resource damage proceedings and assessments, an estimated $661,250 (Hauge and Tucker 1994). However, the portion of such funds allocated to economic analysis is limited. This is because the federal procedures require that as much of the damage award as possible be used for restoration purposes.

Benefits transfers are also especially useful in the NRDA process (Unsworth and Petersen 1995). A "back-of-the-envelope" analysis of preliminary estimates of economic damages is often needed for preliminary damage assessment reports and can allow a trustee to determine if a specific resource damage assessment is warranted (i.e., if the magnitude of loss exceeds estimates of assessment costs). Benefits transfers also have been used successfully in developing final estimates of economic losses in the NRDA process. The NRDA computer assessment model that comprises the type A rule of the Comprehensive Environmental Response, Compensation, and Liability Act is in principle based on a benefits transfer approach and has been used in a number of final resource damage assessments (e.g., *World Prodigy* oil spill). This procedure represents a standardized methodology that requires minimal field data and is meant to provide a fairly simplified straightforward procedure for use in NRDAs at low cost. Furthermore, benefits transfers are useful in cases where the additional cost of an original study is greater than the additional precision gained and in the case where the cost of an original study would not guarantee superior estimates of economic value compared to a benefits transfer.

However, there are issues and concerns that have not been adequately addressed. A number of researchers have concluded that: (1) the existing stock of studies and their reporting (e.g., reporting of data, methods, and results) constrain benefits transfers, (2) replications of previous studies are not conducted, and both editors and reviewers should recognize the merits of replicated studies to provide incentives to conduct replications, and (3) research to date has not addressed the practical aspects of benefits transfers (Bingham et al. 1992, Brookshire and Neill 1992, Smith 1992). Furthermore, the set of assumptions and decisions that resulted in benefit estimates from original studies may also affect their usefulness in transfers (Smith 1992).

A number of issues, in addition, are of concern in conducting benefits transfers:

- The nature of the good or service to be assessed, where similarity of the characteristics of the good across sites (i.e., sites of the original study versus the site to transfer the study to) are important to qualify a benefit transfer as "defensible"
- Identification of all relevant studies to determine the pool from which benefit estimates are developed
- The appropriate units or measures of economic welfare in which to express economic value in (e.g., equivalent surplus measures or compensating surplus measures)
- Recognition of variations in the quality across studies and how to account for this (i.e., how to weigh different studies)
- The effects of the age of the study, and some consensus about how long results remain applicable over time; in other words recognition and treatment of changes in tastes, economic conditions, and site-quality characteristics since the original study was conducted
- Whether benefit estimates based on different nonmarket methods (e.g., indirect vs. direct) can be combined
- Whether benefit estimates based on different economic models (e.g., travel cost demand, random utility model) for a similar generic nonmarket method (e.g., indirect methods) can be combined
- Whether a specific or targeted study is superior to results pooled or averaged over all studies
- Recognition and treatment of the relevant market or population affected (geographic extent of market) in which to transfer benefit estimates to versus that of the original study
- Recognition and treatment of characteristics and similarities of the population within a market area across sites (the site in the original study vs. that in which to transfer the benefit estimate to)
- The effect of environmental change on activities, participation, and use characteristics, and on site quality if not treated in the original study
- The role of judgment in benefits transfers

Aside from these issues the basic steps of a defensible benefits transfer can be summarized as: (1) identify the good or nature of the commodity (e.g., resources or services) to be assessed, (2) identify potentially applicable studies (3) evaluate their relevance to the transfer under consideration, (4) develop benefit estimates based on the applicable studies. This last item can involve a number of steps. For example, it includes: (1) the identification of the market extent affected by a change (e.g., relevant population affected by a closed beach, closed site, newly available site, improvement in water quality), which forms the basis of the expansion of the per unit estimates and can become a critical factor because more error can be associated with the expansion factor versus specific per unit estimates; the development of benefit estimates from the applicable study(ies) (e.g., a single point estimate based on a single study, a range of estimates [i.e., mean and standard deviation] from a number of studies or estimates based on an empirical function [e.g., demand function], or number of such functions from which an average could be determined); (2) the determination of the time period and level of economic losses or gains expected to occur in each period and develop benefit estimates for each period; (3)

expansion of per unit benefit estimates to obtain aggregate benefit estimates; (4) selection of a discount rate or a range of discount rates to determine their sensitivity; (5) compounding the benefit estimates if the time periods correspond to past time periods that losses or gains and damages occurred or discounting the benefit estimates that correspond to future time periods in which losses or gains are expected to occur; (6) adding the compounded or discounted estimates together to determine total economic losses or gains in present value terms.

Common sense dictates preferred practices in benefits transfers in lieu of uniform guidelines. Careful attention to the quality of the study; sound research design, sampling method, appropriate size of the database to ensure statistical reliability of the estimates; appropriate empirical analysis together with treatment of statistical problems if necessary (e.g., collinearity, heteroscedasticity, treatment of outliers, etc.) are all essential to a good study. Similar characteristics of the good or its services and population affected, and careful thought to determination of the market extent are also critical and can determine a well done benefit transfer application. As Brookshire and Neill (1992) point out, benefit transfers will magnify and compound accuracy problems that are implicit in an original investigation.

Recent research in benefits transfer has examined and compared the superiority of using benefit functions (e.g., appropriate demand functions, CV functions) versus simply transferring per unit benefit estimates (e.g., $/trip) (Kirchhoff et al. 1997, Loomis 1992). The argument for the use of benefit functions in benefits transfers is that the functions sometimes take into consideration factors such as demographic information (income, education), and, in the case of two stage estimation procedures, sometimes includes a participation function as the first stage and then a demand or value function as the second stage (e.g., in some form of random utility models). Because specific factors are related to demand, the use of these functions can produce benefit estimates for different areas and regions where such demand factors can differ from the original study site and incorporate this information into the resulting benefit estimates. Estimates developed in this manner might represent "second best" benefit estimates as opposed to "first best" benefit estimates developed from an original research investigation.

What does the literature have to offer in using a simple benefits transfer approach over a benefits function transfer approach? To be frank there is not much literature on the use and preference of the benefits function approach, other than to evaluate the quality of the study and statistical reliability of the estimates. One of the few empirical investigations lends support to the superiority of benefit function transfers under certain situations (Kirchhoff et al. 1997). Their findings suggest that benefit function transfers can be more robust than transfers of per unit benefit estimates; however, circumstances that dictate valid, policy-related information can be very limited and resulting errors from such transfers could be "quite large, even across seemingly similar amenities" (Kirchhoff et al. 1997: 75). They suggest that researchers need to explore the effects of resource quality, market conditions, and other factors on benefits transfer performance. In their study they found that some transfer errors were as high as 228 percent, and of 24 comparisons from previous studies 2 resulted in errors over 100 percent, and 16 involved errors under 50 percent.

Given estimates of the economic value of beach use used by Ofiara and Brown (1999) of $108/individual (1987$), an error of 228 percent would mean an estimate of $354/individual and a significant overestimate of the benefits of beach use. In applications such an error could give biased messages vis à vis public policy responses and the allocation of scarce resources. To further illustrate a benefits function transfer based on the New Jersey–New York Bight case study, use of a benefit function transfer from Bockstael et al. (1989) results in beach use benefit estimates of $129/individual (1987$), an error of 19 percent compared to $108/individual, or possibly an improvement in the original benefit estimate. In general, if one chooses a benefit estimate one should strive to compare that estimate with one obtainable from a benefit function and use estimates that do not differ greatly unless one can justify such an estimate. A superior approach is to develop benefit estimates based on a range of reasonable or possible estimates rather than based on a single point estimate.

A brief example of this follows. Consider a researcher who wants to assess the economic value of trout fishing in the Northeast. After a review of the literature the following studies are summarized in Table 8.12. Based on the extent of the market or the study area, the high estimates associated with the states Tennessee and Minnesota would be excluded (these states are not in the Northeast); the remaining studies yield an average of $24.81 versus $31.94 if all are included (an increase of 29 percent). If further projected for 100,000 anglers in the Northeast, aggregate economic value would be $2.5 million versus $3.2 million, an overstatement of value of 1.28 times if all studies are used. Furthermore this example illustrates that the economic value per trip or day differs based on the economic method. The studies based on the CV method were surprisingly lower than those based on a travel cost demand approach, an average of $16.45 and $43.56, respectively. Section 9.6 of Chapter 9 contains more examples of benefits transfer to illustrate

Table 8.12. Use Values of Freshwater Fishing From Previous Studies.

Study/Date	Method	Source of Data	Scope	Fish-type	Year (Reported)	Value (1992$)	Value
Brown & Hay (1987)	CV	1980 National Survey	U.S.	Trout	1980	12.00	20.23
Brown & Hay (1987)	CV	1980 National Survey	PA	Trout	1980	8.00	13.49
Miller & Hay (1984)	TCD	1980 National Survey	Maine	Freshwater	1980	23.00	38.78
Miller & Hay (1984)	TCD	1980 National Survey	TN	Freshwater	1980	30.00	50.59
Miller & Hay (1984)	TCD	1980 National Survey	MN	Freshwater	1980	29.00	48.90
Vaughn & Russell (1982)	TCD	Private Fee Fishing Sites	U.S.	Trout	1979	19.49	35.97
Connelly et al. (1990)	CV	NY State Angler Survey	NY	Coldwater	1988	13.42	15.62
Average—all							31.94
S.D.							15.50
Average—Northeast							24.82
S.D.							11.76

Note: CV refers to contingent valuation, TCD to travel cost demand, and S.D. standard deviation. Reported value converted to 1992 dollars by the implicit price deflator (i.e., gross domestic product deflator).

Source: Unsworth and Petersen (1995).

application. Further applications of benefits transfer and potential problems are contained in Unsworth and Peterson (1995).

8.6.1. Future of Benefits Transfer

A repeated message from the literature is that one must use caution in unquestioned acceptance of estimated benefits based on transfers from the literature (Naughton and Desvousges 1985, Smith 1992); one must be able to justify the transfer of benefits. Bingham concludes in his summary of a 1992 Association of Environmental and Resource Economists workshop on benefits transfers that "benefit transfers will not have the elegance of pure theory or the rigor of hypothesis testing" (Bingham 1992: ix). Further insights and issues in benefits transfer have been addressed in the literature, and a number of researchers emphasize that uniform procedures and standards are lacking and are needed in benefits transfer practices. Such uniform procedures would have a favorable influence on benefits transfer practices, and possibly minimize criticism of it. Researchers also stress that replications of previous studies should become an active area for research, that both editors and reviewers should recognize the merits of replicated studies, and that research addressing practical questions in benefits transfer is also needed and should become actively pursued (Bingham et al. 1992, Brookshire and Neill 1992, Smith 1992). Research has just begun to evaluate past studies using meta-analysis, which can aid in determining the relative importance of various factors in economic value estimates and models and help target future research efforts; for example Carson et al. (1996) and Smith and Osborne (1996) examined previous CV studies, and Smith and Kaoru (1990) examined past travel cost studies.

8.7. Applications: A Caution

The examples presented here were meant to give the reader an appreciation of the mechanics of each of the techniques: contingent valuation approach, travel cost approach, hedonic price approach, and repeat sales approach, as well as the versatility of these approaches and their applications. The examples were also meant to illustrate the techniques, how they can and have been applied, and how to interpret the results. While the techniques and procedures can be applied to other areas, the results are sometimes not readily or easily transferred to represent other areas. Other issues must also be considered in any application, and the examples provided have been simplified for the purposes of this book. The area of benefits transfer has now become concerned with the transfer of benefit estimates and transfer of benefit function estimates in applied studies, and a large literature has developed in this area.

Furthermore, the examples given are not comprehensive in dealing with the multitude of problems and issues that can arise in applied studies, nor are they exhaustive in the variety of possible applications; they are no substitute for field experience and comprehensive reading. Actual applications and econometric models may be quite different from the examples discussed due to different underlying circumstances and assumptions. Thus the examples are not to be taken literally. It is suggested that any application be conducted with the consultation of economists experienced with these techniques.

8.8. Note

1. This study was conducted in 1981 and included option value as a nonuse value. As discussed in Chapter 2 and in Chapter 5, researchers agree that option value was misunderstood in earlier studies that included it as a component of nonuse values, and the current consensus is not to consider option value as a nonuse value.

8.9. References

Bingham, T.H. 1992. "Forward." In Bingham, T.H., E. David, T. Graham-Tomassi, M.J. Kealy, M. LeBlanc and R. Leeworthy (eds.). *Benefits Transfer: Procedures, Problems, and Research Needs.* 1992 Association of Environmental and Resource Economics Workshop, June 3–5: Snowbird, UT: iii–ix.

Bingham, T.H., E. David, T. Graham-Tomassi, M.J. Kealy, M. LeBlanc and R. Leeworthy (eds.). 1992. *Benefits Transfer: Procedures, Problems, and Research Needs.* 1992 Association of Environmental and Resource Economics Workshop, June 3–5: Snowbird, UT.

Bockstael, N.E. and I.E. Strand. 1987. "The Effect of Common Sources of Regression Error on Benefit Estimates." *Land Economics* 63(1): 11–20.

Bockstael, N.E., W.M. Hanemann and I.E. Strand (eds.). 1986. *Measuring the Benefits of Water Quality Improvements Using, Recreational Demand Models, Volume II.* Prepared for Office of Policy Analysis, Office of Policy and Resource Management, U.S. Environmental Protection Agency: Washington, DC.

Bockstael, N.E., K.E. McConnell and I.E. Strand. 1988. *Benefits from Improvements in Chesapeake Bay Water Quality, Volume III.* Prepared for Office of Policy Analysis, Office of Policy and Resource Management, U.S. EPA: Washington, DC.

———. 1989. "Measuring the Benefits of Improvements in Water Quality: Chesapeake Bay." *Marine Resource Economics* 6: 1–18.

Brookshire, D.S. and H.R. Neill. 1992. "Benefit Transfers: Conceptual and Empirical Issues." *Water Resources Research* 28(3): 651–655.

Brookshire, D.S., R.C. d'Arge, W.D. Schulze and M.A. Thayer. 1979. *Methods Development for Assessing Tradeoffs in Environmental Management, Vol. II, Experiments in Valuing Non-Market Goods: A Case Study of Alternative Benefit Measures of Air Pollution Control in the South Coast Air Basin of Southern California.* EPA-600/6-79-001b. Prepared for Office of Research Development, U.S. EPA: Washington, DC.

Brown, Jr., G.M. and M. Hay. 1987. *Net Economic Recreation Values for Deer and Waterfowl Hunting and Trout Fishing: 1980.* Working Paper 23. U.S. DOI, Fish and Wildlife Service, Division of Policy and Directives Management: Washington, DC.

Burt, O.D. and D. Brewer. 1971. "Evaluation of Net Social Benefits from Outdoor Recreation." *Econometrica* 39: 813–827.

Carson, R.T., N.E. Flores, K.M. Martin and J.L. Wright. 1996. "Contingent Valuation and Revealed Preference Methodologies: Comparing the Estimates for Quasi-Public Goods." *Land Economics* 72(1): 80–99.

Clawson, M. and J. Knetsch. 1966. *Economics of Outdoor Recreation.* Johns Hopkins University Press: Baltimore, MD.

Cochran, W.G. 1977. *Sampling Techniques.* John Wiley and Sons: New York, NY.

Connelly, N.A., T.L. Brown and B.A. Knuth. 1990. *New York Statewide Angler Survey: 1988.* New York State Department of Environmental Conservation: Albany, NY.

Cummings, R.G., D.S. Brookshire and W.D. Schulze. 1986a. *Valuing Public Goods: The Contingent Valuation Method.* Rowman and Allanheld: Totowa, NJ.

Cummings, R.G., L.A. Cox and A.M. Freeman. 1986b. "General Methods for Benefits Assessment." In Bentkover, J.D., V.T. Covello and J. Mumpower (eds.). *Benefits Assessment: The State of the Art.* D. Reidel: Boston, MA.

Desvousges, W.H., V.K. Smith and M.P. McGivney. 1983. *A Comparison of Alternative Approaches for Estimating Recreation and Related Benefits of Water Quality Improvements.* Prepared for Office of Policy Analysis, U.S. Environment Protection Agency: Washington, DC.

Dillman, D.A. 1978. *Mail and Telephone Surveys: The Total Design Method.* John Wiley & Sons: New York, NY.

Dwyer, J.F., J.R. Kelly and M.D. Bowes. 1977. *Improved Procedures for Valuation of the Contribution of Recreation to National Economic Development.* WRC Research Report No. 128. Water Resources Center, University of Illinois: Urbana, IL.

Freeman, A.M. 1979. *The Benefits of Environmental Improvement: Theory and Practice.* Resources for the Future, Inc.: Washington, D.C.

Greene, W.H. 1993. *Econometric Analysis.* Macmillan: New York, NY.

Hanemann W.M. 1984. "Welfare Evaluation in Contingent Valuation Experiments with Discrete Responses." *American Journal of Agricultural Economics* 66(3): 332–341.

Harrison, D. and D.L. Rubinfeld. 1978. "Hedonic Housing Prices and the Demand for Clean Air." *Journal of Environmental Economics and Management* 5: 81–102.

Hauge, P.M. and R.K. Tucker. 1994. "Governmental Cooperation." In Burger, J. (ed.) *Before and After an Oil Spill: The Arthur Kill.* Rutgers University Press: New Brunswick, NJ: 23–43.

Huppert, D.D. and C.J. Thomson. 1984. *Demand Analysis of Partyboat Angling in California Using the Travel Cost Method.* Administrative Report LJ-84-06. Southwest Fisheries Center, NMFS: La Jolla, CA.

Judge, G.G., W.E. Griffiths, R.C. Hill and T.C. Lee. 1988. *Introduction to the Theory and Practice of Econometrics.* John Wiley & Sons: New York, NY.

Kirchhoff, S., B.G. Colby and J.T. LaFrance. 1997. "Evaluating the Performance of Benefit Transfer: An Empirical Inquiry." *Journal of Environmental Economics and Management* 33: 75–93.

Loomis, J. 1992. "The Evolution of a More Rigorous Approach to Benefit Transfer: Benefit Function Transfer." *Water Resources Research* 28(3): 701–705.

McConnell, K.E. 1979. "Values of Marine Recreational Fishing: Measurement and Impact of Measurement." *American Journal of Agricultural Economics* December: 921–925.

McConnell, K.E. and N.E. Bockstael. 1984. "Aggregation in Recreation Economics: Issue of Estimation and Benefit Measurement." *Northeastern Journal of Agriculture and Resource Economics* 13(2): 181–186.

McConnell, K.E and C. Kling. 1986. "Aggregation Issues: Choice among Estimation Approaches." In Bockstael, N.E., W.M. Hanemann and I.E. Strand (eds.). *Measuring the Benefits of Water Quality Improvements Using, Recreational Demand Models, Volume II,* Chapter 3. Prepared for Office of Policy Analysis, Office of Policy and Resource Management, U.S. Environmental Protection Agency: Washington, DC.

McConnell, K.E. and I.E. Strand. 1981. "Measuring the Cost of Time in Recreation Demand Analysis: An Application to Sport Fishing." *American Journal of Agricultural Economics* 63(February): 153–156.

Mendelsohn, R. 1986. *Assessment of Damages by PCB Contamination to New Bedford Harbor*

Amenities Using Residential Property Values. Prepared for Ocean Assessment Division, NOAA: Rockville, MD.

Miller, J.R. and M.J. Hay. 1984. "Estimating Substate Values of Fishing and Hunting." *Transactions of the North American Wildlife and Natural Resource Conference* 49: 345–355.

Mitchell, R.C. and R.T. Carson. 1981. *An Experiment in Determining Willingness to Pay for National Water Quality Improvements.* Draft Report. Prepared for Office of Research and Development, U.S. Environment Protection Agency: Washington, DC.

———. 1989. *Using Surveys to Value Public Goods: The Contingent Valuation Method.* Resources for the Future: Washington, DC.

Naughton, M.C. and W.H. Desvousges. 1985. *Water Quality Benefits of the BCT Regulations for the Pulp and Paper Industry.* Draft Report, July. Research Triangle Institute: Research Triangle Park, NC.

Nelson, J.P. 1979. "Airport Noise, Location Rent, and the Market for Residential Amenities." *Journal of Environmental Economics and Management* 6: 320–331.

———. 1981. "Three Mile Island and Residential Property Values: Empirical Analysis and Policy Implications." *Land Economics* 57(3): 363–372.

O'Byrne, P.H., J.P. Nelson and J.J. Seneca. 1985. "Housing Values, Census Estimates, Disequilibrium, and the Environmental Cost of Airport Noise: A Case Study of Atlanta." *Journal of Environmental Economics and Management* 12: 169–178.

Ofiara, D.D. and B. Brown. 1988. *Economic Assessment of New York Bight Use Impairments on the State of New Jersey.* Institute of Marine and Coastal Sciences, Rutgers University: New Brunswick, NJ.

———. 1999. "Assessment of Economic Losses to Recreational Activities from 1988 Marine Pollution Events and Assessment of Economic Losses from Long-term Contamination of Fish Within the New York Bight to New Jersey." *Marine Pollution Bulletin* 38(11): 990–1004.

Ostle, B. and R.W. Mensing. 1975. *Statistics in Research.* Iowa State University Press: Ames, IO.

Rosenthal, D.H. and J.C. Anderson. 1984. "Travel Cost Models, Heteroskedasticity, and Sampling." *Western Journal of Agricultural Economics* 9(1): 58–65.

Smith, V.K. 1992. "On Separating Defensible Benefits Transfers from Smoke and Mirrors." *Water Resources Research* 28(3): 685–694.

Smith, V.K. and W.H. Desvousges. 1986. *Measuring Water Quality Benefits.* Kluwer, Nijhoff Publishing: Boston, MA.

Smith, V.K. and Y. Kaoru. 1990. "Signals or Noise? Explaining the Variation in Recreation Benefit Estimates." *American Journal of Agricultural Economics* May: 419–433.

Smith, V.K. and L.L.. Osborne. 1996. "Do Contingent Valuation Estimates Pass a "Scope" Test? A Meta-analysis." *Journal of Environmental Economics and Management* 31: 287–301.

Unsworth, R.E. and T.B. Petersen. 1995. *A Manual for Conducting Natural Resource Damage Assessment: The Role of Economics.* Division of Economics, Fish and Wildlife Service, U.S. Department of Interior: Washington, DC.

Vaughn, W.J. and C.S. Russell. 1982. "Valuing a Fishing Day: An Application of a Systematic Varying Parameter Model." *Land Economics* 58(4): 450–463.

CHAPTER 9

Case Studies: Damage to Fish–Shellfish, Public Health, Beach Use, Property Value, and Impairments to Estuaries

9.1. Introduction

This chapter includes a collection of case studies to illustrate the economic effects of damages to marine resources resulting from the degradations in marine water quality identified in Chapter 6. Moreover this examination illustrates concepts, gives readers an appreciation of the complexity of economic damage assessments, and serves as a guide to a range of applications. There are two kinds of cases that are reviewed: (1) cases of specific kinds of losses to show the variety of economic effects that have been examined in the literature, and (2) cases of comprehensive assessments of economic losses and effects pertaining to estuaries in the U.S. Environmental Protection Agency's (U.S. EPA's) National Estuary Program. All the cases discussed were chosen because they demonstrate applications to the marine environment, the focus of this book. In each of these cases, the basic challenge facing the researchers was to isolate the economic effect caused by a specific event from all other possible factors and to express this isolated effect in terms of a dollar value. Researchers use existing or published data, or they collect survey data from a sample of individuals (usually representing users and nonusers of the affected resource), and then use a specific economic method to assess the value of these effects. The studies that used existing data include: Figley et al. 1979, Swartz and Strand 1981, Capps et al. 1984, Lipton 1986, Ofiara and Brown 1989, 1999, Kahn et al. 1989a, Mendelsohn 1986, and Swanson et al. 1991. Others were based on survey data: McConnell and Morrison 1986, McConnell and IE 1986, ERA 1979, Bell and Leeworthy 1986, Strand et al. 1985, Strand et al. 1986, and Bockstael et al. 1989.

Although there are flaws in the methods used in these cases, ranging from summing across uses (and potentially double-counting) to the use of methods not fully tested and controversial, we must weigh the need to develop aggregate economic loss estimates for public policy purposes against the risk of error. It is sometimes unavoidable that due to resource and time constraints applied researchers have no choice but to conduct benefits transfer approaches, however simple or complex, versus original investigations. There has to be a compromise between thoroughness and timeliness that can be acceptable to all in this process and in developing aggregate loss estimates that can approach a reasonable "ballpark" range. These issues beg for future research. With the above concerns pointed out, the case studies that follow were completed using the latest research methods available at the time.

9.2. Damage to Fish–Shellfish

9.2.1. Harvest Closures and Restrictions

Commercial Lobstering. Economic impacts from harvest restrictions because of PCB contamination in New Bedford Harbor to local commercial lobstermen were investigated by McConnell and Morrison (1986). Since 1979, waterbodies in New Bedford Harbor and some areas of Buzzards Bay, Massachusetts, have been closed to the harvest of lobsters because of PCB contamination. As a result, New Bedford inshore lobstermen have been forced to travel to new, more distant fishing grounds or discontinue lobstering. By reallocating effort to grounds outside the closed areas, lobstermen incur increased travel distance and, in turn, increased costs of time, fuel, vessel maintenance, and gear replacement. A survey was used to collect data on each of these elements. The increase in costs was estimated annually at $1093/lobsterman (1985$) and was used to represent economic damages that accrue from harvest closures because of PCB contamination. Total damages were estimated at $53,557/year (1985$) and the present value of economic damages over a 106-year period (the time period damages were expected to last, 1980–2085) is $2 million (1986$). An obvious economic impact that McConnell and Morrison do not address is the effect the pollution advisory and subsequent closure have had on the local demand and price for lobsters. It is suspected that the effect would be a decrease in revenues due to a demand and price reduction (assuming consumers are risk averse and choose to avoid contaminated seafood product; see Capps et al. [1984] for such an approach to hard clams), with lost consumer surplus and lost producer surplus. Thus the damages as estimated are likely to underestimate the true damage.

Sportfishing. In one of the few studies of marine pollution impacts on recreational fishing, McConnell and IE (1986) examined the impact of harvest restrictions because of PCB contamination in New Bedford Harbor and subsequent state health advisories on the local recreational fishery. Damages were identified and measured as increased costs incurred because of increased travel time and distance to alternative sites with relatively cleaner water. Benefits of pollution control were measured as the cost savings to anglers (i.e., anglers saving the increased costs) from removal of PCBs in the harbor and reversing the ban on bottom fishing in the harbor area. A survey was used to collect the data on increased costs. It was estimated that the damage due to increased time and distance traveled was an additional $1.60/trip (1986$) relative to normal trip costs. Total economic damages were estimated at $67,100 for 1986, and a present value of damages of $3.1 million over a 106-year period. Therefore, if PCBs were removed from New Bedford Harbor, benefits to recreational fishermen would amount to a savings of a present value of $3.1 million in additional trip costs.

9.2.2. Mortality—Fish–Shellfish Kills

In 1976 a severe hypoxic event occurred off the New Jersey coast that resulted in a massive shellfish kill or benthic mortality kill (Swanson and Sindermann 1979). Estimated impacts were assessed from estimates of the biomass lost, and the current dockside price commercial fishermen received expanded over time (a 5-year period) and throughout the seafood industry using an impact multiplier of 2.5 (Figley et al. 1979). Estimates of losses to the recreational fishery were developed from an estimate of average expenses from the 1975 National Survey of Hunting, Fishing, and Wildlife Associated Recreation expanded to sportfishing boat anglers, and estimates of anecdotal per vessel losses expanded for the party-charter boat fleet in New Jersey. Researchers estimated the economic impacts to the commercial fishery (surf clam, ocean quahog, scallop, lobster, and finfish) and seafood industry (processors–marketing sector) at $70.3 million (1976$, Figley et al. 1979). Economic impacts to the recreational fishery were estimated at $3.7 million (1976$), bringing the total estimated impacts to $74 million (1976$). Future effects to the commercial sector were projected at $498.6 million (1976$). However, this analysis has several shortcomings.

A major problem is that the entire amount of destroyed product was assessed at the current (1976) prices. This procedure is correct only if the quantity killed represents a small percentage of total landings or the resource. For example, it was estimated that 8.8 percent to 12.9 percent of the sea scallop resource off the New Jersey was lost. If this represents a small or negligible decline in market supply, assessment of the product lost at the current market price is appropriate. Concerning the lobster fishery, a 32 percent decline in New Jersey landings could have some effect on the local market price. For the surf clam and ocean quahog fishery, New Jersey is the largest national producer (MAFMC 1988). In 1976, the New Jersey harvest represented 49 percent of the total U.S. landings. Hence, a sizable decrease in landings in New Jersey would affect market supply and price. It was estimated that the hypoxic event destroyed 283 million pounds of surf clam meats and 102 million pounds of ocean quahogs (Figley et al. 1979). For surf clams, the largest harvest prior to 1976 was in 1974, when the U.S. harvest was 96 million pounds (the 1973–75 average was 88.3 million pounds, and the 5-year 1971–75 average was 76 million pounds). Hence, the amount lost in New Jersey exceeds U.S. landings by a factor of 3! A similar scenario is true for ocean quahogs. Prior to 1976, U.S. landings averaged 1 million pounds annually for the 1972–75 period (MAFMC 1988). In both cases, to assess all the lost New Jersey product at market prices is incorrect. If all of the lost New Jersey product came onto the market, the market would become glutted and the price would collapse. Therefore, only a proportion of the resource lost in the case of surf clams and ocean quahogs should be assessed, and the price used should reflect the decrease in the market price following a supply increase; that is, an estimate of the price that would have prevailed if the resource had entered the market.

Similar problems exist with estimated impacts for future time periods. Figley et al. (1979) estimate future impacts of $498.6 million (1976$) to commercial and recreational fisheries. We believe this estimate is too high for the following reasons. Future damages were not measured in present value or discounted terms, which is necessary for assessments of damages expected to occur over multiple time periods. To give some idea of this potential error, consider losses of $10,000/year over a 10-year period and a discount rate of 5 percent. Losses are overstated by 15 percent if not appropriately discounted and then summed. This would translate into an overestimate in the above case of some $75 million. The study also ignored economic gains (producer surplus, revenues) from corresponding increases in the market price due to reduced landings (i.e., the effect of a decrease in supply relative to demand) in their analysis. How much the future loss from reduced landings was offset by the increase in price would determine overall losses. For example, the value of U.S. landings increased from $13 million in 1975 to $23 million in 1976 and to $27 million in 1977 (MAFMC 1988). Over time, it was also learned that another benefit accrued to the surf clam fishery that was neither expected nor foreseen (this is not a criticism just an observation). Research indicated that along with the surf clam killed, the predators of the surf clam were also destroyed, and the resource has come back to higher levels than before the kill (Haskin, Personal Communication 1990).

9.3. Damage to Public Health

9.3.1. Unsafe Seafood—Demand Effects

Avoidance of Oysters from Kepone Contamination. During the 1975–76 period, the discovery of the pesticide Kepone in oysters in the James River in Virginia caused federal and state officials to prohibit oyster harvesting from the James River. The event was highly publicized. Swartz and Strand (1981) examined demand effects on uncontaminated oyster products from other waterbodies (both inside and outside Virginia) resulting from the publicity of Kepone and the subsequent harvest closings. A simultaneous demand and supply model of the oyster market in Baltimore (the market impacted and chosen for this analysis) using a polynomial distributed lag form (see Judge et al. 1988 for information about these functional equation forms) for the demand model for 64 biweekly periods during the Maryland oyster season (usually September–October) from 1973 to 1976 (a period of time to account for a "before-Kepone-was-discovered" period and an "after-Kepone-was-discovered" period). The demand and supply model was estimated using a two-stage least squares statistical method (see Judge et al. 1988).

Newspaper articles (the only news media examined) were found to have a significant negative impact on demand for uncontaminated oysters. An additional news article was estimated to cause per capita consumption to drop 0.5 gallons/100 residents (or 1 gallon/200 residents). Welfare losses were estimated at $13,000 (1976$), or about 5 percent of the market value, from estimates of consumer surplus and producer surplus based on the difference between a simulated condition with "no news about Kepone" versus the estimated models "with news reporting" (i.e., the welfare losses from a leftward shift of the demand curve). After an 8-week period following the initial news coverage, consumer avoidance wore off, and consumption returned to previous levels. The researchers conclude that both consumer avoidance and welfare losses were due to conveying imperfect information via news articles.

Hard Clam Avoidance from Gastroenteritis Outbreak. Capps et al. (1984) examined the market effects of a gastroenteritis outbreak on the hard clam market, specifically the losses from a decrease in wholesale and ex-vessel prices following a fall in demand. The outbreak occurred over the summer of 1982 in upstate New York and received widespread publicity. In this analysis, a simultaneous model of demand for various clam sizes (littlenecks, cherrystones, and chowder clam sizes) and ex-vessel price formation was estimated using a two-stage statistical method with a ridge regression modification to account for collinearity problems (i.e., where the effects of individual independent variables on the dependent variable cannot be separated from their joint/combined effects due to linear relationships that exist among the dependent variables; see Judge et al. [1988]). Monthly data was used for the 1972–82 period (to isolate the decrease in demand expected in 1982).

It was found that the disease outbreak and media coverage decreased the wholesale and ex-vessel prices of hard clams, a decrease of 50 percent to 74 percent. A loss in revenues of $2.05 million (1982$) was estimated (65 percent at the ex-vessel level and 35 percent at the wholesale level). Furthermore, ex-vessel prices of uncontaminated hard clams were found to be affected in Rhode Island, North Carolina, New Jersey, Virginia, and New York. Results also demonstrated that the downward demand shift was short term in nature for the New York market (consumer avoidance began to disappear a few months after the initial reports), although impacts persisted longer in the other states.

Both of these demonstrate that wider market effects are possible as a result of highly publicized local events. The studies also demonstrate that news of local contaminated seafood products and health effects can influence demand for uncontaminated product and result in significant short-term losses.

Swordfish Avoidance from Mercury Contamination. In another study Lipton (1986) investigated the U.S. swordfish market and the impact of mercury contamination on consumer demand. In 1971 the U.S. Food and Drug Administration (FDA) issued warnings about consuming swordfish containing high mercury concentrations. Prior to the FDA announcement, per capita consumption was estimated at 0.04–0.05 pounds/year. In 1971 after release of the announcement, per capita consumption fell to less than 0.002 pounds/year. It was not until 1983–84 that consumption levels returned to their previous levels of 0.04–0.05 pounds/year, 13–14 years after the FDA warning. By 1985, consumption had increased to almost 0.08 pounds/year. Interestingly, the FDA warning only pertained to imported swordfish products, although the domestic product landed and sold in the same state could have contained mercury concentrations equal to or higher than the limits set on imported product. This type of warning resulted in depressed demand for all swordfish as demonstrated by the consumption data.

Although present consumption is at its highest levels ever, current information about mercury concentration levels are unknown. Is it because the public has forgotten about the FDA warnings (as illustrated by Lipton's findings), or have mercury levels fallen so that increased consumption levels are now safe? It is possible that individuals may not heed advisories or warnings about limiting or avoiding consumption of particular seafood, and instead choose not to alter their present consumption levels because of beliefs and opinions about health risks and contaminated seafood products. Or it could be that they may simply be willing to accept higher risk rather than forgo consumption of a seafood product they enjoy. For example, despite health advisories that had been issued in New Jersey since 1982, many urban–recreational fishermen in northern New Jersey tended to ignore these health advisories (Belton et al. 1986). Findings confirmed this; 60 percent of fishermen surveyed reported eating some of their catch, with 88 percent of these anglers believing that their catch was "somewhat safe but not harmful." Perceptions and beliefs about health risk and safety of seafood partially contribute to the study's findings along with the

fact that the health advisories issued by the state government may have been too technically complicated for the public to understand (Belton et al. 1986).

9.4. Damage to Beach Use—Closures/Restrictions

Beach Avoidance and Cost Impacts from 1976 Pollution Event—Long Island Beaches. In an
assessment of a marine pollution incident that occurred during June 1976 at numerous
Long Island beaches in New York, Economic Research Associates (ERA) (1979) estimated
cost impacts from changes in travel patterns due to this incident. Average expenses of
beach use were expanded based on the loss in beach attendance. The study is important
because it demonstrates that widespread publicity of a fairly localized incident, beach
closings in the western part of Long Island due to washups of marine debris (see Swanson et al. 1978 for an account of this), coupled with imperfect information (i.e., approximate locations of closed beaches) can affect beach use and tourism in areas that did not
experience any marine pollution. ERA recognized that beach users had alternative beach
sites to choose from and could avoid the closed beaches. Because of this, ERA chose to
examine changes in attendance at three different types of beaches within a 100-mile distance of the closed beaches. Jones Beach and Robert Moses State Park, Long Island, represented a severely polluted beach closed during June; Smith Point Beach, Long Island,
represented a moderately polluted beach that was not closed; and Seaside Heights, New
Jersey, a clean beach that was not closed. During the June incident, ERA noted that press
releases exaggerated the incident and did not specify which particular beaches were
affected. As a result, imperfect information contributed to residents' beliefs that all Long
Island and New Jersey beaches were polluted. The study found that beach attendance
declined 50 to 60 percent in 1976 over previous 1975 levels at all three beaches. Impacts
from lost expenditures (excluding beach fees) were estimated at $8,876,800 (1976$) for
Jones and Robert Moses Beaches, $734,100 for Smith Point, and $332,100 for the Seaside
Heights, New Jersey, beach.

Value of Beach Use in Florida. The first comprehensive economic study of recreational
beach use was conducted by Bell and Leeworthy (1986). The study examined both residents' and tourists' characteristics and patterns of beach use in Florida from survey data
of a random sample of residents and nonresidents (tourists). It was the first study to estimate the economic benefits of beach use in terms of consumer surplus using a simple
contingent valuation method (open-ended willingness-to-pay questions) and a linear
travel cost demand model. Results indicated that residents were willing to pay $1.31/day
and tourists $1.45/day for a beach day (1984$). Estimates of consumer surplus from linear demand travel cost models produced the following results: $10.23/trip for residents
and $29.32/trip for tourists (1984$).

Value of Water Quality Improvements—Chesapeake Bay. Three studies have examined
economic benefits from water quality improvements in the Chesapeake Bay. In the first
study, Strand et al. (1985) used a CV approach to assess net economic benefits from
improving water quality levels for all recreational uses in general. A survey of residents in
the Baltimore–Washington SMSA (Standard Metropolitan Statistical Area) was conducted using a CV method (closed-ended willingness-to-pay questions in which dollar

amounts were randomly changed over the sample) coupled with a logit statistical model to obtain net economic value estimates. They found that the average household was willing to pay over $60/year (1984$) in additional taxes to raise water quality to "acceptable" levels (i.e., average of $69/year across users and nonusers, a range of $45 to $138/year for users and $28 to $73/year for nonusers; see Strand et al. [1986] for additional detail of the first study). In a second study, Strand et al. (1986) attempted to substantiate the previous study's finding using actual behavior of recreationists and estimated travel-cost demand models. The economic value of water quality improvements per user for beach use were found to range from $6.91 to $10.67/year (average of $32.59/year) (1984$) based upon a discrete choice model (i.e., logit statistical model) estimated for each of the sample areas, and $18 to $43.41/year (average of $8.81/year) (1984$) based on a Tobit statistical model estimated for all the sample areas (i.e., data pooled over all sample areas). It was concluded that because the discrete choice model did not allow individuals to increase trips with improvements in water quality, the model underestimated benefits.

Then Bockstael et al. (1989) conducted a study that assessed the economic value of improvements of water quality (to swimmable levels) in the Chesapeake Bay based on a CV approach (i.e., closed-ended willingness-to-pay questions in which dollar amounts were randomly changed over the sample) coupled with a logit statistical model for all recreational uses. Data were based on a survey of households in the Baltimore–Washington SMSA. Net economic value was estimated in terms of participation status and racial composition (e.g., a white user was willing to pay $183.63/year, a nonwhite user $34.16/year, a white nonuser $48.13/year and a nonwhite nonuser $8.95/year [1984$]). Aggregate benefits were expanded to represent the entire Baltimore–Washington SMSA population and were estimated at $83.6 million for an average case, $106.976 million for an optimistic case, and $60.275 million for a pessimistic case (1984$). Both previous economic value estimates (those of Strand and others) fall within the range of estimated impacts reported in this latter study and illustrate the wide variation that can be present in expanded economic impact–value estimates.

Beach Use Losses from PCBs—New Bedford Harbor. In a study of improved water quality in New Bedford Harbor, McConnell and IE (1986) examined the effect of PCB contamination in New Bedford Harbor on recreational beach use and estimated the benefits from removal of PCBs. A survey of households was used to collect data on household beach use patterns and perceptions about the PCB problem. Household travel cost to a particular beach in the study area was calculated as the product of the round-trip distance from the center of the census tract to a specific beach and $0.084/mile plus the cost of time spent in travel to the specific beach (i.e., the opportunity cost of time). The opportunity cost of time was valued by associating the occupation of the surveyed household head with an appropriate average pre-tax hourly rate from *Employment and Earnings* (a U.S. Department of Labor publication); in some cases the U.S. minimum wage was used for those occupations/categories not listed. The wage rate was then adjusted by a marginal tax rate to represent the after-tax opportunity cost of time. Travel cost demand curves were estimated using a Tobit statistical approach to account for a large number of 0-observations associated with beach trips (the independent variable) (see Judge et al. 1988 for a discussion of the Tobit model).

Economic damages per trip were estimated at $2.88 to $3.31/household for households which were aware of the PCB contamination problem. Benefits of beach access per trip were estimated for planned 1986 trips, and ranged from $4.25 to $4.61 per user with PCB contamination and $8.44 to $8.71 per user without PCB contamination for households aware of PCB contamination. Benefits from PCB removal (or conversely damages due to PCBs) were calculated from consumer surplus estimates without PCB less those with PCB. This yielded a range from $2.88 to $3.31/household per trip. For households not aware of PCB contamination, benefits of planned 1986 beach use ranged from $4.25 to $6.64 ($5.45 was the midpoint). Overall estimates of the present value of PCB-related damage to beach use over a 107-year period (1979–2085) ranged from $8.3 million with constraints on beach capacity, to $11.4 million without capacity constraints (1985$ discounted to 1986).

Beach Use Losses from 1988 Pollution Events—New York Bight. As part of the U.S. EPA's New York Bight Restoration Plan, Kahn et al. (1989a) assessed economic impacts and economic damage for the New York Bight region for use impairments due to marine pollution events during 1988. A simplified benefits transfer approach was used in which an estimate of the average expense and average economic value was expanded based on a decline in observed beach attendance in New Jersey of 8 to 34 percent from 1987 to 1988. Expenditure impacts were developed using multipliers of 2 to 3 to account for the total effect of spending and responding effects in the economy. As a result of washups of marine debris, lost net economic value for New York and New Jersey was estimated to range from $447 to $1,515 million (1987$). Direct expenditures lost ranged from $539 to $2,165 million (1987$). Lost net economic value as a result of pathogen contamination to the New York–New Jersey area was estimated at $287 million, and losses of direct expenditures $236 million (1987$). This study is discussed in detail below as a case study.

Beach Use Losses from 1988 Pollution Events—New Jersey. In an examination of 1988 marine pollution events in New Jersey, Ofiara and Brown (1999) reassessed economic damages and impacts based on an earlier study (Ofiara and Brown 1989). The study used a simplified benefits transfer approach that expanded average expense and average economic value estimates. During the summer of 1988 numerous beaches along the Jersey shore were closed as a result of periodic washups of marine debris and medical waste and excessive levels of bacteria. Based on an estimated range of decline in beach use attributable to the 1988 event of 9 to 44 percent (average of 26 percent), lost net economic value to beach use was estimated to range from $131.7 million to $643.98 million (a midpoint of $380.5 million), and lost expenditures from $250.9 million to $1,226.9 million (a midpoint of $724.98 million) (1987$).

9.5. Damage to Property Value—Housing, Real Estate

Losses in Property Value from PCBs—New Bedford Harbor. Mendelsohn (1986) conducted an examination of the economic damage caused by PCB contamination in New Bedford Harbor, Massachusetts, to single-family residential homes using a repeat sales approach. A sample of single-family, owner-occupied residences for which repeat sales were available over the 1969–85 period resulted in 1,030 observations. A requirement of the data was that residences had to sell before the 1979–80 period and after the 1979–80 period; that is, sales of residences had to straddle the 1979–80 period (the time period when most residents became aware of the PCB problem). Sales were adjusted for housing improvements to eliminate any effect these improvements might have had on housing values. Sales prices were also corrected for inflation. The results indicated that in the most polluted areas, the adjusted value of homes averaged $5600 less, or 9.8 percent less, than similar homes near cleaner waters. In the next most polluted area, adjusted values averaged $6300 less or 13.9 percent less than similar homes near cleaner waters. On the basis of these results and a sample projection factor, aggregate damages were estimated to range from $27.3 million to $39.8 million (1985$).

9.6. Detailed Assessments of Impairments to Resources or Improvements to Water Quality in Selected Estuaries in the U.S. EPA National Estuary Program

9.6.1. Long Island Sound Study

Long Island Sound was designated a significant national estuary and included in a special study by the U.S. EPA in 1985, referred to as the Long Island Sound Study (LISS); it was one of the first estuaries included in the U.S. EPA's National Estuary Program in 1987. Long Island Sound is approximately 110 miles long, at its widest point 21 miles wide, and it encompasses 1300 square miles of water (U.S. EPA 1989). It is bounded by Long Island on the south, New York City and the East River on the west, Connecticut on the north, and the Atlantic Ocean on the east. It represents a highly urbanized estuary due to the proximity of New York City and the densely populated areas of Queens, Nassau and Suffolk Counties, Westchester County, and Southwestern Connecticut (Fairfield and New Haven Counties) and is impacted by some 14.6 million people from these areas. The LISS identified a number of priority areas to address in their Comprehensive Conservation and Management Plan (CCMP) so as to improve and restore the water quality and integrity of its resources and resource uses. These priority areas were: toxic contamination, pathogens, hypoxia, habitat loss and alteration, and changes in living resources (Altobello 1992; LISS 1988, 1989/90; U.S. EPA 1989).

A study was conducted to determine the economic importance of marine dependent activities as part of the LISS (Altobello 1992). The study used a simplified benefits transfer approach pertaining to recreational uses of previous economic studies. This report and its estimates of economic values are examined below. All dollar values are reported in 1990 dollars.

Commercial Finfishing and Shellfishing Industry. The estimates of economic value consist of the direct or primary value (i.e., value at ex-vessel prices) of landings, and subsequent economic impacts based on multipliers from a previous input–output (I/O) study in a Connecticut coastal county (consisting of "multiplier" effects, i.e., indirect and induced effects or secondary-ripple effects as dollars are respent in the economy, and total impacts, i.e., direct plus indirect and induced effects). The direct value of commercial fishery landings in 1990 was estimated at $53 million (Table 9.1). "Multiplier" or indirect and induced effects were estimated at $95.4 million ($53 million * 1.8 = $95.4 million), and the total impact of the commercial fishery was $148.4 million (based on a multiplier of 2.8; $53 million * 2.8) in 1990.

Table 9.1. Estimated Use Values and Economic Impacts to Long Island Sound, 1990.

Category	Value ($ millions)
COMMERCIAL FISHERIES (FINFISH, SHELLFISH)	
Direct value (ex-vessel)	53.0[a]
Multiplier effects (*2.8)	95.4[b]
Total value	148.4
RECREATIONAL USE	
Use value	303.17[c]
Direct expenditures	2,187.55
Multiplier effects	2,739.47
Total value	5,230.19
INTRINSIC — NONUSE VALUE	151.59[d]
RECREATION USE AND NONUSE VALUE	5,381.78
TOTAL RESOURCE VALUE	5,530.18
VALUE OF COASTAL WETLANDS	93.75[e]

[a]CT DEP – Marine Fisheries Division and NY DEC – Marine Division.
[b]Multiplier of 2.8 from Crawford (1984). Although it is usual practice to report the multiplier in this manner it is somewhat misleading, e.g., the dollar amount of $95.4 mill. is actually $53.0 mill. * 1.8; the total value of $148.4 mill. is based on $53.0 mill. * 2.8. Usually multiplier effects are not listed separately, the usual practice is to report the combined multiplier effect, e.g., $148.4 mill. based on a multiplier of 2.8.
[c]See Tables 9.2 and 9.3.
[d]Estimated as half of use value for recreation following Fisher and Raucher (1984).
[e]Product of $2500/acre and midpoint of 37,500 acres (35,000–40,000 acres) from CT DEP – Marine Fisheries Division.
Source: Altobello (1992).

Recreational Uses: Beach Use and Swimming, Pleasure Boating, and Sportfishing. Before dollar values can be assessed to a use, some indication of its magnitude is necessary. In the case of recreational uses this usually consists of the number of user days or trips (i.e., user days express trips in terms of days as the basic unit, assuming that a trip is equivalent to a day in length versus several hours, etc.). The number of trips (e.g., user days or activity days) for beach use and pleasure boating was estimated from the formula:

$$D = R * P * N * F,$$

where D represents the annual number of trips, R the participation rate, P population estimate, N demand distribution factors, and F facility coefficients. Population estimates and demand distribution factors are contained in Table 9.2 for beach use and boating. Participation rates for beach use were 5.0 to account for reductions from beach closings in the late 1980s (the estimated participation rate was 15.15 days per year for 1980 [NERBC 1975a]) and 4.0 for boating (reduced from 5.5 for 1980 [NERBC 1975a]). Lastly, facility coefficients used were 0.6 for beach use, 0.4 for boat ramps, and 0.3 for boat slips and moorings estimated for 1980 (NERBC 1975b). The product of these variables results in estimated trips (Table 9.2).

Table 9.2. Derivation of Estimated Trips (User or Activity Days), Long Island Sound Region, 1990.

| State: Co. | Population | DEMAND-DISTRIBUTION FACTORS | | |
		Beach Use/Swimming	Boating: Ramps	Boating: Slips and Moorage
CT				
New London	254,957	2.25	1.25	3.0
Middlesex	143,196	2.10	2.20	5.45
New Haven	804,219	1.50	0.45	1.0
Fairfield	827,645	0.50	0.40	1.7
Total	2,030,017			
NY				
Westchester	874,866	0.50	0.20	0.90
Nassau	1,287,348	0.50	0.20	0.90
Suffolk	1,321,864	0.30	0.15	0.30
Queens	1,951,958	0.30	0.15	0.30
Total	5,436,036			
		ESTIMATED TRIPS (USER DAYS)		
CT				
New London		1,720,960	917,845	509,914
Middlesex		920,135	936,502	504,050
New Haven		3,618,986	965,063	579,038
Fairfield		1,241,468	1,688,396	529,693
Total		7,483,549	4,507,806	2,122,695
NY				
Westchester		1,312,299	944,855	279,957
Nassau		1,931,022	1,390,336	411,951
Suffolk		1,189,678	475,871	317,247
Queens		1,756,762	702,705	468,470
Total		6,189,761	3,513,767	1,477,625

Source: Altobello (1992).

The method used to obtain estimates of economic value of recreational uses in this study was based on a simplified benefits transfer approach, where estimates from previous studies were used and adjusted to represent 1990 dollars. Table 9.3 contains both average and aggregate estimates for use values (i.e., net economic value to users) and expenditures together with multiplier effects. For beach use, estimated trips are multiplied by the average use value to obtain an estimate of aggregate use value. Aggregate direct expenditures are obtained in a similar manner, and "multiplier" effects are obtained from the product of direct expenditures and one minus the multiplier (e.g., 2.27186–1 = 1.27186, etc.). The sum of aggregate direct expenditures and multiplier effects gives aggregate total expenditures. Altobello (1992) also obtained an estimate of the total resource value from the sum of aggregate use value and aggregate total expenditures. Aggregate use value for the Long Island region was estimated at $303.17 million, aggregate direct expenditures $2,187.55 million, total expenditures $4,927.02 million, yielding a total resource value of $5,230.19 million (sum of use value and total expenditures) for the three recreational uses (beach use—swimming, pleasure boating, and

Table 9.3. Derivation of Aggregate Economic Value and Expenditure Impacts, Long Island Sound 1990.

						Aggregate			
	Estimated Trips	Average Econ. Value	Average Expense		Economic Value	Multiplier Expenditures	Total Effects	Resource Impacts	Value
Use: State	NO.	$/TRIP	$/TRIP	Multiplier			$ MILLIONS		
Beach Use									
CT	7,483,549	13.34[a]	21.26[d]	2.271186[g]	99.83	159.10	202.35	361.45	461.28
NY	6,189,761	13.34[a]	21.26[d]	2.271186[g]	82.57	131.59	167.36	298.95	381.52
Pleasure Boating									
CT	6,630,501	8.48[b]	126.08[e]	2.20[h]	56.23	836.00	1,003.20	1,839.2	1,895.43
NY	4,991,392	8.48[b]	126.08[e]	2.20[h]	42.33	629.31	755.17	1,384.48	1,426.81
Sportfishing									
CT	1,485,000*	7.46[c]	783.20[f]	2.41674[i]	11.08	258.46	366.17	624.63	635.71
NY	1,491,750*	7.46[c]	783.20[f]	2.41674[i]	11.13	173.09	245.22	418.31	429.44
All Uses									
CT	—	—	—	—	167.14	1,253.56	1,571.72	2,825.28	2,992.42
NY	—	—	—	—	136.03	933.99	1,167.75	2,101.74	2,237.77
Total	—	—	—	—	303.17	2,187.55	2,739.47	4,927.02	5,230.19

Note: All dollars are in 1990 dollars. Resource value is the sum of economic value and total (expenditure) impacts.

*Product of estimated number of individuals participating in marine sportfishing and participation rate: CT 330,000/year * 4.5days/yr, NY 221,000/year (from mid-point of range 484,000–741,000/year times 0.3608 [36.08 are Long Island Sound anglers]) * 6.75days/yr.

[a]Bell and Leeworthy (1986); use values of $10.23/trip for residents and $29.32/trip for nonresidents, Altobello (1992) used $10.23/trip adjusted to 1990 dollars (1990$).

[b]Reiling, Gibbs and Stoevener (1973).

[c]Hushak, Winslow and Dutta (1988).

[d]Average of daily estimated expenses of $23.17/trip (Tyrrell et al. 1982), $18.87/trip and $21.74/trip (Bell and Leeworthy 1986).

[e]CMTA (1987); $728 million in 1987 for boat sales and accessories and services. Average expenditures as $836 mill./6,630,501 = 126.08/day in 1990 dollars.

[f]1985 average estimated expenses of $369/trip or $447.19/trip in 1990 dollars from CT DEP. Kahn (1991) estimated average expenses of NY anglers at $1,119.20/trip in 1990 $; midpoint of $447.19 and $1,119.20 is $783.20/trip.

[g]Average of multiplier ratios for sectors 5, 6, 7, 8, 13, 14 to represent the tourism industry (Crawford 1984).

[h]Rorholm and Burrage (1983).

[i]Average of multiplier ratios for sectors 7, 8, 9, 11, and 14 to represent the sportfishing industry (Crawford 1984).

marine sportfishing) in 1990. In addition intrinsic values of recreational activities were calculated, and consisted of nonuse values such as existence values, assuming nonuse values represented 50 percent of use values (see Fisher and Raucher 1984). Intrinsic values were estimated at a total of $151.59 million in 1990 (Table 9.1).

Coastal Wetlands. A value was also placed on coastal wetlands in the Long Island Sound estimated at 35,000 to 40,000 acres. A value of $2500/acre to represent the value of wetland "services" (services were not defined nor itemized in Altobello [1990] and are taken to mean *all* services) from previous studies was used. The product of the midpoint of acreage (37,500 acres) and $2500/acre resulted in an estimate of $93.75 million for the value of services and benefits from coastal wetlands (Table 9.1).

Overall, the total resource value of Long Island Sound resources selected in this study yielded an aggregate of $5,530.18 million (sum of total value of the commercial fishery [$148.4 million], and the sum of use and nonuse values of selected recreational activities [$5,381.78 million], 1990$).

Criticisms of this study concern the marine sportfishing estimates. The estimate of the average value of a sportfishing trip ($7.46/trip) is somewhat low compared to similar estimates of sportfishing trips in Southern California for party/charter boat trips and for private boat trips, the two most significant fishing modes in Long Island Sound. As a result, economic value should be based on these two boat modes; in Southern California estimates were $47/trip for party/charter boat trips and for private boat trips $89/trip in 1990 dollars (Wegge et al. 1986). In addition, the average expense of a sportfishing trip ($783.20/trip) is rather high compared to average expenses of sportfishing trips in New Jersey (Ofiara and Brown 1999). For party/charter boats average expenses in New Jersey were $112/trip, for private boats $80/trip, and for shore-based trips $40/trip in 1990 dollars. If these changes (for economic value and expenses of boat fishing only) are incorporated into the Long Island Study, estimated use values for recreation would become $420.87 to $545.89 million (midpoint of $483.4 million) compared to Altobello's estimate of $22.2 million a 19- to 24-fold increase. Estimated direct expenditures become $1800.08 to $1,817.71 million, and "multiplier" effects $3,991 to $4,927 million. The intrinsic value would become $210.44 to $272.95 million (midpoint of $241.7 million) for recreational uses.

Another criticism concerns the value of coastal wetlands ($2500/acre) used in the study. This is an area that begs for more research to differentiate and develop estimates of specific services that coastal wetlands provide. Altobello (1992) notes that this estimate was provided for illustrative purposes rather than as a more exact value estimate.

9.6.2. New York Bight Use Impairments

The New York Bight has been described as one of the most used and abused coastal areas in the world (Swanson et al. 1991). Some 20 million people reside within watersheds that empty into the New York Bight. The New York Bight represents the coastal area from a southeast transect from the tip of Long Island (Montauk Point) to the 200-meter contour of the continental shelf; from an east transect from the tip of Cape May, New Jersey, to the 200-meter contour; and a transect joining these two points (Swanson et al. 1991, their Figure 1). Historically the New York Bight has been abused from industrial development and urbanization and has received the waste products of some 20 million people that reside along its shores, nearby land, and watersheds that empty into the New York Bight (Swanson et al. 1991). Garbage and trash was legally dumped into the Bight over the 1888–1934 period (Squires 1983, Swanson 1993). There are a variety of dump sites within the New York Bight. The 12-Mile Sewage Sludge Dump Site, or "12-Mile Site" as it is commonly referred to, received sewage sludge over the 1924–87 period (Mueller and Anderson 1978, Swanson et al. 1991). As late as 1986, some 6.64 million wet metric tons of sewage sludge from 12 New Jersey municipal sewage treatment facilities, 11 New York City, and 3 Nassau County sewage treatment facilities were dumped at this site. As this sludge dumpsite was phased out, an offshore sludge dumpsite (the 106-Mile Sewage Sludge Dump Site) was used, and in 1990 11 million wet metric tons of sewage sludge were dumped there (Massa et al. 1996, Swanson et al. In process). By 1992, ocean dumping of sludge in the New York Bight was phased out.

An Acid Waste Dump Site, 17 miles from the Statue of Liberty established in 1948 and phased out in 1981, was used primarily for industrial waste by-products of hydrochloric acid, and sulfuric acid–iron wastes in recent times (Massa et al. 1996, Squires 1983). A further offshore industrial waste dumpsite, the 106-Mile Industrial Waste Dump Site, which operated from 1965 to 1981, is beyond the boundary of the New York Bight (Massa et al. 1996, Squires 1983). This site received more-toxic materials such as hydrochloric acid–iron; a sodium sulfate solution containing methanol, methylamines, and phenol; waste products from the production of thiabendazole; and by-products from the manufacture of rubber chemicals, paper chemicals, water-treatment chemicals, and nonpersistent organophosphate insecticides, among others (Squires 1983).

Other dumpsites consist of a Cellar Dirt Dump Site that received debris from construction and demolition projects in the New York metropolitan area over the 1940–89 period, which amounted to 180,000 cubic yards per year over the 1973–89 period (Gross 1976, Massa et al. 1996, Squires 1983). Dredge disposal dump sites were also established in the New York Bight to receive dredged material (usually bottom sediment) from harbor and channel projects, among them the Mud Dump Site. The process of dredging and dumping of dredged material has now resulted in a new problem, the resuspension of toxicants, since bottom sediment and dredged material have been found to contain toxic substances. Within the Bight, dredged material contains the largest source of copper, cadmium, lead, and chromium and possibly the largest source of chlorinated hydrocarbons such as PCBs (Squires 1983). Finally, a wood burning site operated by the U.S. EPA from the mid-1960s to 1990 (officially dedesignated in 1997) is located within the New York Bight (Massa et al. 1996). This site received all floatable wooden drift material in the New York–New Jersey Waterways to minimize any hazard from floating drift (Bell 1989). In addition, up to 2.3 billion gallons (8.7 billion liters) of wastewater (primary and secondary treated wastewater) are discharged into the New York Harbor daily (HydroQual 1989).

In spite of this waste load, the New York Bight provides enormous recreational opportunities to its population, including beach use and swimming, ocean sports, pleasure boating, marine sportfishing, and wildlife and bird watching. Additional opportunities include educational and scientific uses, navigation and transportation, commercial fisheries, and summer beach communities for leisure and escape from the pressures of New York City and the surrounding metropolitan areas.

As part of a U.S. EPA investigation to develop a New York Bight Restoration Plan to rehabilitate and restore the water quality of the New York Bight, part of the U.S. EPA's Near Coastal Waters Program, a study was conducted to determine the use impairments and estimate the ecosystem impacts in the New York Bight (WMI, SUNY 1989a) from the pollution just described. Economic activities and uses assessed consisted of the following: recreational beach use–swimming, unsafe seafood products, commercial and recreational navigation and boating, and commercial and recreational fisheries. Economic measures consisted of losses in net economic value (consumer surplus) and losses in expenditures (both direct and multiplier effects, i.e., indirect and induced effects). Results from two main studies are presented and discussed because of different assumptions used and coverage, and because the New York Bight analysis is poorly documented; one study pertains to the the New York Bight region (Kahn 1993, Swanson et al. 1991, WMI, SUNY 1989a), and another to the state of New Jersey (Ofiara and Brown 1988, 1989, 1999; Brown and Ofiara 1993). Both of these investigations use a simplified benefits transfer approach where average use value and expenditures from previous studies adjusted to current prices are expanded based on estimates of trip numbers (i.e., user days). However two of these studies (Swanson et al. 1991 and WMI, SUNY 1989a) present summary information with little discussion of the derivations. Furthermore, the Swanson et al. (1991) paper is a summary of the Waste Management Institute, State University of New York (1989a) report that is concerned with economic impacts in the form of direct expenditures and multiplier effects, and excludes losses of economic welfare such as consumer surplus estimates. The focus of the Kahn (1993) paper is about economic welfare losses.

9.6.2.1. Use Impairments and Economic Impacts to New York Bight from Recent Marine Pollution Events

Recent marine pollution events occurred in 1987 and 1988 within the New York Bight. In particular, beaches in New York and New Jersey were closed due to washups of marine debris and floatable waste, and from excessive levels of pathogens in both years. The 1987 marine pollution events mainly occurred along New Jersey beaches with beach closings reported in all four coastal counties (some 25 miles of beaches in late May and 50 miles of beaches in mid-August) due to marine debris and floatable waste washups and from excessive fecal coliform levels (NJDEP 1988; Ofiara and Brown 1989, 1999; Swanson and Zimmer 1989). By comparison, only two Long Island beaches, some 1.5 miles of beachfront, were closed in New York from waste washups. In 1988 washups of marine debris and floatables along with medical wastes occurred primarily along New York beaches. During July some 58 miles of beaches were closed in Long Island (Swanson and Zimmer 1989), and in New Jersey, beaches were closed in three of the coastal counties, with the majority of closings in the northernmost county (Monmouth Co.) due to debris and floatable waste washups (Ofiara and Brown 1989, 1999). The focus of the investigation of use impairments and economic impacts is due to the 1988 event.

Beach Use. The first step of this investigation involved determining the estimated trip numbers (user days) associated with beach use, and with marine recreational fishing, and then determining a range of probable changes (i.e., changes deemed "most likely" by professional judgment rather than based on probability distributions) attributable to the marine pollution event of 1988. First consider beach use. A baseline level of attendance was estimated to range from 60 million trips to 150 million trips, with an average of 105 million trips for New York with a comparable estimate for New Jersey of 93.6 million trips (Kahn et al. 1989a). Reductions in beach trips from waste washups in 1988 were estimated to range from 30 million to 90 million trips for New York, and 6.7 to 37 million trips for New Jersey assuming a 25 to 50 percent reduction for New York and a 7.9 percent to 34 percent reduction in New Jersey.

Losses in economic value were expanded based on estimates from Bell and Leeworthy (1986), and the estimated decrease in consumer surplus from an inward shift (i.e., decrease) of inferred demand curves (Kahn 1993; see Chapter 5 for more detail on measuring the decrease in consumer surplus following a decrease in the demand curve such as in Figures 5.9, 5.10, and 5.13). For example, for the lower-bound estimate of 60 million trips, consumer surplus is estimated at $660 million (60 million trips * $11/trip). Recall this is the shaded area a in Figures 2.1 and 2.3, Chapter 2, and can be found using the area of a triangle formula where area = 1/2 * base * height, the base is trip numbers and the height is an unknown price in addition to P_0 for inferred demand curves following Kahn (1993). The problem here is that one does not know the price P_0, because the demand curve is inferred and not statistically estimated. However Kahn (1993) shows that one can approximate the loss of consumer surplus assuming linear demand curves and estimate the approximate intercept of the demand curves, the prices P_0 and P_1 in Figure 5.13.

The steps to accomplish this follow; they are a bit technical and may require a second reading to fully understand. The area of consumer surplus as represented by a triangular area under the demand curve (refer to the shaded area a in Figures 2.1 and 2.3, Chapter 2) equals $660 million, where the base is 60 million trips, and the height is unknown. Now refer to Figure 9.1, in Chapter 9, for the remaining steps. Given the formula for the area of a triangle, two variables (i.e., the base-trips and the height-price) are necessary to calculate the area, a third variable. If we know only the area and one other variable—two known variables—then we can find the third variable using the procedure to solve for an unknown, here the intercept of the inferred demand curve D_0 in Figure 9.1; this is as follows: $660 million equals the area, and the base, 60 million trips (i.e., $660 mill. = 1/2 * 60 mill. * h, where h is unknown height; h can be found by transposing all terms to the left-hand side of the equation, giving h = (660 mill. * 2)/60 mill. or $22. The intercept of the inferred demand curve D_0 is now $P_0 + 22$ (see Figure 9.1). Following a 10 percent decrease in trips and a downward parallel shift in the demand curve, the number of trips is estimated to have decreased to 54 million trips (i.e., 60 million–[60 million * 0.10], or 60 million * 0.90) along with a corresponding 10 percent decrease in price (i.e., 22 * 0.90 = $19.80). The estimated consumer surplus now becomes $534.6 million (i.e., [54 million ($19.8]/2) and the loss in consumer surplus is the shaded area in Figure 9.1, $125.4 million, which represents a 19 percent decrease in consumer surplus (i.e., $660 million–$534.6 million = $125.4 million). Such a procedure is appropriate and is used in cases where an empirical demand curve has been estimated, and now Kahn (1993) using simple algebraic tools has shown how the difference in consumer surplus can be obtained even when a demand curve has not been estimated.

On the basis of this procedure, estimated losses in economic value from floatable waste washups were estimated at $300 to $990 million for New York, and $147 to $525 million for New Jersey; a total loss of net economic value of $447 to $1,515 million to the

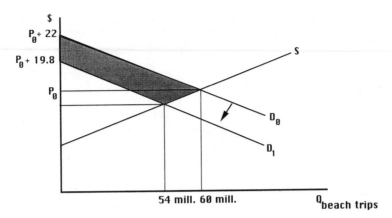

.Figure 9.1
Loss of Consumer Surplus from a 10 Percent Decrease in Demand.

New York Bight associated with beach use–floatable waste (Table 9.4; Kahn et al. 1989a). Such losses represent annual losses given a floatable waste washup of the magnitude experienced in 1988.

Losses of direct expenditures were estimated from previous studies and expanded to reflect the estimated loss from beach use. These estimates were $539 to $2,165 million to the New York Bight associated with the floatable washups in 1988 (Table 9.4). Total impacts were developed based on multipliers of 2.0 to 2.5, which yielded total impacts of $1,078 to $4,333 million for the multiplier of 2.0 and from $1,348 to $5,413 million for a multiplier of 2.5 (Table 9.4; Kahn et al. 1989a, Swanson et al. 1991). Again, these losses represent annual losses of expenditures from floatables that would correspond to an event similar to the 1988 event.

Economic losses and impacts were also estimated for beach use impairments associated with pathogens. Following a similar procedure as used by Kahn for effects from floatables, losses of consumer surplus were estimated at $277 million for the New York Bight (Kahn 1993, Kahn et al. 1989a). Losses of direct expenditure based on average estimates from previous studies were estimated at $236 million, with total impacts of $472 million (multiplier of 2) to $590 million (multiplier of 2.5).

These economic impacts were compared to two independent studies, one conducted for New Jersey and the other for New York, which found that losses of direct expenditures were estimated at $700 million for New Jersey (R.L. Associates 1988) and $700 million for New York (Conoscenti 1989) from marine pollution events, a total of $1,400 million from 1988 marine pollution events in 1988 dollars.

Unsafe Seafoods. Effects of the 1988 marine pollution events on recreational and commercial fishing sectors were analyzed from the perspective of the effects of unsafe seafoods. Toxicants were believed responsible for these effects. Again, estimates were based on previous average economic estimates and expanded.

Consider first the marine recreational fishery. Losses in consumer surplus were estimated at $250 million, losses in direct expenditures $500 million, and total losses of $1,250 million (Table 9.4; Kahn et al. 1989b, Swanson et al. 1991). Now consider the com-

Table 9.4. Use Impairments and Economic Impacts for New York Bight, 1988.

Use Impairment: Cause	Losses of Expenditures ($ millions)		
	NY	NJ	Both
BEACH CLOSURES			
Floatables			
Consumer Surplus	300–990	147-525	447–1,515
Direct Expenditures	300–735	239–1,430	539–2,165
Total Impact (*2.0)	600–1,470	478–2,860	1,078–4,333
Total Impact (*2.5)	750-1,838	598-3,575	1,348-5,413
Pathogens			
Consumer Surplus	180	97	277
Direct Expenditures	80	156	236
Total Impact (*2.0)	160	312	472
Total Impact (*2.5)	200	390	590
UNSAFE SEAFOODS			
Toxicants—Recreational Fishery			
Consumer Surplus			250
Direct Expenditures			500
Total Impact (*2.5)			1,250
Toxicants—Commercial Fishery			
Consumer and Producer Surplus	11.75	18.25	30
Direct Expenditures	11.75	18.25	30
Total Impact (*2.0)	23.50	36.50	60
Total Impact (*3.0)	35.25	54.75	90
Pathogens-Shellfish			
Loss of Landings			36
Impacts (*2 – *3)			72–108
COMMERCIAL AND RECREATIONAL NAVIGATION			
Floatables	250	250	500
Noxious Odors	13	13	26

	probable range
Overall	
Beach Closures—Pathogens	590–590
Beach Closures—Floatables	1,350–5,400
Total	1,940–5,990
Unsafe Seafoods—Toxicants	
Recreational Fishery	1,250–1,250
Commercial Fishery	60–60
Total	1,310–1,310
Unsafe Seafoods—Pathogens	
Commercial Fishery	72–108
Navigation—Floatables	500–500
Navigation—Odors	26– 26
Total	526–526
Total Impacts—w/o Navigation	3,322–7,408
Total Impacts—w Navigation	3,847–7,825

Source: Swanson et al. (1991); Kahn (1993); Kahn, Ofiara and McCay (1989a, 1989b).

mercial fishery. Losses in consumer surplus were estimated at $30 million for the New York Bight in 1988 assuming a 25 percent loss, a loss of $30 million for harvested landings corresponding to a 25 percent loss, with an estimated total impact of $60 to $90 million. Overall, total losses in consumer surplus (net economic value) approach a range of $280 million, direct expenditures $530 million, and total impacts $1,310 to $1,340 million (1988$) to the New York Bight from unsafe seafoods in 1988.

Economic effects were also examined from closing of shellfish beds, mainly due to pathogen contamination. Losses in shellfish landings were estimated at $36 million with impacts estimated to range from $72 million (multiplier of 2.0) to $108 million (multiplier of 3.0) (Table 9.4; Kahn et al. 1989c, Swanson et al. 1991).

Commercial and Recreational Navigation/Boating. Estimates of economic impacts due to floatable wastes were believed to be of similar magnitude to the annual expenditures of the New York–New Jersey Harbor floatable collection and burning program—$500 million/year (Table 9.4; Kahn et al. 1989d, Swanson et al. 1991). Furthermore, economic impacts of noxious odors (more specifically degraded water quality) were estimated at $26 million per year, based on a simplified benefits transfer approach using a study that estimated losses from degraded water quality to recreational boaters in the Chesapeake Bay (McConnell et al. 1986). This estimate was developed from the product of $30/individual/year, 146,266 registered vessels in New York and approximately three individuals per vessel with comparable estimates in New Jersey (i.e., $30 * 146,266 * 3 = $13.16 million * 2 states = $26.33 million) (Table 9.4; Kahn et al. 1989d, Swanson et al. 1991).

Overall, marine pollution events due to washups of floatable waste and excessive pathogen levels have had significant economic effects and impacts on the New York Bight.

9.6.2.2. Economic Assessment of New York Bight Use Impairments to New Jersey

As part of the New York Bight initiative, Ofiara and Brown (1988, 1989, 1999) and Brown and Ofiara (1993) conducted an assessment of losses of net economic value (economic welfare) and expenditures and impacts on the State of New Jersey from use impairments of recent marine pollution events in the New York Bight. Uses or sectors examined included beach use, travel and tourism, commercial and recreational fisheries, unsafe seafoods, disease and fish kills, and effects on shellfish resources. As in the case study of the New York Bight above, a simplified benefits transfer approach was used where average estimates from previous studies were adjusted to reflect the current price level, and expanded to represent effects to the State of New Jersey. In some cases sightly different assumptions were used and are discussed.

Beach Use. As in the case of New York beaches on Long Island, data on beach attendance in New Jersey over time are generally not available nor collected. Beach use in New Jersey consists of federal beaches (beaches at the Sandy Hook Gateway National Park complex), state beaches (e.g., Island Beach State Park), private beaches and beach clubs, and municipal and town beaches. In addition the manner in which beach use is marketed and sold to the public varies greatly. In some communities beach use is free (e.g., the Wildwoods, Atlantic City, for hotel guests), in some communities only private beach clubs are present (e.g., Allenhurst, Bay Head). In many other communities beach users are charged user fees, for example beach fees ranged from $3 to $8 per person per day on weekends, $2 to $6 per person on weekdays, and $10 to $55 per person for the entire season in 1988. At both federal and state beach areas, counts of cars are recorded and a conversion factor is used to estimate beach attendance. At municipal beaches records are only kept of beach tag sales and the number sold, while at private beach clubs members come and go as they please without records on daily use. As a result beach attendance data are absent and the first step was to estimate beach attendance at municipal beaches.

Beach attendance was estimated in the following manner. A study conducted by R.L. Associates (1988) estimated that 8.61 million individuals visited the shore region in New Jersey in 1987 from noncoastal counties and from out of state; this was used as the estimate of beach use by noncoastal residents. A telephone interview was conducted to obtain beach tag sales data for municipal beach use, which serves as a proxy for beach attendance. A total of 46 towns, boroughs, cities, a state park, and a federal park were contacted. Seven beach communities provided beach tag data for the 1984–88 period, which showed that total attendance was down each year from 1985, a 58.1 percent decline from 1985 to 1988. Without information on factors that can influence beach use, one can say little about the cause. But because New Jersey beaches were closed due to pollution events in 1987 and 1988, a greater proportion of the decline was probably attributable to these pollution events, but the relative magnitude is unknown.

Thirty-one beach communities provided information for the 1986–88 seasons representing 67 percent of all beach communities in New Jersey (Table 9.5; Ofiara and Brown 1999). In 1987 and 1988, beaches were closed from marine pollution events. In 1987 beach closing incidents were disproportionate; more closings were reported in the central region than in the northern region (the 44 days that Long Branch beaches were closed involved only private beaches, public/municipal beaches were not closed). The percent decrease in attendance from 1986 to 1987 ranged from 8.9 percent to 18.7 percent over all coastal counties but Cape May County (Cape May did not provide data for 1986). For the 1987–88 period, these data show that attendance decreased from 7.9 to 34 percent.

A range of impacts from the 1988 events was developed from various assumptions because time and financial constraints limited the original investigation. First, there was no information on other factors that could have affected beach use, making it impossible to know the exact effects from the pollution events. Because of the occurrence of pollution events in 1987 and 1988, a very large proportion of the decline in beach use is probably attributable to these events. Second, the effects of the 1987 and 1988 events may not be separable; the impacts of one may not be isolated from that of the other and the timing of the two events further confounds the separability issue, resulting in combined effects and possible lagged effects. Hence, one may only be able to assess the effects of the combined events; the issue of lagged effects must await further investigation.

Evidence on the number of washups, beach closings, and number of days beaches were closed from either event can lend further insight concerning isolation of both effects. On the basis of number of days beaches were closed, 104 in total for both 1987–88 (excluding Long Branch), the 1987 event accounted for 20 percent (21 days) and the 1988 event 80 percent (83 days). A total of 16 beaches were closed in 1987–88 (excluding Long Branch); 1987 accounted for 44 percent of all beaches (7 different beaches) and 1988

Table 9.5. Beach Attendance, Revenue, and Days Closed for Beach Communities by County, New Jersey, 1986–88.

County: Beach	1986 Attend. No.	1986 Revenue $	DC No.	1987 Attend. No.	1987 Revenue $	DC No.	1988 Attend. No.	1988 Revenue $
MONMOUTH CO.:								
Gateway[a]	NA	NA	0	1,667,617	677,462	4,1[b]	1,248,305	452,252
Highlands	*	—	—	*	—	—	*	—
Highlands Beach	**	—	—	**	—	—	**	—
Sea Bright	NA	NA	—	15,078	61,722	—	11,475	47,072
Long Branch[c]	NA	NA	43[4]	27,066	127,0797[d]	15,108	66,396	
Deal	NA	NA	—	NA	NA	—	NA	NA
Allenhurst	**	—	—	**	—	—	**	—
Asbury Park[e]	54,238	205,513	—	43,377	196,405	12	18,816	89,818
Ocean Grove	53,208	379,812	0	34,125	314,000	18	12,980	177,240
Bradley Beach[e]	65,060	418,484	—	62,713	504,061	9	32,829	380,867
Avon	28,677	449,745	—	34,103	476,362	14	28,486	326,362
Belmar[a]	151,225	1,752,196	—	140,919	1,684,960	2	96,742	1,217,899
Spring Lake	7,013	315,585	—	7,000	317,000	—	5,360	296,000
Sea Girt	15,415	334,861	0	15,492	368,593	0	13,528	323,404
Manasquan	73,479	932,202	1	70,764	905,910	0	57,052	823,572
OCEAN CO.:								
Pt. Pleasant Beach	12,030	24,178	—	NA	—	—	NA	—
Bay Head	**	—	—	**	—	—	**	—
Mantoloking	*	—	—	*	—	—	*	—
So. Mantoloking	NA	NA	—	12,687	66,980	—	9,429	61,917
Normandy Beach	NA	NA	—	2,090	6,270	—	1,614	4,842
Chadwick	NA	NA	—	NA	NA	—	NA	NA
Lavalette	NA	NA	0	42,460	443,369	0	34,448	380,220
Ortley Beach	NA	NA	—	NA	NA	—	NA	NA
Seaside Heights	498,905	1,789,535	4	450,551	1,689,981	1	272,779	744,694
Seaside Park	NA	NA	—	131,492	785,469	—	81,197	581,975
Island Beach St. Pk.	NA	NA	3	551,560	415,370	—	520,643	499,638
LONG BEACH ISLAND:								
Barnegat Light	NA	NA	—	NA	NA	—	NA	NA
Long Beach Twnsp.	87,267	379,812	0	34,125	314,000	18	12,980	177,240
Harvey Cedars	11,635	64,526	2	10,588	76,860	0	9,124	67,142
Surf City	NA	NA	—	38,303	285,288	—	32,809	243,296
Ship Bottom	NA	163,656	—	NA	252,272	—	NA	210,669
Beach Haven	NA	NA	0	NA	129,459	0	NA	101,891
ATLANTIC CO.:								
Brigantine	51,332	255,698	—	40,515	170,304	—	34,694	183,284
Atlantic City[f]	2,560,000	NA	6	2,150,000	NA	0	3,630,000	NA
Ventnor City	33,500	200,700	—	32,500	195,900	—	30,820	182,000
Margate City	NA	NA	—	12,687	66,980	—	9,429	61,917
Longport[g]	NA	NA	—	NA	55,498	—	NA	55,037
CAPE MAY CO.:								
Ocean City	NA	NA	—	309,786	1,537,799	5	258,603	1,340,396
Strathmere	*	—	—	*	—	—	*	*
Sea Isle City	NA	NA	—	NA	NA	—	NA	NA
Avalon	NA	NA	—	NA	NA	—	NA	NA
Stone Harbor	NA	NA	—	71,000	306,000	—	42,156	258,571
No. Wildwood	*	—	5	*	—	—	*	*
Wildwood Crest	*	—	—	*	—	—	*	*
Cape May	NA	NA	1	84,907	403,922	—	87,603	410,888

NA refers to not available.

*Beaches are free, no attendance figures are counted.

**No public beaches are located in the community, all are private.

[a]Comparison is from May to August, September (Labor Day weekend) was not available.

[b]Complete unit (bay and ocean beaches) was closed 4 days, 1/2 unit (ocean beaches) closed 1 day.

[c]Comparison is from May to July, August and September were not available.

[d]Private beaches, which were leased from the town, reported closings, public beaches were not closed.

[e]1988 figures are through August 31, 1988.

[f]Beaches were free, lifeguards/beach patrol performs attendance counts.

[g]1987 and 1988 beach fees remained the same.

some 56 percent (9 different beaches). The number of washups is unknown for 1988, but is known for 1987. Assuming that the effects are separable, the 1988 event would account for the largest share, 80 percent of days closed and 56 percent of beaches closed. If this were directly transferable to losses, then the 1988 event would be associated with larger losses than that of 1987. The data on beach use support this claim: Beach use declined 9 to 19 percent over 1986–87 and 8 to 33 percent over 1987–88. Hence, these assumptions were used to form the loss estimates associated with the 1988 event.

Derivation of the estimate of the range of losses follows. A range (low, average, and high) of decreases in beach use over the 1986–88 period over the three counties was first developed (Monmouth, Atlantic Ocean; data from 1986 were not provided by beaches in Cape May and hence were dropped from further analysis) based on the average of the minimum proportionate decline over the three counties (low estimate), the overall average of the proportionate decline in beach use for these counties (average estimate), and an average of the maximum proportionate decline over the three counties (high estimate). This yielded a range of decline of 13.94 to 64.38 percent, an overall average of 38.05 percent (over the average of the three counties). It was further assumed that the 1988 event accounted for 68 percent (i.e., midpoint of 80 percent and 56 percent) of the above decline, which yielded a range of 9.48 to 43.78 percent decline and an overall average decline of 25.88 percent. This procedure was felt to yield a conservative range of losses compared to using 80 percent as an upper-bound of the decline attributable to the 1988 event.

Beach attendance was derived from the RL Associates study (8.61 million noncoastal residents), and from the beach tag data as follows. First an estimate of beach users was derived and then an estimate of beach trips (i.e., user days or trips). Beach use by noncoastal residents was assumed to represent daily and weekly badge sales data, and that of coastal residents was represented by seasonal badge sales. An estimate of total beach users was developed from the product of 1 plus the ratio of seasonal badge sales to total daily and weekly badge sales (1 + 0.3168 = 1.3168) and the attendance of daily and weekly beach users (8.61 million). This yielded 11.34 million users (1.3168 * 8.61 million; Table 9.6). Attendance of coastal residents was then derived as 2.73 million individuals in 1987 (11.34 – 8.61 million).

The total number of trips or user days was derived as follows. Of the 8.61 million individuals, it was assumed that 6.31 million took an average of 4.7 day trips (RL Associates 1988), and it was assumed that the remainder took at least 1 day trip, which yielded 31.96 million trips by nonresidents ([6.31 million * 4.7 trips] + [2.3 million * 1 trip]). Coastal residents were assumed to take as many trips as did Florida residents based on a study by Bell and Leeworthy (1986); 14.68 trips during the summer season. The product of 2.73 million and 14.68 trips yields 40.08 million trips by coastal residents. In total 72.04 million beach trips served as the estimate of aggregate user days for the 1988 season (Table 9.6). This estimate is conservative compared to the estimate of 93.6 million user days for New Jersey from the New York Bight case study (Kahn 1993, Swanson et al. 1991).

Estimates of direct expenditures and consumer surplus attributable to beach use were then developed. Expenditures were developed based on average expenditures from previous studies ($77/day/person for noncoastal residents [RL Associates 1988], $8.17/day/person for coastal residents [NYDEC 1977]) and estimated user days. This yielded an aggregate estimate of $2,788.4 million in direct expenditures associated with

Table 9.6. Economic Effects on Beach Use (1987$).

Category	Noncoastal Residents[a]	Coastal Residents[a]	All Residents
	$ millions[b]		
Users	$6.32^c + 2.3^c$ =	$8.61^c + 2.73^d$ =	11.34
Average Day Trips	4.70^c 1.0	14.68^e	
Estimated Trips (User days)	29.66 + 2.3 =	31.96 + 40.08 =	72.04
Average Expenses ($/trip or $/days)		77.00^c 8.17^f	
Estimated Expenses		2460.92 + 327.45 =	788.37
Average Benefits ($/trip or $/days)		32.00^e 11.00^e	
Estimated Benefits		1022.72 + 440.88 =	1463.60
Gross Economic Value		3483.64 + 768.33 =	4251.97

ESTIMATED ECONOMIC LOSSES

Change	Expenses	Value	Gross Value
	$ millions[b]		
0	2,788.37	1,463.60	4,251.97
−9%	250.953	131.724	382.677
−26%	724.976	380.536	1,105.512
−44%	1,226.883	643.984	1,870.867

[a]Noncoastal Residents comprise residents from noncoastal counties in New Jersey and those from out-of-state, Coastal Residents comprise residents from coastal counties in New Jersey.
[b]In millions unless where indicated.
[c]RL Associates (1988).
[d]Ratio of seasonal badge sales to the sum of daily and weekly badge sales times noncoastal residents.
[e]Bell and Leeworthy (1986).
[f]NYDEC (1977).

beach users in New Jersey in 1987 (Table 9.6). On the basis of a multiplier of 1.899 (slightly less than that used by Kahn and others) from the State of New Jersey Economic I/O Model, multiplier effects were estimated at $2,506.77 million, which yields total expenditure impacts of $5,295.17 million ($2788.4 + $2506.77; direct plus indirect and induced impacts) from beach use. Economic value based on consumer surplus was estimated based on the Bell and Leeworthy (1986) estimate of $11.10/day/person for coastal residents and $32.08 for noncoastal residents in 1987 dollars, resulting in an aggregate estimate of $1,463.6 million associated with enjoyment and satisfaction from beach use (i.e., economic welfare of beach use) (Table 9.6).

Economic losses from the 1988 marine pollution events in New Jersey were then based on the estimated range of decrease in beach use of 9 to 44 percent (midpoint of 26 percent) and thus ranged from an estimated $132 million to $644 million (midpoint of $381 million) associated with lost net economic value, and $251 million to $1,227 million (midpoint of $725 million) associated with lost expenses in 1987 dollars (Table 9.6). Because losses of indirect expenditures (i.e., multiplier effects) were not included these aggregate impact estimates are conservative. If multiplier effects were included, estimated aggregate expenditure impacts to beach use would range from $477 million to $2,330 million (multiplier of 1.899; Table 9.6). In general these loss estimates are conservative when compared to loss estimates produced by Kahn and others (see Table 9.4). If one further defines gross economic value of beach use by the sum of expenditures and net economic value (i.e., the total area under a demand curve, the shaded areas $a + b$ in Figure 2.1, Chapter 2) total losses from marine pollution events in 1988 could be estimated at $383 to $1,871 million in New Jersey (1987$).

To gauge the relative magnitude of these estimates, estimated losses of economic value were extrapolated from a study of beach use and water quality in the Chesapeake Bay (Strand et al. 1986) based on average estimated losses of $19.69/person/year to $47.49/person/year in 1987 dollars. This yields a range of losses of economic welfare from marine pollution of from $223 million to $539 million (midpoint of $381 million) in 1987 dollars (i.e., 11.34 million * $19.69 to 11.34 million * $47.49). Although this range is within the above range of estimated net benefits, the midpoint value of $381 million is identical to Ofiara and Brown's average loss estimate for the 1988 event ($380.9 million vs. $380.5 million); hence, both procedures provide reasonable and fairly similar estimates of losses of net benefits. Furthermore, based on evidence of the nature of beach closings in 1988 in New Jersey (i.e., total number of beach closings due to specific causes), it is possible to disaggregate the estimated losses associated with specific effects (e.g., 82.4 percent due to sewage-bacteria levels, 14.3 percent due to medical waste washups, 2.2 percent due to grease balls, and 1.1 percent due to algae blooms) (McIver 1988).

Travel and Tourism. Statistical data that relate to business unit growth, employment growth, and wage payment growth available for the years 1982, 1986, and 1987 were also examined (Ofiara and Brown 1988, 1989). On the basis of this data, impairments from the marine pollution events of 1987 had little effect on these numbers, indicating that the pollution events were not strong enough to cause macroeconomic-type effects, but were strong enough to cause local effects.

Recreational Fishery. A range of impacts of the 1988 events on sportfishing was developed in the same manner as the range of impacts to beach use, and only a brief discussion follows (Ofiara and Brown 1999). On the basis of information on days beaches were closed (number of days closed) and on number of beaches closed, the 1988 event accounted for the largest share compared to the 1987 event, respectively 80 percent and 56 percent of the totals. However, the decline in sportfishing trips based on National Marine Fisheries Service (NMFS) sportfishing statistical data does not show a similar pattern, with trips declining only 26 percent in the 1986–87 period and 4 percent over the 1987–88 period, a total of 29 percent in 1986–88 (see Ofiara and Brown 1999). The estimate for the 1987–88 period served as the lower-bound estimate of losses, a decline of 4 percent. Derivation of the upper-bound estimate follows. Based on the overall decline of 29 percent for the 1986–88 period, the 1988 event accounted for 68 percent (midpoint of 80 percent and 56 percent) of this decline based on beach use data yielding a decline of 19.7 percent. This represents a conservative upper-bound estimate of losses when compared to an upper-bound of 34 percent (i.e., 68 percent of the decline over the 1986–89 period—0.68 * 0.50).

Economic losses for the sportfishery are developed on the basis of the range of impacts (4–20 percent) and expanded estimates for sportfishing expenditures and net economic value. Average expenses were obtained from survey research of the marine recreational fishery conducted by the New Jersey Department of Environmental Protec-

Table 9.7. Economic Effects on Marine Recreational Fishing (1987$).

Category[a]	Shore	Party/Charter	Private Boat	All
Average Expense ($/trip)[b]	34.71	97.05	69.41	—
Estimated Trips (No.)[c]	2,307,360	857,670	4,424,970	7,590,000
Estimated Expenses ($)	80,088,466	83,236,874	307,137,168	470,462,508
Average Benefits ($/trip)[d]	55	41	77	—
Estimated Benefits ($)	126,904,800	35,164,470	340,722,690	502,791,960
Gross Economic Value ($)	206,993,266	118,401,344	647,859,858	973,254,468

ESTIMATED ECONOMIC LOSSES

Change	Expenses	Value	Gross Value
	$ millions[b]		
0	470.462	502.792	973.254
−4%	18.819	20.112	38.930
−12%	68.455	68.335	116.791
−20%	94.092	100.558	194.651

[a]Refers to shore based fishing, party/charter vessel–based fishing, and private boat–based fishing.
[b]Based on survey data from B. Brown, NJDEP, Marine Fisheries Administration, Trenton, NJ.
[c]NMFS (1987).
[d]Wegge et al. (1986).

tion–Marine Fisheries Administration and expanded based on estimated trips (Table 9.7; Ofiara and Brown 1999). Economic welfare estimates were adapted from a study of marine recreational fishing in Southern California (Wegge et al. 1986; this study was used because it was the only study at the time that expressed net benefits in terms of fishing mode, the only context in which fishing trips could be projected) and expanded on the basis of trips (Table 9.7). Losses in economic welfare were estimated to range from $20 million to $100 million in 1988 (1987$). Losses of direct expenditures were estimated to range from $19 million to $94 million in 1988, and together with multiplier effects (i.e., indirect and induced expenditures based on a multiplier of 1.899), expenditure impacts were estimated to range from $35.7 million to $178.7 million in 1988 (Table 9.7). If the gross economic value of the sportfishery can be represented by the sum of expenditures and net economic value (i.e., the total area under a demand curve), then total losses from marine pollution would range from an estimated $39 million to $195 million (1987$).

Commercial Fishery. Data examined concerned landings, value of landings, unit price of landings for all finfish and shellfish harvested in New Jersey, and landings and subsequent value for bluefish, in particular. However, none of these data indicated any changes in 1987. Hence it was believed that the pollution events had little effect on the annual aggregate level of seafood harvested in New Jersey waters; in fact average finfish prices in 1987 were above those of 1983–1986 in all months (January–December) (Ofiara and Brown 1988, Brown and Ofiara 1993) when one would have suspected that if the 1987 pollution event had had a negative impact on seafood and seafood prices in New Jersey, demand would have decreased relative to supply causing the price to drop. The data support the opposite scenario; that demand increased relative to supply causing the price to rise in recent years.

Unsafe Seafoods. The following section contains estimates of long-term impacts from toxicants in the New York Bight and Hudson River Estuary that could result from continuous eating of contaminated finfish over a period of time. These estimates are not related to the short-term impacts estimated in the preceding text and attributable to the 1988 pollution event. Within the New York Bight, a number of toxicants occur, and several studies have implicated them in cancer mortalities. These studies have developed risk estimates of excess cancer mortalities (i.e., excess risk) from the consumption of contaminated seafood harvested from the New York Bight–Hudson River Estuary (Belton et al. 1985, 1986, Connor et al. 1984; IOM 1991 contains risk estimates not related to location). However, it should be emphasized that these excess risk estimates are *estimates* and that the chemical composition of some toxicants found in seafood product differs from their composition when disposed in marine waters (e.g., for these toxicants their health effects are sometimes less toxic or less known, as is the case with nickel, chromium, arsenic, and PCB) (see IOM [1991] and Chapter 6, this volume), therefore these excess risk estimates could overstate the health risks from the consumption of contaminated seafood. The methods used to assess economic losses due to excess cancer mortalities from toxicants in seafood were based on a human capital (HC) approach that represented a lower-bound estimate, and a willingness-to-pay (WTP) approach (also referred to as contingent valuation [CV]) that represented an upper-bound approach, with adjustments to both based on an adjusted WTP/HC approach (Ofiara and Brown 1999; see Chapter 7 for more detail pertaining to these economic approaches). Previous research was used to develop estimates of the medical costs and forgone earnings associated with the lower-bound estimate of the HC approach (Hartunian et al. 1981), and estimates of the value of a statistical life (i.e., equal to aggregate economic value for a policy that saves b lives divided by the actual number of lives saved; in other words, a policy that reduces the probability of death by the number of lives saved [b] divided by the number of individuals affected [H; i.e., b/H] [Johansson 1995; see also Freeman 1979]) based on the WTP approach from labor market studies to represent a midpoint estimate (Thaler and Rosen 1975) and an upper-bound estimate (Smith 1976). All dollars reported are expressed in 1987 dollars.

Economic estimates were developed for the case of a male, aged 35 to 44 years, assuming continued consumption of contaminated seafood and following a similar procedure as used by Gold and Van Ravenswaay (1984) in an assessment of PCB contamination in fish from the Great Lakes. The average value of saving one life (or value of a statistical life) was estimated at $672,875/life (lower-bound estimate), $990,682/life (middle-bound estimate), and $3,872,471/life or $3.9 million (upper-bound estimate) (Ofiara and Brown 1999). Estimates of excess cancer risk and associated economic value from PCB contamination involve an assumed low consumption rate and a high consumption rate over a 70-year lifetime based on Belton et al. (1986). The species white catfish and white perch found within the New York Bight–Hudson River Estuary were estimated to have the highest risk. The net economic value from excess cancer mortality from PCB for striped bass was estimated to range from $2,490 million to $14,328 million (low consumption rate) to $5,854 to $33,690 million (high consumption rate), the value associated with consumption of contaminated bluefish ranged from $2,490 million to $33,033 million (1987 dollars; Table 9.8).

Estimated excess risk from dioxin-contaminated seafood (Belton et al. 1985) was

Table 9.8. Public Health Impacts from PCBs (1987$).

Contaminant: Seafood	Consumption Rate, lb/yr	Excess Risk (No.)	Economic Losses[a]		
			(1)	(2)	(3)
			millions ($)		
PCB					
Crab (mixed tissue)	12.6	2,200	1,480	2,179	8,519
	29.5	5,200	3,499	5,152	20,137
Crab (muscle)	12.6	160	108	158	620
	29.5	380	256	376	1,472
Bluefish	12.6	3,700	2,490	3,665	14,328
	29.5	8,600	5,787	8,519	33,303
White perch	12.6	5,200	3,499	5,152	20,137
	29.5	12,000	8,075	11,888	46,470
White catfish	12.6	5,200	3,499	5,152	20,137
	29.5	12,000	8,075	11,888	46,470
Striped bass	12.6	3,700	2,490	3,665	14,328
	29.5	8,700	5,854	8,619	33,690
American eel	12.6	3,500	2,355	3,467	13,554
	29.5	8,300	5,585	8,223	32,142

[a](1) is based on Hartunian et al. (1981), (2) is based on Thaler and Rosen (1975), and (3) is based on Smith (1976).
Source: Belton et al. (1986).

highest for blue crab consumption, followed by striped bass consumption (Table 9.9). The value of excess risk associated with consumption of dioxin-contaminated striped bass was found to range from $874 million to $6,037 million (Table 9.9) and shows that dioxin-associated risk was smaller in magnitude compared to PCB-associated risk. Connor et al. (1984) developed estimates of excess risk and estimates of additive risk for several toxic substances from consumption of striped bass, winter flounder, windowpane flounder, mussels, and lobster harvested from the New York Bight. It was not surprising that striped bass, a predator species higher up on the food chain, exhibited the highest levels of excess risk and of additive risk, followed by risk estimates associated with lobster (Table 9.10). Concerning risk estimates for striped bass, of the substances tested, PCB accounted for the highest individual risk, followed by DDT and its metabolites–derivatives, and then Chlordane. The estimated value of the additive risks associated with striped bass ranges from $1,144 million to $6,583 million (low risk) to $3,970 million to

Table 9.9. Public Health Impacts from Dioxin (1987$).

Contaminant: Seafood	Consumption Rate, lb/yr	Excess Risk (No.)	Economic Losses[a]		
			(1)	(2)	(3)
			millions ($)		
DIOXIN					
Blue crab	NA	870–3300	585–2,220	862–3,269	3,367–12,771
Striped bass	NA	1,300–1560	874–1,049	1,288–1,545	5,031–6,037
Lobster	NA	530–1,500	357–1,009	525–1,486	2,051–5,805

[a](1) is based on Hartunian et al. (1981), (2) is based on Thaler and Rosen (1975), and (3) is based on Smith (1976).
Source: Belton et al. (1985).

Table 9.10. Public Health Impacts from Mixed Chemicals (Additive Risk [Σrisk]) (1987$).

| | Excess Risk | | Economic Losses[a] | | | | | |
| | | | Low | | | High | | |
Compound	Low	High	(1)	(2)	(3)	(1)	(2)	(3)
			$ millions					
STRIPED BASS								
Chlordane	22	25	16.8	21.8	96.8	14.8	24.8	85.2
tDDT[b]	390	620	262	386	1,510	417	614	2,401
PCB	1,300	5,200	875	1,288	5,034	3,499	5,152	20,137
Σrisk	1,700	5,900	1,144	1,684	6,583	3,970	5,845	22,848
WINTER FLOUNDER								
Chlordane	1.2	–	0.8	1.2	4.6	–	–	–
tDDT[b]	13	–	8.7	12.9	50.3	–	–	–
PCB	40	–	26.9	39.6	154.9	–	–	–
Σrisk	54	–	36.3	53.5	209.1	–	–	–
WINDOWPANE FLOUNDER								
Chlordane	0.6	0.9	0.4	0.6	2.3	0.6	0.9	3.5
tDDT[b]	10	17	6.7	9.9	38.7	11.4	16.8	65.8
Dieldrin	11	–	7.4	10.9	42.6	–	–	–
Hexachlorobenzene	0.1	–	0.07	0.1	0.4	–	–	–
PCB	31	64	20.9	39.7	120	43.1	82.0	247.8
Σrisk	52	83	35.0	66.7	201	55.8	106.4	321.4
MUSSELS								
Chlordane	1.2	–	1.1	1.2	6.2	–	–	–
tDDT[b]	52	–	34.9	51.5	201.4	–	–	–
PCB	63	–	42.2	62.4	244.0	–	–	–
Σrisk	120	–	80.7	118.9	464.7	–	–	–
LOBSTER								
Chlordane	0.25	0.72	0.2	0.2	1.0	0.5	0.7	2.8
tDDT[b]	8.0	8.8	5.4	7.9	31	5.9	8.7	34.1
Dieldrin	14	18	9.4	13.9	54.2	12.1	17.8	69.7
Hexachlorobenzene	0.05	0.05	0.03	0.05	0.2	0.03	0.05	0.2
Heptachlor	0.21	0.25	0.14	0.2	0.8	0.2	0.2	1.0
PCB	39	140	26	39	151	94	139	542
Σrisk	67	170	45	66	259	114	168	658

[a](1) is based on Hartunian et al. (1981), (2) is based on Thaler and Rosen (1975), and (3) is based on Smith (1976).
[b]DDT and its metabolites.
Source: Connor et al. (1986).

$22,848 million (high risk) (Table 9.10). Ofiara and Brown (1999) conclude that although the data on which these value estimates are based are imprecise, it is apparent that consumption of seafood contaminated with toxic substances, especially PCBs and dioxins, can cause sizable economic losses and that these losses may be disproportionately shared by recreational anglers who consume their catch. Because of findings such as these, researchers are concerned about the health risk to the public from consuming unsafe seafood and urge that continual inspection of seafood for specific toxicants be required as well as ongoing studies of health risk assessments to obtain a more precise range of the estimates of health risk (IOM 1991, U.S. Congress, OTA 1987).

Shellfish Resources. The following section contains estimates of longer-term impacts from both toxicants and bacterial contamination in the New York Bight and Hudson River Estuary that result from closure of once productive shellfishing grounds to commercial harvest. They are not related to the short-term impacts estimated directly above attributable to the 1988 pollution event. Economic impacts to hard clam resources were estimated for waters under "prohibited" and "special restricted" (closed) areas (some 1,323,520 acres), in the New York Bight associated with New Jersey. Estimates of yield and value were based on yield estimates of clams from "approved" and "seasonal" areas and average price received (ex-vessel) assuming the price would not change if these clams were brought to market. The value of landings from "prohibited" areas was estimated at $1.84 million per year, and from "special restricted" areas $294,102 per year, a total of $2.13 million per year for closed areas (Ofiara and Brown 1988). If multiplier effects are included economic impacts could be $4.04 million per year.

Conclusion. The overall magnitudes of the value of economic losses to coastal and marine resources, and the economic impacts from the short-term 1988 marine pollution event and long-term pollution problems that have contaminated finfish and closed productive shellfish grounds to New Jersey are sizable. Although the data on which the above economic assessments were based are imprecise, their magnitude should be apparent. Assessments of losses due to marine pollution can provide justification for public policy responses and continued efforts to mitigate and prevent these effects. Further research is justified to provide more precise estimates of these economic losses and effects.

9.6.3. Buzzards Bay Project—New Bedford Harbor Impairments

The U.S. EPA approved Buzzards Bay for inclusion within the National Estuary Program on January 29, 1988 (Buzzards Bay Project 1988). New Bedford Harbor and Buzzards Bay form the waterbody along the Southeastern part of Massachusetts below Cape Cod. The Buzzards Bay Project identified three problems: closure of shellfish beds, toxic contamination, and eutrophication (U.S. EPA 1989). In addition, New Bedford Harbor is listed as a Superfund site because of PCB contamination of the bottom sediment and involves one of the largest settlements in the United States for damages caused to New Bedford Harbor and Buzzards Bay. Early industrial development in the area has thus left its imprint on the coastal resources from the deposition of historically contaminated "in-place" sediment. An excess of 100 tons of PCBs were dumped into New Bedford Harbor and the Acushnet River, the headwaters of New Bedford Harbor during the 1940–70 period

(Brewster 1990, NBHTC 1997). A number of private businesses (five in total) were identified that represent the surviving or successor business entities which subsequently were
held liable and sued as a result of this industrial waste dumping activity via the Comprehensive Environmental Response, Compensation, and Liability Act in 1980. In 1992, two
of the cases were settled out of court for $99.6 million, comprising $79 million for remediation and cleanup and $21 million for restoration of natural resources (NBHTC 1997).
The cleanup method chosen by the trustees involves dredging and storing the contaminated sediment from the most polluted areas, "hot spots," of the Acushnet River and New
Bedford Harbor. It is estimated that this method will remove as much as half of the 140
tons of PCBs (NBHTC 1997, Pollock 1990).

A number of investigations have examined the economic damages to New Bedford
Harbor and Buzzards Bay. These include effects on recreational activities (beach use and
swimming, and sportfishing), the commercial lobster fishery, and property values adjacent to the waterfront of New Bedford Harbor. The property value study was discussed
in detail in Chapter 8 and will be briefly noted here.

Recreational Use. Recreational activities of beach use and marine sportfishing were examined and economic losses developed for these two recreational uses.

Recreational Use—Beach Use. Economic losses of economic welfare for beach use were
based on survey data from 545 households in the New Bedford area that participated in
a telephone survey during March 1986 (McConnell and IE 1986). In principle, economic
damages (i.e., losses of economic welfare) were defined as the difference in ordinary consumer surplus (OCS) without damage and OCS with damage (i.e., $OCS_{w/oPCB}-OCS_{wPCB}$)
(see Section 5.7 for details). This procedure involves estimation of two demand curves,
one corresponding to a nondamaged state (without PCBs), the other corresponding to a
damaged state; the difference in OCS is then the loss of OCS between the two demand
curves (refer to Figure 5.13, Chapter 5).

McConnell and IE (1986) estimated two linear travel costs demand curves using a
Tobit statistical technique to account for censored data (i.e., where a large number of 0-
dependent variables occur, the data are referred to as being "censored," and censored
regression techniques are used to counter bias in parameter estimates from ordinary least
squares techniques; the Tobit approach is a popular statistical technique [see Judge et al.
1988]). These demand curves were of the following form:

$$x_{ij} = ß_0 + ß_1X1 + ß_2X2 + ß_3X3 + ß_4D1 + e_{ij}, \text{ where}$$

x_{ij} is the number of trips by the *ith* household to the *jth* beach, *X1* is the own-price (i.e.,
travel cost associated with going to a primary beach), *X2* is the substitute price (i.e., the
travel cost of going to alternative beaches), *X3* is the substitute price of a less desirable
substitute beach (i.e., cheaper and less desired beach substitute), *D1* is a dummy variable
to account for the presence of Fort Phoenix beach (where D1 = 1, if site is Fort Phoenix
and 0 otherwise), ß the estimated parameters, and e_{ij} the error term. Results are contained
in Table 9.11. Two additional pieces of information were required: estimates of trip numbers (e.g., median sample estimate used) and the proportion of the sample aware of the
contamination–PCB problem (Table 9.12).

Table 9.11. Estimated Tobit Travel Cost Demand Curves for Planned 1986 Trips with PCBs, and Planned 1986 Trips and without PCBs.

Beach	Constant	X1	X2	X3	D1	Log-likelihood	N
			Variables				
			PLANNED 1986 TRIPS WITH PCBs				
East/West	−11.96	−10.84	2.73	1.05	36.0	−841	495
	(1.5)	(4.73)	(0.98)	(0.40)	(2.8)		
Fort Phoenix	−3.70	−2.94	0.65	0.30	8.3	−620	495
	(1.6)	(3.40)	(1.00)	(0.40)	(2.0)		
			PLANNED 1986 TRIPS WITHOUT PCBs				
East/West	−6.90	−12.91	3.94	3.93	40.4	−1268	495
	(0.8)	(5.30)	(1.30)	(1.40)	(2.8)		
Fort Phoenix	−3.24	−4.80	0.88	2.87	22.7	−1126	495
	(1.1)	(4.40)	(1.0)	(2.70)	(4.1)		

Note: Numbers in parentheses refer to asymptotic *t*-statistics under the null hypothesis of no association. Dependent variable is number of beach trips, X1 is the trip cost to the same beach (i.e., own-price), X2 the trip cost to a substitute beach, X3 the trip cost to a less desirable substitute beach, D1 is 1 if the beach visited is Fort Phoenix beach, and N is the number of observations.
Source: McConnell and Industrial Economics, Inc. (1986).

Table 9.12. Proportion of HHs Aware of PCB Problem and Attend, and Trip Numbers, 1986.

Category	East/West Beach	Fort Phoenix
PROPORTION OF HHs AWARE OF PCB PROBLEM AND ATTEND		
1986 with PCBs	0.275	0.251
1986 without PCBs	0.476	0.518
MEDIAN TRIPS		
1986 with PCBs	10	5
1986 without PCBs	15	9

Source: McConnell and Industrial Economics, Inc. (1986).

Estimates of losses of economic welfare were derived as follows:

1. The first step was to estimate OCS for the case without PCBs (w/o PCB), e.g., for East/West Beach: $OCS_{w/oPCB} = [15^2 / −2(−12.91)] = \$8.71/trip$, etc. (see Table 9.13).
2. Repeat step 1 for the case with PCBs.
3. Then estimate economic damages as the difference in $OCS_{w/oPCB}$ and OCS_{wPCB} adjusted for the proportion of sample population aware of the PCB problem (e.g., for East/West Beach: $\$8.71(0.476) − \$4.61(0.275) = \$2.88$).

Losses of economic welfare due to the damaged state (i.e., PCB occurrence at both beaches) were taken as the sum of welfare losses across both beaches (i.e., $\$2.88 + \$3.31 = \$6.19$). Results of these steps are in Table 9.13. The next phase involved developing a time-series of the proportion of households aware of the PCB problem [P(t)]. This was

Table 9.13. Estimated Economic Damages from PCB Contamination to New Bedford Harbor, 1986.

Category	East/West Beach	Fort Phoenix	All Beaches
OCS without PCB[a]	$8.71	$8.44	—
OCS with PCB[a]	$4.61	$4.25	—
$OCS_{w/oPCB}$ adjusted for HHs that attend[b]	$4.1460	$4.3719	—
OCS_{wPCB} adjusted for HHs that attend[b]	$1.2678	$1.0668	—
Damage without PCB	$2.88	$3.31	$6.19

[a]Estimated based on formula for OCS = $trips^2/(-2ß)$.
[b]Product of proportion of HHs aware of PCB problem and attended these beaches.
Source: McConnell and Industrial Economics, Inc. (1986).

accomplished from an estimated population growth equation based on a logistic form to predict the proportion of households aware estimated as:

$$P(t) = [1 + exp(2.85 - 0.35t)]^{-1},$$

where *exp( )* represents the exponential operator that allowed predictions of P(t) to grow over time as more of the population in the area learns of the problem over time. The telephone survey obtained a past time-series (1979–85) of P(t). The following step involved calculating the present value (PV) of damages [PV(D)] over the 1979–2085 period (107-year period) as:

PV(D) = sum of annual compounded damages for the 1979–85 period

plus the

sum of annual discounted damages for the 1986–2085 period, or,

$$\sum_{t=1979}^{2085} (1 + r)^{1986 - t} P(t)D(1986) = \$11.4 \text{ million (in 1985 dollars).}$$

Economic damages were also computed in the presence of beach capacity constraints, which in general reduces both use and economic value by some proportion k (i.e., net economic value = $trips^2[1-(1-k)^2] / (-2ß)$). Following a similar procedure as above, aggregate damages were estimated at a present value of $8.3 million (1985 dollars).

Recreational Use—Sportfishing. Data for analysis of economic damages pertaining to sportfishing were obtained from a survey of 428 households; of these 83 participated in marine sportfishing in 1986 (McConnell and IE 1986). On September 25, 1979, the State of Massachusetts Department of Public Health banned the taking of any fish but baitfish in the area of New Bedford Harbor that is within the hurricane barrier delineated as Area

I, and the taking of bottomfish in an area adjacent to New Bedford Harbor within Buzzards Bay delineated as Area II.

The conceptually correct measure of losses of economic welfare due to PCB contamination would be estimated as the sum of lost economic welfare from Area I and Area II (i.e., $OCS_I + OCS_{II}$). This would involve the estimation of demand curves for both cases with PCB (in damaged state) and without PCB (in nondamaged state), for both areas I and II. As McConnell and IE (1986) point out, estimation of travel cost demand curves based on survey data of households that reside in the New Bedford area alone probably would contain insufficient variation to yield statistically robust demand curves (i.e., robust in a statistical sense satisfying statistical properties [see Judge et al. 1988 or any good statistics textbook for the meaning of "robust"]). Economic damages were then defined as the cost savings that would result had the damaged state not occurred in Area II. That is, damages were measured as the increased cost of fishing trips to travel to areas outside of Area II in order to avoid PCB-contaminated sites (i.e., avoidance behavior). Specifically, damages were represented as: damages $= \Delta x \Delta c / 2$, where $\Delta x \Delta c$ is cost savings without the PCB state as a result lower costs per trip and shorter distance to travel, Δc is the decease in costs per trip from not having to travel further, Δx is additional trips and estimated as follows:

$$\Delta x = HH * P(t) * P(fish)[P(aware|fish\ in\ Area\ II)_{w/oPCB} * x_{w/oPCB}$$

$$- P(aware|fish\ in\ Area\ II)_{w\ PCB} * x_{w/oPCB}],$$

$$= 51,498\ (0.782)(0.195)[(0.77(12) - 0.65(6)]$$

$$= 41,935,$$

where $x_{w/oPCB}$ is median trips of anglers aware of PCB if PCBs were removed (trips that would be taken in 1986 if PCBs were removed, i.e., without PCBs), and x_{wPCB} is median trips of anglers aware of PCB given PCB contamination—with PCBs—(actual trips taken in 1985),

Cost savings (Δc) was estimated as follows:

$0.72/trip—shore-based trips

$\underline{+ \$2.47/trip—boat-based\ trips}$

$3.19 / 2 = 1.595$ or $1.60/trip = \Delta c$.

Aggregate economic damages were estimated as:

$$damages = \Delta c * No.\ of\ trips$$

$$= 1.60 * 41,935$$

$$= \$67,100\ (in\ 1985\ dollars).$$

Damages were then discounted and summed over the 1979–2085 period (107-year period) as the PV of damages [PV(D)]:

$$PV(D) = \sum_{t=1979}^{2085} (1 + r)^{1986 - t} DF(t) = \$3.1 \text{ million (in 1985 dollars)},$$

where DF(t) is economic damage to sportfishing that depends on the proportion of HHs aware of PCBs estimated from the logistic growth equation in the beach use section.

Overall, the present value of losses of economic welfare due to the damaged state (i.e., damages from PCB contamination) pertaining to recreational activities was estimated at $14.5 million ($11.4 million—beach use + $3.1 million—sportfishing) and $11.4 million ($8.3 million + $3.1 million) given capacity constraints (1985$).

Commercial Lobster Fishery. The first part of this analysis involved development of the estimated number of commercial lobstermen affected (49 in number) by the closure of fishing areas and grounds as a result of PCB contamination (McConnell and Morrison 1986). This was derived in the following manner:

1. Sixty-five lobstermen were identified that held commercial lobster licenses in 1986 from three ports in Southeastern Massachusetts (New Bedford, Fairhaven, and Dartmouth).
2. Interviews of these lobstermen of their past activities yielded estimates of lobstering activities affected by the closure and were translated into estimates of numbers of lobstermen affected (52 in number).
3. Of these, a number of lobstermen changed activities to pursue offshore lobster activities (6 percent); accounting for this adjustment yields an estimate of the number of lobstermen affected 49 (52 * 0.94).

Data for the assessment of economic damages come from field interviews of 35 lobstermen in 1986 who provided information on their activities. The conceptually correct measure of lost economic welfare from changes in production activities is the loss of producer surplus or quasi-rent to the producers. Losses in consumer surplus to local consumers of lobsters as a result of supply reductions and from higher production costs from transporting lobsters greater distances to the local market can also cause a decrease in the supply curve, and subsequent higher prices relative to demand also represent a component of economic damage pertaining to lobster activities (however given the small area closed this effect is probably negligible).

To estimate these losses of economic welfare requires sufficient data to estimate demand and supply curves for the particular activity (commercial lobster fishery), but given the small number of affected lobstermen in southeastern Massachusetts it is probable that this effect would not be translated into noticeable changes in the industry demand and supply curves, and hence changes in producer surplus. Although real losses in economic welfare have occurred at the local level, losses may not be perceptible at the aggregate or industry level. Therefore the measure of economic damages used in this case study was measurable increases in costs (added costs) that resulted from travel to more distant noncontaminated fishing grounds, a type of avoidance behavior (McConnell and Morrison 1986). Such increased costs comprise increases in variable costs pertaining to travel (e.g., increased fuel use, increased travel time), and increases in fixed costs such as maintenance and repair costs, and fishing gear (i.e., lobster traps).

Estimates of these added costs were computed based on data from field interviews as:

1. Increase in travel time costs were estimated from increased travel time (median value

of 1.125 hr/trip), number of affected trips (average of 38 trips/year), and time cost ($8.46/hr) yielding $361.67 per individual per year (i.e., 1.125 * 38 * 8.46);

2. Added fuel costs were based on increased travel (median value of 1.125 hr/trip), added fuel use (median of 3 gal/hr), number of affected trips (38/year), and an estimate of fuel cost (average of $0.88/gal) yielding $112.86/individual/year (i.e., 1.125 * 3 * 38 * 0.88).

3. Added maintenance and repair costs were estimated from increased travel (median of 1.125 hr/trip), number of trips affected (38), and an estimate of added engine maintenance costs of $0.59/hr from such travel, which yielded $25.22/individual/year (i.e., 1.125 * 38 * 0.59).

4. Added costs of fishing gear estimated from the number of lobster traps fished per individual (average of 152 traps/year), an estimate of the cost per trap (average of $32.50/trap), and an estimate of the increase in trap loss or damage (median value of 12 percent per year) yielding $592.80 (i.e., 152 * 0.12 * 32.50).

Added costs per individual per year totaled $1093 (i.e., sum of added costs related to time $362, fuel $113, maintenance and repair $25, fishing gear replacement $593). This cost estimate was then expanded to the entire population of affected lobstermen (49 in number) producing total added costs of $53,557/year.

The final step of the analysis was to determine the present value of damages [PV(D)] over the 1980–2085 (106-year) period as:

PV(D = sum of compounded added costs over the 1980–85 period
plus the sum of discounted added costs over the 1986–2085 period.

This is formally represented as:

$$PV(D) = \sum_{t=1980}^{1985}(1 + r)^{1985 - t} (\$53,557)$$

$$+ \sum_{t=1986}^{2085}(1 + r)^{1985 - t} (\$53,557), \text{ or}$$

$$= \sum_{t=1980}^{2085}(1 + r)^{1980 - t} (\$53,557)$$

$$= \$2,038,771, \text{ where } r = 0.03.$$

Overall the present value of economic damages from PCB contamination to the commercial lobster fishery was estimated at $2 million over the 106-year period.

Residential Property Values. Mendelsohn (1986) conducted an examination of the economic damage to single-family residential homes caused by PCB contamination in New Bedford Harbor, Massachusetts, and in the Buzzards Bay area. The 1979–80 period was chosen as the time period when most residents became aware of the problem. The repeat sales method was preferred to the hedonic property method because its research design allowed for better control of housing characteristics, which makes it possible to isolate and assess more precisely the temporal effects, such as welfare losses, from resource damages (Mendelsohn 1986).

A sample of single-family, owner-occupied residences that sold at least twice since

1969 resulted in 1,030 observations. A complete history of sales for this sample of residences was then obtained for the 1969–85 period. Many different variations of paired sales were then possible—residences that sold once, some twice, and some over three times within the 1969–85 period. In addition, these paired sales could have occurred anytime within this period. The data set, then, was composed of observations of paired sales that sold before and after the 1979–80 period (i.e., sales that straddled the 1979–80 period) and observations of paired sales that did not straddle the 1979–80 period. Because the objective of the study and structure of the model was to examine the difference in sales for residences that sold before the 1979–80 period versus after the 1979–80 period, observations of sales were identified and distinguished among paired sales that did not straddle the 1979–80 period by using a binary-shift variable. (Unfortunately, the original report does not list the breakdown of the number of observations that fall into these groups.)

Both linear and semi-log models were estimated to examine the functional form (Table 9.14). It was not known whether the linear model or semi-log model best represented the data and repeat sales method, so both were used to estimate economic damages. Mendelsohn (1986) found that damages to housing in PCB Zone1 (adjacent to Area I) resulted in $5600/home based on a linear damage effect in 1985 dollars or 9.8 percent (10.3 percent in log values) per home assuming a proportional damage.[1] Housing damages in PCB Zone2 (adjacent to Area II) resulted in estimated damages of $6300/home if

Table 9.14. Repeat Sales Regression Models, New Bedford Harbor 1985.

Variables	Linear Model	Semi-Log Model
CONSTANT	4470	.089
	(6.12)	(6.41)
IMPROVE	1076	.021
	(6.68)	(6.85)
INTEREST	−2711	−.041
	(13.18)	(10.38)
LENGTH1	−1024	−.027
	(3.49)	(4.73)
LENGTH3–4	−839	−.019
	(3.55)	(4.13)
EVENT	16900	.252
	(8.90)	(6.90)
EVPCBZONE1	−5616	−.103
	(1.94)	(1.85)
EVPCBZONE2	−6338	−.150
	(2.43)	(2.98)
HIGHSCHOOL	490	.015
	(2.12)	(3.41)
ADJ–R^2	.218	.177
ERROR^2	$2.210*10^{11}$	81.72

Note: t-statistics are in parentheses, the dependent variable represents the difference in sales price that straddles 1980 (sales before 1980: 1969–79, and sales after 1980: 1980–85). Descriptions of the variables at right.
Source: Mendelsohn (1986).

The independent variables are:

IMPROVE = Value in thousands of dollars of home improvements made, measured in real 1985 dollars between the first and second sale

INTEREST = The difference in annual effective mortgage interest rates between the sale dates

LENGTH1 = Time, in years, between first and second sale multiplied by PCBZONE1, a binary variable to indicate whether the property is located in PCB Zone I or not

LENGTH3–4 = Time, in years, between first and second sale multiplied by PCBZONE3–4, a binary variable to indicate whether the property is located in PCB Zone III or in PCB Zone IV

EVENT = Binary variable (0,1) for whether earlier or later sale dates straddle the 1979–80 period

EVPCBZONE1 = Binary variable (0,1) for whether the sale dates straddle 1979–80 and also whether the nearest water is in PCB Zone I. It is the product of EVENT times PCBZONE1

EVPCBZONE2 = Binary variable (0,1) for whether the sale dates straddle 1979–80 and also whether the nearest water is in PCB Zone II. It is the product of EVENT times PCBZONE2

HIGHSCHOOL = The change in the percentage of adults in the census tract who completed high school in 1970 vs. 1980 weighted by the length of sale

PCBZONE1 = Binary variable (0,1) for those properties whose nearest water lies within PCB Zone I

PCBZONE2 = Binary variable (0,1) for those properties whose nearest water lies within PCB Zone II

Table 9.15. Aggregate Economic Damages of Residential Property, New Bedford Harbor, 1985.

		Category			

ECONOMIC DAMAGE PER HOME

Area	Linear	Semi-log
I	$5,616	9.8%
II	$6,338	13.9%

NO. HOMES AFFECTED

Area	Fairhaven Census tract	Fairhaven	Dartmouth	New Bedford
I	1690	—	—	—
II	—	1,100	900	830

AVG. SELLING PRICE ($)

Area	Fairhaven Census tract	Fairhaven	Dartmouth	New Bedford
I	78,500	—	—	—
II	—	59,000	81,000	66,000

AGGREGATE ECON. DAMAGE ($ MILLIONS)

Linear[a]	Fairhaven Census tract	Fairhaven	Dartmouth	New Bedford	Total
I	9.491	—	—	—	9.5
II	—	6.972	5.704	5.261	17.829
Total					27.329

AGGREGATE ECON. DAMAGE ($ MILLIONS)

Semi-log[b]	Fairhaven Census tract	Fairhaven	Dartmouth	New Bedford	Total
I	13.001	—	—	—	13.0
II	—	9.021	10.133	7.614	26.768
Total					39.769

[a]Product of economic damage per home and number of homes affected.
[b]Product of percentage reduction in sales price (% economic damage per home) and average selling price and number of homes affected (e.g., (.098)*78,500*1690=$13.001 million).
Source: Mendelsohn (1986).

linear damage effect or 13.9 percent (15 percent in log values) per home ($\exp[-0.15]-1 = 0.139$) if proportional damages in 1985 dollars.

Aggregate economic damage estimates were developed by expanding these unit damage estimates by an estimate of the number of homes affected in Areas I and II for the linear model, and the product of the estimated average selling price and number of homes affected in Areas I and II for the semi-log model (Table 9.15). Aggregate economic damages were estimated at $9.5 million to $13 million (1985 dollars) for residences adjacent to Area I and from $17.8 million to $26.8 million for residences adjacent to Area II (1985 dollars). Over both areas aggregate damages range from $27.3 million to $39.8 million in 1985 dollars.

Aggregate Economic Damages. On the basis of the above research, if the separate losses can be summed over use, aggregate economic damages from PCB contamination to the New

Bedford Harbor and adjacent area (Buzzards Bay) would range from $41 million to $56 million in 1985 dollars:

Beach use—$8.3 million–$11.4 million

Sportfishing—$8.3 million

Commercial lobster fishery—$2.0 million

Residential property—$27.3 million–$39.8 million

Epilogue. In addition to these economic damages, there are legal fees and cleanup costs. Altogether these include (in 1985$):

Legal fees—$20 million

Economic damages—$40.7 million–$56.3 million

Cleanup costs—$100 million

Conclusion. In hindsight, had society known the social costs and economic damages of specific toxicants such as PCBs, public policymakers would have been in a position to create appropriate incentives regarding the use and design of optimal public policies. In the case of PCB contamination of Buzzards Bay, it is estimated that over 100 tons of PCB were discharged into New Bedford Harbor waters. If we consider an estimate of the social costs from PCBs on the basis of this one case study and Superfund site, it would be considerably higher than the private costs of producing PCBs.

Strictly for illustrative purposes consider the following example. Suppose that a unit of PCBs was $10,000/ton in 1985. This price would represent the private marginal cost of PCB production and its equilibrium sale price; an aggregate market value of the amount contained in bottom sediment would be $1,000,000 ($10,000 (100 tons). On the basis of economic damages and legal costs of $70 million, aggregate social costs would become $71 million (sum of private costs and value of negative externality) or $710,000/ton; that is, the social marginal costs of PCB production would be an estimated $710,000/ton— over 71 times above the private marginal cost. Of course this estimate is understated because economic damages and other external costs have occurred at other locations that have not been assessed, and other use impairments (e.g., public health damages from PCBs) have not been included. One would also need to include the benefits from PCB use in the electrical industry to complete the exercise. But this simple example serves to motivate the basic concept in externality theory. If the damages and social costs had been known, public policymakers could have implemented a unit tax on PCB use equal to its marginal social cost in the private market, and PCB use would have been limited so as to achieve a social optimum (i.e., oq' in Figure 2.6, Chapter 2), and hence a minimum or optimal level of damages to society. The difficulty facing policymakers and researchers is that problems caused by pollution such as with PCBs are not known nor anticipated, and it is only after damage has occurred that society and policymakers understand and realize the appropriate actions. Such a situation justifies the need for toxicity studies of manufactured chemicals and suspected toxicants and the need for continued monitoring of the fate of waste and toxicants. In general the usefulness of performing economic analyses of damage assessments can serve to motivate and influence public policies about the socially efficient use of toxic contaminants.

9.6.4. Chesapeake Bay Program

The Chesapeake Bay represents the largest estuary in the United States and one of the most productive systems in the world. It is bordered by the states of Maryland and Virginia and is fed by a number of major river systems with the Susquehanna River at its headwaters. Watersheds that drain into the Chesapeake Bay include parts of the states of New York, Pennsylvania, West Virginia, Maryland, Delaware, and Virginia, and its water and related land resources serve over 12 million people (U.S. EPA 1989). The Chesapeake Bay is about 200 miles long and its width varies from 4 miles to 30 miles, yielding a water surface over 2,500 square miles. More than 50 rivers drain into the bay and its shoreline represents over 4,000 miles in Maryland alone (Eichbaum 1987).

The Chesapeake Bay Program, started in 1977, is the second-oldest environmental-estuary protection program directed by the U.S. EPA. The program began as a joint federal–state partnership and has focused on three critical problems of the bay: nutrient enrichment, toxic substances, and the decline of submerged aquatic vegetation (SAV) (U.S. EPA 1989, see also Greer 1996, Harding Jr. et al. 1992, Horton and Eichbaum 1991, Mackiernan 1992, MOG 1988). This program served as one of the model programs for the U.S. EPA's National Estuary Program. Over time a number of innovative solutions for water quality improvements have come from this program due to research that provided evidence of the influence of nutrients on the bay's water quality (Greer 1996; Harding Jr. et al. 1992; Horton and Eichbaum 1991; Leffler 1995, 1997; Mackiernan 1992; MOG 1988). Examples of these innovative solutions acknowledge the link between land use practices and the bay's water quality (e.g., agricultural and urban "best practices," "smart farming," and a "rural legacy program") to preserve open land adjacent to the bay (Eichbaum 1987, Greer 1997, Leffler 1997, MOG 1988). Research has in turn influenced public policy. For example, there have been efforts to reinstate a subsidy to farmers to plant cover crops on agricultural land adjacent to the shoreline of the bay so as to reduce nutrient loads, specifically to reduce excess nitrogen levels from fertilizer use in the root zone or soil substrate before it can leach through the soil and migrate into the bay's waters (Leffler 1997). Another policy initiative involves the protection of farmland and open space via the "Rural Legacy Program" to further control erosion and soil sediment from entering the bay (Greer 1997, MOG 1988). Some of these solutions have reportedly been incorporated into other programs, for example, New Jersey Public Service Electric and Gas Company has incorporated "smart farming" practices into their estuary enhancement program in the Delaware Estuary Program (NJPSE&G 1995).

An economic assessment was conducted regarding the value of improvements in water quality for the activities of beach use, pleasure boating, and sportfishing for striped bass (Bockstael et al. 1989). Portions of this study have been discussed in Chapter 7, about applications of specific economic methods, hence the discussion here is brief.

Improvements in Water Quality. A CV approach using a closed-ended question was used to determine the economic value of improved water quality to be acceptable for swimming. A telephone interview was conducted for a subset of a telephone survey of residents in the Baltimore–Washington SMSA in 1987. A multinomial logit model was used to develop estimates of economic value (see Section 8.2.2.2 for more detail). The average estimate of economic value was expanded on the basis of the population in the Baltimore–Washington SMSA yielding aggregate estimates of net economic value: an average of $67.58 million for users of the Chesapeake Bay (a range of $47.25 million to $87.87 million based on minus or plus one standard error from the average estimate), an average of $23.56 million for nonusers (a range of $18.45 to $28.73 million), a total economic value of $91.14 million (based on the average economic value estimate) with an estimated probable range of $65.7 million to $116.6 million in 1987 (Table 9.16; Bockstael et al. 1989). This estimate was then compared to economic value estimates derived from approaches that used observed behavior (i.e., indirect or revealed preference methods).

Beach Use. Field data from a 1984 survey of beach users on the western shore of Maryland were used to estimate Tobit travel cost demand curves, presented earlier in Table 8.4, Chapter 8. As discussed in Section 8.3.2.4, two methods were used to develop estimates of economic value that were expanded to yield an average aggregate value of $34.66 million for a 20 percent improvement in water quality, and a range of $15.4 million to $44.95 million (Table 9.16, see also Table 8.6, Chapter 8).

Pleasure Boating. Field data were also used to develop economic value estimates of recreational boating in the Chesapeake. Data comprised a survey of boaters who trailered their boats as opposed to those who used marinas, slips, and mooring facilities from a 1983 study. Tobit travel cost demand models were estimated, with results in Table 8.5, Chapter 8. Average welfare values were derived from these demand models based on two methods in which "before" and "after" trip behavior is estimated based on situations that correspond to with versus without improvements in water quality. Aggregate estimates for a 20 percent improvement in water quality were $4.72 million and ranged from $0.65 million to $8.13 million (Table 9.16, see also Table 8.6, Chapter 8).

Table 9.16. Aggregate Economic Benefits from Water Quality Improvements in Chesapeake Bay, 1987.

Approach: Category	Benefit Estimate (1987$)		
	Pessimistic	Average	Optimistic
	$ thousands		
TRAVEL COST APPROACH[a]			
Beach Use (Western Shore)	15,532[c]	34,658	44,950
Pleasure Boating	654	4,717	8,129
Sportfishing (Striped bass)	663	1,368	2,071
CONTINGENT VALUATION[b]			
User	47,254	67,582	87,870
Nonuser	18,446	23,555	28,733
Total	65,700	91,137	116,603

[a]Refers to a 20% improvement in water quality.
[b]Refers to an improvement in water quality to a swimmable level.
[c]Bockstael et al. (1988, 1989) reported a value of $16,853 (thousands). This estimate could not be duplicated following their explanation in footnote *a* of their original Table 7 (Bockstael et al. 1989: 16); 20% improvement values for Sandy Point were $14,084 (method A) and $9,967 (method B) in 1984 dollars (Table 4.6, Bockstael et al. [1988]). Adjusted to 1987 dollars by 1.09 yields $15,352 (method A) and $10,864 (method B); the larger estimate is used.
Source: Bockstael et al. (1989).

Sportfishing—Striped Bass. The economic value associated with sportfishing use of the Chesapeake Bay was developed from the 1980 National Survey of Fishing, Hunting, and Wildlife-Associated Recreation and in particular for the species striped bass. A simplified version of a travel cost demand curve was estimated via a tobit procedure (i.e., a pooled model versus a varying parameter model) (Bockstael et al. 1989). Data limitations precluded estimation of second stage models. Unit economic value estimates were developed from these demand models, and then expanded to yield aggregate estimates of economic value. These aggregate estimates based on the average value were $1.37 million for a 20 percent improvement in water quality, and ranged from $0.66 million to $2.07 million (Table 9.16, see also Table 8.6, Chapter 8).

One will note that the aggregate economic value estimate from all three uses falls short of the aggregate estimate based on the CV method, an average of $40.74 million ($16.67 million–$55.15 million) versus an average of $91.14 million from the CV method ($65.7 million–$116.6 million). Even the upper-bound estimate based on the travel cost demand approach falls below the range of that from the CV method. There are several faults with the comparison and the estimates based on the travel cost approach that can account for underestimates of economic value. In the case of beach use, the data were obtained from beach users along the western shore of Maryland, because water quality improvements would affect this group. As a result, the eastern shore of Maryland, which represents the state's largest beach and summer resort, was not included in the survey, and it is possible that this group may use and value water quality improvements in the Chesapeake Bay differently. Individuals that visit the Eastern Shore usually visit for an entire weekend and beach users in many cases have bought into a summer beach accommodation (condo, house, cottage); few individuals are expected to travel each day during a weekend because of the distance involved (up to three hours from Baltimore, four hours from Washington, DC, without traffic); and possibly represent higher income levels than beach users along the Western Shore. One would expect individuals with higher incomes to be willing to pay more and have higher economic values compared to individuals with lower incomes, everything else being equal. For these reasons, the estimates for beach use could be underestimated.

The data used to generate the economic values for recreational boating were only for individuals who trailer their boats, and hence were limited to smaller-sized boats. Large vessels must be kept at marinas either in slips or at moorings, and again, it is expected that a higher income level is associated with these larger vessels. And it is reasonable to expect that pleasure boaters associated with high income levels would have a higher willingness to pay compared to boaters in a lower income level. The survey of boat use could misrepresent the population of recreational boaters by not including boaters that use slips and mooring facilities at marinas, and is potentially biased toward lower income levels. Hence we suspect economic values associated with recreational boating may also be underestimated.

Concerning the sportfishing use component, striped bass is not the only specie recreational anglers pursue within the Chesapeake Bay. Sportfishing is targeted for bluefish, flounder, and a variety of other species. Hence, the survey and aggregate estimates only represent a component of sportfishing trips and activity and the effect is to underrepresent and underestimate the recreational component in the Chesapeake Bay.

9.6.5. *Delaware Estuary Program*

The Delaware Estuary Program was created on July 18, 1988, when the U.S. EPA recognized and approved the nomination of the Delaware Estuary as a nationally significant estuary and added it to the National Estuary Program (Delaware Estuary Program 1994, Greeley-Polhemus Group, Inc. 1993). The Delaware Estuary is nearly 133 miles long and includes the Delaware Bay and the tidal portion of the Delaware River up to the northern boundary of Trenton, New Jersey (Greeley-Polhemus Group, Inc. 1993, Sutton 1993,). The Delaware River portion is bounded in the north by New Jersey, Pennsylvania, and Delaware, and the Delaware Bay is bounded by New Jersey and Delaware in the south. Some 6000 square miles of land area drains into the estuary and a population of 5 million people (in 1990) resides within the Delaware Estuary region.

Problem areas the Delaware Estuary Program has identified include: point and non-point pollution, toxic contamination, protection of public water supplies, changes in living resources, and managing economic growth. As with the Buzzards Bay Program–New Bedford Harbor, and Narragansett Bay Program early industrial development has left a lasting mark on the ecological health of the Delaware Estuary. Recent health advisories either limiting or banning consumption of selected finfish from the Delaware Estuary have been issued by the states of Pennsylvania, New Jersey, and now Delaware. They are sad reminders of past waste disposal practices and unabated historical industrial development within the Delaware Estuary (Delaware Estuary Program 1994). These health advisories include the species channel catfish, white catfish, white perch, American eel, striped bass, and bluefish. Consumption of these species caught in some areas is limited, especially for high risk groups (i.e., pregnant women, nursing mothers, women of child-bearing age, and young children), and in some areas consumption is banned. Researchers at the State of Delaware Department of Natural Resources and Department of Health and Special Services have calculated lifetime cancer risk for consumption of recreational-size striped bass (i.e., 28 in. and above) at 1 in 36,000 (0.0000278) for one 8 ounce meal/year and one in 670 (0.0015) for one 8 ounce meal/week (or 26 lbs/year) caught between the Pennsylvania state line and Chesapeake and Delaware Canal (Delaware Estuary Program 1994). In addition to the excess cancer risk, children that consume the above fish caught in the specific areas of the advisories are at higher risk for neurobehavioral defects and adults could compromise their immune system (Delaware Estuary Program 1994).

In an effort to characterize both the market and the nonmarket economic structure within the region of the Delaware Estuary and to develop estimates of the value of natural resources in the Delaware Estuary, the Greeley-Polhemus Group (1993) utilized a regional I/O model based on county-level data from the 1990 Bureau of Census *County Business Patterns* to evaluate the market economy, and a benefits transfer approach to assess nonmarket goods and services. To account for the relative importance of the market economy within the Delaware Estuary researchers had to identify only estuary-related economic activities (both direct and indirect effects) to include in the regional I/O model. Based on this approach it was estimated that direct employment resulted in 61,443 jobs linked to estuary-related economic activities in 1990, and total impacts resulted in 122,773 jobs (direct and indirect effects). This employment resulted in an estimated $2,826 million in direct wage income and $4,327 million in total wage impacts (direct and indirect effects included) in 1990 dollars. Output effects of estuary-related economic activity yielded an estimated $18,814 million in direct sales (direct output) and some $24,363 million in total impacts (direct and indirect effects) in 1990 dollars. This activity further generated total impacts of state tax revenues of $358.5 million and of local tax revenues of $202.5 million (1990$).

Nonmarket activities and services were assessed indirectly in terms of the overall value of wetland resources (Greeley-Polhemus 1993). Wetland resources were assessed in terms of values relative to mitigation, preservation, and that of created wetlands. In 1991, the Georgia Department of Transportation estimated that it cost $1442.50/acre to enhance wetlands, $5013.30/acre to preserve wetlands (the exact meaning of "preserve" was not discussed), and $34,620/acre to create wetlands in 1991 dollars. These per acre estimates were expanded based on an estimated 38,868 acres of wetlands lost in the estuary, yielding a value of lost wetlands in the context of mitigation, "mitigation value," of $56.067 million to $194.857 million, and an estimate of $1,345 million if the lost wetlands were to be created, a "restoration/creation value" (in 1991 dollars). Similar "mitigation value" estimates for the remaining 153,986 acres of wetlands within the Delaware Estuary ranged from $22.12 million to $771.98 million (1991$). It is conceivable that a value in the context of created wetlands could be assessed for the remaining wetlands for the purpose of an upper-bound estimate of the value of wetlands but such an estimate may have little basis; it would be an impossible and inconceivable task to create almost 154 thousand acres of wetlands.

Greeley-Polhemus (1993) then developed values of nonmarket resources based on various values associated with specific services of wetlands (e.g., recreational services, pollution removal services, etc.) and expanded these per unit values based on the wetlands lost (38,868 acres) and wetlands remaining (153,986 acres). Although such an expansion can produce reasonable economic value estimates in general, specifically in the case of recreational values such a procedure is not commonly used. It could be that these estimates are superior to those from benefits transfer approaches because all recreational uses are included; however, this is a concern that future research must address. The estimates follow. Per unit values for specific wetland services from previous studies were estimated at $4253/acre for recreational services, $1876/acre for pollution removal, $3685/acre for flood and storm protection, $188/acre for education and research, and $3725/acre for commercial wildlife services in 1991 dollars. Expanding these values to represent losses from lost wetlands (38,868 acres) yielded estimates of $7.3 million to $165.3 million per year and if summed over wetland services or functions yield a total of $533.5 million per year (1991$). Similar expansions of the remaining wetlands (153,986 acres) resulted in estimates of $28.9 million to $654.9 million per year and if summed over all functions $2.11 billion per year (1991$). Overall estimated economic effects were:

Market-economy (in 1990 $)

Direct:	61,443 jobs; $2826 million in wages; $18,814 million output/sales
Direct and indirect:	122,773 jobs; $4327 million in wages; $24,363 million ouput/sales

Nonmarket resources (in 1990 $)

    Recreational services: $165.3 million in losses; $554.9 million current value
    Pollution removal: $72.9 million in losses; $288.9 million current value
    Flood and storm protection: $143.2 million in losses; $567.4 million current value
    Education and research: $7.3 million in losses; $28.9 million current value
    Commercial wildlife: $144.8 million in losses; $573.6 million current value

Total losses and current value for nonmarket resources were $533.5 million and $2,113.8 million, respectively.

Limitations of the Greeley-Polhemus study are that the I/O model was based on county-level data, which could introduce an upward bias and overestimation of the economic impacts for those counties and economic activities that are not primarily estuary-related nor estuary-dependent (that is, located far enough from the boundary of the Delaware Estuary so as not to be affected by the presence or absence of the Delaware Estuary). Municipal-level data could overcome this problem, but many economic series are not available at this level. It is unknown what the magnitude of such an error could be but it is not inconceivable for it to approach over 50 percent. Other concerns are with the procedure and derivation of nonmarket resource values discussed above.

9.6.6. Narragansett Bay Program

The Narragansett Bay Program was created in 1985 as part of the U.S. EPA National Estuary Program (Narragansett Bay Project 1989). The Narragansett Bay forms a major presence in the state of Rhode Island accounting for an area of 102 square miles and a drainage basin of 1820 square miles with 60 percent in Massachusetts and the remainder in Rhode Island (Hayes et al. 1992, Narragansett Bay Project 1989). The program has identified seven issues that are to be addressed in the CCMP (Comprehensive Conservation and Management Plan): (1) fisheries management, (2) excessive nutrients and eutrophication, (3) impacts of pollutants, (4) health of living resources, (5) health risk from seafood consumption, (6) land-use effects on water quality, and (7) recreational issues.

Several of the problems and issues identified in the Narragansett Bay Program are a result of unabated historical industrial activity that dates back to the nineteenth century and the Industrial Revolution. Activity such as textile, dye-works, and metal finishing industries have left their imprint on Narragansett Bay and its drainage basin, which contain historically contaminated "in-place" sediments (Narragansett Bay Project 1989). Furthermore both the states of Rhode Island and Massachusetts have combined sewer overflows (CSOs) that discharge a mix of raw, untreated sewage and storm runoff into tributaries of the Narragansett Bay that partially explain shellfish bed closures.

Given this backdrop, Hayes et al. (1992) conducted a CV study to determine the economic value of water quality improvements to Narragansett Bay. Researchers used a mail survey sent to a random sample of 1500 Rhode Island residents throughout the state. Both open-ended and closed-ended CV questions were used, although Hayes et al. (1992) only present the results of the closed-ended questions. Respondents were asked if they would be willing to pay $x per year, where $x varied randomly between $1 and $100, for improvements in water quality to swimmable quality as well as to allow shellfish beds to be opened for harvesting. A logit model using a linear specification was estimated to obtain net economic value. Because many intermediate steps were not included in their article we cannot reproduce their derivations of aggregate economic values estimates but can only discuss their findings.

Regarding improvements in water quality to swimmable levels, additions to aggregate net economic value were estimated to range from $39.5 million to $61.4 million per year (approximately $40 to $60 million) using a mean value of the statistical distribution, and from $31.6 million to $60.1 million ($30–$60 million) per year based on a median value of the distribution in 1984 dollars; the midpoint of these estimates (up to eight versions) is $50.38 million based on the mean of the distribution, and $45.78 million based on the median of the distribution (1984$).

Concerning improvements in water quality to safe levels of shellfish resources, gains in net economic value were estimated to range from $37.2 million to $64.9 million per year (mean of the distribution) and from $20.9 million to $70.5 million per year (median of the distribution) in 1984 dollars; a midpoint of $53.54 million (mean of the distribution) and $45.55 million (median of the distribution).

In comparison to estimated gains in aggregate net economic value from water quality improvements of the Chesapeake Bay of $60.4 million to $107 million (1984$) from Bockstael et al. (1989), the above figures offer comparable evidence (assuming comparable population bases) that investment in improving water quality can result in significant economic value (i.e., gains in economic welfare).

9.7. Conclusion

As this chapter illustrates there have been a variety of economic effects and economic losses that have been evaluated by economists. Some of these applications used fairly sophisticated economic models and statistical techniques and some, those based on the benefits transfer approach, expanded per unit values from previous studies on the basis of estimates of users. As these assessments also illustrate, society values the services and public policies that maintain and restore the integrity of the water quality and ecosystems in the order of $50 million to $100 million (improvements to swimmable levels in 1991$, Table 9.17). In addition, social values associated with damages from marine pollution are rather significant and can range from $500 million (e.g., Delaware Bay losses) to in excess of $1 billion (New York Bight losses) in 1991 dollars (Table 9.17). Some of the variation in these magnitudes is partly due to the relative size of the population near these estuaries and the subsequent demand placed on the use of the natural resources. Examining per capita social values shows that estimates for improvements in water quality range from $6 to $12/individual in the Chesapeake Bay area and $20 to $40/person in the Narragansett Bay area; the social value of damages ranges from $59 to $121/person in the New York Bight area, and $106/person in the Delaware Bay area (an estimate within the range for New York Bight); while society values the resources of Long Island Sound from $22/person to $32/person (1991$, Table 9.17). One can reasonably say that public policies designed to maintain and improve the integrity of marine environments and estuaries can safely err on the side of protection and restoration of these resources and marine ecosystems.

Table 9.17. Summary of Economic Value and Expenditure Estimates Associated with Specific National Estuaries (1991$)

Area[a]	Pop.[b]	Reported Effects[a]		Adjusted Effects (1991$)		Per Capita Effects (1991$)	
		Economic value	Expenditures	Economic value	Expenditures	Economic value	Expenditures
		$ millions		$ millions		$/person	
New York Bight (1988$)	20	LOSSES					
		1,030–2,098	1,305–2,931	1,186–2,415	1,502–3,3474	59.31–120.75	75.10–168.70
Delaware Bay (1991$)	5	LOSSES					
		533.5	2,113.8	533.5	2,113.8	106.70	422.76
Long Island Sound (1990$)	14.6	RESOURCE VALUE					
		303.2+151.6	2,241–5,075	316+474	2,335–5,289	21.64–32.47	159.93–362.26
Chesapeake Bay (1987$)	12	IMPROVEMENTS FOR SWIMMING					
		65.7–116.6 (mean 91.1)		79–140 (mean 109)		6.56–11.65 (mean 9.11)	
Narragansett Bay (1984$)	2	IMPROVEMENTS FOR SWIMMING					
	2	39.5–61.4[c]		52–80		26–40	
	2	31.6–60.1[d]		41–79		20.50–39.50	
	2	IMPROVEMENTS FOR SHELLFISHING					
	2	37.2–71.1[c]		49–93		24.50–46.50	
	2	20.9–70.5[d]		27–92		13.50–46.00	

[a]The year associated with the reported effects in dollar measures is contained in parentheses below the area-site.
[b]Population estimates (in millions) for the 1980–90 period.
[c]Based on mean estimates.
[d]Based on median estimates.

Source: New York Bight – Swanson et al. (1991), Kahn (1993), Kahn et al. (1989); Chesapeake Bay – Bockstael et al. (1988, 1989); Long Island Sound – Altobello (1992), LISS (1986); Delaware Bay – Greeley-Polhemus Group, Inc. (1993), Sutton (1993); Narragansett Bay – Hayes et al. (1992), NBP (1989); U.S. EPA (1989).

9.8. Note

1. In the semi-log model, dummy variables are expressed in log values and must be appropriately converted to pure numbers by $\exp[x]-1 = \exp[-0.103]-1 = 0.0979$ or 9.8 percent, where *exp[.]* refers to the exponential function.

9.9. References

Altobello, M.A. 1992. *The Economic Importance of Long Island Sound's Water Quality Dependent Activities*. U.S. EPA, Region I: Boston, MA.

Bell, T.M. 1989. "Floatable Hazards and Noxious Conditions." In WMI, SUNY. *Use Impairments and Ecosystem Impacts of the New York Bight*. SUNY: Stony Brook, NY: 150–161.

Bell, F.W. and V.R. Leeworthy. 1986. *An Economic Analysis of the Importance of Saltwater Beaches in Florida*. Florida Sea Grant Report No. 82. Florida State University: Tallahassee, FL.

Belton, T.A., R. Hazen, B.E. Ruppel, K. Lockwood, R. Mueller, E. Stevenson and J.J. Post. 1985. *A Study of Dioxin (2,3,7,8-tetrachlorodibenzo-p-ioxin) Contamination in Select Finfish, Crustaceans and Sediments of New Jersey Waterways*. NJDEP, Office of Science and Research: Trenton, NJ.

Belton, T.A., R. Roundy and N. Weinstein. 1986. "Urban Fishermen: Managing the Risks of Toxic Exposure." *Environment* 28(9): 19–37.

Bockstael, N.E., K.E. McConnell and I.E. Strand. 1988. *Benefits from Improvements in Chesapeake Bay Water Quality, Volume III*. Prepared for Office of Policy Analysis, Office of Policy and Resource Management, U.S. EPA: Washington, DC.

———. 1989. "Measuring the Benefits of Improvements in Water Quality: The Chesapeake Bay." *Marine Resource Economics* 6: 1–18.

Brewster, F. 1990. "PCBs in New Bedford Harbor and Acushnet River." *Buzzards Bay Project Newsletter* 5(1): 6–14.

Brown, B. and D.D. Ofiara. 1993. "The Effect of Recent Marine Pollution Events on New Jersey's Commercial Fisheries." In WMI, SUNY. *Floatable Wastes in the Ocean: Social, Economic, and Public Health Implications*. SUNY: Stony Brook, NY: 53–73.

Buzzards Bay Project. 1988. *The Buzzards Bay Project: 1987 Annual Report*. Lloyd Center for Environmental Studies: South Dartmouth, MA.

Capps, O., L.A. Shabman and J.W. Brown. 1984. "Short-term Effects of Publicized Shellfish Contamination: The Case of Hard Clams." Paper Presented at AAEA Annual Meetings. Department of Agricultural Economics, Virginia Polytechnic Institute and State University: Blacksburg, VA.

Connecticut Marine Trades Association. 1987. *Economic Impact Survey of Boating Industry in Connecticut*.

Connor, M.S., C.E. Werme and K.D. Rosemann. 1984. " Public Health Consequences of Chemical Contaminants in the Hudson River Estuary." In Brateler, R.J. (ed.). *Chemical Pollution of the Hudson River Estuary*. NOAA/NOS Technical Memorandum OMA-7. NOAA/NOS: Rockville, MD.

Conoscenti, T. 1989. "Floatable Wastes and its Impact on the Long Island Tourist Industry." In WMI, SUNY. *Floatable Wastes in the Ocean: Social, Economic, and Public Health Implications, March 21–22, 1989*. Special Report 104, Reference No. 93-1. Marine Sciences Research Center, SUNY: Stony Brook: 74–76.

Crawford, J.S. 1984. *An Economic Input–Output Analysis of the Marine-Oriented Industries of New London County, Connecticut*. M.S. Thesis. University of Connecticut: Storrs, CT.

Delaware Estuary Program. 1994. "State of the Estuary." *Delaware Estuary News* 5(1): 1–16.

Economic Research Associates. 1979. *Cost Impact of Marine Pollution on Recreational Travel Patterns.* PB-290655. National Technical Information Service: Springfield, VA.

Eichbaum, W.M. 1987. "Estuary Reports: Chesapeake Bay." *EPA Journal—Protecting Our Estuaries* 13(6): 28–29.

Falk, J.M. 1996. *1995 Delaware Boating Study: An Analysis of Delaware-Registered Boaters.* University of Delaware Sea Grant: Newark, DE.

Falk, J.M. and A.R. Graefe. 1990. *Citizens' Opinions about the Delaware Estuary: Results of a Public Opinion Survey.* Technical Report DEL-SG-03-90. University of Delaware Sea Grant: Newark, DE.

Falk, J.M., A.R. Graefe and M.E. Suddleson. 1994. *Recreational Benefits of Delaware's Public Beaches: Attitudes and Perceptions of Beach Users and Residents of the Mid-Atlantic Region.* DEL-SG-05-94. University of Delaware, Sea Grant College Program: Newark, DE.

Falk, J.M., D.G. Swartz and A.R. Graefe. 1987. *The 1985 Delaware Recreational Boating Survey: An Analysis of Delaware-Registered Boaters.* Technical Report DEL-SG-06-87. University of Delaware Sea Grant: Newark, DE.

Figley, W., B. Pyle and B. Halgren. 1979. "Socioeconomic Impacts." In Swanson, R.L. and C.J. Sindermann (ed.). *Oxygen Depletion and Associated Benthic Mortalities in New York Bight, 1976.* NOAA Professional Paper 11. U.S. Government Printing Office: Washington, DC.

Fisher, A. and R. Raucher. 1984. "Intrinsic Benefits of Improved Water Quality: Conceptual and Empirical Perspectives." In Smith, V.K. and A.D. Witte (eds.). *Applied Micro-economics,* Vol 3. JAI Press: Greenwich, CT.

Freeman, A.M. 1979. *The Benefits of Environmental Improvement: Theory and Practice.* Johns Hopkins University Press: Baltimore, MD.

Gold, M.S. and E.O. Van Ravenswaay. 1984. *Methods for Assessing the Economic Benefits of Food Safety Regulations: A Case Study of PCBs in Fish.* Agricultural Economics Report No. 460. Michigan State University: East Lansing, MI.

Greeley-Polhemus Group, Inc. 1993. *Assessment of Selected Delaware Estuary Economic and Natural Resource Values.* Delaware Estuary Program, U.S. EPA: Philadelphia, PA.

Greer, J. 1996. "The Trouble with Toxics in the Bay." *Maryland Marine Notes* 14(6): 1–5.

———. 1997. "Preserving Maryland's Open Land." *Maryland Marine Notes* 15(3): 4–5.

Gross, M.G. 1976. *Waste Disposal.* MESA New York Bight Atlas Monograph No. 26. New York Sea Grant Institute: Albany, NY.

Harding Jr., L.W., M. Leffler and G.E. Mackiernan. 1992. *Dissolved Oxygen in the Chesapeake Bay: A Scientific Consensus.* A Workshop Report No. UM-SG-TS-92-03. Maryland Sea Grant College. University of Maryland: College Park, MD.

Hartunian, N.S., C.N. Smart and M.S. Thompson. 1981. *The Incidence and Economic Costs of Major Health Impairments: A Comparative Analysis of Cancer, Motor Vehicle Injuries, Coronary Heart Disease, and Stroke.* Lexington Books, DC Heath and CO.: Lexington, MA.

Haskin, H. 1990. Retired Professor of Biology, Rutgers University: Bivalve, NJ. Personal Communication.

Hayes, K.M., T.J. Tyrrell and G. Anderson. 1992. "Estimating the Benefits of Water Quality Improvements in the Upper Narragansett Bay." *Marine Resource Economics* 7: 75–85.

Horton, T. and W. Eichbaum. 1991. *Turning the Tide.* Island Press: Washington, DC.

Hushak, L., J. Winslow and N. Dutta. 1988. "The Economic Value of Great Lakes Sportfishing: The

Case of Private Boat Fishing in Ohio's Lake Erie." *Transactions of the American Fisheries Society* 117: 363–373.

HydroQual, Inc. 1989. *Assessment of Pollutant Inputs to New York Bight.* Job No. DYNM0100. Dynamac Corporation: Rockville, MD.

Institute of Medicine. 1991. *Seafood Safety.* National Academy Press: Washington, DC.

Johansson, P.O. 1995. *Evaluating Health Risks: An Economic Approach.* Cambridge University Press: New York, NY.

Judge, G.G., W.E. Griffiths, R.C. Hill and T.C. Lee. 1988. *Introduction to the Theory and Practice of Econometrics.* John Wiley & Sons: New York, NY.

Kahn, J.R. 1991. "Economic Value of Long Island Saltwater Recreational Fishing." *New York Economic Review* 21: 3–23.

Kahn, J. 1993. "General Overview of the Economic Impacts of Floatable Wastes on Fisheries, Tourism, and Marine Recreation." In WMI, SUNY. *Floatable Wastes in the Ocean: Social, Economic, and Public Health Implications.* SUNY: Stony Brook, NY: 16–52.

Kahn, J., D. Ofiara and B. McCay. 1989a. "Economic Measures of Beach Closures." In WMI, SUNY. *Use Impairments and Ecosystem Impacts of the New York Bight.* SUNY: Stony Brook, NY: 96–103.

———. 1989b. "Economic Measures of Toxic Seafoods." In WMI, SUNY. *Use Impairments and Ecosystem Impacts of the New York Bight.* SUNY: Stony Brook, NY: 121–126.

———. 1989c. "Economic Measures of Pathogens in Shellfish." In WMI, SUNY. *Use Impairments and Ecosystem Impacts of the New York Bight.* SUNY: Stony Brook, NY: 147–149.

———. 1989d. "Economic Measures of Commercial Navigation and Recreational Boating—Floatable Hazards." In WMI, SUNY. *Use Impairments and Ecosystem Impacts of the New York Bight.* SUNY: Stony Brook, NY: 162–167.

Leffler, M. 1995. "Land Use and Water Quality: Connecting Ecology and Economics." *Maryland Marine Notes* 13(1–2): 1–5.

———. 1997. "Smart Farming for a Cleaner Bay." *Maryland Marine Notes* 15(3): 1–3.

Lipton, D.W. 1986. "The Resurgence of the U.S. Swordfish Market." *Marine Fisheries Review* 48(3): 24–27.

Long Island Sound Study. 1988. *Long Island Sound Study: Annual Report 1988.* U.S. EPA, Region II: New York, NY.

———. 1989/90. *Long Island Sound Study: Annual Report 1989/1990.* U.S. EPA, Region II: New York, NY.

Mackiernan, G. 1992. "Nutrients and Dissolved Oxygen in the Chesapeake: How Much Is Enough?" *Maryland Marine Notes* March: 1–3.

Maryland Office of the Governor. 1988. *Maryland Restoring the Chesapeake: A Progress Report.* Office of the Governor, State House: Annapolis, MD.

Massa, A.A., M. Del Vicario, D. Pabst, P. Pechko, A. Lechich, E.A. Stern, R. Dieterich and B. May. 1996. "Disposal of Wastes and Dredged Sediments in the New York Bight." *Northeastern Geology and Environmental Sciences* 18(4): 265–285.

McConnell, K.E. and Industrial Economics, Inc. 1986. *The Damages to Recreational Activities from PCBs in New Bedford Harbor.* Ocean Assessment Division, NOAA: Rockville, MD.

McConnell, K.E. and B.G. Morrison. 1986. *Assessment of Economic Damages to the Natural Resources of New Bedford Harbor: Damages to the Commercial Lobster Fishery.* Prepared for Ocean Assessment Division, NOAA: Rockville, MD.

McConnell, K.E., N.E. Bockstael, B. Madariaga and I.E. Strand. 1986. "Recreational Boating and the Benefits of Improved Water Quality: Preliminary Results for the Chesapeake." Paper Presented at the Conference on Economics of Chesapeake Bay Management II: Annapolis, MD.

McIver, R.V. 1988. "Jersey Shore: Safe Haven or Danger Zone." *Camden Courier Post.* In "Our Endangered Shore." Tuesday, August 30: 3E.

Mendelsohn, R. 1986. *Assessment of Damages by PCB Contamination to New Bedford Harbor Amenities Using Residential Property Values.* Prepared for Ocean Assessment Division, NOAA: Rockville, MD.

Mid-Atlantic Fishery Management Council. 1988. Catch Statistics for Surfclams, Ocean Quahogs, Sea Scallops.

Mueller, J.A. and A.R. Anderson. 1978. *Industrial Wastes.* MESA New York Bight Atlas Monograph No. 30. New York Sea Grant Institute: Albany, NY.

Narragansett Bay Project. 1989. *Narragansett Bay Project Progress Report: Pollutant Trends in Narragansett Bay.* RI Department of Environmental Management. Narragansett Bay Project: Providence, RI.

National Marine Fisheries Service. 1987. *Marine Recreational Fisheries Statistics Surveys: Atlantic and Gulf Coasts.* NMFS: Rockville, MD.

Naughton, M.C. and W.H. Desvousges. 1985. *Water Quality Benefits of the BCT Regulations for the Pulp and Paper Industry.* Draft Report, July. Research Triangle Institute: Research Triangle Park, NC.

New Bedford Harbor Trustee Council. 1997. *New Bedford Harbor Trustee Council Restoration Plan Environmental Impact Statement.* U.S. DOC, NOAA, DARP: Silver Spring, MD.

New England River Basin Commission. 1975a. *People and the Sound, Outdoor Recreation.* Boston, MA.

———. 1975b. *People and the Sound, Fish and Wildlife.* Boston, MA.

New Jersey Department of Environmental Protection. 1988. *The State of the Ocean—1987: A Report of the Blue Ribbon Panel on Ocean Incidents, 1987.* Division of Science and Research, NJDEP: Trenton, NJ.

New Jersey Public Service Electric and Gas. 1995. *Bayside Tract Management Plan: Greenwich Township, Cumberland County, New Jersey, November 22.* NJPSE&G: Hancocks Bridge, NJ.

New York Department of Environmental Conservation. 1977. *New York State and Outer Continental Development: An Assessment of Impacts.* New York Department of Environmental Conservation: Albany, NY.

Ofiara, D.D. and B. Brown. 1988. *Economic Assessment of New York Bight Use Impairments on the State of New Jersey.* Institute of Marine and Coastal Sciences, Rutgers University: New Brunswick, NJ.

———. 1989. "Marine Pollution Events of 1988 and Their Effect on Travel, Tourism, and Recreational Activities in New Jersey." Presented at the Conference on Floatable Wastes in the Ocean: Social, Economic, and Public Health Implications, March 21–22, SUNY: Stony Brook, NY.

———. 1999. "Assessment of Economic Losses to Recreational Activities from 1988 Marine Pollution Events and Assessment of Economic Losses from Long-term Contamination of Fish Within the New York Bight to New Jersey." *Marine Pollution Bulletin* 38(11): 990–1004..

Pollack, K. 1990. "Around the Bay—PCBs." *Buzzards Bay Project Newsletter* 5(2): 10–11.

Randall, A. 1991. "Total and Nonuse Values." In Braden, J.B. and C.D. Kolstad (eds.). *Measuring the Demand for Environmental Quality.* North Holland: New York, NY: 303–321.

Reiling, S.D., K.C. Gibbs and H.H. Stoevener. 1973. *Economic Benefits from an Improvement in*

Water Quality. EPA-R5-73-008, U.S. EPA: Washington, DC.

R.L. Associates. 1988. *The Economic Impact of Visitors to the New Jersey Shore the Summer of 1988.* R.L Associates: Princeton, NJ.

Rorholm, N. and D. Burrage. 1983. *Economic Impact of the Rhode Island Boating Industry.* Marine Technical Report No. 85. University of Rhode Island: Kingston, RI.

Smith, R.O. 1976. *The Occupational Safety and Health Act.* The American Enterprise Institute: Washington, DC.

Squires, D.F. 1983. *The Ocean Dumping Quandry: Waste Disposal in the New York Bight.* State University of New York Press: Albany, NY.

Strand, I.E., N.E. Bockstael and C.L. Kling. 1986. "Chesapeake Bay Water Quality and Public Beach Use in Maryland." Paper Presented at the Conference on Economics of Chesapeake Bay Management II: Annapolis, MD.

Strand, I.E., K.E. McConnell and C.G. Hall. 1985. "Measuring Benefits from Improvements in Chesapeake Bay Water Quality, Some Preliminary Findings." Paper Presented at the 8th Biennial Estuarine Research Federation Meeting: Durham, NH.

Sutton, C.C. 1993. "The State of the Estuary." In Delaware Estuary Program. *Comprehensive Conservation and Management Plan.* U.S. EPA: Philadelphia, PA.

Swanson, R.L. 1993. "Floatable Wastes in Marine Waters." In WMI, SUNY. *Floatable Wastes in the Ocean: Social, Economic, and Public Health Implications.* SUNY: Stony Brook, NY: 103–111.

Swanson, R.L. and R. Zimmer. 1989. "Beach Closures due to Washup of Floatables." In WMI, SUNY. *Use Impairments and Ecosystem Impacts of the New York Bight.* SUNY: Stony Brook, NY: 45–90.

Swanson, R.L., T.M. Bell, J. Kahn, and J. Olha. 1991. "Use Impairments and Ecosystem Impacts of the New York Bight." *Chemistry and Ecology* 5: 99–127.

Swanson, R.L., M.L. Boetman, T.P. O'Connor and H.M. Stanford. In Process. "Management of Sewage Materials." SUNY: Stony Brook, NY.

Swanson, R.L., H.M. Stanford, J.S. O'Connor, S. Chanesman, C.A. Parker, P.A. Eisen, and G.A. Mayer, 1978. "June 1976 Pollution of Long Island Ocean Beaches." *Journal of the Environmental Engineering Division, ASCE* 10:4(EE6): 1067–1085.

Swanson, R.L. and C.J. Sindermann. (ed.) 1979. *Oxygen Depletion and Associated Benthic Mortalities in New York Bight, 1976.* NOAA Professional Paper 11. U.S. Government Printing Office: Washington, DC.

Swartz, D.G. and I.E. Strand. 1981. "Avoidance Costs Associated with Imperfect Information: The Case of Kepone." *Land Economics* 57(2): 139–150.

Thaler, R. and S. Rosen. 1975. " The Value of Saving a Life: Evidence from the Labor Market." In Terleckj, N.E. (ed.). *Household Production and Consumption, No. 4.* Columbia University Press: New York, NY: 265–298.

Tyrrell, T.J., W.K.B. Emerson and D.E. Molzan. 1982. *The Economic Impact of Tourism on Westerly, Rhode Island.* Agricultural Experiment Station Bulletin No. 433. University of Rhode Island: Kingston, RI.

U.S. Congress, Office of Technology Assessment. 1987. *Wastes in the Marine Environment.* OTA: Washington, DC.

U.S. Environmental Protection Agency. 1989. *Marine and Estuarine Protection: Programs and Activities.* EPA-503/9-89-002. U.S. EPA: Washington, DC.

Wegge, T.C., W.M. Hanemann and I.E. Strand. 1986. *An Economic Assessment of Marine Recre-*

ational Fishing in Southern California. NOAA-TM-NMFS-SWR-015. Southwest Region, National Marine Fisheries Service: Terminal Island, CA.

WMI, SUNY. 1989a *Use Impairments and Ecosystem Impacts of the New York Bight.* SUNY: Stony Brook, NY.

WMI, SUNY. 1989b. *Floatable Wastes in the Ocean: Social, Economic, and Public Health Implications, March 21–22, 1989.* Special Report 104, Reference No. 93-1. Marine Sciences Research Center, SUNY: Stony Brook.

Restoration of Coastal Wetlands, the Role of Trustees, and Scaling Restoration Projects

10.1. Introduction

This chapter addresses two of the latest developments in resource damage assessments, wetlands restorations and approaches to scale restoration projects that pertain only to National Oceanic and Atmospheric Administration Natural Resource Damage Assessment (NOAA–NRDA) rules, and hence, oil spills. In addition it discusses the possible role(s) that trustees can pursue in this process. The restoration of coastal wetlands has become a major initiative for both federal agencies responsible with the NRDA process, the U.S. Department of Interior (DOI) and the U.S. Department of Commerce, National Oceanic and Atmospheric Administration (DOC, NOAA). From the legislative acts that resulted in the development of a set of uniform procedures to perform NRDAs resulting from spills of hazardous substances and of oil, the designated public trustees ultimately seek a damage award. This award is used to cover the costs of cleanup–mitigation and restoration of the aquatic environment–wetlands that were spoiled, where the bulk of the damage award is for restoration purposes.

Two issues now become important, the first of which is the use of public funds to restore the degraded wetland-environment so as to achieve the same or equivalent level of resources-services as in the pre-spill state, or the purchase of wetlands resources equivalent to those degraded. In principle, this is to achieve the same level of economic welfare compared to initial levels so that society remains at the same levels in both pre-spill and post-spill/restored states. The other issue concerns integrating a variety of skills and knowledge from many different disciplines in order to restore or create coastal wetlands. This involves the use of construction techniques to restore soil and hydrology characteristics of wetlands, plant and soil sciences to restore vegetative characteristics, and other sciences (biology, ecology, etc.) to restore other characteristics of wetlands in terms of the functions and services the degraded wetland provided in its pre-spill state, i.e., functional equivalence. In the past 10 to 15 years great strides and advances have pushed this new area into an exploding field and discipline. With the emphasis of federal procedures and the bulk of settlement monies on restoration efforts, this has now become one of the areas of cutting-edge research and application.

Economic analysis in this overall process is crucial in two different senses. On one hand, economic analysis is an important component in determining the magnitude of damages and hence the damage award. It now has a new role assisting with wetlands restoration efforts, providing information to aid decisions about the optimal restoration project and the scaling of restoration projects, and it can assist in monitoring restored wetlands to help ensure that equivalent services measured in terms of net economic value have been achieved compared to the wetland in a pre-spill state. Future research can provide critical guidance and information regarding monitoring efforts and changes to the federal NRDA procedures.

10.2. Insights on Wetlands Restoration Efforts

A relatively new science and discipline has emerged known as wetlands restoration and along with it the allied field of restoration economics. At the same time, new journals and societies have also emerged, including *Restoration Ecology* (the journal of the Society of Ecological Restoration) and *Ecological Economics* (the journal of the International Society of Ecological Economists), as a result of degradations of aquatic environments from oil–hazardous substance spills, development, agricultural conversions, and the like. The field is moving toward quantitative evaluations of created, restored, and rehabilitated wetlands (referred to as "restored" wetlands from now on in this book) compared to pre-spill or natural, undisturbed wetlands that serve as a control or a reference in experimentally designed studies. From such comparisons evaluation criteria have been developed such as specific planting criteria for revegetative purposes, criteria and measures to assess revegetative efforts (e.g., height of plants, basil density of plants, weight of above ground biomass, etc.), criteria for restocking living organisms (e.g., fish, shellfish, etc.), criteria for relative assessments of living organisms, and criteria for assessments of soil sediments of contaminant levels and degradations of contaminants. As with any new science, researchers are learning by doing and rapidly developing new and more accurate techniques and evaluation criteria. From such efforts researchers can address linkages, possible hypotheses, and reasons that account for comparative differences and for temporal changes and development of "restored" wetlands. Sharp attention to detail, research design, and a painstakingly thorough process will advance this science.

Some of the recent interest and motivation behind this new science results from the federal rules and procedures promulgated by the U.S. DOC, NOAA via the Oil Protection Act (OPA) in 1990. As noted in Chapter 3, the federal NRDA rules and procedures developed by NOAA stressed wetlands restoration in their NRDA process, rather than economic damage claims. This emphasis and the fact that all future oil spills will come under OPA ensures that wetlands restoration will become the benchmark and the main tool in the NRDA process as it pertains to oil spills. Rather than base final proceedings on economic damages (where the metric is in terms of dollars) it appears that NOAA wishes that final proceedings be based on the metric of biological and other functions and services of the resources lost.

10.2.1. Factors and Considerations Based on NOAA–NRDA Rules

Because of the emphasis of NOAA–NRDA rules it seems appropriate to include a brief discussion of criteria and factors used in determining suitable restoration projects under an NOAA setting. Trustees are first expected to develop a number (i.e., a reasonable range) of alternative or proposed restoration projects that typically range from natural recovery to enhanced recovery (i.e., the use of methods and techniques that would accelerate the recovery of injured wetlands to baseline or pre-spill conditions). Once a number of alternatives have been developed the alternatives are to be evaluated based on various criteria. Briefly these are as follows (refer to Section 990.54 of OPA for more detail):

- Costs associated with each alternative
- Extent that alternatives can meet expected goals of achieving baseline conditions and compensation of losses
- Probability of success
- Extent that alternatives can prevent future injury and avoid collateral injury from implementation
- Extent that alternatives may benefit more than one resource or service
- Possible effects of alternatives on public health and safety

Based on the above criteria, a trustee must select a "preferred" restoration project. In the case that more than two alternative projects are equally preferable (based on the above criteria), the project chosen must be the least-cost alternative.

10.2.2. Parameters and Criteria in Evaluations of Wetlands Restorations

To ensure and to evaluate the performance or success of a wetlands restoration project in relation to a baseline condition (e.g., historical data of the injured site, comparison to "control" sites, etc.) a number of parameters have been identified from work in wetlands restorations (Bergen et al. 1995, Cairns 1988, Gosselink et al. 1990, Jordan et al. 1987, Kusler and Kentula 1989, Mitsch and Gosselink 1993, NRC 1992, 1995, PERL 1990, Packer 1997, Thayer 1992). Furthermore, criteria useful in evaluations of the relative performance of restored wetlands, also referred to as the degree of functional equivalence (i.e., whether or not restored wetlands perform equivalent functions–services compared to those natural wetlands or wetlands in a pre-spill condition) of restored wetlands, are usually based on historical data from the injured site if possible, or if not, on the basis of a control or reference site that has similar characteristics of the injured site before injury occurred. Such an exercise follows from controlled experimental research designs in statistics. In the case study that follows in some instances it was hard to maintain the integrity of the control or reference sites over a long-term monitoring period, and the researcher must account for this possibility. Monitoring parameters that have been identified and used to provide quantitative statistical evaluations in previous studies include:

- Vegetative parameters
  - Plant height
  - Stem density

- Density of flowers
- Rhizome spread
- Basal area of individual plants
- Above ground biomass
- Below ground biomass
- Marine organism parameters
  - Population density of specific shellfish (e.g., ribbed mussels, oysters, clams)
  - Population density and relative distribution of specific fish (e.g., mummichog, minnows, etc.)
  - Relative importance or distribution of food items from stomach contents of specific fish
  - Relative distribution of benthic organisms (meiofauna and macrofauna) from sediment samples
  - Relative distribution of nesting and visiting waterfowl and shorebirds

As this new science matures it could move toward the use of specific organisms as key parameters to monitor and evaluate such as in the case of bioindicators or biomarkers proposed in monitoring levels of toxic substances.

10.2.3. Restoration of a Coastal Salt Marsh—Exxon Bayway Arthur Kill Oil Spill

One of the few cases in which an evaluation of restoration efforts was available was that of an oiled salt marsh in the Arthur Kill, New York and New Jersey. Only preliminary results, based on the first few years of monitoring efforts, were obtained. It was chosen for inclusion because the case was settled, because an extensive monitoring study phase was incorporated into the final settlement and restoration project, and because comparative results from the first phase monitoring efforts were available (Bergen et al. 1995, Packer 1997). In 1990 an underwater pipeline operated by Exxon cracked and discharged 576,000 gallons of No. 2 heating oil on January 1–2, 1990, into the Arthur Kill, a tidal waterway between New Jersey and Staten Island, New York (Burger 1994a, 1994b). It was determined that the oil spill adversely affected over 125 acres of marine intertidal low marsh and tidal creeks, with a loss of 25 acres of wetlands (Bergen et al. 1995, NYC DP&R, SMRT 1996, Packer 1997).

Following the oil spill, damage, and penal settlement, a multiyear restoration and monitoring project was undertaken by the New York City Department of Parks and Recreation (NYC DP&R) as part of the final restoration plan in 1991 (NYC DP&R, SMRT 1995). To date 6.5 acres of salt marsh composed of 1.25 miles of shoreline located in the most heavily impacted or oiled areas of the Arthur Kill have undergone restoration efforts. This has involved hand planting of over 200,000 plugs of Spartina alterniflora (smooth cordgrass) first propagated in nurseries from Spartina alterniflora that originated from the Arthur Kill (NYC DP&R, SMRT 1995, Packer 1997).

Preliminary monitoring efforts, in the sense that these efforts evaluated progress over a narrow two- to three-year period and are still ongoing, have been conducted and reported by Bergen et al. (1995) and Packer (1997). A variety of monitoring parameters were identified and statistically sampled to provide quantitative evaluations. These parameters include:

- Vegetative parameters
  - Plant height
  - Stem density
  - Density of flowers
  - Rhizome spread
  - Basal area of individual plants
  - Above ground biomass
  - Below ground biomass
- Marine organisms parameters
  - Population density of ribbed mussels
  - Relative importance or distribution of food items from stomach contents of the common mummichog
  - Relative distribution of benthic organisms (meiofauna and macrofauna) from sediment samples

First Phase Results. The focus and objective of the monitoring evaluations of Bergen et al. (1995) concerned the success of revegetation of *Spartina alterniflora* transplants and seedlings in restored areas, concentrations of total petroleum hydrocarbons (TPH) in marsh soil, recolonization of ribbed mussels (*Guekensia demissa*), and the effect of specific heterotrophic bacteria on degrading oil trapped within the soil substrate. Study findings follow.

Regarding TPH concentrations in soil, results appear to indicate the occurrence of other oil spills; TPH concentrations increased over the 1990–93 period in the test sites. Concerning revegetation of *Spartina alterniflora*, all vegetation monitoring parameters increased over the two-year period compared to baseline conditions at the restored marsh sites as shown in Table 10.1. Unrestored sites exhibited more modest increases in the vegetative parameters: above ground biomass (AGB) and stem density, and decreases in all other parameters (Table 10.1). In relation to control sites, increases in all vegetative parameters but below ground biomass (BGB) and plant height were found (Table 10.1). Concentrations of TPH in soils in restored sites showed a 75 percent decrease over the two-year period (17,534 ppm/m^2 to 4,425 ppm/m^2) while soil concentrations of TPH at unrestored sites indicated more modest decreases of 60 percent (6,701 ppm/m^2 to 2,651 ppm/m^2) compared to a 43 percent decline at control sites (583 ppm/m^2 to 330 ppm/m^2) (Table 10.1). Results of recolonization studies of ribbed mussels showed increases from zero to an average of 6/m^2 at restored sites, none were found at unrestored sites over the two-year period, and at control sites the average baseline density of 32/m^2 increased to 41/m^2 over the two-year period (Table 10.1). Evidence of bacterial activity seemed to indicate the presence and abundance of relatively similar magnitudes across control and restored sites within the range of an average of 10^8–10^{10} CFU/gram (Colony-Forming Units).

Based on this preliminary narrow data Bergen et al. (1995) offer some tentative conclusions. In terms of the revegetative parameters the restoration project could be deemed "successful," although soil contaminated with TPH remained at high levels compared to

Table 10.1. Exxon Bayway Arthur Kill Oil Spill Restoration Project: First Phase Results.

Restored Sites

Year	Ribbed Mussel/m²	AGB/m²	BGB/m²	Stems/m²	Flowers/m²	Height/m²	TPH/m²
0	0	0	0	0	0	0	$17,534 \pm 2.3{*}10^4$
1	nc	313 ± 236	540 ± 282	119 ± 63	7 ± 10	0.81 ± 0.4	$6,188 \pm 6.6{*}10^3$
2	6 ± 8	909 ± 443	1,395 ± 807	154 ± 70	30 ± 23	1.38 ± 0.4	$4,425 \pm 4.6{*}10^3$

Unrestored Sites

Year	Ribbed Mussel/m²	AGB/m²	BGB/m²	Stems/m²	Flowers/m²	Height/m²	TPH/m²
0	0	nc	nc	nc	nc	nc	$6,701 \pm 4.7 \times 10^3$
1	nc	183 ± 318	879 ± 1523	14 ± 32	3 ± 5	0.92 ± 0.65	$2,651 \pm 2.8 \times 10^3$
2	0	225 ± 390	283 ± 490	27 ± 50	0.3 ± 0.9	0.64 ± 0.6	nc

Control Sites

Year	Ribbed Mussel/m²	AGB/m²	BGB/m²	Stems/m²	Flowers/m²	Height/m²	TPH/m²
0	32 ± 32	nc	nc	nc	nc	nc	583 ± 319
1	nc	1,072 ± 290	2,065 ± 1,126	165 ± 31	32 ± 12	1.6 ± 0.3	330 ± 106
2	41 ± 24	1,680 ± 90	1,360 ± 203	137 ± 31	44 ± 10	1.4 ± 0.6	<10

Note: m² refers to square meters, AGB is above ground biomass in grams, BGB is below ground biomass in grams, height is in meters, TPH is total petroleum hydrocarbons in ppm, and nc refers to not collected or still to be collected.
Source: Bergen et al. (1995).

control sites, indicating persistence of oil some three years after the spill despite cleanup efforts. Recolonization of ribbed mussels has begun in restored sites although at numbers or densities below those of control sites, and lends support to the hypothesis that recolonization rates are low for those living organisms that are immobile. These researchers remain concerned about the high levels of TPH that remain in marsh soils at restored sites and at unrestored sites. They further speculate that TPH degradation may approach the time frame observed by Burns and Teal (1979) at an oil spill at West Falmouth, Massachusetts. They also wonder if some of the initial dramatic reduction in TPH levels might be attributable to tramping the marsh substrate (similar to squeezing a sponge) and from aerating the soil during restoration and replanting activities (Alderson 1998).

Second Phase Results. Concerns about the ecological viability and functional equivalence of the restored marsh sites in the Arthur Kill shaped the study objectives of the monitoring evaluations of the Salt Marsh Restoration Assessment Team of the National Marine Fisheries Service (NMFS) (Packer 1997). Specific objectives were to explore whether "some ambient or essential ecosystem functions have been lost, altered, degraded or approximately restored," (Packer 1997: 2). These efforts were to complement and further extend monitoring activities of that of the NYC DP&R.

Results pertaining to the food habits of the common mummichog (*Fundulus heteroclitus*) based on the preliminary evidence indicate areas for future research and offer some evidence of changes in dietary habits, and thus evidence regarding ecosystem functions of restoration efforts. On the basis of percentage of occurrence of food items, findings suggest some differences in food habits; fish collected at control sites indicated a similar relative importance of detritus and algal particles when compared to food items found in fish from restored and unrestored sites (Steimle 1997: Table I). At restored and unrestored sites, detritus was found to be a relatively important food item although this was the only food item common to these sites. Results based on mean percent stomach volume support previous findings and offer more conclusive evidence of differences between control and noncontrol sites. Algal parts and detritus were relatively important at both control sites and constituted a large part of the diet of these fish (Steimle 1997: Table II). At the control sites, the amphipod (*Orchestia grillus*) and decapod shrimp were again found to be important food items along with the bait used as an attractant to trap sampled fish. At all restored and unrestored sites, bait, detritus, and unidentified organic matter formed the relative mix of food items in the diets of these fish.

This preliminary evidence suggests that some differences were discernible at control versus noncontrol sites, and could indicate that a lack of specific food sources may be evident at noncontrol sites. Thus, the restored and unrestored sites appear to remain compromised with limited ecological functions.

Vitaliano et al. (1997) examined the relative distribution of the occurrence of various benthic organisms (meiofauna and macrofauna) among restored, unrestored, and control sites. They used a multidimensional scaling technique to examine differences in community structure of benthic organisms among sites. Their preliminary findings suggest that benthic organisms were present and somewhat abundant at oiled sites. The restored sites were found to contain relatively more organisms than the unrestored sites and one of the control sites. In terms of this monitoring parameter it would appear that restoration activities had a noticeable effect, that benthic organisms have begun to repopulate the impacted sites, although at a faster rate at the restored sites compared to unrestored sites, and one of the lowest trophic levels (bottom dwelling organisms that serve as food sources to larger living organisms) has begun to function again.

Deshpande et al. (1997) examined ribbed mussels for concentrations of petroleum hydrocarbons at restored, unrestored, and control sites. These researchers concluded based on the preliminary evidence that low levels (in ppm) of hydrocarbon concentrations were measured and supported the results of Berger and Associates (1991) that correlations between hydrocarbon concentrations in ribbed mussels and in bottom sediment are not present. Hence, the ribbed mussel does not appear to be a representative biomarker or indicator for monitoring petroleum hydrocarbon pollution (Deshpande et al. 1997).

The above preliminary evidence will provide direction to future sampling and monitoring efforts and can provide some indication of preliminary restoration activities as discussed here. However, as these researchers caution, the results are preliminary, more monitoring work is needed, the effects of oil may persist longer than originally thought, and it may take longer than previously thought for restored marshes to achieve various ecological functions (functional equivalence) other than revegetation of *Spartina alterniflora,* which has been demonstrated to be successful within a very short time.

10.3. Insights on Overseers and Trustees in Restoration Efforts: Their Role, Arrangement, and Lifespan

According to the Comprehensive Environmental Response, Compensation, and Liability Act (CERCLA) and OPA, it is not until a spill or discharge of oil or a hazardous substance has occurred, with subsequent injury and economic damage of sufficient levels, that a trustee of the injured and damaged natural resources is designated to address legal proceedings, cleanup activities beyond emergency responses, and restoration efforts. Monitoring activities are becoming more frequently added to this list of responsibilities. What remains uncertain is the lifespan of the trustee's arrangement. The federal policies (CERCLA and OPA) stipulate that as much of the awarded damage claims as possible be devoted to restore injured wetlands and their respective services. This leaves little available for monitoring activities once approved restoration projects have been completed. It also seems to indicate that monitoring activities are not a component of the NRDA process and not important to restoration activities. Clearly this is an oversight. In many conversations we have had, resource trustees, specialists, and research scientists repeatedly voice concerns about monitoring. It is important, necessary, and a critical and integral part of restoration activities; without it one can never determine if "restored" wetlands approach the functional equivalence of nearby natural or undisturbed wetlands, the time span involved, and the degree of functional equivalence achieved. The recent increase in monitoring activities in NRDA cases may demonstrate the importance and the need of this activity. If trustee arrangements last only as long as it takes to process an NRDA case, and ignore monitoring of restoration projects, information regarding the long-term success of restoration efforts will be lost. We feel that, over time, monitoring activities will become a formally integrated component of the NRDA process and federal NRDA policy.[1]

The *Exxon Valdez* Oil Spill Trustee Council (EVOSTC), developed as a result of the *Exxon Valdez* oil spill in Prince William Sound, Alaska, has been the most visible trustee arrangement (EVOSTC 1998a). This council will have an unusually long life span because of the sheer magnitude of the settlement and associated restoration projects and the trustees' establishment of a restoration reserve as a trust fund (i.e., an endowment) whereby the interest generated will be used for future restoration activities, which include monitoring (EVOSTC 1998a, 1998b). In comparison, the trustee arrangement for the Exxon Bayway oil spill had financial support for a period of up to seven years, after which time monitoring activities will be conducted on an infrequent basis with no more funds available if restoration projects do not reach the functional equivalence of nearby undisturbed wetlands. In this scenario one could conclude that the damage settlement may not be adequate, that the restoration projects were not properly designed to achieve restoration, or that further research in wetlands restoration will provide answers to overcome present difficulties and unknowns. Clearly it would have been in the public interest for the trustee arrangement to have had a longer life so that the damaged natural resources held in public trust would have been returned to the public in a pre-spill state, providing all the functions and services lost.

To cite another example of a quasi-trustee arrangement, settlement of disputes and controversies over the environmental impact of electric power plants on the Hudson River between representatives of commercial fishermen (Hudson River Fishermen's

Association), environmental organizations, the U.S. Environmental Protection Agency, the State of New York, and public utilities situated along the Hudson River in New York led to the creation of an independent institution to foster and sponsor research and education programs that could assist in public policies concerning the environmental and ecological integrity of the Hudson River (Barnthouse et al. 1988a, 1988b; HRF 1998). The Hudson River Foundation for Science and Environmental Research was established in 1981 and began operations with an initial endowment of $12 million in May 1982, referred to as the Hudson River Fund (Barnthouse et al. 1988a, HRF 1998). The settlement was placed in an investment-annuity type vehicle (i.e., an endowment) with the interest on the principle used to support scientific and public policy research via competitive research grants and educational programs. From the initial $12 million endowment the Hudson River Fund has grown to over $36 million in 1997 and has allowed the foundation to award almost $20 million to over 350 grants over the 1982–97 period (HRF 1998). Although the settlement award was not used for restoration efforts, one could argue that it has provided scientific evidence and in turn has leveraged and influenced public policy to protect and restore the environmental and ecological health of the Hudson River.

For example, Hudson River Foundation sponsored research on PCB contamination of the Hudson River and of fish in the Hudson River that has contributed to public policy in the management of toxic substances within the sediment of the riverbed and in recent debates over removal of contaminated bottom sediment versus "capping" bottom sediment (Brown et al. 1985, Limburg 1986, O'Connor 1984). A major difference between the structure and arrangement of an independent entity such as the Hudson River Foundation is that the foundation has an indirect effect on protection and restoration activities via influences on public policy, whereas trustee arrangements via NRDA have a direct effect on restoration. The formal arrangement of the Hudson River Foundation ensures it will remain in perpetuity, whereas the arrangement of trustees via NRDAs have a finite life. A number of issues become obvious for research. For example, is the value of scientific and policy information relatively more important than pure restoration efforts—are the payoffs from influencing public policy greater or lesser than actual restoration efforts in the long-run? Which type of arrangement over time has ultimately influenced a greater degree of restoration of a degraded environment? How successful and what role has scientific evidence had in leveraging and influencing further support and public policy that ultimately resulted in cleanup and restoration efforts? And what type and magnitude of tradeoff must be made pursuing an indirect role versus a direct role in the context of lost economic values, impacts, and time period? Consideration of these types of issues and concerns can help ensure that trustee arrangements in the future achieve the goals of the federal NRDA policies.

I0.4. Insights on Scaling Restoration Projects and Determining Optimal Size

This section contains information from the U.S. DOC, NOAA-NRDA rules and procedures to use in determining the scale of restoration projects that meet NOAA criteria. It draws heavily from the NOAA Scaling Guidance Document (U.S. DOC, NOAA 1997a). In general this section applies only to NOAA procedures. It should be noted that the outcomes based on these techniques could diverge from those based on economic efficiency criteria (see Desvousges et al. 1997). The process of scaling suitable restoration projects in general, consists of adjusting the size of a restoration project so that the present value (or discounted value) of project gains is the same as the present value of (compensable) interim losses (i.e., those services lost until a restored project provides services or service gains equal to baseline conditions).

Scaling procedures consist of two main types, resource-to-resource (RtR) or service-to-service (StS) approaches being one type, and valuation approaches (e.g., value-to-value, value-to-cost) the other main type. Specific criteria apply, and in turn, determine which approach to use. RtR or StS is recommended for restoration projects that provide resources or services of the same type and quality and are of comparable value to those resources or services lost and injured (i.e., Class I projects in NOAA terminology). If resources/services are of the same type and quality but not of comparable value (i.e., Class II projects) or are not of the same type and quality nor of comparable value (i.e., Class III projects), then the valuation approach is recommended. In other words the valuation approach is recommended for use when resources are of a different type, quality, and value, or when the RtR or StS approach is not appropriate. If projects are not of comparable type and quality of resources or services as those lost (i.e., Class IV projects), one cannot consider them as alternative projects in restoration plans; these projects have no place in NOAA procedures. Classification of restoration projects provides trustees with a framework to aid in determining how well injured resources or services match proposed replacement resources or services in terms of key characteristics and quality attributes.

10.4.1. Resource-to-Resource or Service-to-Service Scaling Approach

The RtR or StS approach, hereafter StS, consists of an approach wherein a suitable quantity of replacement resources (e.g., vegetative resources, living resources, etc.) and services (e.g., human services such as fishing and recreation, and physical services such as nursery grounds to living organisms, cycling nutrients, flood protection, etc.) are determined where the quantity of discounted services or proxies (e.g., where the number of sportfishing trips represents a proxy to sportfishing "services" in lieu of measures of economic value of sportfishing for a specific wetland area) lost equals the quantity of discounted services or proxies gained or replaced by the restoration project in question. This approach is based on a strong implicit assumption that there is an acceptable one-to-one equivalency between a unit of services lost and a unit of services gained from the restoration project. This assumption does not necessarily imply a one-to-one tradeoff in resources, because services provided by wetlands and quantities of resources in a wetland can differ across locations. NOAA emphasizes that tradeoffs should be evaluated in terms of services (U.S. DOC, NOAA 1997a).

The types of services the injured site had previously provided determine how one implements the StS approach. For example, services lost could be lost human use activities measured as lost user days or trips associated with beach use or sportfishing. Services lost could also be lost ecological services such as lost marsh vegetation (a primary production activity) measured by plant height, stem density, and below ground biomass, or lost finfish–shellfish–bird habitat (secondary production activities) measured by abundance (population density) and variety of species (relative mix). In both cases one must choose some measure (i.e., a metric or proxy) in which to represent and measure the service gains and losses (e.g., user days or number of trips for human uses, and possibly a variety of proxy measures for ecological services such as vegetation proxies [stem density, below ground biomass, etc.], biological proxies [population density, relative distribution]) of various species.

Habitat Equivalency Analysis (HEA) is an StS approach recommended for habitat injuries. In this approach the PV (present value) of services lost is set equal to the PV of services gained by adjusting the size of the restoration project formally represented by Equations (10.1a) and (10.1b) (from a modification of NOAA [1997b]):

$$(10.1a) \quad [\textstyle\sum_{t=0}^{B} p_t \, (b^j - x_t^j)/b^j]^*J = [\textstyle\sum_{t=I}^{L} p_t \, (x_t^P - b^P)/b^j]^*R, \text{ or}$$

with slight modifications (arithmetical corrections) to conform with their example calculations:

$$(10.1b) \quad [\textstyle\sum_{t=0}^{B} p_t \{b^j - [(x_{t+1}^j + x_t^j)/2]\}/b^j]^*J =$$

$$[\textstyle\sum_{t=I}^{L} p_t \{[(x_{t+1}^P + x_t^P)/2] - b^P\}/b^j]^*R.$$

Here p_t is the discount factor, b^j represents the baseline (pre-spill) level of services per area for the injured habitat, x_t^j is the the level of services per area provided by the injured habitat in year t, J corresponds to the area injured (in acres, hectares), x_t^P represents the level of services per area to be provided by the replacement–restored habitat in year t, b^P is the initial level of services per area of replacement–restored habitat, R represents the size or scale of the restoration project, and the time periods t=0 to B represent the time that the injury or spill occurred (t=0) to the time that the injured habitat recovers to baseline (t=B), and the time period t=I to L represents the time in which incremental service gains start, from implementing the habitat restoration project (t=I) to the time where incremental service gains from the restoration project end (t=L).

The appropriately sized restoration project is determined by solving Equations (10.1a or b) for P such as:

$$(10.2a) \quad R = [\textstyle\sum_{t=0}^{B} p_t \, (b^j - x_t^j)/b^j]^*J \, / \, [\textstyle\sum_{t=I}^{L} p_t \, (x_t^P - b^P)/b^j], \text{ or following modifications}$$

$$(10.2b) \quad R = [\textstyle\sum_{t=0}^{B} p_t \{b^j - [(x_{t+1}^j + x_t^j)/2]\}/b^j]^*J \, / \, [\textstyle\sum_{t=I}^{L} p_t \{[(x_{t+1}^P + x_t^P)/2] - b^P\}/b^j].$$

When applied to determine the scale of a project to restore or replace lost services, the HEA and other service-equivalency approaches make economists uncomfortable, especially when such services are strictly ecological services and there is no direct link to human use (in particular, the economic constructs of utility and welfare) and have been so criticized (Desvousges et al. 1997). Unsworth and Bishop (1994) reason that the HEA approach is comparable to setting the money value of service losses to that of the money value of service gains. Desvousges et al. (1997) further claim that a number of restrictive assumptions must be met in order for the quantity of replacement services to equal the quantity of lost services, and ultimately achieve an optimal size restoration project. These include:

- The real unit value of services of injured habitat associated with baseline conditions is constant over time.
- The real unit value of services from restoration or replacement projects is constant over time.

They suggest that for the HEA to become consistent with economic efficiency criteria, the quantity of services should be linked to the economic constructs of utility and welfare.

10.4.2. Valuation Scaling Approach

The valuation scaling approach is suitable for restoration projects when injured and restored or replacement services are of a different type, quality, or value. In these cases, the assumption of a one-to-one tradeoff between units of services of injured and lost resources versus that of replacement or restored resources cannot be met. Restoration projects that meet the above criteria are to be classified as either Class II or III restoration projects.

In these instances, the valuation approach preferred by NOAA is the value-to-value approach, in which the scale of a restoration project is adjusted so that the present value of service gains (from the restoration project) equals the present value of interim losses of services from a spill event. If trustees determine that it is possible to assess a value for lost services, but assessment of a value of replacement or restored resources and services would either exceed a reasonable time limit or a reasonable cost, then a value-to-cost approach must be used. This particular approach involves adjusting the size of the restoration projects so that the cost (i.e., discounted cost) of the restoration project is the same as the value (i.e., discounted value) of interim losses.

Recommended economic procedures to use in valuation approaches involve a number of economic techniques, for example benefits transfer practices, behavioral or revealed preference models (averting-behavior models, hedonic price, travel cost, random utility models), and stated preference models (contingent valuation, conjoint analysis [Mathews et al. 1997]).

10.4.3. Further Insights in Scaling Projects

To illustrate some of the above concepts we consider an application to the New Bedford Harbor case study. Recall that damages caused by PCB contamination resulted in closing off an 18-square-mile area of productive inshore lobster grounds in 1977, which resulted in economic damages estimated at a PV of $2 million (1985$) over a 106-year time period (McConnell and Morrison 1986).

10.4.3.1. Simplified Service-Equivalency Approach

We first consider a simplified approach developed by Unsworth and Bishop (1994), which NOAA considers to be analogous to the HEA (U.S. DOC, NOAA 1997a: D-2). Unsworth and Bishop advance an approach that first determines the discounted quantity of resources or services (i.e., quantity of resources–services expressed in discounted terms) lost over some relevant time period, and then determines the quantity of discounted resources–services needed to compensate those for interim losses formally expressed below. The first step involves:

$$(10.3) \qquad D = \sum_{t=d}^{R} D_t = \sum_{t=d}^{R} NW_t (1+i)^{T-t} = N^*W,$$

where D represents the present value of damages to the public from the loss of W_t acres of wetlands over the time period from d to R, D_t is the present value (in year T) of damages expressed in quantity units of damages to the public beginning in year t due to the loss of W_t acres of wetlands, W_t is the quantity of acres of wetlands lost beginning in year t, N is the total economic value of an acre of wetlands assumed to be constant over time, d represents the year in which damages begin, T is the current year, R represents the year the restored project becomes completed, i is the discount rate, and W represents the present value (in year T) of wetland services lost over the period d to R expressed in wetland acre–years.

In this model, N is assumed to be a constant value over time. As already mentioned, Equation (10.3) determines the discounted quantity of resources or services lost over some relevant time period (t to R). The next step involves solving an equation in one unknown to determine the suitable scale of a restoration project that would compensate the public for interim losses:

$$(10.4) \qquad N^* W = (N^* X/i) / (1+i)^{-r},$$

where X is the quantity of wetlands needed to compensate the public for interim losses, r represents the number of years until full recovery (i.e., R–T). In Equation (10.4) N is assumed constant, appears on both sides of the equation and hence cancels out, leaving one to solve the equation for X as follows:

$$N^* W = (N^* X/i) / (1+i)^{-r},$$

$$W = (X/i) / (1+i)^{-r},$$

$$W^* (1+i)^{-r} {}^* i = X.$$

Application of the above approach to the New Bedford Harbor case study assumes we want to express losses and gains in quantities of resources or services rather than in monetary values. We emphasize that this is for illustrative purposes and is not meant to challenge the previous studies of resource damages. If we use the same time frame as that used by McConnell and Morrison (1986), 106 years, we can express the 18-square-mile area lost in terms of the PV of area–years that would have been lost over the time frame necessary to compensate the public for PCB contamination. This involves the following equation:

$$D = \sum_{t=1980}^{2085} D_t = N^* 18 \text{ sq. miles} / (1 + .03)^{1985-t}, \text{ where } N \text{ is fixed.}$$

Details of the approach are contained in Table 10.2. It shows the derivation for each time period for the 106-year period. An estimated 685 square mile–years of productive inshore lobster grounds in discounted terms as of January 1, 1985, is estimated to have been lost from PCB contamination over this time frame. To find the suitable scale of a restoration project solve the following for the variable X:

$$685 * N = (N * X/0.03) / (1.03)^{-7},$$

where it is assumed that a suitable restoration project can be implemented in areas open to commercial lobster fishing in a seven-year time period rather than that determined from R–T (2085–1985 = 100-year period). This yields a 25.27-square-mile area of equal lobster productivity, compared to a 395-square-mile area if based on 100 years, as the optimal scale of a restoration project. Restoration projects could consist of introducing lobsters and artificial reefs or habitats for lobsters to a 25-square-mile area previously unproductive or not fished so as to equal lobster productivity in open areas, or to double the population of lobsters in a 25-square-mile area of open productive areas by introducing and doubling the number of lobster habitats via artificial reefs or habitats so as to achieve a doubling of productivity. The details of accomplishing these projects are neither simple nor straightforward.

To further show how one would apply valuation approaches to evaluate restoration projects and determine an appropriate scale we again consider the New Bedford Harbor case study. We cannot fully carry out the specific approaches, but instead illustrate how one would begin to think about implementing valuation scaling approaches. Economic damages to the commercial lobster fishery were estimated at $2 million in PV terms. A scaling approach based on the value-to-value approach would be set up to determine an appropriate-sized project where the discounted value of services gained from the restoration project would equal the discounted value of interim losses. In this case, restoration projects capable of providing services expressed in discounted value equivalent to $2 million when completed over the period that interim losses occur are suitable candidates. For example, a restoration project that would return an annual value of services of $425,000 discounted over a five-year period would equal $2 million ($1.95 million with r=0.03); however, one needs to find the scale that would return a discounted value over a 106-year period approaching a discounted value of $55,000 in the initial period extended over 106 years.

If a value-to-cost scaling approach is to be used, one must set the problem up to find the scale of a project such that the cost of the project will equal the discounted value of services lost needed to compensate the public (i.e., value of compensable-interim losses). In the case of New Bedford Harbor, one needs to find the appropriate scale of a project such that the discounted cost over the time it would take to complete the project would be the same as the discounted value of interim losses, here a discounted value of $2 million. If such a restoration project would take five years to complete so its discounted value would be $2 million, a project that involves establishing artificial lobster reef or habitats that would cost $450,000 each year over five years would satisfy this approach.

10.4.3.2. Simplified Habitat Equivalency Approach

The HEA requires a few more steps than the simplified service-equivalency approach developed by Unsworth and Bishop (1994). In calculating interim losses from injury to natural resources and their services, one needs to estimate the proportion of service gains

Table I0.2. Example of Service Equivalency Approach Following Unsworth and Bishop (1994) New Bedford Harbor Case Study, 1980–2085.

Year	Period	$(1.03)^{1985-t}$	D_t	Year	Period	$(1.03)^{1985-t}$	D_t
1980	5	1.1593	20.8669	2032	−47	0.2493	4.4867
1981	4	1.1255	20.2592	2033	−48	0.2420	4.3560
1982	3	1.0927	19.6691	2034	−49	0.2350	4.2291
1983	2	1.0609	19.0962	2035	−50	0.2281	4.1059
1984	1	1.03	18.5400	2036	−51	0.2215	3.9863
1985	0	1.0	18.0	2037	−52	0.2150	3.8702
1986	−1	0.9709	17.4757	2038	−53	0.2088	3.7575
1987	−2	0.9426	16.9667	2039	−54	0.2027	3.6481
1988	−3	0.9151	16.4725	2040	−55	0.1968	3.5418
1989	−4	0.8885	15.9928	2041	−56	0.1910	3.4386
1990	−5	0.8626	15.5270	2042	−57	0.1855	3.3385
1991	−6	0.8375	15.0747	2043	−58	0.1801	3.2413
1992	−7	0.8131	14.6356	2044	−59	0.1748	3.1469
1993	−8	0.7894	14.2094	2045	−60	0.1697	3.0552
1994	−9	0.7664	13.7955	2046	−61	0.1648	2.9662
1995	−10	0.7441	13.3937	2047	−62	0.1600	2.8798
1996	−11	0.7224	13.0036	2048	−63	0.1553	2.7959
1997	−12	0.7014	12.6248	2049	−64	0.1508	2.7145
1998	−13	0.6810	12.2571	2050	−65	0.1464	2.6354
1999	−14	0.6611	11.9001	2051	−66	0.1421	2.5587
2000	−15	0.6419	11.5535	2052	−67	0.1380	2.4842
2001	−16	0.6232	11.2170	2053	−68	0.1340	2.4118
2002	−17	0.6050	10.8903	2054	−69	0.1301	2.3416
2003	−18	0.5874	10.5731	2055	−70	0.1263	2.2734
2004	−19	0.5703	10.2651	2056	−71	0.1226	2.2071
2005	−20	0.5537	9.9662	2057	−72	0.1190	2.1429
2006	−21	0.5375	9.6759	2058	−73	0.1156	2.0804
2007	−22	0.5219	9.3941	2059	−74	0.1122	2.0198
2008	−23	0.5067	9.1205	2060	−75	0.1089	1.9610
2009	−24	0.4919	8.8548	2061	−76	0.1058	1.9039
2010	−25	0.4776	8.5969	2062	−77	0.1027	1.8484
2011	−26	0.4637	8.3465	2063	−78	0.0997	1.7946
2012	−27	0.4502	8.1034	2064	−79	0.0968	1.7423
2013	−28	0.4371	7.8674	2065	−80	0.0940	1.6916
2014	−29	0.4243	7.6382	2066	−81	0.0912	1.6423
2015	−30	0.4120	7.4158	2067	−82	0.0886	1.5945
2016	−31	0.40	7.1998	2068	−83	0.0860	1.5480
2017	−32	0.3883	6.9901	2069	−84	0.0835	1.5030
2018	−33	0.3770	6.7865	2070	−85	0.0811	1.4592
2019	−34	0.3660	6.5888	2071	−86	0.0787	1.4167
2020	−35	0.3554	6.3969	2072	−87	0.0764	1.3754
2021	−36	0.3450	6.2106	2073	−88	0.0742	1.3354
2022	−37	0.3350	6.0297	2074	−89	0.0720	1.2965
2023	−38	0.3252	5.8541	2075	−90	0.0699	1.2587
2024	−39	0.3158	5.6836	2076	−91	0.0679	1.2220
2025	−40	0.3066	5.5180	2077	−92	0.0659	1.2864
2026	−41	0.2976	5.3573	2078	−93	0.0640	1.1519
2027	−42	0.2890	5.2013	2079	−94	0.0621	1.1183
2028	−43	0.2805	5.0498	2080	−95	0.0603	1.0858
2029	−44	0.2724	4.9027	2081	−96	0.0586	1.0541
2030	−45	0.2644	4.7599	2082	−97	0.0569	1.0234
2031	−46	0.2567	4.6213	2083	−98	0.0552	0.9936
				2084	−99	0.0536	0.9647
				2085	−100	0.0520	0.9366
Total	685.2117						

Note: $(1.03)^{1985-t}$ refers to the discount factor.

from a restoration project over time from its beginning until its completion, estimates of the proportion of service losses from the injured habitat for the same time period (from start to completion of the restoration project), and an estimate of the average proportion of annual service losses over the same time period (U.S. DOC, NOAA 1997b). This latter estimate is then combined with the discount factor (i.e., product of the average proportion of annual service losses and the discount factor) to determine an estimate of the discounted average proportion of services lost per square area, which is then used to determine estimates of the quantity of lost services in discounted terms (i.e., habitat area–years).

To determine the appropriate size of the restoration project, one must develop several estimates associated with the service gains from the restoration project (U.S. DOC, NOAA 1997b). One must first develop estimates of the proportion of change in service gains from the restoration project, estimates of the average annual proportionate change in service gains, and then an estimate of the quantity of services gained in discounted terms (i.e., habitat area–years). The size of the restoration project is then determined by dividing the sum of estimated quantity of lost services by the sum of estimated quantity of service gains as shown in Equations (10.2a) and (10.2b).

For example, consider the loss of 4,047 acres of salt marsh from an oil spill in 1995 (U.S. DOC, NOAA 1997b). The level of services in the year of the injury is expected to be zero (i.e., $b^p=0$). The year a potential restoration project would begin is 1997. It would take two years to be completed and is expected to provide 100 percent of the baseline services (initially baseline services provided by the injured resource are 0, but with the restoration project services will become 100 percent within two years, i.e., $b^j=1.0$ at 1999). Furthermore the period over which service gains would accrue is indefinite (i.e., infinite). On the basis of this information, and a discount rate of 3 percent, we can apply the HEA. Table 10.3 contains the detail of each step. The sum of the quantity of lost services in discounted terms is estimated at 11,763 in acre–year units, and the sum of the quantity of service gains in discounted terms is estimated at 30.51 in acre–year units. The scale of the restoration project is then determined as 11,763/30.51 = 385 acres of replacement habitat or resources. Again we emphasize that if the restored wetlands/environs are not functionally equivalent or do not return equivalent economic welfare/surplus to society, we could be short-changing future generations and not investing enough in restoration and monitoring efforts. To ensure against this, monitoring activities should be an essential component of all NRDA projects.

10.5. References

Alderson, C. 1998. Personal Communication on June 3. Salt Marsh Restoration Group, Natural Resources Group, New York City Department of Parks and Recreation: Staten Island, NY.

Barnthouse, L.W., J. Boreman, T.L. Englert, W.L. Kirk and E.G. Horn. 1988a. "Hudson River Settlement Agreement: Technical Rationale and Cost Considerations." In Barnthouse, L.W., R.J. Klauda, D.S. Vaughan and R.L. Kendall (eds.). *Science, Law, and Hudson River Power Plants: A Case Study in Environmental Impact Assessment.* American Fisheries Society Monograph 4. American Fisheries Society: Bethesda, MD: 267–273.

Barnthouse, L.W., R.J. Klauda and D.S. Vaughan. 1988b. "Introduction to the Monograph." In Barnthouse, L.W., R.J. Klauda, D.S. Vaughan and R.L. Kendall (eds.). *Science, Law, and Hudson*

Table 10.3. Example of HEA Approach Following U.S. DOC, NOAA (1997b).

Calculation of Service Losses

Year	Proportion of Services of Injured $x(t)^j$	Proportion of Service Losses (Start of Year)	Average Annual Proportion of Service Loss[a] $z(t)$	Discount Factor $(1.03)^{1995-t}$	Quantity of Average Proportion of Service Loss[b]	Quantity of Services Lost Discounted[c] area-year units
1995	0.0	1.0	1.0	1.0	1.00	4,047.00
1996	0.0	1.0	1.0	0.9709	0.9709	3,929.23
1997*	0.0	1.0	0.75	0.9426	0.7070	2,861.23
1998	0.50	0.50	0.25	0.9151	0.2288	925.85
1999*	1.00	0.0	0.0	0.8885	0.0	0.0
2000	1.00	0.0	0.0	0.8626	0.0	0.0
2001	1.00	0.0	0.0	0.8375	0.0	0.0
Total						11,763.31

Calculation of Service Gains

Year	Change in Proportion of Service Levels at Start of Year $x(t)^p$	Average Annual Change in Service Levels[d] $y(t)$	Discount Factor $(1.03)^{1995-t}$	Quantity of Service Gains Discounted[e] area-year units
1995	0.0	0.0	1.0	0.0
1996	0.0	0.0	0.9709	0.0
1997*	0.0	0.0	0.9426	0.0
1998	0.0	0.25	0.9151	0.2288
1999*	0.50	0.75	0.8885	0.6664
2000	1.00	1.00	0.8626	0.8626
2001	1.00	1.00	0.8375	0.8375
2002–perpetuity	.	.	.	.
Total				30.51

*1997 refers to year when restoration project begins, 1999 when it is completed.

[a] $z_t = \{b^j - [(x_{t+1}^j + x_t^j)/2]\}/b^j$; $.75 = \{1.0 - [(0.5 + 0)/2]\}/1$; $.25 = \{1.0 - [(1.0 + 0.5)]/2\}/1$, where $b^j=1.0$.

[b] Product of $z(t)$ and discount factor.

[c] Product of 4,047 acres lost and the respective discount factor.

[d] $y_t = \{[(x_{t+1}^p + x_t^p)/2] - b^p\}/b^j$; $.75=\{[(1.0 + 0.5)/2] - 0.0\}/1$; $.25=\{[(0.0 + 0.5)/2] - 0.0\}/1$, where $b^p=0$ and $b^j=1.0$.

Source: U.S. DOC, NOAA (1997b).

River Power Plants: A Case Study in Environmental Impact Assessment. American Fisheries Society Monograph 4. American Fisheries Society: Bethesda, MD: 267–273.

Bergen, A., M. Levandowsky, T. Gorrell and C. Alderson. 1995. "Restoration of Heavily Oiled Salt Marsh Using *Spartina alterniflora* Seedlings and Transplants: Effects on Petroleum Hydrocarbon Levels and Soil Microflora." Presented at the 10th Annual Conference on Contaminated Soils: Analysis, Site Assessment, Fate, Environmental and Human Risk Assessment, Remediation, and Regulation, Amherst, MA. Salt Marsh Restoration Group, Natural Resources Group, New York City Department of Parks and Recreation: Staten Island, NY.

Berger, L. and Associates. 1991. *Arthur Kill Oil Discharge Study,* Volume 1—Final Report, Volume 2—Appendices. Prepared for New Jersey Department of Environmental Protection and Energy: Trenton, NJ.

Brown, M.P., M.B. Werner, R.J. Sloan and K.W. Simpson. 1985. "Polychlorinated Biphenyls in the Hudson River." *Environmental Science and Technology* 19(8): 656–661.

Burger, J. (ed.). 1994a. *Before and After An Oil Spill: The Arthur Kill.* Rutgers University Press: New Brunswick, NJ.

———. 1994b. "Introduction." In Burger, J. (ed.). *Before and After An Oil Spill: The Arthur Kill.* Rutgers University Press: New Brunswick, NJ: 1–19.

Burns, K.T. and J.M. Teal. 1979. "The West Falmouth Oil Spill: Hydrocarbons in the Salt Marsh Ecosystem." *Estuarine and Coastal Marine Science* 8: 349–360.

Cairns, J. (ed.). 1988. *Rehabilitating Damages Ecosystems,* vols. 1 and 2. CRC Press: Boca Raton, FL.

Deshpande, A., B. Dockum and A. Tesolin. 1997. "Hydrocarbon Contaminants in Ribbed Mussels (*Geukensia demissa*)." In Packer, D. (ed.). *Assessment of Restored, Unrestored and Reference Salt Marshes Affected by the 1990 Exxon Bayway Oil Spill in the Arthur Kill, New York and New Jersey.* The Salt Marsh Restoration Assessment Team, NOAA, NMFS, James J. Howard Marine Sciences Laboratory: Highlands, NJ: 17–26.

Desvousges, W.H., E.E. Fries, S.P. Hudson and R.W. Dunford. 1997. "Scaling and Selecting Compensatory-Restoration Projects: An Economic Perspective." Presented at the Conference on Restoration of Lost Human Uses of the Environment, Washington, DC, May 7–8, 1997. Triangle Economic Research: Durham, NC.

Exxon Valdez Oil Spill Trustee Council. 1998a. *1998 Status Report.* Exxon Valdez Oil Spill Trustee Council, The Restoration Office: Anchorage, AK.

———. 1998b. "The Restoration Reserve." *Restoration Update* 5(2). *Exxon Valdez* Oil Spill Trustee Council, The Restoration Office: Anchorage, AK.

Gosselink, J.G., L.C. Lee and T.A. Muir. 1990. *Ecological Processes and Cumulative Impacts.* Lewis Publishers: Chelsea MI.

Hudson River Foundation. 1998. *Hudson River Fund: Call for Proposals 1998.* Hudson River Foundation for Science and Environmental Research: New York, NY.

Jordan, W., M. Gilpin and J. Aber. (eds.) 1987. *Restoration Ecology: A Synthetic Approach to Ecological Research.* Cambridge University Press: New York, NY.

Kusler, J.A. and M.E. Kentula. (eds.) 1989. *Wetland Creation and Restoration: The Status of the Science.* Island Press: Washington, DC.

Limburg, K.E. 1986. "PCBs in the Hudson." In Limburg, K.E., M.A. Moran and W.H. McDowell. (eds.). *The Hudson River Ecosystem.* Springer-Verlag: New York, NY: 83–130.

Mathews, K.E., W.H. Desvousges, F.R. Johnson and M.C. Ruby. 1997. *Using Economic Models to Inform Restoration Decisions: The Lavaca Bay, Texas Experience.* Presented at the Conference on Restoration of Lost Human Uses of the Environment, Washington, DC, May 7–8, 1997. Triangle Economic Research: Durham, NC.

McConnell, K.E. and B.G. Morrison. 1986. *Assessment of Economic Damages to the Natural Resources of New Bedford Harbor: Damages to the Commercial Lobster Fishery.* Prepared for Ocean Assessment Division, NOAA: Rockville, MD.

Mitsch, W.J. and J.G. Gosselink. 1993. *Wetlands.* John Wiley and Sons: New York, NY.

National Research Council. 1992. *Restoration of Aquatic Ecosystems.* National Academy Press: Washington, DC.

———. 1995. *Wetlands.* National Academy Press: Washington, DC.

New York City Department of Parks and Recreation, Salt Marsh Restoration Team. 1996. *Project History: Exxon Bayway Oil Spill—January 1st, 1990: Arthur Kill and Kill Van Kull.* Salt Marsh Restoration Group, Natural Resources Group, New York City Department of Parks and Recreation: Staten Island, NY.

O'Connor, J.M. 1984. "Capping of Contaminated Sediments." *Northeastern Environmental Science* 3(1): 35–39.

Pacific Estuarine Research Laboratory. 1990. *A Manual for Assessing Restored and Natural Coastal Wetlands with Examples from Southern California.* California Sea Grant Report No. T-CSGCP-021. California Sea Grant Program: La Jolla, CA.

Packer, D. (ed.). 1997. *Assessment of Restored, Unrestored and Reference Salt Marshes Affected by the 1990 Exxon Bayway Oil Spill in the Arthur Kill, New York and New Jersey.* The Salt Marsh Restoration Assessment Team, NOAA, NMFS, James J. Howard Marine Sciences Laboratory: Highlands, NJ.

Steimle, F. 1997. "Food Habits of the Mummichog, *Fundulus Heteroclitus.*" In Packer, D. (ed.). *Assessment of Restored, Unrestored and Reference Salt Marshes Affected by the 1990 Exxon Bayway Oil Spill in the Arthur Kill, New York and New Jersey.* The Salt Marsh Restoration Assessment Team, NOAA, NMFS, James J. Howard Marine Sciences Laboratory: Highlands, NJ: 5–10.

Thayer, G.W. (ed.). 1992. *Restoring the Nation's Marine Environment.* Maryland Sea Grant Book: College Park, MD.

U.S. Department of Commerce, National Oceanic and Atmospheric Administration. 1997a. *Scaling Compensatory Restoration Actions: Guidance Document for Natural Resource Damage Assessment under the Oil Pollution Act of 1990.* USDOC, NOAA, Damage Assessment and Restoration Program: Silver Spring, MD.

———. 1997b. *Habitat Equivalency Analysis: An Overview.* USDOC, NOAA, Damage Assessment and Restoration Program: Silver Spring, MD.

Unsworth, R.E. and R.C. Bishop. 1994. "Assessing Natural Resource Damages Using Environmental Annuities." *Ecological Economics* 11: 35–41.

Vitaliano, J., R. Reid, A. Frame and J. Sacco. 1997. "Infaunal Benthic Survey." In Packer, D. (ed.). *Assessment of Restored, Unrestored and Reference Salt Marshes Affected by the 1990 Exxon Bayway Oil Spill in the Arthur Kill, New York and New Jersey.* The Salt Marsh Restoration Assessment Team, NOAA, NMFS, James J. Howard Marine Sciences Laboratory: Highlands, NJ: 11–12.

CHAPTER 11

Policy Options and Future Directions: Effectiveness of Liability Rules and Future Directions for the NRDA Process

11.1. Introduction

Whenever negative externalities occur, economists argue for the use of incentives for control of such behavior and to impose various instruments to cause those individuals responsible for such behavior to internalize their actions. Classic instruments suggested have been the use of taxes, abatement fees, and effluent charges (Bohm 1976, Cornes and Sandler 1996, Field 1997, Mishan 1976, Hanley et al. 1997). With the passage of the Comprehensive Environmental Response, Compensation, and Liability Act (CERCLA) in 1980 and the Oil Protection Act (OPA) in 1990, another instrument has been advanced—liability rules based on legal foundations. However, the use of liability rules in controlling external behavior had not been examined before passage of these new laws. This closing chapter focuses its discussion on liability rules because of their importance in terms of CERCLA and OPA.

11.2. Use of Liability Rules in Controlling Random Pollution Events

Theoretical and empirical research has demonstrated that liability rules can influence private behavior so that social costs such as economic losses and damages from oil spills (i.e., random pollution events associated with a low probability of occurrence) become internalized by the responsible party (the polluter) (Conrad 1980; Grigalunas and Opaluch 1988; Opaluch 1984; Opaluch and Grigalunas 1984; Segerson 1986, 1987, 1989; Segerson and Tietenberg 1992). However this research is based on strong assumptions of perfect knowledge of both environmental and economic damages from these random pollution events; that pollution prevention technology is available, known, and can achieve full control; and that the probability of accidents is reasonably well known by the potential polluters. Any violation of these assumptions would result in partial internalization, where the degree of internalization is high when all assumptions are nearly met and low if large errors exist in such knowledge and technology.

For example, Opaluch (1984) showed that under ideal conditions full internalization of social costs can be achieved. A simulation model was also developed based on monte carlo methods and data from offshore drilling activities in the Gulf of Mexico. Results indicated that overconfidence in current prevention technology can result in high levels of economic damages from underestimating the probabilities of spills and insufficient updating of such probabilities as new information is learned.

In an empirical study, Opaluch and Grigalunas (1984) found that liability rules established by the Outer Continental Shelf Lands Act of 1978 (OCSLA) (P.L. 95-372) for offshore oil production caused bids for leasing specific tracts to reflect a high proportion of social costs of economic damage. Data are based on the 1979 Georges Bank Lease Sale. Opaluch and Grigalunas use a model where a private firm's expected profits are reduced following social damages from spills (i.e., the firm subtracts an estimate of economic damage from expected profits in the event spills occur). A robust estimation technique is applied. Results indicate that receipts from all high bids to the U.S. government would have increased some $236.7 million (1979$) had there been no environmental risk associated with oil spills. In other words where environmental risk was high, firms recognized this by bidding low to incorporate reduced profits given economic damages.

II.3. The Effect of Risk and Uncertainty in Liability Rules and Outcomes

However, optimal policy design based on liability rules also depends on the sharing or allocation of risk and the risk characteristics of the public versus private economic agents as well as availability of pollution liability insurance (Segerson 1986, 1987, 1989). What follows is a brief summary based on an economic model of decision making that accounts for risk characteristics and the availability of insurance. In the case of past disposal activities (e.g., Superfund sites) efficient policies for financing cleanup are affected by risk allocation and risk characteristics of economic agents (Segerson 1989). If the public is risk averse and firms are risk neutral, the optimal policy design would be full liability that would efficiently allocate risk across agents. If the risk characteristics were reversed (public risk neutral and firm risk averse) an optimal policy would be a fixed liability rule such that ex post liability (responsibility after the spill) is zero. This would be equal to the case where a tax is imposed on waste generators and waste disposers to pay for cleanup activities with no liability for cleanup costs.

In the case of future damages an optimal policy design would have both efficient incentives and risk allocation. Furthermore this would depend on the the availability of insurance for pollution liability. With insurance an optimal policy rule would be a full liability rule that would achieve an efficient balance between incentives and risk. Without insurance a partial liability rule would be preferred where polluters are held responsible for a portion of cleanup costs. In addition, optimal policy design for random pollution events could also involve some mix of regulations and liability rules (Segerson 1987).

Implications of the results depend on risk characteristics and if policy incentives (e.g., regulations) do not affect actions that, in turn, affect the probability distribution of damages. If both conditions hold and without liability insurance an optimal policy rule would

Table 11.1. Incidents Involving Spills of Oil/Chemicals in the United States, 1991–1997.

Incident Type[a]	1991	1992	1993	1994	1995	1996	1997
Oil/Chemical spills	24,794	25,929	28,263	31,378	30,794	27,499	25,693
Continuous releases	333	323	476	215	184	177	170
Railroad hotline	627	933	1,109	1,109	1,134	1,197	1,451
Generic incidents	0	0	0	236	971	565	113
Total	25,754	27,185	29,848	32,938	33,083	29,438	27,427

[a]Based on U.S. Coast Guard notification of incidents.
Source: U.S. Coast Guard, National Response Center, Washington, D.C.

include a mix of regulations of observable actions (e.g., required use of double hulls in tankers, safe practices) and ex post partial liability (i.e., liability for less than full damages). If liability insurance is available and both conditions hold, optimal policy would be full liability.

The critical question is whether liability rules have in fact resulted in private agents voluntarily (independent of other regulations or laws) adopting spill prevention technologies such as double hulls and if a trend of per unit oil spill measures (number of spills divided by number of shipments–spills per shipments) in U.S. waters has fallen after liability rules went into effect. Evidence from the U.S. Coast Guard National Response Center indicates that the number of identified oil or chemical spills increased from 24,794 incidents in 1991 to approximately 33,000 incidents in 1994 and 1995, and then decreased to about 26,000 in 1997, which is still above 1991 levels (Table 11.1). Without less aggregated data and further information about the adoption of double hull tankers, increased monitoring activities of the condition of captains and crew members, perhaps increased training of captains and crew members, and state laws pertaining to monitoring and safety of tankers and damage compensation, one can say little about the direct influence OPA-1990 may have had. We believe a longer time period or more detailed data are necessary to further examine the hypothesized effectiveness of liability rules pertaining to random low probability pollution events, such as from a regression model that incorporates a binary-shift variable associated with the year 1996 when formal rules were published.

11.4. Future Directions in NRDA and Assessing Losses from Marine Pollution

Areas where future research will direct the path of NRDAs involve the advancement and refinement of economic methods suitable to NRDAs and of wetland restoration efforts. Research in both areas will advance our understanding of the time frames needed for "restored" wetlands to approach functional equivalence, if ever, and thus enable us to consider more appropriate time frames in scaling restoration projects and in assessing economic damages (i.e., compensable values, and time frames of interim losses). In addition, research directed at benefits transfer (e.g., limitations, replications, practical issues, age limit, etc.) will contribute to the advancement of these techniques and possibly resolve differing interpretations between government trustees and the (potentially) responsible party, and minimize court actions in order to further expedite restoration efforts. Here journal editors, reviewers, and sponsors of funded research are urged to consider benefits transfers as research efforts requiring equal place with that of original empirical research. There is more need for guidance documents from both federal agencies responsible for implementing NRDAs (U.S. Department of Interior and U.S. Department of Commerce, National Oceanic and Atmospheric Administraiton) to provide a set of uniform principles and guidelines to direct individuals at all levels in the NRDA process. Such a uniform set of principles and guidelines directed at federal water resource projects played an important role and helped to develop a procedure we now refer to as cost–benefit analysis. Further efforts will help to advance economics in both theoretical and applied areas and can only elevate its stature in applied welfare economics and in the NRDA process.

Our lack of knowledge of both the relative quantitative functions of marine wetlands located throughout the United States and the economic values of the services wetlands perform will continue to frustrate the NRDA process and begs for basic research at all levels. Such information would greatly assist those involved with evaluations of both damaged and "restored" wetlands, should improve the precision of such evaluations, and in general should advance our understanding of wetlands. As results of these types of research become available, they will, in turn, influence public policy and federal NRDA procedures. In this manner scientific research benefits all.

II.5. Note

1. Although monitoring activities are a part of the federal NOAA–NRDA rules and procedures (see Section 990.55), our conversations with researchers indicated that monitoring was not a common factor in restoration projects. It could be that not enough time has passed between the published NOAA–NRDA rules and procedures (published in 1996) and implementation of these rules and procedures (e.g., the *North Cape* oil spill of 1990 is the first oil spill processed under OPA, and material has not been widely distributed by NOAA concerning the restoration plan nor has the restoration plan been completed).

II.6. References

Bohm, P. 1976. *Social Efficiency: A Concise Introduction to Welfare Economics.* Macmillan: Surry, Great Britain.

Conrad, J. 1980. "Oil Spills: Policies for Prevention, Recovery, and Compensation." *Public Policy* 28: 143–170.

Cornes, R. and T. Sandler. 1996. *The Theory of Externalities, Public Goods and Club Goods.* Cambridge University Press: New York, NY.

Field, B.C. 1997. *Environmental Economics: An Introduction.* Irwin/McGraw-Hill: New York, NY.

Grigalunas, T.A. and J.J. Opaluch. 1988. "Assessing Liability for Damages under CERCLA: A New Approach for Providing Incentives for Pollution Avoidance?" *Natural Resources Journal* 28(Summer): 509–533.

Hanley, N., J.F. Shogren and B. White. 1997. *Environmental Economics: In Theory and Practice.* Oxford University Press: New York, NY.

Mishan, E.J. 1976. *Cost–Benefit Analysis.* Praeger: New York, NY.

Opaluch, J.J. 1984. "The Use of Liability Rules in Controlling Hazardous Waste Accidents: Theory and Practice." *Northeast Journal of Agricultural and Resource Economics* 13(2): 210–217.

Opaluch, J.J. and T.A. Grigalunas. 1984. "Controlling Stochastic Pollution Events with Liability Rules: Some Evidence from OCS Leasing." *Rand Journal of Economics* 15: 142–151.

Segerson, K. 1986. "Risk-Sharing in the Design of Environmental Policy." *American Journal of Agricultural Economics* 68(5): 1261–1265.

———. 1987. "Risk-Sharing and Liability in the Control of Stochastic Externalities." *Marine Resource Economics* 4(3): 175–192.

———. 1989. "Risk and Incentives in the Financing of Hazardous Waste Cleanup." *Journal of Environmental Economics and Management* 16: 1–8.

Segerson, K. and T. Tietenberg. 1992. "The Structure of Penalties in Environmental Enforcement: An Economic Analysis." *Journal of Environmental Economics and Management* 23: 179–200.

Appendix A

NOAA's Damage Assessment and Restoration Program Settlements and Restoration Status (as of May 4, 1998)

Case Name/ Location/ Type	Civil Act No./ Court/DOJ No.	Federal Statute(s)[1]	Participating Trustees	Status	Settlement Terms[2]
American Trader **TransAlaska Pipeline Fund British Petroleum** US v. Steam Tanker American Trader Huntington Beach, CA Oil Spill – 2/7/90	CV-91-3363 RJK D.C. CA 90-5-1-1-3602	CWA 311 TAPAA	NOAA DOI State of California	Complaint filed: 04/21/92 1)Trans Alaska Consent Decree entered 4/19/95 2)BP Consent Decree entered 3/5/97	1.) TransAlaska Pipeline Fund Total: $90,000 $45,000 for NOAA past assessment costs $45,000 for DOI past assessment costs 2.) British Petroleum Total: $3,894,247 **$2,884,567: bird restoration** **$400,000: fish hatchery** $300,000: coastal pollution mitigation $79,680: CA Parks lost revenue $630,000 for CA response costs (money still in escrow)
Apex Galveston Golnoy Barge Co. And Apex R.E.&T., Inc. V. M/T Shinoussa Houston Ship Channel, TX Oil Spill – 7/28/90	90-2414 S.D. TX 90-11-3-670	CWA 311	NOAA DOI State of Texas	Complaint filed: 08/09/90 Joint Stipulation entered: 10/26/94	Total: $1,700,000 **$1,312,962: restoration** $66,630: DOI and NOAA past assessment costs $75,199: Texas past assessment costs $245,209: Texas response costs

Case Name/ Location/ Type	Civil Act No./ Court/DOJ No.	Federal Statute(s)[1]	Participating Trustees	Status	Settlement Terms[2]
Apex Houston US v. Apex Oil Co. San Francisco, CA Oil Spill – 1/28/86	89-0246 89-0685 89-0250 N.D. CA 90-5-1-1- 3298A	NMSA CWA 311	NOAA DOI State of California	Complaint filed: 01/27/89 Consent Decree entered: 08/31/94	Total: $6,400,000 **$4,916,430: common murre recolonization project** **$500,000: habitat acquisition trust fund** $450,570: NOAA past assessment costs and NMSA response and assessment fund $97,500: DOI past assessment costs $144,000: CA past assessment and response $36,500: USCG response $5,000: USCG civil penalty $250,000: CA Water Code civil penalty
Blackbird Mine State of Idaho, et al. v. The M.A. Hanna Company et. el. Panther Creek , ID Hazardous Material Release	83-4179 (R) D. ID 90-11-2-816	CERCLA 107 CWA ESA	NOAA USDA/Forest Service State of Idaho	Complaint filed: 06/14/93 Consent Decree entered: 09/05/95	Total: $14,091,842 (estimated) paid to Trustees to implement: **$2,500,000 - hatchery operation trust fund** **$2,714,000 (est.) - smolt survival plan** **$1,364,000 - livestock exclusion on private lands** **$225,000 - off-channel ponds** **$350,000 (est.) - environmental plans & compliance** $1,500,000 - environmental monitoring $2,000,000 - oversight $4,699,100 - reimburse Trustees for past damage assessment costs. $328,742 - response costs

Case Name/ Location/ Type	Civil Act No./ Court/DOJ No.	Federal Statute(s)[1]	Participating Trustees	Status	Settlement Terms[2]
R/V Columbus Iselin Florida Keys National Marine Sanctuary, Florida Vessel Grounding – 8/10/94	N/A	NMSA 312, 307	NOAA	Settlement Agreement signed 11/22/97	Total: $3,760,488 (estimated) **$2.2 million (approx.): physical and biological restoration** **$536,000: compensatory restoration** **$306,800: project management and oversight** $240,000: past damage assessment and emergency response costs
Commencement Bay: Simpson, Champion, WDNR US v. Simpson Tacoma Kraft, Co., Champion International Corp. & Washington Dept. of Natural Resources. (Nearshore/Tideflats) Commencement Bay, WA (St. Paul Waterway) Hazardous Material Release	91-5260TC W.D. WASH 90-11-3-363	CERCLA 106-107 CWA 311	NOAA DOI Puyallup Tribe of Indians Muckleshoot Indian Tribe State of Washington	Complaint filed: 06/24/91 Consent Decree entered: 12/13/91 Amendment No.1: 4/1/96	Civil Penalty: $200,000 Total: $1,000,000 plus $200,000 in-kind WDNR aquatic land **$500,000: additional restoration (Middle Waterway)** **$200,000: WDNR donated aquatic lands for habitat restoration projects** **$75,000: for future restoration oversight costs** $25,000: contingent future NRDA contribution $100,000: trustee past assessment costs $100,000: future damage assessment contribution

Case Name/ Location/ Type	Civil Act No./ Court/DOJ No.	Federal Statute(s)[1]	Participating Trustees	Status	Settlement Terms[2]
Commencement Bay: Port of Tacoma US v. Port of Tacoma (Nearshore/Tideflats) Commencement Bay, WA Hazardous Material Release	93-5462 W.D. WASH 90-11-3-711	CERCLA 107	NOAA DOI State of Washington Puyallup Tribe of Indians Muckleshoot Indian Tribe	Complaint filed: 08/16/93 Consent Decree entered: 10/08/93	Total: $12,335,000 **$12,000,000 for restoration** (of which $1,950,000 could be used for future damage assessment costs) $335,000: trustee past assessment costs (including $157,000 NOAA)
Commencement Bay: City of Tacoma U.S. et al. v. City of Tacoma & the Tacoma Public Utility (Nearshore/Tideflats) Commencement Bay, WA Hazardous Material Release	97-5336RJB W.D. WASH.	CERCLA	NOAA DOI State of Washington Puyallup Tribe of Indians Muckleshoot Indian Tribe	Consent Decree entered 12/30/97	Property, cash and in-kind services valued at over $7 million - will be used to implement 5 negotiated projects on 37 acres. Total project expenditures = $3,364,929 Funds and Services = $4,916,929 **$500,000: Trustee oversight of restoration** **$500,000: tribal trustee oversight** **$75,000: pollution-reporting hotline** **$250,000: in-kind services for restoration planning & implementation** **$2,721,818: real property** $227,000: Trustees' past assessment costs

Case Name/ Location/ Type	Civil Act No./ Court/DOJ No.	Federal Statute(s)[1]	Participating Trustees	Status	Settlement Terms[2]
Commencement Bay: Washington Dept. Of Natural Resources U.S. et al. v. State of Washington through WDNR. (Nearshore/Tideflats) Commencement Bay, WA Hazardous Material Release	97-5337 RJB W.D. WASH.	CERCLA	NOAA DOI State of Washington Puyallup Tribe of Indians Muckleshoot IndianTribe	Consent Decree entered 12/30/97	Total: 8.3 acres of state-owned aquatic lands for habitat projects In-kinds services for consultation activities
Dixon Bay Mississippi River Delta, LA Oil Spill – 1/95	N/A	OPA	NOAA State of Louisiana DOI	Administrative Settlement signed: 02/15/96	Total: In-kind creation of 5 acres of fresh-to-brackish-water marsh habitat on existing federal wildlife refuge. Performance monitoring, and payment of past and future trustee costs totaling $65,314.
Elliott Bay: City of Seattle and Metro US v. The City of Seattle, and Municipality of Metropolitan Seattle (Metro) Elliott Bay, WA Hazardous Material Release	90-395WD W.D. WA 90-11-2-527	CERCLA 107	NOAA DOI State of Washington Suquamish Indian Tribe Muckleshoot Indian Tribe	Complaint filed: 03/19/90 Consent Decree entered: 12/23/91	Total: $24,250,000 to be paid in six payments over 6 years **$12,000,000: sediment remediation $5,000,000: habitat development up to $2,000,000: pollution source control up to $5,000,000: Real property for projects habitat** $250,000 for NOAA past costs

Case Name/ Location/ Type	Civil Act No./ Court/DOJ No.	Federal Statute(s)[1]	Participating Trustees	Status	Settlement Terms[2]
M/V Elpis US v. M/V Elpis et al. Key Largo National Marine Sanctuary, FL Vessel Grounding Nov. 1989	90-10011-CIV-JLK S.D. FL Admiralty	NMSA	NOAA	Settlement and Release 8/14/91	Total: $2,375,000 Total of $2,275,000 distributed to NOAA: **$1,660,000 restoration** $100,000: forfeiture claim $100,000: civil penalties $415,000: emergency response and future damage assessment $100,000 response costs to USCG
Exxon Bayway US v. Exxon Corp. Arthur Kill, NY/NJ Oil Spill – 1/1/90	91-1003 E.D. NY 90-5-1-1-3519	CWA 311	NOAA DOI State of New York State of New Jersey Cities of New York and Elizabeth	Complaint filed: 03/20/91 Consent Decree entered: 06/14/91	Total: $15,000,000 $10,000,000 to be paid in 6 payments over 5 years **$9,250,000 for restoration (approx. $5.92M to NYC and NYS, and approx. $3.33M, for NJ)** $750,000 for cost recovery $5,000,000 paid as criminal settlement **$3,209,333 for restoration ($1,733,333 to NJ and $1,476,000 to NY State)** **$1,562,580 in fines paid into the Arthur Kill Trust Fund for restoration** $18,315.07: for NOAA past damage assessment costs $200,125: criminal fines $9,647: DOI reimbursement

[1]Settled under the Marine Protection, Research and Sanctuaries Act

Case Name/ Location/ Type	Civil Act No./ Court/DOJ No.	Federal Statute(s)[1]	Participating Trustees	Status	Settlement Terms[2]
MV Fortuna Reefer Mona Island. Puerto Rico Oil Spill/Vessel Grounding - 7/23/97	N/A	OPA	NOAA Puerto Rico DNER	Administrative settlement signed 9/11/97	Total: $1,250,000 **$650,000: emergency restoration project to rescue corals dislodged by vessel stabilization efforts** **$400,000: compensatory restoration for crushed coral** $200,000: trustee administrative costs
Greenhill Well Blowout Administrative Settlement Timbalier Bay, LA Oil Spill – 9/29/92	N/A	OPA	NOAA DOI State of Louisiana	Administrative Settlement signed: 01/18/94	Total: $991,000 (estimated) $102,500: NOAA past costs and future monitoring costs $43,600: Louisiana past cost and future monitoring costs **21.7 acres of created intertidal wetlands (estimated construction and monitoring costs of: $845,000)**
Jahre Spray West Deptford, NJ Oil Spill – 7/22/95	N/A	OPA	NOAA DOI State of New Jersey State of Pennsylvania	Administrative Settlement signed 10/31/96 Final 2/97	Total: $179,634 (estimated) **$20,000 for restoration to New Jersey (Type A NRDA settlement)** **$22,000 New Jersey lost recreational boating opportunities** **$75,000 Pennsylvania lost recreational boating opportunities** $54,674 past assessment costs ($6,612 to NOAA) $4,000 Pennsylvania penalties $3,960 Pennsylvania law

Case Name/ Location/ Type	Civil Act No./ Court/DOJ No.	Federal Statute(s)[1]	Participating Trustees	Status	Settlement Terms[2]
Jacquelyn L U.S. and State of Florida v. Jacquelyn L.. et al. Florida Keys National Marine Sanctuary, Florida Vessel Grounding – 7/7/91	CV 91-10067 S.D. FL	NMSA	NOAA State of Florida	Complaint filed 7/91 Settled 8/14/97 Voluntary dismissal w/prejudice 9/10/97	Total $257,500 **$125,127 restoration** $126,427 NOAA past assessment costs $ 5,946 Florida past assessment costs
M/T Kentucky Administrative Settlement Paulsboro, NJ (Delaware River) Oil Spill – 7/94	N/A	OPA	NOAA DOI State of New Jersey State of Pennsylvania	Administrative Settlement signed: 12/6/95	Total: $66,571 **$34,500: restoration** $4,415: NOAA past assessment costs $1,514: DOI past assessment costs $8,845: PA past assessment costs $6,097: NJ past assessment costs $4,000: PA/Fish and Boat Commission penalty $$7,200: PA/Dept. Oi Environmental Protection penalty
M/V Alec Owen Maitland US v. M/V Alec Owen Maitland, et al. Key Largo National Marine Sanctuary, FL Vessel Grounding - 10/25/89	90-10081 S.D FL Admiralty Consolidated with 90-0125 (King) S.D. FL	NMSA	NOAA	Settled 9/91 Released 10/23/91 Final 12/91	Total: $1,450,000 **$1,080,000: restoration** $100,000: civil penalty account $270,000: NMSA Emergency Response and Damage Assessment accounts

Case Name/ Location/ Type	Civil Act No./ Court/DOJ No.	Federal Statute(s)[1]	Participating Trustees	Status	Settlement Terms[2]
Mini Laurel					
Key Largo National Marine Sanctuary, FL Vessel Grounding - 1989					Total $30,000 $12,500: Civil penalty **$14,000: restoration** $3,500: NMSA Damage Assessment and Emergency Response accounts
Miss Beholden					
Florida Keys National Marine Sanctuary Vessel Grounding – 3/13/93	93-10024 S.D.FL	NMSA	NOAA State of Florida	Summary Judgment entered 12/1/95	Judgment entered in favor of U.S. for Total $1,873,741: **$1,671,337: primary and compensatory restoration encompassing reef creation and rehabilitation.** **$202,404: performance monitoring and trustee administrative costs.**
Mobil Gypsum					
US v. Mobil Mining and Mineral, Co. Pasadena, Texas Hazardous material spill (phosphoric acid) – 4/6/92	H96-0605 S.D. TX	CERCLA 107, 113	NOAA DOI State of Texas	Complaint filed: 02/21/96 Consent Decree Settlement lodged 2/21/96 Consent Decree Final 6/13/96	Total: $2,430,102 (Estimated) **$2,200,000: (estimated) in-kind services: Wetlands Restoration Project includes: Creation of 17 acres of intertidal estuarine marsh Enhancement of 15 acres of upland habitat Establishment of conservation easement or deed restriction for the restoration site $100,000: Site maintenance $25,000, (not to exceed): Restoration project monitoring** $73,140: NOAA past assessment costs $3,761: DOI past assessment costs $53,201: Texas past assessment costs

Case Name/ Location/ Type	Civil Act No./ Court/DOJ No.	Federal Statute(s)[1]	Participating Trustees	Status	Settlement Terms[2]
T.V Mormac Star Sandy Hook, NJ Oil Spill – 2/10/95	N/A	OPA	NOAA State of New Jersey	Administrative Settlement signed 4/16/97	Total: $25,320.01 **$22,000 for restoration** $3,320.01 NOAA's past assessment costs
B/T Nautilus In re Nautilus Motor Tanker Co., Ltd. Kill Van Kull, NY/NJ Oil Spill – 6/7/90	90-2419 NJ 90-5-1-1-3575	CWA 311	NOAA DOI State of New York State of New Jersey City of New York	Claim filed: 10/01/90 Consent Decree entered: 03/30/94	Total: $4,000,000 **$3,300,000: restoration** $700,000 for trustee past costs including $145,673 for NOAA.

Case Name/ Location/ Type	Civil Act No./ Court/DOJ No.	Federal Statute(s)[1]	Participating Trustees	Status	Settlement Terms[2]
New Bedford Harbor **Aerovox/Belleville** **AVX** **FPE/CDE** US v. AVX Corp., New Bedford Harbor, MA Hazardous Material Release	83-3882 83-3889 MA 90-11-2-78	CERCLA 106, 107 RCRA 7003 CWA 504 Rivers and Harbors Act of 1899, 13	NOAA DOI Commonwealth of Massachusetts	Complaints filed: 12/09/83 Aerovox/ Belleville Consent Decree entered: 07/16/91 Appeal resolved: 06/22/92 2) AVX Consent Decree entered: 02/03/92 Appeal resolved: 06/22/92 3) FPE/CDE Consent Decree entered: 11/13/92	Aerovox/Belleville Settlement: Total: $12,600,000 **$2,584,000: restoration** $550,000: NOAA past assessment costs $16,000: MA past costs $2,370,000: EPA past response costs $130,000: MA past response costs $6,950,000: EPA future response costs AVX Settlement: Total: $66,000,000 **$6,700,000: restoration** $59,000,000: EPA and MA past and future response costs $205,946: NOAA past assessment cost FPE/CDE Settlement: Total: $10,999,808 **$9,670,192: restoration** $54,228: NOAA past costs $275,580: MA past costs $1,000,000: EPA and MA past and future response costs Overall total: $21,300,000 plus $10,000,000 in escrow to be used by either EPA or trustees to clean up the outer harbor.

Case Name/ Location/ Type	Civil Act No./ Court/DOJ No.	Federal Statute(s)[1]	Participating Trustees	Status	Settlement Terms[2]
Presidente Rivera US v. Oriental Republic of Uruguay Delaware River, PA Oil Spill – 6/24/89	90-404-SLR DE 90-5-11-3609	CWA 311	NOAA DOI State of Delaware State of New Jersey State of Pennsylvania	Claim filed: 02/06/90 Consent Decree entered: 12/06/93	Total: $2,650,000 **$2,141,000: restoration** $100,000: NOAA past assessment costs $107,000: Delaware past costs $295,000: New Jersey past costs $7,000: DOI past costs
RTC 380 Barge Administrative Settlement Long Island Sound, NY/CT Oil Spill – 12/21/92	N/A	OPA 1990	NOAA DOI State of Connecticut State of New York	Administrative settlement signed: 11/10/94	Total: $230,972 **$100,000: CT for restoration** **$100,000: NY for restoration** $10,199: NOAA past assessment costs $5,560: DOI past assessment costs $2,677: CT past assessment costs $12,536: NY past assessment costs
Rancocas Creek Rancocas Creek, NJ Oil Spill – 1/1/94	N/A	OPA	NOAA State of New Jersey	Administrative Settlement signed: 2/13/97	Total: $50,487 (est.) **$6,000 (approx.) public access and habitat improvement** $2,770: NOAA past assessment costs $10,717: NJI's assessment costs **Purchase a 27-acre parcel of land (valued at $31,000)**

Case Name/ Location/ Type	Civil Act No./ Court/DOJ No.	Federal Statute(s)[1]	Participating Trustees	Status	Settlement Terms[2]
Salvors Inc.	92-10027-CIV	NMSA	NOAA	Complaint filed 4/22/92	Total: $589,331
Florida Keys National Marine Sanctuary, Florida				Trial held 5/12- 5/13/97 & 5/19- 5/22/97	**$351,648: Seagrass restoration** $211,130: U.S. for response and assessment costs
Seagrass Injury – prior to 5/22/92				Judgment for U.S. entered 9/3/97	$26,553: interest on costs.
				On Appeal	
Santa Clara	2:92-0389-18	CERCLA	NOAA	Complaint filed: 02/07/92	Total: $1,400,000
US v. M/V Santa Clara, et al.	SC			Stipulation of Compromise Settlement entered: 02/07/94	**$200,000: restoration** $5,000: NOAA past assessment costs $100,000: civil penalties $500,000: retire the magnesium claim $595,000: past response costs
Offshore Cape May, NJ	90-11-3-915				
Hazardous Material Spill – 1/4/92					

Case Name/ Location/ Type	Civil Act No./ Court/DOJ No.	Federal Statute(s)[1]	Participating Trustees	Status	Settlement Terms[2]
Southern California: Potlatch/Simpson US v. Montrose Chemical Corp. Palos Verdes Shelf, CA Hazardous Material Release	90-3122-AAH C.D. CA	CERCLA 107	NOAA DOI State of California	Complaint filed: 06/18/90; Count one dismissed 4/22/95; appeal pending. Potlatch/ Simpson Consent Decree entered: 05/11/92	Total: $12,000,000 to be paid in 3 payments over 4 years.
Southern California: LACSD plus 155 municipalities Palos Verdes Shelf, CA Hazardous Material Release (*Litigation continuing with other defendants*)		CERCLA	NOAA DOI State of California	LACSD Amended Consent Decree lodged 3/25/97	Total: $45,700,000 $21,860,000 to U.S. EPA to investigate contamination $140,000 to CA Dept. Of Toxic Substances Control $23,700,000 to trustees

Case Name/ Location/ Type	Civil Act No./ Court/DOJ No.	Federal Statute(s)[1]	Participating Trustees	Status	Settlement Terms[2]
Tenyo Maru US v. Maruha Corp. Olympic Peninsula, WA Oil Spill – 7/22/91	94-1537 W.D. WASH 90-11-3-829	OPA	NOAA DOI State of Washington Makah Indian Tribe	Complaint filed: 10/14/94 Consent Decree entered: 12/23/94	Total: $9,000,000 **$5,160,000: restoration** $10,500: NOAA past assessment costs $162,000: DOI past assessment costs $83,800: WA DOE past assessment costs $31,300: WA DWF past assessment costs $52,400: Makah Indian Tribe past assessment costs $3,000,000: USCG OSLTF (response costs) $500,000: civil penalties
United Heckathorn (a.k.a.) **Levin Richmond** Richmond, CA Hazardous Materials Release	C84-66273CW C84-6324CW C85-4776 C86-2103 (N.D. Cal)	CERCLA	NOAA DOI State of California	Complaint filed 6/6/96 Consent Decree lodged 6/7/96 Consent Decree entered 7/19/96	Total: $400,000 **$380,000 for restoration** $20,000 for NOAA past assessment costs

Case Name/ Location/ Type	Civil Act No./ Court/DOJ No.	Federal Statute(s)[1]	Participating Trustees	Status	Settlement Terms[2]
M/V Wellwood U.S. v. Wellwood Shipping Company, et al. Key Largo National Marine Sanctuary, FL Vessel Grounding - 8/4/84	84-1888-CIV (Atkins) S.D. FL. (ALJ Docket Nos. 455-225, 455-226; and 455-227)	NMSA	NOAA	Complaint filed 8/10/84 Settled 12/22/86 Voluntary release from liability: 1/8/87 Wellwood Shipping Co. Ltd., and Hanseatic Shipping Co. Ltd.	Total: $6,275,000 The RPs provided $3,000,000 for the purchase of an annuity from Allstate Life Insurance Co. to generate $6,275,000 which was to be used to pay specific annual payments to U.S./NOAA over a 15 year payment period. **$4,654,297: restoration** $750,000: NMSA funding for future emergency response and damage assessment account $250,000: civil penalty $620,772: U.S. Coast Guard response costs
World Prodigy Matter of Ballard Shipping Co. Narragansett Bay, RI Oil Spill – 6/23/89	89-0685 RI 62-66-22 Admiralty	CWA 311	NOAA DOI State of Rhode Island	Claim filed: 2/23/90 Stipulation of Dismissal entered: 06/19/91	Total: $3,900,000 **$567,319: NOAA for restoration** $3,256,643.72: USCG response costs $76,037.28: NOAA past damage assessment and other costs

Cost Recoveries Only

Case Name/ Location/ Type	Civil Act No./ Court/DOJ No.	Federal Statute(s)[1]	Participating Trustees	Status	Settlement Terms[2]
Chiltipin Creek San Patricio County, TX Oil Spill – 1/7/92	N/A	N/A	NOAA DOI State of Texas	Cost recovery final: 08/19/94	Total: $3,085 for NOAA's past assessment costs
Golden Hill Port Everglades, FL Oil Spill – 6/19/91	N/A	N/A	NOAA State of Florida	Cost recovery final: 06/24/94	Total: $4,985 for NOAA's past assessment costs
Prime Trader Jacksonville, FL Oil Spill – 5/19/93	N/A	N/A	NOAA	Cost recovery final: 6/24/94	Total: $1,872 for NOAA's past assessment costs
Barge Sea Robin/TMI-11 Flagler Beach, FL Caustic Soda Spill - 3/11/96	N/A	CERCLA	NOAA	Costs paid 7/97	Total: $9,124.18 for NOAA's past assessment costs

CRC Case: Assistance by DARP

Case	Docket	Statute	Agencies	Dates	Est. cost/value of restoration	Status
Army Creek US v. BP America Inc. New Castle Co., DE Hazardous Material Release	91-409 (Consolidated with H-90-2476 H-90-2488 H-91-180 in Admiralty) DE 90-11-2-411	CERCLA 106, 107	NOAA DOI State of Delaware	Complaint filed: 07/22/91 Consent Decree entered: 09/12/91	Total: $800,000 **$600,000: for restoration** **$200,000: for groundwater remediation in Delaware**	The state of Delaware has completed surveys of marshes, hydrological modeling of surface waters in the watershed, and hydraulic evaluations of the existing water control structure.
Conoco/EDC Release, Calcasieu estuary, LA. Westlake, LA Hazardous Material Release – 4/31/94	97-0445 W.D. LA	CERCLA	NOAA DOI State of Louisiana	Consent Decree entered 10/8/97	**Est. cost/value of restoration:** Convert and enhance 41 acres of agricultural lands into bottomland hardwood swamp habitat. With a conservation servitude, protect and maintain 4.5 acres in perpetuity, and the remaining 36.5 acres as a buffer for 50 years. $51,178: Performance monitoring, and payment of past and future trustee costs.	Land preparation and planting of native trees completed. Performance monitoring to begin in May, 1998.
French Limited US v. French Limited Inc. Crosby City, TX Hazardous Material Release	89-2544 S.D. TX 90-11-3-46A	CERCLA 106	NOAA SOI State of Texas	Complaint filed: 07/31/89 Consent Decree entered: 03/16/93	Total value: $1,060,000 includes $93,262 + wetlands creation project **$966,738(est. cost): 21-25 acres of created tidal wetlands** **$30,000: restoration of wetlands in event of damage within 5 years of creation** $30,000: wetland maintenance beyond 5 years after creation $13,180: NOAA past assessment costs and future oversight costs $16,800: DOI past assessment costs $3,282: Texas past assessment costs	Successful completion of the Construction Phase of the 21-25 acre Brownwood Subdivision marsh creation/restoration project by the French Limited Group was confirmed by the Trustee Project Review Group on October 1, 1995. The beginning of the five-year monitoring/maintenance phase of the project was initiated on this same date. The $30K Restoration Fund has been formally established as required by the Consent Decree.

[1] OPA - Oil Pollution Act of 1990
CWA - Clean Water Act
TAPAA - Trans Alaska Pipeline Act
CERCLA - Comprehensive Environmental Response, Compensation, and Liability Act of 1980
NMSA - National Marine Sanctuaries Act
ESA - Endangered Species Act

[2] **Bolded** amounts represent restoration funding

APPENDIX B

Benefits Measures

Source: Desvousges et al. 1983. *A Comparison of Alternative Approaches for Estimating Recreation and Related Benefits of Water Quality Improvements.* Prepared for Office of Policy Analysis, U.S. Environmental Protection Agency: Washington, DC.

B.   BENEFITS MEASURES

B-1   The next group of questions is about the quality of water in the Monongahela River. Congress passed water pollution control laws in 1972 and in
1977 to improve the nation's water quality. The states of Pennsylvania
and West Virginia have also been involved in water quality improvement
programs of their own. These programs have resulted in cleaner rivers
that are better places for fishing, boating, and other outdoor activities
which people take part in near water. We all pay for these water quality
improvement programs both as taxpayers and as consumers.

In this study we are concerned with the water quality of only the Monongahela River. Keep in mind that people take part in all of the activities on Card 1 both on and near the water.

Generally, the better the water quality, the better suited the water is
for recreational activities and the more likely people will take part in
outdoor recreational activities on or near the water. Here is a picture
of a ladder that shows various levels of water quality. GIVE RESPONDENT
CARD 4, "WATER QUALITY LADDER".

The top of the ladder stands for the best possible quality of water. The
bottom of the ladder stands for the worst possible water quality. On the
ladder you can see the different levels of the quality of the water. For
example: (POINT TO EACH LEVEL -- E, D, C, B, A -- AS YOU READ THE STATE-
MENTS BELOW.)

Level "E" (POINTING) is so polluted that it has oil, raw sewage and
other things like trash in it; it has no plant or animal life and
smells bad.

Water at level "D" is okay for boating but not fishing or swimming.

Level "C" shows where the water is clean enough so that game fish
like bass can live in it.

Level "B" shows where the water is clean enough so that people can
swim in it safely.

And at level "A", the quality of the water is so good that it would
be possible to drink directly from it if you wanted to.

a.   Now, think about the water quality of the Monongahela River on the
whole. In terms of this scale from zero to ten, how would you rate
the water quality of the Monongahela River at the present time?
POINT TO THE ZERO-TO-TEN SCALE ON THE LADDER AND CIRCLE NUMBER.

    00 01 02 03 04 05 06 07 08 09 10 (GO TO B-1.b.)

    DON'T KNOW. . . . . 11 (GO TO B-2)

Card 5

1-22
Dup.

(23-24)

b.   Is your rating for a particular site on the river? CIRCLE NUMBER.

    YES . . . . 01 (GO TO B-1.c.)

    NO . . . . 02 (GO TO B-2)

(25)

c.   On the map, please show me which river site your rating applies to.

Site Code: ☐☐   *(26-27)*

IF NOT ON LIST OF RECREATIONAL SITES, SPECIFY:

_____

B-2   Another important purpose of this study is to learn how much the quality
of water of the Monongahela River is worth to the people who live in the
river basin. In answering this question, there are three ways of think-
ing about water quality that might influence your decision. GIVE RESPON-
DENT CARD 5, "VALUE CARD". The three ways are shown on this card.

a.   One, you might think about how much water quality is worth to you
because you use the river for recreation. POINT TO PART I OF VALUE
CARD AND GIVE RESPONDENT TIME TO READ THAT PART.

How important a factor is your actual use of the river in making a
decision about how much clean water is worth to you? CIRCLE NUMBER.

        VERY IMPORTANT 01   *(28-29)*

        SOMEWHAT IMPORTANT 02

        NEITHER IMPORTANT NOR
            UNIMPORTANT 03

        NOT VERY IMPORTANT 04

        NOT IMPORTANT AT ALL . . . 05

b.   Another way you might think about how much clean water is worth to
you is that it is worth something to you to know that a clean water
river is being maintained for your use if you should decide, in the
future, that you want to use it. POINT TO PART II OF VALUE CARD AND
GIVE RESPONDENT TIME TO READ THAT PART. For example, you might buy
an advance ticket for the Steelers or Pirates just to be able to go
to a home game if you later decide you want to go. Likewise, you
might pay some amount each year to have a clean water river available to use if you should decide to use it.

In deciding how much clean water is worth to you, how important a
factor is knowing that a clean water river is being maintained for
your use, if you should decide to use it? CIRCLE NUMBER.

        VERY IMPORTANT 01   *(30-31)*

        SOMEWHAT IMPORTANT 02

        NEITHER IMPORTANT NOR
            UNIMPORTANT 03

        NOT VERY IMPORTANT 04

        NOT IMPORTANT AT ALL . . . 05

c. A third thing you might think about in deciding how much clean water
    is worth to you is the satisfaction of knowing that a clean water
    river is there. POINT TO PART III OF VALUE CARD AND GIVE RESPONDENT
    TIME TO READ THAT PART. For example, you might be willing to pay
    something to maintain a public park even though you know you won't
    use it. The same thing could be true for clean water in the Monon-
    gahela; that is, you might pay something just for the satisfaction
    of knowing that it is clean and that others can use it.

    In deciding how much clean water is worth to you, how important is
    knowing that a clean water river is being maintained? CIRCLE
    NUMBER.

      VERY IMPORTANT 01

      SOMEWHAT IMPORTANT 02

      NEITHER IMPORTANT NOR
        UNIMPORTANT 03

      NOT VERY IMPORTANT 04

      NOT IMPORTANT AT ALL . . . 05

(32-33)

INTRODUCTION TO QUESTION B-3

Now, we would like for you to think about the relationship between improving the quality of water in the Monongahela River and what we all have to
pay each year as taxpayers and as consumers. We all pay directly through our
tax dollars each year for cleaning up all rivers. We also pay indirectly each
year through higher prices for the products we buy because it costs companies
money to clean up water they use in making their products. Thus, each year,
we are paying directly and indirectly for improvements in the water quality of
the Monongahela River.

I want to ask you a few questions about what amount of money you would be
willing to pay each year for different levels of water quality in the Monongahela River. Please keep in mind that the amounts you would pay each year
would be paid in the form of taxes or in the form of higher prices for the
products that companies sell.

We are talking about different levels of water quality for only the
Monongahela River, with water quality at other sites on Card 2 staying the
same as it is now.

I also want you to keep in mind the recreational activities that you now
do and that you might do in the future on the Monongahela River or at other
sites. That is, keep in mind the first two parts of the value card. (POINT
TO THE VALUE CARD, CARD 5.) Your actual use or possible use can involve
activities in the water or near the water, or both, as we talked about earlier.

We know that for the Monongahela River as a whole the current water
quality is at level "D", but that it may vary at different points along the
river. At level "D" it is clean enough for boating, but not clean enough for
catching game fish or for swimming.

HAVE REMINDER CARD READY. RECORD DOLLAR AMOUNTS GIVEN FOR EACH PART
ASKED.

B-3 a.   What is the most it is worth to you (and your family) on a yearly basis to keep the water quality in the Monongahela River from slipping back from level "D" to level "E", where it is not even clean enough for boating?

$_____ DOLLARS (IF ANY AMOUNT, GO TO B-3.b.; IF ZERO DOLLARS, ASK ⌐ .)   (34-36)

> Would it be worth something to you (and your family) to raise the water quality level from level "D" to a higher level? CIRCLE NUMBER.
>
> YES . . . . 01 (GO TO B-3.b.)
>
> NO . . . . 02 (GO TO B-3.e.)

b.   (In addition to the amount you just told me,) What is the most that you would be willing to pay each year in higher taxes and prices for products that companies sell to raise the water quality from level "D" to level "C", where game fish can live in it and it is improved for other activities?

$ _____ DOLLARS (IF ANY AMOUNT, GO TO B-3.c.; IF ZERO DOLLARS, GO TO B-3.d.)   (37-39)

c.   How much more than (READ AMOUNT FROM b.) would you be willing to pay each year in higher taxes and prices for products that companies sell to raise the water quality from level "C" to level "B", where it is clean enough for swimming and it is improved for other activities?

$ _____ DOLLARS (GO TO B-4)   (40-42)

d.   What is the most that you would be willing to pay each year in higher taxes and prices for products that companies sell to raise the water quality from level "D" to level "B", where it is clean enough for swimming and it is improved for other activities?

$ _____ DOLLARS

    ⎛ IF ANY AMOUNT IN a., GO TO B-4;   ⎞
    ⎜ IF ZERO DOLLARS IN a. AND: ⎟   (43-45)
    ⎜   · ANY AMOUNT IN d., GO TO B-4.d.;   ⎟
    ⎝   · ZERO DOLLARS IN d., GO TO B-3.e.   ⎠

e.   We have found in studies of this type that people have a lot of different reasons for answering as they do. Some people felt they did not have enough information to give a dollar amount, some did not want to put dollar values on environmental quality, and some objected to the way the question was presented. Others gave a zero dollar amount because that was what it was worth to them.

Which of these reasons best describes why you answered the way you did? REPEAT REASONS IF NECESSARY AND CIRCLE NUMBER.

                                                              (46-47)

NOT ENOUGH INFORMATION . . 01 ⎤

DID NOT WANT TO PLACE
   DOLLAR VALUE . . . . . . 02 ⎥

OBJECTED TO WAY QUESTION   ⎬ (GO TO B-6)
   WAS PRESENTED . . . . . 03 ⎥

THAT IS WHAT IT IS WORTH . 04 ⎥

OTHER (SPECIFY) . . . . . 05 ⎦

_____

B-3 a.   This payment card shows different yearly amounts people might be
          willing to pay for different levels of water quality. HAND RESPON-
          DENT CARD 6, "PAYMENT CARD," AND ALLOW RESPONDENT TIME TO LOOK AT
          IT.

0	100	200	300	400	500	600	700
25	125	225	325	425	525	625	725
50	150	250	350	450	550	650	750
75	175	275	375	475	575	675	775

What is the most it is worth to you (and your family) on a yearly
basis to keep the water quality in the Monongahela River from
slipping back from level "D" to level "E", where it is not even
clean enough for boating? Please pick any amount on the card, any
amount in between, or any other amount you think is appropriate.

$ _____ DOLLARS (IF ANY AMOUNT, GO TO B-3.b.;   (34-36)
                          IF ZERO DOLLARS, ASK ⌐ .)

Would it be worth something to you (and your family) to raise the
water quality level from level "D" to a higher level? CIRCLE
NUMBER.

   YES . . . . 01 (GO TO B-3.b.)

   NO . . . . 02 (GO TO B-3.e.)

b.   (In addition to the amount you just told me,) What is the most that
     you would be willing to pay each year in higher taxes and prices for
     products that companies sell to raise the water quality from level
     "D" to level "C", where game fish can live in it and it is improved
     for other activities?

     $ _____ DOLLARS (IF ANY AMOUNT, GO TO B-3.c.;   (37-39)
                               IF ZERO DOLLARS, GO TO B-3.d.)

c.   How much more than (READ AMOUNT FROM b.) would you be willing to pay
     each year in higher taxes and prices for products that companies
     sell to raise the water quality from level "C" to level "B", where
     it is clean enough for swimming and it is improved for other activi-
     ties?

     $ _____ DOLLARS (GO TO B-4)   (40-42)

d. What is the most that you would be willing to pay each year in higher taxes and prices for products that companies sell to raise the water quality from level "D" to level "B", where it is clean enough for swimming and it is improved for other activities?

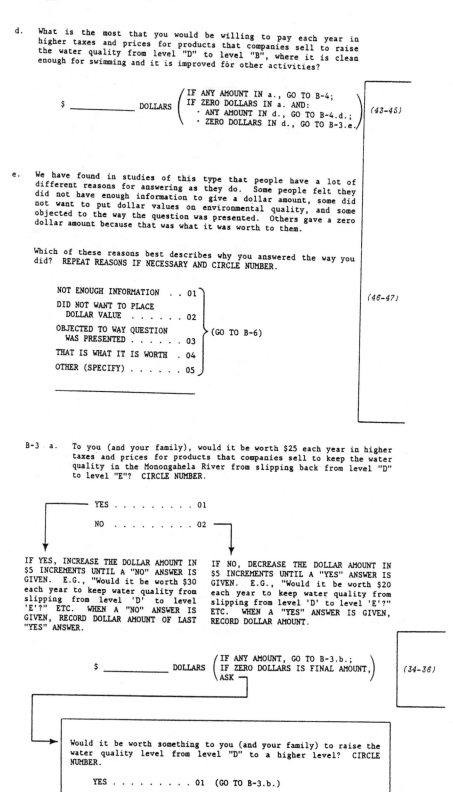

$ _____ DOLLARS (IF ANY AMOUNT IN a., GO TO B-4;
IF ZERO DOLLARS IN a. AND:
· ANY AMOUNT IN d., GO TO B-4.d.;
· ZERO DOLLARS IN d., GO TO B-3.e.)   (43-45)

e. We have found in studies of this type that people have a lot of different reasons for answering as they do. Some people felt they did not have enough information to give a dollar amount, some did not want to put dollar values on environmental quality, and some objected to the way the question was presented. Others gave a zero dollar amount because that was what it was worth to them.

Which of these reasons best describes why you answered the way you did? REPEAT REASONS IF NECESSARY AND CIRCLE NUMBER.

NOT ENOUGH INFORMATION . . 01
DID NOT WANT TO PLACE
    DOLLAR VALUE 02
OBJECTED TO WAY QUESTION
    WAS PRESENTED . . . . . 03 } (GO TO B-6)   (46-47)
THAT IS WHAT IT IS WORTH . 04
OTHER (SPECIFY) 05

_____

B-3 . a. To you (and your family), would it be worth $25 each year in higher taxes and prices for products that companies sell to keep the water quality in the Monongahela River from slipping back from level "D" to level "E"? CIRCLE NUMBER.

YES 01
NO 02

IF YES, INCREASE THE DOLLAR AMOUNT IN $5 INCREMENTS UNTIL A "NO" ANSWER IS GIVEN. E.G., "Would it be worth $30 each year to keep water quality from slipping from level 'D' to level 'E'?" ETC. WHEN A "NO" ANSWER IS GIVEN, RECORD DOLLAR AMOUNT OF LAST "YES" ANSWER.

IF NO, DECREASE THE DOLLAR AMOUNT IN $5 INCREMENTS UNTIL A "YES" ANSWER IS GIVEN. E.G., "Would it be worth $20 each year to keep water quality from slipping from level 'D' to level 'E'?" ETC. WHEN A "YES" ANSWER IS GIVEN, RECORD DOLLAR AMOUNT.

$ _____ DOLLARS (IF ANY AMOUNT, GO TO B-3.b.;
IF ZERO DOLLARS IS FINAL AMOUNT,)   (34-36)
ASK

Would it be worth something to you (and your family) to raise the water quality level from level "D" to a higher level? CIRCLE NUMBER.

YES . . . . 01 (GO TO B-3.b.)

NO . . . . 02 (GO TO B-3.e.)

b. Would you (and your family) be willing to pay (an additional) $25 each year in higher taxes and prices for products that companies sell to raise the water quality from level "D" to level "C", where game fish can live in it and it is improved for other activities? CIRCLE NUMBER.

YES 01

NO 02

IF YES, INCREASE THE DOLLAR AMOUNT IN $5 INCREMENTS UNTIL A "NO" ANSWER IS GIVEN. E.G., "Would you be willing to pay $30 (more) each year to raise the water quality from level 'D' to level 'C'?" ETC. WHEN A "NO" ANSWER IS GIVEN, RECORD DOLLAR AMOUNT OF LAST "YES" ANSWER.

IF NO, DECREASE THE DOLLAR AMOUNT IN $5 INCREMENTS UNTIL A "YES" ANSWER IS GIVEN. E.G., "Would you be willing to pay $20 (more) each year to raise the water quality from level 'D' to level 'C'?" ETC. WHEN A "YES" ANSWER IS GIVEN, RECORD DOLLAR AMOUNT.

$ _____ DOLLARS (IF ANY AMOUNT, GO TO B-3.c.; IF ZERO DOLLARS IS FINAL AMOUNT, GO TO B-3.d.)   (37-39)

c. Would you (and your family) be willing to pay an additional $25 each year in higher taxes and prices for products that companies sell to raise the water quality from level "C" to level "B", where you can swim in it and it is improved for other activities? CIRCLE NUMBER.

YES 01

NO 02

IF YES, INCREASE THE DOLLAR AMOUNT IN $5 INCREMENTS UNTIL A "NO" ANSWER IS GIVEN. E.G., "Would you be willing to pay $30 more each year to raise the water quality from level 'C' to level 'B'?" ETC. WHEN A "NO" ANSWER IS GIVEN, RECORD DOLLAR AMOUNT OF LAST "YES" ANSWER.

IF NO, DECREASE THE DOLLAR AMOUNT IN $5 INCREMENTS UNTIL A "YES" ANSWER IS GIVEN. E.G., "Would you be willing to pay $20 more each year to raise the water quality from level 'C' to level 'B'?" ETC. WHEN A "YES" ANSWER IS GIVEN, RECORD DOLLAR AMOUNT.

$ _____ DOLLARS (GO TO B-4)   (40-42)

d.   Would you (and your family) be willing to pay $25 each year in higher taxes and prices for products that companies sell to raise the water quality from level "D" to level "B", where you can swim in it and it is improved for other activities?   CIRCLE NUMBER.

YES 01

NO 02

IF YES, INCREASE THE DOLLAR AMOUNT IN $5 INCREMENTS UNTIL A "NO" ANSWER IS GIVEN.   E.G., "Would you be willing to pay $30 each year to raise the water quality from level 'D' to level 'B'?" ETC.   WHEN A "NO" ANSWER IS GIVEN, RECORD DOLLAR AMOUNT OF LAST "YES" ANSWER.

IF NO, DECREASE THE DOLLAR AMOUNT IN $5 INCREMENTS UNTIL A "YES" ANSWER IS GIVEN.   E.G., "Would you be willing to pay $20 each year to raise the water quality from level 'D' to Level 'B'?" ETC.   WHEN A "YES" ANSWER IS GIVEN, RECORD DOLLAR AMOUNT.

$ _____ DOLLARS

IF ANY AMOUNT IN a., GO TO B-4;
IF ZERO DOLLARS IN a. AND:
· ANY AMOUNT IN d., GO TO B-4.d.;
· ZERO DOLLARS IN d., GO TO B-3.e.

(43-45)

e.   We have found in studies of this type that people have a lot of different reasons for answering as they do.   Some people felt they did not have enough information to give a dollar amount, some did not want to put dollar values on environmental quality, and some objected to the way the question was presented.   Others gave a zero dollar amount because that was what it was worth to them.

Which of these reasons best describes why you answered the way you did?   REPEAT REASONS IF NECESSARY AND CIRCLE NUMBER.

NOT ENOUGH INFORMATION . . 01

DID NOT WANT TO PLACE
    DOLLAR VALUE 02

OBJECTED TO WAY QUESTION
    WAS PRESENTED 03

THAT IS WHAT IT IS WORTH . 04

OTHER (SPECIFY) 05

(GO TO B-6)

(46-47)

_____

Index